From the Height of Elegance to the Depths of Human Tragedy

Maj. Arthur Peuchen, first-class passenger: Sunday evening I dined with my friends, Markelham Molson, Mr. Allison and Mrs. Allison; and their daughter was there for a short time. The dinner was an exceptionally good dinner. It seemed to be a better bill of fare than usual, although they are all good. After dinner my friends and I went to the sitting-out room and had some coffee. . . . I then went to the smoking room and joined Mr. Beatty, Mr. McCaffery and another English gentleman who was going to Canada. We sat chatting and smoking there until probably twenty minutes after 11, or it may have been a little later than that. I then bid them good night. . . . I had only reached my room and was starting to undress when I felt as though a heavy wave had struck our ship. . . . Knowing that it was a calm night and that it was an unusual thing to occur on a calm night, I immediately put my overcoat on and went up on deck. As I started to go through the grand stairway I met a friend who said, "Why, we have struck an iceberg. . . ."

62d Congress }   SENATE   { Document
2d Session }   { No. 726

"TITANIC" DISASTER

HEARINGS

BEFORE A

SUBCOMMITTEE OF THE
COMMITTEE ON COMMERCE
UNITED STATES SENATE

SIXTY-SECOND CONGRESS
SECOND SESSION

PURSUANT TO

S. RES. 283

DIRECTING THE COMMITTEE ON COMMERCE TO INVES-
TIGATE THE CAUSES LEADING TO THE WRECK
OF THE WHITE STAR LINER "TITANIC"

WASHINGTON
GOVERNMENT PRINTING OFFICE
1912

Title page of the 1912 Senate transcript of the *Titanic* disaster hearings.

THE
TITANIC
DISASTER HEARINGS:

The Official Transcripts of the 1912 Senate Investigation

Edited and with an introduction by
TOM KUNTZ

POCKET BOOKS
New York   London   Toronto   Sydney   Tokyo   Singapore

For orders other than by individual consumers, Pocket Books grants a discount on the purchase of **10 or more** copies of single titles for special markets or premium use. For further details, please write to the Vice-President of Special Markets, Pocket Books, 1633 Broadway, New York, NY 10019-6785 8th Floor.

For information on how individual consumers can place orders, please write to Mail Order Department, Simon & Schuster, Inc., 200 Old Tappan Road, Old Tappan, NJ 07675.

An *Original* Publication of POCKET BOOKS

POCKET BOOKS, a division of Simon & Schuster Inc.
1230 Avenue of the Americas, New York, NY 10020

Introduction and compilation copyright © 1998 by Tom Kuntz

ISBN: 0-671-02553-8

First Pocket Books printing March 1998

10 9 8 7 6 5 4 3 2 1

POCKET and colophon are registered trademarks of Simon & Schuster Inc.

Cover art courtesy of Corbis/Bettmann

Printed in the U.S.A.

For Tess and Katy
         —T.K.

CONTENTS

Without any pretension to experience or special knowledge of nautical affairs, nevertheless I am of the opinion that very few important facts which were susceptible of being known escaped our scrutiny.

—Senator William Alden Smith,
Chairman of the Senate Subcommittee
on the *Titanic* "Disaster"
May 12, 1912

INTRODUCTION

The *Titanic* steams onward in the popular imagination, most recently in James Cameron's critically acclaimed and award-winning film epic. For decades after its sinking in 1912, the lure of the doomed White Star liner remained powerful as its wreckage lay lost and undisturbed two miles beneath the surface of the North Atlantic. With the discovery of its remains in 1985 by a team led by Dr. Robert Ballard, one doubt was cleared up—the ship had in fact broken in two—but the *Titanic* mystique only grew: deep-sea mini-submarines brought back artifacts and murky, dreamlike images from its once-elegant recesses. With public fascination rekindled, documentaries, books, even a Broadway musical soon followed—and now Cameron's *Titanic,* the most expensive movie ever made and among the biggest box-office draws of all time.

Despite all this, the essential story of the *Titanic* stands unchanged. Most of its key details, themes, characters and enigmas emerged in a dramatic United States Senate investigation begun the very day after survivors arrived in New York. Those hearings were sensationally covered by newspapers of the day, and the records of them have long been an indispensable resource to *Titanic* historians. The London press bristled at their anti-British tone, but the Senate hearings prompted (and set much of the agenda for) a more formal and detached British royal inquiry that, while longer in duration, covered much of the same ground and reached many of the same conclusions. Without question, the portrait of the disaster that first emerged in the 1912 Senate

Titanic hearings informs all narratives and dramatizations of the catastrophe since then—from Walter Lord's classic, *A Night to Remember,* to, yes, *Titanic,* the movie.

But, as I discovered in researching the column on the Senate sessions for *The New York Times* Week in Review that inspired this book, the transcripts of the hearings themselves are largely inaccessible to the public, available only in the Senate archives and some libraries, typically on microfiche. Here, for the first time, the more than 1,100 pages of testimony and evidence, along with the Senate inquiry's conclusions, are extensively excerpted in book form. Reading them, you can learn of history's greatest sea disaster much as the story unfolded in the spring of 1912, through the questions of those struggling to comprehend its enormity and the answers of those who just days earlier lived through it.

In these sessions the lookout Frederick Fleet first recounted his fateful alarm of an "iceberg right ahead" and disclosed the lack of binoculars in the crow's nest (page 177). Here the world first learned of Isidor and Ida Straus's decision to die together rather than separate under the "women and children first" evacuation tradition (page 72). Here Fifth Officer Harold Lowe acknowledged firing warning shots along the *Titanic*'s decks as his lifeboat was being lowered, to prevent men from jumping in (page 226). In these sessions, passenger Archibald Gracie vividly described people swarming up the *Titanic*'s rear decks as the ship plunged deeper into the sea (page 412) and Olaus Abelseth, a steerage passenger, told of diving off the stern at the last minute (page 454). And in these Senate hearings, Seaman Edward Buley told of going back to search for survivors in the frigid North Atlantic and finding bobbing victims in life preservers, not drowned but "frozen altogether" (page 263). These transcripts have a rawness and immediacy that became the stuff of legend.

This is the background: On the night of April 14–15, 1912, the R.M.S. *Titanic*—a mammoth new British liner of incomparable luxury, three football fields long and eleven stories high from its bottom—struck an iceberg and sank on its maiden voyage from Southampton to New York with the loss of more than two-thirds of the more than 2,200 people aboard, claiming aristocrats and immigrants alike. People on both sides of the Atlantic clamored for answers.

How could the world's largest and purportedly safest vessel have foundered? What about the ice warnings undoubtedly available to its captain, and the well-known threat of icebergs at that time of year? Why were there not nearly enough lifeboats and why were even those few underloaded? Why had J. Bruce Ismay, the head of the *Titanic's* parent conglomerate (and an obvious target of the rampant anti-trust fervor of the day) left the ship before its senior officers? Why were there so many conflicting and, as it turned out, blatantly erroneous reports about the ship's fate? What exactly had gone so terribly wrong?

Senator William Alden Smith, a white-haired, populist Republican lawyer from Michigan with something of a Horatio Alger background, set out to find answers. On Wednesday, April 17—two days after the sinking, when the extent of the disaster had only just become clear—he rose on the floor of the Senate to propose a special investigation under the auspices of the Senate Commerce Committee, of which he was a member. His resolution, unanimously approved, authorized a panel "to investigate the causes leading to the wreck of the White Star liner *Titanic,* with its attendant loss of life so shocking to the civilized world." It empowered the panel "to summon witnesses, send for persons and papers, to administer oaths, and to take such testimony as may be necessary to determine the responsibility therefor." The resolution stressed the need to determine whether the ship had adequate lifeboats and had undergone proper inspections. And it directed the panel to study whether new laws or an international treaty was needed to prevent a repetition. Smith was named chairman.

There was little time to waste. The rescue ship *Carpathia,* a Cunard liner, was due in New York the next day with the *Titanic's* more than 700 survivors. According to Wyn Craig Wade in *The Titanic: End of a Dream* (Penguin, 1986), the Navy informed the Senator on the day of the ship's expected arrival that a Navy wireless operator had intercepted troubling messages sent from the *Carpathia* by Ismay. His messages suggested that he was trying to spirit himself and surviving crew members back to England on another White Star liner without setting foot on American soil. Smith wanted to make sure that no one culpable in the disaster escaped American jurisdiction.

So, according to Wade's account, the Senator headed over to the White House and got President William Howard

Taft's authorization for a Treasury revenue cutter to intercept the *Carpathia* before it docked, to thwart any effort by Ismay to evade American authorities. (Taft was distraught over a personal connection to the disaster: a close aide and friend, Maj. Archibald Butt, was a passenger but hadn't turned up among the survivors.)

Senator Smith next rushed to Washington's Union Station and boarded a mid-afternoon train north with a small entourage. Arriving in New York just as the *Carpathia* was docking at the Cunard pier that evening, he took a cab straight from the station to the ship, where throngs of reporters, friends and relatives of *Titanic* passengers as well as curious onlookers had gathered. He made his way through to the ship, and aboard the *Carpathia* spoke briefly with a weary Ismay in the doctor's cabin. The Senator emerged to tell reporters that he anticipated full cooperation from Ismay and his employees when the hearings got under way the next morning.

The inquiry, which Smith dominated as its chief interrogator, opened at the Waldorf-Astoria Hotel, symbol of the Gilded Age, whose demise the *Titanic* now seems to have augured. The next week it moved down to Washington, where it christened the new caucus room of the Russell Senate Office Building, site of all the famous televised Senate investigations since. Later the sessions—there were seventeen in all—were moved around as needed, even back to New York, sometimes with Smith and the other Senators questioning witnesses and taking statements on their own. Held in the era before tape recorders, the sessions had to be transcribed by a stenographer, and for the most part this was William McKinstry, a beleaguered young aide to Senator Smith. In his account of the Senate hearings, Wade cautions that McKinstry sometimes misapprehended British accents, transcribing "40" for "14," for example. It is possible that such errors appear here.

That aside, the excerpts that follow make fascinating reading mainly for their unscripted drama. The testimony of the wireless operator Harold Bride, for example, amounts to one of the most thrilling sea stories of all time (page 77). The transcripts also evoke an era of pre-suffrage gender roles that will strike many today as tragically absurd (as it did many then). Senator Smith noted at one point that he hadn't called more women as witnesses out of deference to their fresh grief over the loss of their husbands.

Nobody on the panel—and certainly not Senator Smith, a Midwesterner—was a maritime expert (though, coincidentally, Smith had once dined with the *Titanic's* ill-fated captain on a ship earlier under his command). Smith's clipped method of questioning, in which he frequently skipped randomly from topic to topic, lent a kinetic, improvisational air to the tense proceedings, especially at the beginning. That interrogative method may reflect the Senator's initial grappling with the unfamiliar issues at hand, but later in the transcripts he makes clear his ability to absorb and process huge amounts of information.

He does so when the inquiry focuses on complex or subsidiary aspects of the disaster that have not lent themselves easily to popular dramatization. These include the scandal of the steamer *Californian,* the ship close to the *Titanic* that did nothing to help her; the heroic and risky steps taken by the captain of the *Carpathia* to rescue survivors; and the role of Marconi wireless telegraphy in the disaster, which posed the same sorts of questions about new forms of media and the responsible handling of information that persist today. The transcripts also convey the press frenzy surrounding the catastrophe, including checkbook journalism practiced by *The New York Times* in collusion with Guglielmo Marconi, the wireless inventor. The *Times* was out in front on the story in part because it joined in the excesses of the day.

In the end the Senators could recommend no prosecutorial action because shipping and shipping-safety laws were so lax that no one could be found culpable (and, in any case, the operators of the British-registered *Titanic* had to answer primarily to the British authorities, whose regulations were also lax). The inquiry's main contribution was to recommend corrective legislation—and to provide a gripping first draft of history. That story of wealth, poverty, hubris, and loss at the dawn of a century of progress and promise unfulfilled has evolved at its end into a defining myth of modern times.

—Tom Kuntz,
Word for Word Editor,
The New York Times Week in Review

A note on lifeboats: The transcripts often refer to the *Titanic*'s 16 main lifeboats by their numbers, which indicate where they were located on the ship before lowering. Even-numbered lifeboats were on the port side, or to the left if facing forward on the ship. Odd-numbered boats were on the starboard side, or to the right if facing forward on the ship. Lifeboats 1 through 8 were near the front of the ship, with lifeboats 1 and 2 nearest to the bow, 3 and 4 next nearest, and so on. Lifeboats 9 through 16 were near the stern, with 15 and 16 the farthest back, and so on. There were also four smaller lifeboats on the ship, one of which slid, overturned, off the top of the officers' quarters and figures prominently in survivors' accounts.

—T.K.

THE
TITANIC
DISASTER HEARINGS

FIRST DAY
Friday, April 19, 1912
The Waldorf-Astoria Hotel, New York

The opening session was called to order by Senator William Alden Smith at 10:30 in the morning in the hotel's crystal-chandeliered East Room—a Gilded Age setting if ever there was one—now crammed to standing-room-only capacity with reporters and curious spectators, many from New York's upper class.

Seated next to Senator Smith, on one side of a conference table, were Senator Francis G. Newlands, Democrat of Nevada, the Senate subcommittee's vice chairman; and George Uhler, inspector general of the Commerce Department's steamboat inspection service, an advisor to Smith.

Across from them at the table was the first witness, J. Bruce Ismay, head of White Star, the Titanic's cruise line, also president of the International Mercantile Marine Co., White Star's American parent, financed by J. P. Morgan Jr. (who had canceled his trip on the Titanic). Seated with Ismay were his American vice president, Philip A. S. Franklin; the Titanic's senior surviving officer, Second Officer Charles Lightoller; IMM attorneys; and bodyguards detailed to protect Ismay, who in the four days since the disaster had been villainized in the American press for not staying with his ship.

Witness: J. Bruce Ismay, 49
Managing director of the White Star Line and first-class passenger, from Liverpool, England

Key testimony: Ismay, who later would be summoned back before the panel, elicited broad skepticism in his initial appearance with evasive statements like, "More than that I do not know." He denied that the Titanic had been pushed to its maximum speed, though Senator Smith would ultimately conclude that Ismay's presence on the ship was a factor

1

encouraging Capt. Edward J. Smith to go faster. Asked how he managed to get away in a lifeboat when many passengers, including women and children, were unable to, Ismay said there were no more women or children in the vicinity of the boat that he had been helping to load and the boat still had room, so he got in. He said that as the Titanic *sank, he did not look back because he was "pulling away" with his back to the ship: "I did not wish to see her go down." Asked to explain why he wouldn't be facing the wreck if he were rowing away from it, Ismay said that on his lifeboat the oars had to be pushed.*

. . . SENATOR SMITH: Will you kindly tell the committee the circumstances surrounding your voyage, and, as succinctly as possible, beginning with your going aboard the vessel at Liverpool, your place on the ship on the voyage, together with any circumstances you feel would be helpful to us in this inquiry?

MR. ISMAY: In the first place, I would like to express my sincere grief at this deplorable catastrophe.

I understand that you gentlemen have been appointed as a committee of the Senate to inquire into the circumstances. So far as we are concerned, we welcome it. We court the fullest inquiry. We have nothing to conceal; nothing to hide. The ship was built in Belfast. She was the latest thing in the art of shipbuilding; absolutely no money was spared in her construction. She was not built by contract. She was simply built on a commission.

She left Belfast, as far as I remember—I am not absolutely clear about these dates—I think it was on the 1st of April.

She underwent her trials, which were entirely satisfactory. She then proceeded to Southampton; arriving there on Wednesday.

SENATOR SMITH: Will you describe the trials she went through?

MR. ISMAY: I was not present.

She arrived at Southampton on Wednesday, the 3d, I think, and sailed on Wednesday, the 10th. She left Southampton at 12 o'clock. She arrived in Cherbourg that evening, having run over at 68 revolutions [propeller revolutions per minute].

We left Cherbourg and proceeded to Queenstown. We arrived there, I think, about midday on Thursday.

We ran from Cherbourg to Queenstown at 70 revolutions.

After embarking the mails and passengers, we proceeded at 70 revolutions. I am not absolutely clear what the first day's run was, whether it was 464 miles or 484 miles.

The second day the number of revolutions was increased. I think the number of revolutions on the second day was about 72. I think we ran on the second day 519 miles.

The third day the revolutions were increased to 75, and I think we ran 546 or 549 miles.

The weather during this time was absolutely fine, with the exception, I think, of about 10 minutes' fog one evening.

The accident took place on Sunday night. What the exact time was I do not know. I was in bed myself, asleep, when the accident happened.

The ship sank, I am told, at 2:20.

That, sir, I think is all I can tell you.

I understand it has been stated that the ship was going at full speed. The ship never had been at full speed. The full speed of the ship is 78 revolutions. She works up to 80. So far as I am aware, she never exceeded 75 revolutions. She had not all her boilers on. None of the single-ended boilers were on.

It was our intention, if we had fine weather on Monday afternoon or Tuesday, to drive the ship at full speed. That, owing to the unfortunate catastrophe, never eventuated.

SENATOR SMITH: Will you describe what you did after the impact or collision?

MR. ISMAY: I presume the impact awakened me. I lay in bed for a moment or two afterwards, not realizing, probably, what had happened. Eventually I got up and walked along the passageway and met one of the stewards, and said, "What has happened?" He said, "I do not know, sir."

I then went back into my room, put my coat on, and went up on the bridge, where I found Capt. Smith. I asked him what had happened, and he said, "We have struck ice." I said, "Do you think the ship is seriously damaged?" He said, "I am afraid she is."

I then went down below, I think it was, where I met Mr. Bell, the chief engineer, who was in the main companion-

3

way. I asked if he thought the ship was seriously damaged, and he said he thought she was, but was quite satisfied the pumps would keep her afloat.

I think I went back onto the bridge. I heard the order given to get the boats out. I walked along to the starboard side of the ship, where I met one of the officers. I told him to get the boats out——

SENATOR SMITH: What officer?

MR. ISMAY: That I could not remember, sir.

I assisted, as best I could, getting the boats out and putting the women and children into the boats.

I stood upon that deck practically until I left the ship in the starboard collapsible boat, which is the last boat to leave the ship, so far as I know. More than that I do not know.

SENATOR SMITH: Did the captain remain on the bridge?

MR. ISMAY: That I could not tell you, sir.

SENATOR SMITH: Did you leave him on the bridge?

MR. ISMAY: Yes, sir.

SENATOR SMITH: His first statement to you was that he felt she was seriously damaged?

MR. ISMAY: Yes, sir.

SENATOR SMITH: And the next statement of the chief engineer was what?

MR. ISMAY: To the same effect.

SENATOR SMITH: To the same effect?

MR. ISMAY: Yes.

SENATOR SMITH: But that he hoped the pumps might keep her afloat?

MR. ISMAY: Yes.

SENATOR SMITH: Did you have any talk with any officer other than the captain or the chief engineer and the steward that you met?

MR. ISMAY: Not that I remember.

SENATOR SMITH: Did the officers seem to know the serious character of this collision?

MR. ISMAY: That I could not tell, sir, because I had no conversation with them.

SENATOR SMITH: Did any officer say to you that it evidently was not serious?

MR. ISMAY: No, sir.

SENATOR SMITH: All the officers with whom you talked expressed the same fear, saying that it was serious?

4

MR. ISMAY: I did not speak to any of them, sir.

SENATOR SMITH: Except the captain?

MR. ISMAY: Except the captain and the chief engineer. I have already stated that I had spoken to them; but to no other officer that I remember.

SENATOR SMITH: You went to the bridge immediately after you had returned to your room?

MR. ISMAY: After I had put on my coat I went up to the bridge.

SENATOR SMITH: And you found the captain there?

MR. ISMAY: The captain was there.

SENATOR SMITH: In what part of the ship were your quarters?

MR. ISMAY: My quarters were on B deck, just aft of the main companionway.

SENATOR SMITH: I wish you would describe just where that was.

MR. ISMAY: The sun deck is the upper deck of all. Then we have what we call the A deck, which is the next deck, and then the B deck.

MR. UHLER: The second passenger deck?

MR. ISMAY: We carry very few passengers on the A deck. I think we have a diagram here that will show you these decks. Here it is, and there is the room I was occupying [indicating on diagram].

SENATOR SMITH: What is the number of that room?

MR. ISMAY: B-52 is the room I had.

SENATOR SMITH: You had the suite?

MR. ISMAY: I had the suite; I was sleeping in that room [indicating on diagram], as a matter of fact.

SENATOR SMITH: Do you know whether there were any passengers on that deck?

MR. ISMAY: I have no idea sir.

SENATOR SMITH: You say that the trip was a voluntary trip on your part?

MR. ISMAY: Absolutely.

SENATOR SMITH: For the purpose of viewing this ship in action, or did you have some business in New York?

MR. ISMAY: I had no business to bring me to New York at all. I simply came in the natural course of events, as one is apt to, in the case of a new ship, to see how she works, and with the idea of seeing how we could improve on her for the next ship which we are building.

5

SENATOR SMITH: Were there any other executive officers of the company aboard?

MR. ISMAY: None.

SENATOR SMITH: Was the inspector or builder on board?

MR. ISMAY: There was a representative of the builders on board.

SENATOR SMITH: Who was he?

MR. ISMAY: Mr. Thomas Andrews.

SENATOR SMITH: In what capacity was he?

MR. ISMAY: I do not quite follow you.

SENATOR SMITH: What was the occasion for his coming to make this trial trip?

MR. ISMAY: As a representative of the builders, to see that everything was working satisfactorily, and also to see how he could improve the next ship.

SENATOR SMITH: Was he a man of large experience?

MR. ISMAY: Yes.

SENATOR SMITH: Had he had part in the construction of this ship himself?

MR. ISMAY: Yes.

SENATOR SMITH: Was he among the survivors?

MR. ISMAY: Unfortunately, no.

SENATOR SMITH: How old a man was he?

MR. ISMAY: It is difficult to judge a man's age, as you know, but I should think he was perhaps 42 or 43 years of age. He may have been less. I really could not say.

SENATOR SMITH: Then, you were the only executive officer aboard representing your company, aside from the ship's customary complement of officers?

MR. ISMAY: Yes, sir.

SENATOR SMITH: Did you have occasion to consult with the captain about the movement of the ship?

MR. ISMAY: Never.

SENATOR SMITH: Did he consult you about it?

MR. ISMAY: Never. Perhaps I am wrong in saying that. I should like to say this: I do not know that it was quite a matter of consulting him about it, or of his consulting me about it, but what we had arranged to do was that we would not attempt to arrive in New York at the lightship before 5 o'clock on Wednesday morning.

SENATOR SMITH: That was the understanding?

MR. ISMAY: Yes. But that was arranged before we left Queenstown.

SENATOR SMITH: Was it supposed that you could reach New York at that time without putting the ship to its full running capacity?

MR. ISMAY: Oh, yes, sir. There was nothing to be gained by arriving at New York any earlier than that.

SENATOR SMITH: You spoke of the revolutions on the early part of the voyage.

MR. ISMAY: Yes, sir.

SENATOR SMITH: Those were increased as the distance was increased?

MR. ISMAY: The *Titanic* being a new ship, we were gradually working her up. When you bring out a new ship you naturally do not start her running at full speed until you get everything working smoothly and satisfactorily down below.

SENATOR SMITH: Did I understand you to say that she exceeded 70 revolutions?

MR. ISMAY: Yes, sir; she was going 75 revolutions on Tuesday.

SENATOR SMITH: On Tuesday?

MR. ISMAY: No; I am wrong—on Saturday. I am mixed up as to the days.

SENATOR SMITH: The day before the accident?

MR. ISMAY: The day before the accident. That, of course, is nothing near her full speed.

SENATOR SMITH: During the voyage, do you know, of your own knowledge, of your proximity to icebergs?

MR. ISMAY: Did I know that we were near icebergs?

SENATOR SMITH: Yes.

MR. ISMAY: No, sir; I did not. I know ice had been reported.

SENATOR SMITH: Ice had been reported?

MR. ISMAY: Yes.

SENATOR SMITH: Did you personally see any icebergs, or any large volume of ice?

MR. ISMAY: No; not until after the accident.

SENATOR SMITH: Not until after the wreck?

MR. ISMAY: I had never seen an iceberg in my life before.

SENATOR SMITH: You never saw one before.

MR. ISMAY: No, sir.

7

SENATOR SMITH: Had you ever been on this so-called northern route before?

MR. ISMAY: We were on the southern route, sir.

SENATOR SMITH: On this Newfoundland route?

MR. ISMAY: We were on the long southern route; not on the northern route.

SENATOR SMITH: You were not on the extreme northern route?

MR. ISMAY: We were on the extreme southern route for the west-bound ships.

SENATOR SMITH: What was the longitude and latitude of this ship? Do you know?

MR. ISMAY: That I could not tell you; I am not a sailor.

SENATOR SMITH: Were you cognizant of your proximity to icebergs at all on Saturday?

MR. ISMAY: On Saturday? No, sir.

SENATOR SMITH: Do you know anything about a wireless message from the [German liner] *Amerika* to the *Titanic*——

MR. ISMAY: No, sir.

SENATOR SMITH: Saying that the *Amerika* had encountered ice in that latitude?

MR. ISMAY: No, sir.

SENATOR SMITH: Were you aware of the proximity of icebergs on Sunday?

MR. ISMAY: On Sunday? No; I did not know on Sunday. I knew that we would be in the ice region that night sometime.

SENATOR SMITH: That you would be or were?

MR. ISMAY: That we would be in the ice region on Sunday night.

SENATOR SMITH: Did you have any consultation with the captain regarding the matter?

MR. ISMAY: Absolutely none.

SENATOR SMITH: Or with any other officer of the ship?

MR. ISMAY: With no officer at all, sir. I was absolutely out of my province. I am not a navigator. I was simply a passenger on board the ship.

SENATOR SMITH: Do you know anything about the working of the wireless service on this ship?

MR. ISMAY: In what way? We had wireless on the ship.

SENATOR SMITH: Had you taken any unusual precaution to have a reserve power for this wireless?

MR. ISMAY: I believe there was, but I have no knowledge of that myself.

SENATOR SMITH: Do you know how long the wireless continued to operate after the blow or collision?

MR. ISMAY: No, sir; I do not.

SENATOR SMITH: Did you, at any time, see the operator of the wireless?

MR. ISMAY: I did not.

SENATOR SMITH: Did you attempt to send any messages yourself?

MR. ISMAY: I did not.

SENATOR SMITH: Were you outside on the deck, or on any deck, when the order was given to lower the lifeboats?

MR. ISMAY: I heard Capt. Smith give the order when I was on the bridge.

SENATOR SMITH: You heard the captain give the order?

MR. ISMAY: Yes, sir.

SENATOR SMITH: Will you tell us what he said.

MR. ISMAY: It is very difficult for me to remember exactly what was said, sir.

SENATOR SMITH: As nearly as you can.

MR. ISMAY: I know I heard him give the order to lower the boats. I think that is all he said. I think he simply turned around and gave the order.

SENATOR SMITH: Was there anything else said, as to how they should be manned or occupied?

MR. ISMAY: No, sir; not that I heard. As soon as I heard him give the order to lower the boats, I left the bridge.

SENATOR SMITH: You left the bridge?

MR. ISMAY: Yes.

SENATOR SMITH: Did you see any of the boats lowered?

MR. ISMAY: Yes, sir.

SENATOR SMITH: How many?

MR. ISMAY: Certainly three.

SENATOR SMITH: Will you tell us, if you can, how they were lowered?

MR. ISMAY: They were swung out, people were put into the boats from the deck, and then they were simply lowered away down to the water.

SENATOR SMITH: Were these lifeboats on the various decks?

MR. ISMAY: They were all on one deck.

SENATOR SMITH: On what deck?

Mr. Ismay: On the sun deck; the deck above this [indicating on diagram]. I do not think it is shown on this plan.

Senator Smith: That is, the second deck above yours?

Mr. Ismay: On this deck here, on the big plan [indicating].

Senator Smith: On the sun deck?

Mr. Ismay: Yes; on what we call the sun deck or the boat deck.

Senator Smith: They were on the boat deck, which would be the upper deck of all?

Mr. Ismay: The upper deck of all, yes.

Senator Smith: Was there any order or supervision exercised by the officers of the ship in loading these lifeboats?

Mr. Ismay: Yes, sir.

Senator Smith: I wish you would tell just what that was.

Mr. Ismay: That I could not say. I could only speak from what I saw for myself.

Senator Smith: That is all I wish you to do.

Mr. Ismay: The boats that were lowered where I was were in charge of the officer and were filled and lowered away.

Senator Smith: They first put men into the boats for the purpose of controlling them?

Mr. Ismay: We put in some of the ship's people.

Senator Smith: Some of the ship's people?

Mr. Ismay: Yes.

Senator Smith: How many?

Mr. Ismay: That I could not say.

Senator Smith: About how many?

Mr. Ismay: I could not say.

Senator Smith: About three or four?

Mr. Ismay: The officer who was there will be able to give you that information, sir. My own statement would be simply guesswork. His statement would be reliable.

Senator Smith: In the boat in which you left the ship how many men were on board?

Mr. Ismay: Four.

Senator Smith: Besides yourself?

Mr. Ismay: I thought you meant the crew.

Senator Smith: I did mean the crew.

Mr. Ismay: There were four of the crew.

Senator Smith: What position did these men occupy?

Mr. Ismay: I do not know, sir.

Senator Smith: Were any of them officers?

MR. ISMAY: No.

SENATOR SMITH: Or seamen?

MR. ISMAY: I believe one was a quartermaster.

SENATOR SMITH: One was a quartermaster?

MR. ISMAY: I believe so, but I do not know.

SENATOR SMITH: You saw three of the boats lowered yourself?

MR. ISMAY: Yes.

SENATOR SMITH: And three of them loaded?

MR. ISMAY: Yes.

SENATOR SMITH: As they were loaded, was any order given as to how they should be loaded?

MR. ISMAY: No.

SENATOR SMITH: How did it happen that the women were first put aboard these lifeboats?

MR. ISMAY: The natural order would be women and children first.

SENATOR SMITH: Was that the order?

MR. ISMAY: Oh, yes.

SENATOR SMITH: That was followed?

MR. ISMAY: As far as practicable.

SENATOR SMITH: So far as you observed?

MR. ISMAY: So far as I observed.

SENATOR SMITH: And were all the women and children accommodated in these lifeboats?

MR. ISMAY: I could not tell you, sir.

SENATOR SMITH: How many passengers were in the lifeboat in which you left the ship?

MR. ISMAY: I should think about 45.

SENATOR SMITH: Forty-five?

MR. ISMAY: That is my recollection.

SENATOR SMITH: Was that its full capacity?

MR. ISMAY: Practically.

SENATOR SMITH: How about the other two boats?

MR. ISMAY: The other three, I should think, were fairly loaded up.

SENATOR SMITH: The three besides the one you were in?

MR. ISMAY: Yes.

SENATOR SMITH: They were fairly well filled?

MR. ISMAY: Yes.

SENATOR SMITH: Was there any struggle or jostling?

MR. ISMAY: I saw none.

SENATOR SMITH: Or any attempt by men to get into the boats?

MR. ISMAY: I saw none.

SENATOR SMITH: Were these women passengers designated as they went into the lifeboat?

MR. ISMAY: No, sir.

SENATOR SMITH: Those that were nearest the lifeboat were taken in?

MR. ISMAY: We simply picked the women out and put them in the boat as fast as we could.

SENATOR SMITH: You picked them from among the throng?

MR. ISMAY: We took the first ones that were there and put them in the lifeboats. I was there myself and put a lot in.

SENATOR SMITH: You helped put some of them in yourself?

MR. ISMAY: I put a great many in.

SENATOR SMITH: Were children shown the same consideration as the women?

MR. ISMAY: Absolutely.

SENATOR SMITH: Did you see any lifeboat without its complement of oarsmen?

MR. ISMAY: I did not.

SENATOR SMITH: Did you see the first lifeboat lowered?

MR. ISMAY: That I could not answer, sir. I saw the first lifeboat lowered on the starboard side. What was going on on the port side I have no knowledge of.

SENATOR SMITH: It has been intimated, Mr. Ismay, that the first lifeboat did not contain the necessary number of men to man it.

MR. ISMAY: As to that I have no knowledge, sir.

SENATOR SMITH: And that women were obliged to row the boat.

MR. HUGHES: That is the second lifeboat, Senator.

SENATOR SMITH: The second lifeboat; and that women were obliged to row that boat from 10:30 o'clock at night until 7:30 o'clock the next morning.

MR. ISMAY: The accident did not take place until 11——

SENATOR SMITH: Well, from after 11:30 o'clock at night until between 6 and 7 o'clock the next morning.

MR. ISMAY: Of that I have no knowledge.

SENATOR SMITH: Until the *Carpathia* overtook them. You have no knowledge of that?

MR. ISMAY: Absolutely none, sir.

12

SENATOR SMITH: So far as your observation went, would you say that was not so?

MR. ISMAY: I would not say either yes or no; but I did not see it.

SENATOR SMITH: When you first went on to the deck, you were only partially clothed?

MR. ISMAY: That is all, sir.

SENATOR SMITH: And, as I understand, you went as far as to encounter an officer or steward?

MR. ISMAY: Yes, sir.

SENATOR SMITH: And then returned?

MR. ISMAY: That is right.

SENATOR SMITH: How long were you on the ship after the collision occurred?

MR. ISMAY: That is a very difficult question to answer, sir. Practically until the time—almost until she sank.

SENATOR SMITH: How long did it take to lower and load a lifeboat?

MR. ISMAY: I could not answer that.

SENATOR SMITH: Can you approximate it?

MR. ISMAY: It is not possible for me to judge the time. I could not answer that.

SENATOR SMITH: Were you on the *Titanic* an hour after the collision?

MR. ISMAY: Oh, yes.

SENATOR SMITH: How much longer?

MR. ISMAY: I should think it was an hour and a quarter.

SENATOR SMITH: An hour and a quarter?

MR. ISMAY: I should think that was it; perhaps longer.

SENATOR SMITH: Did you, during this time, see any of the passengers that you knew?

MR. ISMAY: I really do not remember; I saw a great many passengers, but I do not think I paid much very attention to who they were. I do not remember recognizing any of them.

SENATOR SMITH: Did you know [the Canadian railroad magnate] Charles M. Hayes?

MR. ISMAY: Yes, sir.

SENATOR SMITH: Did you know of the presence of other Americans and Canadians of prominence?

MR. ISMAY: No, sir; I knew Mr. Hayes was on board the ship.

SENATOR SMITH: You knew he was on the ship?

13

MR. ISMAY: Yes; I have known him for some years.

SENATOR SMITH: But you did not see him after the accident occurred?

MR. ISMAY: I never saw him after the accident; no.

SENATOR SMITH: And he is unaccounted for?

MR. ISMAY: Yes, sir.

SENATOR SMITH: He was not among the saved?

MR. ISMAY: No, sir.

SENATOR SMITH: What were the circumstances, Mr. Ismay, of your departure from the ship?

MR. ISMAY: In what way?

SENATOR SMITH: Did the last boat that you went on leave the ship from some point near where you were?

MR. ISMAY: I was immediately opposite the lifeboat when she left.

SENATOR SMITH: Immediately opposite?

MR. ISMAY: Yes.

SENATOR SMITH: What were the circumstances of your departure from the ship? I ask merely that——

MR. ISMAY: The boat was there. There was a certain number of men in the boat, and the officer called out asking if there were any more women, and there was no response, and there were no passengers left on the deck.

SENATOR SMITH: There were no passengers on the deck?

MR. ISMAY: No, sir; and as the boat was in the act of being lowered away, I got into it.

SENATOR SMITH: At that time the *Titanic* was sinking?

MR. ISMAY: She was sinking.

SENATOR SMITH: Where did this ship collide? Was it a side blow?

MR. ISMAY: I have no knowledge, myself. I can only state what I have been told, that she hit the iceberg somewhere between the breakwater and the bridge.

SENATOR SMITH: State that again.

MR. ISMAY: Between the breakwater and the bridge.

SENATOR SMITH: On the starboard side?

MR. ISMAY: Yes.

SENATOR SMITH: Did you see any of the men passengers on that ship with life preservers on?

MR. ISMAY: Nearly all passengers had life preservers on.

SENATOR SMITH: All that you saw?

MR. ISMAY: All that I saw had life preservers on.

SENATOR SMITH: All of them that you saw?

MR. ISMAY: Yes; as far as I can remember.

SENATOR SMITH: Naturally, you would remember that if you saw it? When you entered the lifeboat yourself, you say there were no passengers on that part of the ship?

MR. ISMAY: None.

SENATOR SMITH: Did you, at any time, see any struggle among the men to get into these boats?

MR. ISMAY: No.

SENATOR SMITH: Was there any attempt, as this boat was being lowered past the other decks, to have you take on more passengers?

MR. ISMAY: None, sir. There were no passengers there to take on.

SENATOR SMITH: Before you boarded the lifeboat, did you see any of the passengers jump into the sea?

MR. ISMAY: I did not.

SENATOR SMITH: After you had taken the lifeboat did you see any of the passengers or crew with life-saving apparatus on them in the sea?

MR. ISMAY: No, sir.

SENATOR SMITH: What course was taken by the lifeboat in which you were after leaving the ship?

MR. ISMAY: We saw a light some distance off to which we attempted to pull and which we thought was a ship.

SENATOR SMITH: Can you give the direction of it?

MR. ISMAY: I could not give that.

SENATOR SMITH: But you saw a light?

MR. ISMAY: Yes, sir.

SENATOR SMITH: And you attempted to pull this boat toward it?

MR. ISMAY: Yes, sir.

SENATOR SMITH: How long were you in the open sea in this lifeboat?

MR. ISMAY: I should think about four hours.

SENATOR SMITH: Were there any other lifeboats in that vicinity?

MR. ISMAY: Yes.

SENATOR SMITH: How many?

MR. ISMAY: That I could not answer. I know there was one, because we hailed her. She had a light, and we hailed her, but got no answer from her.

SENATOR SMITH: You got no answer?

MR. ISMAY: No, sir.

SENATOR SMITH: Did you see any rafts in the open sea?

MR. ISMAY: No, sir; none.

SENATOR SMITH: Were there any other rafts on the *Titanic* that could have been utilized?

MR. ISMAY: I believe not.

SENATOR SMITH: Were all of the lifeboats of one type?

MR. ISMAY: No; there were four that are called collapsible boats.

SENATOR SMITH: What were the others?

MR. ISMAY: Ordinary wooden boats.

SENATOR SMITH: How many were there?

MR. ISMAY: I think there were 20 altogether.

SENATOR SMITH: Including both designs?

MR. ISMAY: Yes. Sixteen wooden boats and four collapsible boats, I think. I am not absolutely certain.

SENATOR SMITH: When you reached the *Carpathia,* was your lifeboat taken aboard the *Carpathia?*

MR. ISMAY: That I do not know.

SENATOR SMITH: Did you see any other lifeboats taken aboard the *Carpathia?*

MR. ISMAY: I did not.

SENATOR SMITH: What was the method of getting you aboard the *Carpathia?*

MR. ISMAY: We simply walked up a Jacob's ladder.

SENATOR SMITH: What was the condition of the sea at that time?

MR. ISMAY: There was a little ripple on it, nothing more.

SENATOR SMITH: Do you know whether all the lifeboats that left the *Titanic* were accounted for?

MR. ISMAY: I believe so. I do not know that of my own knowledge.

SENATOR SMITH: I think it has been suggested that two of them were engulfed.

MR. ISMAY: Of that I know nothing.

SENATOR SMITH: You would know if that were true, would you not?

MR. ISMAY: I have had no consultation with anybody since the accident with the exception of one officer.

SENATOR SMITH: Who was that?

MR. ISMAY: Mr. Lightoller. I have spoken to no member of the crew or anybody since in regard to the accident.

SENATOR SMITH: What was Mr. Lightoller's position?

MR. ISMAY: He was the second officer of the *Titanic*.

SENATOR SMITH: How many officers of the ship's crew were saved?

MR. ISMAY: I am told four.

SENATOR SMITH: Can you give their names?

MR. ISMAY: I can not.

SENATOR SMITH: Or their occupation?

MR. ISMAY: I could not. The only one I know is Mr. Lightoller, who was the second officer.

SENATOR SMITH: I understand they are here.

MR. ISMAY: I believe so; I do not know.

SENATOR SMITH: Mr. Ismay, what can you say about the sinking and disappearance of the ship? Can you describe the manner in which she went down?

MR. ISMAY: I did not see her go down.

SENATOR SMITH: You did not see her go down?

MR. ISMAY: No, sir.

SENATOR SMITH: How far were you from the ship?

MR. ISMAY: I do not know how far we were away. I was sitting with my back to the ship. I was rowing all the time I was in the boat. We were pulling away.

SENATOR SMITH: You were rowing?

MR. ISMAY: Yes; I did not wish to see her go down.

SENATOR SMITH: You did not care to see her go down?

MR. ISMAY: No. I am glad I did not.

SENATOR SMITH: When you last saw her, were there indications that she had broken in two?

MR. ISMAY: No, sir.

SENATOR SMITH: When did you last see her?

MR. ISMAY: I really could not say. It might have been 10 minutes after we left her. It is impossible for me to give any judgment of the time. I could not do it.

SENATOR SMITH: Was there much apparent confusion on board when you saw her last?

MR. ISMAY: I did not look to see, sir. My back was turned to her. I looked around once only, to see her red light—her green light, rather.

SENATOR SMITH: You never saw the captain again after you left him on the bridge?

17

MR. ISMAY: No, sir.

SENATOR SMITH: Did you have any message from him?

MR. ISMAY: Nothing.

SENATOR SMITH: Do you know how many wireless operators there were on board the ship?

MR. ISMAY: I do not; but I presume there were two. There is always one on watch.

SENATOR SMITH: Do you know whether they survived?

MR. ISMAY: I am told one of them did, but I do not know whether it is true or not. I really have not asked.

SENATOR SMITH: Were any of this crew enlisted men in the English Navy?

MR. ISMAY: I do not know, sir. The ship's articles will show that.

SENATOR SMITH: Can you tell us anything about the inspection, and the certificate that was made and issued before sailing?

MR. ISMAY: The ship receives a board of trade passenger certificate; otherwise she would not be allowed to carry passengers.

SENATOR SMITH: Do you know whether that was done?

MR. ISMAY: You could not sail your ship without it; you could not get your clearance.

SENATOR SMITH: Do you know whether this ship was equipped with its full complement of lifeboats?

MR. ISMAY: If she had not been, she could not have sailed. She would not have received her passenger certificate; therefore she must have been fully equipped.

SENATOR SMITH: Do you know whether these lifeboats were the lifeboats that were planned for the *Titanic?*

MR. ISMAY: I do not quite understand what you mean, sir. I do not think lifeboats are ever built for the ship. Lifeboats are built to have a certain cubic capacity.

SENATOR SMITH: I understand that; but I mean whether these lifeboats were completed for the ship coincident with the completion of the ship, or whether the lifeboats, or any of them, were borrowed from the other ships of the White Star Line?

MR. ISMAY: They certainly would not be borrowed from any other ship.

SENATOR SMITH: Do you recollect whether the lifeboat in

18

which you left the ship was marked with the name *Titanic* on the boat or on the oars?

MR. ISMAY: I have no idea. I presume oars would be marked. I do not know whether the boat was marked or not. She was a collapsible boat.

SENATOR SMITH: Can you recollect whether that was so?

MR. ISMAY: I did not look to see whether the oars were marked. It would be a natural precaution to take?

SENATOR SMITH: Mr. Ismay, do you know about the boiler construction of the *Titanic?*

MR. ISMAY: No, sir; I do not.

May I suggest, gentlemen, if you wish any information in regard to the construction of the ship, in any manner, shape, or form, that I shall be only too pleased to arrange for one of the Harlan & Wolf's people to come here and give you all the information you require; the plans and everything.

SENATOR SMITH: We are much obliged to you.

There has been some suggestion by passengers who left the ship in lifeboats, that an explosion took place after this collision. Have you any knowledge on that point?

MR. ISMAY: Absolutely none.

SENATOR SMITH: Do you think you would have known about that if it had occurred?

MR. ISMAY: Yes; I should. Do you mean to say before the ship went down?

SENATOR SMITH: Yes.

MR. ISMAY: Absolutely.

SENATOR SMITH: Mr. Ismay, do you know anything about the action of the amidship turbine; the number of revolutions?

MR. ISMAY: No.

MR. UHLER: The reciprocating engines, you say, were going at 75 or 72 revolutions at one time?

MR. ISMAY: Yes.

MR. UHLER: Have you any knowledge as to how many revolutions the amidship turbine was making?

MR. ISMAY: No, sir. Those are all technical questions which can be answered by others, if you desire.

SENATOR NEWLANDS: What speed would 75 revolutions indicate?

MR. ISMAY: I should think about 21 knots.

SENATOR NEWLANDS: What is that in miles?

MR. ISMAY: It is in the ratio of 11 to 13; about 26 miles, I think.

SENATOR NEWLANDS: Mr. Ismay, did you have anything to do with the selection of the men who accompanied you in the last boat?

MR. ISMAY: No, sir.

SENATOR NEWLANDS: How were they designated?

MR. ISMAY: I presume by the officer who was in charge of the boat.

SENATOR NEWLANDS: Who was that?

MR. ISMAY: Mr. Weyl [Chief Officer Henry Wilde].

SENATOR NEWLANDS: And he was what officer?

MR. ISMAY: Chief officer.

SENATOR NEWLANDS: Was that done by lot or by selection?

MR. ISMAY: I think these men were allotted certain posts.

SENATOR NEWLANDS: Indiscriminately?

MR. ISMAY: No; I fancy at the time they had what they called, I think, the boat's crew list. That is all arranged beforehand.

SENATOR SMITH: Can you describe those rafts?

MR. ISMAY: There were none on board the ship.

SENATOR SMITH: Did you see any rafts actually in service?

MR. ISMAY: No, sir.

SENATOR SMITH: Is it customary for the White Star Line to carry rafts?

MR. ISMAY: I believe in the olden days we carried rafts.

SENATOR SMITH: Recently that has not been done?

MR. ISMAY: Not in the recent ships; no, sir.

SENATOR SMITH: Why?

MR. ISMAY: I presume because they are not considered suitable.

SENATOR SMITH: Do you know what water capacity there was on that ship?

MR. ISMAY: I do not, sir.

SENATOR SMITH: I mean, when she was stove in, how many compartments could be flooded with safety?

MR. ISMAY: I beg your pardon, sir. I misunderstood your question. The ship was especially constructed to float with two compartments full of water.

SENATOR SMITH: She was constructed to float with two compartments full of water?

MR. ISMAY: The ship was specially constructed so that she would float with any two compartments full of water. I think I am right in saying that there are very few ships—perhaps I had better not say that, but I will continue, now that I have begun it—I believe there are very few ships today of which the same can be said.

When we built the *Titanic* we had that especially in mind. If this ship had hit the iceberg stem on, in all human probability she would have been here to-day.

SENATOR SMITH: If she had hit the iceberg head on, in all probability she would be here now?

MR. ISMAY: I say in all human probability that ship would have been afloat to-day.

SENATOR NEWLANDS: How did the ship strike the iceberg?

MR. ISMAY: From information I have received, I think she struck the iceberg a glancing blow between the end of the forecastle and the captain's bridge, just aft of the foremast, sir.

SENATOR SMITH: I understood you to say a little while ago that you were rowing, with your back to the ship. If you were rowing and going away from the ship, you would naturally be facing the ship, would you not?

MR. ISMAY: No; in these boats some row facing the bow of the boat and some facing the stern. I was seated with my back to the man who was steering, so that I was facing away from the ship.

SENATOR SMITH: You have stated that the ship was specially constructed so that she could float with two compartments filled with water?

MR. ISMAY: Yes.

SENATOR SMITH: Is it your idea, then, that there were no two compartments left entire?

MR. ISMAY: That I can not answer, sir. I am convinced that more than two compartments were filled. As I tried to explain to you last night, I think the ship's bilge was ripped open.

SENATOR NEWLANDS: The ship had 16 compartments?

MR. ISMAY: I could not answer that, sir.

SENATOR NEWLANDS: Approximately?

MR. ISMAY: Approximately. That information is absolutely at your disposal. Our shipbuilders will give it to you accurately.

SENATOR NEWLANDS: She was so built that if any two of these compartments should be filled with water she would still float?

MR. ISMAY: Yes, sir; if any two of the largest compartments were filled with water she would still float.

SENATOR SMITH: Mr. Ismay, what time did you dine on Sunday evening?

MR. ISMAY: At 7:30.

SENATOR SMITH: With whom?

MR. ISMAY: With the doctor.

SENATOR SMITH: Did the captain dine with you?

MR. ISMAY: He did not, sir.

SENATOR SMITH: When you went to the bridge after this collision, was there any ice on the decks?

MR. ISMAY: I saw no ice at all, and no icebergs at all until daylight Monday morning.

SENATOR SMITH: Do you know whether any people were injured or killed from ice that came to the decks?

MR. ISMAY: I do not, sir. I heard ice had been found on the decks, but it is only hearsay.

SENATOR SMITH: I think I asked you, but in case it appears that I have not, I will ask you again: Were all of the women and children saved?

MR. ISMAY: I am afraid not, sir.

SENATOR SMITH: What proportion were saved?

MR. ISMAY: I have no idea. I have not asked. Since the accident I have made very few inquiries of any sort.

SENATOR SMITH: Did any of the collapsible boats sink, to your knowledge, after leaving the ship?

MR. ISMAY: No, sir.

SENATOR NEWLANDS: What was the full equipment of life-boats for a ship of this size?

MR. ISMAY: I could not tell you that, sir. That is covered by the board of trade regulations. She may have exceeded the board of trade regulations, for all I know. I could not answer that question. Anyhow, she had sufficient boats to obtain her passenger certificate, and therefore she must have been fully boated, according to the requirements of the English Board of Trade, which I understand are accepted by this country. Is not that so, General?

MR. UHLER: Yes.

SENATOR SMITH: Mr. Ismay, did you in any manner attempt

to influence or interfere with the wireless communication between the *Carpathia* and other stations?

MR. ISMAY: No, sir. I think the captain of the *Carpathia* is here, and he will probably tell you that I was never out of my room from the time I got on board the *Carpathia* until the ship docked here last night. I never moved out of the room.

SENATOR SMITH: How were you dressed? Were you completely dressed when you went into the lifeboat?

MR. ISMAY: I had a suit of pajamas on, a pair of slippers, a suit of clothes, and an overcoat.

SENATOR SMITH: How many men, officers and crew, were there on this boat?

MR. ISMAY: There were no officers.

SENATOR SMITH: I mean the officers of the ship.

MR. ISMAY: How many officers were there on the ship?

SENATOR SMITH: Yes, and how many in the crew?

MR. ISMAY: I think there were seven officers on the ship.

SENATOR SMITH: And how many in the crew?

MR. ISMAY: I do not know the full number of the crew. There were seven officers—or nine officers; there are always three officers on watch.

SENATOR SMITH: And how many men were in the lifeboat with you?

MR. ISMAY: Oh, I could not tell. I suppose nine or ten.

SENATOR SMITH: Do you know who they were?

MR. ISMAY: I do not. Mr. [William] Carter, a passenger [a wealthy Philadelphian], was one. I do not know who the others were; third-class passengers, I think. In fact, all the people on the boat, as far as I could see, were third-class passengers.

SENATOR SMITH: Did they all survive, and were they all taken aboard the *Carpathia*?

MR. ISMAY: They all survived, yes.

Witness: Arthur Henry Rostron
Captain of the Cunard liner *Carpathia,* the only ship to come to the aid of *Titanic* survivors

Key testimony: The hero of the disaster testifying right on the heels of its scapegoat (Ismay), Rostron described the elabo-

rate steps that he had ordered for the rescue and care of survivors. He said the Carpathia, *bound to Gibraltar from New York, had been at sea three and a half days and was 58 miles away from the* Titanic *when it received its distress signal. (The* Carpathia's *wireless operator had been about to turn in for the night, yet happened to be still wearing his headphones as he was undressing.) Rostron answered general questions from Senator Smith about a captain's authority at sea that appeared to reflect the Senator's suspicion that Ismay had exerted undue influence over the* Titanic's *captain.*

. . . MR. ROSTRON: At 12:35 A.M. on Monday I was informed of the urgent distress signal from the *Titanic.*

SENATOR SMITH: By whom?

MR. ROSTRON: By our wireless operator, and also by the first officer.

The wireless operator had taken the message and run with it up to the bridge, and gave it to the first officer who was in charge, with a junior officer with him, and both ran down the ladder to my door and called me. I had only just turned in. It was an urgent distress signal from the *Titanic,* requiring immediate assistance and giving me his position.

The position of the *Titanic* at the time was 41° 46′ north, 50° 14′ west. I can not give you our correct position, but we were then——

SENATOR SMITH: Did you give the hour?

MR. ROSTRON: Yes, 12:35; that was our apparent time. I can give you the New York time, if you would rather have it?

SENATOR SMITH: Yes; please do so.

MR. ROSTRON: The New York time at 12:35 was 10:45 P.M. Sunday night.

Immediately on getting the message, I gave the order to turn the ship around, and immediately I had given that order I asked the operator if he was absolutely sure it was a distress signal from the *Titanic.* I asked him twice.

SENATOR SMITH: Just what was that signal?

MR. ROSTRON: I did not ask him. He simply told me that he had received a distress signal from the *Titanic,* requiring immediate assistance, and gave me his position; and he assured me he was absolutely certain of the message.

In the meantime I was dressing, and I picked up our position on my chart, and set a course to pick up the *Titanic*. The course was north 52 degrees west true 58 miles from my position.

I then sent for the chief engineer. In the meantime I was dressing and seeing the ship put on her course. The chief engineer came up. I told him to call another watch of stokers and make all possible speed to the *Titanic*, as she was in trouble.

He ran down immediately and told me my orders would be carried out at once.

After that I gave the first officer, who was in charge of the bridge, orders to knock off all work which the men were doing on deck, the watch on deck, and prepare all our lifeboats, take out the spare gear, and have them all ready for turning outboard.

Immediately I had done that I sent for the heads of the different departments, the English doctor, the purser, and the chief steward, and they came to my cabin, and then I issued my orders. I do not know whether you care to hear what my orders were exactly.

SENATOR SMITH: Yes, sir; we would like to hear them.

MR. ROSTRON: As a matter of fact, I have them all written down here.

We carry an English doctor, an Italian doctor, and a Hungarian doctor. My orders were these:

English doctor, with assistants, to remain in first-class dining room.

Italian doctor, with assistants, to remain in second-class dining room.

Hungarian doctor, with assistants, to remain in third-class dining room.

Each doctor to have supplies of restoratives, stimulants, and everything to hand for immediate needs of probable wounded or sick.

Purser, with assistant purser and chief steward, to receive the passengers, etc., at different gangways, controlling our own stewards in assisting *Titanic* passengers to the dining rooms, etc.; also to get Christian and surnames of all survivors as soon as possible to send by wireless.

Inspector, steerage stewards, and master at arms to

25

control our own steerage passengers and keep them out of the third-class dining hall, and also to keep them out of the way and off the deck to prevent confusion.

Chief steward: That all hands would be called and to have coffee, etc., ready to serve out to all our crew.

Have coffee, tea, soup, etc., in each saloon, blankets in saloons, at the gangways, and some for the boats.

To see all rescued cared for and immediate wants attended to.

My cabin and all officials' cabins to be given up. Smoke rooms, library, etc., dining rooms, would be utilized to accommodate the survivors.

All spare berths in steerage to be utilized for *Titanic*'s passengers, and get all our own steerage passengers grouped together.

Stewards to be placed in each alleyway to reassure our own passengers, should they inquire about noise in getting our boats out, etc., or the working of engines.

To all I strictly enjoined the necessity for order, discipline, and quietness and to avoid all confusion.

Chief and first officers: All the hands to be called; get coffee, etc. Prepare and swing out all boats.

All gangway doors to be opened.

Electric sprays in each gangway and over side.

A block with line rove hooked in each gangway.

A chair sling at each gangway, for getting up sick or wounded.

Boatswains' chairs. Pilot ladders and canvas ash bags to be at each gangway, the canvas ash bags for children.

I may state the canvas and bags were of great assistance in getting the infants and children aboard.

Cargo falls with both ends clear; bowlines in the ends, and bights secured along ship's sides, for boat ropes or to help the people up.

Heaving lines distributed along the ship's side, and gaskets handy near gangways for lashing people in chairs, etc.

Forward derricks, topped and rigged, and steam on winches; also told off officers for different stations and for certain eventualities.

Ordered company's rockets to be fired at 2:45 A.M. and every quarter of an hour after to reassure *Titanic*.

This is a copy of what I am sending to our own company.

SENATOR SMITH: We would like to have you leave a copy of that with the committee, if you can.

MR. ROSTRON: Yes, sir; I shall do it with pleasure.

One more thing:

As each official saw everything in readiness, he reported to me personally on the bridge that all my orders were carried out, enumerating the same, and that everything was in readiness.

This was at 3:45. That was a quarter of an hour before we got up to the scene of the disaster.

The details of all this work I left to the several officials, and I am glad to say that they were most efficiently carried out.

SENATOR SMITH: I should judge from what you say that you made 19¼ knots from the time you got the signal of distress from the *Titanic*, until you reached the scene of the wreck or loss?

MR. ROSTRON: No, it was 58 miles, and it took us three and a half hours.

MR. UHLER: From 12:35 to 3:45?

MR. ROSTRON: No; 3:45 is when they reported to me. I have not got to the time of arrival at the scene of action yet.

I stopped my engines at 4 o'clock, and I was then close to the first boat.

SENATOR SMITH: Just proceed, in your own way.

MR. ROSTRON: After interviewing the heads of the departments, I went on the bridge and remained there. While I was up there I made inquiries making sure that my orders were all being carried out, and that everything possible was being done.

At 2:40, I saw a flare, about half a point on the port bow, and immediately took it for granted that it was the *Titanic* itself, and I remarked that she must be still afloat, as I knew we were a long way off, and it seemed so high.

However, soon after seeing the flare I made out an

iceberg about a point on the port bow, to which I had to port to keep well clear of. Knowing that the *Titanic* had struck ice, of course I had to take extra care and every precaution to keep clear of anything that might look like ice.

Between 2:45 and 4 o'clock, the time I stopped my engines, we were passing icebergs on every side and making them ahead and having to alter our course several times to clear the bergs.

At 4 o'clock I stopped.

At 4:10 I got the first boat alongside.

Previous to getting the first boat alongside, however, I saw an iceberg close to me, right ahead, and I had to starboard to get out of the way. And I picked him up on the weather side of the ship. I had to clear this ice.

I am on the scene of action now. This is 4:10 with the first boat alongside.

SENATOR SMITH: You are picking up these people now?

MR. ROSTRON: Yes.

SENATOR SMITH: Please describe that in your own way.

MR. ROSTRON: We picked up the first boat, and the boat was in charge of an officer. I saw that he was not under full control of this boat, and the officer sung out to me that he only had one seaman in the boat, so I had to maneuver the ship to get as close to the boat as possible, as I knew well it would be difficult to do the pulling. However, they got alongside, and they got them up all right.

By the time we had the first boat's people it was breaking day, and then I could see the remaining boats all around within an area of about 4 miles. I also saw icebergs all around me. There were about 20 icebergs that would be anywhere from about 150 to 200 feet high and numerous smaller bergs; also numerous what we call "growlers." You would not call them bergs. They were anywhere from 10 to 12 feet high and 10 to 15 feet long above the water.

I maneuvered the ship and we gradually got all the boats together. We got all the boats alongside and all the people up aboard by 8:30.

I was then very close to where the *Titanic* must have gone down, as there was a lot of hardly wreckage but small pieces of broken-up stuff; nothing in the way of anything large.

At 8 o'clock the Leyland Line steamer *Californian* hove up, and we exchanged messages. I gave them the notes by semaphore about the *Titanic* going down, and that I had got all the passengers from the boats; but we were then not quite sure whether we could account for all the boats. I told them: "Think one boat still unaccounted for." He then asked me if he should search around, and I said, "Yes, please." It was then 10:50.

I want to go back again, a little bit.

At 8:30 all the people were on board. I asked for the purser, and told him that I wanted to hold a service, a short prayer of thankfulness for those rescued and a short burial service for those who were lost. I consulted with Mr. Ismay. I ran down for a moment and told them that I wished to do this, and Mr. Ismay left everything in my hands.

I then got an Episcopal clergyman, one of our passengers, and asked him if he would do this for me, which he did, willingly.

While they were holding the service, I was on the bridge, of course, and I maneuvered around the scene of the wreckage. We saw nothing except one body.

SENATOR SMITH: Floating?

MR. ROSTRON: Floating, sir.

SENATOR SMITH: With a life preserver on?

MR. ROSTRON: With a life preserver on. That is the only body I saw.

SENATOR SMITH: Was it male or female?

MR. ROSTRON: Male. It appeared to me to be one of the crew. He was only about 100 yards from the ship. We could see him quite distinctly, and saw that he was absolutely dead. He was lying on his side like this [indicating] and his head was awash. Of course he could not possibly have been alive and remain in that position. I did not take him aboard. For one reason, the *Titanic*'s passengers then were knocking about the deck and I did not want to cause any unnecessary excitement or any more hysteria among them, so I steamed past, trying to get them not to see it.

From the boats we took three dead men, who had died of exposure.

SENATOR SMITH: From the lifeboats?

MR. ROSTRON: From the lifeboats; yes, sir.

SENATOR SMITH: Do you know from which boats they were taken?

MR. ROSTRON: No, sir; I am only giving you the general news now. We took three dead men from the boats, and they were brought on board. Another man was brought up—I think he was one of the crew—who died that morning about 10 o'clock, I think, and he, with the other three, were buried at 4 o'clock in the afternoon.

SENATOR SMITH: At sea?

MR. ROSTRON: At sea.

SENATOR SMITH: Did they have anything on their persons by which they could be identified?

MR. ROSTRON: One of my own officers and the *Titanic*'s officers identified the bodies, as far as possible, and took everything from them that could be of the slightest clue or use. Nothing was left but their clothes. There was very little taken, of course. But, as regards details, I can not give you much. I have been too busy. . . .

SENATOR SMITH: Did you see any bodies afloat, except as you have described?

MR. ROSTRON: Only one; no more—no others.

SENATOR SMITH: Did you have any information as to whether the passengers or crew of the *Titanic* had made use of their life preservers?

MR. ROSTRON: I had very little opportunity of being amongst the passengers or any of them. . . . They had all been supplied with life belts.

SENATOR SMITH: I assume that you kept watch to see whether there was any of these people afloat?

MR. ROSTRON: Precisely. I was cruising all around the vicinity of the disaster.

SENATOR SMITH: How long did you cruise around there?

MR. ROSTRON: In the actual vicinity of the disaster?

SENATOR SMITH: Yes.

MR. ROSTRON: Half an hour.

SENATOR SMITH: During that time was there a swirl or any unnatural condition of the sea?

MR. ROSTRON: Nothing whatever. The wind and sea were then beginning to get up. There was a moderate breeze blowing then, and a little slop of the sea.

SENATOR SMITH: Have you any idea how much depth of water there was about that point?

MR. ROSTRON: Yes; about two thousand and odd fathoms.

SENATOR SMITH: Two thousand and odd fathoms?

MR. ROSTRON: Yes; I looked on the chart.

SENATOR SMITH: Have you concluded that you did not see the ill-fated ship at all?

MR. ROSTRON: Oh, no; we arrived an hour and a half after she went down; after the last of her was seen. . . .

SENATOR SMITH: Would you regard the course taken by the *Titanic* in this trial trip as appropriate and safe and wise at this time of the year?

MR. ROSTRON: Quite so.

SENATOR SMITH: What would be a safe, reasonable speed for a vessel of that size on such a course and in proximity of icebergs?

MR. ROSTRON: Of course I do not know the ship. I know absolutely nothing about her.

SENATOR SMITH: How would you have felt yourself about it? Suppose you had been taking that course with your ship; how fast would you have felt it prudent to go in such a situation?

MR. ROSTRON: I can only tell you this, gentlemen, I knew there was ice about——

SENATOR SMITH: How did you know it?

MR. ROSTRON: From the *Titanic*.

SENATOR SMITH: From the *Titanic's* message?

MR. ROSTRON: Precisely. He told me he had struck ice.

SENATOR SMITH: Did you know it any other way?

MR. ROSTRON: No, sir; that was the first intimation I had that there was ice there.

SENATOR SMITH: You did not know it until you saw it yourself?

MR. ROSTRON: I knew the *Titanic* had struck ice. Therefore, I was prepared to be in the vicinity of ice when I was getting near him, because if he had struck a berg and I was going to his position I knew very well that there must be ice about. I went full speed, all we could——

SENATOR SMITH: You went full speed?

MR. ROSTRON: I did, and doubled my lookouts, and took extra precautions and exerted extra vigilance. Every possible care was taken. We were all on the qui vive.

SENATOR SMITH: You had a smaller ship, however, and it would respond more readily to a signal?

MR. ROSTRON: No.

SENATOR SMITH: Would it not?

MR. ROSTRON: No, sir; it would not. I do not maintain that, for one moment.

SENATOR SMITH: How many men were on the bridge, on the lookout, so to speak, in that situation, on your ship?

MR. ROSTRON: There were three officers with me: A quartermaster, one man in the crow's nest, and two men in the eyes of the ship—that is, right forward on the deck, nearer to the water than the crow's nest.

SENATOR SMITH: Was that the ordinary complement, or did you put them there because of that danger?

MR. ROSTRON: I put an extra lookout on forward.

SENATOR SMITH: An extra lookout?

MR. ROSTRON: Yes; and the officer came up extra with me. I had another officer up with me, extra. He came up voluntarily.

SENATOR SMITH: What would be the ordinary complement?

MR. ROSTRON: The ordinary complement of a night lookout, two men. We keep one in the crow's nest and one in the eyes—that is, right forward. . . .

SENATOR SMITH: How many lifeboats do you carry on the *Carpathia?*

MR. ROSTRON: We carry 20.

SENATOR SMITH: What is their capacity?

MR. ROSTRON: I am not prepared to say at the present moment. I can not say; I really forget.

SENATOR SMITH: Do you carry 20 in obedience to certain regulations of the British Board of Trade?

MR. ROSTRON: I think it is 20; yes.

SENATOR SMITH: What is your gross tonnage?

MR. ROSTRON: Thirteen thousand six hundred tons.

SENATOR SMITH: That is the total capacity of your ship, the tonnage?

MR. ROSTRON: Thirteen thousand six hundred.

SENATOR SMITH: What is it as to passengers?

MR. ROSTRON: I can not tell you. I have not come here with any data. I have not looked up anything, and was absolutely unprepared for any questions. I have been too busy.

SENATOR SMITH: What did you say was the tonnage of your ship?

MR. ROSTRON: Thirteen thousand six hundred tons.

Senator Smith: What was the tonnage of the *Titanic?*

Mr. Uhler: It was 45,629 tons.

Senator Smith: Are these regulations of the British Board of Trade new regulations or old regulations?

Mr. Rostron: They are of recent date.

Senator Smith: The fact that, under these regulations, you are obliged to carry 20 lifeboats and the *Titanic* was only obliged to carry 20, with her additional tonnage, indicates either that these regulations were prescribed long ago——

Mr. Rostron (interposing): No, sir; it has nothing to do with that. What it has to do with is the ship itself.

The ships are built nowadays to be practically unsinkable, and each ship is supposed to be a lifeboat in itself. The boats are merely supposed to be put on as a standby. The ships are supposed to be built, and the naval architects say they are, unsinkable under certain conditions. What the exact conditions are, I do not know, as to whether it is with alternate compartments full, or what it may be. That is why in our ship we carry more lifeboats, for the simple reason that we are built differently from the *Titanic;* differently constructed. . . .

Senator Smith: You say the captain of a ship is vested ordinarily with absolute control and discretion over the movements of his vessel?

Mr. Rostron: Absolutely. I wish to qualify that, however. By law, the captain of the vessel has absolute control, but suppose we get orders from the owners of the vessel to do a certain thing and we do not carry it out. The only thing is then that we are liable to dismissal.

I shall give you an illustration of what I mean by that, as regards receiving orders, and so on. When I turned back to New York, I sent my message to the Cunard Co. telling them that I was proceeding to New York unless otherwise ordered. You see what I mean there? I said, "For many considerations, consider New York most advisable."

Senator Smith: And you immediately reversed your course?

Mr. Rostron: I came right around for New York immediately, and returned to New York.

Would you like to know my reasons for coming back to New York?

SENATOR SMITH: Yes.

MR. ROSTRON: The first and principal reason was that we had all these women aboard, and I knew they were hysterical and in a bad state. I knew very well, also, that you would want all the news possible. I knew very well, further, that if I went to Halifax, we could get them there all right, but I did not know how many of these people were half dead, how many were injured, or how many were really sick, or anything like that. I knew, also, that if we went to Halifax, we would have the possibility of coming across more ice, and I knew very well what the effect of that would be on people who had had the experience these people had had. I knew what that would be the whole time we were in the vicinity of ice. I took that into consideration. I knew very well that if we went to Halifax it would be a case of railway journey for these passengers, as I knew they would have to go to New York, and there would be all the miseries of that.

Furthermore, I did not know what the condition of the weather might be, or what accommodation I could give them in Halifax, and that was a great consideration—one of the greatest considerations that made me turn back. . . .

SENATOR SMITH: You say, Captain, that you ran under a full head of steam?

MR. ROSTRON: Yes.

SENATOR SMITH: Toward the *Titanic?*

MR. ROSTRON: Yes, sir.

SENATOR SMITH: Would you have done so in the nighttime?

MR. ROSTRON: It was in the nighttime. I can confess this much, that if I had known at the time there was so much ice about, I should not; but I was right in it then. I could see the ice. I knew I was perfectly clear.

There is one other consideration: Although I was running a risk with my own ship and my own passengers, I also had to consider what I was going for.

SENATOR SMITH: To save the lives of others?

MR. ROSTRON: Yes; I had to consider the lives of others.

SENATOR SMITH: You were prompted by your interest in humanity?

MR. ROSTRON: Absolutely.

SENATOR SMITH: And you took the chance?

MR. ROSTRON: It was hardly a chance. Of course it was a chance, but at the same time I knew quite what I was doing. I considered that I was perfectly free, and that I was doing perfectly right in what I did.

SENATOR SMITH: I suppose no criticism has been passed upon you for it?

MR. ROSTRON: No.

SENATOR SMITH: In fact, I think I may say, for my associates, that your conduct deserves the highest praise.

MR. ROSTRON: I thank you, sir. . . .

SENATOR SMITH: How far can you communicate [using the *Carpathia*'s short-range wireless]?

MR. ROSTRON: Under good conditions, 200 miles. We only reckon, under ordinary conditions, on 150 miles. Fog, mist, haze, snow, or any other unfavorable weather conditions make it so that we may not get more than 90 to 100 miles.

SENATOR SMITH: It was rather accidental, then, that you happened to be within the radius of your instrument when you got the *Titanic*?

MR. ROSTRON: Yes; we were only 58 miles away then.

SENATOR SMITH: It was providential?

MR. ROSTRON: The whole thing was absolutely providential. I will tell you this, that the wireless operator was in his cabin, at the time, not on official business at all, but just simply listening as he was undressing. He was unlacing his boots at the time. He had this apparatus on his ear, and the message came. That was the whole thing. In 10 minutes maybe he would have been in bed, and we would not have heard the message.

SENATOR SMITH: It was a very remarkable coincidence. . . .

Witness: Charles Herbert Lightoller, 38
Titanic's Second Officer, from Hampshire, England

Key testimony: The scattershot questioning of Lightoller, in which Senator Smith jumped from topic to topic, illustrated the fact that the Senator had had little time to prepare for the

*hearings. A career seaman, Lightoller spoke with some
pride of lifesaving precautions aboard the Titanic. It had the
maximum number of lifeboats stipulated in British regulations, but the rules hadn't kept pace with the growing size of
ships. Like other officers, Lightoller underfilled the few lifeboats there were, making subjective judgments on how
much weight the boats and their davits could withstand
while being lowered, regardless of their capacity in the
water. He explained the difficulty in finding enough women
and children for the boats. And he told of diving off the top
of the sinking ship, getting sucked underwater against a
funnel and finally climbing to safety aboard an overturned
lifeboat.*

. . . SENATOR SMITH: When did you go aboard the *Titanic?*
MR. LIGHTOLLER: In Belfast.
SENATOR SMITH: When?
MR. LIGHTOLLER: March 19 or 20.
SENATOR SMITH: Did you make the so-called trial trips?
MR. LIGHTOLLER: Yes, sir.
SENATOR SMITH: Of what did they consist?
MR. LIGHTOLLER: Turning circles and adjusting compasses.
SENATOR SMITH: In what waters?
MR. LIGHTOLLER: Belfast Lough. . . .
SENATOR SMITH: From the time you boarded the *Titanic* did
   you at any time encounter any rough weather?
MR. LIGHTOLLER: No, sir.
SENATOR SMITH: You were always in smooth water, so called?
MR. LIGHTOLLER: Yes, sir.
SENATOR SMITH: Does that include up to the time of this
   collision?
MR. LIGHTOLLER: Yes, sir.
SENATOR SMITH: Of what do these trial tests consist?
MR. LIGHTOLLER: Turning circles.
SENATOR SMITH: I wish you would describe that a little more
   fully. Under what head of steam and how fast would the
   boat be moving?
MR. LIGHTOLLER: Under various speeds.
SENATOR SMITH: In how large a radius would these circles be
   made?
MR. LIGHTOLLER: Turning circles consists of seeing in what

space the ship will turn under certain helms with the engines at various speeds.

SENATOR SMITH: Was this boat tested at its maximum speed?

MR. LIGHTOLLER: That I could not say, sir.

SENATOR SMITH: What was the maximum speed of this boat?

MR. LIGHTOLLER: That I could not say, sir. She was never put, to my knowledge, to her maximum speed. . . .

SENATOR SMITH: I want to be sure I get the results of these trial tests accurately. I want you to tell me how long it took to make these tests. The straightaway tests and the circle tests altogether consumed how much time?

MR. LIGHTOLLER: Approximately six or seven hours. I could not say any nearer than that. . . .

SENATOR SMITH: Was the life-saving equipment complete?

MR. LIGHTOLLER: Yes, sir.

SENATOR SMITH: Of what did it consist?

MR. LIGHTOLLER: The necessary number of lifeboats.

SENATOR SMITH: I wish you would say how that is determined, if you can.

MR. LIGHTOLLER: By the number of people on board.

SENATOR SMITH: You do not know how many there are on board until you are ready to start?

MR. LIGHTOLLER: No sir.

SENATOR SMITH: Is it not determined by the number of accommodations rather than by the number of people who get aboard?

MR. LIGHTOLLER: There must be life-saving apparatus for every one on board, regardless of accommodations.

SENATOR SMITH: Yes; but what I desire to know is whether in each stateroom on each deck, in all classes, whether there is any rule, and whether it was followed at that time, so far as you know, in equipping this boat with life preservers and life belts and anything else that might appropriately go into the rooms and be upon the decks of a boat of that character?

MR. LIGHTOLLER: She was perfectly complete throughout, sir.

SENATOR SMITH: How many lifeboats were there?

MR. LIGHTOLLER: Sixteen.

SENATOR SMITH: All of the same type?

MR. LIGHTOLLER: Consisting of 14 lifeboats, 2 emergency boats, and 4 collapsible boats.

37

SENATOR SMITH: Tell us whether they were new entirely.

MR. LIGHTOLLER: Entirely new.

SENATOR SMITH: And in their proper places?

MR. LIGHTOLLER: In their proper places.

SENATOR SMITH: With the necessary lowering apparatus?

MR. LIGHTOLLER: Everything complete, examined by the officers of the ship.

SENATOR SMITH: Was a test of the lifeboats made before you sailed for Southampton?

MR. LIGHTOLLER: All the gear was tested. . . .

SENATOR SMITH: Had you ever seen one of those ocean liners inspected by the British Board of Trade representative before?

MR. LIGHTOLLER: Frequently.

SENATOR SMITH: How thorough are they about it?

MR. LIGHTOLLER: Speaking of Capt. Clark, we call him a nuisance because he is so strict.

SENATOR SMITH: Capt. Clark?

MR. LIGHTOLLER: Yes, sir.

SENATOR SMITH: Is he the marine officer?

MR. LIGHTOLLER: That is the board of trade representative.

SENATOR SMITH: In what respect is he a nuisance?

MR. LIGHTOLLER: Because he makes us fork out every detail.

SENATOR SMITH: I should suppose you would be quite willing to do that?

MR. LIGHTOLLER: Perfectly willing.

SENATOR SMITH: Do you mean by that that he would call attention to the absence of tools, implements, and devices necessary for the ship's full equipment?

MR. LIGHTOLLER: No, sir. He would insist upon them all being absolutely brought out on deck every time.

SENATOR SMITH: On what?

MR. LIGHTOLLER: Everything that contributes to the ship's equipment.

SENATOR SMITH: What would that consist of?

MR. LIGHTOLLER: The whole of the ship's life-saving equipment.

SENATOR SMITH: Life preservers?

MR. LIGHTOLLER: Life preservers throughout the ship, all the boats turned out, uncovered, all the tanks examined, all

38

the breakers examined, oars counted, boats turned out, rudders tried, all the davits tried—there was innumerable detail work.

SENATOR SMITH: And the boats lowered?

MR. LIGHTOLLER: The boats lowered, put in the water, and pulled out, and brought back again, and if he was not satisfied, sent back again.

SENATOR SMITH: And the ropes and chains tested?

MR. LIGHTOLLER: Yes, sir.

SENATOR SMITH: When he inspected your ship, about where would he find these life preservers?

MR. LIGHTOLLER: Life belts in every room, in every compartment, where, as we say, there was habitation, where a man could live. . . .

SENATOR SMITH: I wish you would describe a life belt.

MR. LIGHTOLLER: It consists of a series of pieces of cork—allow me to show you by illustration—a hole is cut in there [illustrating] for the head to go through and this falls over front and back, and there are tapes from the back then tied around the front. It is a new idea and very effective, because no one can make a mistake in putting it on.

SENATOR SMITH: Is there cork on both sides?

MR. LIGHTOLLER: On both sides.

SENATOR SMITH: Are the arms free?

MR. LIGHTOLLER: Free, absolutely.

SENATOR SMITH: And when in the water does this adhere or extend?

MR. LIGHTOLLER: It is tied to the body.

SENATOR SMITH: It is tied to the body?

MR. LIGHTOLLER: Yes, sir.

SENATOR SMITH: Have you ever had one of these on?

MR. LIGHTOLLER: Yes, sir.

SENATOR SMITH: Have you ever been into the sea with one of them?

MR. LIGHTOLLER: Yes, sir.

SENATOR SMITH: Where?

MR. LIGHTOLLER: From the *Titanic*.

SENATOR SMITH: In this recent collision?

MR. LIGHTOLLER: Yes, sir.

SENATOR SMITH: How long were you in the sea with a life belt on?

MR. LIGHTOLLER: Between half an hour and an hour.

SENATOR SMITH: What time did you leave the ship?

MR. LIGHTOLLER: I didn't leave it.

SENATOR SMITH: Did the ship leave you?

MR. LIGHTOLLER: Yes, sir.

SENATOR SMITH: Did you stay until the ship had departed entirely?

MR. LIGHTOLLER: Yes, sir.

SENATOR SMITH: I wish you would tell us whether the suction incidental to the sinking of this vessel was a great deterrent in making progress away from the boat?

MR. LIGHTOLLER: It was hardly noticeable.

SENATOR SMITH: From what point on the vessel did you leave it?

MR. LIGHTOLLER: On top of the officers' quarters.

SENATOR SMITH: And where were the officers' quarters?

MR. LIGHTOLLER: Immediately abaft the bridge.

SENATOR SMITH: Immediately abaft the bridge?

MR. LIGHTOLLER: Abaft the wheelhouse.

SENATOR SMITH: Was that pretty well toward the top of the vessel?

MR. LIGHTOLLER: Yes, sir. . . .

SENATOR SMITH: Had the passengers the right to go on [the boat] deck from below?

MR. LIGHTOLLER: Every right.

SENATOR SMITH: There was no restraint at the staircase?

MR. LIGHTOLLER: None.

SENATOR SMITH: Was that true as to the steerage?

MR. LIGHTOLLER: The steerage have no right up there, sir.

SENATOR SMITH: Did they on that occasion?

MR. LIGHTOLLER: Oh, yes.

SENATOR SMITH: There was no restraint?

MR. LIGHTOLLER: Oh, absolutely none.

SENATOR SMITH: There must have been considerable confusion.

MR. LIGHTOLLER: Not that I noticed.

SENATOR SMITH: Was everybody orderly?

MR. LIGHTOLLER: Perfectly. . . .

SENATOR SMITH: Did you believe the boat was in danger [after hitting the iceberg]?

MR. LIGHTOLLER: No, sir.

SENATOR SMITH: You felt that it was not a serious accident?

MR. LIGHTOLLER: I did not think it was a serious accident.

SENATOR SMITH: What was the force of the impact?

MR. LIGHTOLLER: A slight jar and a grinding sound.

SENATOR SMITH: From front or side?

MR. LIGHTOLLER: Well, naturally I should think it was in front, whether I could tell or not.

SENATOR SMITH: You could not tell exactly?

MR. LIGHTOLLER: No, sir.

SENATOR SMITH: Was there a noise?

MR. LIGHTOLLER: Very little.

SENATOR SMITH: Very little?

MR. LIGHTOLLER: Very little.

SENATOR SMITH: Did you go back to your room under the impression that the boat had not been injured?

MR. LIGHTOLLER: Yes, sir.

SENATOR SMITH: Didn't you tell Mr. Ismay that that night?

MR. LIGHTOLLER: I had not seen Mr. Ismay then.

SENATOR SMITH: Did you tell him that afterwards?

MR. LIGHTOLLER: Really, I could not say, sir.

SENATOR SMITH: Where were you when the impact occurred?

MR. LIGHTOLLER: In my berth.

SENATOR SMITH: Asleep?

MR. LIGHTOLLER: No, sir; I was just getting off asleep.

SENATOR SMITH: You arose?

MR. LIGHTOLLER: Yes, sir.

SENATOR SMITH: Did you dress yourself?

MR. LIGHTOLLER: No, sir.

SENATOR SMITH: What did you put on, if anything?

MR. LIGHTOLLER: Nothing.

SENATOR SMITH: You went out of your room?

MR. LIGHTOLLER: Yes, sir.

SENATOR SMITH: Forward?

MR. LIGHTOLLER: Out on deck.

SENATOR SMITH: On deck?

MR. LIGHTOLLER: Yes; I walked forward.

SENATOR SMITH: You walked forward how far?

MR. LIGHTOLLER: A matter of 10 feet, until I could see the bridge distinctly.

SENATOR SMITH: You could see the bridge distinctly; and the captain was on the bridge?

MR. LIGHTOLLER: The captain and first officer.

SENATOR SMITH: Did you see any other officers at that time?

MR. LIGHTOLLER: I did not notice them.

SENATOR SMITH: Had no alarm been given at that time?

MR. LIGHTOLLER: None.

SENATOR SMITH: How much time elapsed after the impact and your appearance on the deck?

MR. LIGHTOLLER: I should say about two or three minutes.

SENATOR SMITH: Two or three minutes?

MR. LIGHTOLLER: Two minutes.

SENATOR SMITH: Then you returned? How long did you remain on deck?

MR. LIGHTOLLER: About two or three minutes.

SENATOR SMITH: At that time who else was on deck at that point?

MR. LIGHTOLLER: Excluding the bridge, I saw no one except the third officer, who left his berth shortly after I did.

SENATOR SMITH: Did he join you?

MR. LIGHTOLLER: Yes.

SENATOR SMITH: Did you confer about what had happened?

MR. LIGHTOLLER: Yes, sir.

SENATOR SMITH: What did you conclude had happened?

MR. LIGHTOLLER: Nothing much.

SENATOR SMITH: You knew there had been a collision?

MR. LIGHTOLLER: Not necessarily a collision.

SENATOR SMITH: You knew you had struck something?

MR. LIGHTOLLER: Yes, sir.

SENATOR SMITH: What did you assume it to be?

MR. LIGHTOLLER: Ice.

SENATOR SMITH: Ice?

MR. LIGHTOLLER: Yes, sir.

SENATOR SMITH: Why?

MR. LIGHTOLLER: That was the conclusion one naturally jumps to around the Banks there.

SENATOR SMITH: Had you seen ice before?

MR. LIGHTOLLER: No, sir.

SENATOR SMITH: Had there been any tests taken of the temperature of the water?

MR. LIGHTOLLER: A test is taken of the water every two hours from the time the ship leaves until she returns to port.

SENATOR SMITH: Do you know whether these tests were made?

MR. LIGHTOLLER: They were.

SENATOR SMITH: Did you make them?

MR. LIGHTOLLER: Oh, no, sir.

SENATOR SMITH: Were they made under your direction?

MR. LIGHTOLLER: No, sir.

SENATOR SMITH: How do you know they were made?

MR. LIGHTOLLER: It is the routine of the ship.

SENATOR SMITH: You assume they were made?

MR. LIGHTOLLER: Yes, sir.

SENATOR SMITH: But you can not say of your own knowledge that they were?

MR. LIGHTOLLER: Not of my own actually seeing; no, sir.

SENATOR SMITH: How were these tests made?

MR. LIGHTOLLER: By drawing water from over the side in a canvas bucket and placing a thermometer in it.

SENATOR SMITH: How far down did you dip this water; did you try to get surface water, or did you try to get below?

MR. LIGHTOLLER: It is impossible to get water below; just the surface.

SENATOR SMITH: You get surface water entirely?

MR. LIGHTOLLER: Yes, sir.

SENATOR SMITH: Those tests had been made that day?

MR. LIGHTOLLER: Yes.

SENATOR SMITH: At intervals of two hours?

MR. LIGHTOLLER: Yes, sir.

SENATOR SMITH: This was on Sunday?

MR. LIGHTOLLER: Yes, sir.

SENATOR SMITH: Did you hear anything about the rope or chain or wire to which the test basins were attached not reaching the water at any time during those tests?

MR. LIGHTOLLER: The bucket, you speak of?

SENATOR SMITH: Yes.

MR. LIGHTOLLER: No, sir.

SENATOR SMITH: Would a complaint of that character come to you if it had been true?

MR. LIGHTOLLER: Very quickly, I should think, sir.

SENATOR SMITH: How would it come to you?

MR. LIGHTOLLER: From the person who saw it, I should think.

SENATOR SMITH: It would be his duty to report to you?

MR. LIGHTOLLER: Undoubtedly.

43

SENATOR SMITH: Directly to you?

MR. LIGHTOLLER: Directly to the officer in charge of the ship at the time.

SENATOR SMITH: Who was in charge of the ship on Sunday?

MR. LIGHTOLLER: Each officer kept his own watch, sir.

SENATOR SMITH: Were you in charge?

MR. LIGHTOLLER: During my watch.

SENATOR SMITH: What hours were your watch?

MR. LIGHTOLLER: Six o'clock until 10 o'clock.

SENATOR SMITH: At night?

MR. LIGHTOLLER: And morning.

SENATOR SMITH: So that from 6 o'clock in the evening on Sunday——

MR. LIGHTOLLER: Yes, sir.

SENATOR SMITH: Until 10 o'clock you were in charge?

MR. LIGHTOLLER: Yes, sir.

SENATOR SMITH: And during that time two tests should have been made of the temperature of the water for the purpose of ascertaining whether you were in the vicinity of icebergs?

MR. LIGHTOLLER: No, sir.

SENATOR SMITH: For what purpose were the tests made?

MR. LIGHTOLLER: They were routine, sir. It is customary to make them.

SENATOR SMITH: Do you mean that you take these tests when you are not in the vicinity of the Grand Banks?

MR. LIGHTOLLER: From the time we leave port, any port in the world, until the time we get to the next port in any part of the world, these tests are taken by the White Star Line. . . .

SENATOR SMITH: Did you know of the wireless message from the *Amerika* to the *Titanic,* warning you that you were in the vicinity of icebergs?

MR. LIGHTOLLER: From the *Amerika* to the *Titanic*?

SENATOR SMITH: Yes.

MR. LIGHTOLLER: I can not say that I saw that individual message.

SENATOR SMITH: Did you hear of it?

MR. LIGHTOLLER: I could not say, sir.

SENATOR SMITH: Would you have heard of it?

MR. LIGHTOLLER: Most probably, sir.

SENATOR SMITH: If that had been the case?

MR. LIGHTOLLER: Most probably, sir.

SENATOR SMITH: In fact, it would have been the duty of the person receiving this message to communicate it to you, for you were in charge of the ship?

MR. LIGHTOLLER: Under the commander's orders, sir.

SENATOR SMITH: But you received no communication of that kind?

MR. LIGHTOLLER: I do not know whether I received the *Amerika's*; I knew that a communication had come from some ship; I can not say that it was the *Amerika*.

SENATOR SMITH: Giving the latitude and the longitude of those icebergs?

MR. LIGHTOLLER: No; no latitude.

SENATOR SMITH: And that they were prevalent?

MR. LIGHTOLLER: Speaking of the icebergs and naming their longitude. . . .

SENATOR SMITH: From whom did you get that information?

MR. LIGHTOLLER: From the captain.

SENATOR SMITH: That night?

MR. LIGHTOLLER: Yes. . . .

SENATOR SMITH: Who succeeded you as officer of the ship?

MR. LIGHTOLLER: The first officer, Mr. Murdoch.

SENATOR SMITH: Did you communicate to him this information that the captain had given you on the bridge?

MR. LIGHTOLLER: I communicated that when I was relieving him at 1 o'clock.

SENATOR SMITH: What did you tell him?

MR. LIGHTOLLER: Exactly what was in the telegram.

SENATOR SMITH: What did he say?

MR. LIGHTOLLER: "All right." . . .

SENATOR SMITH: How fast was the boat going at that time?

MR. LIGHTOLLER: About 21½ or 22.

SENATOR SMITH: 21½ or 22 knots?

MR. LIGHTOLLER: Yes, sir.

SENATOR SMITH: Was that her maximum speed?

MR. LIGHTOLLER: I do not know, sir. I could not say, sir. . . .

SENATOR SMITH: Did you have any instructions from anybody to exhaust that power?

MR. LIGHTOLLER: None.

SENATOR SMITH: Did you have any ambition of your own to see it exhausted?

MR. LIGHTOLLER: Yes; I dare say.

SENATOR SMITH: You wanted her to go as fast as she could?

MR. LIGHTOLLER: At some time or other; yes. . . .

SENATOR SMITH: You were anxious to see it tested?

MR. LIGHTOLLER: Not necessarily anxious.

SENATOR SMITH: Interested, however?

MR. LIGHTOLLER: Interested; yes. . . .

SENATOR SMITH: Was the lookout increased that evening after you took the watch?

MR. LIGHTOLLER: No, sir.

SENATOR SMITH: What was the complement of your ship that night, in officers?

MR. LIGHTOLLER: You mean on deck, sir?

SENATOR SMITH: Yes, sir.

MR. LIGHTOLLER: Myself and two juniors.

SENATOR SMITH: Where were those two juniors stationed?

MR. LIGHTOLLER: They have various duties to perform, taking the various parts of the ship; sometimes in the wheelhouse; at different periods one has to go the whole rounds of the ship and see that everything is in order.

SENATOR SMITH: When you came on watch at 6 o'clock, was the captain on the bridge, or did you see him?

MR. LIGHTOLLER: I didn't see him at 6 o'clock.

SENATOR SMITH: When did you next see him?

MR. LIGHTOLLER: About five minutes to 9 was the next time I saw him.

SENATOR SMITH: About five minutes to 9?

MR. LIGHTOLLER: Yes, sir.

SENATOR SMITH: In his absence, who was on the bridge?

MR. LIGHTOLLER: Myself.

SENATOR SMITH: Did you relieve him?

MR. LIGHTOLLER: The captain?

SENATOR SMITH: Yes.

MR. LIGHTOLLER: No, sir. The first officer. I beg your pardon; I relieved the chief.

SENATOR SMITH: You relieved the chief?

MR. LIGHTOLLER: Yes, sir.

SENATOR SMITH: And went to the bridge?

MR. LIGHTOLLER: I relieved the chief. The chief's watch was from 2 until 6. I relieved the chief officer at 6 o'clock and carried on the watch until 10.

SENATOR SMITH: Did you remain on the bridge?

MR. LIGHTOLLER: Yes, sir.

SENATOR SMITH: From 6 until 10 o'clock?

MR. LIGHTOLLER: Yes, sir. . . .

SENATOR SMITH: Who was there, and where were they stationed?

MR. LIGHTOLLER: Two men in the crow's nest, one man at the wheel, one man standing by.

SENATOR SMITH: What was the weather that night?

MR. LIGHTOLLER: Clear and calm.

SENATOR SMITH: Were you at all apprehensive about your proximity to these icebergs?

MR. LIGHTOLLER: No, sir.

SENATOR SMITH: And for that reason you did not think it necessary to increase the official lookout?

MR. LIGHTOLLER: No, sir. . . .

SENATOR SMITH: From 6 until 10 o'clock was the captain on the bridge at all?

MR. LIGHTOLLER: Yes, sir.

SENATOR SMITH: When did he arrive?

MR. LIGHTOLLER: Five minutes to 9.

SENATOR SMITH: Five minutes to 9?

MR. LIGHTOLLER: Yes, sir.

SENATOR SMITH: But he was not there from 6 o'clock until five minutes of 9?

MR. LIGHTOLLER: I did not see him, sir.

SENATOR SMITH: You would have seen him if he had been there, would you not?

MR. LIGHTOLLER: If he had been actually on the bridge, yes, I should have seen him.

SENATOR SMITH: You did not see him?

MR. LIGHTOLLER: I did not see him.

SENATOR SMITH: And you were there during all that time?

MR. LIGHTOLLER: During all that time.

SENATOR SMITH: When he came to the bridge at five minutes of 9 what did he say to you or what did you say to him? Who spoke first?

MR. LIGHTOLLER: I could not say, sir. Probably one of us said "Good evening."

SENATOR SMITH: But you do not know who?

MR. LIGHTOLLER: No.

SENATOR SMITH: Was anything else said?

Mr. LIGHTOLLER: Yes. We spoke about the weather; calmness of the sea; the clearness; about the time we should be getting up toward the vicinity of the ice and how we should recognize it if we should see it—freshening up our minds as to the indications that ice gives of its proximity. We just conferred together, generally, for 25 minutes.

SENATOR SMITH: For 20 or 25 minutes?

Mr. LIGHTOLLER: Yes, sir.

SENATOR SMITH: Was any reference made at that time to the wireless message from the *Amerika?*

Mr. LIGHTOLLER: Capt. Smith made a remark that if it was in a slight degree hazy there would be no doubt we should have to go very slowly.

SENATOR SMITH: Did you slow up?

Mr. LIGHTOLLER: That I do not know, sir. . . .

SENATOR SMITH: Do you know where you were at the hour that you turned over the watch to Mr. [First Officer William] Murdoch?

Mr. LIGHTOLLER: Not now, sir.

SENATOR SMITH: Did you know at the time?

Mr. LIGHTOLLER: Yes, sir.

SENATOR SMITH: Can you give us any idea?

Mr. LIGHTOLLER: When I ended the watch we roughly judged that we should be getting toward the vicinity of the ice, as reported by that Marconigram that I saw, somewhere about 11 o'clock.

SENATOR SMITH: That you would be in that latitude?

Mr. LIGHTOLLER: Longitude.

SENATOR SMITH: At 11 o'clock.

Mr. LIGHTOLLER: Somewhere about 11; yes.

SENATOR SMITH: Did you talk with Mr. Murdoch about that phase of it when you left the watch?

Mr. LIGHTOLLER: About what?

SENATOR SMITH: I say, did you talk with Mr. Murdoch about the iceberg situation when you left the watch?

Mr. LIGHTOLLER: No, sir.

SENATOR SMITH: Did he ask you anything about it?

Mr. LIGHTOLLER: No, sir.

SENATOR SMITH: What was said between you?

Mr. LIGHTOLLER: We remarked on the weather, about its being calm, clear. We remarked the distance we could see.

We seemed to be able to see a long distance. Everything was very clear. We could see the stars setting down to the horizon.

SENATOR SMITH: It was cold, was it not?

MR. LIGHTOLLER: Yes, sir. . . .

SENATOR SMITH: When you came out of your room after the impact, did you see any ice on the decks?

MR. LIGHTOLLER: No, sir.

SENATOR SMITH: Did you see or hear any exclamations of pain?

MR. LIGHTOLLER: No, sir.

SENATOR SMITH: Do you know whether anyone was injured?

MR. LIGHTOLLER: No, sir.

SENATOR SMITH: By ice on deck?

MR. LIGHTOLLER: No, sir.

SENATOR SMITH: Tell us, as nearly as you can, just where you saw the captain last, with reference to the sinking of this ship.

MR. LIGHTOLLER: I think the bridge was the last place I saw him, sir; I am not sure. I think he was crossing the bridge.

SENATOR SMITH: What do you mean by that?

MR. LIGHTOLLER: Walking across.

SENATOR SMITH: From one side to the other?

MR. LIGHTOLLER: No, sir; just coming across. I merely recognized a glimpse. I have a slight recollection of having seen him whilst I was walking. It is my recollection that I saw him crossing the bridge. I think that was the last. . . .

SENATOR SMITH: What were the last orders you heard him give?

MR. LIGHTOLLER: When I asked him, "Shall I put the women and children in the boats?" he replied, "Yes; and lower away." Those were the last orders he gave.

SENATOR SMITH: Where was he at that time?

MR. LIGHTOLLER: About abreast the No. 6 boat.

SENATOR SMITH: How long was that before the ship sunk?

MR. LIGHTOLLER: Approximately somewhere about a quarter to 1, say. I don't know what time it was, sir. It would be only a guess.

SENATOR SMITH: It was after this impact?

MR. LIGHTOLLER: Yes, sir.

SENATOR SMITH: After the collision?

MR. LIGHTOLLER: Yes, sir.

SENATOR SMITH: And about how long after? What time did the collision occur?

MR. LIGHTOLLER: I do not know. I understand—I only gather it—that it occurred shortly before 12 o'clock.

SENATOR SMITH: When you heard it, did you look at your watch or make a note of it?

MR. LIGHTOLLER: No, sir.

SENATOR SMITH: How long was the vessel afloat after this collision?

MR. LIGHTOLLER: That I do not know either, only from what I was told.

SENATOR SMITH: What were you told?

MR. LIGHTOLLER: I was told she sunk at 2:20. . . .

SENATOR SMITH: Were all the boats lowered on the port side?

MR. LIGHTOLLER: They were all lowered with the exception of one, the last boat, which was stowed on top of the officers' quarters. We had not time to launch it nor yet to open it. . . .

SENATOR SMITH: What type of boat was it?

MR. LIGHTOLLER: Collapsible.

SENATOR SMITH: Did you see it afterwards?

MR. LIGHTOLLER: Eventually. It was the boat that I got on.

SENATOR SMITH: Eventually that was the boat that you got on?

MR. LIGHTOLLER: Yes, sir; bottom up. . . .

SENATOR SMITH: This lifeboat which was taken from the top of the officers' quarters, and that you finally reached, contained how many people?

MR. LIGHTOLLER: When it floated off the ship?

SENATOR SMITH: Yes.

MR. LIGHTOLLER: I could not say how many.

SENATOR SMITH: How many after you had gotten into it?

MR. LIGHTOLLER: We were thrown off a couple of times. It was cleared; it was a flat, collapsible boat. When I came to it, it was bottom up, and there was no one on it.

SENATOR SMITH: No one on it?

MR. LIGHTOLLER: And it was on the other side of the ship.

SENATOR SMITH: What did you do when you came to it?

MR. LIGHTOLLER: I hung on to it.

SENATOR SMITH: You floated with it merely?

MR. LIGHTOLLER: Yes, sir.

SENATOR SMITH: Was that all the service it ever rendered? Was that the only service this lifeboat performed?

MR. LIGHTOLLER: No, sir. Eventually about 30 of us got in it.

SENATOR SMITH: Tell us just how it occurred.

MR. LIGHTOLLER: From the time the ship went down, you mean?

SENATOR SMITH: No; from the time you found this overturned lifeboat.

MR. LIGHTOLLER: Yes, sir. Immediately after finding that overturned lifeboat, and when I came up alongside of it, there were quite a lot of us in the water around it preparatory to getting up on it.

SENATOR SMITH: With life preservers?

MR. LIGHTOLLER: Yes, sir. Then the forward funnel fell down——

SENATOR SMITH: Were there any persons there without life preservers?

MR. LIGHTOLLER: No, sir. Not that I know of. The forward funnel falling down, it fell alongside of the lifeboat, about 4 inches clear of it.

SENATOR SMITH: What was this that fell?

MR. LIGHTOLLER: The forward funnel.

SENATOR SMITH: Did it strike the boat?

MR. LIGHTOLLER: It missed the boat.

SENATOR SMITH: Then what?

MR. LIGHTOLLER: It fell on all the people there were alongside of the boat, if there were any there.

SENATOR SMITH: Injure any of them seriously?

MR. LIGHTOLLER: I could not say, sir.

SENATOR SMITH: Did it kill anybody?

MR. LIGHTOLLER: I could not say, sir.

SENATOR SMITH: Was this vessel sinking pretty rapidly at that time?

MR. LIGHTOLLER: Pretty quickly, sir.

SENATOR SMITH: Do you know any of the men who were in the water as you were and who boarded this lifeboat?

MR. LIGHTOLLER: Yes, sir.

SENATOR SMITH: Give their names.

MR. LIGHTOLLER: Mr. [Jack] Thayer, a first-class passenger;

the second Marconi operator—I can tell you his name in a minute—Bride.

Senator Smith: Was that the boat that Col. [Archibald] Gracie——

Mr. Lightoller: Oh, yes; and Col. Gracie.

Senator Smith: Col. Gracie, of the United States Army?

Mr. Lightoller: I think I have his card.

Senator Smith: It was Col. Gracie, anyway?

Mr. Lightoller: Col. Gracie was on the upturned boat with me; yes.

Senator Smith: Was he on the upturned boat before you got it righted around?

Mr. Lightoller: We never righted it.

Senator Smith: You never righted it?

Mr. Lightoller: No, sir; we could not.

Senator Smith: Who else was there?

Mr. Lightoller: I think all the rest were firemen taken out of the water, sir. Those are the only passengers that I know of.

Senator Smith: No other passengers?

Mr. Lightoller: There were two or three that died. I think there were three or four who died during the night.

Senator Smith: Aboard this boat with you?

Mr. Lightoller: Yes, sir; I think the senior Marconi operator was on the boat and died. The Marconi junior operator told me that the senior was on this boat and died.

Senator Smith: From the cold?

Mr. Lightoller: Presumably.

Senator Smith: Not from the blow of this——

Mr. Lightoller: No; not that I know of.

Senator Smith: How many persons altogether?

Mr. Lightoller: I should roughly estimate about 30. She was packed standing from stem to stern at daylight.

Senator Smith: Was there any effort made by others to board her?

Mr. Lightoller: We took all on board that we could.

Senator Smith: I understand, but I wanted to know whether there was any effort made by others to get aboard?

Mr. Lightoller: Not that I saw.

Senator Smith: There must have been a great number of people in the water?

MR. LIGHTOLLER: But not near us. They were some distance away from us.

SENATOR SMITH: How far?

MR. LIGHTOLLER: It seemed about a half a mile.

SENATOR SMITH: Was not this the only raft or craft in sight?

MR. LIGHTOLLER: It was dark, sir.

SENATOR SMITH: Yes. But this was the only thing there was to get on at that time?

MR. LIGHTOLLER: With the exception of the wreckage.

SENATOR SMITH: With the exception of what floated off the ship?

MR. LIGHTOLLER: Yes, sir.

SENATOR SMITH: In the form of wreckage?

MR. LIGHTOLLER: Yes, sir. . . .

SENATOR SMITH: When you left the ship, did you see any women or children on board?

MR. LIGHTOLLER: None whatever.

SENATOR SMITH: Could you give us any estimate whatever as to the number of first and second class passengers that were on board when the ship went down?

MR. LIGHTOLLER: No, sir.

SENATOR SMITH: Were there any on the so-called boat deck?

MR. LIGHTOLLER: Yes, sir.

SENATOR SMITH: Were there quite a number, in your opinion?

MR. LIGHTOLLER: A number of people—what they were, first, second, or third, crew or firemen, I could not say, sir.

SENATOR SMITH: But there were many people still on the ship?

MR. LIGHTOLLER: Yes, sir.

SENATOR SMITH: And, so far as you could observe, could you tell whether they were equipped with life preservers?

MR. LIGHTOLLER: As far as I could see, throughout the whole of the passengers, or the whole of the crew, everyone was equipped with a life preserver, for I looked for it especially.

SENATOR SMITH: Were the passengers on those decks instructed at any time to go to one side or the other of the ship?

MR. LIGHTOLLER: Yes.

SENATOR SMITH: What do you know about that?

MR. LIGHTOLLER: When the ship was taking a heavy list—

not a heavy list—but she was taking a list over to port, the order was called, I think, by the chief officer. "Everyone on the starboard side to straighten her up," which I repeated.

SENATOR SMITH: How long before you left the ship?

MR. LIGHTOLLER: I could not say, sir.

SENATOR SMITH: About how long?

MR. LIGHTOLLER: Half an hour or three quarters of an hour.

SENATOR SMITH: Before you left?

MR. LIGHTOLLER: Yes.

SENATOR SMITH: How were these passengers selected in going to the lifeboats?

MR. LIGHTOLLER: By their sex.

SENATOR SMITH: Whenever you saw a woman?

MR. LIGHTOLLER: Precisely. . . .

SENATOR SMITH: . . . altogether there were how many lifeboats actually used?

MR. LIGHTOLLER: Nineteen.

SENATOR SMITH: How many actually picked up by the *Carpathia?*

MR. LIGHTOLLER: All accounted for.

SENATOR SMITH: One, however, was badly injured, and another lifeboat took the passengers from it, did they not?

MR. LIGHTOLLER: That was the upturned one that I was on.

SENATOR SMITH: That was the upturned one that you were on?

MR. LIGHTOLLER: Yes, sir.

SENATOR SMITH: And they took you into another lifeboat?

MR. LIGHTOLLER: Yes, sir.

SENATOR SMITH: All of those who were with you?

MR. LIGHTOLLER: Yes, sir.

SENATOR SMITH: Was the lifeboat full at that time?

MR. LIGHTOLLER: I counted 65 heads, not including myself or any that were in the bottom of the boat. I roughly estimated about 75 in the boat.

SENATOR SMITH: Was the boat safe with that number of people in it?

MR. LIGHTOLLER: Safe in smooth water only.

SENATOR SMITH: How many of those lifeboats did you help load?

MR. LIGHTOLLER: All except one or two on the port side.

SENATOR SMITH: Who determined the number of people who should go into the lifeboats?

MR. LIGHTOLLER: I did.

SENATOR SMITH: How did you reach a conclusion as to the number that should be permitted to go in?

MR. LIGHTOLLER: My own judgment about the strength of the tackle.

SENATOR SMITH: How many did you put in each boat?

MR. LIGHTOLLER: In the first boat I put about 20 or 25. Twenty, sir.

SENATOR SMITH: How many men?

MR. LIGHTOLLER: No men.

SENATOR SMITH: How many seamen?

MR. LIGHTOLLER: Two.

SENATOR SMITH: In the first boat?

MR. LIGHTOLLER: Yes, sir. . . .

SENATOR SMITH: What happened to that lifeboat, the first one loaded?

MR. LIGHTOLLER: It was loaded and sent away from the ship.

SENATOR SMITH: Did it not return to the ship because it was only half loaded?

MR. LIGHTOLLER: Not to my knowledge, sir.

SENATOR SMITH: As a matter of fact it was not much more than half loaded, was it?

MR. LIGHTOLLER: You mean its floating capacity?

SENATOR SMITH: Yes.

MR. LIGHTOLLER: Floating capacity; no.

SENATOR SMITH: How did it happen you did not put more people into that boat?

MR. LIGHTOLLER: Because I did not consider it safe.

SENATOR SMITH: In a great emergency like that, where there were limited facilities, could you not have afforded to try to put more people into that boat?

MR. LIGHTOLLER: I did not know it was urgent then. I had no idea it was urgent.

SENATOR SMITH: You did not know it was urgent.

MR. LIGHTOLLER: Nothing like it.

SENATOR SMITH: Supposing you had known it was urgent, what would you have done?

MR. LIGHTOLLER: I would have acted to the best of my judgment then.

SENATOR SMITH: Tell me what you would have thought wise.

55

MR. LIGHTOLLER: I would have taken more risks. I should not have considered it wise to put more in, but I might have taken risks.

SENATOR SMITH: As a matter of fact are not these lifeboats so constructed as to accommodate 40 people?

MR. LIGHTOLLER: Sixty-five in the water, sir.

SENATOR SMITH: Sixty-five in the water, and about 40 as they are being put into the water?

MR. LIGHTOLLER: No, sir.

SENATOR SMITH: How?

MR. LIGHTOLLER: No, sir; it all depends on your gears, sir. If it were an old ship, you would barely dare to put 25 in.

SENATOR SMITH: But this was a new one?

MR. LIGHTOLLER: And therefore I took chances with her afterwards.

SENATOR SMITH: You put 25 in?

MR. LIGHTOLLER: In the first.

SENATOR SMITH: And two men?

MR. LIGHTOLLER: And two men.

SENATOR SMITH: How were those two men selected; arbitrarily by you?

MR. LIGHTOLLER: No, sir. They were selected by me; yes.

SENATOR SMITH: Who were they?

MR. LIGHTOLLER: I could not say, sir.

SENATOR SMITH: How did you happen to choose those particular men?

MR. LIGHTOLLER: Because they were standing near.

SENATOR SMITH: Did they want to go?

MR. LIGHTOLLER: I did not ask them.

SENATOR SMITH: You did not call for volunteers?

MR. LIGHTOLLER: They went by my orders. . . .

SENATOR SMITH: Were the people ready to go?

MR. LIGHTOLLER: Perfectly quiet and ready.

SENATOR SMITH: Any jostling or pushing or crowding?

MR. LIGHTOLLER: None whatever.

SENATOR SMITH: The men all refrained from asserting their strength and crowding back the women and children?

MR. LIGHTOLLER: They could not have stood quieter if they had been in church. . . .

SENATOR SMITH: How many women were you caring for? How many did you have aboard the ship?

MR. LIGHTOLLER: I could not say.

SENATOR SMITH: Do you know whether they were all cared for?

MR. LIGHTOLLER: I could not say, sir.

SENATOR SMITH: All that would go?

MR. LIGHTOLLER: In the case of the last boat I got out, I had the utmost difficulty in finding women. It was the very last boat of all, after all the other boats were put out and we came forward to put out the collapsible boats. In the meantime the forward emergency boat had been put out by one of the other officers. So we rounded up the tackles and got the collapsible boat to put that over. Then I called for women and could not get hold of any. Somebody said, "There are no women." With this, several men——

SENATOR SMITH: Who said that?

MR. LIGHTOLLER: I do not know, sir.

SENATOR SMITH: On what deck was that?

MR. LIGHTOLLER: On the boat deck.

SENATOR SMITH: Were all the women supposed to be on the boat deck?

MR. LIGHTOLLER: Yes, sir; they were supposed to be. . . .

SENATOR SMITH: How about the sixth boat?

MR. LIGHTOLLER: That is the collapsible, the surfboat?

SENATOR SMITH: That is the collapsible. Did you take the same course with that?

MR. LIGHTOLLER: That is a much smaller boat. . . .

SENATOR SMITH: How many people were put into this sixth boat?

MR. LIGHTOLLER: Fifteen or perhaps 20. Between 15 and 20.

SENATOR SMITH: And two seamen?

MR. LIGHTOLLER: I do not know what seamen——

SENATOR SMITH: Or one?

MR. LIGHTOLLER: I think one seaman probably, if I had one seaman there. Perhaps it was two stewards. I do not know, sir.

SENATOR SMITH: Would the two stewards answer the same purpose?

MR. LIGHTOLLER: They would have to.

SENATOR SMITH: Did you select the men to take that boat the same as you had before?

MR. LIGHTOLLER: You mean whether I ordered them in?

SENATOR SMITH: Yes.

MR. LIGHTOLLER: I ordered them in.

SENATOR SMITH: But you can not recall who they were?

MR. LIGHTOLLER: I was just thinking. No, not with any degree of certainty.

SENATOR SMITH: Were any of them officers?

MR. LIGHTOLLER: No, sir.

SENATOR SMITH: Did you have any difficulty in filling it?

MR. LIGHTOLLER: With women; yes, sir; great difficulty.

SENATOR SMITH: But you filled it to its capacity?

MR. LIGHTOLLER: I filled it with about 15 or 20 eventually mustered up. It took longer to fill that boat than it did any other boat, notwithstanding that the others had more in them. On two occasions the men thought there were no more women and commenced to get in and then found one or two more and then got out again.

SENATOR SMITH: How long a time do you think you had been in loading these six boats?

MR. LIGHTOLLER: I don't know, sir.

SENATOR SMITH: If it took 15 to 20 minutes to a boat?

MR. LIGHTOLLER: About an hour and a half. . . .

SENATOR SMITH: You must have been painfully aware of the fact that there were not enough boats there to care for that large passenger list, were you not?

MR. LIGHTOLLER: Yes, sir. . . .

SENATOR SMITH: From what you have said, you discriminated entirely in the interest of the passengers—first the women and children—in filling those lifeboats?

MR. LIGHTOLLER: Yes, sir.

SENATOR SMITH: Why did you do that? Because of the captain's orders, or because of the rule of the sea?

MR. LIGHTOLLER: The rule of human nature.

SENATOR SMITH: The rule of human nature? And there was no studied purpose, as far as you know, to save the crew?

MR. LIGHTOLLER: Absolutely not. . . .

SENATOR SMITH: In sinking, did the ship tilt?

MR. LIGHTOLLER: Yes, sir.

SENATOR SMITH: To the fore?

MR. LIGHTOLLER: Yes, sir.

SENATOR SMITH: How much?

MR. LIGHTOLLER: Well, roughly, the crow's nest was level with the water when the bridge went under water.

SENATOR SMITH: The crow's nest, at the fore point?

MR. LIGHTOLLER: That is on the foremast. The lookout cage.

SENATOR SMITH: The crow's nest at the highest point?

MR. LIGHTOLLER: Yes, sir.

SENATOR SMITH: Was in the water?

MR. LIGHTOLLER: Was just about level with the water.

SENATOR SMITH: When the bridge was submerged?

MR. LIGHTOLLER: Yes, sir.

SENATOR SMITH: And about what was the angle?

MR. LIGHTOLLER: I am afraid I could hardly tell you the angle, sir. . . .

SENATOR SMITH: I ask you again. There must have been a great number of passengers and crew still on the boat, the part of the boat that was not submerged, probably on the high point, so far as possible. Were they huddled together?

MR. LIGHTOLLER: I could not say, sir. They did not seem to be. I could not say, sir; I did not notice; there were a great many of them; there was a great many of them, I know, but as to what condition they were in, huddled or not, I do not know.

SENATOR SMITH: Did they make any demonstration?

MR. LIGHTOLLER: None.

SENATOR SMITH: Was there any lamentation?

MR. LIGHTOLLER: No, sir; not a sign of it.

SENATOR SMITH: There must have been about 2,000 people there on that part—the unsubmerged part of the boat?

MR. LIGHTOLLER: All the engineers and other men and many of the firemen were down below and never came on deck at all.

SENATOR SMITH: They never came on deck?

MR. LIGHTOLLER: No, sir; they were never seen. That would reduce it by a great number.

SENATOR SMITH: After this impact, did you hear any explosion of any kind?

MR. LIGHTOLLER: None whatever, sir.

SENATOR SMITH: What would be the effect of water at about zero——

MR. LIGHTOLLER (interposing): At about freezing?

SENATOR SMITH: What would be the effect of water at about freezing on the boilers?

MR. LIGHTOLLER: It is an open question. I have heard it said that they will explode, and others say they will not.

SENATOR SMITH: Have you ever known of a case?

Mr. Lightoller: Of a case in point?

Senator Smith: Where they have exploded?

Mr. Lightoller: I was sucked down, and I was blown out with something pretty powerful when the ship went down.

Senator Smith: After the ship went down?

Mr. Lightoller: Yes.

Senator Smith: Just describe that a little more fully. You were sucked down?

Mr. Lightoller: I was sucked against the blower first of all. As I say, I was on top of the officers' quarters, and there was nothing more to be done. The ship then took a dive, and I turned face forward and also took a dive.

Senator Smith: From which side?

Mr. Lightoller: From on top, practically midships; a little to the starboard side, where I had got to; and I was driven back against a blower—which is a large thing that shape [indicating] which faces forward to the wind and which then goes down to the stokehole. But there is a grating there, and it was against this grating that I was sucked by the water and held there.

Senator Smith: Was your head above water?

Mr. Lightoller: No, sir.

Senator Smith: You were under water?

Mr. Lightoller: Yes, sir. And then this explosion, or whatever it was, took place. Certainly, I think it was the boilers exploded. There was a terrific blast of air and water, and I was blown out clear.

Senator Smith: Was there any debris that was blown above the surface?

Mr. Lightoller: That I could not say.

Senator Smith: At least you took your head out of the water?

Mr. Lightoller: I came up above the water; yes.

Senator Smith: And how far from the sinking ship did it throw you?

Mr. Lightoller: Barely threw me away at all; barely threw me away at all, because I went down again against these fiddley gratings immediately abreast of the funnel over the stokehole.

Senator Smith: Was anybody else sucked down at the time?

Mr. Lightoller: Col. Gracie, I believe, was sucked down in

identically the same manner. He was sucked down on the fiddley gratings.

SENATOR SMITH: There must have been considerable suction?

MR. LIGHTOLLER: That was the water rushing down below as she was going down.

SENATOR SMITH: Going down into the ship?

MR. LIGHTOLLER: Exactly.

SENATOR SMITH: How did you get released from that?

MR. LIGHTOLLER: Oh, I don't know, sir. I think it was the boilers again, but I do not distinctly remember. I do not know.

SENATOR SMITH: Where did you next find yourself?

MR. LIGHTOLLER: Alongside of that raft.

SENATOR SMITH: Where?

MR. LIGHTOLLER: Alongside of that upturned boat that had been launched on the other side. . . .

SENATOR SMITH: Were there any water-tight compartments in that ship?

MR. LIGHTOLLER: Yes, sir.

SENATOR SMITH: How many?

MR. LIGHTOLLER: I could not tell you offhand, sir: 40 or 50.

SENATOR SMITH: Nearly 50?

MR. LIGHTOLLER: I say 40 or 50; I can not tell you offhand.

SENATOR SMITH: How were they constructed?

MR. LIGHTOLLER: They were divisional bulkheads; water-tight doors, operated by electricity or mechanically.

SENATOR SMITH: Were those water-tight compartments known to the passengers or crew?

MR. LIGHTOLLER: They must have been.

SENATOR SMITH: How would they know it?

MR. LIGHTOLLER: By the plans distributed about the ship.

SENATOR SMITH: Were they advised at any time that there were water-tight compartments—about how many?

MR. LIGHTOLLER: Forty or fifty.

SENATOR SMITH: Were they advised that there were 40 or 50 water-tight compartments?

MR. LIGHTOLLER: I could not say, sir.

SENATOR SMITH: You heard nothing of that kind and gave no such warning yourself?

MR. LIGHTOLLER: No, sir.

SENATOR SMITH: Are you able to say whether any of the crew

or passengers took to these upper water-tight compartments as a final, last resort; I mean as a place to die?

MR. LIGHTOLLER: I am quite unable to say, sir.

SENATOR SMITH: Is that at all likely?

MR. LIGHTOLLER: No, sir; very unlikely.

SENATOR SMITH: As for yourself, you preferred to take your chance in the open sea?

MR. LIGHTOLLER: Undoubtedly. . . .

Witness: Harold Thomas Cottam, 21
Wireless operator on the rescue ship *Carpathia*

Key testimony: Cottam afforded the hearings what must have seemed an odd (if not comical) encounter with the new, unfamiliar, and largely unregulated world of wireless radio communications. He recounted hearing the Titanic's *distress call just as he was about to take off his clothes and turn in for the night.*

. . . SENATOR SMITH: How did you happen to catch this communication from the *Titanic*?

MR. COTTAM: I was looking out for the *Parisian*, to confirm a previous communication with the *Parisian*.

SENATOR SMITH: You had been in communication with the *Parisian* that day?

MR. COTTAM: Yes, sir.

SENATOR SMITH: At what time?

MR. COTTAM: I can not say. At some time in the afternoon, sir.

SENATOR SMITH: Not a distress signal?

MR. COTTAM: Oh, no, sir.

SENATOR SMITH: Some commercial or business communication?

MR. COTTAM: Yes, sir. . . .

SENATOR SMITH: Did you hear the captain of the *Carpathia* to-day?

MR. COTTAM: No, sir.

SENATOR SMITH: He said you were about to retire.

MR. COTTAM: Yes, sir.

SENATOR SMITH: And caught this message rather providentially?

MR. COTTAM: Yes, sir.

SENATOR SMITH: How far had you gotten along in your arrangements to retire?

MR. COTTAM: Well, I was about to retire.

SENATOR SMITH: Had you disrobed—taken off your clothes?

MR. COTTAM: No, sir.

SENATOR SMITH: Had you taken off your shoes?

MR. COTTAM: No, sir.

SENATOR SMITH: Had you taken off any of your clothing?

MR. COTTAM: I had my coat off.

SENATOR SMITH: When you took your coat off, did you have any instruments attached to your head?

MR. COTTAM: Yes, sir.

SENATOR SMITH: What?

MR. COTTAM: Telephones.

SENATOR SMITH: How did you happen to leave that on?

MR. COTTAM: I was waiting for the *Parisian*.

SENATOR SMITH: How long would you have waited; just long enough to undress?

MR. COTTAM: I would have waited a couple of minutes. I had just called the *Parisian* and was waiting for a reply, if there was one. . . .

SENATOR SMITH: So you kept this telephone on your ears, on your head?

MR. COTTAM: Yes, sir.

SENATOR SMITH: On your head?

MR. COTTAM: Yes.

SENATOR SMITH: With the hope that before you got into bed you might have your message confirmed?

MR. COTTAM: Yes, sir.

SENATOR SMITH: Was that what you had in mind?

MR. COTTAM: Yes, sir.

SENATOR SMITH: What did you hear at that time?

MR. COTTAM: I heard nothing, sir.

SENATOR SMITH: How soon? You heard something pretty quick, did you not?

MR. COTTAM: No, sir; I went back onto Cape Cod again.

SENATOR SMITH: And still left this apparatus on?

MR. COTTAM: Yes, sir.

SENATOR SMITH: Did you send a message to Cape Cod?

MR. COTTAM: No, sir.

SENATOR SMITH: Did Cape Cod send a message to you?

MR. COTTAM: No, sir.

SENATOR SMITH: Then, as a matter of fact, you did not get back to Cape Cod?

MR. COTTAM: Yes, sir.

SENATOR SMITH: How?

MR. COTTAM: They were sending it for the trans-Atlantic two-man ships. They were sending the news to the senior ships.

SENATOR SMITH: Where?

MR. COTTAM: These ships that contribute to the Marconi press. . . .

SENATOR SMITH: You got into communication?

MR. COTTAM: Yes, sir.

SENATOR SMITH: With one of the Marconi stations?

MR. COTTAM: I did not establish it. I was receiving the press communications from Cape Cod.

SENATOR SMITH: While you were undressing there?

MR. COTTAM: I was not undressing.

SENATOR SMITH: After you had taken off your coat?

MR. COTTAM: Yes, sir.

SENATOR SMITH: And then did you sit down to your instrument?

MR. COTTAM: Yes, sir.

SENATOR SMITH: And received this message?

MR. COTTAM: I received about four.

SENATOR SMITH: In how many minutes?

MR. COTTAM: About seven or eight minutes.

SENATOR SMITH: You received four in seven or eight minutes?

MR. COTTAM: Yes, sir.

SENATOR SMITH: Did that include anything from the *Parisian?*

MR. COTTAM: No, sir.

SENATOR SMITH: Simply this Cape Cod relay service?

MR. COTTAM: Yes, sir; sending messages for the *Titanic.* I was taking the messages down with the hope of retransmitting them the following morning.

SENATOR SMITH: Let us understand that a little. When did you first know anything about the *Titanic?*

MR. COTTAM: I had had communication with her late in the afternoon, half past 5 or 6.

SENATOR SMITH: A stray communication, or one addressed to the *Carpathia*?

MR. COTTAM: One addressed to the *Carpathia*.

SENATOR SMITH: What did it say?

MR. COTTAM: It was a message for one of our passengers aboard.

SENATOR SMITH: For whom?

MR. COTTAM: Mrs. Marshal.

SENATOR SMITH: A commercial message, an official message?

MR. COTTAM: A commercial message.

SENATOR SMITH: So that was the only message you received from the *Titanic* in the afternoon. Was the message answered?

MR. COTTAM: Yes, sir.

SENATOR SMITH: Do you know anything about how far you were from her at that time?

MR. COTTAM: No, sir.

SENATOR SMITH: Have you no means of knowing?

MR. COTTAM: No, sir.

SENATOR SMITH: After you got through with this regular business, then what did you do?

MR. COTTAM: I called the *Titanic*.

SENATOR SMITH: You called the *Titanic* yourself?

MR. COTTAM: Yes, sir.

SENATOR SMITH: Who told you to do it?

MR. COTTAM: I did it of my own free will.

SENATOR SMITH: You did it of your own accord?

MR. COTTAM: Yes, sir.

SENATOR SMITH: What did you say?

MR. COTTAM: I asked him if he was aware that Cape Cod was sending a batch of messages for him.

SENATOR SMITH: And did they reply?

MR. COTTAM: Yes, sir.

SENATOR SMITH: What did they say?

MR. COTTAM: "Come at once."

SENATOR SMITH: Did you gather from that that they had received your communication?

MR. COTTAM: Yes, sir.

SENATOR SMITH: And this was the reply?

MR. COTTAM: He said, "Come at once. It is a distress message; C. Q. D."

SENATOR SMITH: Only the three words were used?

MR. COTTAM: No, sir; all the lot. The whole message was for me.

SENATOR SMITH: When you received that message, what did you do?

MR. COTTAM: I confirmed it by asking him if I was to report it to the captain.

SENATOR SMITH: Before you reported to the captain you asked him if you were to report it to the captain?

MR. COTTAM: Yes, sir.

SENATOR SMITH: Did you get an answer?

MR. COTTAM: Yes, sir.

SENATOR SMITH: What did it say?

MR. COTTAM: It said, "Yes."

SENATOR SMITH: How did you happen to confirm it?

MR. COTTAM: By asking him if——

SENATOR SMITH (interrupting): I know, but what prompted you to confirm it before you delivered it to the captain?

MR. COTTAM: Because it is always wise to confirm a message of that description.

SENATOR SMITH: Do you always do it?

MR. COTTAM: Yes, sir.

SENATOR SMITH: Are you instructed to do it?

MR. COTTAM: No, sir.

SENATOR SMITH: Or is that a matter of discretion?

MR. COTTAM: It is a matter of discretion.

SENATOR SMITH: Had you been misled by messages that were without foundation that prompted you to confirm that message?

MR. COTTAM: No, sir.

SENATOR SMITH: What would you have done if you had not received any confirmation?

MR. COTTAM: I should have reported the communication.

SENATOR SMITH: You would have reported it to the captain?

MR. COTTAM: Yes, sir.

SENATOR SMITH: How much time elapsed between the time when you received that distress call and the time you communicated it to the captain?

MR. COTTAM: A matter of a couple of minutes.

SENATOR SMITH: Only a couple of minutes?

MR. COTTAM: Yes, sir.

SENATOR SMITH: Did you send any messages after that to the *Titanic?*

MR. COTTAM: Yes, sir.

SENATOR SMITH: For whom?

MR. COTTAM: For the *Titanic.*

SENATOR SMITH: At the instance of the captain?

MR. COTTAM: Yes, sir.

SENATOR SMITH: What messages?

MR. COTTAM: Our position.

SENATOR SMITH: What did you say?

MR. COTTAM: I simply sent him our position.

SENATOR SMITH: Can you state it to the reporter?

MR. COTTAM: I can not remember what the position was now.

SENATOR SMITH: You can not remember it?

MR. COTTAM: No, sir.

SENATOR SMITH: But you gave the position of your ship, its longitude; is that the idea?

MR. COTTAM: Yes, sir.

SENATOR SMITH: And you did that at the suggestion of the captain?

MR. COTTAM: Yes, sir.

SENATOR SMITH: Did he write out a formal message for you?

MR. COTTAM: No, sir.

SENATOR SMITH: He told you?

MR. COTTAM: Yes, sir.

SENATOR SMITH: And you sent it?

MR. COTTAM: Yes, sir; he wrote the position out on a little slip of paper.

SENATOR SMITH: And you sent that?

MR. COTTAM: Yes, sir.

SENATOR SMITH: Did you get any reply to that?

MR. COTTAM: Yes, sir.

SENATOR SMITH: How long afterwards?

MR. COTTAM: Immediately, sir.

SENATOR SMITH: Signed by anyone?

MR. COTTAM: No, sir.

SENATOR SMITH: What did it say?

MR. COTTAM: It simply gave me "Received."

SENATOR SMITH: Is that all?

MR. COTTAM: Yes, sir.

SENATOR SMITH: Signed by the operator or signed by anybody?

MR. COTTAM: No, sir.

SENATOR SMITH: When did you next hear from the *Titanic,* or communicate with her?

MR. COTTAM: About four minutes afterwards.

SENATOR SMITH: Did you communicate with her, or she with you?

MR. COTTAM: We communicated with each other.

SENATOR SMITH: Who sent the first message?

MR. COTTAM: I did.

SENATOR SMITH: Four minutes after this last message giving your position?

MR. COTTAM: Yes, sir.

SENATOR SMITH: You sent another?

MR. COTTAM: Yes.

SENATOR SMITH: What did you say in that?

MR. COTTAM: Confirmed both positions, that of the *Titanic* and ours.

SENATOR SMITH: Did you get anything back from that?

MR. COTTAM: No, sir; only an acknowledgment.

SENATOR SMITH: What did it say?

MR. COTTAM: "All right."

SENATOR SMITH: When did you next communicate or receive a communication?

MR. COTTAM: A few minutes afterwards.

SENATOR SMITH: How many minutes?

MR. COTTAM: I could not say, sir, because there was another ship calling the *Titanic.*

SENATOR SMITH: How do you know?

MR. COTTAM: Because I heard it.

SENATOR SMITH: What did you hear?

MR. COTTAM: I heard him calling the *Titanic.*

SENATOR SMITH: I understand, but what was said?

MR. COTTAM: There was nothing but the call, sir.

SENATOR SMITH: A distress call?

MR. COTTAM: No, sir.

SENATOR SMITH: Do you know what boat it was?

MR. COTTAM: The *Frankfurt.*

SENATOR SMITH: A North German Lloyd boat?

MR. COTTAM: I do not know whether it is the North German Lloyd. It is some German line; I do not know which one.

SENATOR SMITH: You heard this call?

MR. COTTAM: Yes.

SENATOR SMITH: The German boat was calling the *Titanic?*

MR. COTTAM: Yes, sir.

SENATOR SMITH: And did that disarrange your signals?

MR. COTTAM: No, sir.

SENATOR SMITH: But after that call was finished, then what did you get, if anything?

MR. COTTAM: I heard the *Olympic* calling the *Titanic.*

SENATOR SMITH: Did you hear the *Titanic* calling the *Olympic?*

MR. COTTAM: No, sir; not at first.

SENATOR SMITH: But you heard the *Olympic* calling the *Titanic?*

MR. COTTAM: Yes, sir.

SENATOR SMITH: What did the *Olympic* say?

MR. COTTAM: He was calling him and offering a service message.

SENATOR SMITH: Offering their service?

MR. COTTAM: Offering a service message.

SENATOR SMITH: Offering a service message?

MR. COTTAM: Yes.

SENATOR SMITH: Then what followed?

MR. COTTAM: Nothing, for about a half a minute. Everything was quiet.

SENATOR SMITH: Nothing for about half a minute?

MR. COTTAM: Yes.

SENATOR SMITH: By this time you were quite alert to the situation, were you?

MR. COTTAM: I was in communication with some station or other the whole way from the time of the wreck right to New York.

SENATOR SMITH: You were in communication with some ship?

MR. COTTAM: Yes, sir.

SENATOR SMITH: All the way?

MR. COTTAM: Yes, sir.

SENATOR SMITH: All the way?

MR. COTTAM: Yes, sir.

SENATOR SMITH: And often?

MR. COTTAM: Yes, sir. . . .

SENATOR SMITH: After this minute, then what?

MR. COTTAM: I asked the *Titanic* if he was aware that the *Olympic* was calling him, sir.

SENATOR SMITH: What was the reply?

MR. COTTAM: He said he was not.

SENATOR SMITH: He was not aware of it?

MR. COTTAM: No, sir.

SENATOR SMITH: Then what followed?

MR. COTTAM: He told me he could not read him because of the rush of air and the escape of steam.

SENATOR SMITH: That he could not read him?

MR. COTTAM: That he could not read him; yes, sir.

SENATOR SMITH: Could not read what?

MR. COTTAM: The *Olympic*.

SENATOR SMITH: That he could not read the message from the *Olympic* because of the rush of air?

MR. COTTAM: Yes, sir.

SENATOR SMITH: And the escape of steam?

MR. COTTAM: Yes, sir.

SENATOR SMITH: What was the next thing you heard?

MR. COTTAM: Then the *Titanic* called the *Olympic*.

SENATOR SMITH: Was there anything urgent about that or anything related to the *Titanic*?

MR. COTTAM: No, sir.

SENATOR SMITH: What did you do then?

MR. COTTAM: I told the *Titanic* to call the *Baltic*.

SENATOR SMITH: What followed?

MR. COTTAM: The communication was apparently unsatisfactory.

SENATOR SMITH: It was apparently unsatisfactory?

MR. COTTAM: Yes.

SENATOR SMITH: Well, go right ahead now and tell us just what occurred as long as you were aboard that ship doing work to the time of the rescue of these people.

MR. COTTAM: I was in communication at regular intervals the whole of the time until the last communication I gained with the *Titanic*.

SENATOR SMITH: You heard that?

MR. COTTAM: Yes, sir.

SENATOR SMITH: What was said in that message?

MR. COTTAM: He told him to come at once; that he was head down. And he sent his position.

SENATOR SMITH: And do you know whether he got any reply to that message?

MR. COTTAM: Yes, sir.

SENATOR SMITH: What was it?

MR. COTTAM: "Received." He told him the message was received.

SENATOR SMITH: Is that all?

MR. COTTAM: Yes, sir.

SENATOR SMITH: When did you hear anything again? What happened next?

MR. COTTAM: I heard the *Baltic* calling Cape Race [Newfoundland].

SENATOR SMITH: You were in regular communication?

MR. COTTAM: Yes, sir.

SENATOR SMITH: With the *Titanic?*

MR. COTTAM: Yes, sir.

SENATOR SMITH: Until the last communication was heard?

MR. COTTAM: Yes; until the last communication was heard.

SENATOR SMITH: What was the last one?

MR. COTTAM: The last one was, "Come quick; our engine room is filling up to the boilers."

SENATOR SMITH: That was the last communication you received?

MR. COTTAM: Yes, sir. . . .

SENATOR SMITH: I thought I understood the captain to say that one of the last messages told the sinking ship that they were within a certain distance and coming hard, or coming fast.

MR. COTTAM: I called him with that message, but I got no acknowledgment.

SENATOR SMITH: Just tell us what that message was. You called him with that message?

MR. COTTAM: Yes, sir.

SENATOR SMITH: We would like to know about that; just tell what it was.

MR. COTTAM: The captain told me to tell the *Titanic* that all our boats were ready and we were coming as hard as we could come, with a double watch on in the engine room, and to be prepared, when we got there, with lifeboats. I got no acknowledgment of that message.

SENATOR SMITH: But you sent it?

MR. COTTAM: Yes, sir.

SENATOR SMITH: Whether it was received or not, you don't know?

MR. COTTAM: No, sir.

SENATOR SMITH: Let us understand. When you received that last call from the *Titanic*, that her engine room was filling with water, you say you acknowledged its receipt and took that message to the captain. Did you acknowledge its receipt before you took it to the captain?

MR. COTTAM: Yes, sir.

SENATOR SMITH: Then, after you had taken this message to the captain, you came back to your instrument and sent the message that you have just described?

MR. COTTAM: Yes, sir.

SENATOR SMITH: And to that you received no reply?

MR. COTTAM: No, sir.

SENATOR SMITH: And you never received any other reply?

MR. COTTAM: No, sir.

SENATOR SMITH: Or any other word from the ship?

MR. COTTAM: No, sir. . . .

Witness: Alfred Crawford, 41
A bedroom steward in first class, from Southampton, England

Key testimony: Crawford was the first to tell the world of the elderly Isidor and Ida Straus, wealthy from their New York department stores and the most famous of several couples on the Titanic *who elected to die together.*

. . . SENATOR SMITH: Did you know Mr. and Mrs. Straus?

MR. CRAWFORD: I stood at the boat where they refused to get in.

SENATOR SMITH: Did Mrs. Straus get into the boat?

MR. CRAWFORD: She attempted to get into the boat first and she got back again. Her maid got into the boat.

SENATOR SMITH: What do you mean by "she attempted" to get in?

MR. CRAWFORD: She went to get over from the deck to the boat, but then went back to her husband.

SENATOR SMITH: Did she step on the boat?

MR. CRAWFORD: She stepped on to the boat, on to the gunwales, sir; then she went back.

SENATOR SMITH: What followed?

MR. CRAWFORD: She said, "We have been living together for many years, and where you go I go."

SENATOR SMITH: To whom did she speak?

MR. CRAWFORD: To her husband.

SENATOR SMITH: Was he beside her?

MR. CRAWFORD: Yes; he was standing away back when she went from the boat.

SENATOR SMITH: You say there was a maid there also?

MR. CRAWFORD: A maid got in the boat and was saved; yes, sir.

SENATOR SMITH: Did the maid precede Mrs. Straus into the boat?

MR. CRAWFORD: Mrs. Straus told the maid to get into the boat and she would follow her; then she altered her mind and went back to her husband. . . .

SENATOR SMITH: How many seamen or men of the crew were put into boat No. 8?

MR. CRAWFORD: Four, sir; two were in and Capt. Smith told me to get in.

SENATOR SMITH: Two were in?

MR. CRAWFORD: Two sailors were in the boat at first.

SENATOR SMITH: And Capt. Smith told you to get in?

MR. CRAWFORD: Yes, sir; myself and a cook got in. We were the last to get in the boat—there were so many ladies that there wasn't room for any more.

SENATOR SMITH: How many passengers were in that boat?

MR. CRAWFORD: I should say about 35, sir.

SENATOR SMITH: Was that a regular lifeboat or one of these canvas collapsible boats?

MR. CRAWFORD: No, sir; it was a regular lifeboat.

SENATOR SMITH: When you were lowered to the water, who assumed charge of this lifeboat?

MR. CRAWFORD: The man in the afterpart of the lifeboat, a sailor.

SENATOR SMITH: A sailor?

MR. CRAWFORD: Yes, sir.

SENATOR SMITH: And what was done?

MR. CRAWFORD: We all took an oar and pulled away from the ship. A lady—I don't know her name—took the tiller.

SENATOR SMITH: A lady took the tiller and the men took the oars?

MR. CRAWFORD: Four men took the oars and pulled away.

SENATOR SMITH: Did you know any of the women or men in that boat?

MR. CRAWFORD: No, sir; there were only ladies. There were no men, except four of the crew.

SENATOR SMITH: What about Mr. and Mrs. Bishop?

MR. CRAWFORD: They weren't in that boat.

SENATOR SMITH: What boat were they in?

MR. CRAWFORD: I couldn't say what boat they got into. I saw them afterwards on the *Carpathia*.

SENATOR SMITH: Did each of the boats forward on the port side have four men?

MR. CRAWFORD: I think they did, sir; I couldn't say. I was out loading all the boats as we got along.

SENATOR SMITH: So far as you observed, was there any struggle——

MR. CRAWFORD: No, sir; none whatever.

SENATOR SMITH (continuing): To get into the lifeboats, by men or women?

MR. CRAWFORD: No, sir; none whatever.

SENATOR SMITH: Was the ship sinking at this time?

MR. CRAWFORD: She was making water fast at the bows; yes, sir.

SENATOR SMITH: And was there any noticeable suction?

MR. CRAWFORD: No, sir.

SENATOR SMITH: About the boat?

MR. CRAWFORD: No, sir; I do not think so.

SENATOR SMITH: As she began to sink?

MR. CRAWFORD: No, sir.

SENATOR SMITH: Just tell what you did from that time that you were lowered to the water.

MR. CRAWFORD: Kept pulling and trying to make a light, and we could not seem to get any closer to it. We kept pulling and pulling until daybreak. Then we saw the *Carpathia* coming up, and we turned around and came back to her.

SENATOR SMITH: What time did the day break on Monday?

MR. CRAWFORD: About 4 o'clock, I should say, it began to get light.

SENATOR SMITH: You were in the boat and pulling?

MR. CRAWFORD: Yes, sir; until the time we were picked up. . . .

SENATOR SMITH: Where were you when this collision occurred?

MR. CRAWFORD: I was right forward in B deck.

SENATOR SMITH: Where is that?

MR. CRAWFORD: Two decks underneath the boat deck.

SENATOR SMITH: Tell what you experienced.

MR. CRAWFORD: I was on watch until 12 o'clock, and I was waiting for my relief to come up. I was to be relieved at 12 o'clock. I heard the crash, and I went out on the outer deck and saw the iceberg floating alongside. I went back, and there were a lot of passengers coming out.

SENATOR SMITH: You went out on the outer deck?

MR. CRAWFORD: Yes, sir.

SENATOR SMITH: On which side?

MR. CRAWFORD: On the starboard side.

SENATOR SMITH: And saw the iceberg?

MR. CRAWFORD: I saw the iceberg going by.

SENATOR SMITH: Was there any ice on the deck?

MR. CRAWFORD: I did not go so far forward as that, sir.

SENATOR SMITH: Was there anybody injured that you know anything about?

MR. CRAWFORD: No, sir; I went to all the ladies' cabins. They were all rushing out, and I told them I didn't think there was any immediate danger, and after the order was passed for the life belts, I tied the life belts on the ladies, and an old gentleman by the name of Stewart, and tied his shoes on for him. . . .

SENATOR SMITH: Did you see the ship go down?

MR. CRAWFORD: We saw her at a distance; yes, sir.

SENATOR SMITH: What shape was she in when you saw her last?

MR. CRAWFORD: It seemed as if her bow was going down first.

SENATOR SMITH: At how much of an angle?

MR. CRAWFORD: We saw all the lights going out on the forward part of her.

SENATOR SMITH: And still burning on the after part?

75

MR. CRAWFORD: Yes, sir.

SENATOR SMITH: How much of the aft part was out of the water?

MR. CRAWFORD: There was a good bit of the stern part out of water.

SENATOR SMITH: How many decks?

MR. CRAWFORD: I could not say how many decks there, sir, but it seemed all clear right from amidships to aft.

SENATOR SMITH: Did you see many people?

MR. CRAWFORD: I saw a great number on deck.

SENATOR SMITH: On board of her at that time.

MR. CRAWFORD: Yes, sir.

SENATOR SMITH: What were they doing?

MR. CRAWFORD: When we left they were trying to lower the other boats; the farther-aft boats. . . .

SECOND DAY
Saturday, April 20
The Waldorf-Astoria Hotel, New York

The hearings were moved to the Waldorf-Astoria's larger Myrtle Room so as to better handle the overflow crowd of spectators. Among them was Inez Milholland, the suffragette extolled in the press for her beauty, who was attending with Guglielmo Marconi, the wireless-telegraph pioneer and magnate, and her onetime fiancé. Marconi's operations were a prime focus of the investigators.

Witness: Harold S. Bride of London, 22
Only surviving Marconi wireless operator from the *Titanic* and among the last to leave the ship

Key testimony: Bride transfixed those present, first with his dramatic entrance in a wheelchair, his left foot in a bandage, and then with his account, one of the most astonishing sea stories ever told. It was at once a primer on the still unfamiliar world of wireless communications at sea (with testimony from Marconi at key moments), a tale of human obstinacy, and a firsthand chronicle of disaster foretold and dramatically realized. In sending distress signals to nearby ships, the Titanic's *senior wireless operator, Jack Phillips, grew frustrated with the wireless operator on the* Frankfurt, *the German ship believed at the time to be closest to the* Titanic *(it turned out that it wasn't). Phillips messaged the* Frankfurt *operator that he was a "fool" and in effect told him to get lost, Bride testified. When the* Titanic *sank, Bride wound up in the water, at first under and then on top of the same overturned lifeboat that Lightoller, the Second Officer, and others, including Phillips, climbed aboard. Phillips died of exposure at sea. Bride also described the last moments of the* Titanic's *captain, E. J. Smith, offering a haunting image of a solitary figure diving at the last moment off the bridge.*

77

. . . SENATOR SMITH: Were you on duty when the wireless message was received from the *Amerika* regarding the proximity of icebergs in that longitude?

MR. BRIDE: I have no knowledge of a wireless message received from the *Amerika* regarding any iceberg. There may have been received by Mr. Phillips, but I did not see one myself.

SENATOR SMITH: Have you heard that such a message was received?

MR. BRIDE: No, sir.

SENATOR SMITH: Did Mr. Phillips say that such a message had been received?

MR. BRIDE: No, sir.

SENATOR SMITH: Did you ever talk with the captain about such a message?

MR. BRIDE: There was a message delivered to the captain in the afternoon, sir, late in the afternoon, regarding——

SENATOR SMITH: Of Sunday?

MR. BRIDE: Yes, sir.

SENATOR SMITH: Go ahead.

MR. BRIDE: Regarding the ice field.

SENATOR SMITH: From whom?

MR. BRIDE: From the *Californian,* sir.

SENATOR SMITH: At what hour Sunday?

MR. BRIDE: It may not have been the *Californian,* but I can give you the call signal of the ship; it is "M. W. L." You can ascertain that later.

SENATOR SMITH: Go ahead.

MR. BRIDE: I received that message myself and delivered it to the captain. It stated that there were three large icebergs that the ship had just passed, and it gave their position.

SENATOR SMITH: What was the hour of the day?

MR. BRIDE: Late in the afternoon, but I can not say the hour of the day. . . .

SENATOR SMITH: Now, I would like to know just what that message said?

MR. BRIDE: In the first place the *Californian* had called me, sir, with an ice report. I was rather busy just for the minute, and I did not take it. She did not call again. She transmitted the ice report to the *Baltic,* and as she was transmitting it to the *Baltic* I took it down. I took it to the captain; but it was not official, because it was not intended for me afterwards.

SENATOR SMITH: Was the attempt made first upon you?

MR. BRIDE: First on me; yes, sir.

SENATOR SMITH: And being unable to get you, they tried to get the *Baltic?*

MR. BRIDE: It was about half an hour after that they transmitted it to the *Baltic.*

SENATOR SMITH: Why were they unable to get you?

MR. BRIDE: I was doing some writing at the time, sir.

SENATOR SMITH: You mean you were taking some messages?

MR. BRIDE: No, sir; I was writing some accounts.

SENATOR SMITH: You were writing some accounts?

MR. BRIDE: Yes, sir.

SENATOR SMITH: Where?

MR. BRIDE: On the operating table.

SENATOR SMITH: On the operating table?

MR. BRIDE: Yes, sir.

SENATOR SMITH: Did you have this instrument off your head at the time?

MR. BRIDE: No, sir.

SENATOR SMITH: Were you aware that the *Californian* was trying to get you?

MR. BRIDE: Yes, sir.

SENATOR SMITH: You continued your work on the accounts, if I understand you correctly?

MR. BRIDE: Yes, sir.

SENATOR SMITH: And did not respond to the *Californian's* call?

MR. BRIDE: No, sir.

SENATOR SMITH: For 30 minutes?

MR. BRIDE: I do not think it was quite 30 minutes.

SENATOR SMITH: How long a time was it?

MR. BRIDE: It may have been. It would have been somewhere between 20 and 30 minutes. I can not say definitely.

SENATOR SMITH: Just what hour was this?

MR. BRIDE: Late in the afternoon.

SENATOR SMITH: Of Sunday?

MR. BRIDE: Yes, sir. I should say it was about 5 o'clock.

SENATOR SMITH: About six hours before that calamity occurred?

79

Mr. Bride: Yes, sir.

Senator Smith: Did your work continue for about 20 or 30 minutes on the accounts?

Mr. Bride: Yes, sir.

Senator Smith: After you had finished, what did you do?

Mr. Bride: I still remained on watch until dinner time.

Senator Smith: Had you had any other wireless communications regarding the proximity of icebergs?

Mr. Bride: No, sir.

Senator Smith: This information that you got from the *Californian* was the first information?

Mr. Bride: Yes, sir.

Senator Smith: And that you received about half past 5 o'clock, the afternoon of Sunday?

Mr. Bride: I should say it was nearer 5 o'clock, sir.

Senator Smith: When you took it?

Mr. Bride: Yes, sir.

Senator Smith: Then, when the first call was made it must have been about half past 4 o'clock?

Mr. Bride: Yes.

Senator Smith: The ship being under steam and moving all the time?

Mr. Bride: Yes, sir.

Senator Smith: When you got this call from the *Californian* which was intended for the *Baltic*, what did you do?

Mr. Bride: I simply waited until she informed the *Baltic*. It was an ice report. Then I knew it would be the same one she had for me, so I took it down.

Senator Smith: And delivered it?

Mr. Bride: Yes, sir. I acknowledged it to the *Californian* before I delivered it.

Senator Smith: You acknowledged it?

Mr. Bride: I acknowledged the receipt of it. . . .

Senator Smith: Now, once more I would like to have you tell the exact language of that message.

Mr. Bride: It stated the *Californian* had passed three large icebergs, and gave their latitude and longitude.

Senator Smith: That they had passed three large icebergs?

Mr. Bride: Yes, sir.

Senator Smith: And gave their latitude and longitude?

Mr. Bride: Yes; that she had passed very close to them.

SENATOR SMITH: Do you recollect what the latitude and longitude were?

MR. BRIDE: No, sir; indeed I do not.

SENATOR SMITH: Did you make a record of this communication?

MR. BRIDE: No, sir; I made it on a slip of paper and handed it to the bridge.

SENATOR SMITH: Intending to make a permanent record of it?

MR. BRIDE: No, sir.

SENATOR SMITH: Are you not obliged to make a record of it?

MR. BRIDE: No, sir.

SENATOR SMITH: The reason you made no record of this message was because it was not official?

MR. BRIDE: It was not official, sir. If we kept a record of all these messages we should never be able to get through our work.

SENATOR SMITH: If it had been official you would have preserved it?

MR. BRIDE: I should have preserved it.

SENATOR SMITH: And made permanent record of it?

MR. BRIDE: Yes, sir. . . .

SENATOR SMITH: Did you communicate this message to the captain?

MR. BRIDE: No, sir; I gave it to the officer on watch, sir.

SENATOR SMITH: I just wanted to know whether you communicated it to the captain, yourself?

MR. BRIDE: No, sir.

SENATOR SMITH: You communicated it to the officer in charge of the watch who had charge of the ship at the time?

MR. BRIDE: Yes, sir.

SENATOR SMITH: Did you receive any other communications regarding icebergs?

MR. BRIDE: No, sir.

SENATOR SMITH: From any ship, that afternoon or evening?

MR. BRIDE: No, sir.

SENATOR SMITH: Did Mr. [Jack] Phillips [the *Titanic's* senior wireless operator] receive a message from the *Amerika?*

MR. BRIDE: Not to my knowledge, sir.

SENATOR SMITH: You did not receive one from the *Amerika*?

MR. BRIDE: No, sir.

SENATOR SMITH: You are very certain about that?

MR. BRIDE: Yes, sir.

SENATOR SMITH: Are you also very certain that the only message you received regarding icebergs was received from the *Californian?*

MR. BRIDE: Personally; yes, sir. As to what Mr. Phillips received, I can not say.

SENATOR SMITH: No; I am not asking you that. Now, once more: Did Mr. Phillips at any time say to you that a message had been received from any other ship on that subject?

MR. BRIDE: No, sir.

SENATOR SMITH: Who was on duty at the wireless station from 6 o'clock Sunday evening until the collision or impact?

MR. BRIDE: I was on duty for half an hour, sir, while Mr. Phillips went and had his dinner.

SENATOR SMITH: At what hour?

MR. BRIDE: From 7 o'clock until half past.

SENATOR SMITH: Where were you after that, up to the time of the collision?

MR. BRIDE: At the time of the collision?

SENATOR SMITH: Up to the time of the collision.

MR. BRIDE: I was in bed.

SENATOR SMITH: You had retired?

MR. BRIDE: Yes, sir.

SENATOR SMITH: In a room adjacent to the apparatus?

MR. BRIDE: Yes, sir.

SENATOR SMITH: Did you and Mr. Phillips both occupy that room?

MR. BRIDE: Yes, sir.

SENATOR SMITH: How far was it from the apparatus?

MR. BRIDE: Just next door to it.

SENATOR SMITH: With a door between?

MR. BRIDE: There was a door between; yes, sir.

SENATOR SMITH: Could you enter immediately from the apparatus, or operating room, to the bedroom?

MR. BRIDE: Yes, sir.

SENATOR SMITH: You retired at what time?

Mr. BRIDE: It was just about 8 o'clock.

SENATOR SMITH: Were you in bed when this collision occurred?

Mr. BRIDE: Yes, sir.

SENATOR SMITH: Were you asleep?

Mr. BRIDE: Yes, sir.

SENATOR SMITH: Were you awakened by it?

Mr. BRIDE: No, sir.

SENATOR SMITH: How were you awakened?

Mr. BRIDE: I woke up of my own accord.

SENATOR SMITH: No one aroused you after that impact?

Mr. BRIDE: No, sir.

SENATOR SMITH: How long did you lie in bed after the collision?

Mr. BRIDE: I could not tell you, sir.

SENATOR SMITH: Did Mr. Phillips not arouse you?

Mr. BRIDE: No, sir.

SENATOR SMITH: Or attempt to do so?

Mr. BRIDE: No, sir.

SENATOR SMITH: Do you know what time you arose from your bed?

Mr. BRIDE: It must have been about a quarter to 12, sir; about 5 minutes to 12, ship's time.

SENATOR SMITH: Five minutes to 12, ship's time?

Mr. BRIDE: Yes, sir.

SENATOR SMITH: What time did the collision occur?

Mr. BRIDE: I could not say, sir.

SENATOR SMITH: You remained in bed until 12:05?

Mr. BRIDE: I think it was this side of 12, sir; it was about 5 minutes to 12.

SENATOR SMITH: Then you must have been aroused somewhat by this impact?

Mr. BRIDE: No; I had promised to relieve Mr. Phillips earlier than usual, you see.

SENATOR SMITH: Earlier than usual, that night?

Mr. BRIDE: Yes.

SENATOR SMITH: And you awakened yourself?

Mr. BRIDE: Yes.

SENATOR SMITH: Did you arise immediately?

Mr. BRIDE: Yes, sir.

SENATOR SMITH: And dress yourself?

MR. BRIDE: I went out to speak to him before I dressed. I only had pajamas on.

SENATOR SMITH: Before you put your clothes on?

MR. BRIDE: Yes, sir.

SENATOR SMITH: What did you say to him?

MR. BRIDE: I asked him how he was getting on.

SENATOR SMITH: What did he say?

MR. BRIDE: He had a big batch of telegrams from Cape Race [wireless station in Newfoundland] that he had just finished.

SENATOR SMITH: He told you that?

MR. BRIDE: Yes.

SENATOR SMITH: Had he finished his work?

MR. BRIDE: Yes.

SENATOR SMITH: This was after the collision?

MR. BRIDE: After the collision.

SENATOR SMITH: Did you remain in the operating room?

MR. BRIDE: I got dressed first.

SENATOR SMITH: You returned to the bedroom and got dressed?

MR. BRIDE: Yes, sir.

SENATOR SMITH: During that time did Mr. Phillips tell you that the boat had been injured?

MR. BRIDE: He told me that he thought she had got damaged in some way and that he expected that we should have to go back to Harlan & Wolff's.

SENATOR SMITH: Those are the builders, at Belfast?

MR. BRIDE: Yes.

SENATOR SMITH: What did you do then?

MR. BRIDE: I took over the watch from him.

SENATOR SMITH: You took the watch from him?

MR. BRIDE: Yes, sir.

SENATOR SMITH: Where did he go?

MR. BRIDE: He was going to retire, sir.

SENATOR SMITH: Did he retire?

MR. BRIDE: He got inside of the other room when the captain came in, then.

SENATOR SMITH: The captain came in?

MR. BRIDE: Yes, sir.

SENATOR SMITH: Personally?

MR. BRIDE: Yes, sir.

SENATOR SMITH: To the operating room?

MR. BRIDE: Yes, sir.

SENATOR SMITH: What did the captain say?

MR. BRIDE: He told us that we had better get assistance.

SENATOR SMITH: Can you tell us in his language?

MR. BRIDE: That is exactly what he said. He said, "You had better get assistance." When Mr. Phillips heard him he came out and asked him if he wanted him to use a distress call. He said, "Yes; at once."

SENATOR SMITH: Who sent this call?

MR. BRIDE: Mr. Phillips.

SENATOR SMITH: He responded to the captain's desire?

MR. BRIDE: Yes, sir.

SENATOR SMITH: And you turned the apparatus over to him?

MR. BRIDE: Yes, sir.

SENATOR SMITH: Was the message sent immediately?

MR. BRIDE: Immediately.

SENATOR SMITH: Do you know what the message was?

MR. BRIDE: Yes.

SENATOR SMITH: Please state it.

MR. BRIDE: C. Q. D. about half a dozen times; M. G. Y. half a dozen times.

SENATOR SMITH: Will you kindly explain the meaning of these letters or that code?

MR. BRIDE: C. Q. D. is a recognized distress call; M. G. Y. is the code call of the *Titanic*.

SENATOR SMITH: Is C. Q. D. in itself composed of the first letters of three words, or merely a code?

MR. BRIDE: Merely a code call, sir.

SENATOR SMITH: But one recognized by operators as important and as a distress call?

MR. BRIDE: Yes, sir.

SENATOR SMITH: How long after that call was sent out was it before you got a reply?

MR. BRIDE: As far as I know, immediately, sir.

SENATOR SMITH: Within two or three minutes?

MR. BRIDE: You see I could read what Mr. Phillips was sending, but I could not get the answers because he had the telephones.

SENATOR SMITH: You knew what he had sent, but you did not know what he received in reply?

MR. BRIDE: No, sir.

SENATOR SMITH: Right at this point I am going to ask Mr. Marconi if he will tell us what C. Q. D. means, literally.

MR. MARCONI: It is a conventional signal.

SENATOR SMITH: You mean it is in accordance with the international convention?

MR. MARCONI: No; it is not. It is a conventional signal which was introduced originally by my company to express a state of danger or peril of a ship that sends it.

MR. UHLER: It is an arbitrary signal?

MR. MARCONI: It is arbitrary, but it is conventional. Everyone understands it.

"C. Q." means "All stations," does it not, Mr. Bride?

MR. BRIDE: Yes, sir.

MR. MARCONI: C. Q. is the call for all stations. If you call C. Q. on a ship it means, "All other stations stand at attention and reply."

I did not make the signal originally. I presume the object was to indicate, in a certain way, to all stations, the danger . . . that existed.

MR. KIRLIN: Or distress?

MR. MARCONI: Or distress, yes.

I should add that the international danger signal, introduced or decided on by the Berlin convention, is S. O. S.

SENATOR SMITH: What does that mean?

MR. MARCONI: I do not know what it means. It denotes danger or distress. I believe that was sent, too, from the *Titanic;* but, of course, Mr. Bride will tell you, if it is the fact.

SENATOR SMITH: What is the silent signal?

MR. MARCONI: I do not know it, personally.

SENATOR SMITH: Under the international convention, I mean.

MR. MARCONI: I do not know it.

MR. BRIDE: It is D. D. D.

MR. MARCONI: D. D. D.

SENATOR SMITH: That is the silent signal?

MR. MARCONI: Yes, sir; that means "shut up."

SENATOR SMITH: All other stations must cease?

MR. MARCONI: All other stations must cease.

SENATOR SMITH: But the danger signal, C. Q. D., is the recognized signal for a ship in distress?

MR. MARCONI: Yes.

SENATOR SMITH: You received a reply within three or four minutes, but you only know that from what——
MR. BRIDE: Mr. Phillips told me.
SENATOR SMITH: Just what did he tell you?
MR. BRIDE: He told me to go to the captain and report the *Frankfurt*.
SENATOR SMITH: What do you mean by the *Frankfurt*?
MR. BRIDE: He was in communication with the *Frankfurt*, sir; he had sent the *Frankfurt* our position.
SENATOR SMITH: Was the *Frankfurt* the first ship that picked up the C. Q. D.?
MR. BRIDE: Yes, sir.
SENATOR SMITH: And you delivered that message to the captain?
MR. BRIDE: Yes, sir.
SENATOR SMITH: Personally?
MR. BRIDE: Yes, sir.
SENATOR SMITH: Where was he at the time?
MR. BRIDE: He was on the boat deck, sir.
SENATOR SMITH: On the boat deck?
MR. BRIDE: Yes, sir.
SENATOR SMITH: Not on the bridge?
MR. BRIDE: No, sir.
SENATOR SMITH: The boat deck being the sun deck, or upper deck?
MR. BRIDE: Being the decks where the boats are.
SENATOR SMITH: Where the lifeboats are.
MR. BRIDE: Yes, sir.
SENATOR SMITH: What did he say in reply when you handed him this message?
MR. BRIDE: He wanted to know where she was, sir.
SENATOR SMITH: Her latitude?
MR. BRIDE: And longitude, sir. I told him we would get that as soon as we could.
SENATOR SMITH: What did you do then?
MR. BRIDE: I went back to the cabin with Mr. Phillips.
SENATOR SMITH: What did you tell him?
MR. BRIDE: I told him I had reported to the captain.
SENATOR SMITH: And the captain wished that the position of the boat should be ascertained?
MR. BRIDE: Mr. Phillips was waiting for the position of the boat then, sir.

SENATOR SMITH: What was the next message received by Mr. Phillips?

MR. BRIDE: A reply from the *Carpathia.*

SENATOR SMITH: A reply to the C. Q. D. call?

MR. BRIDE: Yes, sir.

SENATOR SMITH: From the *Carpathia?*

MR. BRIDE: Yes, sir.

SENATOR SMITH: Did the *Carpathia* give her location?

MR. BRIDE: Yes, sir; after she had obtained it from the bridge.

SENATOR SMITH: What did the *Carpathia* message say?

MR. BRIDE: She sent her latitude and longitude and told him she was coming along as quickly as possible. She turned around and was steaming full speed, or words to that effect.

SENATOR SMITH: That she had reversed her course?

MR. BRIDE: Yes, sir.

SENATOR SMITH: And was steaming at full speed toward the *Titanic?*

MR. BRIDE: Yes, sir.

SENATOR SMITH: What was done with this message?

MR. BRIDE: It was taken to the captain, sir. I took it to the captain.

SENATOR SMITH: Where did you find him then?

MR. BRIDE: He was in the wheelhouse.

SENATOR SMITH: What?

MR. BRIDE: In the wheelhouse, upon the bridge.

SENATOR SMITH: In the pilot house?

MR. BURLINGHAM: The wheelhouse.

SENATOR SMITH: The wheelhouse?

MR. BRIDE: Yes, sir.

SENATOR SMITH: On the bridge?

MR. BRIDE: Yes, sir.

SENATOR SMITH: He could enter the wheelhouse from the bridge?

MR. BRIDE: Yes, sir.

SENATOR SMITH: What did the captain say when you delivered that message?

MR. BRIDE: He came back with me to the cabin, sir.

SENATOR SMITH: He came back with you to the cabin?

MR. BRIDE: Yes, sir.

SENATOR SMITH: What took place?

MR. BRIDE: He asked Mr. Phillips what other ships he was in communication with, sir.

SENATOR SMITH: He asked Mr. Phillips what other ships he was in communication with?

MR. BRIDE: Yes, sir.

SENATOR SMITH: And what was said?

MR. BRIDE: He interrupted Mr. Phillips when Mr. Phillips was establishing communication with the *Olympic,* so he was told the *Olympic* was there.

SENATOR SMITH: Then what took place, Mr. Bride?

MR. BRIDE: Why, he worked out the difference between the *Carpathia's* position and ours, sir.

SENATOR SMITH: Who did?

MR. BRIDE: The captain.

SENATOR SMITH: The captain worked out the difference?

MR. BRIDE: He roughly estimated it.

SENATOR SMITH: Worked out the difference between the *Carpathia's* position and that of the *Olympic?*

MR. BRIDE: No; the *Titanic.*

SENATOR SMITH: Between the *Carpathia's* position and that of the *Titanic?*

MR. BRIDE: Yes, sir.

SENATOR SMITH: And then what occurred?

MR. BRIDE: He went out to the cabin then, and we still continued to exchange.

SENATOR SMITH: He went out to the cabin?

MR. BRIDE: Yes, sir.

SENATOR SMITH: And the operator continued what?

MR. BRIDE: To exchange messages, sir.

SENATOR SMITH: To exchange messages?

MR. BRIDE: Yes, sir.

SENATOR SMITH: What was the next message, so far as you can recollect?

MR. BRIDE: Well, after the *Olympic,* sir, we did not get any replies, and I asked Mr. Phillips outside—well, he went outside to see how they were getting on, and I took the phones.

SENATOR SMITH: I understand from you that the first response to the C. Q. D. call of distress was from the *Frankfurt?*

MR. BRIDE: Yes, sir.

SENATOR SMITH: What line of boats?

MR. BRIDE: German line, as far as I can remember, sir.

MR. MARCONI: The North German Lloyd.

SENATOR SMITH: Did you receive any other communication from the *Frankfurt?*

MR. BRIDE: Not then, sir. We had transmitted to the *Frankfurt* our position, but we had received nothing from him in return.

SENATOR SMITH: You transmitted to the *Frankfurt* your position in the sea?

MR. BRIDE: Yes, sir.

SENATOR SMITH: And never received any further acknowledgment?

MR. BRIDE: He told us to stand by, sir. That means to wait.

SENATOR SMITH: The *Frankfurt* told you to stand by?

MR. BRIDE: Yes, sir.

SENATOR SMITH: Does that mean "I am coming?"

MR. BRIDE: It means wait; he is coming back again.

SENATOR SMITH: Where was the *Frankfurt* headed for?

MR. BRIDE: I believe she was bound east, sir; but I can not say for certain.

SENATOR SMITH: Had you been in communication with the *Frankfurt* during that day or the preceding day?

MR. BRIDE: I can not say, sir, as to that.

SENATOR SMITH: What is your best recollection about it?

MR. BRIDE: I can not say, sir. We were in communication with several ships during the afternoon and evening. . . .

SENATOR SMITH: Did anyone say in your hearing that they thought the *Frankfurt* was in closer proximity to the *Titanic* than any other ship?

MR. BRIDE: Yes, sir; Mr. Phillips told me so.

SENATOR SMITH: Who said that?

MR. BRIDE: Mr. Phillips told me that, judging by the strength of the signals received from the two ships, the *Frankfurt* was the nearer.

SENATOR SMITH: Did Mr. Phillips tell you that he was trying to establish such communication with the *Frankfurt* as would bring that ship to your relief?

MR. BRIDE: Well, Mr. Phillips was under the impression that when the *Frankfurt* had heard the C. Q. D. and got our position, he would immediately make it known to his commander and take further steps. Apparently he did not.

SENATOR SMITH: Did the captain of the *Titanic* make any personal reference to that matter to you, or within your hearing, or to Mr. Phillips?

MR. BRIDE: No, sir; he asked us where the *Frankfurt* was, but we told him we could not tell him. . . .

SENATOR SMITH: Did any officer on the *Titanic* at any time express the hope that the *Frankfurt* would come first to their relief?

MR. BRIDE: No, sir.

SENATOR SMITH: Did you have any other communication with the *Frankfurt* after that ship responded to the distress call?

MR. BRIDE: Yes, sir.

SENATOR SMITH: What was it?

MR. BRIDE: He called us up at a considerably long period afterwards and asked us what was the matter.

SENATOR SMITH: How long after?

MR. BRIDE: I should say it would be considerably over 20 minutes afterwards.

SENATOR SMITH: Twenty minutes after the message giving your position, the position of the *Titanic*——

MR. BRIDE: And the C. Q. D.

SENATOR SMITH (continuing): And the C. Q. D. distress call, you got another message from the *Frankfurt* saying, "What is the matter?"

MR. BRIDE: Yes, sir.

SENATOR SMITH: Did they say anything else?

MR. BRIDE: He merely inquired, sir, as to what was the matter with us.

SENATOR SMITH: To that message what did you say?

MR. BRIDE: I think Mr. Phillips responded rather hurriedly.

SENATOR SMITH: What did he say? I would like to know?

MR. BRIDE: Well, he told him to the effect that he was a bit of a fool.

SENATOR SMITH: Just give it in his language.

MR. BRIDE: Well, he told him he was a fool, sir.

SENATOR SMITH: Is that all?

MR. BRIDE: Yes, sir.

SENATOR SMITH: Did he preface that word with anything more severe?

MR. BRIDE: No, sir.

SENATOR SMITH: Did Mr. Phillips then tell him what was the matter?

MR. BRIDE: No, sir.

SENATOR SMITH: Did he have any further communication with the *Frankfurt?*

MR. BRIDE: No, sir. He told him to stand by, sir—finish.

SENATOR SMITH: In the interim you had got into communication with the *Carpathia?*

MR. BRIDE: And the *Olympic.*

SENATOR SMITH: And the *Olympic?*

MR. BRIDE: Yes, sir.

SENATOR SMITH: Both of whom assured you they were coming?

MR. BRIDE: Yes, sir.

SENATOR SMITH: To your relief?

MR. BRIDE: Yes, sir.

SENATOR SMITH: To what line does the *Olympic* belong?

MR. BRIDE: White Star, sir.

SENATOR SMITH: And the *Carpathia* belongs to the Cunard Line?

MR. BRIDE: The Cunard; yes, sir.

SENATOR SMITH: Did you ever learn the position of the *Frankfurt?*

MR. BRIDE: No, sir.

SENATOR SMITH: After she had first responded to your call?

MR. BRIDE: No, sir.

SENATOR SMITH: Did Mr. Phillips ask for it?

MR. BRIDE: Yes, sir.

SENATOR SMITH: How often?

MR. BRIDE: When she first answered our C. Q. D. he said, "Go and get your position." The *Frankfurt* replied "Stand by."

SENATOR SMITH: Did the *Frankfurt* at that time know your position?

MR. BRIDE: Yes, sir.

SENATOR SMITH: What was your interpretation of "stand by," in that connection?

MR. BRIDE: To wait for his position and what he was going to do about the matter.

SENATOR SMITH: Did you ever get the position of the *Frankfurt?*

MR. BRIDE: No, sir.

SENATOR SMITH: Did Mr. Phillips?

MR. BRIDE: No, sir.

SENATOR SMITH: Did you and Mr. Phillips talk about it?

MR. BRIDE: Yes, sir.

SENATOR SMITH: What did you say to one another about it?

MR. BRIDE: We expressed our opinions of the operator on the *Frankfurt*.

SENATOR SMITH: Was it critical?

MR. BRIDE: Yes, sir.

SENATOR SMITH: And uncomplimentary?

MR. BRIDE: Very.

SENATOR SMITH: Was it based upon any knowledge or suspicion that the operator was personally derelict in his duty?

MR. BRIDE: Yes, sir.

SENATOR SMITH: Was it based upon any suspicion that the *Frankfurt* had not responded to this distress call as that ship should have done?

MR. BRIDE: Yes, sir.

SENATOR SMITH: Was it a matter of deep regret between you and Mr. Phillips?

MR. BRIDE: Well, it was at the time when the *Frankfurt* asked us what the matter was with us, because we realized then that we were getting into—we realized what had happened to the ship.

SENATOR SMITH: But you realized at that time that all the lives on that ship depended upon getting relief from some other vessel?

MR. BRIDE: At the time the *Frankfurt* asked us what was the matter with us; yes, sir.

SENATOR SMITH: After you told him that he was a fool, did you tell him the ship was going down?

MR. BRIDE: No, sir; we told him to stand by, sir; to keep out of it.

SENATOR SMITH: Keep out of what?

MR. BRIDE: Not to interfere with his instrument, sir; because we were in communication with the *Carpathia,* and we knew that the *Carpathia* was the best thing doing.

SENATOR SMITH: Did you tell that to the operator of the *Frankfurt?*

MR. BRIDE: No, sir.

SENATOR SMITH: When you said "Keep out of it," could that be interpreted as in any way changing the first distress call?

MR. BRIDE: Merely told him not to interfere with our communications.

SENATOR SMITH: He had not responded as you felt he ought to respond?

MR. BRIDE: Yes, sir.

SENATOR SMITH: He had not indicated that they were coming?

MR. BRIDE: No, sir.

SENATOR SMITH: He had impressed you with the lack of appreciation for your situation? Stop me if I am not interpreting you correctly; I am summarizing what you have said. Am I correct about that?

MR. BRIDE: It struck me so—that he did not seem to be able to realize the position we were in.

SENATOR SMITH: And you are quite sure that you gave him all the information necessary?

MR. BRIDE: We made it very clear to him.

SENATOR SMITH: You mean in referring to the condition you were in, you referred to the sinking of the *Titanic?*

MR. BRIDE: If you call C. Q. D. and give your position, then there is no necessity for another ship to inquire further into the matter, if he is coming to your assistance, because you could not call C. Q. D. unless you were in need of assistance.

SENATOR SMITH: Now, C. Q. D. was the strongest language that you could use under your wireless regulations to apprise any station that you needed help immediately; is that right?

MR. BRIDE: Any operator hearing a C. Q. D., giving a ship's position, when on the job would immediately, without inquiring further into the matter, go to his captain and inform his captain. It would be a waste of time asking anything about it. The less time spent in talking, the more time can be spent in getting to the ship. . . .

SENATOR SMITH: After you told this operator he was a fool, and 20 minutes had gone by, did you tell him that your ship was sinking?

MR. BRIDE: No, sir.

SENATOR SMITH: Did you give him any additional information?

MR. BRIDE: No, sir. He ought not to have wanted any in the first place.

SENATOR SMITH: Upon the information you did give him, are you ready to say whether the ship responded or not?

MR. BRIDE: There ought not to have been any doubt about the information we gave him at all, sir; he ought to have known what to do with it immediately.

SENATOR SMITH: So far as you know, the *Frankfurt* did not respond?

MR. BRIDE: No, sir.

SENATOR SMITH: Will you tell us what confirmation you have that the operator of the *Frankfurt* received your C. Q. D. distress call correctly?

MR. BRIDE: Mr. Phillips had the telephones on at the time, sir. He called "C. Q. D." The *Frankfurt* answered. He gave the *Frankfurt* our position. He said, "Come at once." The *Frankfurt* said, "Stand by." We waited, and that is the last we heard of the *Frankfurt* until he said, "What was the matter with you?" a considerable period afterwards.

SENATOR SMITH: After he said, "What was the matter with you?" then what was said?

MR. BRIDE: We told him he was a fool, sir.

SENATOR SMITH: Was that the last thing you said to him?

MR. BRIDE: To the *Frankfurt,* yes, sir.

SENATOR SMITH: You recall that you said later to him to keep out, not to interfere with your insulation, or——

MR. BRIDE: We told him to keep out and not interfere with our communication.

SENATOR SMITH: Was that all in the one message?

MR. BRIDE: That was all in the one message.

SENATOR SMITH: "You are a fool. Keep out and do not interfere with our communication."

MR. BRIDE: Yes, sir.

SENATOR SMITH: That was all in the one message?

MR. BRIDE: Yes, sir.

SENATOR SMITH: And that was the last thing you said to the *Frankfurt?*

MR. BRIDE: Yes, sir.

SENATOR SMITH: Now, did you see the *Frankfurt* in the

95

vicinity of the wreck of the *Titanic,* or after you were taken on board the *Carpathia?*

MR. BRIDE: The only ship I saw, sir, was the *Carpathia.* . . .

SENATOR SMITH: Mr. Bride, do you know whether the operator on the *Frankfurt* understood the English language?

MR. BRIDE: There was no necessity for him to understand the English language, sir.

SENATOR SMITH: Because this call——

MR. BRIDE: Was an international call.

SENATOR SMITH: And C. Q. D. means the same in the German language and the French language and the English language?

MR. BRIDE: Yes, sir.

SENATOR SMITH: And is the international code signal of distress?

MR. BRIDE: Yes, sir.

SENATOR SMITH: Under the Berlin convention?

MR. BRIDE: I can not say, sir.

SENATOR SMITH: Under the regulations of the Marconi Co.?

MR. BRIDE: It is recognized by all ships' operators as being a signal of distress.

SENATOR SMITH: Mr. Bride, I want this record to be as complete as possible, and I desire to know why, after a message was received from the *Frankfurt* asking "What is the matter" you did not reply "We are sinking and the lives of our passengers and crew are in danger"?

MR. BRIDE: You see, it takes a certain amount of time to transmit that information, sir. If the man had understood properly, as he ought to have, C. Q. D. would have been sufficient, sir. C. Q. D. is the whole thing in a nutshell, you see.

SENATOR SMITH: Yes; but it did not seem to move him.

MR. BRIDE: Well, he did not know his business, that is all, sir.

SENATOR SMITH: But in such an emergency do you not think that a more detailed statement might have been sent? Take, for instance, the message from the *Titanic* to the *Carpathia* that the boiler rooms were filling with water and the ship sinking; that could have been sent with perfect propriety to a boat that was in proximity, could it not?

MR. BRIDE: No, sir; I do not think it could have been, under the circumstances.

SENATOR SMITH: Do you mean to say that the regulations under which you operate are such that in a situation of this character you have such discretionary power that you may dismiss an inquiry of that character——

MR. BRIDE: You use your common sense.

SENATOR SMITH (continuing): Without further word?

MR. BRIDE: You use your common sense, and the man on the *Frankfurt* apparently was not using his at the time.

SENATOR SMITH: I know, but the theory upon which you were angered was that the *Frankfurt* was closer to you than any other ship?

MR. BRIDE: The *Frankfurt* was the first one. We had not got the position. We could not say he was nearer. The signals were stronger.

SENATOR SMITH: Now, Mr. Bride, I would like to ask you whether your dismissing the somewhat tardy inquiry of the *Frankfurt* was due to the fact that you were in constant communication with the *Carpathia;* understand me?

MR. BRIDE: Well, it appeared to Mr. Phillips and me, sir, that the *Carpathia* was the only thing we could hope for at the time we told the *Frankfurt* to keep out of it.

SENATOR SMITH: In other words, you held on to a certainty rather than an uncertainty?

MR. BRIDE: Yes, sir.

SENATOR SMITH: The results of your communications with the *Carpathia* were such as led you to believe that the operator on the *Carpathia* and the officers of that ship understood fully your position and the danger you were in?

MR. BRIDE: Yes, sir.

SENATOR SMITH: And were coming toward you at full speed?

MR. BRIDE: Yes, sir.

SENATOR SMITH: In that situation, if the *Frankfurt* had been 20 miles nearer the *Titanic* than the *Carpathia,* would you still have thought, from what you knew of the ship's condition, that it was wise to confine your communications to the *Carpathia?*

MR. BRIDE: Had we known the *Frankfurt's* position, having already got the *Carpathia's* position, we should have used our judgment, and had the *Frankfurt* been any reasonable distance nearer we should have informed the *Frankfurt* of the whole business and repeated each word we sent to him about a dozen times, to make sure he got it.

SENATOR SMITH: Her position, however, was an object of some speculation?

MR. BRIDE: Yes, sir. . . .

SENATOR SMITH: Mr. Marconi, do you know how the *Frankfurt* is equipped?

MR. MARCONI: The *Frankfurt* is, I believe, a ship belonging to the North German Lloyd. She is equipped by a German company, called the Debed Co. It means a lot of things in German, each letter, which I will not go into, of which I am a director.

SENATOR SMITH: You are a director in the German company?

MR. MARCONI: Yes.

SENATOR SMITH: And you are familiar with the wireless equipment or apparatus?

MR. MARCONI: I am not familiar with the wireless equipment of that particular ship.

SENATOR SMITH: So that you would be unable to make a comparative statement—to make a comparison between the equipment or apparatus on the *Carpathia* and the apparatus on the *Frankfurt?*

MR. MARCONI: I would be unable, sir, to do it.

SENATOR SMITH: Would the fact that the *Frankfurt* is equipped with an apparatus of German type in any way lessen their interest in calls made through the Marconi machine or apparatus?

MR. MARCONI: No; because it is a Marconi apparatus. It is made in Germany, but it is made under my patents under an arrangement which we have with German interests.

SENATOR SMITH: Let me ask you: Are the regulations of Germany, with reference to the operation and use of wireless telegraphy, in perfect harmony with the Berlin convention?

MR. MARCONI: Absolutely. They were enacted at Berlin and most of them were inspired by the German Government.

SENATOR SMITH: Are these calls that are recognized prescribed in the Berlin convention?

MR. MARCONI: The call of the Berlin convention, which has

only been recently introduced, is this S. O. S. call, but the Marconi companies have used and use the C. Q. D. call. The *Frankfurt,* which was equipped with wireless, belonged to one of what I may call the Marconi companies, because I would not be a director of the company if it was not associated with us.

SENATOR SMITH: Would you think that any confusion would arise, growing out of this international arrangement of signal, with the Marconi signal?

MR. MARCONI: No; I should state that the international signal is really less known than the Marconi Co.'s signal.

SENATOR SMITH: So that the C. Q. D. call must have been understood in its full significance by the *Frankfurt* operator?

MR. MARCONI: I have got absolutely no doubt as to that.

SENATOR SMITH: And under the regulations would that be sufficient?

MR. MARCONI: That would be sufficient.

SENATOR SMITH: To bring relief?

MR. MARCONI: Yes.

SENATOR SMITH: I want to know this, before I get away from it. I want to know whether the communications between the *Titanic* and the *Carpathia* were not also within the radius of the *Frankfurt?* I would like to know whether these communications could have been picked up by the *Frankfurt?*

MR. BRIDE: Certainly they could have been.

SENATOR SMITH: Had the operator on the *Frankfurt* shown vigilance.

MR. BRIDE: Certainly. He ought have heard every word that passed between us.

SENATOR SMITH: When you told him to keep out you were guarding against that thing?

MR. BRIDE: We were guarding against his interfering with other communications which we might establish, and we had already established.

SENATOR SMITH: How could it interfere with you?

MR. BRIDE: Because you can not read two ships at once. . . .

SENATOR SMITH: In order that the record may contain the answer, I would like to know whether it would have taken any longer or any more effort for you to have sent the same message to the *Frankfurt* that was sent to the *Carpathia,* when you realized that you were in imminent danger? Is there any code signal for "fool"?

MR. BRIDE: No, sir.

SENATOR SMITH: It would have taken no more time to apprise the *Frankfurt* of your perilous condition, growing more so all the time since the C. Q. D. call?

MR. BRIDE: He did not acknowledge the receipt of that when we told him he was a fool and told him to keep out.

SENATOR SMITH: As a matter of fact it would not have taken any more time to say "we are sinking" than it would have taken to have told him "you are a fool"?

MR. BRIDE: I assume Mr. Phillips thought that if he did not get our first C. Q. D., which was sent slowly and carefully by Mr. Phillips, he would not get anything else.

SENATOR SMITH: Do you think he understood your message that he was a fool?

MR. BRIDE: I doubt it. I think it was sent too fast for him. . . .

SENATOR SMITH: Did you continue to send messages, or Mr. Phillips, up to the time you left the cabin?

MR. BRIDE: When we had finished with the *Frankfurt,* and we had thoroughly informed the *Carpathia* of our position, Mr. Phillips again went out to look and see how things were going outside. I tried to establish a communication with the *Baltic,* and it was not very satisfactory, and I judged myself, from the strength of her signals, that she was too far away to do any good and it was not worth taking any trouble, and I told her we were sinking fast and there was no hope of saving the ship.

SENATOR SMITH: Told who?

MR. BRIDE: The *Baltic.*

SENATOR SMITH: Did Mr. Phillips return from the deck?

MR. BRIDE: Yes, sir.

SENATOR SMITH: To the room?

MR. BRIDE: Yes, sir.

SENATOR SMITH: What did he say to you then?

MR. BRIDE: He told us he thought it was time we put on our life belts.

SENATOR SMITH: Did you act upon his suggestion?

MR. BRIDE: Yes, sir.

SENATOR SMITH: And both of you put on life belts?

MR. BRIDE: Yes, sir.

SENATOR SMITH: At that time had all the lifeboats been lowered?

MR. BRIDE: I could not say, sir.

SENATOR SMITH: You paid no attention to the lifeboats?

MR. BRIDE: Mr. Phillips told me that things looked very queer outside. Beyond that I knew nothing.

SENATOR SMITH: How did you interpret the word "queer"?

MR. BRIDE: The sooner we were out of it the better.

SENATOR SMITH: What did you do then, Mr. Bride?

MR. BRIDE: Mr. Phillips sat down again at the telephone and gave a general call of C. Q. D., but I think that our lamps were running down; we did not get a spark. We could not tell, because the spark of our wireless was in an inclosed room. We could not hear at any time whether it was sparking.

SENATOR SMITH: When Mr. Phillips sat down to the instrument did he have a life preserver on, and did you put one on?

MR. BRIDE: Yes, sir.

SENATOR SMITH: And did you put one on?

MR. BRIDE: Yes, sir.

SENATOR SMITH: Immediately?

MR. BRIDE: Yes, sir.

SENATOR SMITH: But after he had put the life preserver on he tried and succeeded, as I understand you, in sending a last message, and that message was C. Q. D.; and anything else?

MR. BRIDE: General C. Q. D., M. G. Y.; waiting for some one to answer.

SENATOR SMITH: What did you do then, Mr. Bride?

MR. BRIDE: On Mr. Phillips's request I started to gather up his spare money and put on another coat, and made general preparations for leaving the ship.

SENATOR SMITH: How did you expect to leave the ship?

MR. BRIDE: We had to wait until the captain told us, first.

SENATOR SMITH: You had to wait until the captain told you?

MR. BRIDE: Yes, sir. He came along in a very short period afterwards and told us we had better look out for ourselves.

SENATOR SMITH: You waited until the captain told you that you could leave the ship?

MR. BRIDE: Yes, sir.

SENATOR SMITH: How long was that before the ship disappeared?

MR. BRIDE: I should say it was just about a quarter of an hour.

SENATOR SMITH: About 15 minutes?

MR. BRIDE: About 15 minutes.

SENATOR SMITH: And the captain said you had better take care of yourselves?

MR. BRIDE: Yes, sir.

SENATOR SMITH: Did he indicate what he was going to do?

MR. BRIDE: No, sir.

SENATOR SMITH: Where was he when he said this?

MR. BRIDE: He came around to the cabin to tell us.

SENATOR SMITH: He came around to the cabin?

MR. BRIDE: Yes, sir.

SENATOR SMITH: Was there anyone else on the deck?

MR. BRIDE: Oh, there were other people on the deck.

SENATOR SMITH: With you?

MR. BRIDE: Yes; they were running around all over the place.

SENATOR SMITH: How running around?

MR. BRIDE: Several people looking for life belts and looking for refreshments.

SENATOR SMITH: I want to locate exactly the position of this operating room of yours with reference to the boat deck or upper deck. Is it at the rear of the A or B deck?

MR. BRIDE: I believe on the *Titanic,* sir, the boat deck was called A deck. There was no deck above that, with the exception of a little deck which covered the roofs of the houses that were on A deck.

SENATOR SMITH: These people that you say were running around were running around these decks, all of them?

MR. BRIDE: The officers' quarters were situated together with the Marconi cabin, the officers' rooms, and other places, and the people were running around through these cabins. We had a woman in our cabin who had fainted.

SENATOR SMITH: A woman in your cabin who had fainted?

MR. BRIDE: And we were giving her a glass of water there and a chair. We set her down on a chair, which she wanted badly, and then her husband took her away again.

SENATOR SMITH: You gave her a glass of water and revived her, and her husband took her away?

MR. BRIDE: Yes, sir.

SENATOR SMITH: Did they have on life preservers?

MR. BRIDE: Yes, sir.

SENATOR SMITH: But some of these passengers or person were without life belts at that time, and were looking for them?

MR. BRIDE: Yes, sir.

SENATOR SMITH: You and your assistant had on life belts, and after this final message, C. Q. D. and M. G. Y., that was the last you saw of the wireless apparatus?

MR. BRIDE: Yes, sir.

SENATOR SMITH: Did you see any lifeboats after that?

MR. BRIDE: No, sir.

SENATOR SMITH: Do you know whether there was any on the ship at that time?

MR. BRIDE: There were no big lifeboats on the ship at that time. There was a collapsible boat on the top deck at the side of the forward funnel.

SENATOR SMITH: You mean over the officers' quarters?

MR. BRIDE: Over the officers' cabin, sir.

SENATOR SMITH: Do you know what was done with that?

MR. BRIDE: Yes, sir.

SENATOR SMITH: What was done with it?

MR. BRIDE: It was pushed over on to the boat deck.

SENATOR SMITH: What was done then with it?

MR. BRIDE: Went over the side.

SENATOR SMITH: You never saw it?

MR. BRIDE: Yes; I went over with it.

MR. BURLINGHAM: He says it went over the side.

SENATOR SMITH: I understand what the second officer said about it. I want to know whether you saw it again?

MR. BRIDE: Yes, sir; it went over the side of the ship. It was washed off by a wave.

SENATOR SMITH: It was washed over the side of the ship by a wave?

MR. BRIDE: Yes, sir.

SENATOR SMITH: And fell into the water?

MR. BRIDE: Yes, sir.

SENATOR SMITH: Bottom side upward?

MR. BRIDE: Yes, sir.

SENATOR SMITH: And how far were you from the water when you saw this boat fall?

MR. BRIDE: I was in the boat.

SENATOR SMITH: You were in the boat?

MR. BRIDE: Yes, sir.

SENATOR SMITH: It fell, the bottom side upward?

MR. BRIDE: Yes, sir.

SENATOR SMITH: What became of you?

MR. BRIDE: I was inside the boat.

SENATOR SMITH: You were under the boat?

MR. BRIDE: Yes.

SENATOR SMITH: How long did you remain in the boat?

MR. BRIDE: I could not tell you.

SENATOR SMITH: About how long?

MR. BRIDE: It seemed a lifetime to me, really.

SENATOR SMITH: I understand, but I would like to know, if possible, if at any time you got on top of the boat?

MR. BRIDE: I got on top of the boat eventually.

SENATOR SMITH: Eventually?

MR. BRIDE: Yes, sir.

SENATOR SMITH: Before anyone else got on top of it?

MR. BRIDE: No, sir.

SENATOR SMITH: Who was on top of the boat when you got on?

MR. BRIDE: There was a big crowd on top when I got on. I had to get away from under the bottom.

SENATOR SMITH: You remained under the boat how long?

MR. BRIDE: I should say about three-quarters of an hour, or a half.

SENATOR SMITH: Was there breathing space under the boat when it was turned over in that way?

MR. BRIDE: Yes, sir.

SENATOR SMITH: So that you got away from it as quickly as you could?

MR. BRIDE: Yes, sir.

SENATOR SMITH: You got out free from it, or did you cling to it, pulling yourself up to the side?

MR. BRIDE: I freed myself from it and cleared out of it.

SENATOR SMITH: How did you get back to it, then?

MR. BRIDE: Swam back, eventually.

SENATOR SMITH: Which side of the boat was that on, port or starboard?

MR. BRIDE: On the port side of the *Titanic*.

SENATOR SMITH: Did you hear the second officer yesterday say that that boat came around from the starboard to the port side?

MR. BRIDE: I was not here yesterday.

SENATOR SMITH: You can not say as to that?

MR. BRIDE: It went straight over the port side, sir.

SENATOR SMITH: It went straight over the port side?

MR. BRIDE: It was on the port side of the forward funnel. We pushed it on the port side of the boat deck, and it went over the port side of the *Titanic*.

SENATOR SMITH: Did it at any time get on the starboard side?

MR. BRIDE: Not to my knowledge.

SENATOR SMITH: You say there were a number of people on the boat, on the bottom of the boat that was bottom-up when you got there?

MR. BRIDE: Yes.

SENATOR SMITH: Do you know any of them?

MR. BRIDE: I heard afterwards that the senior operator was on board.

SENATOR SMITH: Mr. Phillips?

MR. BRIDE: Mr. Phillips.

SENATOR SMITH: Was on the boat?

MR. BRIDE: Yes; I heard so afterwards.

SENATOR SMITH: He did not survive, however?

MR. BRIDE: He did not survive.

SENATOR SMITH: Do you know whether he died going from the *Titanic* to the *Carpathia*?

MR. BRIDE: He died on the way; yes. He died on board the upturned boat.

SENATOR SMITH: What became of his body?

MR. BRIDE: As far as I know, it was taken on board the *Carpathia* and buried from the *Carpathia*.

SENATOR SMITH: Buried at sea?

MR. BRIDE: Buried from the *Carpathia*.

SENATOR SMITH: Did any one else die on that boat between the wreck and the *Carpathia*?

MR. BRIDE: There was a man lying aft that they said was dead when they took him onto the ship's boat.

SENATOR SMITH: What did they do with his body?

MR. BRIDE: He was taken on board the *Carpathia,* as far as I know.

SENATOR SMITH: They took his body to the *Carpathia?*

MR. BRIDE: Yes.

SENATOR SMITH: How many people were on that boat?

MR. BRIDE: It was estimated between 30 and 40.

SENATOR SMITH: Were there any women on the boat?

MR. BRIDE: No, sir.

SENATOR SMITH: How many people were in the boat or on the boat when it fell from the upper deck on to the lower deck?

MR. BRIDE: There was not anybody in it. It was pushed over intentionally.

SENATOR SMITH: Was it fastened to the boat davits?

MR. BRIDE: No, sir; it was resting on a proper bed there for it.

SENATOR SMITH: How did you get in it?

MR. BRIDE: When it was pushed over on to the A deck, we all scrambled down on to A deck again.

SENATOR SMITH: You all scrambled in?

MR. BRIDE: We did not scramble in. We scrambled down on to A deck and were going to launch it properly.

SENATOR SMITH: Then what happened?

MR. BRIDE: It was washed overboard before we had time to launch it.

SENATOR SMITH: The boat was washed over?

MR. BRIDE: Yes, sir.

SENATOR SMITH: You then went down with it?

MR. BRIDE: I happened to be nearest it and I grabbed it.

SENATOR SMITH: You grabbed it and went down with it?

MR. BRIDE: Yes, sir.

SENATOR SMITH: Did anyone else grab it?

MR. BRIDE: No, sir.

SENATOR SMITH: You went down with it alone?

MR. BRIDE: Yes, sir.

SENATOR SMITH: It fell in such shape that you were under it?

MR. BRIDE: Yes, sir.

SENATOR SMITH: You say there were no women on that boat?

MR. BRIDE: No, sir.

SENATOR SMITH: When it reached the *Carpathia* or at any other time?

MR. BRIDE: No, sir.

SENATOR SMITH: And there were about 35 or 40 people all together?

MR. BRIDE: Yes, sir.

SENATOR SMITH: Do you know any of the people that were on that boat besides Mr. Phillips and yourself?

MR. BRIDE: There was an officer, I believe, on the boat.

SENATOR SMITH: An officer?

MR. BRIDE: And there was a passenger; I could not see whether he was first, second, or third.

SENATOR SMITH: What kind of a looking man?

MR. BRIDE: I could not say, sir.

SENATOR SMITH: Have you learned who it was?

MR. BRIDE: No, sir; I heard him say at the time he was a passenger.

SENATOR SMITH: Was it Col. Gracie?

MR. BRIDE: I could not say. He merely said he was a passenger.

SENATOR SMITH: Where did he get on?

MR. BRIDE: I could not say. I was the last man they invited on board.

SENATOR SMITH: Were there others struggling to get on?

MR. BRIDE: Yes, sir.

SENATOR SMITH: How many?

MR. BRIDE: Dozens.

SENATOR SMITH: Dozens. In the water?

MR. BRIDE: Yes, sir.

SENATOR SMITH: With life preservers on?

MR. BRIDE: Yes, sir.

SENATOR SMITH: Was this one man the only passenger?

MR. BRIDE: I could not say.

SENATOR SMITH: Did anyone say to you that anyone else was a passenger?

MR. BRIDE: No, sir; we did not have much to say to each other.

SENATOR SMITH: You did not talk to one another?

MR. BRIDE: No, sir.

SENATOR SMITH: Do you know whether the other occupants of that boat were officers or seamen or stewards or employees?

MR. BRIDE: I should judge they were all employees. They were all part of the boat's crews.

SENATOR SMITH: They were all in the water?

MR. BRIDE: They had all been in the water some time or other.

SENATOR SMITH: They had been in the water at some time when they got onto the upturned boat?

MR. BRIDE: Yes. . . .

SENATOR SMITH: When did you last see the captain? When he told you to take care of yourself?

MR. BRIDE: The last I saw of the captain he went overboard from the bridge, sir.

SENATOR SMITH: Did you see the *Titanic* sink?

MR. BRIDE: Yes, sir.

SENATOR SMITH: And the captain was at that time on the bridge?

MR. BRIDE: No, sir.

SENATOR SMITH: What do you mean by overboard?

MR. BRIDE: He jumped overboard from the bridge. He jumped overboard from the bridge when we were launching the collapsible lifeboat.

SENATOR SMITH: I should judge from what you have said that this was about three or four minutes before the boat sank.

MR. BRIDE: Yes. It would be just about five minutes before the boat sank.

SENATOR SMITH: About five minutes?

MR. BRIDE: Yes.

SENATOR SMITH: Do you know whether the captain had a life belt on?

MR. BRIDE: He had not when I last saw him.

SENATOR SMITH: He had not?

MR. BRIDE: No, sir.

SENATOR SMITH: Did the bridge go under water at about the same time?

MR. BRIDE: Yes, sir. The whole of the ship was practically under water to the forward funnel, and when I saw her go down the stern came out of the water and she slid down fore and aft.

SENATOR SMITH: The captain at no time went over until the vessel sank?

MR. BRIDE: No, sir.

SENATOR SMITH: He went with the vessel?

MR. BRIDE: Practically speaking; yes, sir.

SENATOR SMITH: I would like to ask you, before I forget it,

whether as this vessel went down there was much suction there?

MR. BRIDE: No, sir.

SENATOR SMITH: There was not?

MR. BRIDE: No, sir.

SENATOR SMITH: The fact that so few of the passengers and crew were picked up [from the water] by the *Carpathia* with life preservers on would seem to indicate that they were sucked under these waves or this water as the ship disappeared. What is your judgment about that?

MR. BRIDE: I estimate I was within 150 feet of the *Titanic;* I was swimming when she went down, and I felt practically no suction at all. . . .

THIRD DAY
Monday, April 22
Washington, D.C.

After the necessary subpoenas had been served in New York to keep crucial witnesses like Ismay in the country, the hearings resumed in Washington before the full, seven-member Senate subcommittee. The initial venue was the immense new caucus room of the Russell Senate Office Building, a room that ever since has been the setting for defining moments in American political history, from the McCarthy hearings to the Watergate hearings to the Clinton-era campaign finance hearings. Later, for acoustic and other reasons, the Titanic hearings were moved to other rooms, where attendance was restricted. On this day, however, there was again a huge throng of spectators.

The full panel for the Titanic inquiry: Chairman Smith and Vice Chairman Newlands (both of whom had returned from New York), as well as Senators George C. Perkins, Republican of California; Jonathan Bourne Jr., Republican of Oregon; Theodore E. Burton, Republican of Ohio; F. M. Simmons, Democrat of North Carolina; and Duncan U. Fletcher, Democrat of Florida.

Witness: Philip A. S. Franklin, 41
American vice president of the International Mercantile Marine Co., the White Star Line's parent company

Key testimony: Franklin shed light on wireless messages that had haunted the disaster and its aftermath, and on Ismay's behavior and motives. He described the confused effort in New York to ascertain the fate of the Titanic in the hours and days after the accident, but did not know the source of a

110

*fraudulent cable the day after, signed "White Star Line,"
that said the* Titanic *was steaming toward Halifax with "all
passengers safe." (This aroused suspicions that someone was
seeking to reinsure the* Titanic *or its cargo before the truth
about the disaster became known.) Franklin disclosed repeated cables from Ismay, aboard the rescue ship* Carpathia,
seeking to rush the Titanic*'s surviving officers and crew back
to England aboard another White Star liner, the* Cedric. *The
cables aroused the Senators' suspicions that Ismay was
seeking to avoid legal action in the United States.*

. . . SENATOR SMITH: I show you a telegram which I will read
in order that the record may contain it. It is dated New
York, N. Y., April 15, 1912. It is addressed to "J. A.
Hughes, Huntington, W. Va." It reads as follows:

> *Titanic* proceeding to Halifax. Passengers will probably
> land there Wednesday; all safe.
>
> WHITE STAR LINE.

I ask you whether you know anything about the sending of that message, or by whom it was authorized, or
from whom it emanated?

MR. FRANKLIN: I do not, sir. And since this was mentioned
at the meeting in New York on Saturday, we have had our
entire passenger staff in No. 9 Broadway office asked, and
we can not find out who sent that message. Now, what we
would appreciate your committee doing is to have the
telegraph company deliver to you the message received
from the White Star Line, and let us see where they got it
and when they got it, and what station it was delivered to.
I think it is only fair for us to explain, in connection with
that, that we have a great many people naturally employed in the passenger department of our No. 9 Broadway office. The office was very crowded on Monday
morning, and a good many of the juniors were answering
communications, to the best of their ability, by telephone, and otherwise, and it might be, possibly, that that
telegram was sent by one of these juniors, from something he had gotten, either from the newspaper or something of that kind, but so far as the White Star Line or its
officials were concerned, the officials did not authorize

anything of that kind, nothing of that kind was authorized, and we were very guarded in advising everybody that the only authentic information we were receiving about the horrible disaster was what we were getting— and we had gotten one message—through Capt. Haddock, of the *Olympic*.

SENATOR SMITH: At the time that telegram was sent did you know the actual condition of the *Titanic?*

MR. FRANKLIN: What is the time of that telegram? I think we ought to fix that question of time. It is headed 8:27 P.M. At 8:27 P.M. on Monday I knew that the *Titanic* sank at 2:20 A.M.

SENATOR SMITH: Monday morning?

MR. FRANKLIN: Monday morning.

SENATOR SMITH: When did you first get that information, and from whom? . . .

MR. FRANKLIN: Would you like me to give you a statement, to the best of my ability, of how we heard and when we heard and what we did?

SENATOR SMITH: I would, from the first. If you have any memoranda or any of the telegrams I wish you would have them marked for identification and filed with the committee.

MR. FRANKLIN: I would like to put them right in the record.

SENATOR SMITH: Go ahead.

MR. FRANKLIN: At about 2 minutes of 2 on Monday morning I was aroused by the telephone bell ringing. I went to the telephone, and a reporter—I could not tell from what paper—said that they had just heard that the *Titanic* was sinking, and that she had sent out a call for assistance. I asked them how they had gotten this message, and they told me that they had received it through the steamship *Virginian* and from Montreal. I immediately called up our dock and asked them if they had heard anything at all. They told me that several reporters had called them up.

SENATOR SMITH: Where were you at this time?

MR. FRANKLIN: At my own house, No. 41 East Sixty-first Street. They told me that the reporters had been trying to give them some information about the *Titanic.* I said, "Have you heard anything authentic about the *Titanic?*"

112

He told me "No." I then called up the Associated Press, the office of the Associated Press; they reported to me practically about what the reporter had told me. I then asked them whether they could not hold the matter and not give out such an alarming report until they could see whether it could be confirmed. They said, "No; it has gone out." I then called up Montreal on the long-distance telephone. I got our representative on the telephone in Montreal and asked him if he could not get the Allan Line office and find out if this could be confirmed, and what they had, and call me on the telephone immediately. I then called up about four or five of our own people and told them I had this information. I wanted to get in touch with them and have them stand by. I got Mr. Ridgway, the head of our steamship department, who lived in Brooklyn, and I asked him to at once go out and send a Marconigram to the captain of the *Olympic* [the *Titanic*'s nearly identical sister ship]. I did not want to alarm the captain of the *Olympic*. So all I asked in that telegram was, "Can you get the position of the *Titanic*? Wire us immediately her position." I can read you that telegram. I then asked all of our important people to immediately report at the office. When we got to the office the first thing that I found there was this memorandum. [Reading from memorandum:]

Titanic. Received from Associated Press from Cape Race 3:05 A.M. Monday, April 15. 10:25 P.M. E. S. T., *Titanic* called C. Q. D.; reported having struck iceberg and required immediate assistance. Half an hour afterwards, reported that they were sinking by the head. Women were being put off in boats and weather calm and clear. Gave position as 41.46 north, 50.14 west. Stop this station. Notified Allan liner *Virginian*, who immediately advised he was proceeding toward scene of disaster. Stop. *Virginian* at midnight stated was about 170 miles distant from *Titanic* and expected reach there about 10 A.M. *Olympic*, at 4:24 A.M. G. M. T. in latitude 40.32 north, longitude 61.18 west, was in direct communication with *Titanic* and is now making all haste toward her. *Baltic*, at 1:15 A.M. E. S. T. reported himself as about 200 miles east of *Titanic*, and was also making toward her. Last signals from *Titanic* were heard by *Virginian* at 12:25 A.M. E. S. T. He reported them blurred and ending abruptly.

Then we worked out the positions. In the first place, I received before leaving the house a reply from Montreal, saying that the Allan Line unfortunately confirmed the record. We worked out the positions then to the best of our ability, and the *Titanic* we found 1,080 miles from New York, about 600 miles from Halifax; the *Olympic* we found, in our opinion, to be about 364 miles from the *Titanic,* and the *Baltic* we thought could reach her at 4 P.M. I do not know how far the *Baltic* was away.

SENATOR SMITH: How did you find the location of these various ships?

MR. FRANKLIN: We worked out the *Olympic* roughly in our own minds.

SENATOR SMITH: On a scale?

MR. FRANKLIN: We had the chart.

SENATOR SMITH: And from the chart you worked them out? But did any of these ships report their exact location?

MR. FRANKLIN: We had no communication at that time from any ship or anybody which in our opinion was authentic. We had numerous rumors from all sources.

SENATOR SMITH: Did they pretend to give you their location?

MR. FRANKLIN: They did not. I will read you the first message sent to the *Olympic,* the one I referred to a few minutes ago. This was sent at 3 A.M.:

Make every effort to communicate *Titanic* and advise position and time. Reply to Ismay, New York [meaning company offices].

SENATOR SMITH: Please say to whom that was addressed.

MR. FRANKLIN: To Haddock [Capt. Herbert Haddock], *Olympic.*

SENATOR SMITH: Please give the date.

MR. FRANKLIN: April 15, 3 A.M.

SENATOR SMITH: And give the hour in each case. Now, in order that we may be sure the committee understands that, please read that again.

MR. FRANKLIN: This was our first endeavor to communicate with any of our steamers, and the first attempt that we

114

know, either one way or the other. This was our telegram to Capt. Haddock, of the *Olympic,* sent at 3 A.M. on April 15, as follows:

Make every endeavor to communicate *Titanic* and advise position and time. Reply to Ismay, New York.

The telegram was sent from Brooklyn by Mr. F. W. Ridgway. I telephoned it to him and asked him to go right out and send it.

SENATOR SMITH: Proceed.

SENATOR FLETCHER: Where was Capt. Haddock—where was the *Olympic?*

MR. FRANKLIN: The *Olympic* had sailed from New York Saturday afternoon at 3 o'clock, bound east.

SENATOR SMITH: What was the position of the boat?

MR. FRANKLIN: I can only give you our estimate of the position which, at 3 o'clock, was 320 miles east of Sandy Hook and about 360 miles, in our estimate, from the *Titanic.*

SENATOR SMITH: Proceed.

MR. FRANKLIN: All during the morning from that time on——

SENATOR SMITH: Monday morning?

MR. FRANKLIN: Monday morning. We were endeavoring to communicate or get some information from Montreal, from Halifax, from the various papers, and we wired to the commander of the *Olympic:*

Keep us fully posted regarding *Titanic.*

That was 6:05 A.M. We had received no reply from him at all. Then we got a telegram from the *Olympic.*

Since midnight, when her position was 41.46 north, 50.14 west, have been unable to communicate. We are now 310 miles from her, 9 A.M. under full power. Will inform you at once if hear anything.

COMMANDER

SENATOR SMITH: Did you understand from that that they were headed toward the *Titanic?*

MR. FRANKLIN: I understood that they were headed toward the *Titanic,* without any question. That was 9 A.M.

SENATOR SMITH: Monday?

MR. FRANKLIN: Monday, 310 miles from the *Titanic*.

SENATOR SMITH: Proceed.

MR. FRANKLIN: We followed that with a telegram, as follows:

Can you ascertain damage *Titanic?*

SENATOR SMITH: What hour was that?

MR. FRANKLIN: That is not the original of that. There is no hour on that, but that was sent in the morning.

SENATOR SMITH: Sent by whom?

MR. FRANKLIN: That was sent by me.

SENATOR SMITH: Had you no information at that time regarding the sinking of the *Titanic?*

MR. FRANKLIN: Absolutely none; most emphatically. I have read you off the first telegram from Haddock. Now, this is the second telegram.

SENATOR SMITH: Give the date and hour.

MR. FRANKLIN: April 15. We do not know what hour this was received, but it was after noon. It was between 12 and 1 o'clock, or around 1 o'clock. That could probably be traced—exactly when that was delivered to us.

Parisian reports *Carpathia* in attendance and picked up 20 boats of passengers and *Baltic* returning to give assistance. Position not given.

SENATOR SMITH: Position of *Baltic* not given?

MR. FRANKLIN: Position of *Baltic* not given. This message was received along about 1 o'clock.

SENATOR SMITH: Signed by whom?

MR. FRANKLIN: Signed by Haddock.

SENATOR SMITH: All right, proceed.

MR. FRANKLIN: We replied to that as follows:

APRIL 15, 1912.

HADDOCK, *Olympic:*

Thanks your message. We have received nothing from *Titanic,* but rumored here that she proceeding slowly Halifax, but we can not confirm this. We expect *Virginian* alongside *Titanic;* try and communicate her.

SENATOR SMITH: Who signed that?

MR. FRANKLIN: I did.

SENATOR SMITH: What hour was that?

MR. FRANKLIN: That was in reply to the other message, immediately after we got it. It must have been about 2 o'clock——

SENATOR SMITH: Capt. Haddock's message?

MR. FRANKLIN: Yes. About 2 o'clock, I would say.

SENATOR SMITH: Tell the committee upon what rumor you based that statement.

MR. FRANKLIN: We based that statement on rumors that we were having from all sources. The press and telegrams from Montreal; but nothing we could put our hands on as being authentic at any time.

SENATOR SMITH: Had you not received anything from the *Carpathia* at that time?

MR. FRANKLIN: No, sir; we had not heard of the *Carpathia* up to that time at all—except this Haddock telegram.

SENATOR SMITH: Let us see what you based that rumor on?

MR. FRANKLIN: I do not know that. I could tell exactly on what I based that. I might by going through those telegrams.

SENATOR SMITH: I wish you would go through them and tell us what you based that on.

MR. FRANKLIN: We had it from all sources—from the newspapers particularly.

SENATOR SMITH: And it was rumor merely?

MR. FRANKLIN: Absolutely. We announced it to everybody that these were rumors, but we could not confirm them, and that we had nothing authentic but one message from Capt. Haddock.

SENATOR SMITH: Did you confer with Mr. Marconi during the early morning of Monday, personally?

MR. FRANKLIN: No, sir; I never conferred with Mr. Marconi.

SENATOR SMITH: Do you know whether any messages went from the Marconi office or from the White Star office to the *Carpathia* enjoining secrecy until they were in communication with you?

MR. FRANKLIN: We know absolutely nothing about such a communication; had nothing at all to do with it, if it was sent.

SENATOR SMITH: Do you know whether such a communication was sent?

MR. FRANKLIN: I do not know anything about it.

SENATOR SMITH: Have you ever conferred with Mr. Marconi about it?

MR. FRANKLIN: I never have mentioned it——

SENATOR SMITH: Or Mr. Sammis [Frederick Sammis, Marconi's chief engineer in the U.S.]?

MR. FRANKLIN: No.

SENATOR SMITH: Or the operator of the *Carpathia?*

MR. FRANKLIN: No; I never talked to either one of the two gentlemen in my life.

SENATOR SMITH: Neither with the captain nor the operator nor an officer of any other ship?

MR. FRANKLIN: Never. Our whole effort—I would like to say this—was to get the *Carpathia* to give to us the names of the passengers, of the people aboard the *Carpathia.* That is the only thing we wanted, and we were pressing for that all the time.

SENATOR SMITH: That is wherever she was bound, and under whatever circumstances?

MR. FRANKLIN: We tried to get it through the *Olympic.* We told the *Olympic* to stand by her and pass it along to us.

SENATOR SMITH: Proceed.

MR. FRANKLIN: I had better get back to the cables, had I not? This message that I have just read is as follows:

APRIL 15, 1912

HADDOCK, *Olympic:*
Thanks, your message. We have received nothing from *Titanic,* but rumored that she proceeding slowly Halifax, but we can not confirm this. We expect *Virginian* alongside *Titanic.* Try and communicate her.

SENATOR SMITH: Are you giving the dates and hours?

MR. FRANKLIN: I have not the dates [sic] on this, but on the next one I have. The next is 2:40, which shows this must have been before 2:40.

SENATOR SMITH: And what is the signature?

MR. FRANKLIN: This is signed "Franklin." Now, our next telegram was to Haddock. . . .

SENATOR SMITH: Give the hour in each case and who signs it, whether by name or cipher or initial.

MR. FRANKLIN: I will give them in the order they are here.

HADDOCK, *Olympic:*
Endeavor ascertain where Ismay is. Advise me and convey him deepest sympathy from us all.

FRANKLIN

SENATOR SMITH: What hour is that?
MR. FRANKLIN: 2:40 in the afternoon.
SENATOR SMITH: And addressed to whom?
MR. FRANKLIN: Capt. Haddock.
SENATOR SMITH: And signed by whom?
MR. FRANKLIN: Signed by "Franklin."
SENATOR SMITH: Do not forget to give the date, the hour, the name, and the signature in each case. . . .
MR. FRANKLIN: The difficulty is that these are not in order exactly.
SENATOR SMITH: Take your time and give the date and hour and name in each case.
MR. FRANKLIN: The trouble about it is that they are not all in order. Here is a Marconigram, dated April 15, 1912.
SENATOR SMITH: From New York?
MR. FRANKLIN: New York.

APRIL 15, 1912.

HADDOCK, *Olympic:*
Do utmost to ascertain immediately and advise us fully disposition *Titanic's* passengers and where they will be landed.

SENATOR SMITH: Signed by whom?
MR. FRANKLIN: "Franklin." I think the best way to do it is to get the time these telegrams were filed—a statement from the Marconi company or the Postal Telegraph Co. here— the time they were filed with them, to confirm all these.
SENATOR SMITH: That is all right; but we had better take what the telegrams show, in so far as they do show anything.
MR. FRANKLIN: The only trouble is they have not the times on them.
SENATOR SMITH: In so far as they do show the dates and hours, give us whatever the telegrams contain.
MR. FRANKLIN: Now, at about 6:20 or 6:30 P.M., April 15, the following telegram was handed to me.

SENATOR SMITH: By whom, and where were you?

MR. FRANKLIN: Handed to me by Mr. Toppin at No. 9 Broadway.

SENATOR SMITH: Who is he?

MR. FRANKLIN: Assistant to the vice president. The record here shows this was received at 6:16 P.M. This is addressed to Ismay, New York, and is as follows:

> *Carpathia* reached *Titanic's* position at daybreak. Found boats and wreckage only. *Titanic* had foundered about 2:20 A.M. in 41.16 north, 50.14 west. All her boats accounted for. About 675 souls saved, crew and passengers, latter nearly all women and children. Leyland Line S. S. *Californian* remaining and searching position of disaster. *Carpathia* returning to New York with survivors; please inform Cunard.
>
> HADDOCK.

SENATOR SMITH: That is from the captain of the *Olympic?*

MR. FRANKLIN: Of the *Olympic*.

SENATOR SMITH: Addressed to Ismay?

MR. FRANKLIN: New York; that is our cable address. Immediately that telegram was received by me it was such a terrible shock that it took us a few minutes to get ourselves together. Then at once I telephoned, myself, to two of our directors, Mr. Steele and Mr. Morgan, jr., and at the same time sent downstairs for the reporters. I started to read the message, holding it in my hands, to the reporters. I got off the first line and a half, where it said, "The *Titanic* sank at 2 o'clock A.M.," and there was not a reporter left in the room—they were so anxious to get out to telephone the news. . . .

SENATOR SMITH: I wish the reporter might mark these telegrams for identification.

MR. FRANKLIN: I will hand the whole bundle to him in a moment. [Reading:]

> Inexpressible sorrow. Am proceeding straight on voyage. *Carpathia* informs me no hope in searching. Will send names survivors as obtainable. Yamsi on *Carpathia*.

This telegram was addressed to "Franklin, Care Ismay, New York," and signed "Haddock."

SENATOR SMITH: The "Yamsi" referred to is——

MR. FRANKLIN: Mr. Ismay ["Yamsi" was his British wireless cipher].

SENATOR SMITH: Was that the first information you had that he was on the *Carpathia?*

MR. FRANKLIN: The first information that we had that he was on the *Carpathia.*

MR. BURLINGHAM: Give the hour of its receipt.

MR. FRANKLIN: These were both received very close to the same time; I would say about 6:30 that evening.

SENATOR SMITH: By whom was that signed?

MR. FRANKLIN: By Haddock, of the *Olympic.* . . .

I want to say this: That during the entire day we considered the ship unsinkable, and it never entered our minds that there had been anything like a serious loss of life. We of course thought there might have been something in transferring passengers or handling the passengers; but it never entered our minds that there had been a serious loss of life until we got this Haddock message at 6:30. . . .

SENATOR SMITH: I would like this record to show whether yourself or any officer of your company, at any time before the landing of the *Carpathia,* received any message from any person asking that the *Cedric* should be held in New York until the arrival of the *Carpathia?*

MR. FRANKLIN: Yes, sir.

SENATOR SMITH: From whom?

MR. FRANKLIN: Here is a telegram: "Steamship *Carpathia,* April 17, 1912."

SENATOR SMITH: What is the hour?

MR. FRANKLIN: 5:35 P.M. is stamped on here.

Most desirable *Titanic* crew aboard *Carpathia* should be returned home earliest moment possible. Suggest you hold *Cedric,* sailing her daylight Friday unless you see any reason contrary. Propose returning in her myself. Please send outfit of clothes, including shoes, for me to *Cedric.* Have nothing of my own. Please reply.

YAMSI.

One word in this telegram reads "and." I have read it as "any," because there is no doubt that that is what it was. It was underscored when it was handed to me, showing that it was evidently a mistake.

SENATOR SMITH: Whose code or cipher signature is that?

MR. FRANKLIN: That is Mr. Ismay's signature or cipher.

SENATOR SMITH: Was any reply made to that?

MR. FRANKLIN: To "Ismay, *Carpathia.*" April 17, 1912, 8 P.M., we sent it.

SENATOR SMITH: What date is that?

MR. FRANKLIN: April 17. That is in reply to this other one.

SENATOR SMITH: That was Wednesday?

MR. FRANKLIN: That was Wednesday evening. Do you want me to read it?

SENATOR SMITH: Yes, please.

MR. FRANKLIN: (reading):

> ISMAY, *Carpathia:*
> Have arranged forward crew *Lapland,* sailing Saturday, calling Plymouth. We all consider most unwise delay *Cedric,* considering all circumstances.

SENATOR SMITH: Who sent that?

MR. FRANKLIN: It is signed "Franklin."

SENATOR SMITH: Did you get any reply to that?

MR. FRANKLIN: I think the best way is just to read all these telegrams as they come.

SENATOR SMITH: I wish you would.

MR. FRANKLIN: They are a little mixed up.

SENATOR SMITH: I want that story in the record.

MR. FRANKLIN: The best way to do that is to read all these telegrams as they come here, and not say which is the reply.

SENATOR SMITH: All right. Just proceed, keeping in mind that we want the date and the person to whom and from whom the telegram was sent, and the signature.

MR. FRANKLIN: I will.

SENATOR SMITH: Give them in chronological order, if possible. . . .

MR. FRANKLIN: [reading more messages from Ismay]:

> STEAMSHIP "CARPATHIA," VIA SIASCONSETTS, MASS.
> ISLEFRANK, *New York:*
> Very important you should hold *Cedric* daylight Friday for *Titanic* crew. Reply.
>
> YAMSI.

> STEAMSHIP "CARPATHIA," *New York*
> ISLEFRANK, *New York:*

Very important you should hold *Cedric* daylight Friday for *Titanic* crew. Answer.

YAMSI.

STEAMSHIP "CARPATHIA," VIA SIASCONSETTS, MASS.
ISLEFRANK, *New York:*
Think most unwise keep *Titanic* crew until Saturday. Strongly urge detain *Cedric* sailing her midnight if desirable.

YAMSI.

That is April 18. All of these are April 18.
SENATOR SMITH: That was Thursday, the 18th.
MR. FRANKLIN: Yes, sir. [Continuing reading:]

"CARPATHIA," VIA SIASCONSETTS, MASS.

And there are just the two figures there, "18", after that. It does not say anything else. It reads:

ISLEFRANK, *New York:*
Unless you have good and substantial reason for not holding *Cedric,* please arrange to do so. Most undesirable have crew New York so long.

No signature.
SENATOR SMITH: To whom was that addressed?
MR. FRANKLIN: That is addressed in the usual way: "Islefrank, New York."
Then this telegram:

ISMAY, *Carpathia:*
Regret after fullest consideration decided *Cedric* must sail as scheduled. Expect join *Carpathia* at quarantine, but can not remove boats, as everything arranged for steamer proceed docs immediately.

Signed "Franklin."
That is all on that subject, sir. . . .
MR. KIRLIN: May we make a suggestion, Senator? I think Mr. Franklin has omitted one message, from Mr. Ismay himself, announcing the loss. That was not received for two or three days.
MR. FRANKLIN: That was a message not in connection with this *Cedric* matter at all. This was a message received from Mr. Ismay.

123

MR. KIRLIN: When?

MR. FRANKLIN: This message was dated "Steamship *Carpathia,* April 15," and addressed to "Islefrank."

MR. BURLINGHAM: And received when?

MR. FRANKLIN: Received on the 17th. [Reading:]

> Deeply regret advise you *Titanic* sank this morning after collision iceberg, resulting serious loss life. Further particulars later.
>
> BRUCE ISMAY.

9:58 A.M.

That was evidently sent by Mr. Ismay.

SENATOR SMITH: On what date?

MR. FRANKLIN: I shall give it to you. That was evidently sent by Mr. Ismay immediately or very shortly after the accident, but was not received by us until 9 A.M. of the 17th, Wednesday. . . .

SENATOR BOURNE: From the experience incident to the *Titanic* disaster, have you or your associates come to any conclusion as to laws, policies, or regulations which, if internationally adopted, would minimize the possibility of repetitions of such a catastrophe?

MR. FRANKLIN: I think the fairest way for me to answer that question is this: That since the accident to the *Titanic* we have been absolutely overwhelmed, first in distress matters, to do everything we could for everybody, and the only precaution or action that we have taken is that Mr. Ismay authorized, last Friday, and instructed the managers abroad to immediately equip all of the I. M. M. Co.'s steamers with lifeboats and life rafts enough to carry every passenger and every member of the crew. Further than that we have not gone.

SENATOR BOURNE: Those new instructions were based upon your conclusions, I assume, that it was impossible to make a nonsinkable ship?

MR. FRANKLIN: Based upon a conclusion that nobody ever for one moment realized that an accident of this kind could have happened. There was nothing further from the minds of everybody than that an accident of this kind could take place. We never thought, until we got Capt. Haddock's message in the first place, that the ship could go down, and, in the next place, that there would be any material loss of life. This has demonstrated an entirely new proposition that has to be dealt with—something that nobody had ever thought of before. These steamers were considered tremendous lifeboats in themselves. This vessel was constructed as only three other ships have been constructed, and they are all owned by the White Star Line.

SENATOR BOURNE: Have you come to any conclusion in your own mind that any individual was responsible in any direction or in any manner for this catastrophe?

MR. FRANKLIN: I do not see how you can blame anybody. You have the best commander; you have everybody aboard that was interested in the ship; there is no reason to feel that every precaution would not be taken. You had no instructions to force the ship; you had nothing for which you can blame yourself at all.

SENATOR BOURNE: You say the *Titanic* cost, complete, one million and a half pounds, in round numbers. What was she insured for?

MR. FRANKLIN: She was insured for, in round numbers, £1,000,000, the balance being carried by the I. M. M. Co., under our own underwriting scheme.

SENATOR BOURNE: You say Harland & Wolff build your ships on a percentage basis. They construct plans and submit them to you, and you determine; and then your representatives, I presume, oversee the construction of the ship, and they get an added percentage of the cost? So it is to their advantage to make the ship, from a dollar standpoint, cost as much as possible, is it not?

MR. FRANKLIN: Right, sir.

When you say that I do this, you mean, of course, that the company, in its ramifications, does this. The owner of the ship does this; the owning company.

SENATOR BOURNE: Yes.

MR. FRANKLIN: There is every reason why Harland & Wolff would be very glad to put anything under heaven on the ship, because the more they put on it the more they would make.

SENATOR BOURNE: What percentage is it customary for Harland & Wolff to receive on the cost?

MR. FRANKLIN: I think it is 5 per cent. It is covered by an agreement.

SENATOR BOURNE: Have you any knowledge as to whether precautionary measures were taken by the officers of the ship after word was received of the vicinity of icebergs and ice floes?

MR. FRANKLIN: I have no doubt of that, because of what we have gotten from the testimony before you. As I say, I have not had any talk about the matter with any of the officers and men. I have not had any conversation with them about the matter.

SENATOR BOURNE: Have you or your associates come to any conclusion as to improvements that can be made in legislation that would minimize the possibility of the repetition of a catastrophe of this nature?

MR. FRANKLIN: No, sir; because, as I have just said, we have had no time to thoroughly discuss that.

SENATOR BOURNE: You have not had the time?

MR. FRANKLIN: We have not had the time to do it. We can only say this, that everything we have is open, and we will give you every assistance that we possibly can, in every way. If there are any suggestions that we can make, or any matters in regard to which you desire our opinion, or anything of that kind, we will get our experts to give it to you. We are not experts ourselves. That is what I would like to have you understand.

SENATOR BOURNE: The only deduction you have made is that it is impossible to build a nonsinkable ship?

MR. FRANKLIN: It looks so to-day, from this experience. If you had asked me that a week ago I would have said no. I would have said we had them. . . .

Senator, have you cleared up as much as you want to in regard to this *Cedric* matter? A good deal has been said about that, and I there; and I would like to clear it up if you care to go into it further.

SENATOR SMITH: Right now?

MR. FRANKLIN: If you wish; yes.

SENATOR SMITH: We will take it up after luncheon, or now.

SENATOR BOURNE: I suggest that the gentleman clear up the matter on his own statement, stating what he thinks is necessary to do.

SENATOR SMITH: Now?

SENATOR BOURNE: Let him state where the misunderstanding is and what he thinks is necessary to clear it up.

MR. FRANKLIN: Criticism has been seriously made to the effect that those messages were sent entirely with the idea of getting the crew away, and of Mr. Ismay's also getting away on account of what information might come out from the crew.

I want to say that that was not in Mr. Ismay's mind. Everybody realizes the importance of getting these members of the crew away from the country at the earliest possible moment. . . .

As far as Mr. Ismay personally is concerned, he left his own personal movements entirely to us.

As far as the crew are concerned, it is the duty of everybody connected with the steamers to get a crew, under such circumstances, out of the country just as quickly as it can be done. We have always tried to do that. . . .

SENATOR SMITH: I think you had better put into the record your motive in wanting to get these men out of the country.

MR. FRANKLIN: Men arriving under these extraordinary circumstances, not being on articles, are very difficult, at times, to control, because a great many people are running after them for stories, and making them presents, and taking them out in the street. They stray away, and they get into endless trouble; and they are not controllable as are seamen and firemen ordinarily from a ship when it is in the dock under the command of an officer, and everything of that sort.

It is the duty of every owner or representative of an owner of a steamship, under similar circumstances, to get those men out of these temptations, and to get them away to their own homes and their own people, and where they can go back again and sign on another ship, and go to sea.

SENATOR SMITH: Is that the sole motive that you had in wanting to get them out of the country?

MR. FRANKLIN: That is the only motive I had. I never thought anything about anything else.

SENATOR BOURNE: In a case like that, if you have a sister ship, or a ship of the same company, it is used as the home of your employees, and the method of transporting them to their homes?

MR. FRANKLIN: Yes. As quickly as we can get them back.

SENATOR BOURNE: That is quite the custom?

MR. FRANKLIN: Yes. If we have a steamer coming in from the Mediterranean, and we do not need the crew, we send them on somebody else's line, or get them to Boston; we get them away. We do not want to have them a minute longer than we have to.

SENATOR SMITH: So far as you know, are these men who are survivors of the *Titanic* to be reemployed by your company?

MR. FRANKLIN: They will certainly be reemployed if they appear for service.

SENATOR SMITH: Are they still in your service?

MR. FRANKLIN: No, sir; technically speaking, they are not, for the reason that the moment a ship goes down, the men's wages cease. But we, of course, take care of them.

There is one other thing I would like to say, and that is this: I think you gentlemen will realize that, under the conditions of this fearful disaster, no man in the crew could tell any story that could do us any harm. Here were all the passengers, and everybody else, who were there, and what difference would it make to us what the crew said? The worst thing they could say could not remedy the matter; could not help the matter, in any way, shape or form. . . .

Witness: Joseph Groves Boxhall, 28
Titanic's Fourth Officer, from Hull, England

Key testimony: Among Boxhall's duties were helping chart the ship's position. He testified that he fired distress rockets and flashed Morse signals to attract an unidentified steamer whose lights he'd spotted in the distance. Other authoritative witnesses would also report seeing a light or lights, but the officer provided the first strong hint of an emerging scandal that there was a ship within sight of the Titanic *that did nothing to help it. The Senate panel concluded that this was the* Californian, *also controlled by International Mercantile Marine. Boxhall also gave a description of the iceberg that differed from others' recollections (themselves hardly uniform). He went down to G Deck after the collision and saw mailbags afloat.*

... Senator Smith: Did the captain tell you that the *Californian* had wired the *Titanic* that they were in the vicinity of icebergs?

Mr. Boxhall: No. The captain gave me some wireless messages from Southampton, I think, that we had had before we had sailed, and asked me to put these positions on the chart.

Senator Smith: Did you know whether a wireless had been received from the *Amerika* that the *Titanic* was in the vicinity of icebergs?

Mr. Boxhall: No; I could not say.

Senator Smith: Do you want us to understand that you had no knowledge of the proximity of this ship to icebergs immediately preceding the——

Mr. Boxhall: I had no knowledge.

Senator Smith: One moment. [Continuing.] Immediately preceding the collision, or during the hours of your watch from 8 o'clock until the collision occurred?

Mr. Boxhall: I did not realize the ship was so near the ice field.

Senator Smith: You knew you were in the vicinity of the Grand Banks?

Mr. Boxhall: I knew we were in the vicinity of the Grand Banks.

Senator Smith: What was the weather at that time?

Mr. Boxhall: Very fine and clear.

Senator Smith: Cold?

Mr. Boxhall: Yes; very cold. . . .

Senator Smith: When did you last see the captain?

Mr. Boxhall: When he told me to go away in the boat.

Senator Smith: How long was that after the collision?

Mr. Boxhall: I do not know what time I left the ship. I have been trying to find the time or trying to calculate, but I can not think what time it was.

Senator Smith: Where were you when the collision took place?

Mr. Boxhall: I was just approaching the bridge.

Senator Smith: On the port or the starboard side?

Mr. Boxhall: Starboard side.

Senator Smith: Did the collision occur on the port or the starboard side?

Mr. Boxhall: On the starboard side, sir.

129

SENATOR SMITH: And you were on deck at that time?

MR. BOXHALL: On the deck, sir.

SENATOR SMITH: Approaching the bridge?

MR. BOXHALL: Just approaching the bridge.

SENATOR SMITH: Could you see what had occurred?

MR. BOXHALL: No, sir; I could not see what had occurred.

SENATOR SMITH: Did you know what had occurred?

MR. BOXHALL: No, not at all. I heard the sixth officer say what it was.

SENATOR SMITH: What did he say that it was?

MR. BOXHALL: He said we had struck an iceberg.

SENATOR SMITH: Was there any evidence of ice on any of the decks, to your knowledge, after that collision?

MR. BOXHALL: Just a little on the lower deck. On the open deck I saw just a little, not much.

SENATOR SMITH: Do you know whether anyone was injured by that impact?

MR. BOXHALL: No, I do not know; I never heard.

SENATOR SMITH: Did you continue to go toward the bridge after the impact?

MR. BOXHALL: Yes, sir.

SENATOR SMITH: How far did you go?

MR. BOXHALL: At the time of the impact I was just coming along the deck and almost abreast of the captain's quarters, and I heard the report of three bells.

SENATOR SMITH: What kind of a report? Describe it.

MR. BOXHALL: The lookout's report.

SENATOR SMITH: What was said?

MR. BOXHALL: Three bells were struck.

SENATOR SMITH: Three bells?

MR. BOXHALL: That signifies something has been seen ahead. Almost at the same time I heard the first officer give the order "Hard astarboard," and the engine telegraph rang.

SENATOR SMITH: What did the order mean?

MR. BOXHALL: Ordering the ship's head to port.

SENATOR SMITH: Did you see this iceberg at that time?

MR. BOXHALL: Not at that time.

SENATOR SMITH: Did it extend above the deck that you were on?

MR. BOXHALL: Oh, no, sir; it did not extend there.

SENATOR SMITH: A little lower?

130

MR. BOXHALL: Yes, sir.

SENATOR SMITH: Do you know whether it struck the bow squarely?

MR. BOXHALL: It seemed to me to strike the bluff of the bow.

SENATOR SMITH: Describe that.

MR. BOXHALL: It is in the forward part of the ship, but almost on the side.

SENATOR SMITH: On which side?

MR. BOXHALL: It is just where the ship begins to widen out on the starboard side.

SENATOR SMITH: How far would that be from the front of the ship?

MR. BOXHALL: I do not know.

SENATOR SMITH: About how far?

MR. BOXHALL: I could not say in feet.

SENATOR SMITH: How far would it be from the eyes?

MR. BOXHALL: I do not know. I could not say.

SENATOR SMITH: You could not describe that?

MR. BOXHALL: No; you could measure it on the plans, though.

SENATOR SMITH: About how far?

MR. BOXHALL: I could not say how many feet. I have no idea of the number of feet.

SENATOR SMITH: But it was not a square blow on the bow of the ship?

MR. BOXHALL: No, sir.

SENATOR SMITH: In ordinary parlance, would it be a glancing blow?

MR. BOXHALL: A glancing blow.

SENATOR SMITH: Was the blow felt immediately?

MR. BOXHALL: A slight impact.

SENATOR SMITH: How slight?

MR. BOXHALL: It did not seem to me to be very serious. I did not take it seriously.

SENATOR SMITH: Slight enough to stop you in your walk to the bridge?

MR. BOXHALL: Oh, no, no, no.

SENATOR SMITH: Heavy enough to stop you, I mean?

MR. BOXHALL: No, sir.

SENATOR SMITH: So slight that you did not regard it as serious?

MR. BOXHALL: I did not think it was serious.

SENATOR SMITH: Did you proceed to the bridge?

MR. BOXHALL: Yes, sir.

SENATOR SMITH: Whom did you find there?

MR. BOXHALL: I found the sixth officer and the first officer and captain.

SENATOR SMITH: The sixth officer, the first officer, and the captain?

MR. BOXHALL: Yes, sir.

SENATOR SMITH: All on the bridge together?

MR. BOXHALL: Yes, sir.

SENATOR SMITH: What, if anything, was said by the captain?

MR. BOXHALL: Yes, sir. The captain said, "What have we struck?" Mr. Murdoch, the first officer, said, "We have struck an iceberg."

SENATOR SMITH: Then what was said?

MR. BOXHALL: He followed on to say—Mr. Murdoch followed on to say, "I put her hard astarboard and run the engines full astern, but it was too close; she hit it."

SENATOR FLETCHER: That was before she struck?

MR. BOXHALL: No; after.

SENATOR SMITH: That was after she struck?

MR. BOXHALL: Yes.

SENATOR SMITH: He said that he put her hard astarboard?

MR. BOXHALL: Yes, sir.

SENATOR SMITH: But it was too late?

MR. BOXHALL: Yes, sir.

SENATOR SMITH: And he hit it?

MR. BOXHALL: Yes, sir.

SENATOR SMITH: What did the captain say?

MR. BOXHALL: Mr. Murdoch also said, "I intended to port around it."

SENATOR SMITH: "I intended to port around it"?

MR. BOXHALL: "But she hit before I could do any more."

SENATOR SMITH: Did he say anything more?

MR. BOXHALL: "The water-tight doors are closed, sir."

SENATOR SMITH: What did the captain say?

MR. BOXHALL: Mr. Murdoch continued to say, "The water-tight doors are closed, sir."

SENATOR SMITH: Mr. Murdoch continued to say, "Are they closed"?

MR. BOXHALL: No; "They are closed."

SENATOR SMITH: "The water-tight doors are closed"?

MR. BOXHALL: "Are closed."

SENATOR SMITH: Do you understand by that that he had applied the——

MR. BOXHALL (interrupting): I saw him close them.

SENATOR SMITH: He had applied the electricity?

MR. BOXHALL: Yes, sir.

SENATOR SMITH: And by that had closed the water-tight compartments?

MR. BOXHALL: Yes, sir; and the captain asked him if he had rung the warning bell.

SENATOR SMITH: What did he say?

MR. BOXHALL: He said, "Yes, sir."

SENATOR SMITH: What is the warning bell?

MR. BOXHALL: It is a small electric bell which rings at every water-tight door.

SENATOR SMITH: And he said that that had been done?

MR. BOXHALL: Yes, sir.

SENATOR SMITH: What else did he say?

MR. BOXHALL: We all walked out to the corner of the bridge then to look at the iceberg.

SENATOR SMITH: The captain?

MR. BOXHALL: The captain, first officer, and myself.

SENATOR SMITH: Did you see it?

MR. BOXHALL: I was not very sure of seeing it. It seemed to me to be just a small black mass not rising very high out of the water, just a little on the starboard quarter.

SENATOR SMITH: How far out of the water should you judge?

MR. BOXHALL: I could not judge the size of it, but it seemed to me to be very, very low lying.

SENATOR SMITH: Did it extend up to B deck?

MR. BOXHALL: Oh, no; the ship was past it then. It looked to me to be very, very low in the water.

SENATOR FLETCHER: Give us an idea; do not leave it there.

SENATOR SMITH: How far do you think it was above the water?

MR. BOXHALL: That is hard to say. In my own opinion I do not think the thing extended above the ship's rail.

SENATOR SMITH: Above the ship's rail?

MR. BOXHALL: No.

SENATOR SMITH: And how far was this rail above the water's edge?

MR. BOXHALL: Probably about 30 feet.

SENATOR SMITH: About 30 feet?

MR. BOXHALL: No; hardly 30 feet.

SENATOR SMITH: The distance from the water's edge to the boat deck was how far?

MR. BOXHALL: I could get that measurement from the plan.

SENATOR SMITH: About 70 feet, was it not?

MR. BOXHALL: From the boat deck it was about 70 feet to the water's edge. The boat deck is one deck above A. This rail I mean is on the C deck.

SENATOR SMITH: You say this looked like a black object?

MR. BOXHALL: Yes.

SENATOR SMITH: Were the stars shining that night?

MR. BOXHALL: The stars were shining.

SENATOR SMITH: And the moon?

MR. BOXHALL: No moon.

SENATOR SMITH: No moon?

MR. BOXHALL: No.

SENATOR SMITH: Was it clear?

MR. BOXHALL: Clear.

SENATOR SMITH: And yet you wish to be understood as saying that, standing in the bow of the ship as far forward as you could get, and looking over directly at this obstacle, you were unable to determine exactly what it was?

MR. BOXHALL: I was not standing in the bow of the ship, sir; I was standing on the bridge.

SENATOR SMITH: On the bridge?

MR. BOXHALL: Yes.

SENATOR SMITH: But you could see this object, could you?

MR. BOXHALL: I am not sure of seeing it; that is what I say, I would not swear to seeing it. But I fancied seeing this long-lying growler.

SENATOR SMITH: And that it looked dark?

MR. BOXHALL: It looked to me as if it was very, very low.

SENATOR SMITH: And dark?

MR. BOXHALL: Yes.

SENATOR SMITH: Did the captain seem to know what you had struck?

MR. BOXHALL: No.

SENATOR SMITH: Did Mr. Murdoch?

MR. BOXHALL: Mr. Murdoch saw it when we struck it.

SENATOR SMITH: Did he say what it was?

MR. BOXHALL: Yes, sir.

SENATOR SMITH: What did he say it was?

MR. BOXHALL: He said it was an iceberg.

SENATOR SMITH: After these signals were turned in, what was done?

MR. BOXHALL: I do not know what was done, because I left the bridge then.

SENATOR SMITH: Where did you go?

MR. BOXHALL: I went right down below, in the lowest steerage, as far as I could possibly get without going into the cargo portion of the ship, and inspected all the decks as I came up, in the vicinity of where I thought she had struck.

SENATOR SMITH: What did you find?

MR. BOXHALL: I found no damage. I found no indications to show that the ship had damaged herself.

SENATOR SMITH: On the inside?

MR. BOXHALL: On the inside.

SENATOR SMITH: Did you say you went to the steerage?

MR. BOXHALL: I went down to the steerage.

SENATOR SMITH: But found no evidence of injury there?

MR. BOXHALL: No, sir.

SENATOR SMITH: Then where did you go?

MR. BOXHALL: Then I went on the bridge and reported to the captain that I could not see any damage.

SENATOR SMITH: One moment. Did you look farther, beyond the steerage?

MR. BOXHALL: I looked in all the decks. I worked my way up to the top deck.

SENATOR SMITH: Looking at all of them in the forward part?

MR. BOXHALL: In the forward part of the ship; that is, abreast of No. 2 and 3 hatches.

SENATOR SMITH: Then what did you do?

MR. BOXHALL: I came right up to the bridge and reported that I could find no damage.

SENATOR SMITH: What did the captain say?

MR. BOXHALL: He said, "Go down and find the carpenter and get him to sound the ship."

SENATOR SMITH: Did you do so?

MR. BOXHALL: I was proceeding down, but I met the carpenter.

SENATOR SMITH: What did you say to him?

MR. BOXHALL: I said, "The captain wants you to sound the ship."

He said, "The ship is making water," and he went on the bridge to the captain, and I thought I would go down forward again and investigate; and then I met a mail clerk, a man named Smith, and he asked where the captain was. I said, "He is on the bridge." He said, "The mail hold is full" or "filling rapidly." I said, "Well, you go and report it to the captain and I will go down and see," and I proceeded right down into the mail room.

SENATOR SMITH: What did you find there?

MR. BOXHALL: I went down as far as the sorting room deck and found mail clerks down there working.

SENATOR SMITH: Doing what?

MR. BOXHALL: Taking letters out of the racks, they seemed to me to be doing.

SENATOR SMITH: Taking letters out of the racks and putting them into pouches?

MR. BOXHALL: I could not see what they were putting them in.

SENATOR SMITH: You could not see what disposition they were making of them?

MR. BOXHALL: I looked through an open door and saw these men working at the racks, and directly beneath me was the mail hold, and the water seemed to be then within 2 feet of the deck we were standing on.

SENATOR SMITH: What did you do in that situation?

MR. BOXHALL (continuing): And bags of mail floating about. I went right on the bridge again and reported to the captain what I had seen.

SENATOR SMITH: What did he say?

MR. BOXHALL: He said all right, and then the order came out for the boats.

SENATOR SMITH: You mean the order was given to man or lower the lifeboats?

MR. BOXHALL: To clear the lifeboats. . . .

SENATOR SMITH: When the order was given to clear the lifeboats, what did you do?

MR. BOXHALL: I went around the decks and was clearing the lifeboats; helping take the covers off.

SENATOR SMITH: Covers off?

MR. BOXHALL: Covers off of the boats, and clearing them generally.

SENATOR SMITH: Were they all covered?

MR. BOXHALL: Yes, sir; except the sea boats; and assisting generally around the decks. Then I went into the chart room and worked out the ship's position. I was clearing boats for a little while, and then went in and worked the position out.

SENATOR SMITH: Did you report her position?

MR. BOXHALL: I submitted her position to the captain.

SENATOR SMITH: What did he say?

MR. BOXHALL: He said, "Take it to the Marconi room."

SENATOR SMITH: Did you do so?

MR. BOXHALL: Yes, sir.

SENATOR SMITH: Did you find the operator in charge?

MR. BOXHALL: I found the two operators there.

SENATOR SMITH: Who?

MR. BOXHALL: Phillips and Bride.

SENATOR SMITH: What did you do with your information?

MR. BOXHALL: There was too much noise of the steam escaping, so I wrote the position down for them and left it.

SENATOR SMITH: You simply wrote the position down?

MR. BOXHALL: Yes.

SENATOR SMITH: And handed it to the operator?

MR. BOXHALL: Left it on his table there. He saw it. He made a call, and he was listening, and I did not interrupt him.

SENATOR SMITH: Did you remain to see what disposition was made of it?

MR. BOXHALL: No.

SENATOR SMITH: Did you keep a copy of that, or do you know exactly what that showed?

MR. BOXHALL: That position?

SENATOR SMITH: Yes.

MR. BOXHALL: Yes; I have the position.

SENATOR SMITH: Have you a memorandum of it?

MR. BOXHALL: No; I have it in my head.

SENATOR SMITH: Give it to the reporter.

MR. BOXHALL: Forty-one, forty-six; fifty, fourteen.

SENATOR BURTON: Give that again.

MR. BOXHALL: Forty-one, forty-six, north; fifty, fourteen west.

SENATOR SMITH: Was that the last time the ship's position was taken?

MR. BOXHALL: That is the position I worked out.

SENATOR SMITH: Was that the last time it was taken so far as you know?

MR. BOXHALL: Yes; that was the position at the time she struck.

SENATOR SMITH: Was that where she sank, do you know?

MR. BOXHALL: I do not know. She would just drift a little way farther on, probably half a mile or so.

SENATOR SMITH: What did you do after you left the operator's room?

MR. BOXHALL: Went around the decks assisting to clear the decks and send distress signals off.

SENATOR SMITH: What do you mean by clearing the decks?

MR. BOXHALL: Clearing the boats, I should say.

SENATOR SMITH: At that time were passengers on these decks?

MR. BOXHALL: Yes.

SENATOR SMITH: Men and women?

MR. BOXHALL: Men and women, yes, coming up.

SENATOR SMITH: What were they doing?

MR. BOXHALL: I was too busy to take notice, as a matter of fact.

SENATOR SMITH: Did they have life preservers on, or life belts?

MR. BOXHALL: Yes; I think all of them had life preservers that I saw.

SENATOR SMITH: Would you be willing to say that, so far as your observation went——

MR. BOXHALL: They all had them, I should say, as far as my observation went.

SENATOR SMITH: Men and women?

MR. BOXHALL: Yes, sir.

SENATOR SMITH: Children?

MR. BOXHALL: I was around the bridge most of the time.

SENATOR SMITH: I want to get your best information about it.

MR. BOXHALL: I was around the bridge most of the time, sending off distress signals and endeavoring to signal to a ship that was ahead of us.

SENATOR SMITH: Taking the signals from the captain?

MR. BOXHALL: No, sir.

SENATOR SMITH: Carrying them yourself to the operator?

MR. BOXHALL: No; distress signals—rockets.

SENATOR SMITH: On the ship?

MR. BOXHALL: Yes, sir.

SENATOR SMITH: Did you return again to the wireless room?

MR. BOXHALL: No.

SENATOR SMITH: You say these passengers were gathered about on all decks?

MR. BOXHALL: I did not leave the boat deck after that.

SENATOR SMITH: You remained on the upper deck?

MR. BOXHALL: On the upper deck.

SENATOR SMITH: Where these lifeboats were?

MR. BOXHALL: Where these lifeboats were.

SENATOR SMITH: And did you take part in clearing?

MR. BOXHALL: Generally assisting.

SENATOR SMITH: Assisting in lowering these lifeboats?

MR. BOXHALL: Not in lowering them, sir.

SENATOR SMITH: In manning them?

MR. BOXHALL: Yes, sir, in manning them; but my attention until the time I left the ship was mostly taken up with firing off distress rockets and trying to signal a steamer that was almost ahead of us.

SENATOR SMITH: How far ahead of you?

MR. BOXHALL: It is hard to say. I saw his masthead lights and I saw his side light.

SENATOR SMITH: In what direction?

MR. BOXHALL: Almost ahead of us.

SENATOR SMITH: On the same course, apparently?

MR. BOXHALL: No; oh, no.

SENATOR SMITH: On the same general course?

MR. BOXHALL: By the way she was heading she seemed to be meeting us.

SENATOR SMITH: Coming toward you?

MR. BOXHALL: Coming toward us.

SENATOR SMITH: Do you know anything about what boat that was?

MR. BOXHALL: No, sir.

SENATOR SMITH: Have you had any information since about it?

MR. BOXHALL: None whatever.

SENATOR SMITH: You say you fired these rockets and otherwise attempted to signal her?

MR. BOXHALL: Yes, sir. She got close enough, as I thought, to read our electric Morse signal, and I signaled to her; I told her to come at once, we were sinking; and the captain was standing——

SENATOR SMITH: This was the signal?

MR. BOXHALL: Yes, sir.

SENATOR SMITH: Go ahead.

MR. BOXHALL: I told the captain about this ship, and he was with me most of the time when we were signaling.

SENATOR SMITH: Did he also see it?

MR. BOXHALL: Yes, sir.

SENATOR SMITH: Did he tell you to do anything else to arrest its attention?

MR. BOXHALL: I went over and started the Morse signal. He said, "Tell him to come at once, we are sinking."

SENATOR SMITH: You were sinking already, you say?

MR. BOXHALL: Yes, sir.

SENATOR SMITH: "Come at once, we are sinking"?

MR. BOXHALL: Yes.

SENATOR SMITH: What would be that signal?

MR. BOXHALL: It was sent in the Morse key, the Morse code.

SENATOR SMITH: And you did that?

MR. BOXHALL: Yes, sir.

SENATOR SMITH: And did you get any reply?

MR. BOXHALL: I can not say I saw any reply. Some people say she replied to our rockets and our signals, but I did not see them.

SENATOR SMITH: Was any attempt made to get in wireless communication after you saw this boat—what you took to be a boat?

MR. BOXHALL: I do not know what was transpiring in the wireless room.

SENATOR SMITH: These signals you utilized were Morse signals?

MR. BOXHALL: Yes.

140

SENATOR SMITH: Are they recognized as standard for the sea?

MR. BOXHALL: Oh, yes.

SENATOR SMITH: Are they a part of the British regulations?

MR. BOXHALL: Yes, sir.

SENATOR SMITH: Did you see any signals from this ship at all?

MR. BOXHALL: No; I can not say that I saw any signals, except her ordinary steaming light. Some people say they saw signals, but I could not.

SENATOR SMITH: In referring to "some people," whom do you mean?

MR. BOXHALL: People who were around the bridge.

SENATOR SMITH: Passengers?

MR. BOXHALL: No; I should not say passengers.

SENATOR SMITH: Officers?

MR. BOXHALL: I think it was stewards.

SENATOR SMITH: Stewards; the crew?

MR. BOXHALL: And people waiting in the boats, or something.

SENATOR SMITH: They saw some of these signals?

MR. BOXHALL: Some men said they saw her signals.

SENATOR SMITH: From what you saw of that vessel, how far would you think she was from the *Titanic?*

MR. BOXHALL: I should say approximately the ship would be about 5 miles.

SENATOR SMITH: What lights did you see?

MR. BOXHALL: The two masthead lights and the red light.

SENATOR SMITH: Were the two masthead lights the first lights that you could see?

MR. BOXHALL: The first lights.

SENATOR SMITH: And what other lights?

MR. BOXHALL: And then, as she got closer, she showed her side light, her red light.

SENATOR SMITH: So you were quite sure she was coming in your direction?

MR. BOXHALL: Quite sure.

SENATOR SMITH: How long was this before the boat sank?

MR. BOXHALL: It is hard to tell. I had no idea of the time then; I do not know what time it was then.

SENATOR SMITH: Can you recall about how long it was after the collision?

MR. BOXHALL: No.

SENATOR SMITH: Was this information communicated to the wireless operators?

MR. BOXHALL: What communication, sir?

SENATOR SMITH: Was this information communicated to the wireless operators?

MR. BOXHALL: Not to my knowledge.

SENATOR SMITH: Did you know that they had sent out a distress signal?

MR. BOXHALL: Oh, yes.

SENATOR SMITH: And you would expect that this boat would pick it up if they had a wireless on it?

MR. BOXHALL: If she had a wireless installation.

SENATOR SMITH: You busied yourself with the Morse signals?

MR. BOXHALL: Yes, sir.

SENATOR SMITH: Did they continue up to the time you assisted in clearing the lifeboats?

MR. BOXHALL: I would signal with the Morse and then go ahead and send off a rocket, and then go back and have a look at the ship, until I was finally sent away.

SENATOR SMITH: Suppose you had had a searchlight on the bow of that boat, and could have thrown it strongly against this object that you seemed to see, do you think that would have apprised the vessel of its proximity to you and of your distress?

MR. BOXHALL: Well, no doubt a searchlight might have called attention to it then.

SENATOR SMITH: This ship was not equipped with a searchlight?

MR. BOXHALL: The *Titanic* was not; no.

SENATOR SMITH: Have you ever been employed on a ship that was so equipped?

MR. BOXHALL: Not in the merchant service.

SENATOR SMITH: Not in the merchant service?

MR. BOXHALL: No, sir.

SENATOR SMITH: Any other service?

MR. BOXHALL: Yes.

SENATOR SMITH: In the naval service?

MR. BOXHALL: In the naval service.

SENATOR SMITH: Is that a part of the equipment of the British naval service?

MR. BOXHALL: Yes; all the ships that I have seen have a searchlight.

SENATOR SMITH: But not in the merchant service?

MR. BOXHALL: Not in the merchant service. . . .

SENATOR SMITH: How are the rockets exploded?

MR. BOXHALL: The rockets are exploded by a firing lanyard.

SENATOR SMITH: They shower?

MR. BOXHALL: They go right up into the air and they throw stars.

SENATOR SMITH: How strong rockets do they have on these boats—what is the charge; do you know?

MR. BOXHALL: I do not know, sir; the Board of Trade regulations govern that.

SENATOR SMITH: Did they work satisfactorily?

MR. BOXHALL: Oh, yes.

SENATOR SMITH: So that, so far as your manipulation of these signals and rockets was concerned——

MR. BOXHALL: They were quite satisfactory.

SENATOR SMITH: The failure to arouse the attention of this ship was not due to any impaired or partial success of these signals?

MR. BOXHALL: Not at all, sir.

SENATOR SMITH: You say you continued to fire the rockets and give the signals?

MR. BOXHALL: Yes, sir.

SENATOR SMITH: And then returned to the side of the ship?

MR. BOXHALL: Yes, sir.

SENATOR SMITH: And assisted in the work of the lifeboats?

MR. BOXHALL: Yes, sir.

SENATOR SMITH: All about the same time?

MR. BOXHALL: Yes, sir. . . .

SENATOR SMITH: Where did you go; to which side of the boat?

MR. BOXHALL: I went on the port side.

SENATOR SMITH: Amidship, or aft, or forward?

MR. BOXHALL: Around forward.

SENATOR SMITH: Were there any lifeboats forward?

MR. BOXHALL: Oh, yes.

SENATOR SMITH: On each side?

MR. BOXHALL: Yes.

SENATOR SMITH: How many?

MR. BOXHALL: When I left the ship?

SENATOR SMITH: When the ship left Southampton, if you can tell? I want to find out the location of the lifeboats.

MR. BOXHALL: They were equally divided on the boat deck, the port side and the starboard side.

SENATOR SMITH: Fore and aft?

MR. BOXHALL: Fore and aft.

SENATOR SMITH: How many would be forward?

MR. BOXHALL: There were 14 lifeboats. That would be 7 on either side.

SENATOR SMITH: Were these lifeboats all along the side?

MR. BOXHALL: Yes, sir.

SENATOR SMITH: Continuously? There was no division between those amidship and those forward?

MR. BOXHALL: No, sir.

SENATOR SMITH: You say there were how many on a side?

MR. BOXHALL: Seven on either side. I never counted them, but I think there were 7. There were 14 lifeboats and 2 sea boats. They were equally divided.

SENATOR SMITH: Did you see any of these lifeboats filled or lowered on the starboard side, either forward or aft?

MR. BOXHALL: I saw some one filling the starboard emergency boat at the time that I went and was firing off rockets. I fired them just close to the bows of this emergency boat.

SENATOR SMITH: There were only two emergency boats?

MR. BOXHALL: That is all; but that one I noticed, because these distress rockets are dangerous things if they explode, and I had to keep people away clear while I fired the rockets.

SENATOR SMITH: On the port side you could have seen but one. There was one on each side?

MR. BOXHALL: Yes.

SENATOR SMITH: You could have seen but one, and that was at the boat deck. Was it being lowered?

MR. BOXHALL: I saw it just before it was lowered, and then I fired a rocket after it was lowered. . . .

SENATOR SMITH: . . . Did you see the other boats of the same type lowered?

MR. BOXHALL: I was in it when it was lowered.

SENATOR SMITH: You were in it. When was it lowered?

MR. BOXHALL: I do not know the time.

SENATOR SMITH: Could you tell the order in which they were lowered, whether this was the second or third or fourth?

MR. BOXHALL: When I was lowered away I was the last boat but one on the port side. There was one of the lifeboats lowered away after I left, a few minutes after I left, and then there were no more boats hanging in the davits on the port side. . . .

SENATOR SMITH: And all of the lifeboats had been lowered when the boat that you got in was lowered?

MR. BOXHALL: All but one.

SENATOR SMITH: Where was that one?

MR. BOXHALL: That was the next boat to me, aft.

SENATOR SMITH: A lifeboat or a collapsible?

MR. BOXHALL: A lifeboat.

SENATOR SMITH: Did you have anything to do with filling these boats?

MR. BOXHALL: I was assisting to get people along there, but I was not standing at the side of the boat, lifting them in, actually.

SENATOR SMITH: What can you say about the anxiety of people to get into these boats; was there great anxiety?

MR. BOXHALL: No, sir; I can not say that I saw that.

SENATOR SMITH: What can you say as to whether they were reluctant to get in?

MR. BOXHALL: I did not notice that, either.

SENATOR SMITH: Were there many people on the boat deck when you got into this boat?

MR. BOXHALL: No, sir.

SENATOR SMITH: Were there any people at all?

MR. BOXHALL: There were some around by the other boat. . . .

SENATOR SMITH: Where was the captain?

MR. BOXHALL: The captain was standing by this emergency boat.

SENATOR SMITH: The one you got in?

MR. BOXHALL: Yes, sir.

SENATOR SMITH: How far from it?

MR. BOXHALL: He was standing by the wheelhouse door, just abreast of this boat.

SENATOR SMITH: By the wheelhouse door, just abreast of this boat?

MR. BOXHALL: Yes.

SENATOR SMITH: What was he doing?

MR. BOXHALL: Supervising the boats being loaded, I think.

SENATOR SMITH: Loaded?

MR. BOXHALL: Supervising passengers being put into the boat.

SENATOR SMITH: Did he tell you to get in?

MR. BOXHALL: Yes, sir.

SENATOR SMITH: What did he say?

MR. BOXHALL: He told me I had to get into that boat and go away.

SENATOR SMITH: Did any other officer get into that boat?

MR. BOXHALL: No, sir.

SENATOR SMITH: Any other member of the crew?

MR. BOXHALL: One man was in it.

SENATOR SMITH: Who was that?

MR. BOXHALL: I do not know his name, sir; I forgot.

SENATOR SMITH: What was his occupation?

MR. BOXHALL: Sailorman.

SENATOR SMITH: But you do not know who he was?

MR. BOXHALL: There was one sailorman, one steward, and one cook; that is all.

SENATOR SMITH: There were four men in that boat?

MR. BOXHALL: And one passenger.

SENATOR SMITH: A sailorman, a steward, a cook, yourself, and one male passenger?

MR. BOXHALL: One male passenger.

SENATOR SMITH: Who was that passenger?

MR. BOXHALL: He was a saloon passenger who did not speak English. He had a black beard.

SENATOR SMITH: How old a man, apparently?

MR. BOXHALL: A middle-aged man.

SENATOR SMITH: Did he seem to have any family there?

MR. BOXHALL: I think he had his wife there, and some children.

SENATOR SMITH: Did she get in?

MR. BOXHALL: The boat was already loaded; I did not see the passengers being put in.

SENATOR SMITH: The boat was full?

MR. BOXHALL: Yes, it seemed to me to be pretty full. The order was given to lower the boats away when I was sent to her.

SENATOR SMITH: How long was this before the ship sank?

MR. BOXHALL: As near as I can judge, it seems to me about 20 minutes to half an hour.

SENATOR SMITH: Before the ship sank?

MR. BOXHALL: Yes, sir.

SENATOR SMITH: Did you see the captain after that?

MR. BOXHALL: No, sir.

SENATOR SMITH: Not at all?

MR. BOXHALL: No, sir.

SENATOR SMITH: How far were you from the ship when it sank?

MR. BOXHALL: I suppose I was about a half a mile away.

SENATOR SMITH: Going in what direction?

MR. BOXHALL: Resting on the oars.

SENATOR SMITH: Did all the men in that boat handle oars?

MR. BOXHALL: Yes, sir.

SENATOR SMITH: Did any women handle oars?

MR. BOXHALL: I was handling one oar and a lady was assisting me with it. But she was not compelled to do it; she was not asked to do it.

SENATOR SMITH: Do you know who she was?

MR. BOXHALL: No, sir.

SENATOR SMITH: Did you find out afterwards who she was?

MR. BOXHALL: No; I did not find out, at all.

SENATOR SMITH: You did not ask her to do that, you say?

MR. BOXHALL: No, sir.

SENATOR SMITH: It was a voluntary service?

MR. BOXHALL: Voluntary service.

SENATOR SMITH: You were resting on your oars about half a mile from the place where the ship went down?

MR. BOXHALL: About half a mile.

SENATOR SMITH: When you left the ship's side, were there others trying to get into your boat?

MR. BOXHALL: No, sir.

SENATOR SMITH: Men or women?

MR. BOXHALL: No, sir.

SENATOR SMITH: As you proceeded from the ship's side did you see anyone in the water?

MR. BOXHALL: No; not at all.

SENATOR SMITH: Did you encounter anyone in the water, at all, after you entered the boat?

MR. BOXHALL: No, sir.

SENATOR SMITH: Did you ever return to the *Titanic* after leaving its side?

MR. BOXHALL: I pulled around the ship's stern and was intending to go alongside, and tried to see if I could get alongside of the ship again.

SENATOR SMITH: What for?

MR. BOXHALL: I reckoned I could take about three more people off the boat with safety.

SENATOR SMITH: Who made that suggestion to you, anyone?

MR. BOXHALL: No.

SENATOR SMITH: Did the suggestion come from a woman passenger, or did you do it of your own motion?

MR. BOXHALL: I did it of my own accord. I was in charge of the boat.

SENATOR SMITH: And you swung it around how close to the side?

MR. BOXHALL: I kept a little distance off the ship.

SENATOR SMITH: How far off?

MR. BOXHALL: Well, probably a hundred yards or so.

SENATOR SMITH: Did anyone make any attempt to get into the boat?

MR. BOXHALL: No. Oh, no; there was no rush.

SENATOR SMITH: And did you halloo to anyone to come?

MR. BOXHALL: No. I was hoping to be able to get alongside of the ship again.

SENATOR SMITH: Why did you not get close?

MR. BOXHALL: Because when I got so close as that I thought it was wiser not to go any closer, and I put it to the people——

SENATOR SMITH: Wiser for what?

MR. BOXHALL: Because there was only one man who understood my orders as to how to handle a boat.

SENATOR SMITH: Did you feel you were in danger from suction?

MR. BOXHALL: Yes.

SENATOR SMITH: Was there any suction?

MR. BOXHALL: Yes; I think there was a little suction.

SENATOR SMITH: How much?

MR. BOXHALL: The boat seemed to be drawn closer to the ship. I think, myself, that there was more suction while the ship was settling bodily. That was shortly after we

148

were lowered into the boat. I think there was more suction then than there was when she actually went down, because I pulled some distance off then.

SENATOR SMITH: You were not close enough to know actually what the suction was when she actually sank, or as she actually sank?

MR. BOXHALL: No.

SENATOR SMITH: As a matter of fact, there was not much suction, was there?

MR. BOXHALL: No; I do not think there was the suction that the people really thought there was. I was really surprised, myself.

SENATOR SMITH: You were rather surprised, and all these officers were rather surprised, were they not, that there was so little suction?

MR. BOXHALL: By hearsay, it seems to have been a general surprise to everybody that there was so little suction.

SENATOR SMITH: Do you know who the passenger was who got into the boat—the man?

MR. BOXHALL: No.

SENATOR SMITH: Have you ever seen him since then?

MR. BOXHALL: No; I have not.

SENATOR SMITH: You did not see him aboard the *Carpathia?*

MR. BOXHALL: No, sir. There was a lady there whom I asked to steer the boat according to my orders. I asked her to pull the tiller toward her or away.

SENATOR SMITH: Was that Mrs. [Mahala] Douglas?

MR. BOXHALL: Mrs. Douglas, and she assisted me greatly in doing that.

SENATOR SMITH: Then you were in Mrs. Douglas's boat?

MR. BOXHALL: Yes.

SENATOR SMITH: Did you see her afterwards?

MR. BOXHALL: Yes; on board the *Carpathia.*

SENATOR SMITH: And you talked with her?

MR. BOXHALL: Yes; I had a talk with her.

SENATOR SMITH: Have you seen her since?

MR. BOXHALL: No, sir.

SENATOR SMITH: Her husband did not survive?

MR. BOXHALL: No; he did not.

SENATOR SMITH: She took the tiller of the lifeboat and steered it?

MR. BOXHALL: Yes, sir.

SENATOR SMITH: And you pulled on an oar?

MR. BOXHALL: Yes.

SENATOR SMITH: Do you know, with reference to the other lifeboats, when yours reached the side of the *Carpathia?*

MR. BOXHALL: Yes; it was the first one there.

SENATOR SMITH: Who was the first person to step out of your boat?

MR. BOXHALL: That I do not know.

SENATOR SMITH: You do not remember whether it was Mrs. Douglas or yourself——

MR. BOXHALL: It was not myself, because I handed everybody out before I came out.

SENATOR SMITH: Did you step onto a little bridge there on the side of the *Carpathia?*

MR. BOXHALL: No.

SENATOR SMITH: On some little steps that went up the side?

MR. BOXHALL: There was a stepladder up the side.

SENATOR SMITH: A direct ladder?

MR. BOXHALL: Yes; a direct ladder.

SENATOR SMITH: And you assisted the passengers to that ladder?

MR. BOXHALL: Yes, put the rope over their heads; put their arms through a rope, and then assisted them up in that way.

SENATOR SMITH: Did you land all the passengers in your boat?

MR. BOXHALL: Yes, everyone.

SENATOR SMITH: Aboard the *Carpathia?*

MR. BOXHALL: Yes.

SENATOR SMITH: Can you give the hour when you went alongside?

MR. BOXHALL: No, sir. They told me on board the *Carpathia* afterwards that it was about 10 minutes after 4, approximately.

SENATOR SMITH: Had you been rowing or lying on your oars from the time you left the *Titanic* until——

MR. BOXHALL: No; I had been showing green lights most of the time. I had been showing pyrotechnic lights on the boat.

SENATOR SMITH: Your boat was equipped with lights?

MR. BOXHALL: Yes, sir.

SENATOR SMITH: Were any of the other lifeboats so equipped,

or did you see any lights of that character on the other boats?

MR. BOXHALL: Not of that character; no, sir.

SENATOR SMITH: Between the time you left the *Titanic* and the time you reached the *Carpathia,* I mean?

MR. BOXHALL: No. . . .

SENATOR SMITH: Did you see the *Titanic* sink?

MR. BOXHALL: No; I can not say that I saw her sink. I saw the lights go out, and I looked two or three minutes afterwards and it was 25 minutes past 2. So I took it that when she sank would be about 20 minutes after 2.

SENATOR SMITH: How far were you from her then?

MR. BOXHALL: I would say we were then about three-fourths of a mile from her.

SENATOR SMITH: So you are unable to tell what scenes were then transpiring on the *Titanic?*

MR. BOXHALL: Yes, sir.

SENATOR SMITH: Did you have any conversation with Mr. Ismay that night?

MR. BOXHALL: Yes, sir.

SENATOR SMITH: Where?

MR. BOXHALL: On board of the ship.

SENATOR SMITH: At what time?

MR. BOXHALL: On the bridge, probably about ten minutes or a quarter of an hour before I came away in the boat.

SENATOR SMITH: On the bridge, about ten minutes or a quarter of an hour before you went down over the side in the lifeboat?

MR. BOXHALL: Yes, sir.

SENATOR SMITH: Did you know him personally?

MR. BOXHALL: Yes, sir.

SENATOR SMITH: How long had you known him?

MR. BOXHALL: I had known him by sight for about three years. He has crossed before in some ships I have been in.

SENATOR SMITH: What did he say to you?

MR. BOXHALL: He asked me why I did not get the people in the boat and get away?

SENATOR SMITH: What did you say to him?

MR. BOXHALL: I told him the boat's crew were ready, and the boat was ready to be put away when the captain's order was given.

SENATOR SMITH: And the order had not yet been given?

MR. BOXHALL: No, sir.

SENATOR SMITH: Was that all that was said?

MR. BOXHALL: That is all.

SENATOR SMITH: Did he say anything about himself?

MR. BOXHALL: No, sir; he passed on, then. . . .

SENATOR SMITH: You say you did not see Mr. Ismay after you saw him on the bridge and before the order had been given to clear the lifeboats or lower the lifeboats?

MR. BOXHALL: I did not see him; no, sir.

SENATOR SMITH: When did you next see him?

MR. BOXHALL: When he came alongside in the collapsible boat outside of the *Carpathia*.

SENATOR SMITH: Do you know what boat that was?

MR. BOXHALL: I do not know any number; it was a collapsible boat.

SENATOR SMITH: How soon after you reached there did it appear at the side of the *Carpathia?*

MR. BOXHALL: It was one of the last boats that came. . . .

SENATOR SMITH: Do you know who was in it?

MR. BOXHALL: Mr. Carter was in it. I saw Mr. Carter. . . .

SENATOR SMITH: Were there any other men in that boat?

MR. BOXHALL: Yes; I saw some men who looked to me like Filipinos.

SENATOR SMITH: Foreigners?

MR. BOXHALL: Yes.

SENATOR SMITH: How many?

MR. BOXHALL: I do not know whether there were three or four of them.

SENATOR SMITH: Were there any women or children in the boat?

MR. BOXHALL: Yes; it was full of them.

SENATOR SMITH: How many were in the boat?

MR. BOXHALL: I will not say that it was full of women and children. Now I come to think of it, there was a foreigner there, a steerage passenger who could not speak English—a man.

SENATOR SMITH: How many of these Filipinos were there?

MR. BOXHALL: Three or four.

SENATOR SMITH: And Mr. Ismay, Mr. Carter, and this foreigner who could not speak English?

MR. BOXHALL: Yes. . . .

SENATOR SMITH: As a matter of fact, were there any other lights visible on the lifeboats except those on your boat?

MR. BOXHALL: I saw some lifeboat lights, but the usual lifeboat's lights. They were very dim, small lamps.

SENATOR SMITH: If all those lifeboats had been lighted, it would have impressed itself upon you, would it not?

MR. BOXHALL: Lighted the same——

SENATOR SMITH: The same as yours?

MR. BOXHALL: But this was a box of green lights that happened to be thrown into the boat.

SENATOR SMITH: Accidentally?

MR. BOXHALL: No, sir; not accidentally.

SENATOR SMITH: Intentionally?

MR. BOXHALL: Yes, sir; because I told the man to put them in.

SENATOR SMITH: Was it a part of the equipment of the boat?

MR. BOXHALL: No; it was not a part of the equipment; but I told him to put them in for anybody that would happen to find them.

SENATOR SMITH: I see. And after the boat was lowered you lighted them?

MR. BOXHALL: Yes.

SENATOR SMITH: Did they make a brilliant light?

MR. BOXHALL: Yes; a very brilliant light.

SENATOR SMITH: You think the *Carpathia* steamed toward these lights?

MR. BOXHALL: They did.

SENATOR SMITH: And you say that is the reason they reached you first?

MR. BOXHALL: Yes. . . .

SENATOR SMITH: Now, Mr. Boxhall, did you personally become acquainted with any of the American passengers on that boat?

MR. BOXHALL: On what boat?

SENATOR SMITH: On the *Titanic.*

MR. BOXHALL: No, sir; not until after the accident. After we got on board the *Carpathia* I met one or two.

SENATOR SMITH: But were you aware at any time between Southampton and the place of this accident of the presence on shipboard of a large number of Americans?

MR. BOXHALL: Yes, sir.

SENATOR SMITH: Did you at any time learn who they were?

MR. BOXHALL: Yes; by glancing through the passenger list.

SENATOR SMITH: Can you tell any names that you now particularly recall?

MR. BOXHALL: Yes; I recall that Col. Astor and his wife were aboard.

SENATOR SMITH: You recall that you saw Col. Astor's name on this list?

MR. BOXHALL: Yes.

SENATOR SMITH: Did you personally see him or his wife?

MR. BOXHALL: I have seen him walking on the top deck.

SENATOR SMITH: Did you know who he was?

MR. BOXHALL: One of the officers—I think it was one of the officers who told me. . . .

SENATOR SMITH: Did you see Col. Astor after this collision occurred?

MR. BOXHALL: No, sir.

SENATOR SMITH: Or his wife?

MR. BOXHALL: I never saw his wife at all. . . .

SENATOR SMITH: After you boarded the *Carpathia* during that early morning, Monday morning, or after you left the *Titanic*'s side, did you see any icebergs?

MR. BOXHALL: Not until I got within about two or three ship's lengths of the *Carpathia*, when I saw her engines were stopped—then I saw the icebergs; it was just breaking daylight then.

SENATOR SMITH: Where were they?

MR. BOXHALL: Close to the *Carpathia*.

SENATOR SMITH: How close?

MR. BOXHALL: He seemed to have stopped within half a mile or quarter of a mile of the berg.

SENATOR SMITH: How many did you see?

MR. BOXHALL: Numerous bergs. As daylight broke I saw them.

SENATOR SMITH: About how many?

MR. BOXHALL: I would not like to say.

SENATOR SMITH: More than two?

MR. BOXHALL: Certainly more than two. Several bergs.

SENATOR SMITH: That is four or five or six?

MR. BOXHALL: And field ice. I could see field ice then as far as the eye could see. . . .

SENATOR SMITH: Can you tell what the theory of the navigator is as to where the icebergs and growlers and field ice come from?

MR. BOXHALL: As far as I understand, they come from the Arctic region.

SENATOR SMITH: What are they composed of, if you know?

MR. BOXHALL: Some people who have been very close to them tell me that they have seen sand and gravel and rocks and things of that kind in them.

SENATOR SMITH: Rocks and other substances?

MR. BOXHALL: And earth. I have never been close enough to see that.

SENATOR SMITH: I suppose you mean the icebergs, when you say that?

MR. BOXHALL: The icebergs; yes, sir.

SENATOR SMITH: And those icebergs are supposed to come from the Arctic regions?

MR. BOXHALL: Yes; so I believe.

SENATOR SMITH: And float down into the open sea?

MR. BOXHALL: Yes.

SENATOR SMITH: How far east have you ever seen them?

MR. BOXHALL: I do not know how far east I have seen them. It has been many years since I have seen any, until this time.

SENATOR SMITH: Is it understood by mariners and navigators that they are more frequent in the latitude of the Grand Banks?

MR. BOXHALL: Around 50 west; 47 to 50 west, I think, as near as I can remember.

SENATOR SMITH: From 47 to 50 west they are known to exist?

MR. BOXHALL: Yes.

SENATOR SMITH: And it is customary to be particularly careful in that vicinity?

MR. BOXHALL: Oh, yes, sir.

SENATOR SMITH: Well, how did it happen that in that identical vicinity it was not thought necessary to increase the lookout?

MR. BOXHALL: I do not know. The lookout may have been increased; I can not say. I was busy most of the watch in the chart room, making calculations.

SENATOR SMITH: As far as you know of your own knowledge, it was not?

MR. BOXHALL: I did not hear any extra lookouts reported as being put on.

SENATOR SMITH: You did not see any extra officers that night, forward on the bridge deck?

MR. BOXHALL: No. . . .

SENATOR SMITH: Do you know what precautions the captain of the *Carpathia* took when he found himself among ice?

MR. BOXHALL: No, sir.

SENATOR SMITH: Do you know whether he doubled his lookout?

MR. BOXHALL: I do not know.

SENATOR SMITH: He proceeded toward New York how long after all the lifeboats had been raised?

MR. BOXHALL: It was approximately, I should say, well on in the forenoon, when he set the course to New York.

SENATOR SMITH: That is, 9 or 10 o'clock?

MR. BOXHALL: No; I think it was well after that. We were steaming around the wreckage for quite a long time. I did not notice the time, but it must have been quite late in the forenoon.

SENATOR SMITH: Steaming around——

MR. BOXHALL: Steaming around the scene of disaster.

SENATOR SMITH: Where were you when they were steaming around?

MR. BOXHALL: I was on the bridge for a few minutes, shortly after we got the boats on board.

SENATOR SMITH: For how long?

MR. BOXHALL: About a quarter of an hour, I think.

SENATOR SMITH: And remained on the bridge of the *Carpathia* after the boats were all raised?

MR. BOXHALL: Yes.

SENATOR SMITH: Did you see any bodies floating in the water?

MR. BOXHALL: I remained on the bridge until he started off for New York direct. I do not know what time that was.

SENATOR SMITH: Did you see any floating bodies?

MR. BOXHALL: I saw one floating body, sir.

SENATOR SMITH: That of a man or woman?

MR. BOXHALL: A man, sir.

SENATOR SMITH: Did you see the face distinctly?

MR. BOXHALL: No; I could not. It had a life preserver on.

SENATOR SMITH: Dead?

MR. BOXHALL: Oh, yes; quite dead.

SENATOR SMITH: How do you know?

MR. BOXHALL: We could see by the way the body was lying.

SENATOR SMITH: What is the ordinary position of a dead body in the water with a life preserver on?

MR. BOXHALL: This body looked as if the man was lying as if he had fallen asleep with his face over his arm.

SENATOR SMITH: On his side?

MR. BOXHALL: On his side.

SENATOR SMITH: Were you near enough to describe his features?

MR. BOXHALL: Not at all, sir.

SENATOR SMITH: Is that the only body you saw?

MR. BOXHALL: That is the only body I saw.

SENATOR SMITH: The only body you saw either dead or alive?

MR. BOXHALL: Yes; dead or alive.

SENATOR SMITH: There must have been hundreds of bodies in the water about the *Titanic*.

MR. BOXHALL: No one ever saw any, at all.

SENATOR SMITH: You say they were all equipped with life belts?

MR. BOXHALL: I do not remember seeing anybody without a life belt.

SENATOR SMITH: Did you know of any persons refusing to enter the lifeboats?

MR. BOXHALL: No; only by hearsay.

SENATOR SMITH: Did you hear that many had refused to enter the lifeboats?

MR. BOXHALL: I heard it on board the *Carpathia,* that some of them had refused.

SENATOR SMITH: Well, those on board the *Carpathia* had not refused. You heard that others had refused?

MR. BOXHALL: I heard that others had refused. . . .

SENATOR SMITH: Did you see any person—man, woman, or child—who refused to get into a lifeboat?

MR. BOXHALL: No, sir.

SENATOR SMITH: Did you see any man, woman, or child refused permission to get into a lifeboat?

MR. BOXHALL: No, sir.

SENATOR SMITH: Did you see any man, woman, or child ejected from a lifeboat?

MR. BOXHALL: No, sir.

SENATOR SMITH: Did you see any man or woman attempt to reach a lifeboat while you were on the deck or when your lifeboat was in the water?

MR. BOXHALL: Do you mean to rush it, or get in quietly?

SENATOR SMITH: To struggle to get in?

MR. BOXHALL: No, sir; I did not.

SENATOR SMITH: To try to get in or attempt to get in?

MR. BOXHALL: I saw several get in, but all I saw try to get in got in.

SENATOR SMITH: Did you see any get in from the water?

MR. BOXHALL: No.

SENATOR SMITH: Did you see anyone in the water attempt to get in?

MR. BOXHALL: I did not see anyone in the water. It was dark, sir.

SENATOR SMITH: So you could not see anyone?

MR. BOXHALL: I could not see anybody in the water. I was looking around for them, keeping my eyes open, but I did not see anyone.

SENATOR SMITH: If you had seen some one in the water, what would you have done?

MR. BOXHALL: Taken them in the boat at once.

SENATOR SMITH: No matter whether its capacity was apparently taxed or not?

MR. BOXHALL: I should have taken them in the boat.

SENATOR SMITH: You would not have left them?

MR. BOXHALL: No, sir.

SENATOR SMITH: If you had seen any struggling man or woman in the water——

MR. BOXHALL: I should have taken them in as far as safety would allow; but I did not see anyone in the water. . . .

FOURTH DAY
Tuesday, April 23
Washington, D.C.

Witness: Herbert John Pitman, 34
Titanic's **Third Officer, from Somerset, England**

Key testimony: Pitman claimed he wanted to row the lifeboat in his command, No. 5, back to the scene of the wreck, but passengers opposed him. So his men lay on their oars while screaming victims froze to death in the water.

. . . SENATOR SMITH: Where were you on Sunday evening immediately preceding the collision?

MR. PITMAN: In my bunk; in bed.

SENATOR SMITH: What were the hours of your watch that night?

MR. PITMAN: I was on the bridge from 6 to 8 o'clock P.M.

SENATOR SMITH: Whom did you see on the bridge, if anyone, that night between 6 and 8 o'clock?

MR. PITMAN: The commander and the second officer.

SENATOR SMITH: The captain?

MR. PITMAN: Yes, sir.

SENATOR SMITH: You call him the commander in that event?

MR. PITMAN: Some do.

SENATOR SMITH: I just wanted to be sure that you referred to the captain. What time was he on the bridge; all the time that you were on watch?

MR. PITMAN: No; I could not say that, sir, because I was inside, working out observations.

SENATOR SMITH: Whenever you went to the bridge, from 6 to 8 o'clock, do you recall having seen the captain?

MR. PITMAN: I saw him once, sir.

SENATOR SMITH: Do you recall the hour?

MR. PITMAN: Previous to 7 o'clock.

SENATOR SMITH: You did not see him after 7 o'clock on the bridge?

MR. PITMAN: I did not, sir, no; because I did not go on the bridge myself.

SENATOR SMITH: Who was on the bridge?

MR. PITMAN: The second officer, sir.

SENATOR SMITH: Mr. Lightoller?

MR. PITMAN: Mr. Lightoller.

SENATOR SMITH: Did you talk with Mr. Lightoller between 6 and 8 o'clock that night?

MR. PITMAN: I did not, sir.

SENATOR SMITH: Did you learn from him that the *Californian* had warned the *Titanic* that she was in the vicinity of icebergs?

MR. PITMAN: I did not, sir. We had no conversation whatever.

SENATOR SMITH: Did you hear anything about the wireless from the *Californian* on the direction of icebergs?

MR. PITMAN: I did not, sir.

SENATOR SMITH: No one mentioned that to you?

MR. PITMAN: No, sir.

SENATOR SMITH: Did you have any conversation with the captain on Sunday?

MR. PITMAN: None whatever, sir. I never had any.

SENATOR SMITH: You never spoke to him?

MR. PITMAN: I never spoke to him; no, sir.

SENATOR SMITH: Did he say anything to you?

MR. PITMAN: Not on Sunday, he did not.

SENATOR SMITH: But you had spoken to him before, on the voyage?

MR. PITMAN: Oh, yes, sir; in reference to work.

SENATOR SMITH: But on Sunday you did not?

MR. PITMAN: No, sir.

SENATOR SMITH: If I recollect what you have said, you saw the icebergs, or evidence of ice, when you were on the watch from 6 to 8 o'clock Sunday evening?

MR. PITMAN: I saw none whatever, sir, until I was in the boat, and that was about half past 3 Monday morning. That was the first ice I saw.

SENATOR SMITH: Did you look for it?

MR. PITMAN: We were keeping a special lookout for ice.

SENATOR SMITH: Who was?

MR. PITMAN: The officer of the watch from 10 o'clock on.

SENATOR SMITH: Who was the officer of the watch from 10 o'clock on?

MR. PITMAN: Mr. Murdoch [First Officer William Murdoch].

SENATOR SMITH: How do you know he was keeping a special lookout?

MR. PITMAN: Because he was warned.

SENATOR SMITH: Who warned him?

MR. PITMAN: Well, I know that Mr. Lightoller passed the word along to him.

SENATOR SMITH: How do you know that? I merely want to get at the fact. I am not pressing you for unnecessary detail.

MR. PITMAN: Because I had heard some one mention it.

SENATOR SMITH: Mention it before the collision or since?

MR. PITMAN: Oh, since.

SENATOR SMITH: Exactly. What did you do after you left the watch at 8 o'clock on Sunday evening?

MR. PITMAN: I went to bed, sir.

SENATOR SMITH: Immediately?

MR. PITMAN: Within a very few minutes.

SENATOR SMITH: What time did you dine that evening?

MR. PITMAN: At 6 o'clock.

SENATOR SMITH: Just before going on watch?

MR. PITMAN: Yes. Well, no; just after I went on the bridge and left the bridge, then I had my dinner.

SENATOR SMITH: You had your dinner where?

MR. PITMAN: On the boat deck.

SENATOR SMITH: Is there a dining room up there, or anything of that kind?

MR. PITMAN: Yes.

SENATOR SMITH: For the officers?

MR. PITMAN: Our own mess.

SENATOR SMITH: After 8 o'clock you retired?

MR. PITMAN: Exactly, sir. . . .

SENATOR SMITH: And when did you next appear outside of your berth?

MR. PITMAN: About 10 minutes to 12, or a quarter to 12, sir.

SENATOR SMITH: What occasion was there for rising at that time?

MR. PITMAN: Well, the collision woke me up.

SENATOR SMITH: Was there any special impact to awaken you?

MR. PITMAN: No; there was a sound that I thought seemed like the ship coming to an anchor—the chain running out over the windlass.

SENATOR SMITH: Did this impact jar the ship?

MR. PITMAN: No; it gave just a little vibration. I was about half awake and about half asleep. It did not quite awaken me.

SENATOR SMITH: Did you arouse yourself?

MR. PITMAN: I did, after a little thinking, wondering where we were anchoring.

SENATOR SMITH: You lay in bed a while after the impact?

MR. PITMAN: Oh, yes.

SENATOR SMITH: How long?

MR. PITMAN: Maybe three or four minutes.

SENATOR SMITH: Then did you get up and dress?

MR. PITMAN: No; I got up and walked on deck without dressing.

SENATOR SMITH: How far on deck?

MR. PITMAN: Just went outside of our quarters, had a look around, and could not see anyone.

SENATOR SMITH: Where were your quarters; on what deck?

MR. PITMAN: On the boat deck, close to the bridge.

SENATOR SMITH: Close to the bridge?

MR. PITMAN: Close to the bridge.

SENATOR SMITH: Forward?

MR. PITMAN: Forward, yes.

SENATOR SMITH: How far did you walk?

MR. PITMAN: Just outside the door, I should say 3 or 4 paces across the deck.

SENATOR SMITH: What did you do when you got out there; look around?

MR. PITMAN: Yes. I can describe to you what I did.

SENATOR SMITH: Do so, please.

MR. PITMAN: I had a look around, and I could not see anything, and could not hear any noise, so I went back to the room and sat down and lit my pipe. I thought that nothing had really happened, that perhaps it might have been a dream, or something like that. A few minutes afterwards I thought I had better start dressing, as it was near my watch, so I started dressing, and when I was partly dressed Mr. Boxhall [Fourth Officer Joseph Boxhall] came in and said the mail room—there was water in the mail room. I said, "What happened?" He said, "We struck an iceberg." So I put a coat on and went on deck, and saw the men uncovering the boats and clearing them away. I walked along to the after end of the boat deck, and met Mr. [James] Moody, the sixth officer. I asked him if he had seen the iceberg. He said no; but he said, "There is some ice on the forward well deck." So, to satisfy my curiosity, I went down there myself.

SENATOR SMITH: How far down?

MR. PITMAN: On the well deck. So I saw a little ice there. I went further, to the forecastle head, to see if there was any damage there. I could not see any at all. On my return, before emerging from under the forecastle head, I saw a crowd of firemen coming out with their bags, bags of clothing. I said, "What is the matter?" They said, "The water is coming in our place." I said, "That is funny." I looked down No. 1 hatch, then, and saw the water flowing over the hatch. I then immediately went to the boat deck, and assisted in getting boats uncovered and ready for swinging out. I stood by No. 5 boat. They would not allow the sailors to get anything, as they thought we should get it again in the morning. In the act of clearing away this boat a man said to me, that was dressed in a dressing gown, with slippers on, he said to me very quietly, "There is no time to waste." I thought he did not know anything about it at all. So we carried on our work in the usual way.

SENATOR SMITH: Do you know who that was?

MR. PITMAN: I did not then.

SENATOR SMITH: Do you now?

MR. PITMAN: I do now.

SENATOR SMITH: Who was it?

MR. PITMAN: Mr. Ismay. I did not know who it was then; I had never seen the man in my life before. So I continued on getting this boat uncovered and swinging out. It struck me at the time the easy way the boat went out, the great improvement the modern davits were on the old-fashioned davits. I had about five or six men there, and the boat was out in about two minutes.

SENATOR SMITH: You are referring now to No. 5 boat?

MR. PITMAN: No. 5 boat.

SENATOR SMITH: The boat at your station?

MR. PITMAN: At my station; yes. The boat went out in two or three minutes. I thought what a jolly fine idea they were, because with the old-fashioned davits it would require about a dozen men to lift her, a dozen men at each end. I got her overboard all right, and lowered level with the rail.

SENATOR SMITH: You lowered her level with the rail of the boat deck?

MR. PITMAN: Of the boat deck; yes. Then this man in the dressing gown said we had better get her loaded with women and children. So I said, "I await the commander's orders," to which he replied, "Very well," or something like that. It then dawned on me that it might be Mr. Ismay, judging by the description I had had given me. So I went along to the bridge and saw Capt. Smith, and I told him that I thought it was Mr. Ismay that wished me to get the boat away with women and children in it. So he said, "Go ahead; carry on." I came along and brought in my boat. I stood on it and said, "Come along, ladies." There was a big crowd. Mr. Ismay helped to get them along; assisted in every way. We got the boat nearly full, and I shouted out for any more ladies.

SENATOR SMITH: You shouted?

MR. PITMAN: I shouted. None were to be seen. So I allowed a few men to get into it. Then I jumped on the ship again. So Murdoch said, "You go in charge of this boat."

SENATOR SMITH: Murdoch said that to you?

MR. PITMAN: Yes; he said, "You go away in this boat, old man, and hang around the after gangway." I did not like the idea of going away at all, because I thought I was better off on the ship.

SENATOR SMITH: That is, these passengers thought so or you thought so?

MR. PITMAN: I thought so.

SENATOR SMITH: You thought they were better off on the ship?

MR. PITMAN: I thought I was.

SENATOR SMITH: That you were better off on the ship?

MR. PITMAN: Sure.

SENATOR SMITH: Were the passengers reluctant to get into this boat?

MR. PITMAN: Oh, no; I filled my boat fairly easily.

SENATOR SMITH: How many? Just go right ahead.

MR. PITMAN: About 40.

SENATOR SMITH: Were there about 40?

MR. PITMAN: Yes, sir.

SENATOR SMITH: How many men and how many women? Just tell it in your own way.

MR. PITMAN: I should say about half a dozen men there; there would not have been so many men there had there been any women around, but there were none. So Murdoch told me. He said, "You go ahead in this boat, and hang around the after gangway." He shook hands with me and said, "Good-by; good luck;" and I said, "Lower away."

SENATOR SMITH: Murdoch did?

MR. PITMAN: Murdoch shook hands good-by, and said, "Good luck to you."

SENATOR SMITH: Did you ever see him after that?

MR. PITMAN: Never. We then cast the boat off and pulled away some safe distance from the ship. It was not for an hour that I realized she would go—an hour after we got into the water. I quite thought we would have to return to the ship again, perhaps at daylight. My idea was that if any wind sprang up we should drift away from the ship and have a job to get back again.

SENATOR SMITH: This boat was the first lifeboat lowered?

MR. PITMAN: Oh, no, it was the second one; the second one on the starboard side.

SENATOR SMITH: And had you seen the first one lowered?

MR. PITMAN: Yes; it was the next boat to me.

SENATOR SMITH: You saw that lowered?

MR. PITMAN: I saw that lowered, yes.

SENATOR SMITH: Was it filled from the boat deck?

MR. PITMAN: Every boat, as far as I know, was filled from the boat deck.

SENATOR SMITH: Is that customary?

MR. PITMAN: Well, to put a certain amount in, yes.

SENATOR SMITH: Does not that give the passengers on the boat deck a decided advantage in the escape from danger?

MR. PITMAN: I had some saloon passengers, of the second class.

SENATOR SMITH: What is that?

MR. PITMAN: I do not think it does.

SENATOR SMITH: I simply wanted your judgment. Who were the men in No. 5 lifeboat, beside yourself?

MR. PITMAN: What do you mean; of the crew?

SENATOR SMITH: Yes; men, whoever they were; crew or passengers.

MR. PITMAN: Five of the crew, and there may have been five or six passengers—male passengers.

SENATOR SMITH: And the balance were——

MR. PITMAN: Women and children. . . .

SENATOR SMITH: Did you have any direction over the number of people who were put into that lifeboat?

MR. PITMAN: Well, not at the end, I did not, because Mr. Murdoch was there and he was the senior officer. It was for him to decide.

SENATOR SMITH: Mr. Lightoller, who had charge of the loading of the boats on the port side, has said that he put only two of the crew into the lifeboats he loaded. How did it happen that you had so many of the crew?

MR. PITMAN: I thought I had only four at the time.

SENATOR SMITH: You thought you had four?

MR. PITMAN: Four.

SENATOR SMITH: But you discovered you had more than that?

MR. PITMAN: I did not discover I had five until some time on the *Carpathia,* during the trip on the *Carpathia.*

SENATOR SMITH: Were there five with yourself?

MR. PITMAN: No; six.

SENATOR SMITH: Six with yourself. Then, as a matter of fact, there were six of the crew, officers and crew, in No. 5 boat?

MR. PITMAN: In No. 5 boat, yes.

SENATOR SMITH: Can you give us the names of the six?

MR. PITMAN: I can not just now, sir. I can get them for you.

SENATOR SMITH: Did they all survive until they reached the *Carpathia?*

MR. PITMAN: Oh, yes, sir. . . .

SENATOR SMITH: Besides those you had about 30 passengers?

MR. PITMAN: I had about 40 passengers.

SENATOR SMITH: Besides the crew?

MR. PITMAN: Yes.

SENATOR SMITH: This was a large lifeboat, was it?

MR. PITMAN: Yes, sir.

SENATOR SMITH: Was that lifeboat equipped with food?

MR. PITMAN: Yes; it had biscuits and water in it.

SENATOR SMITH: Did you have occasion to use either?

MR. PITMAN: No.

SENATOR SMITH: How do you know they were in; did you see them?

MR. PITMAN: They were put there in Southampton; and we also went through all the boats on the *Carpathia*.

SENATOR SMITH: Did you find that to be the case?

MR. PITMAN: That they were full. The boats had bread and water.

SENATOR SMITH: Did you have any lights on No. 5 lifeboat?

MR. PITMAN: I did not have a light in my boat; no.

SENATOR SMITH: Do you know of any boats that did have lights on them?

MR. PITMAN: Yes; there were several of them that had.

SENATOR SMITH: But they did not all have lights?

MR. PITMAN: No.

SENATOR SMITH: Do the regulations of the British Board of Trade prescribe lights?

MR. PITMAN: Yes, sir.

SENATOR SMITH: You say you got into this boat and it was lowered and you were told to go?

MR. PITMAN: To stand by the after gangway.

SENATOR SMITH: Did you do it?

MR. PITMAN: I did it as near as possible. I kept within a safe distance of the ship, if anything did happen.

SENATOR SMITH: You kept far enough away so that if anything happened you would not be involved in it? Is that the idea?

MR. PITMAN: Exactly.

SENATOR SMITH: What did you expect to happen?

MR. PITMAN: I thought she still had about three of the compartments and still would remain afloat.

SENATOR SMITH: And if she did not float and went down, were you expecting a suction that would draw the lifeboats down?

MR. PITMAN: Well, yes; I thought we might get into a bit of a wash.

SENATOR SMITH: And that you were seeking to avoid?

MR. PITMAN: Seeking to avoid; yes.

SENATOR SMITH: Did any persons, men, women, or children, attempt to get into your lifeboat in the water?

MR. PITMAN: No.

SENATOR SMITH: Did any attempt to get out of it?

MR. PITMAN: None whatever, sir; and I had no trouble whatever with my boat. The women all behaved admirably.

SENATOR SMITH: Did any of the women pull on the oars, or handle the tiller?

MR. PITMAN: No, sir; although they wanted to.

SENATOR SMITH: Row?

MR. PITMAN: Yes; to keep themselves warm.

SENATOR SMITH: It was very cold that morning?

MR. PITMAN: It was chilly; yes.

SENATOR SMITH: Zero weather?

MR. PITMAN: Oh, no.

SENATOR SMITH: How cold was it?

MR. PITMAN: It may have been 40—35 to 40.

SENATOR SMITH: Did you ever return to the side of the *Titanic?*

MR. PITMAN: No; we did not.

SENATOR SMITH: Did you see the *Titanic* go down?

MR. PITMAN: Yes, sir.

SENATOR SMITH: Describe, if you can, how she sank?

MR. PITMAN: Judging by what I could see from a distance, she gradually disappeared until the forecastle head was submerged to the bridge. Then she turned right on end and went down perpendicularly.

SENATOR SMITH: At about what angle?

MR. PITMAN: She went straight.

SENATOR SMITH: Right straight down?

MR. PITMAN: Absolutely. That was the last I saw of her.

SENATOR SMITH: Did she seem to be broken in two?

MR. PITMAN: Oh, no.

SENATOR SMITH: Or was she entirely intact? Did you hear any explosions?

MR. PITMAN: Yes; four reports.

SENATOR SMITH: What kind of reports?

MR. PITMAN: They sounded like the reports of a big gun in the distance.

SENATOR SMITH: What did you assume they were?

MR. PITMAN: I assumed it was bulkheads going, myself.

SENATOR SMITH: Did you hear anything like boiler explosions?

MR. PITMAN: Yes; I heard a lot of people say that; but I have my doubts about that. I do not see why the boilers should burst, because there was no steam there. They should have been stopped about two hours and a half. The fires had not been fed, so there was very little steam there.

SENATOR SMITH: Are we to understand that you do not believe that boilers exploded?

MR. PITMAN: I do not believe it.

SENATOR SMITH: And from the distance you were from the ship, you would have known it if that had occurred?

MR. PITMAN: I think so.

SENATOR SMITH: As the ship went down, what did you observe on the afterdeck or decks?

MR. PITMAN: I could not see that, sir.

SENATOR SMITH: You could not see the people?

MR. PITMAN: Oh, no.

SENATOR SMITH: From what you saw of the people aboard this ship when you went down and after you got to the water, and when you went around close to the stern of the ship, were they fitted with life belts?

MR. PITMAN: Everyone I saw before I left the ship had a life belt on.

SENATOR SMITH: Did you see anyone without a life belt?

MR. PITMAN: There may have been a stray one of the crew without one.

SENATOR SMITH: But that was a rare thing?

MR. PITMAN: Yes. I did not have one myself; I did not want it.

SENATOR SMITH: How long before going down were there explosions or noises?

MR. PITMAN: Not until she was submerged.

SENATOR SMITH: Not until she was entirely submerged?

MR. PITMAN: Yes.

SENATOR SMITH: The after part of the ship as well as the forward part?

MR. PITMAN: Yes; the whole of her.

SENATOR SMITH: She had gone under water before these explosions were heard?

MR. PITMAN: Yes, sir.

SENATOR SMITH: And you are quite sure that the explosions you heard came from the ship?

MR. PITMAN: Oh, yes; perfectly sure.

SENATOR SMITH: When did you last see the captain?

MR. PITMAN: When I went to the bridge and asked him if I should fill No. 5 boat with women and get her away.

SENATOR SMITH: And what did he tell you?

MR. PITMAN: "Carry on," or words to that effect.

SENATOR SMITH: Did you ever see him again?

MR. PITMAN: No, sir.

SENATOR SMITH: Was he visible when the boat went down?

MR. PITMAN: I was not there to the last, sir.

SENATOR SMITH: You were unable to see from your point of view?

MR. PITMAN: Yes, sir.

SENATOR SMITH: When you shook hands with Murdoch and bade him good bye, did you ever expect to see him again?

MR. PITMAN: Certainly; I did.

SENATOR SMITH: Do you think, from his manner, he ever expected to see you again?

MR. PITMAN: Apparently not. I expected to get back to the ship again, perhaps two or three hours afterwards.

SENATOR SMITH: But he, from his manner, did not expect that?

MR. PITMAN: Apparently not.

SENATOR SMITH: Did you take leave of any other officers in a similar way?

MR. PITMAN: No. I did not, sir.

SENATOR SMITH: When you were passing from the side of the *Titanic* to the *Carpathia,* did you see any people in the water—men, women, or children?

MR. PITMAN: None, sir.

SENATOR SMITH: When you went around the after part of the ship?

MR. PITMAN: After? I did not go around the stern.

SENATOR SMITH: You did not go back there?

MR. PITMAN: No.

SENATOR SMITH: What did Murdoch tell you to go back there for? Do you know?

MR. PITMAN: Just to be handy, I suppose.

SENATOR SMITH: To be handy to pick up?

MR. PITMAN: To pick up again; to pick the boat up again.

SENATOR SMITH: And you saw no people in the water?

MR. PITMAN: None, sir.

SENATOR SMITH: Did you hear any cries of distress?

MR. PITMAN: Oh, yes.

SENATOR SMITH: What were they, cries for help?

MR. PITMAN: Crying, shouting, moaning.

SENATOR SMITH: From the ship, or from the water?

MR. PITMAN: From the water, after the ship disappeared; no noises before.

SENATOR SMITH: There were no noises from the ship's crew, or officers, or passengers, just preceding the sinking?

MR. PITMAN: None.

SENATOR SMITH: Immediately following the sinking of the ship you heard these cries of distress?

MR. PITMAN: Yes.

SENATOR SMITH: But, as I understand you, you were not in close proximity to those who were uttering the cries?

MR. PITMAN: I may have been three or four hundred yards away; four or five hundred yards away.

SENATOR SMITH: Did you attempt to get near them?

MR. PITMAN: As soon as she disappeared I said, "Now, men, we will pull toward the wreck." Everyone in my boat said it was a mad idea, because we had far better save what few we had in my boat than go back to the scene of the wreck and be swamped by the crowds that were there.

SENATOR SMITH: As a matter of fact, do you not know your boat would have accommodated 20 or 25 more people?

MR. PITMAN: My boat would have accommodated a few more, yes; certainly.

SENATOR SMITH: According to the testimony of your fellow officers——

MR. PITMAN: My boat would have held more.

SENATOR SMITH: (continuing). Your boat would have held about 60 or 65 people.

MR. PITMAN: About 60.

SENATOR SMITH: Tell us about your fellow passengers on that lifeboat. You say they discouraged you from returning or going in the direction of these cries?

MR. PITMAN: They did. I told my men to get their oars out, and pull toward the wreck—the scene of the wreck.

SENATOR SMITH: Yes.

MR. PITMAN: I said, "We may be able to pick up a few more."

SENATOR SMITH: Who demurred to that?

MR. PITMAN: The whole crowd in my boat. A great number of them did.

SENATOR SMITH: Women?

MR. PITMAN: I could not discriminate whether women or men. They said it was rather a mad idea.

SENATOR SMITH: I ask you if any woman in your boat appealed to you to return to the direction from which the cries came?

MR. PITMAN: No one.

SENATOR SMITH: You say that no woman passenger in your boat urged you to return?

MR. PITMAN: None.

MR. BURLINGHAM [Charles Burlingham, attorney for White Star]: It would have capsized the boat. Senator.

SENATOR SMITH: Pardon me, I am not drawing any unfair conclusion from this. One of the officers told us that a woman in his boat urged him to return to the side of the ship. I want to be very sure that this officer heard no woman asking the same thing. [To the witness.] Who demurred, now, that you can specifically recall?

MR. PITMAN: I could not name any one in particular.

SENATOR SMITH: The men with the oars?

MR. PITMAN: No. They did not; no. They started to obey my orders.

SENATOR SMITH: You were in command. They ought to have obeyed your orders?

MR. PITMAN: So they did.

SENATOR SMITH: They did not, if you told them to pull toward the ship.

MR. PITMAN: They commenced pulling toward the ship, and the passengers in my boat said it was a mad idea on my part to pull back to the ship, because if I did, we should be swamped with the crowd that was in the water, and it would add another 40 to the list of drowned, and I decided I would not pull back.

SENATOR SMITH: Officer, you really turned this No. 5 boat around to go in the direction from which these cries came?

MR. PITMAN: I did.

SENATOR SMITH: And were dissuaded from your purpose by your crew——

MR. PITMAN: No, not crew; passengers. . . .

SENATOR SMITH: One moment; by your crew and by the passengers in your boat?

MR. PITMAN: Certainly.

SENATOR SMITH: Then did you turn the boat toward the sea again?

MR. PITMAN: No; just simply took our oars in and lay quiet.

SENATOR SMITH: You mean you drifted?

MR. PITMAN: We may have gone a little bit.

SENATOR SMITH: Drifted on your oars?

MR. PITMAN: We may have drifted along. We just simply lay there doing nothing.

SENATOR SMITH: How many of these cries were there? Was it a chorus, or was it——

MR. PITMAN: I would rather you did not speak about that.

SENATOR SMITH: I would like to know how you were impressed by it.

MR. PITMAN: Well, I can not very well describe it. I would rather you would not speak of it.

SENATOR SMITH: I realize that it is not a pleasant theme, and yet I would like to know whether these cries were general and in chorus, or desultory and occasional?

MR. PITMAN: There was a continual moan for about an hour.

SENATOR SMITH: And you lay in the vicinity of that scene for about an hour?

MR. PITMAN: Oh, yes; we were in the vicinity of the wreck the whole time.

SENATOR SMITH: And drifted or lay on your oars during that time?

MR. PITMAN: We drifted toward daylight, as a little breeze sprang up.

SENATOR SMITH: Did this anguish or those cries of distress die away?

MR. PITMAN: Yes; they died away gradually.

SENATOR SMITH: Did they continue during most of the hour?

MR. PITMAN: Oh, yes; I think so. It may have been a shorter time. Of course I did not watch every five minutes——

SENATOR SMITH: I understand that, and I am not trying to ask about a question of five minutes. Is that all you care to say?

MR. PITMAN: I would rather that you would have left that out altogether.

SENATOR SMITH: I know you would; but I must know what efforts you made to save the lives of passengers and crew under your charge. If that is all the effort you made, say so——

MR. PITMAN: That is all, sir.

SENATOR SMITH (continuing): And I will stop that branch of my examination.

MR. PITMAN: That is all, sir; that is all the effort I made. . . .

SENATOR SMITH: Did you see the light of the *Carpathia,* or know she was approaching?

MR. PITMAN: We saw her lights about half past 3, as near as I can recollect.

SENATOR SMITH: Did you row toward the light?

MR. PITMAN: Well, we waited until we were certain it was a steamer, and then we pulled toward her.

SENATOR SMITH: How far away did you see her, do you think?

MR. PITMAN: We could see the masthead light over 5 miles on a clear night.

SENATOR SMITH: When the *Carpathia* was about 5 miles away did you row toward her?

MR. PITMAN: No; I waited to make certain it was a steamer, until I could see both masthead lights.

SENATOR SMITH: You knew it was an object?

MR. PITMAN: Yes; but I did not know what it was. It might have been a star.

SENATOR SMITH: Could it have been a star—could you have taken it for a star?

MR. PITMAN: Oh, quite possibly.

SENATOR SMITH: But when you satisfied yourself from the number of lights that it was a relief boat——

MR. PITMAN: We pulled toward it.

SENATOR SMITH: You pulled toward it. At that time were there any people in the water?

MR. PITMAN: There were no noises; no sounds then.

SENATOR SMITH: All moaning and cries of distress had ceased?

MR. PITMAN: Yes; that must have been about 4 o'clock.

SENATOR SMITH: Daybreak?

MR. PITMAN: It was just breaking day; yes.

SENATOR SMITH: As you pulled your boat toward the *Carpathia* I understood you to say you saw icebergs?

MR. PITMAN: Yes, sir.

SENATOR SMITH: Several of them. Did you see any bodies in the water?

MR. PITMAN: None whatever, sir.

SENATOR SMITH: After that time?

MR. PITMAN: None whatever, at any time. . . .

Witness: Frederick Fleet, 24
Able seaman and *Titanic* lookout, from
Southampton, England

Key testimony: In a Cockney accent he described raising the alarm about the iceberg, though it was too late. To murmurs of astonishment, he admitted he had no idea of distances. And he revealed that for the trans-Atlantic crossing, lookouts in the Titanic's crow's nest hadn't been given binoculars, which he said could have allowed them to see the iceberg in time.

. . . SENATOR SMITH: I want to get on the record the place where you were stationed in the performance of your duty.

MR. FLEET: I was on the lookout.

SENATOR SMITH: On the lookout?

MR. FLEET: At the time of the collision.

SENATOR SMITH: In the crow's nest?

MR. FLEET: Yes.

SENATOR SMITH: At the time of the collison?

MR. FLEET: Yes, sir.

SENATOR SMITH: Can you tell how high above the boat deck that is?

MR. FLEET: I have no idea.

SENATOR SMITH: Can you tell how high above the crow's nest the masthead is?

MR. FLEET: No, sir.

SENATOR SMITH: Do you know how far you were above the bridge?

MR. FLEET: I am no hand at guessing.

SENATOR SMITH: I do not want you to guess; but, if you know, I would like to have you tell.

MR. FLEET: I have no idea.

SENATOR FLETCHER [Duncan Fetcher, Democrat of Florida]: You hardly mean that; you have some idea?

MR. FLEET: No; I do not.

SENATOR FLETCHER: You know whether it was a thousand feet or two hundred?

SENATOR SMITH: Was there any other officer or employee stationed at a higher point on the *Titanic* than you were?

MR. FLEET: No, sir.

SENATOR SMITH: You were the lookout?

MR. FLEET: Yes, sir.

SENATOR SMITH: Where are the eyes of the ship?

MR. FLEET: The eyes of the ship?

SENATOR SMITH: The ship's eyes?

MR. FLEET: Forward.

SENATOR SMITH: At the extreme bow?

MR. FLEET: Yes, sir.

SENATOR SMITH: And on the same level as the boat deck or below it?

MR. FLEET: Below it.

SENATOR SMITH: How far below it?

MR. FLEET: I do not know, sir.

SENATOR SMITH: Mr. Fleet, can you tell who was on the forward part of the *Titanic* Sunday night when you took your position in the crow's nest?

MR. FLEET: There was nobody.

SENATOR SMITH: Nobody?

MR. FLEET: No, sir.

SENATOR SMITH: Who was on the bridge?

MR. FLEET: When I went up to relieve the others?

SENATOR SMITH: Yes.

MR. FLEET: Mr. Murdoch.

SENATOR SMITH: Officer Murdoch?

MR. FLEET: First officer.

SENATOR SMITH: Who else?

MR. FLEET: I think it was the third officer.

SENATOR SMITH: What was his name?

MR. FLEET: The man that was here, Pitman.

SENATOR SMITH: Mr. Pitman, the man who just left the stand?

MR. FLEET: I do not know the officers on the bridge.

SENATOR SMITH: You do not recall any more of them?

MR. FLEET: No; I do not know whether he was there or not.

SENATOR SMITH: I do not want any confusion if I can help it. I want to get this down right. Was the captain on the bridge?

MR. FLEET: I do not know, sir.

SENATOR SMITH: You did not see him?

MR. FLEET: No, sir.

SENATOR SMITH: What time did you take your watch Sunday night?

MR. FLEET: Ten o'clock.

SENATOR NEWLANDS: Whom did you relieve?

MR. FLEET: [George] Symons and [Archie] Jewell.

SENATOR SMITH: Who was with you on the watch?

MR. FLEET: [Reginald] Lee.

SENATOR SMITH: What, if anything, did Symons and Jewell, or either one, say to you when you relieved them of the watch?

MR. FLEET: They told us to keep a sharp lookout for small ice.

SENATOR SMITH: What did you say to them?

MR. FLEET: I said "All right."

SENATOR SMITH: What did Lee say?

MR. FLEET: He said the same.

SENATOR SMITH: And you took your position in the crow's nest?

MR. FLEET: Yes, sir.

SENATOR SMITH: Did you keep a sharp lookout for ice?

MR. FLEET: Yes, sir.

SENATOR SMITH: Tell what you did?

MR. FLEET: Well, I reported an iceberg right ahead, a black mass.

SENATOR SMITH: When did you report that?

MR. FLEET: I could not tell you the time.

SENATOR SMITH: About what time?

MR. FLEET: Just after seven bells.

SENATOR SMITH: How long after you had taken your place in the crow's nest?

MR. FLEET: The watch was nearly over. I had done the best part of the watch up in the nest.

SENATOR SMITH: How long a watch did you have?

MR. FLEET: Two hours; but the time was going to be put back—that watch.

177

SENATOR SMITH: The time was to be set back?

MR. FLEET: Yes, sir.

SENATOR SMITH: Did that alter your time?

MR. FLEET: We were to get about 2 hours and 20 minutes.

SENATOR SMITH: How long before the collision or accident did you report ice ahead?

MR. FLEET: I have no idea.

SENATOR SMITH: About how long?

MR. FLEET: I could not say, at the rate she was going.

SENATOR SMITH: How fast was she going?

MR. FLEET: I have no idea.

SENATOR SMITH: Would you be willing to say that you reported the presence of this iceberg an hour before the collision?

MR. FLEET: No, sir.

SENATOR SMITH: Forty-five minutes?

MR. FLEET: No, sir.

SENATOR SMITH: A half hour before?

MR. FLEET: No, sir.

SENATOR SMITH: Fifteen minutes before?

MR. FLEET: No, sir.

SENATOR SMITH: Ten minutes before?

MR. FLEET: No, sir.

SENATOR SMITH: How far away was this black mass when you first saw it?

MR. FLEET: I have no idea, sir.

SENATOR SMITH: Can you not give us some idea? Did it impress you as serious?

MR. FLEET: I reported it as soon as ever I seen it.

SENATOR SMITH: I want a complete record of it, you know. Give me, as nearly as you can, how far away it was when you saw it. You are accustomed to judging distances, are you not, from the crow's nest? You are there to look ahead and sight objects, are you not?

MR. FLEET: We are only up there to report anything we see.

SENATOR SMITH: But you are expected to see and report anything in the path of the ship, are you not?

MR. FLEET: Anything we see—a ship, or anything.

SENATOR SMITH: Anything you see?

MR. FLEET: Yes; anything we see.

SENATOR SMITH: Whether it be a field of ice, a "growler," or an iceberg, or any other substance?

MR. FLEET: Yes, sir.

SENATOR SMITH: Have you trained yourself so that you can see objects as you approach them with fair accuracy?

MR. FLEET: I do not know what you mean, sir.

SENATOR SMITH: If there had been a black object ahead of this ship, or a white one, a mile away, or 5 miles away, 50 feet above the water or 150 feet above the water, would you have been able to see it, from your experience as a seaman?

MR. FLEET: Yes, sir.

SENATOR SMITH: When you see these things in the path of the ship, you report them?

MR. FLEET: Yes, sir.

SENATOR SMITH: What did you report when you saw this black mass Sunday night?

MR. FLEET: I reported an iceberg right ahead.

SENATOR SMITH: To whom did you report that?

MR. FLEET: I struck three bells first. Then I went straight to the telephone and rang them up on the bridge.

SENATOR SMITH: You struck three bells and went to the telephone and rang them up on the bridge?

MR. FLEET: Yes.

SENATOR SMITH: Did you get anyone on the bridge?

MR. FLEET: I got an answer straight away—what did I see, or "What did you see?"

SENATOR SMITH: Did the person who was talking to you tell you who he was?

MR. FLEET: No. He just asked me what did I see. I told him an iceberg right ahead.

SENATOR SMITH: What did he say then?

MR. FLEET: He said: "Thank you."

SENATOR SMITH: Do you know to whom you were talking?

MR. FLEET: No; I do not know who it was.

SENATOR SMITH: What was the object in sending the three bells?

MR. FLEET: That denotes an iceberg right ahead.

SENATOR SMITH: It denotes danger?

MR. FLEET: No; it just tells them on the bridge that there is something about.

SENATOR SMITH: You took both precautions; you gave the three bells, and then you went and telephoned to the bridge?

MR. FLEET: Yes, sir.

SENATOR SMITH: Where did you have to go to telephone?

MR. FLEET: The telephone is in the nest.

SENATOR SMITH: The telephone is right in the crow's nest?

MR. FLEET: Yes.

SENATOR SMITH: You turned and communicated with the bridge from the nest?

MR. FLEET: Yes, sir.

SENATOR SMITH: Did you get a prompt response?

MR. FLEET: I did.

SENATOR SMITH: And you made the statement that you have indicated?

MR. FLEET: Yes.

SENATOR SMITH: Then what did you do?

MR. FLEET: After I rang them up?

SENATOR SMITH: Yes, sir.

MR. FLEET: I kept staring ahead again.

SENATOR SMITH: You remained in the crow's nest?

MR. FLEET: I remained in the crow's nest until I got relief.

SENATOR SMITH: And Lee remained in the nest?

MR. FLEET: Yes.

SENATOR SMITH: How long did you stay there?

MR. FLEET: About a quarter of an hour to 20 minutes after.

SENATOR SMITH: After what?

MR. FLEET: After the accident.

SENATOR SMITH: And then did you leave this place?

MR. FLEET: We got relieved by the other two men.

SENATOR SMITH: The other two men came?

MR. FLEET: Yes.

SENATOR SMITH: Did they go up?

MR. FLEET: They came up in the nest.

SENATOR SMITH: And you got down?

MR. FLEET: We got down; yes.

SENATOR SMITH: Can you not indicate, in any way, the length of time that elapsed between the time that you first gave this information by telephone and by bell to the bridge officer and the time the boat struck the iceberg?

MR. FLEET: I could not tell you, sir.

SENATOR SMITH: You can not say?

MR. FLEET: No, sir.

SENATOR SMITH: You can not say whether it was five minutes or an hour?

MR. FLEET: I could not say, sir.

SENATOR SMITH: I wish you would tell the committee whether you apprehended danger when you sounded these signals and telephoned; whether you thought there was danger?

MR. FLEET: No; no, sir. That is all we have to do up in the nest; to ring the bell, and if there is any danger ring them up on the telephone.

SENATOR SMITH: The fact that you did ring them up on the telephone indicated that you thought there was danger?

MR. FLEET: Yes, sir.

SENATOR SMITH: You thought there was danger?

MR. FLEET: Well, it was so close to us. That is why I rang them up.

SENATOR SMITH: How large an object was this when you first saw it?

MR. FLEET: It was not very large when I first saw it.

SENATOR SMITH: How large was it?

MR. FLEET: I have no idea of distances or spaces.

SENATOR SMITH: Was it the size of an ordinary house? Was it as large as this room appears to be?

MR. FLEET: No; no. It did not appear very large at all.

SENATOR SMITH: Was it as large as the table at which I am sitting?

MR. FLEET: It would be as large as those two tables put together, when I saw it at first.

SENATOR SMITH: When you first saw it, it appeared about as large as these two tables put together?

MR. FLEET: Yes, sir.

SENATOR SMITH: Did it appear to get larger after you first saw it?

MR. FLEET: Yes; it kept getting larger as we were getting nearer it.

SENATOR SMITH: As it was coming toward you and you were going toward it?

MR. FLEET: Yes.

SENATOR SMITH: How large did it get to be, finally when it struck the ship?

MR. FLEET: When we were alongside, it was a little bit higher than the forecastle head.

SENATOR SMITH: The forecastle head is how high above the water line?

MR. FLEET: Fifty feet, I should say.

SENATOR SMITH: About 50 feet?

MR. FLEET: Yes.

SENATOR SMITH: So that this black mass, when it finally struck the boat, turned out to be about 50 feet above the water?

MR. FLEET: About 50 or 60.

SENATOR SMITH: Fifty or sixty feet above the water?

MR. FLEET: Yes.

SENATOR SMITH: And when you first saw it it looked no larger than these two tables?

MR. FLEET: No, sir.

SENATOR SMITH: Do you know whether the ship was stopped after you gave that telephone signal?

MR. FLEET: No, no; she did not stop at all. She did not stop until she passed the iceberg.

SENATOR SMITH: She did not stop until she passed the iceberg?

MR. FLEET: No, sir.

SENATOR SMITH: Do you know whether her engines were reversed?

MR. FLEET: Well, she started to go to port while I was at the telephone.

SENATOR SMITH: She started to go to port?

MR. FLEET: Yes; the wheel was put to starboard.

SENATOR SMITH: How do you know that?

MR. FLEET: My mate saw it and told me. He told me he could see the bow coming around.

SENATOR SMITH: They swung the ship's bow away from the object?

MR. FLEET: Yes; because we were making straight for it.

SENATOR SMITH: But you saw the course altered? And the iceberg struck the ship at what point?

MR. FLEET: On the starboard bow, just before the foremast.

SENATOR SMITH: How far would that be from the bow's end?

MR. FLEET: From the stem?

SENATOR SMITH: From the stem.

MR. FLEET: About 20 feet.

SENATOR SMITH: About 20 feet back from the stem?

MR. FLEET: From the stem to where she hit.

SENATOR SMITH: When she struck this obstacle, or this black mass, was there much of a jar to the ship?

MR. FLEET: No, sir.

SENATOR SMITH: Was there any?

MR. FLEET: Just a slight grinding noise.

SENATOR SMITH: Not sufficient to disturb you in your position in the crow's nest?

MR. FLEET: No, sir.

SENATOR SMITH: Did it alarm you seriously when it struck?

MR. FLEET: No, sir; I thought it was a narrow shave.

SENATOR SMITH: You thought it was a narrow shave?

MR. FLEET: Yes, sir.

SENATOR SMITH: Did any of this ice break onto the decks?

MR. FLEET: Yes; some on the forecastle light and some on the weather deck.

SENATOR SMITH: How much?

MR. FLEET: Not much; only where she rubbed up against it.

SENATOR SMITH: Did Lee and you talk over this black object that you saw?

MR. FLEET: Only up in the nest.

SENATOR SMITH: What did you say about it? What did he say about it to you or what did you say about it to him?

MR. FLEET: Before I reported, I said, "There is ice ahead," and then I put my hand over to the bell and rang it three times, and then I went to the phone.

SENATOR SMITH: What did he say?

MR. FLEET: He said nothing much. He just started looking. He was looking ahead while I was at the phone and he seen the ship go to port.

SENATOR SMITH: Did Lee survive this wreck, or was he drowned?

MR. FLEET: He is one that survived it.

SENATOR SMITH: You can not recollect just what he said to you when she struck?

MR. FLEET: No, sir.

SENATOR SMITH: Nor when you first sighted this black mass?

MR. FLEET: No, sir.

SENATOR SMITH: Who sighted the black mass first; you or Lee?

MR. FLEET: I did. I say I did, but I think he was just as soon as me.

SENATOR SMITH: Were you both looking ahead?

MR. FLEET: We were looking all over the place, all around.

SENATOR SMITH: All over the sea?

MR. FLEET: Yes, sir.

SENATOR SMITH: Had you been especially directed to look carefully?

MR. FLEET: Yes, sir.

SENATOR SMITH: By whom?

MR. FLEET: By the mates we relieved; by the other two lookout men.

SENATOR SMITH: Were you told to do so by Officer Murdoch?

MR. FLEET: No, sir. We got our order from Mr. Lightoller, and passed it on to the lookouts as they get relieved.

SENATOR SMITH: Mr. Lightoller gave the order to your mates?

MR. FLEET: And they passed it on to us.

SENATOR SMITH: Is that usual?

MR. FLEET: Yes, sir; as we get relieved we pass it on to the other men.

SENATOR SMITH: If any orders come in the meantime to you, you pass them on?

MR. FLEET: To the next two lookout men.

SENATOR SMITH: Do you know what time it was when you saw that iceberg?

MR. FLEET: I have no idea, sir.

SENATOR SMITH: Did you carry a watch?

MR. FLEET: No, sir.

SENATOR SMITH: You made no record of it in any way?

MR. FLEET: No, sir.

SENATOR SMITH: You went to the lookout at 10 o'clock?

MR. FLEET: Yes, sir.

SENATOR SMITH: Whom did you relieve?

MR. FLEET: Symons and Jewell.

SENATOR SMITH: Did they tell you they had seen icebergs?

MR. FLEET: No, sir; they only gave us the orders to look out for them.

SENATOR SMITH: But they did not say they had seen any?

MR. FLEET: No, sir.

SENATOR SMITH: Were you four men the only men that occupied this position in the boat?

MR. FLEET: There were six.

SENATOR SMITH: Who were the other two?

MR. FLEET: [lookout George] Hogg and Evans.

SENATOR SMITH: Did they survive the wreck?

MR. FLEET: Yes, sir.

SENATOR SMITH: All of the lookouts survived?

MR. FLEET: Yes, sir.

SENATOR SMITH: Where do these last two men live? Do you know?

MR. FLEET: No, sir; there is one here.

SENATOR SMITH: Which one?

MR. FLEET: Hogg and Symons are here besides me. The other three have gone home.

SENATOR SMITH: Lee?

MR. FLEET: I do not know where Lee is. He got detained in New York.

SENATOR SMITH: What is the watch? It is two hours on and——

MR. FLEET: And four hours off.

SENATOR SMITH: Who was on watch from 8 to 10 that night in the crow's nest or lookout?

MR. FLEET: Symons and Jewell.

SENATOR SMITH: Who was on watch from 6 to 8?

MR. FLEET: Hogg and Evans.

SENATOR SMITH: Did either of these mates of yours say anything about having seen icebergs Sunday or Sunday evening?

MR. FLEET: No, sir.

SENATOR SMITH: Your last watch before 10 o'clock was from 4 to 6, was it not?

MR. FLEET: From four to six; yes, sir.

SENATOR SMITH: And from four to six did you see any icebergs?

MR. FLEET: No, sir.

SENATOR SMITH: Up there in the crow's nest, are there any indications of the presence of ice off the Grand Banks of Newfoundland?

MR. FLEET: No, sir.

SENATOR SMITH: Does the weather change on the Newfoundland Banks?

MR. FLEET: No, sir. It is all open in the nest, sir.

SENATOR SMITH: Was that a cold night—Sunday?

MR. FLEET: Yes, sir.

SENATOR SMITH: What protection against the weather have you in the crow's nest?

MR. FLEET: We have nothing ahead, and there are just two bits of screen behind us.

SENATOR SMITH: Canvas?

MR. FLEET: Yes, sir.

SENATOR SMITH: And nothing ahead?

MR. FLEET: Nothing in front.

SENATOR SMITH: So your view is unobstructed?

MR. FLEET: Yes, sir.

SENATOR SMITH: Are you given glasses of any kind?

MR. FLEET: We had none this time. We had nothing at all, only our own eyes, to look out.

SENATOR SMITH: On the *Oceanic* you had glasses, had you not?

MR. FLEET: Yes, sir.

SENATOR SMITH: Each of you?

MR. FLEET: There is one pair in the nest.

SENATOR SMITH: One pair of glasses?

MR. FLEET: Yes, sir.

SENATOR SMITH: What kind of glasses are they; strong, powerful glasses?

MR. FLEET: No, not always, sir.

SENATOR SMITH: What were those on the *Oceanic?*

MR. FLEET: Very poor; you could see about from here to that looking-glass [indicating].

SENATOR SMITH: Did you make any request for glasses on the *Titanic?*

MR. FLEET: We asked them in Southampton, and they said there was none for us.

SENATOR SMITH: Whom did you ask?

MR. FLEET: They said there was none intended for us.

SENATOR SMITH: Whom did you ask?

MR. FLEET: We asked Mr. Lightoller, the second officer.

SENATOR SMITH: Did you make the request yourself?

MR. FLEET: No; the station lookout men did, Hogg and Evans.

SENATOR SMITH: How do you know they made it?

MR. FLEET: Because they told us.

SENATOR SMITH: Where did they tell you; after leaving Southampton?

MR. FLEET: In Southampton, and afterwards.

SENATOR SMITH: You expected glasses?

MR. FLEET: We had a pair from Belfast to Southampton.

SENATOR SMITH: You had a pair of glasses from Belfast to Southampton?

MR. FLEET: Yes, sir; but none from Southampton to New York.

SENATOR SMITH: Where did those go that you had from Belfast to Southampton?

MR. FLEET: We do not know that. We only know we never got a pair.

SENATOR SMITH: And you had none from Southampton to the place of this accident?

MR. FLEET: No, sir.

SENATOR SMITH: Suppose you had had glasses such as you had on the *Oceanic,* or such as you had between Belfast and Southampton, could you have seen this black object a greater distance?

MR. FLEET: We could have seen it a bit sooner.

SENATOR SMITH: How much sooner?

MR. FLEET: Well, enough to get out of the way. . . .

SENATOR SMITH: Tell the committee what you did after you left the crow's nest that night.

MR. FLEET: I went down below and I found there was nobody down there, and the quartermaster come down and said we were all wanted on the bridge.

SENATOR SMITH: Did you go up to the bridge?

MR. FLEET: I went up on the boat deck.

SENATOR SMITH: What did they say to you up there?

MR. FLEET: I did not see anyone there; I seen them all at the boats, getting them ready and putting them out.

SENATOR SMITH: The lifeboats?

MR. FLEET: Yes, sir.

SENATOR SMITH: What did you do?

MR. FLEET: I helped to get the port boat out.

SENATOR SMITH: The fourth one?

MR. FLEET: The port-side lifeboat. I got No. 6 out.

SENATOR SMITH: How many of those boats did you help lower?

MR. FLEET: I lowered No. 6 to the rail.

SENATOR SMITH: How many sailors or men of the crew were put into No. 6?

MR. FLEET: There was me and one quartermaster.

SENATOR SMITH: Yourself and one quartermaster?

MR. FLEET: Yes, sir.

SENATOR SMITH: Was that all of the crew or officers that were in that boat?

MR. FLEET: That is all. No officers; just us two.

SENATOR SMITH: You and the quartermaster?

MR. FLEET: Me and Quartermaster [Robert] Hitchens.

SENATOR SMITH: Did he survive?

MR. FLEET: Yes, sir; he is staying in New York.

SENATOR SMITH: After lowering the lifeboat to the boat deck, did he get in first or you?

MR. FLEET: I was told by Mr. Lightoller to get in the boat and help the women in.

SENATOR SMITH: You got in by direction of the second officer?

MR. FLEET: Yes, sir.

SENATOR SMITH: And helped the women in?

MR. FLEET: Yes, sir.

SENATOR SMITH: How many men were in that boat?

MR. FLEET: Five.

SENATOR SMITH: Who were they?

MR. FLEET: Three men passengers and two of the crew.

SENATOR SMITH: Who were the passengers?

MR. FLEET: I do not know. There was one steerage and two first.

SENATOR SMITH: You do not know who they were?

MR. FLEET: No, sir.

SENATOR SMITH: Have you ever seen them since?

MR. FLEET: No, sir.

SENATOR SMITH: How many women or children were there in the boat?

MR. FLEET: There was no children. They were all women. I could not tell how many because I did not count them.

SENATOR SMITH: Was the boat full?

MR. FLEET: It was full up, but it could have took a few more forward, where I was.

SENATOR SMITH: How many do you think you had in it all together?

MR. FLEET: About 30.

SENATOR SMITH: Was it the regular lifeboat, the large size?

MR. FLEET: One of the wooden lifeboats.

SENATOR SMITH: You got about 30 people in there, and then it was lowered to the water?

MR. FLEET: Yes, sir.

SENATOR SMITH: And what did you do then?

MR. FLEET: We got the oars and pulled for the light that was on the port bow.

SENATOR SMITH: Did you see it?

MR. FLEET: Yes, sir.

SENATOR SMITH: What happened there?

MR. FLEET: We could not get up to it.

SENATOR SMITH: Why not?

MR. FLEET: There were only two of us pulling.

SENATOR SMITH: You could not get up to it?

MR. FLEET: No, sir.

SENATOR SMITH: How close could you get to it?

MR. FLEET: She was getting away off.

SENATOR SMITH: At that time were there any persons in the water?

MR. FLEET: No, sir.

SENATOR SMITH: Did you hear any cries of distress?

MR. FLEET: No, sir.

SENATOR SMITH: When you found you could not get up to it, what did you do?

MR. FLEET: We kept on pulling; that is all.

SENATOR SMITH: In that direction; away from the boat?

MR. FLEET: Away from the boat.

SENATOR SMITH: Away from the *Titanic?*

MR. FLEET: Yes, sir.

SENATOR SMITH: Did you keep right on pulling away?

MR. FLEET: We kept on pulling.

SENATOR SMITH: And did not stop?

MR. FLEET: No, sir.

SENATOR SMITH: Toward what did you pull?

MR. FLEET: We thought we could get up to this light, but we could not. It seemed to be getting away from us all the time.

SENATOR SMITH: What light was it?

MR. FLEET: It was a light on the port bow. She seemed to be abreast of us.

SENATOR SMITH: Are you now talking of the *Titanic?*

MR. FLEET: Abreast of the *Titanic.*

SENATOR SMITH: From the time you started to pull away from the *Titanic's* side, did anyone try to get into your boat?

MR. FLEET: No, sir.

SENATOR SMITH: Did anyone try to get out of it?

MR. FLEET: No, sir.

SENATOR SMITH: Did anyone step into your boat, man or woman, and then step out of it?

MR. FLEET: No, sir. There was just one passenger, when we was lowering away, come in the boat.

SENATOR SMITH: Who was that?

MR. FLEET: One of the men passengers.

SENATOR SMITH: Who was it; do you know?

MR. FLEET: I do not know who he was, sir.

SENATOR SMITH: When you were lowering away?

MR. FLEET: Yes, sir.

SENATOR SMITH: How far had you gotten below the boat deck?

MR. FLEET: It was not very far; just about the length of the table down. He got over the life lanyard and swung in and come down the fall.

SENATOR SMITH: You took no other persons aboard this lifeboat from that time?

MR. FLEET: No, sir.

SENATOR SMITH: And landed all of your occupants of that boat alongside the *Carpathia?*

MR. FLEET: Yes, sir.

SENATOR SMITH: During the time you were waiting for the *Carpathia,* were you rowing the boat away or lying on your oars?

MR. FLEET: We pulled until we were clear of the suction of the *Titanic.*

SENATOR SMITH: Pulled away from the *Titanic?*

MR. FLEET: Yes, sir.

SENATOR SMITH: Assuming there would be suction when she went down?

MR. FLEET: Yes, sir.

SENATOR SMITH: Was there any?

MR. FLEET: No, sir; we were too far off.

SENATOR SMITH: Did you see her go down?

MR. FLEET: No, sir.

SENATOR SMITH: Why not?

MR. FLEET: The lights were out, and we were too far away.

SENATOR SMITH: You could not see her when she disappeared?

MR. FLEET: No, sir.

SENATOR SMITH: Where were you picked up by the *Carpathia*, near the *Titanic*?

MR. FLEET: When we sighted the lights of the *Carpathia*, we pulled toward her again.

SENATOR SMITH: And were picked up by her?

MR. FLEET: Yes, sir; right alongside.

SENATOR SMITH: After getting alongside the *Carpathia* you did not take your lifeboat back to the scene of the wreck?

MR. FLEET: No, sir.

SENATOR SMITH: You got aboard the *Carpathia?*

MR. FLEET: Yes, sir. . . .

SENATOR SMITH: Did you see any rockets fired from the deck of the *Titanic?*

MR. FLEET: Yes, sir; when we were in the boat and when we were on the deck before I went in the boat.

SENATOR SMITH: But you saw no lights ahead that indicated the presence of another vessel?

MR. FLEET: No, sir.

SENATOR SMITH: Or while you were in the crow's nest?

MR. FLEET: No, sir.

SENATOR SMITH: Nor any other object except the one you have described?

MR. FLEET: No, sir.

SENATOR SMITH: Did you see any other icebergs, field ice, or growlers while you were in the crow's nest Sunday or Sunday night?

MR. FLEET: Only the one I reported right ahead.

SENATOR SMITH: Only that one?

MR. FLEET: That is all.

SENATOR SMITH: I think that is all at this time, and if I want you again I will send you word. Will you just remain subject to the committee's call?

MR. FLEET: Yes, sir. . . .

Witness: Maj. Arthur G. Peuchen, 53
First-class passenger, a chemical manufacturer and Canadian militiaman, from Toronto

Key testimony: An amateur yachtsman pressed into service as an oarsman on lifeboat No. 6, he said women on the boat wanted to go back for more survivors. But the man in charge

191

of the boat, Robert Hitchens, the Titanic's *helmsman, headed instead toward a light he sighted in the distance.*

... SENATOR SMITH: Major, I wish you would tell the committee ... as nearly as you can, in your own way, what took place from the time the *Titanic* sailed. You may proceed in your own way and take your own time, and you will not be interrupted until you finish.

MAJ. PEUCHEN: ... The weather up to the time of Sunday was pleasant. There was very little wind; it was quite calm. Everything seemed to be running very smoothly on the steamer, and there was nothing that occurred. There was no mention of fire in any way. In fact, it was a very pleasant voyage up to Sunday evening. We were all pleased with the way the new steamer was progressing, and we had hopes of arriving in New York quite early on Wednesday morning.

Do you wish me to go on further?

SENATOR SMITH: Go right along. I wish you to complete your statement, in your own way, up to the time you went on board the *Carpathia*.

MAJ. PEUCHEN: It would be a rather long story.

SENATOR SMITH: Well, I want it in the record, Major.

MAJ. PEUCHEN: Sunday evening I dined with my friends, Markleham Molson, Mr. Allison, and Mrs. Allison; and their daughter was there for a short time. The dinner was an exceptionally good dinner. It seemed to be a better bill of fare than usual, although they are all good. After dinner my friends and I went to the sitting-out room and had some coffee. I left the friends I had dined with about 9 o'clock, I think, or a little later. I then went up to the smoking room and joined Mr. Beatty, Mr. McCaffery, and another English gentleman who was going to Canada. We sat chatting and smoking there until probably 20 minutes after 11, or it may have been a little later than that. I then bid them good night and went to my room. I probably stopped, going down, but I had only reached my room and was starting to undress when I felt as though a heavy wave had struck our ship. She quivered under it somewhat. If there had been a sea running I would simply have thought it was an unusual wave which had struck the boat; but knowing that it was a calm night and that it was an unusual thing to occur on a calm night, I immediately put my overcoat on and went up on deck. As I started to go through the grand stairway I met a friend, who said, "Why, we have struck an iceberg."

SENATOR SMITH: Give his name, if you can.

MAJ. PEUCHEN: I can not remember his name. He was simply a casual acquaintance I had met. He said, "If you will go up on the upper deck," or "If you will go up on A deck, you will see the ice on the fore part of the ship." So I did so. I went up there. I suppose the ice had fallen inside the rail, probably 4 to 4½ feet. It looked like shell ice, soft ice. But you could see it quite plainly along the bow of the boat. I stood on deck for a few minutes, talking to other friends, and then I went to see my friend, Mr. Hugo Ross, to tell him that it was not serious; that we had only struck an iceberg. I also called on Mr. Molson at his room, but he was out. I afterwards saw Mr. Molson on deck and we chatted over the matter, and I suppose 15 minutes after that I met Mr. Hays, his son-in-law, and I said to him, "Mr. Hays, have you seen the ice?" He said, "No." I said, "If you care to see it I will take you up on the deck and show it to you." So we proceeded from probably C deck to A deck and along forward, and I showed Mr. [Charles M.] Hays the ice forward. I happened to look and noticed the boat was listing, probably half an hour after my first visit to the upper deck. I said to Mr. Hays, "Why, she is listing; she should not do that, the water is perfectly calm, and the boat has stopped." I felt that looked rather serious. He said, "Oh, I don't know; you can not sink this boat." He had a good deal of confidence. He said, "No matter what we have struck, she is good for 8 or 10 hours."

I hardly got back in the grand staircase—I probably waited around there 10 minutes more—when I saw the ladies and gentlemen all coming in off the deck looking very serious, and I caught up to Mr. Beatty, and I said, "What is the matter?" He said, "Why the order is for life belts and boats." I could not believe it at first, it seemed so sudden. I said, "Will you tell Mr. Ross?"

He said, "Yes; I will go and see Mr. Ross." I then went

to my cabin and changed as quickly as I could from evening dress to heavy clothes. As soon as I got my overcoat on I got my life preserver and I came out of my cabin.

In the hallway I met a great many people, ladies and gentlemen, with their life belts on, and the ladies were crying, principally, most of them. It was a very serious sight, and I commenced to realize how serious matters were. I then proceeded up to the boat deck, and I saw that they had cleared away——

SENATOR SMITH (interposing): Pardon me one moment. Were you still on C deck?

MAJ. PEUCHEN: I was on C deck when I came out and saw the people standing in the corridor near the grand stairway. I then proceeded upstairs to the boat deck, which is the deck above A.

I saw the boats were all ready for action; that is, the covers had been taken off of them, and the ropes cleared, ready to lower. This was on the port side. I was standing near by the second officer, and the captain was standing there as well, at that time. The captain said—I do not know whether it was the captain or the second officer said—"We will have to get these masts out of these boats, and also the sail." He said, "You might give us a hand," and I jumped in the boat, and we got a knife and cut the lashings of the mast, which is a very heavy mast, and also the sail, and moved it out of the boat, saying it would not be required. Then there was a cry, as soon as that part was done, that they were ready to put the women in; so the women came forward one by one. A great many women came with their husbands. . . . They would only allow women in that boat, and the men had to stand back.

SENATOR SMITH: Was there any order to that effect given?

MAJ. PEUCHEN: That was the order. The second officer stood there and he carried out that to the limit. He allowed no men except the sailors, who were manning the boat, but there were no passengers that I saw got into that boat.

SENATOR SMITH: How many sailors?

MAJ. PEUCHEN: I am not sure, but I imagine there were about four. As far as my memory serves me, there were about four. I was busy helping and assisting to get the ladies in. After a reasonable complement of ladies had got aboard, she was lowered, but I did not see one single passenger get in that first boat.

SENATOR FLETCHER: You mean male passenger.

MAJ. PEUCHEN: Yes; male passenger.

SENATOR SMITH: Did you see any attempt to get in?

MAJ. PEUCHEN: No; I never saw such order. It was perfect order. The discipline was splendid. The officers were carrying out their duty and I think the passengers behaved splendidly. I did not see a cowardly act by any man.

SENATOR SMITH: Was the boat safely lowered?

MAJ. PEUCHEN: The boat was loaded, but I think they could have taken more in this boat. They took, however, all the ladies that offered to get in at that point.

SENATOR SMITH: Was the boat safely lowered?

MAJ. PEUCHEN: Oh, very; the boat was safely lowered.

SENATOR SMITH: Who was in it that you know of?

MAJ. PEUCHEN: I should say about—I do not know—I imagine about 26 or 27. There was room for more.

Then, as soon as that boat was lowered, we turned our attention to the next.

I might say I was rather surprised that the sailors were not at their stations, as I have seen fire drill very often on steamers where they all stand at attention, so many men at the bow and stern of these lifeboats. They seemed to be short of sailors around the lifeboats that were being lowered at this particular point. I do not know what was taking place in other parts of the steamer.

There was one act, sir, I would like to mention a little ahead of my story. When I came on deck first, on this upper deck, there were, it seems to me, about 100 stokers came up with their dunnage bags, and they seemed to crowd this whole deck in front of the boats. One of the officers—I do not know which one, but a very powerful one—came along and drove these men right off that deck. It was a splendid act.

SENATOR SMITH: Off the boat deck?

MAJ. PEUCHEN: Off the boat deck. He drove them, every man, like a lot of sheep, right off the deck.

SENATOR SMITH: Where did they go?

MAJ. PEUCHEN: I do not know. He drove them right ahead of

him, and they disappeared. I do not know where they
went, but it was a splendid act. They did not put up any
resistance. I admired him for it.

I had finished with the lowering of the first boat from
the port side. We then proceeded to boat No. 2 or No. 4
or No. 6; I do not know which it is called.

SENATOR SMITH: You had stepped into the boat to assist in
lowering it?

MAJ. PEUCHEN: Yes; and then got out of it again.

SENATOR SMITH: And you stepped out of it?

MAJ. PEUCHEN: I only got into the boat to assist in taking out
the mast and the sail.

SENATOR SMITH: I understand. Then you got out again?

MAJ. PEUCHEN: Then I got out again, and I assisted in
putting the ladies into the boat. We then went to the next
boat and we did the same thing—got the mast and the
sail out of that. There was a quartermaster in the boat,
and one sailor, and we commenced to put the ladies in
that boat. After that boat had got a full complement of
ladies, there were no more ladies to get in, or if there were
any other ladies to get in they did not wish to do so,
because we were calling out for them—that is, speaking
of the port side—but some would not leave their husbands.

SENATOR SMITH: Do you know who they were?

MAJ. PEUCHEN: I only saw one or two stand by who would
not get in. Whether they afterwards left them I can not
say, but I saw one or two women refuse to get in on that
account.

SENATOR SMITH: Did you see any woman get in and then get
out because her husband was not with her?

MAJ. PEUCHEN: No, I do not think I did. I saw one lady
where they had to sort of pull her away from her husband,
he insisting upon her going to the boat and she did not
want to go.

This boat was then lowered down, and when it got——

SENATOR SMITH (interposing): Pardon me a moment. How
many were put into this second boat?

MAJ. PEUCHEN: I did not know at the time of the lowering,
but as I happened to be a passenger later on, they were
counted and there were exactly 20 women, 1 quartermas-

ter, 1 sailor, and 1 stowaway that made his appearance after we had been out about an hour.

SENATOR SMITH: Twenty-three all together?

MAJ. PEUCHEN: Twenty-three all together; before I was a passenger.

After that the boat was lowered down some distance, I should imagine probably parallel with C deck, when the quartermaster called up to the officer and said, "I can not manage this boat with only one seaman."

SENATOR SMITH: Where was this call from?

MAJ. PEUCHEN: As the boat was going down, I should think about the third deck. So he made this call for assistance, and the second officer leaned over and saw he was quite right in his statement, that he had only one man in the boat, so they said, "We will have to have some more seamen here," and I did not think they were just at hand, or they may have been getting the next boat ready. However, I was standing by the officer, and I said, "Can I be of any assistance? I am a yachtsman, and can handle a boat with an average man." He said, "Why, yes. I will order you to the boat in preference to a sailor."

SENATOR SMITH: Pardon me right there. Who was this man then in the boat?

MAJ. PEUCHEN: He was one of the quartermasters. The captain was standing still by him at that time, and I think, although the officer ordered me to the boat, the captain said, "You had better go down below and break a window and get in through a window, into the boat."

SENATOR SMITH: The captain said that?

MAJ. PEUCHEN: Yes. That was his suggestion; and I said I did not think it was feasible, and I said I could get in the boat if I could get hold of a rope. However, we got hold of a loose rope in some way that was hanging from the davit, near the block anyway, and by getting hold of this I swung myself off the ship, and lowered myself into the boat.

SENATOR SMITH: How far did you have to swing yourself?

MAJ. PEUCHEN: The danger was jumping off from the boat. It was not after I got a straight line; it was very easy lowering. But I imagine it was opposite the C deck at the time. On getting into the boat I went aft in the lifeboat, and said to the quartermaster, "What do you want me to do?" He said, "Get down and put that plug in," and I made a dive down for the plug, and the ladies were all sitting pretty well aft, and I could not see at all. It was dark down there. I felt with my hands, and I said it would be better for him to do it and me do his work, and I said, "Now, you get down and put in the plug, and I will undo the shackles," that is, take the blocks off. So he dropped the blocks, and he got down, and he came rushing back to assist me, and he said, "Hurry up." He said "This boat is going to founder." I thought he meant our lifeboat was going to founder. I thought he had had some difficulty in finding the plug, or he had not gotten it in properly. But he meant the large boat was going to founder, and that we were to hurry up and get away from it. So we got the rudder in, and he told me to go forward and take an oar. I went forward and got an oar on the port side of the lifeboat; the sailor was on my left, on the starboard side. But we were just opposite each other in rowing.

SENATOR SMITH: Who was the sailor?

MAJ. PEUCHEN: He was the man who gave evidence just before me.

SENATOR SMITH: Mr. Fleet, from the lookout.

MAJ. PEUCHEN: From the lookout, yes; sitting next to me on my left. He told us to row as hard as possible away from the suction. Just as we got rowing out part of the way, this stowaway, an Italian——

SENATOR SMITH: Pardon me. Did the officer say to row away, so as to get away from the suction?

MAJ. PEUCHEN: The quartermaster who was in charge of our boat told us to row as hard as we could to get away from this suction, and just as we got a short distance away this stowaway made his appearance. He was an Italian by birth, I should think, who had a broken wrist or arm, and he was of no use to us to row. He got an oar out, but he could not do much, so we got him to take the oar in.

SENATOR SMITH: Where did he make his appearance from, Major?

MAJ. PEUCHEN: Underneath; I think he was stowed away underneath. I should imagine if there was any room for him to get underneath the bow of the boat he would be there. I imagine that was where he came from. He was not visible when looking at the boat. There were only two men when she was lowered.

SENATOR SMITH: Would you know him if you should see him?

MAJ. PEUCHEN: No, it was dark. At daylight I was rowing very hard—in the morning—and I did not notice. As we rowed, pulled away from the *Titanic,* there was an officer's call of some kind. We stopped rowing.

SENATOR SMITH: A whistle?

MAJ. PEUCHEN: A sort of a whistle. Anyway, the quartermaster told us to stop rowing so he could hear it, and this was a call to come back to the boat. So we all thought we ought to go back to the boat. It was a call. But the quartermaster said, "No, we are not going back to the boat." He said, "It is our lives now, not theirs," and he insisted upon our rowing farther away.

SENATOR SMITH: Who made the rebellion against it?

MAJ. PEUCHEN: I think the rebellion was made by some of the married women that were leaving their husbands.

SENATOR SMITH: And did you join in that?

MAJ. PEUCHEN: I did not say anything. I knew I was perfectly powerless. He was at the rudder. He was a very talkative man. He had been swearing a good deal, and was very disagreeable. I had had one row with him. I asked him to come and row, to assist us in rowing, and let some woman steer the boat, as it was a perfectly calm night. It did not require any skill for steering. The stars were out. He refused to do it, and he told me he was in command of that boat, and I was to row.

SENATOR SMITH: Did he remain at the tiller?

MAJ. PEUCHEN: He remained at the tiller, and if we wanted to go back while he was in possession of the tiller, I do not think we could have done so. The women were in between the quartermaster and myself and the other seaman. The night was cold and we kept rowing on. Then he imagined he saw a light. I have done a good deal of yachting in my life, I have owned a yacht for six years and have been out on the Lakes, and I could not see these lights. I saw a reflection. He thought it was a boat of some kind. He thought probably it might be a buoy out there of some kind, and he called out to the next boat, which was within hearing, asking if he knew if there was any buoy around there. This struck me as being perfectly absurd, and showed me the man did not know anything about navigating, expecting to see a buoy in the middle of the Atlantic. However, he insisted upon us rowing. We kept on rowing toward this imaginary light and, after a while, after we had gone a long distance—I am ahead of my story. We commenced to hear signs of the breaking up of the boat.

SENATOR SMITH: Of the *Titanic?*

MAJ. PEUCHEN: Of the *Titanic.* At first I kept my eyes watching the lights, as long as possible.

SENATOR SMITH: From your position in the boat, did you face it?

MAJ. PEUCHEN: I was facing it at this time. I was rowing this way [indicating], and afterwards I changed to the other way. We heard a sort of a call for help after this whistle I described a few minutes ago. This was the officer calling us back. We heard a sort of a rumbling sound and the lights were still on at the rumbling sound, as far as my memory serves me; then a sort of an explosion, then another. It seemed to be one, two, or three rumbling sounds, then the lights went out. Then the dreadful calls and crys.

SENATOR SMITH: For help?

MAJ. PEUCHEN: We could not distinguish the exact cry for assistance; moaning and crying; frightful. It affected all the women in our boat whose husbands were among these; and this went on for some time, gradually getting fainter, fainter. At first it was horrible to listen to.

SENATOR SMITH: How far was it away?

MAJ. PEUCHEN: I think we must have been five-eighths of a mile, I should imagine, when this took place. It was very hard to guess the distance. There were only two of us rowing a very heavy boat with a good many people in it, and I do not think we covered very much ground.

SENATOR SMITH: While these cries of distress were going on, did anyone in the boat urge the quartermaster to return?

MAJ. PEUCHEN: Yes; some of the woman did. But, as I said before, I had had a row with him, and I said to the women, "It is no use you arguing with that man, at all. It is best not to discuss matters with him." He said it was no use going back there, there was only a lot of stiffs there, later on, which was very unkind, and the women resented it very much. I do not think he was qualified to be a quartermaster.

SENATOR SMITH: As a matter of fact, you did not return to the boat?

MAJ. PEUCHEN: We did not return to the boat.

SENATOR SMITH: After you left its side?

MAJ. PEUCHEN: No.

SENATOR SMITH: And when the boat went down, were you looking toward it?

MAJ. PEUCHEN: I was looking toward the boat; yes.

SENATOR SMITH: Did you see it?

MAJ. PEUCHEN: I saw it when the lights went out. You could not tell very much after the lights went out.

SENATOR SMITH: You were not close enough to recognize anyone aboard?

MAJ. PEUCHEN: Oh, no.

SENATOR SMITH: Could you see the outlines of the people on the deck?

MAJ. PEUCHEN: No; you could not. I could only see the outline of the boat, you might say.

SENATOR SMITH: Do you know how she went down?

MAJ. PEUCHEN: While the lights were burning, I saw her bow pointing down and the stern up; not in a perpendicular position, but considerable.

SENATOR SMITH: About what angle?

MAJ. PEUCHEN: I should think an angle of not as much as 45°.

SENATOR SMITH: From what you saw, do you think the boat was intact, or had it broken in two?

MAJ. PEUCHEN: It was intact at that time. I feel sure that an explosion had taken place in the boat, because in passing the wreck the next morning—we steamed past it—I just happened to think of this, which may be of some assistance to this inquiry—I was standing forward, looking to see if I could see any dead bodies, or any of my friends, and to my surprise I saw the barber's pole floating. The barber's pole was on the C deck, my recollection is—the barber shop—and that must have been a tremendous explosion to allow this pole to have broken from its fastenings and drift with the wood.

SENATOR SMITH: Did you hear the explosions?

MAJ. PEUCHEN: Yes, sir; I heard the explosions.

SENATOR SMITH: How loud were they?

MAJ. PEUCHEN: Oh, a sort of a rumbling sound. It was not a sharp sound—more of a rumbling kind of a sound, but still sharp at the same time. It would not be as loud as a clap of thunder, or anything that way, or like a boiler explosion, I should not think.

SENATOR SMITH: Were these explosions evidently from under the water?

MAJ. PEUCHEN: I should think they were from above. I imagined that the decks had blown up with the pressure, pulling the boat down, bow on, this heavy weight and the air between the decks; that is my theory of the explosion. I do not know whether it is correct or not, but I do not think it was the boilers. I think it was the pressure, that heavy weight shoving that down, the water rushing up, and the air coming between the decks; something had to go.

SENATOR SMITH: How many explosions did you hear?

MAJ. PEUCHEN: I am not absolutely certain of this, because there was a good deal of excitement at the time, but I imagine there were three, one following the other very quickly.

SENATOR SMITH: Did you see the captain after he told you to go below and get through the window into the lifeboat?

MAJ. PEUCHEN: No; I never saw him after that.

SENATOR SMITH: From what you saw of the captain, was he alert and watchful?

MAJ. PEUCHEN: He was doing everything in his power to get women in these boats, and to see that they were lowered properly. I thought he was doing his duty in regard to the lowering of the boats, sir.

SENATOR SMITH: Did you see the officer of the watch that night?

MAJ. PEUCHEN: Whom do you mean? I hardly know what you mean?

SENATOR SMITH: Who was the officer with you on your side of the boat?

MAJ. PEUCHEN: The second officer.

SENATOR SMITH: Mr. Lightoller?

MAJ. PEUCHEN: Yes, sir.

SENATOR SMITH: Had you seen the captain before that night?

MAJ. PEUCHEN: I passed him in one of the companionways some place, just about dinner time.

SENATOR SMITH: What time?

MAJ. PEUCHEN: I can not be very certain as to the hour; around 7 o'clock, I imagine. I generally come out to dress about 7 o'clock.

SENATOR SMITH: What time did you dine that night?

MAJ. PEUCHEN: I dined a little after 7; I think it was a quarter after.

SENATOR SMITH: In the main dining room?

MAJ. PEUCHEN: In the main dining room; yes.

SENATOR SMITH: Did the captain dine in that room?

MAJ. PEUCHEN: I do not think so. I think he dined in the other—in the restaurant.

SENATOR SMITH: But you did not see him?

MAJ. PEUCHEN: I did not see him dining.

SENATOR SMITH: I wish you would say whether or not these lifeboats were equipped with food and water and lights.

MAJ. PEUCHEN: As far as I could tell, our boat was equipped with everything in that respect. I heard some talk that there was not proper food in some of the boats, and when I was on the *Carpathia* I made it my business to go down and look at one or two, and I found hard-tack in this sealed box.

SENATOR SMITH: In both of them?

MAJ. PEUCHEN: On the boat. I did not go all around the fleet.

SENATOR SMITH: You say you looked at one or two?

MAJ. PEUCHEN: One or two.

SENATOR SMITH: Did you find provisions and water in both?

MAJ. PEUCHEN: I did not examine the kegs, but I was assured by the sailors there was water in them.

SENATOR SMITH: Did you see lights in them?

MAJ. PEUCHEN: We had lights in our boat, but some of the other boats did not. I know there was a boat that hung near us that had not lights. Whether it was on account of not being able to light their lights I do not know.

SENATOR SMITH: You say there were 36 or 37 people in your boat?

MAJ. PEUCHEN: No, sir.

SENATOR SMITH: In the first boat that was lowered?

MAJ. PEUCHEN: No; I said I thought about 26 or 27.

SENATOR SMITH: In the first one?

MAJ. PEUCHEN: Yes; I think so.

SENATOR SMITH: And 23 in the second boat before you got in?

MAJ. PEUCHEN: Including the stowaway there would be 23. I made the twenty-fourth.

SENATOR SMITH: Twenty women?

MAJ. PEUCHEN: Twenty women, yes; the quartermaster, one seaman, the stowaway, and then when I got in there were 24.

SENATOR SMITH: Any children?

MAJ. PEUCHEN: No; I do not think we had any children. Later on we tied up to another boat, toward morning, for a very short time—I think for about 15 minutes.

SENATOR SMITH: What boat was that?

MAJ. PEUCHEN: I do not know. Our quartermaster did not know the number of our boat. I do not know the other. I know they called out and asked the number of our boat and our quartermaster did not know which it was.

SENATOR SMITH: Did you hear the testimony given this morning by the third officer?

MAJ. PEUCHEN: I heard part of it, sir. I was out in the hall while he was giving some of it.

SENATOR SMITH: Did you hear him say that a lifeboat was attached to his lifeboat for a while?

MAJ. PEUCHEN: Yes; but, then, let me see; did he not say he took some people off of that boat?

SENATOR SMITH: I was going to come to that.

MAJ. PEUCHEN: No; that was not our boat.

SENATOR SMITH: He said he took three people out of his lifeboat.

MAJ. PEUCHEN: And put them into the one attached.

SENATOR FLETCHER: On the starboard side of No. 7.

SENATOR SMITH: That was not done in your boat?

MAJ. PEUCHEN: No. The only thing that occurred with the boat we were tied up with was, we asked how many men they had in their boat, and this quartermaster said he had about seven sailors, or something like that—six or seven. Then we said, "Surely you can spare us one man, if you have so many," and we got a fireman.

SENATOR SMITH: You got a fireman?

MAJ. PEUCHEN: One more man out of that boat.

SENATOR SMITH: They transferred one more man to you?

MAJ. PEUCHEN: Yes; one more man.

SENATOR SMITH: What did he do?

MAJ. PEUCHEN: He assisted in rowing on the starboard side of the lifeboat, and I rowed on the port side.

SENATOR SMITH: Did any of the women help with the oars?

MAJ. PEUCHEN: Yes; they did, very pluckily, too. We got the oars. Before this occurred we got a couple of women rowing aft, on the starboard side of our boat, and I got two women to assist on our side; but of course the woman with me got sick with the heavy work, and she had to give it up. But I believe the others kept on rowing quite pluckily for a considerable time.

SENATOR SMITH: Do you know who these women were at the oars?

MAJ. PEUCHEN: I know one of them.

SENATOR SMITH: Give the name.

MAJ. PEUCHEN: If you will excuse me, I will have to look it up. [Referring to memorandum.] Miss M. E. A. Norton, Apaley Villa, Horn Lane, Acton, London.

SENATOR SMITH: Is that the only one of the women who handled the oars that you know by name?

MAJ. PEUCHEN: No; I think there is another.

SENATOR SMITH: The other two women who handled the oars you do not know?

MAJ. PEUCHEN: I do not know their names. . . .

SENATOR SMITH: Major, at any time between leaving the side of the *Titanic* and reaching the *Carpathia,* did Mrs. Douglas [Mahala Douglas, first-class passenger] hold the tiller?

MAJ. PEUCHEN: In our lifeboat?

SENATOR SMITH: Yes.

MAJ. PEUCHEN: I think the quartermaster was at the tiller all the time, with the exception probably of a couple of minutes. I know he asked one of the ladies for some brandy, and he also asked for one of her wraps, which he got.

SENATOR SMITH: The officer did?

MAJ. PEUCHEN: The quartermaster, not the officer. . . .

SENATOR SMITH: You say when the impact occurred, the ship shuddered?

MAJ. PEUCHEN: When the impact occurred, describing it I

would say it would be like a wave striking it, a very heavy wave.

SENATOR SMITH: How soon after that did the boat begin to list?

MAJ. PEUCHEN: I should think about 25 minutes afterwards.

SENATOR SMITH: So far as you could observe, did the passengers have on life belts?

MAJ. PEUCHEN: They had. . . .

SENATOR SMITH: I believe you said you have had considerable experience as a mariner?

MAJ. PEUCHEN: Yes, sir.

SENATOR SMITH: Can you say whether the *Titanic* listed to the starboard or port side?

MAJ. PEUCHEN: She listed to the starboard side; the side she was struck on.

SENATOR SMITH: Did she go down by the bow or by the head?

MAJ. PEUCHEN: Eventually, you mean?

SENATOR SMITH: Yes.

MAJ. PEUCHEN: She was down by the bow. You mean the head by the bow, do you not?

SENATOR SMITH: Exactly.

MAJ. PEUCHEN: It is the same thing.

SENATOR SMITH: No; not exactly the same thing. Where was this impact on the bow of the ship?

MAJ. PEUCHEN: It was aft of the bow about 40 feet, I should imagine, on the starboard side—about 40 or 50 feet, I should imagine—from where the ice started to come off the iceberg.

SENATOR SMITH: You say you saw some ice on the deck?

MAJ. PEUCHEN: Yes, sir.

SENATOR SMITH: Do you know of anyone being injured by ice on the deck?

MAJ. PEUCHEN: No; but I know a great many of the passengers were made afraid by this iceberg passing their portholes. The ship shoved past this ice, and a great many of them told me afterwards they could not understand this thing moving past them—those that were awakened at the time. In fact, it left ice on some of the portholes, they told me.

SENATOR SMITH: Do you know of your own knowledge whether any alarm was sounded to arouse the passengers from their rooms after the impact?

MAJ. PEUCHEN: There was no alarm sounded whatever. In fact, I talked with two young ladies who claimed to have had a very narrow escape. They said their stateroom was right near the Astors, I think almost next to it, and they were not awakened.

SENATOR SMITH: They were not awakened?

MAJ. PEUCHEN: They slept through this crash, and they were awakened by Mrs. Astor. She was in rather an excited state, and their door being open—and I think the Astor door was open—they think that was the means of their being saved.

SENATOR SMITH: On what deck were they?

MAJ. PEUCHEN: I do not know, sir. It was only conversation told me on the *Carpathia*.

SENATOR SMITH: I think you said that from your judgment and from your own observation there was no general alarm given?

MAJ. PEUCHEN: No, I did not hear one. I was around the boat all the time. . . .

SENATOR FLETCHER: Major, do you mean for us to understand that at the time lifeboat No. 4 and lifeboat No. 6 on the port side of the ship were loaded and lowered every woman in sight was given an opportunity?

MAJ. PEUCHEN: Every woman on the port side was given an opportunity. In fact, we had not enough women to put into the boats. We were looking for them. I can not understand why we did not take some men. The boats would have held more.

SENATOR FLETCHER: If there had been more women there they could have found room in those boats?

MAJ. PEUCHEN: Plenty of room. . . .

SENATOR FLETCHER: Is it your idea that the water was so cold that a person could not live in it except for a short time?

MAJ. PEUCHEN: I feel quite sure that a person could not live in that water very long. Those who had been in the water had their feet frozen; that is, those who were standing up in a boat in the water. I happened to have the cabin with three of them who were rescued, and they said they sustained their life by punching each other during the two or three hours they stood up. The minute any one got tired and sat down in the water, or at least very shortly thereafter, he floated off the raft, dead, I believe.

SENATOR FLETCHER: What was the temperature of the water, if you know?

MAJ. PEUCHEN: I do not know, sir.

SENATOR FLETCHER: You say people were frozen?

MAJ. PEUCHEN: Their feet were frozen; yes, sir.

SENATOR FLETCHER: Was that by exposure, after being taken out of the water on the boat?

MAJ. PEUCHEN: Yes, sir. A number of them swam, I know of three cases, at least, where they jumped from the big boat and swam and got on to a raft which was partly submerged in the water, and they stood up in the raft, and those are the ones whose feet were badly swollen or frozen.

SENATOR FLETCHER: You assume from that that the water was very cold?

MAJ. PEUCHEN: I am sure it was.

SENATOR FLETCHER: Was it below the freezing point?

MAJ. PEUCHEN: It must have been very near the freezing point, anyway. It probably would not be quite freezing; but it being salt water, of course it would not freeze very readily.

SENATOR FLETCHER: Was there any floating ice, aside from these icebergs?

MAJ. PEUCHEN: Oh, yes; when we started to steam away we passed a lot of floating ice, I suppose several miles long.

SENATOR FLETCHER: You mean the *Carpathia* steamed through the ice?

MAJ. PEUCHEN: Yes.

SENATOR FLETCHER: Did you come into contact with floating ice while you were on the lifeboat?

MAJ. PEUCHEN: No, sir; we did not.

SENATOR FLETCHER: Have you any idea as to how long a person could live in water like that?

MAJ. PEUCHEN: It depends on his constitution, but I should imagine that if a person could stay in the water a half an hour he would be doing very well.

SENATOR FLETCHER: Would not the effort to swim, and exercise, prevent one getting numb for several hours?

MAJ. PEUCHEN: Up to a certain point; yes. But I do not think a man could live an hour in that water. . . .

FIFTH DAY
Wednesday, April 24
Washington, D.C.

Witness: Harold Godfrey Lowe, 28
Titanic's Fifth Officer, from North Wales, England

Key testimony: He hotly denied a claim that he had been drinking. He said Ismay got in the way of loading lifeboat No. 5 so Lowe told him to "get the hell out of that," whereupon Ismay moved to another lifeboat. (Ismay was present as he testified.) Lowe said that as his lifeboat was being lowered, he fired his pistol along the side of each deck level to prevent men, particularly "Italians," from jumping on.

. . . SENATOR SMITH: Are you a temperate man?

MR. LOWE: I am, sir. I never touched it in my life. I am an abstainer.

SENATOR SMITH: I am very glad to have you say that.

MR. LOWE: I say it, sir, without fear of contradiction.

SENATOR SMITH: I am not contradicting you, and I congratulate you upon it; but so many stories have been circulated; one has just been passed up to me now, from a reputable man, who says it was reported that you were drinking that night.

MR. LOWE: Me, sir?

SENATOR SMITH: That is the reason I asked the question.

MR. LOWE: No, sir; this [indicating a glass of water] is the strongest drink I ever take.

SENATOR SMITH: That there might not be any misunderstanding about it, I asked that question. You retired at 8 o'clock that night?

MR. LOWE: I was supposed to retire.

SENATOR SMITH: You retired from your duty?

MR. LOWE: I was relieved from the ship at 8 o'clock. . . .

SENATOR SMITH: What time did you go to bed that Sunday night?

Mr. Lowe: I went between 8:15 and 8:30.

Senator Smith: What time were you awakened?

Mr. Lowe: I do not know. I was awakened by hearing voices, and I thought it was very strange, and somehow they woke me up and I realized there must be something the matter; so I looked out and I saw a lot of people around, and I jumped up and got dressed and went up on deck.

Senator Smith: What did you find when you got up there?

Mr. Lowe: I found that all the passengers were wearing belts.

Senator Smith: Life belts?

Mr. Lowe: Yes, sir; I also found that they were busy getting the boats ready to go overboard.

Senator Smith: What did you do?

Mr. Lowe: I met somebody, and they said she had struck an iceberg, and I could feel by my feet that there was something wrong.

Senator Smith: What—a listing?

Mr. Lowe: No. I heard that term applied yesterday, and it is wrong. It is not listing; it is tipping.

Senator Smith: I suppose he meant tipping when he said listing; but did she tip?

Mr. Lowe: This is sideways [indicating].

Senator Smith: Could you feel her tip sideways?

Mr. Lowe: No; there was no listing. Listing is the side motion and tipping is the end motion. She was by the bow; she was very much by the bow. She had a grade downhill; a grade like that [indicating].

Senator Smith: The bow, you say, was down?

Mr. Lowe: Down, and the stern was up.

Senator Smith: Could you tell at about what angle she was at that time?

Mr. Lowe: Do you want the perpendicular angle or the horizontal angle?

Senator Smith: The horizontal angle.

Mr. Lowe: I should say she was about 12° to 15° by the head.

Senator Smith: How long was that after the impact?

Mr. Lowe: I do not know, sir.

Senator Smith: You did not feel the impact?

Mr. Lowe: I never felt anything.

Senator Smith: You do not know how long that was?

MR. LOWE: I have not the slightest idea of the time, sir, because I had Greenwich time on me, and I did not look at my watch.

SENATOR SMITH: You were not aroused from your slumber by anyone?

MR. LOWE: No, sir. Mr. Boxhall, the fourth officer, told me that he told me that we had struck an iceberg, but I do not remember it.

SENATOR SMITH: You do not remember his telling you that?

MR. LOWE: I do not remember his telling me that.

SENATOR SMITH: That is, while you were——

MR. LOWE: It must have been while I was asleep. You must remember that we do not have any too much sleep and therefore when we sleep we die.

SENATOR SMITH: Now, what did you do after you went out on the deck and ascertained the position of the ship in the water, and saw what had occurred?

MR. LOWE: I first of all went and got my revolver.

SENATOR SMITH: What for?

MR. LOWE: Well, sir; you never know when you will need it.

SENATOR SMITH: All right; go ahead.

MR. LOWE: Then I went and helped everybody all around. Let us see; I crossed over to the starboard side. I lowered away. The first boat I helped to lower was No. 5, starboard boat. I lowered that boat away——

SENATOR SMITH: You lowered No. 5 boat?

MR. LOWE: Yes. That is, under the orders of Mr. Murdoch.

SENATOR SMITH: Did Mr. Murdoch assist you?

MR. LOWE: No; he was the senior officer; I was the junior.

SENATOR SMITH: On that side of the ship?

MR. LOWE: Yes.

SENATOR SMITH: Was he superintending?

MR. LOWE: He was superintending that deck.

SENATOR SMITH: The loading?

MR. LOWE: He was in charge of everything there.

SENATOR SMITH: The loading and the lowering of the lifeboats?

MR. LOWE: Yes, sir.

SENATOR SMITH: How many officers or men were there to assist you with lifeboat No. 5?

MR. LOWE: I could not very well answer that; but I should

say that there were about 6. No; more than 6; there must have been more than 6. There were about 10, I should say.

SENATOR SMITH: All around the station?

MR. LOWE: It takes 2 at each winch. Then there were 2 jumped in each boat. Then there were some clearing the falls—that is, the ropes—and you can roughly estimate it at 10 men.

SENATOR SMITH: Who got into the boat, do you know?

MR. LOWE: How do you mean?

SENATOR SMITH: You say two got into the boat? Who were the two?

MR. LOWE: Oh, I do not know, sir.

SENATOR SMITH: Do you know any of the men who assisted you in lowering that lifeboat?

MR. LOWE: No, sir; I do not, by name. But there is a man here, and had he not been here I should not have known that I had ordered Mr. Ismay away from the boat.

SENATOR SMITH: Did you order Mr. Ismay away from the boat?

MR. LOWE: I did, sir.

SENATOR SMITH: What did you say to him?

MR. LOWE: This was on the starboard side. I don't know his name, but I know him by sight. He is a steward. He spoke to me on board the *Carpathia*. He asked me if I knew what I had said to Mr. Ismay. I said, "I don't know Mr. Ismay." "Well," he said, "you used very, very strong language with him." I said, "Did I?" I said, "I can not help it if I did." He said, "Yes, you did," and he repeated the words. If you wish me to repeat them I will do so; if you do not, I will not.

SENATOR SMITH: I will first ask you this: What was the occasion for your using this harsh language to Mr. Ismay?

MR. LOWE: The occasion for using the language I did was because Mr. Ismay was overanxious and he was getting a trifle excited. He said, "Lower away! Lower away! Lower away!" I said—well, let it be——

MR. ISMAY: Give us what you said.

MR. LOWE: The chairman is examining me.

SENATOR SMITH: Mr. Ismay, you asked the witness to give the language?

MR. ISMAY: I have no objection to his giving it. It was not very parliamentary.

SENATOR SMITH: If the language is inappropriate——

MR. LOWE: There is only one word that might be so considered.

MR. ISMAY: May I suggest that it be put on a piece of paper and given to you, Mr. Chairman, and you decide.

SENATOR SMITH: All right; write it down. [The witness, Mr. Lowe, wrote something on a piece of paper and handed it to the chairman.]

SENATOR SMITH: You may put that into the record. You said you——

MR. LOWE: You wish me to repeat it, sir?

SENATOR SMITH: You uttered this to Mr. Ismay?

MR. LOWE: Yes; that was in the heat of the moment.

SENATOR SMITH: What was the occasion of it; because of his excitement, because of his anxiety?

MR. LOWE: Because he was, in a way, interfering with my duties, and also, of course, he only did this because he was anxious to get the people away and also to help me.

SENATOR SMITH: What did you say to him?

MR. LOWE: Do you want me to repeat that statement?

SENATOR SMITH: Yes, sir.

MR. LOWE: I told him, "If you will get to hell out of that I shall be able to do something."

SENATOR SMITH: What reply did he make?

MR. LOWE: He did not make any reply. I said, "Do you want me to lower away quickly?" I said, "You will have me drown the whole lot of them." I was on the floor myself lowering away.

SENATOR SMITH: You were on the boat deck, standing on the deck of the boat, the upper deck; and where did he stand?

MR. LOWE: He was at the ship's side, like this [indicating]. This is the ship—he was hanging on the davit like this [indicating]. He said, "Lower away, lower away, lower away," and I was slacking away just here at his feet [indicating].

SENATOR SMITH: The boat was being lowered?

MR. LOWE: I was lowering away the boat myself, personally.

SENATOR SMITH: I want you to say what he did after you said this to him?

Mr. Lowe: He walked away; and then he went to No. 3 boat.

Senator Smith: Alongside of yours?

Mr. Lowe: The next boat forward of mine; that is, on the same side; and I think he went ahead there on his own hook, getting things ready there, to the best of his ability. . . .

Senator Smith: From what you saw, was that boat loaded carefully, to its proper capacity, that night?

Mr. Lowe: The lowering of that boat was not up to me.

Senator Smith: I am not asking that; I did not ask you that at all. Read the question. If you will answer my questions we will make much better progress.

[The reporter repeated the question as follows:
From what you saw, was that boat loaded carefully, to its proper capacity, that night?]

Mr. Lowe: You pull me up about going around explaining matters to you, so I do not see how I can very well get at it if you pull me up on it.

Senator Smith: I am not pulling you up.

Mr. Lowe: I say, it is a matter of opinion whether that boat was properly filled or not.

Senator Smith: I want your opinion.

Mr. Lowe: And that depends on the man in charge of that said boat.

Senator Smith: Let me say this to you, Mr. Lowe: Nobody is on trial here, and this is not a court; this is an inquiry. You stood there and helped load this boat, and the man who had charge of it did not survive. Now I ask you whether, in your judgment, No. 5 lifeboat was properly loaded to its capacity for safety, considering the condition of the weather and the condition of the sea? You certainly can answer that.

Mr. Lowe: Yes; she was, as regards lowering.

Senator Smith: What is the capacity of a lifeboat like that under the British regulations?

Mr. Lowe: Sixty-five point five.

Senator Smith: What do you mean by "point five"? Do you mean a little more?

Mr. Lowe: A boy, or something like that.

Senator Smith: A little below 65 or a little above it?

Mr. Lowe: More than 65; 65.5.

Senator Smith: I want that understood. Do you wish the

committee to understand that a lifeboat whose capacity is 65 under the British regulations could not be lowered with safety, with new tackle and equipment, containing more than 50 people?

MR. LOWE: The dangers are that if you overcrowd the boat the first thing that you will have will be that the boat will buckle up like that [indicating] at the two ends, because she is suspended from both ends and there is no support in the middle.

SENATOR SMITH: These lifeboats were all on the upper deck?

MR. LOWE: Yes, sir.

SENATOR SMITH: If it is dangerous to lower a boat from the upper deck, filled to the capacity prescribed by the British regulations——

MR. LOWE: Yes; that is the floating capacity.

SENATOR SMITH: Sixty-five plus is the floating capacity?

MR. LOWE: That is the floating capacity; that is, in the water, when she is at rest in the water. That is not when she is in the air.

SENATOR SMITH: I am coming to that. Then 50 would be the lowering capacity, in your judgment?

MR. LOWE: Yes; I should not like to put more than 50 in. . . .

SENATOR SMITH: Did you see families separated?

MR. LOWE: I did.

SENATOR SMITH: Do you know who they were?

MR. LOWE: Yes.

SENATOR SMITH: Was there anything special that occurred at such times?

MR. LOWE: Well, when I was going in my boat—that is, No. 14—do you wish me to go on and tell it?

SENATOR SMITH: No; I am talking about No. 3 and No. 5, when they were being loaded and families were being separated.

MR. LOWE: I did not see any at those boats; no.

SENATOR SMITH: And was there any demonstration?

MR. LOWE: No.

SENATOR SMITH: Everything was quiet?

MR. LOWE: Everything was quiet and orderly.

SENATOR SMITH: Was there any weeping or lamentation?

MR. LOWE: No, not that I heard.

SENATOR SMITH: And with everything quiet and orderly, who selected the persons to fill these boats?

215

Mr. Lowe: Let us see. Mr. Murdoch was on No. 5 and No. 3. Then I took one——

Senator Smith: No, do not get away from these two. I will get to the other later. Was it a part of your duty to select the people who were to get into lifeboat No. 3 and lifeboat No. 5?

Mr. Lowe: Yes; I aided Mr. Murdoch generally, but——

Senator Smith: What did you do about it yourself? Did you arbitrarily select from the deck?

Mr. Lowe: You say "select." There was no such thing as selecting. It was simply the first woman, whether first class, second class, third class, or sixty-seventh class. It was all the same; women and children were first.

Senator Smith: You mean that there was a procession of women——

Mr. Lowe: The first woman was first into the boat, and the second woman was second into the boat, no matter whether she was a first-class passenger or any other class.

Senator Smith: So there was a procession——

Mr. Lowe: A procession at both ends of the boat.

Senator Smith: Coming toward these lifeboats?

Mr. Lowe: Yes.

Senator Smith: Did that extend beyond the upper deck?

Mr. Lowe: No; no; there were only little knots around the deck, little crowds.

Senator Smith: Now, as they came along, you would pass them, one at a time, into the lifeboat? What orders did you have; to pass women and children?

Mr. Lowe: I simply shouted, "Women and children first; men stand back."

Senator Smith: Do you know how many women there were on the boat?

Mr. Lowe: I do not, sir.

Senator Smith: You put them aboard as they came along, the first being served first?

Mr. Lowe: The first, first; second, second.

Senator Smith: Regardless of class?

Mr. Lowe: Regardless of class, or nationality, or pedigree.

Senator Smith: If it happened to be a stewardess——

Mr. Lowe: Yes; just the same, if she was a woman.

Senator Smith: Or other woman employee?

Mr. Lowe: Any women.

SENATOR SMITH: Or passenger; you made no distinction, but put them into the lifeboat?

MR. LOWE: No distinction whatsoever. Even if we had wished to draw a distinction, to select them, as you might call it, we would not know who were the stewardesses and who were not.

SENATOR SMITH: I have not asked you to go into that at all. I think you stated it very clearly, that you took the first woman who came and asked no questions. Now, when you filled lifeboat No. 5, did the women hesitate or demur about going in, or were they anxious to go?

MR. LOWE: Well, I do not remember about that particular boat; but during the course of the evening I distinctly remember saying "One more woman," or "Two more women," or "Three more women," and they would step forward and I would pass them into the boat.

SENATOR SMITH: Did you not ever call for women passengers and not get any?

MR. LOWE: Mr. Murdoch said, "That will do," and it was stopped. Then, "Lower away."

SENATOR SMITH: But you feel quite confident that there were 50 people in lifeboat No.——

MR. LOWE (interposing): I do not, sir. I want you to understand that I can not judge with any degree of accuracy how many people there were in it.

SENATOR SMITH: Let it stand that way. We will not talk about it; we will just let it stand that way.

MR. LOWE: That was simply as near as I can judge.

SENATOR SMITH: In loading boat No. 3, did you take the same course?

MR. LOWE: Yes; the same proceedings.

SENATOR SMITH: Did Officer Murdoch have charge of that boat?

MR. LOWE: Yes; he was there up to the finishing of No. 3.

SENATOR SMITH: Did Mr. Ismay assist in filling that boat?

MR. LOWE: Yes; he assisted there, too.

SENATOR SMITH: You found him there when you turned from No. 5 to No. 3?

MR. LOWE: He was there, and I distinctly remember seeing him alongside of me—that is, by my side—when the first detonator went off. I will tell you how I happen to remember it so distinctly. It was because the flash of the detonator lit up the whole deck. I did not know who Mr. Ismay was then, but I learned afterwards who he was, and he was standing alongside of me.

SENATOR SMITH: Did you say anything to him?

MR. LOWE: I did not. . . .

SENATOR SMITH: I want to get the number of women, if you can tell, who were put into lifeboat No. 3.

MR. LOWE: I can not tell. I do not know.

SENATOR SMITH: Or the number of men?

MR. LOWE: I do not know, sir. I can not tell.

SENATOR SMITH: Or the number of sailors?

MR. LOWE: I know there must have been pretty nearly an equal percentage of men and women in No. 3.

SENATOR SMITH: How do you know that?

MR. LOWE: Because there were not many women there.

SENATOR SMITH: Not many women there to respond?

MR. LOWE: No, sir.

SENATOR SMITH: And so you took men?

MR. LOWE: Yes, sir; so as to get the lifeboats away.

SENATOR SMITH: And you do not know what men were in No. 3?

MR. LOWE: No, sir.

SENATOR SMITH: Were there any officers in it?

MR. LOWE: No. As I told you before, Mr. Pitman was either in No. 3 or No. 5; which one I do not know.

SENATOR SMITH: But there were no other officers in lifeboat No. 3?

MR. LOWE: No, sir.

SENATOR SMITH: It was about equally filled with men and women, you say?

MR. LOWE: I should say so.

SENATOR SMITH: Any children in lifeboat No. 3?

MR. LOWE: I do not know; I do not remember.

SENATOR SMITH: Do you know whether any of those men who filled lifeboat No. 3 were of the crew; or were they passengers?

MR. LOWE: I can not say.

SENATOR SMITH: What is your judgment in regard to that?

MR. LOWE: As far as I know—of course I gave preference to the male passengers, I should say, to the passengers rather than the crew. Do you understand me?

SENATOR SMITH: Yes. How many were there in lifeboat No. 3, in your opinion?

MR. LOWE: I do not know, sir.

SENATOR SMITH: Was it loaded?

MR. LOWE: She was not very heavily loaded. I should say 40 to 45, maybe. We will say 40.

SENATOR SMITH: The same sized boat as No. 5?

MR. LOWE: The same sized boat; yes.

SENATOR SMITH: Did you have any difficulty in lowering it?

MR. LOWE: No, sir; absolutely none.

SENATOR SMITH: Did you have any difficulty in manning her?

MR. LOWE: No, sir; none.

SENATOR SMITH: How did it happen that you did not put more people into lifeboat No. 3 than 45?

MR. LOWE: There did not seem to be any people there.

SENATOR SMITH: You did not find anybody that wanted to go?

MR. LOWE: Those that were there did not seem to want to go. I hollered out, "Who's next for the boat?" and there was no response. . . .

SENATOR SMITH: Where did you next go?

MR. LOWE: I next went across the dock.

SENATOR SMITH: To the other side?

MR. LOWE: To the other side, that is, the port side, and I met the sixth officer, [James] Moody, and asked Moody, "What are you doing?" He said, "I am getting these boats away." So we filled both 14 and 16 with women and children.

SENATOR SMITH: Which one did you fill first?

MR. LOWE: No. 14. I did not fill 16; Moody filled 16.

SENATOR SMITH: You filled 14?

MR. LOWE: Yes.

SENATOR SMITH: Was Mr. Lightoller, the second officer, there?

MR. LOWE: He was there a part of the time, and he went away somewhere else. He must have gone to the second boat forward.

SENATOR SMITH: Who had charge of the loading of lifeboat No. 14?

MR. LOWE: I had.

SENATOR SMITH: And how many people did you put into it?

MR. LOWE: Fifty-eight.

SENATOR SMITH: How many women; do you know?

MR. LOWE: They were all women and children, bar one passenger, who was an Italian, and he sneaked in, and he was dressed like a woman.

SENATOR SMITH: Had woman's clothing on?

MR. LOWE: He had a shawl over his head, and everything else; and I only found out at the last moment. And there was another passenger that I took for rowing.

SENATOR SMITH: Who was that?

MR. LOWE: That was a chap by the name of C. Williams. . . .

SENATOR SMITH: You say there were how many people in your boat?

MR. LOWE: Fifty-eight, sir.

SENATOR SMITH: And that was when you left the davits?

MR. LOWE: That was when I left the davits.

SENATOR SMITH: How many people got into that boat after it reached the water, or at any other deck?

MR. LOWE: None, sir. You see, I chased all of my passengers out of my boat and emptied her into four other boats that I had. I herded five boats all together.

SENATOR SMITH: Yes; what were they?

MR. LOWE: I was in No. 14. Then I had 10, I had 12, and I had another collapsible, and one other boat the number of which I do not know. I herded them together and roped them—made them all tie up—and of course I had to wait until the yells and shrieks had subsided—for the people to thin out—and then I deemed it safe for me to go amongst the wreckage. So I transferred all my passengers—somewhere about 53 passengers—from my boat, and I equally distributed them between my other four boats. Then I asked for volunteers to go with me to the wreck, and it was at this time that I found this Italian. He came aft, and he had a shawl over his head and I suppose he had skirts. Anyhow, I pulled this shawl off his face and saw he was a man. He was in a great hurry to get into the other boat, and I caught hold of him and pitched him in.

SENATOR SMITH: Pitched him in?

MR. LOWE: Yes; because he was not worthy of being handled better.

SENATOR SMITH: You pitched him in among the women?

MR. LOWE: No, sir; in the fore part of the lifeboat in which I transferred my passengers.

SENATOR SMITH: Did you use some pretty emphatic language when you did that?

MR. LOWE: No, sir; I did not say a word to him.

SENATOR SMITH: Just picked him up and pitched him into this other lifeboat?

MR. LOWE: Yes. Then I went off and I rowed off to the wreckage and around the wreckage and I picked up four people.

SENATOR SMITH: Dead or alive?

MR. LOWE: Four alive.

SENATOR SMITH: Who were they?

MR. LOWE: I do not know.

SENATOR SMITH: Have you ever found out?

MR. LOWE: I do not know who those three live persons were; they never came near me afterwards, either to say this, that, or the other. But one died, and that was a Mr. Hoyt, of New York, and it took all the boat's crew to pull this gentleman into the boat, because he was an enormous man, and I suppose he had been soaked fairly well with water, and when we picked him up he was bleeding from the mouth and from the nose. So we did get him on board and I propped him up at the stern of the boat, and we let go his collar, took his collar off, and loosened his shirt so as to give him every chance to breathe; but, unfortunately, he died. I suppose he was too far gone when we picked him up. But the other three survived. I then left the wreck. I went right around and, strange to say, I did not see a single female body, not one, around the wreckage.

SENATOR SMITH: Did you have a light in your boat?

MR. LOWE: No, sir. I left my crowd of boats somewhere, I should say, about between half past 3 and 4 in the morning, and after I had been around it was just breaking day, and I am quite satisfied that I had a real good look around, and that there was nothing left.

SENATOR SMITH: Now, I am going to stop you there just for a moment. You can tell what you did then?

MR. LOWE: Then what?

SENATOR SMITH: After you looked around, then what did you do?

MR. LOWE: I then thought—well, the thought flashed

through my mind, "Perhaps the ship has not seen us in the semigloom."

SENATOR SMITH: The *Carpathia?*

MR. LOWE: Yes. I could see her coming up, and I thought, "Well, I am the fastest boat of the lot," as I was sailing, you see. I was going through the water very nicely, going at about, well, I should say, four knots, five knots, maybe; it may have been a little more; it may have been six; but, anyhow, I was bowling along very nicely.

SENATOR SMITH: In the direction of the *Carpathia?*

MR. LOWE: In the direction of the *Carpathia.* And I thought, "I am the fastest boat, and I think if I go toward her, for fear of her leaving us to our doom"—that is what I was scared about, and you will understand that day was dawning more and more as the time came on.

SENATOR SMITH: I assume that to be so.

MR. LOWE: And by and by, I noticed a collapsible boat, and it looked rather sorry, so I thought, "Well, I will go down and pick her up and make sure of her." So I went about and sailed down to this collapsible, and took her in tow. . . .

SENATOR SMITH: I want to take you back a moment. Before you transferred the 53 people from your lifeboat, No. 14, to other lifeboats, including this Italian in woman's attire, you say you lay off a bit. Where; how far from the *Titanic?*

MR. LOWE: I lay off from the *Titanic,* as near as I could roughly estimate, about 150 yards, because I wanted to be close enough in order to pick up anybody that came by.

SENATOR SMITH: I understand; but you said you lay off a bit to wait until it quieted down.

MR. LOWE: Yes.

SENATOR SMITH: Until what quieted down?

MR. LOWE: Until the drowning people had thinned out.

SENATOR SMITH: You lay off a bit until the drowning people had quieted down?

MR. LOWE: Yes.

SENATOR SMITH: Then you went to the scene of the wreck?

MR. LOWE: Yes.

SENATOR SMITH: Had their cries quieted down before you started?

MR. LOWE: Yes; they had subsided a good deal. It would not have been wise or safe for me to have gone there before, because the whole lot of us would have been swamped and then nobody would have been saved.

SENATOR SMITH: But your boat had, according to your own admission, a water capacity of 65 people?

MR. LOWE: Yes; but then what are you going to do with a boat of 65 where 1,600 people are drowning?

SENATOR SMITH: You could have saved 15.

MR. LOWE: You could not do it, sir.

SENATOR SMITH: At least, you made no attempt to do it?

MR. LOWE: I made the attempt, sir, as soon as any man could do so, and I am not scared of saying it. I did not hang back or anything else.

SENATOR SMITH: I am not saying you hung back. I am just saying that you said you lay by until it had quieted down.

MR. LOWE: You had to do so. It was absolutely not safe. You could not do otherwise, because you would have hundreds of people around your boat, and the boat would go down just like that [indicating].

SENATOR SMITH: About how long did you lay by?

MR. LOWE: I should say an hour and a half; somewhere under two hours.

SENATOR SMITH: On your oars?

MR. LOWE: No; we did not. We unshipped our oars, and I made the five boats fast together and we hung on like that.

SENATOR SMITH: Did you see the *Titanic* sink?

MR. LOWE: I did, sir.

SENATOR SMITH: How long after you left her side in the lifeboat did she sink?

MR. LOWE: I suppose about half an hour. No—yes; somewhere about half an hour.

SENATOR SMITH: Then you laid an hour after she sank?

MR. LOWE: An hour after she sank.

SENATOR SMITH: Before going to the scene of the wreck?

MR. LOWE: Before going to the scene of the wreck.

SENATOR SMITH: You were about 150 yards off?

MR. LOWE: I was just on the margin. If anybody had struggled out of the mass, I was there to pick them up; but it was useless for me to go into the mass.

SENATOR SMITH: You mean for anybody?

Mr. Lowe: It would have been suicide. . . .

Senator Smith: . . . When you went alongside the *Carpathia,* how many people were in your boat?

Mr. Lowe: There were about 45.

Senator Smith: Where did you get them?

Mr. Lowe: I got them out of the sinking collapsible.

Senator Smith: An overturned collapsible?

Mr. Lowe: No, sir; it was a collapsible that some wreckage had pierced. I was coming to that when you stopped me.

Senator Smith: I would like to have you come to it now.

Mr. Lowe: I had taken this first collapsible in tow, and I noticed that there was another collapsible in a worse plight than this one that I had in tow. I was just thinking and wondering whether it would be better for me to cut this one adrift and let her go, and for me to travel faster to the sinking one, but I thought, "No, I think I can manage it"; so I cracked on a bit, and I got down there just in time and took off, I suppose, about 20 men and 1 lady out of this sinking collapsible.

Senator Smith: Did you leave any bodies on there?

Mr. Lowe: I left three bodies on it.

Senator Smith: What was the number of that boat?

Mr. Lowe: I do not know, sir; it was one of the collapsibles.

Senator Smith: But you took off of it 20 men?

Mr. Lowe: About 20 men.

Senator Smith: And three women?

Mr. Lowe: One woman?

Senator Smith: And left on board how many?

Mr. Lowe: Three male bodies.

Senator Smith: So that in this damaged collapsible there were 24 people, all together?

Mr. Lowe: Twenty-one and three are twenty-four, all together; yes, sir.

Senator Smith: What became of the other three that you left on it?

Mr. Lowe: As to the three people that I left on her—of course, I may have been a bit hard hearted, I can not say—but I thought to myself, "I am not here to worry about bodies; I am here for life, to save life, and not to bother about bodies," and I left them.

Senator Smith: Were they dead when you left them?

Mr. Lowe: They were dead; yes, sir. The people on the raft

told me they had been dead some time. I said, "Are you sure they are dead?" They said, "Absolutely sure." I made certain they were dead, and questioned them one and all before I left this collapsible.

SENATOR SMITH: Did you attempt to find anything on their persons that would identify them?

MR. LOWE: No, sir; I did not.

SENATOR SMITH: Do you know whether anyone did?

MR. LOWE: No, sir; nobody; because they were all up to their ankles in water when I took them off. Another three minutes and they would have been down.

SENATOR SMITH: From what you saw of these three persons would you say, or could you say, whether they were old or young?

MR. LOWE: No, sir; I would not like to state anything. All that I can state is that they were male.

SENATOR SMITH: They were men?

MR. LOWE: Yes.

SENATOR SMITH: Were they of the crew or passengers?

MR. LOWE: That I would not like to say.

SENATOR SMITH: You could not tell?

MR. LOWE: No, sir.

SENATOR SMITH: Did they have life preservers on, or did they not?

MR. LOWE: I think they had life belts on.

SENATOR SMITH: Have you ever learned since that night who those three people were?

MR. LOWE: No, sir.

SENATOR SMITH: Mr. Lowe, after taking these passengers from that collapsible that was injured, you headed in the direction of the *Carpathia?*

MR. LOWE: Yes; I left for the *Carpathia.*

SENATOR SMITH: Did you succeed in landing them?

MR. LOWE: I landed everybody.

SENATOR SMITH: All of them?

MR. LOWE: And the corpse included.

SENATOR SMITH: Including the corpse of the man that had died on your boat?

MR. LOWE: Yes.

SENATOR SMITH: What, if anything, did you do after that?

MR. LOWE: There was nothing to do, sir. What was there to do?

225

SENATOR SMITH: I did not say there was anything. I simply asked what you did.

MR. LOWE: No, sir; there was nothing to do. . . .

SENATOR SMITH: . . . One more question and I will let you go. Did you hear any pistol shots?

MR. LOWE: Yes.

SENATOR SMITH: And by whom were they fired Sunday night?

MR. LOWE: I heard them, and I fired them.

SENATOR SMITH: Where?

MR. LOWE: As I was going down the decks, and that was as I was being lowered down.

SENATOR SMITH: In lifeboat——

MR. LOWE: Lifeboat No. 14.

SENATOR SMITH: What did you do?

MR. LOWE: As I was going down the decks I knew, or I expected every moment, that my boat would double up under my feet. I was quite scared of it, although of course it would not do for me to mention the fact to anybody else. I had overcrowded her, but I knew that I had to take a certain amount of risk. So I thought, "Well, I shall have to see that nobody else gets into the boat or else it will be a case"——

SENATOR SMITH: That was as it was being lowered?

MR. LOWE: Yes; I thought if one additional body was to fall into that boat, that slight jerk of the additional weight might part the hooks or carry away something, no one would know what. There were a hundred and one things to carry away. Then, I thought, well, I will keep an eye open. So, as we were coming down the decks, coming down past the open decks, I saw a lot of Italians, Latin people, all along the ship's rails—understand, it was open—and they were all glaring, more or less like wild beasts, ready to spring. That is why I yelled out to look out, and let go, bang, right along the ship's side.

SENATOR SMITH: How far from the ship's side was the lifeboat you were in?

MR. LOWE: I really do not know. I should say—oh, 3 or 4 feet. . . .

SENATOR SMITH: And as you went down you fired these shots?

MR. LOWE: As I went down I fired these shots and without intention of hurting anybody and also with the knowledge that I did not hurt anybody.

226

SENATOR SMITH: You are positive of that?

MR. LOWE: I am absolutely positive.

SENATOR SMITH: How do you know?

MR. LOWE: How do I know? Because I looked where I fired.

SENATOR SMITH: It was a dark night, was it not, to see?

MR. LOWE: Oh, but I could see where I was shooting. A man does not want to shoot over here and look over here [indicating], or to shoot here and look here [indicating], but to look where he shoots. I shot between the boat and the ship's side, so these people would hear and see the discharge.

SENATOR SMITH: You shot this revolver through that 3-foot space?

MR. LOWE: Yes; I think I fired three times. There were three decks. . . .

SENATOR SMITH: You are positive you did not hit anybody?

MR. LOWE: I am absolutely positive I hit nobody. . . .

Witness: Charles Lightoller
Titanic's Second Officer

Key testimony: In his second appearance before the inquiry, he defended Ismay, his boss and the man who held sway over his seagoing career. After the sinking, the White Star director had tried, via wireless from the rescue ship Carpathia, *to detain the White Star liner* Cedric *in New York so he and the* Titanic's *surviving crew could catch it for a hasty return trip home. That raised suspicions that Ismay was trying to avoid American investigators. But Lightoller told the skeptical Senators that the surviving crew members needed to return to their livelihoods right away. He added that Ismay was actually in anguish over the fact he had survived while some women passengers hadn't. And he said Ismay in fact had been ordered into a lifeboat by the* Titanic's *chief officer, who did not survive.*

. . . SENATOR BURTON [Theodore E. Burton, Republican of Ohio]: I understand you have some information in regard to the messages to the *Cedric,* and in regard to some conversations with Mr. Ismay. Please state them both.

MR. LIGHTOLLER: Previous to having the conversation with Mr. Ismay in regard to any telegrams that were sent to our office in New York with reference to holding the *Cedric*, the other three officers and myself had spoken about it casually, saying we knew the *Cedric* was in, and we thought it a jolly good idea if we could get home with her if we were in time to catch her. We were very much disappointed at the delay through fog. We were saying all the time, "It is a great pity if we will miss the *Cedric*. If we could only get home in time to get everybody on board the *Cedric*, we shall probably be able to keep the men together as much as possible." Otherwise, you understand, once the men get in New York, naturally these men are not going to hang around New York or hang around anywhere else. They want to get to sea to earn money to keep their wives and families, and they would ship off. You can not find a sailor but what will ship off at once if he gets the opportunity. They simply would stand this off as a loss or stand it off as a bad debt, and probably try to ship off somewhere. Its a case like this, where the men are brought into prominence, they are very frequently offered berths immediately. Certain of the steerage passengers were offered berths by the saloon passengers. They were offered berths to go and be servants, or whatever it was until they found employment.

Our crew would in all probability have done the same and we would have lost a number of them, probably some very important witnesses. They would perhaps ship on some yacht, which very often they do. A great many of them, quartermasters especially, ship on gentlemen's yachts in New York, because they know they are thoroughly capable men. They are just as good men as they can obtain in the world, and there is great demand for them; much to our regret, because we lose them.

On having a conversation with Mr. Ismay he also mentioned about the *Cedric* and asked me my opinion about it, and I frankly stated that it was the best thing in the world to do if we could catch the *Cedric*.

Later on he remarked that owing to weather conditions it was very doubtful if we would catch the *Cedric*. I said, "Yes; it is doubtful. It will be a great pity if she sails without us." "Do you think it will be advisable to hold her up?" I said, "Most undoubtedly; the best thing in the world to hold her up."

A telegram was dispatched asking them to hold the *Cedric* until we got in, to which we received the reply that it was not advisable to hold the *Cedric*. He asked what I thought about it. I said, "I think we ought to hold her, and you ought to telegraph and insist on their holding her and preventing the crew getting around in New York." We discussed the pros and cons and deemed it advisable to keep the crew together as much as we could, so we could get home, and we might then be able to choose our important witnesses and let the remainder go to sea and earn money for themselves. So I believe the other telegram was sent.

I may say that at that time Mr. Ismay did not seem to me to be in a mental condition to finally decide anything. I tried my utmost to rouse Mr. Ismay, for he was obsessed with the idea, and kept repeating, that he ought to have gone down with the ship because he found that women had gone down. I told him there was no such reason; I told him a very great deal; I tried to get that idea out of his head, but he was taken with it; and I know the doctor tried, too; but we had difficulty in arousing Mr. Ismay, purely owing to that wholly and solely, that women had gone down in the boat and he had not.

You can call the doctor of the *Carpathia*, and he will verify that statement. . . .

SENATOR SMITH: As I understood you in your testimony in New York, your watch expired at 10 o'clock Sunday night?

MR. LIGHTOLLER: That is so.

SENATOR SMITH: If I recollect correctly, you took charge of the loading of the lifeboats.

MR. LIGHTOLLER: On the port side.

SENATOR SMITH: On the port side.

MR. LIGHTOLLER: The chief officer also loaded some of the boats on the port side. I may also say, in regard to the testimony in regard to Mr. Ismay, although I can not vouch for the source, yet it was given to me from a source such that I have every reason to believe its truth——

SENATOR SMITH: Before or since this occurred?

MR. LIGHTOLLER: Since.

SENATOR SMITH: When?

MR. LIGHTOLLER: On the *Carpathia*.

SENATOR SMITH: En route to New York?

MR. LIGHTOLLER: Yes.

SENATOR SMITH: Or after she had arrived?

MR. LIGHTOLLER: Before she arrived in New York.

SENATOR SMITH: Give the information.

MR. LIGHTOLLER: It is that Chief Officer [Henry] Wilde was at the starboard collapsible boat in which Mr. Ismay went away, and that he told Mr. Ismay, "There are no more women on board the ship." Wilde was a pretty big, powerful chap, and he was a man that would not argue very long. Mr. Ismay was right there. Naturally he was there close to the boat, because he was working at the boats and he had been working at the collapsible boat, and that is why he was there, and Mr. Wilde, who was near him, simply bundled him into the boat.

SENATOR SMITH: You did not say that before?

MR. LIGHTOLLER: No; but I believe it is true. I forget the source. I am sorry I have forgotten it.

SENATOR SMITH: Did Mr. Wilde survive?

MR. LIGHTOLLER: He did not.

SENATOR SMITH: Who relieved you on watch that night at 10 o'clock?

MR. LIGHTOLLER: The first officer, Mr. [William] Murdoch.

SENATOR SMITH: Did he survive?

MR. LIGHTOLLER: He did not.

SENATOR SMITH: Who told you that this powerful officer, Mr. Wilde, ordered Mr. Ismay to get into the boat?

MR. LIGHTOLLER: I do not know.

SENATOR SMITH: As I now recollect your testimony—and I have it here—you said you were not acquainted with Mr. Ismay.

MR. LIGHTOLLER: I have known Mr. Ismay for 14 years, since I first met him.

SENATOR SMITH: You did not speak to him that night?

MR. LIGHTOLLER: I did.

SENATOR SMITH: You told me that you looked at one another, and said nothing.

MR. LIGHTOLLER: I might not have spoken and I might have said "Good evening."

SENATOR SMITH: I mean after the collision——

MR. LIGHTOLLER: After the collision; no.

SENATOR SMITH: One moment. After the collision, you said, you saw Mr. Ismay standing on the deck?

MR. LIGHTOLLER: Yes.

SENATOR SMITH: Looking out at the sea?

MR. LIGHTOLLER: I do not know what he was looking at.

SENATOR SMITH: You were standing out on the deck about 20 feet from him?

MR. LIGHTOLLER: No, sir.

SENATOR SMITH: You say now that you did not say that?

MR. LIGHTOLLER: No, sir.

SENATOR SMITH: Would not that be true?

MR. LIGHTOLLER: I do not think so. I was walking along that side of the deck.

SENATOR SMITH: How far from Mr. Ismay?

MR. LIGHTOLLER: I walked past him, within a couple of feet of him.

SENATOR SMITH: And he said nothing to you, and you said nothing to him?

MR. LIGHTOLLER: I might have said "Good evening." Beyond that I said nothing. I had work on hand; something else to do.

SENATOR SMITH: Did he say anything else to you?

MR. LIGHTOLLER: Not that I know of. He may have said "Good evening." Perhaps I said that, and perhaps I did not. I do not remember.

SENATOR SMITH: In a great peril like that, passing the managing director of the company that owned the ship, you passed him on the ship, and said "Good evening"?

MR. LIGHTOLLER: I would, as I would to any passenger that I knew.

SENATOR SMITH: And he passed you and said "Good evening"?

MR. LIGHTOLLER: He was standing still.

SENATOR SMITH: And he said "Good evening"?

MR. LIGHTOLLER: I could not say. I say I may have said "Good evening" and may not, and he may have said it and may not.

SENATOR SMITH: I only want to know as well as you can recollect.

MR. LIGHTOLLER: I can not say for certain.

SENATOR SMITH: My recollection of the testimony is that you said you did not speak to him.

MR. LIGHTOLLER: I am not certain. If I did speak, it was purely to say "Good evening" and nothing more and nothing less. I spoke to Mr.——

SENATOR SMITH: How long was that after the collision?

MR. LIGHTOLLER: I think you will find that in the testimony.

SENATOR SMITH: I know I will find it there, but I want it again. Your recollection is just a little better to-day than it was the other day, and I would like to test it out a little.

MR. LIGHTOLLER: My mind was fresher on it then, perhaps, than it is now.

[The question was read by the stenographer, as follows: How long was that after the collision?]

MR. LIGHTOLLER: Oh, perhaps half an hour. . . .

SENATOR SMITH: You made a statement a few minutes ago about Mr. Ismay which evidently was a voluntary statement. No one asked you about it. Why did you not make that statement in New York?

MR. LIGHTOLLER: Because the controversy in regard to the telegram had not been brought up then, or brought to my knowledge; I mean all this paper talk there has been about this telegram.

SENATOR SMITH: Has there been paper talk about a telegram?

MR. LIGHTOLLER: Undoubtedly there has.

SENATOR SMITH: And that is the reason you were prompted to make this disclosure?

MR. LIGHTOLLER: Because I think I am principally responsible for the telegram being sent.

SENATOR SMITH: And you sent it?

MR. LIGHTOLLER: I did not.

SENATOR SMITH: You delivered it to the wireless?

MR. LIGHTOLLER: I did not.

SENATOR SMITH: Who did?

MR. LIGHTOLLER: I do not know.

SENATOR SMITH: Did you write it out?

MR. LIGHTOLLER: I did not.

SENATOR SMITH: Did you speak to the operator about it?

MR. LIGHTOLLER: I did not.

SENATOR SMITH: Have you spoken to him about it since?

MR. LIGHTOLLER: I have not.

SENATOR SMITH: But you wish to be understood as saying that you urged Mr. Ismay to send it?

MR. LIGHTOLLER: I did.

SENATOR SMITH: Do you know whether it was sent or not?

MR. LIGHTOLLER: I know it was sent.

SENATOR SMITH: How do you know it?

MR. LIGHTOLLER: Because Mr. Ismay told me it had been, and showed me the reply. . . .

Witness: Robert Hitchens, 30
Titanic's helmsman, at the wheel when the iceberg struck

Key testimony: He disputed passenger Peuchen's testimony about what happened in the lifeboat under his command, No. 6. He denied that women had pleaded with him to go back toward the wreck.

. . . SENATOR SMITH: I wish you would tell now, in your own way, what occurred that night from the time you went on watch until the collision occurred.

MR. HITCHENS: I went on watch at 8 o'clock. The officers on the watch were the second officer, Mr. Lightoller, senior in command; the fourth officer, Mr. Boxhall; and the sixth officer, Mr. Moody. My first orders when I got on the bridge was to take the second officer's compliments down to the ship's carpenter and inform him to look to his fresh water; that it was about to freeze. I did so. On the return to the bridge, I had been on the bridge about a couple of minutes when the carpenter came back and reported the duty carried out. Standing by waiting for another message—it is the duty of the quartermaster to strike the bell every half hour—as the stand-by quartermaster, sir, I heard the second officer repeat to Mr. Moody, the sixth officer, to speak through the telephone, warning the lookout men in the crow's nest to keep a sharp lookout for small ice until daylight and pass the word along to the other lookout men. The next order I received from the second officer was to go and find the deck engineer and bring him up with a key to open the heaters up in the corridor of the officers' quarters, also the wheelhouse and the chart room, on account of the intense cold. At a quarter to 10 I called the first officer, Mr. Murdoch, to let him know it was one bell, which is part of our duty; also took the thermometer and barometer, the temperature of the water, and the log. At 10 o'clock I went to the wheel, sir. Mr. Murdoch come up to relieve Mr. Lightoller. I had the course given me from the other quartermaster, north 71° west, which I repeated to him, and he went and reported it to the first officer or the second officer in charge, which he repeated back—the course, sir. All went along very well until 20 minutes to 12, when three gongs came from the lookout, and immediately afterwards a report on the telephone, "Iceberg right ahead." The chief officer rushed from the wing to the bridge, or I imagine so, sir. Certainly I am inclosed in the wheelhouse, and I can not see, only my compass. He rushed to the engines. I heard the telegraph bell ring; also give the order "Hard astarboard," with the sixth officer standing by me to see the duty carried out and the quartermaster standing by my left side. Repeated the order, "Hard astarboard. The helm is hard over, sir."

SENATOR SMITH: Who gave the first order?

MR. HITCHENS: Mr. Murdoch, the first officer, sir; the officer in charge. The sixth officer repeated the order, "The helm is hard astarboard, sir." But, during the time, she was crushing the ice, or we could hear the grinding noise along the ship's bottom. I heard the telegraph ring, sir. The skipper came rushing out of his room—Capt. Smith—and asked, "What is that?" Mr. Murdoch said, "An iceberg." He said, "Close the emergency doors."

SENATOR SMITH: Who said that, the captain?

MR. HITCHENS: Capt. Smith, sir, to Mr. Murdoch; "Close the emergency doors." Mr. Murdoch replied, "The doors are already closed." The captain sent then for the carpenter to sound the ship. He also came back to the wheelhouse and looked at the commutator in front of the compass, which is a little instrument like a clock to tell you how the ship is listing. The ship had a list of 5° to the starboard.

SENATOR SMITH: How long after the impact, or collision?

MR. HITCHENS: I could hardly tell you, sir. Judging roughly, about 5 minutes; about 5 to 10 minutes. I stayed to the wheel, then, sir, until 23 minutes past 12. I do not know whether they put the clock back or not. The clock was to go back that night 47 minutes, 23 minutes in one watch and 24 in the other.

SENATOR SMITH: Had the clock been set back up to the time you left the wheel?

MR. HITCHENS: I do not know, sir. I did not notice it.

SENATOR SMITH: When do you say you left the wheel, at 20 minutes after 12?

MR. HITCHENS: I left the wheel at 23 minutes past 12, sir. I was relieved by Quartermaster Perkins. He relieved me at 23 minutes past 12. I think the first officer, or one of the officers said, "That will do with the wheel; get the boats out." I went out to get the boats out on the port side. I think I got in No. 6 boat, sir; put in charge of her by the second officer, Mr. Lightoller. We lowered away from the ship, sir, and were told to "Pull toward that light," which we started to do, to pull for that light. I had 38 women in the boat, sir, 1 seaman and myself, with 2 male passengers, 1 Italian boy and a Canadian major who testified here yesterday.

SENATOR SMITH: Were you in charge of the boat?

MR. HITCHENS: I was; yes, sir. Everybody seemed in a very bad condition in the boat, sir. Everybody was quite upset, and I told them somebody would have to pull; there was no use stopping there alongside of the ship, and the ship gradually going by the head. We were in a dangerous place, so I told them to man the oars, ladies and all, "All of you do your best." We got away about a mile, I suppose, from the ship, going after this light, which we expected to be a "codbanker," a schooner that comes out on the Banks.

SENATOR SMITH: A fisherman's boat?

MR. HITCHENS: Yes, sir; we expected her to be that, sir; but we did not get any nearer the light. There were several other boats around us at this time and one boat that had no light came close up to us. He had four to six men in his boat and I borrowed one fireman from him to put in my boat, to enable me to pull. We did not seem to get any nearer the light, so we conversed together, and we tied our boats side by side. We stopped there until we saw the *Carpathia* heave in sight about daybreak. The wind had sprung up a bit then, and it got very choppy. I relieved one of the young ladies with the oar, and told her to take the tiller. She immediately let the boat come athwart, and the ladies in the boat got very nervous. So I took the tiller back again and told them to manage the best way they could.

SENATOR SMITH: Do you know who that woman was?

MR. HITCHENS: I do not, sir. They were all entire strangers to me, sir. But the lady I refer to, Mrs. Mayer, she was rather vexed with me in the boat and I spoke rather straight to her, and she accused me of wrapping myself up in the blankets in the boat, using bad language, and drinking all the whisky, which I deny, sir. I was standing to attention, exposed, steering the boat all night, which is a very cold billet. I would rather be pulling the boat than be steering. 0But I seen no one there to steer, so I thought, being in charge of the boat, it was the best way to steer myself, especially when I seen the ladies get very nervous with the nasty tumble on. We got down to the *Carpathia* and I seen every lady and everybody out of the boat, and I seen them carefully hoisted on board the *Carpathia*, and I was the last man to leave the boat. That is all I can tell you, sir.

SENATOR SMITH: I want to ask you a few questions. I would like to ask you whether you had any trouble with the major, between the *Titanic* and the *Carpathia*?

MR. HITCHENS: I had no trouble with him at all, sir, only once. He was not in the boat more than 10 minutes before he wanted to come and take charge of the boat.

SENATOR SMITH: What did you say to him?

MR. HITCHENS: I told him, "I am put here in charge of the boat." I said, "You go and do what you are told to do."

SENATOR SMITH: Did he say anything more to you?

MR. HITCHENS: He did not answer me, sir, but sat down; went forward on the starboard bow, alongside of Seaman Fleet, who was working very hard. He done most of the work himself; Fleet was doing most of the work.

SENATOR SMITH: That was the man who was in the crow's nest at the time the boat struck?

MR. HITCHENS: Yes, sir.

SENATOR SMITH: He was in your lifeboat, too?

MR. HITCHENS: Yes, sir.

SENATOR SMITH: Did you lie on your oars off the *Titanic* at any time before the *Titanic* went down?

MR. HITCHENS: Yes, sir.

SENATOR SMITH: How long?

MR. HITCHENS: Well, we had no time, sir; I could hardly tell you.

SENATOR SMITH: About how long?

MR. HITCHENS: That I could hardly tell you, sir, because our minds was thinking of other things, sir. I do know we did it, sir.

SENATOR SMITH: How far were you from the *Titanic* at the time she went down?

MR. HITCHENS: When we sighted the *Carpathia* we were about a mile from her.

SENATOR SMITH: No; when you were lying on your oars?

MR. HITCHENS: About 1 mile, sir.

SENATOR SMITH: About a mile from the *Titanic*?

MR. HITCHENS: Yes, sir.

SENATOR SMITH: Could you see the *Titanic*?

MR. HITCHENS: I could not see her; not after the lights went out; no, sir.

SENATOR SMITH: You could see the lights?

MR. HITCHENS: We could see the lights go out; yes, sir.

SENATOR SMITH: And you knew the location of the boat?

MR. HITCHENS: We heard the cries for an interval of about two or three minutes.

SENATOR SMITH: As the ship disappeared?

MR. HITCHENS: As the ship disappeared; yes, sir.

SENATOR SMITH: The major, who was in that boat with you, said yesterday that you were lying on your oars, drifting, and before the *Titanic* went down you heard cries of distress, and for help. Is that true?

MR. HITCHENS: I did not hear any cries as regarding distress. We heard a lot of crying and screaming. At one time we were made fast to another boat. We were not lying on our oars at all.

SENATOR SMITH: You made fast to another boat. What boat?

MR. HITCHENS: The boat the master-at-arms was in, sir. I think it was No. 8 boat. He left about the same time as we did.

SENATOR SMITH: You had 38 women in your boat?

MR. HITCHENS: Yes, sir; I counted them, sir.

SENATOR SMITH: And how many men?

MR. HITCHENS: I had [lookout Frederick] Fleet, myself——

SENATOR SMITH: Fleet, the major, and yourself?

MR. HITCHENS: And an Italian boy, sir.

SENATOR SMITH: That is four men?

MR. HITCHENS: Four, sir. But the Italian boy had a broken arm, sir.

SENATOR SMITH: Was he the one who was hid away?

MR. HITCHENS: I do not know how he managed to get on the boat at all sir; I do not know.

SENATOR SMITH: Was he dressed in woman's clothing?

MR. HITCHENS: No; I do not think so, sir.

SENATOR SMITH: During the time that you were lying off on your oars, and before the *Titanic* sank, did the women in your boat urge you to go toward the *Titanic*?

MR. HITCHENS: Not that I remember, sir. I am not aware of it.

SENATOR SMITH: Did they urge you not to go toward the *Titanic*?

MR. HITCHENS: Not that I am aware of, sir.

SENATOR SMITH: So far as you can recollect, did the women say nothing either one way or the other about it?

MR. HITCHENS: No, sir; not that I remember. In fact, under the conditions, with one seaman in the boat and myself to pull a big boat like that, and being a mile away from the *Titanic*—I did not know what course to take, we had no compass in the boat—it seemed impossible, sir.

SENATOR SMITH: The major said yesterday when you were asked to return to the source from which these distress cries came——

MR. HITCHENS: I read it in the paper, but that is continually false, sir.

SENATOR SMITH: That you said, "We are to look out for ourselves now, and pay no attention to those stiffs."

MR. HITCHENS: I never made use of that word, never since I have been born, because I use other words in preference to that.

SENATOR SMITH: Did you say anything about it?

MR. HITCHENS: Not that I am aware of, sir.

SENATOR SMITH: And you wish the committee to understand that you did not refuse to go to the relief of people in the water, either before or after the *Titanic* disappeared?

MR. HITCHENS: I could not, sir. I was too far away, and I had no compass to go back, to enable me to find where the cries came from. The cries I heard lasted about two minutes, and some of them were saying, "It is one boat aiding the other." There was another boat aside of me, the boat the master-at-arms was in, full right up.

SENATOR SMITH: How long after you were lying on your oars was it that the *Titanic* went down?

MR. HITCHENS: I could hardly tell you, sir.

SENATOR SMITH: Did you instruct the men in your boat to row away from the *Titanic* after it went down?

MR. HITCHENS: I did, sir.

SENATOR SMITH: Why did you not row toward the scene of the *Titanic?*

MR. HITCHENS: The suction of the ship would draw the boat, with all her occupants, under water, I thought, sir.

SENATOR SMITH: Is that the sole reason you did not go toward the *Titanic?*

MR. HITCHENS: I did not know which way to go back to the *Titanic.* I was looking at all the other boats; I was among all the other boats.

SENATOR SMITH: What other boats; the lifeboats?

MR. HITCHENS: We were all together; yes, sir.

SENATOR SMITH: Why were you looking at the lifeboats?

MR. HITCHENS: We were looking at each other's lights.

SENATOR SMITH: Did you have a light?

MR. HITCHENS: I did; yes, sir. We all had lights and were showing them to one another.

SENATOR SMITH: The lifeboats all had lights?

MR. HITCHENS: Most all of us. We kept all showing our lights now and then to let them know where we were, too.

SENATOR SMITH: Do you mean to tell me you would pass your time in showing one another your own lights, but did not go toward the *Titanic?*

MR. HITCHENS: Yes; but before the *Titanic* sank we were all pulling for a light which we thought was to be a cod banker. We all made for this light.

SENATOR SMITH: You made up your mind it was not the boat you thought it was? You thought it was a fishing boat?

MR. HITCHENS: We all thought so, and all pulled for that light.

SENATOR SMITH: You then pulled for that light, and finally discovered you were making no progress toward it?

Mr. Hitchens: Yes, sir.

Senator Smith: And you stopped?

Mr. Hitchens: We stopped then; yes, sir.

Senator Smith: And at that time you were a mile away from the *Titanic?*

Mr. Hitchens: Yes, sir; a mile or more, sir.

Senator Smith: And was the *Titanic* stil afloat?

Mr. Hitchens: The *Titanic* was still afloat, sir, and her lights all showing.

Senator Smith: How long after that did you see her go down?

Mr. Hitchens: I could hardly tell you. Probably 10 minutes after that her lights disappeared, but I did not see her go down.

Senator Smith: You, yourself, did not see her disappear?

Mr. Hitchens: No, sir.

Senator Smith: Was your back toward her?

Mr. Hitchens: We could not see her at all. When I seen the lights disappear, that was all I could see, because it was very dark.

Senator Smith: You sat at the tiller?

Mr. Hitchens: I was standing at the tiller.

Senator Smith: With your back to the ship?

Mr. Hitchens: Yes, sir.

Senator Smith: And you did not see her go down?

Mr. Hitchens: No, sir.

Senator Smith: After the lights disappeared and went out, did you then hear cries of distress?

Mr. Hitchens: We did hear cries of distress, or I imagined so, sir, for two or three minutes. Some of the men in the boat said it was the cries of one boat hailing the other. I suppose the reason they said this was not to alarm the women—the ladies in the boat.

Senator Smith: Did the Italian say that?

Mr. Hitchens: The Italian could not speak. I am not talking of our own men, but the boat close, near by.

Senator Smith: Some other boat?

Mr. Hitchens: Yes, sir; we were having conversation with them and the master-at-arms.

Senator Smith: You desire the committee to understand that you kept a safe distance from the *Titanic* after you got into the lifeboat; you made fast to the other lifeboat;

you went away from the *Titanic* about a mile; you lay there on your oars; you saw the *Titanic* go down, or saw the lights go out, and you did not go in that direction at all?

MR. HITCHENS: We did not know what direction to go, sir.

SENATOR SMITH: Did you, after the lights went out, go in the direction in which the lights were?

MR. HITCHENS: When the lights were gone out, we were still heading toward this cod banker, all of us.

SENATOR SMITH: That fishing boat was away from the *Titanic's* position?

MR. HITCHENS: Yes, sir, a good ways, sir.

SENATOR SMITH: You were heading for that?

MR. HITCHENS: Yes, sir.

SENATOR SMITH: When you left the *Titanic* in the lifeboat, did anyone tell you to take that load off and come back to the *Titanic?*

MR. HITCHENS: Yes, sir.

SENATOR SMITH: Who told you that?

MR. HITCHENS: I think it was the first officer or the second officer. I am not sure which officer it was.

SENATOR SMITH: Mr. Murdoch or Mr. Lightoller?

MR. HITCHENS: One of them; I am not sure which.

SENATOR SMITH: What did you say?

MR. HITCHENS: All right, we was willing to pull away for this light; but when we got down we told him we had to have one more man in the boat.

SENATOR SMITH: You wanted another man?

MR. HITCHENS: We wanted two or three more men if we could get them.

SENATOR SMITH: But you did not get them?

MR. HITCHENS: No, sir; only this major; he came down. He got in then, and that is all.

SENATOR SMITH: He swung himself out and got in, didn't he?

MR. HITCHENS: Yes, sir.

SENATOR BURTON: Did that call come back before the major got into the boat, or was it when you were away from the ship and rowing away?

MR. HITCHENS: When I got down to the bottom, when we were lowered down in the water, we only had one man there, one seaman besides myself.

SENATOR BURTON: Then you say it was the first or second officer called you to come back?

MR. HITCHENS: He told us to go away and make for the light. We had them orders before we went down below. We had no orders when we got to the water at all; we couldn't hear then.

SENATOR SMITH: The orders you got were to take that boat to the water?

MR. HITCHENS: To that light.

SENATOR SMITH: To the light and return?

MR. HITCHENS: Yes, sir; that is right.

SENATOR SMITH: And that order was given to you by the first or second officer?

MR. HITCHENS: Yes, sir.

SENATOR SMITH: Was your lifeboat lowered from the port or from the starboard side?

MR. HITCHENS: The port, sir.

SENATOR SMITH: You did not carry out that order?

MR. HITCHENS: Yes; I did sir.

SENATOR SMITH: What did you do?

MR. HITCHENS: I pulled for that light—this imaginary light. We were pulling for it all the time.

SENATOR SMITH: You pulled for this imaginary light?

MR. HITCHENS: Yes, sir.

SENATOR SMITH: And never returned to the side of the *Titanic?*

MR. HITCHENS: We could not return, sir.

SENATOR SMITH: I think I understand you. . . .

SIXTH DAY
Thursday, April 25
Washington, D.C.

Witness: Guglielmo Marconi, late 30s
Wireless-radio pioneer and head of an international communications monopoly

Key testimony: The inventor, who had testified briefly about his shipboard wireless operations during the first two days of the hearings, was recalled and confronted by Senator Smith over his role in checkbook journalism: agreeing to the sale of his poorly paid operators' exclusive stories to The New York Times *when they arrived in port aboard the* Carpathia.

. . . SENATOR SMITH: What is the pay of a wireless operator, generally speaking, in this country?

MR. MARCONI: I am not aware of the exact pay in this country.

SENATOR SMITH: What is it in England?

MR. MARCONI: In England it is from, I should say, beginning at $4 a week to $10 or $12 a week, with board and lodging. Of course, you have not asked me this, but I might say it is fairly easy to get operators on those terms in England because it is a rate of pay which is considerably higher than what they get on the shore telegraphs; and, of course, the fact of going to sea is very attractive to a great number of young men.

SENATOR SMITH: The hazard does not seem to deter them from that service?

MR. MARCONI: No; it does not. . . .

SENATOR SMITH: Was Mr. [Harold] Bride, who survived the *Titanic* disaster, employed in England or in America?

MR. MARCONI: He was employed in England.

SENATOR SMITH: And the same is true of Mr. [Jack] Phillips, who perished?

MR. MARCONI: The same is true of Mr. Phillips. . . .

SENATOR SMITH: Where were you on Sunday, April 14, last?

MR. MARCONI: I was in New York. . . .

SENATOR SMITH: Where were you when the *Carpathia* landed at the Cunard dock with the survivors of the *Titanic* wreck?

MR. MARCONI: I was dining with Mr. [John] Bottomley [Marconi's American manager]. . . . I had the intention of going on board the *Carpathia* as soon as she reached dock, but she happened to get in sooner than we expected. I therefore left the house where I was dining and proceeded to the dock, and we got on board.

SENATOR SMITH: What time?

MR. MARCONI: At about half past 9, just when the survivors were leaving, or just when the last survivors were leaving.

SENATOR SMITH: You got on board?

MR. MARCONI: I got on board.

SENATOR SMITH: What did you do when you got on board?

MR. MARCONI: I went to the wireless operating room.

SENATOR SMITH: Did you find the operator there?

MR. MARCONI: I found the operator there.

SENATOR SMITH: What did you say to him?

MR. MARCONI: I said I was glad to see him, and congratulated him on what I had heard he had done. I inquired after his senior operator, Phillips.

SENATOR SMITH: That is, you inquired of Bride about his senior operator, Phillips?

MR. MARCONI: About Phillips. The operator of the *Carpathia,* Cottam, was not there.

SENATOR SMITH: Where was he?

MR. MARCONI: He had gone ashore immediately the ship arrived. . . .

SENATOR SMITH: Did you send a wireless to the operator on the *Carpathia* and ask him to meet you and [Frederick] Sammis [Marconi's chief engineer in the United States] at the Strand Hotel, 502 West Fourteenth Street, saying "Keep your mouth shut"?

MR. MARCONI: No, sir; I did not.

SENATOR SMITH: If any message of that kind was sent in your name, you did not send it?

MR. MARCONI: I did not send it.

SENATOR SMITH: And you know nothing of it?

MR. MARCONI: I know nothing of it, except some statements or rumors I have heard of it in the press.

SENATOR SMITH: Do you know the naval vessel *Florida*?

MR. MARCONI: Yes; I have heard of her.

SENATOR SMITH: Is she equipped with wireless apparatus?

MR. MARCONI: Yes, sir; I think so. I think they all are.

SENATOR SMITH: I am going to read to you the following, and ask whether you know anything about any fact or circumstance connected with it.

This is from the commanding officer of the *Florida* to the Secretary of the Navy, dated April 22, and reads as follows:

On the evening of the steamship *Carpathia's* arrival in New York, the four following radiograms were intercepted by the chief operator, J. R. Simpson, chief electrician, United States Navy. They appear to me to be significant enough to be brought to the attention of the department:

"SEAGATE TO CARPATHIA—8:12 P.M.
"Say, old man, Marconi Co. taking good care of you. Keep your mouth shut, and hold your story. It is fixed for you so you will get big money. Now, please do your best to clear."

That was 8:12 P.M. Then follows this one:

8:30 P.M.

To Marconi officer, Carpathia and Titanic:
Arranged for your exclusive story for dollars in four figures, Mr. Marconi agreeing. Say nothing until you see me. Where are you now?

J. M. SAMMIS, *Opr. C.*

9 P.M.

From Seagate to *Carpathia* operator: Go to Strand Hotel, 502 West Fourteenth Street. To meet Mr. Marconi.

C.

From Seagate to *Carpathia*: A personal to operator *Carpathia*. Meet Mr. Marconi and Sammis at Strand Hotel, 502 West Fourteenth Street. Keep your mouth shut.

MR. MARCONI.

What can you say about that, Mr. Marconi?

MR. MARCONI: I do not know anything whatever about any of those messages. They are not in the phraseology which I would have approved of if I had passed them. I should, however, say that I told Mr. Sammis or Mr. Bottomley— I do not remember which—that I, as an officer of the British company, would not prohibit or prevent these operators from making anything which they reasonably could make out of selling their story of the wreck. I was anxious that, if possible, they might make some small amount of money out of the information they had.

SENATOR SMITH: Is that a custom of your company?

MR. MARCONI: It is not a custom; it is a thing that is done——

SENATOR SMITH: Is it a habit?

MR. MARCONI: No; it is not a habit. It is done on very special occasions. . . .

SENATOR SMITH: Mr. Marconi, do you wish the committee to understand that you approve that method?

MR. MARCONI: I was in favor of it, or at least I approved of or consented to his getting something out of this story.

SENATOR SMITH: I know, but let me ask you this. With the right to exact compensation for an exclusive story detailing the horrors of the greatest sea disaster that ever occurred in the history of the world, do you mean that an operator under your company's direction shall have the right to prevent the public from knowing of that calamity——

MR. MARCONI (interrupting): No.

SENATOR SMITH: Hold on a moment [continuing]. From knowing of that calamity except through the exclusive appropriation of the facts by the operator who is cognizant of them?

MR. MARCONI: I say, not at all. I gave no instructions in regard to withholding any information, and I gave no advice or instructions in regard to any exclusive story to anybody. The only thing I did say or did authorize was that if he was offered payment for a story of the disaster, he was permitted, so far as the English company went, to take that money. . . .

SENATOR SMITH: You have seen the rumors of this matter, have you not, in the papers?

MR. MARCONI: Yes.

SENATOR SMITH: I have not seen those rumors; but after seeing those rumors did you talk with Sammis about the matter?

MR. MARCONI: I saw Mr. Sammis for a few moments some time ago, and I told him—I said, "You know that I did not authorize that message."

SENATOR SMITH: When did you tell him that?

MR. MARCONI: I told him that since the survivors were landed. I do not remember the exact date.

SENATOR SMITH: About what time?

MR. MARCONI: Three or four days ago, I should say.

SENATOR SMITH: Have you talked with him about it since?

MR. MARCONI: No, sir. I should state in explanation, also, of this matter——

SENATOR SMITH: Please do; I would like to have you, in your own way. I am not seeking to embarrass you, at all. I simply feel it my duty to get the information I have asked for.

MR. MARCONI: What I meant and intended when I stated to the operator that he could take something for a story or for an account of the disaster was that newspapers and reporters would be so interested in what he had to say, and in himself personally, in view of the fact especially that Bride had behaved in such a brave and gallant manner, that, without withholding any general information, they would be ready to pay him an amount for a story or a description which he could give them.

SENATOR SMITH: Have you finished?

MR. MARCONI: Yes, sir.

SENATOR SMITH: Mr. Marconi, did you expect the operator to syndicate this information, or to give it exclusively to one newspaper?

MR. MARCONI: I did not expect him to give it exclusively.

SENATOR SMITH: Did you expect him to put the story up to the highest bidder?

MR. MARCONI: No, sir. . . .

SENATOR SMITH: If I understand you correctly, you did not

247

seek to control the operator, at all, in what he would say or to whom he would say it?

MR. MARCONI: No; I did not.

SENATOR SMITH: Do you know what the use of the words, "Arranged for your exclusive story for dollars in four figures, Mr. Marconi agreeing. Say nothing until you see me. J. M. Sammis," would indicate? What did he mean by "four figures"?

MR. MARCONI: I suppose it was something over a thousand dollars; but if you will allow me to repeat again——

SENATOR SMITH: Please do. I wish you would say anything you want to about it.

MR. MARCONI (continuing): For the fourth or fifth or sixth time, I say that I know nothing whatever about those messages.

SENATOR SMITH: And you understand I am not saying that you do.

MR. MARCONI: Thank you.

SENATOR SMITH: I am simply inquiring. Do you know whether [Harold] Cottam [the *Carpathia*'s wireless operator] or Bride sold their story?

MR. MARCONI: I think they received remuneration for it, and that may be called "sold," I presume. I mean that they were paid for it.

SENATOR SMITH: Do you know how much they got?

MR. MARCONI: I do not know how much Cottam got.

SENATOR SMITH: Do you know how much Bride got?

MR. MARCONI: I was told that Bride got $500.

SENATOR SMITH: From whom?

MR. MARCONI: From the New York Times.

SENATOR SMITH: Who told you that?

MR. MARCONI: I think it was Mr. Bottomley.

SENATOR SMITH: The general manager of your company?

MR. MARCONI: Yes. I should also say, I believe, one of the editors of the New York Times, either Mr. [Adolph S.] Ochs [the publisher] or [Carr] Van Ander [the managing editor]. . . .

SENATOR SMITH: Is any officer of the Marconi Co. interested in the New York Times?

MR. MARCONI: I do not know. I do not think so, because if anyone was I would probably hear of it in some way.

SENATOR SMITH: Is any director of your company interested in the New York Times?

MR. MARCONI: No.

SENATOR SMITH: Have you heard from any source any statement given as to the amount Cottam received for his story?

MR. MARCONI: No; I have not.

SENATOR SMITH: Did you see his story?

MR. MARCONI: I saw the headlines of his story; I did not read it through.

SENATOR SMITH: In the New York Times?

MR. MARCONI: In the Times. . . .

To move more expeditiously on Day 6, the Senators broke apart to interview many crew members individually.

Witness: Frank Osman, 38
Seaman

Key testimony: He, too, saw the light of a ship off in the distance. In his lifeboat, "the women were all nervous and we pulled as far as we could get from her, so that the women would not see, and it would not cause a panic." The Titanic "exploded, broke in halves, and . . . all the engines and everything that was in the afterpart slid out into the forward part, and the afterpart came up right again."

. . . SENATOR BURTON: Where were you when the collision occurred?

MR. OSMAN: Outside the seamen's dining room.

SENATOR BURTON: Tell what happened.

MR. OSMAN: I was waiting for one bell, which they strike, one bell just before the quarter of the hour, before the four hours, when you get a call to relieve; and I heard three bells strike, and I thought there was a ship ahead. Just after that I heard the collision, and I went out in the foresquare, that is, the forewell deck, just against the seamen's mess room. Looking in the forewell square I saw ice was there. I went down below and stepped down there, and seen the ship was getting a bit of a list. Then they passed the order that all the seamen had to go up and clear away all the boats. All of us went up and cleared away the boats. After that we loaded all the boats there were, and I went away in No. 2 boat, the fourth from the last to leave the ship.

SENATOR BURTON: Was yours lowered first, second, or third?

MR. OSMAN: Fourth from the last, about the sixteenth boat to lower.

SENATOR BURTON: Who had command of that boat?

MR. OSMAN: The fourth officer, Mr. Boxhall.

SENATOR BURTON: Did he direct the loading of the boat?

MR. OSMAN: No, sir; the chief officer, Mr. Murdoch.

SENATOR BURTON: How many were in that boat? First the seamen and then the passengers.

MR. OSMAN: There was one able seaman, sir, a cook, and a steward, and an officer. That was all the men there was in the boat out of the crew. There was one man, a third-class passenger, and the remainder were women and children.

SENATOR BURTON: You were the able seaman?

MR. OSMAN: Yes, sir.

SENATOR BURTON: How many women were in the boat?

MR. OSMAN: I could not say exactly how many there were, but there were between 25 and 30, all told.

SENATOR BURTON: Including the seamen?

MR. OSMAN: Including the crew. This was one of the emergency boats.

SENATOR BURTON: Did you have any trouble in lowering the boat?

MR. OSMAN: No, sir; the boat went down very easy, very steady indeed.

SENATOR BURTON: Was it full?

MR. OSMAN: Yes, sir; full right up.

SENATOR BURTON: Did you get along comfortably or was there suffering?

MR. OSMAN: There was only one lady there, a first-class passenger—I did not know her name—who was worrying. That was the only thing that was said.

SENATOR BURTON: In what order were you taken onto the *Carpathia?*

MR. OSMAN: I was the first boat back, sir. After I got in the boat the officer found a bunch of rockets, which was put in the boat by mistake for a box of biscuits. Having them in the boat, the officer fired some off, and the *Carpathia* came to us first and picked us up a half an hour before anybody else.

SENATOR BURTON: Did you steer for a light?

MR. OSMAN: No, sir; we saw a light; but the other boats were making for it, and the officer was not sure whether it was a light or whether it was not, and as he had the rockets they could repeat the signals.

SENATOR BURTON: Did you see that light?

MR. OSMAN: Yes, sir.

SENATOR BURTON: What did you think it was?

MR. OSMAN: I thought it was a sailing vessel from the banks.

SENATOR BURTON: When did you last have a sight of that light?

MR. OSMAN: About an hour afterwards.

SENATOR BURTON: What do you think about it? Did it sail away?

MR. OSMAN: Yes, sir; she sailed right away.

SENATOR BURTON: You are sure you saw that light?

MR. OSMAN: Yes, sir; quite sure, sir.

SENATOR BURTON: What was it, a stern light?

MR. OSMAN: No, sir; a masthead light.

SENATOR BURTON: Does a sailing ship have a white light on her masthead?

MR. OSMAN: Yes, sir.

SENATOR BURTON: You are sure that light was not a star?

MR. OSMAN: I am sure it was not a star.

SENATOR BURTON: Just what happened when you were on the boat? Did you see this iceberg?

MR. OSMAN: Not until the morning.

SENATOR BURTON: Are you sure it was the one?

MR. OSMAN: Yes, sir; you could see it was the one, sir.

SENATOR BURTON: How high was it?

MR. OSMAN: At a rough estimate it was 100 feet out of the water.

SENATOR BURTON: What shape was it?

MR. OSMAN: It was round, and then had one big point sticking up on one side of it.

SENATOR BURTON: What was its color?

MR. OSMAN: It was apparently dark, like dirty ice.

SENATOR BURTON: How far away from it were you when you saw it?

MR. OSMAN: About 100 yards.

SENATOR BURTON: How did you know that was the one you struck?

MR. OSMAN: We could see it was the biggest berg there, and the other ones would not have done so much damage, I think.

SENATOR BURTON: Was there any mark on the side, as if it had collided with something?

MR. OSMAN: It looked as if there was a piece broken off after she struck, and the ice fell on board. I went and picked up a piece of ice and took it down below in my sleeping room.

SENATOR BURTON: There was some little time that you were down below, was there not?

MR. OSMAN: Yes sir; a matter of 10 minutes.

SENATOR BURTON: Not more than 10 minutes?

MR. OSMAN: Not more than 10 minutes.

SENATOR BURTON: I do not see, quite, how you account for all the time after the collision before you took to the boat.

MR. OSMAN: It is only just like walking out of the door.

SENATOR BURTON: About what time was this boat lowered in which you went away?

MR. OSMAN: I could not say exactly the time.

SENATOR BURTON: About how long after the collision?

MR. OSMAN: About an hour, I suppose—an hour and a half.

SENATOR BURTON: You say the boat listed. Did it list to the port or the starboard?

MR. OSMAN: To the starboard.

SENATOR BURTON: How much?

MR. OSMAN: A matter of about that angle [indicating]. A gradual list, it was; four or five degrees.

SENATOR BURTON: Did you take any part in loading any of the other boats?

MR. OSMAN: Yes; I helped load four of the boats on the starboard side.

SENATOR BURTON: Was there any panic?

MR. OSMAN: No; there was no panic at all. I was helping women and children in the boat and the crew was lowering boats.

SENATOR BURTON: Was there any panic?

MR. OSMAN: I never seen no panic there.

SENATOR BURTON: When you were down on that lower deck, did you see persons moving about there?

MR. OSMAN: No; there was nobody there at all, because Mr. Murdoch was singing out, "Is there any more women and children here to put in my boat?"

SENATOR BURTON: I mean, before you went up to man the boat, were there any people moving about where you were, down on the lower deck?

MR. OSMAN: Oh, no, sir; there was nobody there. . . .

SENATOR BURTON: How far were you away from the boat when she sank?

MR. OSMAN: Sixty to 100 yards.

SENATOR BURTON: Was there much suction?

MR. OSMAN: There was no suction whatever. When we were in the boat we shoved off from the ship, and I said to the officer, "See if you can get alongside to see if you can get any more hands, to see if you can squeeze any more hands in." So the women then started to getting nervous after I said that, and the officer said "All right." The women disagreed to that. We pulled around to the starboard side of the ship and found we could not get to the starboard side because it was listing too far. We pulled astern that way again, and after we got astern we lay on our oars and saw the ship go down. After she got to a certain angle she exploded, broke in halves, and it seemed to me as if all the engines and everything that was in the after part slid out into the forward part, and the after part came up right again, and as soon as it came up right down it went again.

SENATOR BURTON: What do you think those explosions were?

MR. OSMAN: The boilers bursting.

SENATOR BURTON: What makes you think that?

MR. OSMAN: The cold water coming under the red-hot boilers caused the explosions.

SENATOR BURTON: You reasoned that out?

MR. OSMAN: Yes; but you could see the explosions by the smoke coming right up the funnels.

SENATOR BURTON: Did you see any steam and smoke coming?

MR. OSMAN: Yes.

SENATOR BURTON: Did you see any sparks?

MR. OSMAN: It was all black; looked like as if it was lumps of coal, and all that.

SENATOR BURTON: Coming up through the funnels?

MR. OSMAN: Through the funnels.

SENATOR BURTON: That is, there was a great amount of black

smoke coming up through the funnels just after this explosion?

Mr. Osman: Just after the explosion.

Senator Burton: And there were lumps of coal, etc., coming up?

Mr. Osman: Yes; pretty big lumps. I do not know what it was.

Senator Burton: Did any water come up?

Mr. Osman: I never seen no water; only the steam and very black smoke.

Senator Burton: Why did you not go back to the place where the boat had sunk after she had gone down?

Mr. Osman: The women were all nervous and we pulled around as far as we could get to her, so that the women would not see, and it would not cause a panic, and we got as close as we would dare to by the women. We could not have taken any more hands into the boat; it was impossible. We might have got one in. That is about all. The steerage passengers were all down below, and after she got a certain distance it seemed to me all the passengers climbed up her.

Senator Burton: Steerage passengers, too?

Mr. Osman: All the passengers there were.

Senator Burton: That were left on board?

Mr. Osman: Yes.

Senator Burton: Did you see any of them climb up there?

Mr. Osman: It looked blacker. She was white around there [indicating], and it looked like a big crowd of people.

Senator Burton: Then you think the passengers, first, second, and third class, went up on the top deck?

Mr. Osman: On the top deck; yes.

Senator Burton: Do you think there were any passengers down in here when she went down [indicating on diagram]?

Mr. Osman: I do not think so. I could not say as to that.

Senator Burton: Was there any panic amongst these steerage passengers when they started manning the boats?

Mr. Osman: No. I saw several people come up from there, and go straight up on the boat deck. That is one thing I saw; and the men stood back while the women and children got in the boat.

Senator Burton: Steerage passengers, as well as others?

MR. OSMAN: One steerage passenger, a man, and his wife and two children, were in my boat; all belonged to the one family.

SENATOR BURTON: You took the man?

MR. OSMAN: Yes; that was the only man passenger we had in the boat.

SENATOR BURTON: What do you think? Do you think they believed the ship would float?

MR. OSMAN: I thought so, myself. I thought it was going down a certain depth, and would float after that.

SENATOR BURTON: Did you hear any conversation around among the passengers as to whether she would sink or not?

MR. OSMAN: No; I never heard anything amongst the passengers as to whether she would sink. The only thing I heard was one passenger was saying he was going in the boat, and stand by the ship.

SENATOR BURTON: You heard one passenger say that?

MR. OSMAN: Yes.

SENATOR BURTON: Would you rather have gotten into the boat, or stayed on the ship?

MR. OSMAN: I was put into the boat.

SENATOR BURTON: Which would you rather have done?

MR. OSMAN: You see it was rather dangerous to stop aboard.

SENATOR BURTON: The *Titanic* was dangerous?

MR. OSMAN: Yes.

SENATOR BURTON: So in your judgment it was safer to have gone in the boat than to have stayed on the *Titanic*?

MR. OSMAN: Oh, yes, sir.

SENATOR BURTON: That was when you left?

MR. OSMAN: Yes, sir.

SENATOR BURTON: What did you think when the first boat was launched?

MR. OSMAN: I did not think she was going down then. . . .

Witness: George A. Hogg
Lookout, from Hull, near Yorkshire, England

Key testimony: The women manned the oars admirably, he testified: "I think all the women ought to have a gold medal on their breasts."

. . . Senator Perkins: Were you on the ship's articles as the lookout man in this case?

Mr. Hogg: Yes, sir.

Senator Perkins: What watch were you on?

Mr. Hogg: My watch was from 12 to 2, sir.

Senator Perkins: Were you in the crow's nest when the vessel struck the iceberg?

Mr. Hogg: No, sir.

Senator Perkins: What time did she strike this iceberg?

Mr. Hogg: I woke up about 20 minutes to 12.

Senator Perkins: You were in your bunk at that time?

Mr. Hogg: Yes, sir.

Senator Perkins: Did you turn out?

Mr. Hogg: I turned out, with the confusion in the forecastle.

Senator Perkins: What boat were you assigned to?

Mr. Hogg: No. 6 was my boat.

Senator Perkins: By the way, I will ask you this first: After leaving Southampton you were divided into watch and watch; and then the detail of the lookouts was also made, was it not?

Mr. Hogg: I signed on the ship as a lookout man.

Senator Perkins: You did?

Mr. Hogg: Yes, sir.

Senator Perkins: You received £5 a month and 10 shillings extra?

Mr. Hogg: Five pounds a month and 5 shillings extra, sir.

Senator Perkins: And 5 shillings extra, for a lookout man?

Mr. Hogg: Yes, sir.

Senator Perkins: Tell us, in your own way, what happened next, after the ship collided with the iceberg.

Mr. Hogg: I waked up, at 20 minutes to 12, with the confusion in the forecastle. I rushed up on the deck, and I saw there was not much confusion on deck, and I went below again, with some of my shipmates.

I asked the time, then, of my mate Evans, and he said, "It is a quarter to 12. We will get dressed and get ready to go on the lookout."

Senator Perkins: Go on and tell us, in your own way, just what happened.

Mr. Hogg: Very good, sir. I have started it, right now.

I dressed myself, and we relieved the lookout at 12 o'clock, me and my mate Evans.

We stopped about 20 minutes, and lifted up the back cover of the nest, the weather cover, and I saw people running about with life belts on.

I went to the telephone then, to try to ring up on the bridge and ask whether I was wanted in the nest, when I saw this. I could get no answer on the telephone. Also my mate——

SENATOR PERKINS: Who was your shipmate?

MR. HOGG: My shipmate was a man by the name of Evans, sir. He has gone home.

SENATOR PERKINS: Go ahead; continue to tell your story, as to what boat you went to, and what happened.

MR. HOGG: Yes, sir.

I went straight on the boat deck. I assisted in starting to uncover the boats. Then I was sent for a Jacob's ladder.

SENATOR PERKINS: You have not said to what particular boat you were assigned?

MR. HOGG: No. 6 was my proper boat; what I signed for.

SENATOR PERKINS: As to this Jacob's ladder: Did you put it over the side and go down that?

MR. HOGG: No, sir.

SENATOR PERKINS: Who sent you for the Jacob's ladder?

MR. HOGG: The boatswain. I was told to drop it. As I got past the No. 7 boat on the starboard side, Mr. Murdoch, chief officer, said: "See that those plugs are in that boat." I put the plugs in, and I said: "The plugs are all correct," and I jumped out again.

SENATOR PERKINS: Who lowered away at the falls?

MR. HOGG: I jumped out to assist with the falls; and he said: "You step in that boat." I said, "Very good, sir." Mr. Murdoch lowered one end, and I am trying to think of the man that lowered the other end. Evans lowered the other end.

SENATOR PERKINS: How many people were in this other boat at this time, when it was hanging in the davits?

MR. HOGG: As soon as I unhooked her, I mustered her people to see how many I had. I must have had 42.

SENATOR PERKINS: While she was hanging in the davits?

MR. HOGG: No, sir; when I shoved away.

SENATOR PERKINS: When you shoved her from the ship's side?

257

MR. HOGG: Yes, sir.

SENATOR PERKINS: This was on the port side?

MR. HOGG: On the starboard side, sir. I asked a lady if she could steer, and she said she could. I said: "You may sit here and do this for me, and I will take the stroke oar."

I pulled a little way from the ship, about a quarter of a mile, I should think, sir. I went alongside another boat. I can not think of the number of the boat now, sir—and they transferred some of the passengers to my boat.

SENATOR PERKINS: You had how many, all told, then?

MR. HOGG: I think they transferred four ladies and a baby and one gentleman—I think it was—as I wanted an extra gentleman for oar pulling.

SENATOR PERKINS: That made, all told, how many?

MR. HOGG: About 47, and the ladies objected to having those men.

SENATOR PERKINS: This was one of the lifeboats, was it?

MR. HOGG: It was one of the big ones; yes.

SENATOR PERKINS: She is measured to carry 65 people, is she not?

MR. HOGG: I could not answer that, sir. I did not know at the time what they were capable of carrying.

SENATOR PERKINS: She rode the sea cleverly? It was smooth, though.

MR. HOGG: It was very, very smooth, sir. The sea was very smooth.

SENATOR PERKINS: Of your own judgment as a sailor man, would you have permitted any more people to get into the boat if they had been alongside of you?

MR. HOGG: Yes, sir.

SENATOR PERKINS: You were ordered to pull away from the ship?

MR. HOGG: Yes, sir; I was ordered to pull away from the ship for safety, for the time being. One lady said I should not take any more in that boat. I said: "I will take all I can get."

SENATOR PERKINS: Go on with your story. Tell us the balance of that.

MR. HOGG: I stopped alongside those two. As soon as she went down, I went to try to assist them in picking up anybody if I could.

I met another boat on my way, and they said to pull

away. They said: "We have done all in our power and we can not do any more." I can not remember the number of the boat or who the man was who spoke to me. I laid off, then, until I saw the lights of the *Carpathia*.

SENATOR PERKINS: But you pulled around in search of other people?

MR. HOGG: I pulled around in search of other people before I could pull to the wreck. One man said: "We have done our best. There are no more people around. We have pulled all around." I said: "Very good. We will get away now."

SENATOR PERKINS: And you were then within about half a mile of the *Titanic?*

MR. HOGG: About that, sir.

SENATOR PERKINS: From what quarter was the wind drawing then?

MR. HOGG: I did not exactly take notice, sir.

SENATOR PERKINS: Was it cold?

MR. HOGG: It was bitter cold.

SENATOR PERKINS: There was quite a ripple on the water?

MR. HOGG: Not a ripple on the water, sir. It was as smooth as glass.

SENATOR PERKINS: After that, what did you do?

MR. HOGG: I saw the lights of the *Carpathia*. I said: "It is all right, now, ladies. Do not grieve. We are picked up. Now, gentlemen, see what you can do in pulling these oars for this light." It was practically daylight then. Then the passengers could see for themselves that there was a ship there. I pulled up and went alongside, and I assisted in putting a bowline around all the ladies, to haul them up aboard. After I saw all aboard the boat, me and my friend went aboard, and I put some blankets around myself and went to sleep.

SENATOR PERKINS: After this accident happened, you pulled away, and did all you could to save life?

MR. HOGG: I thought of suction, first. . . .

SENATOR PERKINS: Could anything have been done to save more lives than were saved?

MR. HOGG: No, sir. The only thing I can suggest is in regard to the glasses. If we had had the glasses, we might have seen the berg before. . . .

SENATOR PERKINS: In an ordinary way, can you not see better with your plain eyes than you can with artificial glasses?

MR. HOGG: But the idea of the glasses, sir, is that if you happen to see something on the horizon you can pick your ship out, if it is a ship, for instance.

SENATOR PERKINS: As soon as you see anything, you signal the officer on the bridge, do you not?

MR. HOGG: Yes, sir; you would strike the bell. But you would make sure, if you had the glasses that it was a vessel and not a piece of cloud on the horizon.

On a very nice night, with the stars shining, sometimes you might think it was a ship when it was a star on the horizon. If you had glasses, you could soon find out whether it was a ship or not.

SENATOR SMITH: As soon as you discover anything unusual, however, you call the attention of the officer on the bridge to it, do you not?

MR. HOGG: Quite so.

SENATOR PERKINS: And he has glasses, of course?

MR. HOGG: He has glasses, sir; yes, sir. . . .

SENATOR PERKINS: Unless you have something more to state that you think will throw light on this subject, that will be all; and we thank you for what you have said.

MR. HOGG: That is all I have to say, except this: I think all the women ought to have a gold medal on their breasts. God bless them. I will always raise my hat to a woman, after what I saw.

SENATOR PERKINS: What country women were they?

MR. HOGG: They were American women that I had in mind. They were all Americans.

SENATOR PERKINS: Did they man the oars? Did they take the oars and pull?

MR. HOGG: Yes, sir. I took the oar all the time, myself, and one lady steered. Then I got another lady to steer, and she gave me a hand on the oar, to keep herself warm. . . .

Witness: Edward John Buley
Able seaman and British Royal Navy veteran, from Itchen, England

Key testimony: He said he saw a steamer passing the bow of the Titanic *three miles away. Crew members told many*

*aboard that "there is a steamer coming to our assistance,"
Buley said, which may have persuaded them to wait for
rescue rather than risk taking to lifeboats. He described
finding bodies in the water in life preservers, not drowned but
"frozen altogether."*

. . . SENATOR FLETCHER: Did you observe anything out of the
ordinary or usual on board ship up to the time of this
accident?

MR. BULEY: No, sir. I was sitting in the mess, reading, at the
time when she struck.

SENATOR FLETCHER: Were you on duty?

MR. BULEY: I was in the watch on deck, the starboard watch.
At 12 o'clock we relieved the other watch.

SENATOR FLETCHER: You were then on your watch?

MR. BULEY: Yes, sir.

SENATOR FLETCHER: Where were you sitting, reading?

MR. BULEY: On the mess deck. If it was Sunday night, we
never had anything to do. Ordinary nights we should have
been scrubbing the decks.

SENATOR FLETCHER: What was your first notice of the
collision?

MR. BULEY: The slight jar. It seemed as though something
was rubbing alongside of her, at the time. I had on my
overcoat and went up on deck, and they said she had
struck an iceberg.

SENATOR FLETCHER: Who said that?

MR. BULEY: I think it was a couple of firemen. They came
down. One of our chaps went and got a handful of ice and
took it down below. They turned in again.

The next order from the chief officer, Murdoch, was to
tell the seamen to get together and uncover the boats and
turn them out as quietly as though nothing had happened. They turned them out in about 20 minutes. . . .

SENATOR FLETCHER: Did you lower the boats?

MR. BULEY: I helped lower all the starboard boats.

SENATOR FLETCHER: That is, to lower them as far as the boat
deck, to get the gunwales in line?

MR. BULEY: Yes, sir.

SENATOR FLETCHER: That is the deck on which the boats
were?

Mr. Buley: Yes, sir.

Senator Fletcher: Not to any lower deck?

Mr. Buley: No, sir; not to the lower deck. We lowered all the starboard boats, and went over and done the same to the port boats. There was No. 10 boat, and there was no one there, and the chief officer asked what I was, and I told him, and he said, "Jump in and see if you can find another seaman to give you a hand." I found Evans, and we both got in the boat, and Chief Officer Murdoch and Baker also was there. I think we were the last lifeboat to be lowered. We got away from the ship.

Senator Fletcher: How many people were in that boat?

Mr. Buley: From 60 to 70.

Senator Fletcher: Mostly women?

Mr. Buley: Women and children. . . .

Senator Fletcher: Were any ladies on the deck when you left?

Mr. Buley: No, sir. Ours was the last boat up there, and they went around and called to see if there were any, and they threw them in the boat at the finish, because they didn't like the idea of coming in.

Senator Fletcher: Pushed them in, you mean?

Mr. Buley: Threw them in. One young lady slipped, and they caught her by the foot on the deck below, and she came up then and jumped in.

We got away from the ship, and about an hour afterwards Officer Lowe came alongside, and he had his boat filled up, and he distributed them among the other boats, and he said to all the seamen in the boat to jump in his boat until he went back among the wreckage to see if there were any people that had lived.

Senator Fletcher: Did you go in the last boat?

Mr. Buley: Yes, sir.

Senator Fletcher: Who had charge of the boat you were in?

Mr. Buley: I was in charge of that.

Senator Fletcher: But when you left that?

Mr. Buley: I left that, and I believe he put some more stewards in the boat to look after the women. All the boats were tied together.

SENATOR FLETCHER: You were then with Lowe in his boat and went back to where the *Titanic* sank?

MR. BULEY: Yes, sir; and picked up the remaining live bodies.

SENATOR FLETCHER: How many did you get?

MR. BULEY: There were not very many there. We got four of them. All the others were dead.

SENATOR FLETCHER: Were there many dead?

MR. BULEY: Yes, sir; there were a good few dead, sir. Of course you could not discern them exactly on account of the wreckage; but we turned over several of them to see if they were alive. It looked as though none of them were drowned. They looked as though they were frozen. The life belts they had on were that much [indicating] out of the water, and their heads laid back, with their faces on the water, several of them. Their hands were coming up like that [indicating].

SENATOR FLETCHER: They were head and shoulders out of the water?

MR. BULEY: Yes, sir.

SENATOR FLETCHER: With the head thrown back?

MR. BULEY: Yes, sir.

SENATOR FLETCHER: And the face out of the water?

MR. BULEY: Yes, sir.

SENATOR FLETCHER: They were not, apparently, drowned?

MR. BULEY: It looked as though they were frozen altogether, sir.

In the morning, after we picked up all that was alive, there was a collapsible boat we saw with a lot of people, and she was swamped, and they were up to their knees in water. We set sail and went over to them, and in a brief time picked up another one.

SENATOR FLETCHER: Another boat?

MR. BULEY: Another boat filled with women and children, with no one to pull the oars, and we took her in tow. We went over to this one and saved all of them. There was one woman in that boat. After that we seen the *Carpathia* coming up, and we made sail and went over to her. I think we were about the seventh or eighth boat alongside. During the time I think there was two died that we had saved; two men.

SENATOR FLETCHER: How far were you from the *Titanic* when she went down?

MR. BULEY: About 250 yards.

SENATOR FLETCHER: Could you see people on the decks before she went down?

MR. BULEY: No. All the lights were out.

SENATOR FLETCHER: Could you hear the people?

MR. BULEY: Yes; you could hear them.

SENATOR FLETCHER: Calling?

MR. BULEY: Yes, sir.

SENATOR FLETCHER: Before she went down?

MR. BULEY: Yes, sir; and we laid to, not because we could give any assistance, but because the boat I was in was full up, and we had no one to pull the oars. There was three only to pull the oars, and one could not pull at all. He was a fireman. That left but two people to pull the oars, so I directed the steward to take the coxswain's watch.

SENATOR FLETCHER: Before she went down, you could hear people calling for help?

MR. BULEY: Yes, sir.

SENATOR FLETCHER: Was there very much of that?

MR. BULEY: Yes, sir; it was terrible cries, sir.

SENATOR FLETCHER: Most of the witnesses have said they could hear no cries for help until after the ship went down.

MR. BULEY: This was after the ship went down when we heard them.

SENATOR FLETCHER: I have been asking you about hearing cries before the ship went down.

MR. BULEY: No, sir; there was no signs of anything before that at all.

SENATOR FLETCHER: Before the ship went down you did not hear any cries for help?

MR. BULEY: No cries whatever, sir. Her port bow light was under water when we were lowered.

SENATOR FLETCHER: How long after you were lowered and put in the water was it before she went down?

MR. BULEY: I should say about 25 minutes to half an hour.

SENATOR FLETCHER: Was yours the last boat?

MR. BULEY: Mine was the last lifeboat, No. 10.

SENATOR FLETCHER: Were the collapsibles lowered after that?

MR. BULEY: The collapsibles were washed off the deck, I believe, sir. The one we picked up that was swamped, I think they dropped her and broke her back, and that is why they could not open her.

SENATOR FLETCHER: Were there people in that collapsible?

MR. BULEY: She was full up, sir; that is the one we rescued the first thing in the morning.

SENATOR FLETCHER: How soon after the *Titanic* went down was it before you got back there with Lowe to help rescue people?

MR. BULEY: From an hour to an hour and a half.

SENATOR FLETCHER: And your idea is that the people were frozen.

MR. BULEY: Yes, frozen.

SENATOR FLETCHER: Frozen in the meantime?

MR. BULEY: If the water had been warm, I imagine none of them would have been drowned, sir.

SENATOR FLETCHER: Then you got some people out of the water, and some of those died after you rescued them, did they?

MR. BULEY: Yes, sir.

SENATOR FLETCHER: Were they injured in any way?

MR. BULEY: No, sir. I think it was exposure and shock.

SENATOR FLETCHER: On account of the cold?

MR. BULEY: Yes, sir. We had no stimulants in the boat to revive them, at all.

SENATOR FLETCHER: They seemed to be very cold when you got them out of the water?

MR. BULEY: Yes, sir, and helpless.

SENATOR FLETCHER: Numb?

MR. BULEY: Yes, sir. There were several in the broken boat that could not walk. Their legs and feet were all cramped. They had to stand up in the water in that boat.

SENATOR FLETCHER: Do you know of any banquets or drinking on board the ship that night?

MR. BULEY: No, sir.

SENATOR FLETCHER: So far as you know, the crew were sober.

MR. BULEY: The crew were all asleep, sir. . . .

SENATOR FLETCHER: Do you know when the water began to come into the ship?

Mr. Buley: Yes, sir; a little after she struck. You could hear it.

Senator Fletcher: Immediately?

Mr. Buley: You could hear it immediately. Down where we were, there was a hatchway, right down below, and there was a tarpaulin across it, with an iron batten. You could hear the water rushing in, and the pressure of air underneath it was such that you could see this bending. In the finish I was told it blew off.

Senator Fletcher: What part of the ship would you call that?

Mr. Buley: The forecastle head.

Senator Fletcher: How far was that from the bow?

Mr. Buley: About 20 yards, I should think.

Senator Fletcher: That condition could not have obtained unless the steel plates had been torn off from the side of the ship?

Mr. Buley: From the bottom of the ship. It was well underneath the water line.

Senator Fletcher: And the plates must have been ripped off by the iceberg?

Mr. Buley: Yes, sir.

Senator Fletcher: There was no way of closing that up so as to prevent water coming in?

Mr. Buley: It was already closed up. The carpenter went down and tested the wells, and found she was making water, and the order was given to turn the boats out as well as possible, and then to get the life belts on.

Senator Fletcher: Could not that ship take a great deal of water and still float?

Mr. Buley: She ought to be able to do it, sir.

Senator Fletcher: There was no way of filling one compartment completely, and still not affecting the other part of it?

Mr. Buley: No. I should think if that had been a small hole, say about 12 by 12 feet square, in a collision, or anything like that, it would have been all right; but I do not think they carried collision mats.

Senator Fletcher: What is a collision mat?

Mr. Buley: It is a mat to shove over the hole to keep the water from rushing in.

SENATOR FLETCHER: You think she did not carry collision mats?

MR. BULEY: I do not believe she did. I never saw one.

SENATOR FLETCHER: Did you ever see collision mats used on merchant ships?

MR. BULEY: I had never been on a merchant ship before. I have seen them frequently used in the navy.

SENATOR FLETCHER: You think if she had had collision mats, she might have been saved?

MR. BULEY: That would not have done much good with her, because I believe she was ripped up right along.

SENATOR FLETCHER: For what distance?

MR. BULEY: I should say half way along, according to where the water was. I should say the bottom was really ripped open altogether.

SENATOR FLETCHER: The steel bottom?

MR. BULEY: Yes, sir.

SENATOR FLETCHER: So no amount of mats would have done any good?

MR. BULEY: It would not have done any good in that case. Should the ship have had a collision or anything like that, it would have done some good.

SENATOR FLETCHER: You did not see the iceberg?

MR. BULEY: No, sir. I never saw any ice until morning. We thought it was a full-rigged ship. We were right in amongst the wreckage, and we thought it was a sailing ship, until the light came on and we saw it was an iceberg.

SENATOR FLETCHER: Did you get very far away from where the *Titanic* went down before the *Carpathia* was in sight?

MR. BULEY: No, sir. When the *Carpathia* came and hove to, we were still amongst the wreckage looking for bodies.

SENATOR FLETCHER: By that time there were none of those afloat who were alive, so far as you could see?

MR. BULEY: No, sir; there were no more alive, then. . . .

SENATOR FLETCHER: Were there any passengers jumping overboard?

MR. BULEY: I never seen anyone jump overboard, sir.

SENATOR FLETCHER: Did you see any passengers on the deck when you left?

MR. BULEY: Only men, sir.

SENATOR FLETCHER: Were there many of those?

MR. BULEY: Yes, sir; there were plenty of them, sir. If she had had sufficient boats I think everyone would have been saved.

SENATOR FLETCHER: Were these men that you saw on deck desiring or wanting to get into the boats?

MR. BULEY: No, sir.

SENATOR FLETCHER: Or did they seem to think the ship was going to float?

MR. BULEY: I think that is what the majority thought, that the ship would float. They thought she would go down a certain distance and stop there.

SENATOR FLETCHER: Did you hear any of them say that?

MR. BULEY: Yes, several of them. They said they were only getting the boats out for exercise and in case of accident.

SENATOR FLETCHER: After you left her, her bow continued to go under?

MR. BULEY: Settled down; yes, sir. She went down as far as the afterfunnel, and then there was a little roar, as though the engines had rushed forward, and she snapped in two, and the bow part went down and the afterpart came up and stayed up five minutes before it went down.

SENATOR FLETCHER: Was that perpendicular?

MR. BULEY: It was horizontal at first, and then went down.

SENATOR FLETCHER: What do you mean by saying she snapped in two?

MR. BULEY: She parted in two.

SENATOR FLETCHER: How do you know that?

MR. BULEY: Because we could see the afterpart afloat, and there was no forepart to it. I think she must have parted where the bunkers were. She parted at the last, because the afterpart of her settled out of the water horizontally after the other part went down. First of all you could see her propellors and everything. Her rudder was clear out of the water. You could hear the rush of the machinery, and she parted in two, and the afterpart settled down again, and we thought the afterpart would float altogether.

SENATOR FLETCHER: The afterpart kind of righted up horizontally?

MR. BULEY: She uprighted herself for about five minutes, and then tipped over and disappeared.

SENATOR FLETCHER: Did it go on the side?

MR. BULEY: No, sir; went down headforemost.

SENATOR FLETCHER: That makes you believe the boat went in two?

MR. BULEY: Yes, sir. You could see she went in two, because we were quite near to her and could see her quite plainly.

SENATOR FLETCHER: You were near and could see her quite plainly?

MR. BULEY: Yes, sir.

SENATOR FLETCHER: Did you see any people on her?

MR. BULEY: I never saw a soul.

SENATOR FLETCHER: You must have been too far away to see that?

MR. BULEY: It was dark.

SENATOR FLETCHER: Were there lights on that half part?

MR. BULEY: The lights were all out. The lights went out gradually before she disappeared.

SENATOR FLETCHER: Notwithstanding the darkness you could see the outline of the ship?

MR. BULEY: Yes, sir; we could see the outline of the ship.

SENATOR FLETCHER: You could see the funnel?

MR. BULEY: Quite plainly.

SENATOR FLETCHER: Were there any cinders or sparks or anything of that sort from the funnel?

MR. BULEY: No, sir. We were lying to there. The people in the boat were very frightened that there would be some suction. If there had been any suction we should have been lost. We were close to her. We couldn't get away fast enough. There was nobody to pull away.

SENATOR FLETCHER: How far were you when she went down?

MR. BULEY: We were about 200 yards. . . .

SENATOR FLETCHER: Your opinion is, if they had had enough lifeboats here, these people could all have been saved?

MR. BULEY: Yes, sir; they could all have been saved.

There was a ship of some description there when she struck, and she passed right by us. We thought she was coming to us; and if she had come to us, everyone could have boarded her. You could see she was a steamer. She had her steamer lights burning.

She was off our port bow when we struck, and we all started for the same light, and that is what kept the boats together.

269

SENATOR FLETCHER: But you never heard of that ship any more?

MR. BULEY: No; we could not see anything of her in the morning when it was daylight. She was stationary all night; I am very positive for about three hours she was stationary, and then she made tracks.

SENATOR FLETCHER: How far away was she?

MR. BULEY: I should judge she was about 3 miles.

SENATOR FLETCHER: Why could not she see your skyrockets?

MR. BULEY: She could not help seeing them. She was close enough to see our lights and to see the ship itself, and also the rockets. She was bound to see them.

SENATOR FLETCHER: You are quite certain that it was a ship?

MR. BULEY: Yes, sir; it was a ship.

SENATOR FLETCHER: How many lights did you see?

MR. BULEY: I saw two masthead lights.

SENATOR FLETCHER: No stern lights?

MR. BULEY: You could not see the stern lights. You could not see her bow lights. We were in the boat at the time.

SENATOR FLETCHER: Did you see that ship before you were in the water?

MR. BULEY: Yes, sir; I saw it from the ship. That is what we told the passengers. We said, "There is a steamer coming to our assistance." That is what kept them quiet, I think.

SENATOR FLETCHER: Did she come toward you bow on?

MR. BULEY: Yes, sir; bow on toward us; and then she stopped, and the lights seemed to go right by us.

SENATOR FLETCHER: If she had gone by you, she would have been to your stern?

MR. BULEY: She was stationary there for about three hours, I think, off our port, there, and when we were in the boat we all made for her, and she went by us. The northern lights are just like a searchlight, but she disappeared. That was astern of where the ship went down.

SENATOR FLETCHER: She gave no signal?

MR. BULEY: No signal whatever. I could not say whether she gave a signal from the bridge or not. You could not see from where we were, though.

SENATOR FLETCHER: Do you suppose she was fastened in the ice?

MR. BULEY: I could not say what she was.

SENATOR FLETCHER: She must have known the *Titanic* was in distress?

MR. BULEY: She must have known it. They could have seen the rockets and must have known there was some distress on.

SENATOR FLETCHER: The *Titanic* had sirens?

MR. BULEY: Yes; she had sirens, but she never blew them. They fired rockets.

SENATOR FLETCHER: They did not blow the siren or whistle?

MR. BULEY: No, sir.

SENATOR FLETCHER: But the steam was escaping and making quite a noise?

MR. BULEY: Yes, sir; you could not hear yourself speak then. That had quieted down. The firemen went down and drew nearly all the fires.

SENATOR FLETCHER: When she went down, she had no fire in her of any consequence?

MR. BULEY: She might have had fire, but very little.

SENATOR FLETCHER: When did you first see that boat on the bow? How long was it before you launched?

MR. BULEY: When we started turning the boats out. That was about 10 minutes after she struck.

SENATOR FLETCHER: Did that boat seem to be getting farther away from you?

MR. BULEY: No; it seemed to be coming nearer.

SENATOR FLETCHER: You are possessed of pretty good eyes?

MR. BULEY: I can see a distance of 21 miles, sir.

SENATOR FLETCHER: This was a clear night and no fog?

MR. BULEY: A clear night and no fog.

SENATOR FLETCHER: A smooth sea?

MR. BULEY: Yes, sir.

SENATOR FLETCHER: You are quite positive there was no illusion about that boat ahead?

MR. BULEY: It must have been a boat, sir. It was too low down in the sea for a star. Then we were quite convinced afterwards, because we saw it go right by us when we were in the lifeboats. We thought she was coming toward us to pick us up.

SENATOR FLETCHER: How far away was she?

MR. BULEY: Three miles, sir, I should judge. . . .

271

Witness: George Frederick Crowe, 30
Steward, from Southampton, England

Key testimony: Crowe reported that just after the accident, "the stewards were making quite a joke of it." He said that as his lifeboat was being lowered it got hung up; the ropes had to be slashed and it fell into the water. People on his lifeboat, commanded by Fifth Officer Lowe, pulled some out of the water, but one later died. The Titanic "broke clean in two" as she went down.

. . . SENATOR BOURNE: What were the duties of steward on the *Titanic*?

MR. CROWE: To act in general and wait on tables.

SENATOR BOURNE: Under what officer of the ship were you directly located, or to whom were you responsible?

MR. CROWE: The chief steward.

SENATOR BOURNE: Will you please state in your own way what knowledge you have in reference to the accident to the *Titanic*?

MR. CROWE: I was on duty up until about 10:30 on the night of the disaster, and I turned in about 11 o'clock; it might have been a little later. About 11:40 there was a kind of shaking of the ship and a little impact, from which I thought one of the propellers had been broken off.

SENATOR BOURNE: You were in your berth at the time?

MR. CROWE: I was in my berth; yes.

SENATOR BOURNE: And had gone to sleep?

MR. CROWE: No; I was just dozing.

SENATOR BOURNE: Did it shake you out of your berth?

MR. CROWE: No, sir.

SENATOR BOURNE: How much of a shock was it?

MR. CROWE: Well, had I been asleep I do not think it would have awakened me; that is, had I been in a heavy sleep.

SENATOR BOURNE: What deck were you sleeping on?

MR. CROWE: On "E" deck.

SENATOR BOURNE: How far away from the bow of the ship; amidship?

MR. CROWE: About amidship; yes. Probably 50 feet forward of amidship.

SENATOR BOURNE: Now will you kindly go on?

MR. CROWE: I got out of my bed. I came out into the alleyway and saw quite a number of stewards and steerage passengers carrying their baggage from forward to aft. I inquired of the trouble and was told it was nothing, and to turn in again.

SENATOR BOURNE: Who told you this, the steerage passengers?

MR. CROWE: No; somebody amongst the boys. The stewards were making quite a joke of it. They did not think of the seriousness of it at the time. I went back to my bunk again, and a saloon steward came down shortly afterwards and told me to come up on the upper deck with as much warm clothes on as I could get. I went up on the boat deck; when I got outside of the companionway, I saw them working on boat No. 1. After that I went to boat No. 14, the boat allotted to me—that is, in the case of fire or boat drill—and I stood by according to the proceedings of the drill. I assisted in handing the women and children into the boat, and was asked if I could take an oar, and I said "Yes," and was told to man the boat.

SENATOR BOURNE: Who told you to man the boat?

MR. CROWE: The senior officer. I am not sure whether it was the first officer or the chief officer, sir, but I believe the man's name was Murdoch.

SENATOR BOURNE: Was that his boat?

MR. CROWE: I do not think so, sir; no.

SENATOR BOURNE: Who was in charge, during the drills, of boat No. 14; which officer?

MR. CROWE: The fifth officer, Mr. Lowe.

SENATOR BOURNE: That was his boat?

MR. CROWE: That was his boat; yes, sir. After getting the women and children in, we lowered down within 4 or 5 feet of the water and found the block and tackle had gotten twisted in some way, causing us to have to cut the ropes to allow the boat to get into the water.

SENATOR BOURNE: Who called to you to do that?

MR. CROWE: The fifth officer, sir.

SENATOR BOURNE: He was in the boat with you?

MR. CROWE: Yes, sir. I stood by the lever. The lever releases the blocks from the hooks in the boat, and he told me to wait, to get away and cut the line to raise the lever, thereby causing the hooks to open and allow the boat to drop in the water. After getting into the water we pushed out to the other boats. Fifth Officer Lowe suggested standing by in case of any necessity for us to do so.

SENATOR BOURNE: How many occupants were in there in boat No. 14?

MR. CROWE: Fifty-seven women and children and about 6 men, including 1 officer; and I may have been 7; I am not quite sure about that.

SENATOR BOURNE: How did you come to know there were 57 women and children?

MR. CROWE: When we got out a distance the officer asked me how many people we had in the boat, thinking the other boats had not got their number, and it was his idea to put our people into their boats and return back.

SENATOR BOURNE: Feeling that you were overcrowded?

MR. CROWE: No, sir; his idea was to stand by in case of an emergency; that is, anybody coming over the sides, with the idea of picking them up. I might state in between there the boat had sprung a leak and taken in water, probably 8 inches of water. That is, when the boat was released and fell, I think she must have sprung a leak.

SENATOR BOURNE: How long after the boat fell in the water did you discover that there was probably 8 inches of water in the boat?

MR. CROWE: Well, sir, we did not keep time or anything like that, but I should imagine when we transferred our people was when we discovered the amount of water that was in the boat, because just prior to getting to the other boat a lady stated that there was some water coming over her ankles, and two men and this lady—I believe the lady—assisted in bailing it out with bails that were kept in the boat for that purpose.

SENATOR BOURNE: Explain what you mean by when you transferred your people.

MR. CROWE: The officer on one of the boats that was near to us told them to stand by, and he got, I think, four or maybe five boats together. We transferred so many people from one boat to the other boats; we distributed from here to there.

SENATOR BOURNE: Your reason for transferring was because of this 8 inches of water?

MR. CROWE: No; he decided to return to the wreckage and see if he could pick anybody up.

SENATOR BOURNE: You had 57 men, women, and children in your boat, and 7 men in addition. You were pretty well loaded, were you not?

MR. CROWE: The officer said we could take 80 people in all, but the ladies seemed to make a protest at his idea of going back again with these people in the boat.

SENATOR BOURNE: Would it not have been easier to take one of these boats that was not nearly as full as your boat and have them stand by the wreckage and have them try to pick up people?

MR. CROWE: No, because the other boats were without an officer. We were the only boat out of the bunch that was there with an officer.

SENATOR BOURNE: Then it was discipline?

MR. CROWE: Just a matter of discipline.

SENATOR BOURNE: Now, if you will go on with the story.

MR. CROWE: Returning back to the wreckage, we heard various cries, and endeavored to get among them, and we were successful in doing so and in picking one body up that was floating around in the water; when we got him into the boat—after great difficulty, he being such a heavy man—he expired shortly afterwards. Going farther into the wreckage we came across a steward or one of the crew, and we got him into the boat, and he was very cold and his hands were kind of stiff, but we got him in and he recovered by the time we got back to the *Carpathia*.

SENATOR BOURNE: Did he survive?

MR. CROWE: Yes, sir; also a Japanese or Chinese young fellow that we picked up on top of some of the wreckage—it might have been a sideboard or table—that was floating around. We stopped until daybreak, and we saw in the distance a raft or Berthon boat submerged, in the distance, with a crowd of men on it. We went over to the boat and found probably 20, or there might have been 25, men and 1 woman; also 3 or 4 dead bodies, which we left. Returning again under canvas sail—we stepped our mast at night—we took in tow a collapsible boat containing fully 60 people—women, children, and men.

SENATOR BOURNE: How much water was there in your boat at that time? Was there still 8 inches, or had you any water in there at that time?

MR. CROWE: After we got some people out of our boat and returned to the wreck we did not take in so much water, because we bailed a certain amount of water out and no more seemed to come in.

SENATOR BOURNE: Then you infer that the strain was among the upper timbers, near the gunwale?

MR. CROWE: Yes, sir; I think, the boat being new, the wood had warped sufficiently to not prevent the water from coming in. Then we returned alongside the *Carpathia*, and then we landed our people. That is the story, sir.

SENATOR BOURNE: You were in boat No. 14 when it was lowered?

MR. CROWE: Yes, sir.

SENATOR BOURNE: Was there any shooting that occurred at the time the boat was lowered?

MR. CROWE: Yes, sir.

SENATOR BOURNE: Explain to the committee what knowledge or information you have relative to that?

MR. CROWE: There were various men passengers, probably Italians or some foreign nationality other than English or American, who attempted to rush the boats. The officers threatened to shoot any man who put his foot into the boat. He fired the revolver, but either downward or upward, not shooting at any of the passengers at all and not injuring anybody. He fired perfectly clear, upward or downward.

SENATOR BOURNE: Did that stop the rush?

MR. CROWE: Yes, sir.

SENATOR BOURNE: There was no disorder after that?

MR. CROWE: No disorder. Well, one woman was crying, but that was all; no panic or anything in the boat. . . .

SENATOR BOURNE: Did you and boat No. 14, with those that were with you manning the boat, return to the wreck as soon as your passengers were shifted into the other boat?

MR. CROWE: Yes, sir; almost immediately. There might have been a lapse of 5 or 10 minutes, perhaps.

SENATOR BOURNE: For what reason was that lapse; for the purpose of shifting your passengers to the other boat so you could return to the wreckage?

MR. CROWE: Because, endeavoring to get the other boats together, we were making a circle after each other, and consequently we lost our bearings, and we did not know in which direction to go.

SENATOR BOURNE: Did you know of any water on E deck?

MR. CROWE: Only from hearing other people speak of it.

SENATOR BOURNE: Would you state what you heard in reference to water being on E deck?

MR. CROWE: A stewardess—I do not know her name—said that as she came from her cabin she could see the water coming up.

SENATOR BOURNE: Could see it coming up?

MR. CROWE: Yes, sir.

SENATOR BOURNE: On E deck?

MR. CROWE: On E deck.

SENATOR BOURNE: And that was all?

MR. CROWE: That was all; yes.

SENATOR BOURNE: Did you see the ship sink?

MR. CROWE: I did, sir.

SENATOR BOURNE: Would you explain in your own way how it appeared to you?

MR. CROWE: When we left the ship her head was down in the water probably several feet; I could not say the distance, or any angle.

SENATOR BOURNE: And you left the ship how many minutes or hours after she struck?

MR. CROWE: It might have been an hour; it might have been more. After getting clear of the ship the lights were still burning very bright, but as we got away she seemed to go lower and lower, and she almost stood up perpendicular, and her lights went dim, and presently she broke clean in two, probably two-thirds of the length of the ship.

SENATOR BOURNE: That is, two-thirds out of the water or two-thirds in the water?

MR. CROWE: Two-thirds in the water, one-third of the aft funnel sticking up.

SENATOR BOURNE: How long did that third stick up?

MR. CROWE: After she floated back again.

SENATOR BOURNE: She floated back?

MR. CROWE: She broke, and the after part floated back.

SENATOR BOURNE: And the bow part, two-thirds of the ship, sank.

MR. CROWE: Yes, sir; then there was an explosion, and the aft part turned on end and sank.

SENATOR BOURNE: Then you attribute the sinking to the explosion. You believe it would have floated, had it not been for the explosion?

MR. CROWE: That I can not say, sir.

SENATOR BOURNE: Did the officer in charge of your boat express any opinion on that, at all?

MR. CROWE: He said he thought it best to return back to the wreckage and see if we could save any lives. At that time we had not put our people into the other boats.

SENATOR BOURNE: How long a time after you left the ship did it break and the explosion and sinking of the aft part of the ship take place, would you judge?

MR. CROWE: She sank around half past 2, from statements made by a man that was supposed to have jumped from the poop of the ship—that is, the quarter deck—into the water. He had a watch on, and as his watch stopped at 20 minutes past 2, he said she was in a sinking condition then and her stern on end—a man named Burnett, a storekeeper aboard ship.

SENATOR BOURNE: Did you, yourself, hear the explosion?

MR. CROWE: Yes, sir.

SENATOR BOURNE: Was there one, or more?

MR. CROWE: There were several explosions.

SENATOR BOURNE: Were they loud, like a cannon?

MR. CROWE: Not so loud as that, sir.

SENATOR BOURNE: Muffled?

MR. CROWE: A kind of muffled explosion. It seemed to be an explosion at a very great distance, although we were not very far away.

SENATOR BOURNE: How far, would you judge; about a quarter of a mile?

MR. CROWE: About a mile.

SENATOR BOURNE: You were about a mile away?

MR. CROWE: Yes, sir.

SENATOR BOURNE: Officer Lowe, you say, was in charge of your boat?

MR. CROWE: Yes, sir; I am certain of it.

SENATOR BOURNE: The fifth officer?

MR. CROWE: The fifth officer, Mr. Lowe. . . .

SENATOR BOURNE: Did Officer Lowe call for volunteers to return to the wreck?

MR. CROWE: No, sir; he impressed upon us that we must go back to the wreck.

SENATOR BOURNE: Was there any protest?

MR. CROWE: None whatever, sir. A second-class passenger named [C.] Williams, the champion racket player of England, returned with us.

SENATOR BOURNE: He volunteered his service?

MR. CROWE: Yes, sir.

SENATOR BOURNE: He was not requested by Officer Lowe?

MR. CROWE: Not at all, sir.

SENATOR BOURNE: He did so of his own volition?

MR. CROWE: Yes.

SENATOR BOURNE: Did you find ice on the ship before you left it?

MR. CROWE: I did not find it myself, sir. Another man brought a piece along from the forward part of the ship.

SENATOR BOURNE: On what deck?

MR. CROWE: On E deck. . . .

Witness: John Collins, 17
Assistant cook in the first-class galley, from Belfast, Ireland

Key testimony: He took a child in his arms but, apparently as the ship was breaking up, a "wave washed us off the deck—washed us clear of it—and the child was washed out of my arms."

. . . SENATOR BOURNE: I wish you would tell the committee just what you were doing immediately prior to, and what you did after, the time that the catastrophe on the *Titanic* took place, in your own language?

MR. COLLINS: I stopped work at 9 o'clock in Sunday night, and I came up again and walked up and down the alleyway. I went into my bunk and fell asleep. That was about 10 o'clock—about a quarter to 10. I fell asleep, and was sound asleep, and exactly at a quarter past 11 I was wakened up. I had a clock by me, by my bed, and my clock was five minutes fast, and it was exactly a quarter past 11 when the ship struck the iceberg, and it wakened me. I put on my trousers, got out of bed, and they were letting off steam in the stoke hole. I asked what was the matter, and it seemed she struck an iceberg. The word came down the alleyway that there was no harm, and everyone returned to their bunks.

SENATOR BOURNE: How long was that after the ship struck, which you say according to your clock was——

MR. COLLINS: About 10 or 15 minutes, sir.

SENATOR BOURNE: You are certain from your clock you saw at the time of the accident took place at exactly 30 minutes past 11, not according to that clock, but allowing for the five minutes that the clock was slow?

MR. COLLINS: No; the clock was fast, sir.

SENATOR BOURNE: I thought you said the clock showed 11:15, and the accident took place at 11:20?

MR. COLLINS: No, sir; the clock was 20 minutes past 11, and the accident took place at a quarter past 11, if my clock was right. I could not exactly say. I put on my trousers and went up on to the deck, up forward, and I saw the deck almost packed with ice on the starboard side.

SENATOR BOURNE: What deck was this?

MR. COLLINS: I could not say what deck it was; it was on the same deck we slept on. Coming from the funnels it would be C deck, I think. I am not exactly sure. I was not too well acquainted with the decks.

SENATOR BOURNE: You say the deck was packed with ice?

MR. COLLINS: Yes; on the starboard side.

SENATOR BOURNE: How far aft from the bow?

MR. COLLINS: Well, it was just—I could not say exactly how far, but the deck came up like this [indicating] and then came down like this [indicating] to No. 1 alley. It was all along. I could not exactly explain right to tell you how far it was from the back.

SENATOR BOURNE: Now, go on with your description.

MR. COLLINS: I went back into the bedroom and was told to lie down, and I got up again. I did not take off any of my clothes, and I came out again and saw the stewards in their white jackets in the passageway; the passengers were running forward, the stewards were steering them, and they made a joke of it, and we all turned in then and the word came in that we were to get out of our beds and get the life belts on and get up to the upper deck.

SENATOR BOURNE: At what time was it that this word came? How long after the ship struck?

MR. COLLINS: Well, it was exactly—I am sure—half an hour, sir. Quite half an hour, it was.

SENATOR BOURNE: Go on.

MR. COLLINS: We went up to the deck when the word came. Then I met a companion of mine, a steward, and I asked him what number my boat was, and he said No. 16; so I went up to No. 16 boat, and I seen sailors with their bags ready for No. 16 boat. I said to myself, "There is no chance there," and I ran back to the deck, ran to the port side on the saloon deck with another steward and a woman and two children, and the steward had one of the children in his arms and the woman was crying. I took the child off of the woman and made for one of the boats. Then the word came around from the starboard side there was a collapsible boat getting launched on the starboard side and that all women and children were to make for it. So me and another steward and the two children and the woman came around on that side, the starboard side, and when we got around there we saw then that it was forward. We saw the collapsible boat taken off of the saloon deck, and then the sailors and the firemen that were forward seen the ship's bow in the water and seen that she was intending to sink her bow, and they shouted out for all [that] we were to go aft, and the word came there was a boat getting launched, so we were to go aft, and we were just turning around and making for the stern end when the wave washed us off the deck—washed us clear of it—and the child was washed out of my arms; and the wreckage and the people that was around me, they kept me down for at least two or three minutes under the water.

SENATOR BOURNE: Two or three minutes?

MR. COLLINS: Yes; I am sure.

SENATOR BOURNE: Were you unconscious?

MR. COLLINS: No; not at all. It did not affect me much, the salt water.

SENATOR BOURNE: But you were under the water. You can not stay under the water two or three minutes, can you?

MR. COLLINS: Well, it seemed that to me. I could not exactly state how long, but it seemed that to me. When I came to

281

the surface I saw this boat that had been taken off. I saw a man on it. They had been working on it taking it off of the saloon deck, and when the waves washed it off the deck they clung to that; then I made for it when I came to the surface and saw it, and I swam over to it.

SENATOR BOURNE: Did you have a life belt on?

MR. COLLINS: I had, sir. I was only about 4 or 5 yards off of it, and I swam over to it and I got on to it.

SENATOR BOURNE: How many were on the collapsible boat?

MR. COLLINS: Well, sir, I could not exactly say; but I am sure there was more than 15 or 16.

SENATOR BOURNE: Did those who were on help you get on?

MR. COLLINS: No, sir; they were all watching the ship. I had not much to do. All I had to do was to give a spring and I got onto it; and we were drifting about for two hours on the water.

SENATOR BOURNE: When you had the child in your arms and went to this collapsible boat that you understood was being launched, why did you not get into it?

MR. COLLINS: Sir, we had not time, sir; they had not got it off the deck until we were washed off the deck.

SENATOR BOURNE: After the ship struck did you see any lights over the water anywhere before any of your boats were lowered?

MR. COLLINS: No, sir.

SENATOR BOURNE: After the boats were lowered did you see any lights that you believed was a ship coming to your relief?

MR. COLLINS: Yes, sir; there was three boats lowered.

SENATOR BOURNE: I do not mean of your own boats, but I mean any lights away from your own boats or your own ship. Did you see any light in the distance?

MR. COLLINS: I had the child in my arms, and I looked back at her stern end and I saw a green light.

SENATOR BOURNE: What did you think it was, one of your own boats?

MR. COLLINS: No, sir; I did not really think of what it was until the firemen and sailors came up and said that it was a boat.

SENATOR BOURNE: That is, a ship?

MR. COLLINS: Yes, sir.

SENATOR BOURNE: What became of it?

MR. COLLINS: Sir, it disappeared.

SENATOR BOURNE: How long was it visible?

MR. COLLINS: About 20 minutes or half an hour, I am sure it was.

SENATOR BOURNE: How far away, would you think, from the *Titanic?*

MR. COLLINS: I guess it would be about 4 miles; I am sure, 3 or 4 miles.

SENATOR BOURNE: You say you were swept off the *Titanic's* deck by a wave?

MR. COLLINS: Yes, sir.

SENATOR BOURNE: How long after the accident occurred or at what time would you judge it was that you were swept off of the deck?

MR. COLLINS: Well, sir, I could not say; I am sure it was close on to 1 o'clock.

SENATOR BOURNE: Was the ship sinking when you were swept off?

MR. COLLINS: She was, sir.

SENATOR BOURNE: When you came up from the water and got on this collapsible boat, did you see any evidence of the ship as she sunk, then?

MR. COLLINS: I did, sir; I saw her stern end.

SENATOR BOURNE: Were you on the boat at the time that you were washed off the ship?

MR. COLLINS: Amidships, sir.

SENATOR BOURNE: You say you saw the stern end after you got on the collapsible boat?

MR. COLLINS: Yes, sir.

SENATOR BOURNE: Did you see the bow?

MR. COLLINS: No, sir.

SENATOR BOURNE: How far were you from the stern end of the ship when you came up and got into the collapsible boat, would you judge?

MR. COLLINS: We were about—I could not exactly state how far I was from the *Titanic* when I came up to the surface. I was not far, because here lights went out then. Her lights went out until the water almost got to amidships on her.

SENATOR BOURNE: As I understand, you were amidships on the bow as the ship sank?

MR. COLLINS: Yes, sir.

SENATOR BOURNE: You were washed off by a wave. You were

under water, as you think, for two or three minutes, and then swam 5 or 6 yards to the collapsible boat and got aboard—and got into the boat. The stern of the ship was still afloat?

MR. COLLINS: The stern of the ship was still afloat.

SENATOR BOURNE: The lights were burning?

MR. COLLINS: I came to the surface, sir, and I happened to look around and I just saw the lights and nothing more, and I looked in front of me and I saw the collapsible boat and I made for it.

SENATOR BOURNE: After you got in the boat, did you see any lights on the *Titanic?*

MR. COLLINS: No, sir.

SENATOR BOURNE: When you were in the water, after you came up above the surface of the water, you saw the lights on the *Titanic?*

MR. COLLINS: Just as I came up to the surface, sir. Her bow was in the water. She had not exploded then. Her bow was in the water, and I just looked around and saw the lights.

SENATOR BOURNE: Had she broken in two?

MR. COLLINS: Her bow was in the water and her stern was up.

SENATOR BOURNE: But you did not see any break? You did not think she had parted, and broken in two?

MR. COLLINS: Her bow was in the water. She exploded in the water. She exploded once in the water, and her stern end was up out of the water; and with the explosion out of the water it blew her stern up.

SENATOR BOURNE: You saw it while it was up?

MR. COLLINS: Yes, sir; saw her stern up.

SENATOR BOURNE: How long?

MR. COLLINS: I am sure it floated for at least a minute.

SENATOR BOURNE: The lights were still burning?

MR. COLLINS: No, sir; the lights was out.

SENATOR BOURNE: How could you see it?

MR. COLLINS: I was on the collapsible boat at the time.

SENATOR BOURNE: If it was dark, how could you see?

MR. COLLINS: We were not too far off. I saw the white of the funnel. Then she turned over again, and down she went.

SENATOR BOURNE: There was not much of a sea on at the time of the accident?

MR. COLLINS: It was as calm as that board.

SENATOR BOURNE: How do you account for this wave that washed you off amidships?

MR. COLLINS: By the suction which took place when the bow went down in the water.

SENATOR BOURNE: And the waves broke over the deck and washed you off?

MR. COLLINS: Washed the decks clear.

SENATOR BOURNE: How many were around you at that time that were washed off?

MR. COLLINS: There were hundreds on the starboard side.

SENATOR BOURNE: And you think every one of the hundreds were washed in the water?

MR. COLLINS: Yes, sir; they were washed off into the water.

SENATOR BOURNE: The order had been given that every passenger and member of the crew should put on a life belt?

MR. COLLINS: Yes, sir.

SENATOR BOURNE: What became of those hundreds that were washed off at the same time you were?

MR. COLLINS: I got on to the raft. I could see when I got on to the raft. I saw the stern of the boat, and I saw a mass of people and wreckage, and heard cries.

SENATOR BOURNE: In the water?

MR. COLLINS: In the water.

SENATOR BOURNE: How many were rescued from the water beside yourself, on the boat you got into, which I understand was No. 16?

MR. COLLINS: No, sir; the boat we got into was not No. 16.

SENATOR BOURNE: What was the number?

MR. COLLINS: It was a collapsible boat.

SENATOR BOURNE: Was it not numbered?

MR. COLLINS: No, sir; not that I know of.

SENATOR BOURNE: The collapsible boats were not numbered?

MR. COLLINS: No, sir.

SENATOR BOURNE: How many of the hundreds that were washed off of the ship at the same time with you got into the collapsible boat with you?

MR. COLLINS: Well, sir, the boat was taken off the saloon deck, and the wave came up and washed the boat right off, and she was upside down, sir, and the water washed over her. She was turned over, and we were standing on her.

SENATOR BOURNE: You were standing on the bottom of the boat?

MR. COLLINS: Yes, sir.

SENATOR BOURNE: The boat being upset?

MR. COLLINS: Yes, sir.

SENATOR BOURNE: How many got on to the bottom of the boat with you?

MR. COLLINS: We lifted four people.

SENATOR BOURNE: There were five on there; four beside yourself?

MR. COLLINS: Oh, sir, there was more.

SENATOR BOURNE: There were probably 15 on there at the time you got on?

MR. COLLINS: Exactly, sir.

SENATOR BOURNE: Then what did you do?

MR. COLLINS: We were drifting about there; we drifted, I am sure, a mile and a half from the *Titanic,* from where she sank, and there was some lifeboat that had a green light on it, and we thought it was a boat after the *Titanic* had sunk. We thought this green light was some boat, and we commenced to shout. All we saw was the green light. We were drifting about for two hours, and then we saw the lights of the *Carpathia.* We saw her topmast lights. Then came daylight, and we saw our own lifeboats, and we were very close to them. We were about from this window here to over there, almost opposite them; but in the dark we could not see them. When it became daylight, we spied them and shouted to them, and they came over to us, and there was two of our lifeboats that lifted the whole lot that were on the collapsible boats. Then the *Carpathia* came into sight. We saw her masthead lights first and saw her starboard and port side lights. When she came near us, we saw her, and we did not know what boat it was. Then there was one of our own boats had got a sail, and we put up the sail. The fellow that was guiding this boat put up the sail. When he put up the sail, he told us he would come back and take us in tow. He did what he said; but we rowed for the *Carpathia,* and whenever we got in amongst a lot of wreckage we rowed on ahead. The wind rose, and the waves were coming up, and we were rowing for all we were worth. Then the *Carpathia* blew her horn, and we all seen the *Carpathia*. She stopped in the one place. We were at this time within a mile of her, and she did not make any sign of coming over near to us. She stopped in the one place, and, I think, lowered two or three of her own boats, and her own boats were kept in the water when one of our boats, the sailboat, went up alongside of her.

SENATOR BOURNE: Why did the *Carpathia* lower any of her boats as long as none of your boats were in distress?

MR. COLLINS: To take up some of the bodies that had been washed up by the side of her. . . .

SENATOR BOURNE: Did the men on the bottom of the collapsible boat refuse to let others get on from the water?

MR. COLLINS: Only one, sir. If a gentleman had got on we would all have been turned over. We were all on the boat. One was running from one side to the other to keep her steady. If this man had caught hold of her he would have tumbled the whole lot of us off.

SENATOR BOURNE: Who prevented him?

MR. COLLINS: We were all telling him not to get on. He said, "That is all right, boys, keep cool," he said; "God bless you," and he bid us good-by and he swam along for about two minutes and we seen him, but did not see him moving off; we saw his head, but we did not see him moving his hands. Then we were washed out of his road.

SENATOR BOURNE: There was only this one instance, then, when one tried to get on?

MR. COLLINS: There were others that tried to get on, but we would not let them on. A big foreigner came up; I think he was a Dutchman. He came up to the stern and he hung on to me all the time.

SENATOR BOURNE: Was he saved?

MR. COLLINS: He was, sir.

SENATOR BOURNE: Then all those who wanted to get on and tried to get on, got on, with the exception of only one?

MR. COLLINS: Only one, sir.

SENATOR BOURNE: That was when you had all on the boat that she could support?

MR. COLLINS: Yes, sir.

SENATOR BOURNE: He was not pushed off by anyone, but those on the boat asked him not to try to get on?

MR. COLLINS: Yes, sir.

SENATOR BOURNE: And he acquiesced?

MR. COLLINS: Yes, sir.

SENATOR BOURNE: You do not know whether he was saved or not?

MR. COLLINS: No, sir; I do not think he was.

SENATOR BOURNE: You say this was your first cruise?

MR. COLLINS: It was.

SENATOR BOURNE: On any ship?

MR. COLLINS: On any ship. . . .

Witness: Frederick Clench
Able seaman, from Southampton, England

Key testimony: Fifth Officer Lowe fired warning shots to control crowds at lifeboats, Clench said. A Frenchman jumped off the ship into his lifeboat. His lifeboat came to the aid of the overturned lifeboat carrying Second Officer Lightoller and Bride, the wireless operator.

. . . SENATOR BOURNE: Will you kindly explain in your own way what occurred just prior and subsequent to the catastrophe?

MR. CLENCH: I was asleep in my bunk when the accident occurred, and I was awakened by the crunching and jarring, as if it was hitting up against something.

SENATOR BOURNE: Were you sound asleep?

MR. CLENCH: I was sound asleep.

SENATOR BOURNE: Are you a heavy sleeper?

MR. CLENCH: No, sir; it did not take much to wake me. I am a light sleeper. If anybody touches me, I will jump quick. Of course I put on my trousers and I went on deck on the starboard side of the well deck and I saw a lot of ice.

SENATOR BOURNE: On the deck itself?

MR. CLENCH: On the deck itself.

SENATOR BOURNE: What deck was that?

MR. CLENCH: The well deck, sir. With that, I went in the alleyway again under the forecastle head to come down and put on my shoes. Some one said to me, "Did you hear the rush of water?" I said, "No." They said, "Look down under the hatchway." I looked down under the hatchway and I saw the tarpaulin belly out as if there was a lot of wind under it, and I heard the rush of water coming through.

SENATOR BOURNE: You heard that?

MR. CLENCH: Yes.

SENATOR BOURNE: How soon after you struck? How many minutes, would you think?

MR. CLENCH: I should say about 10 minutes, sir.

SENATOR BOURNE: After you were awake?

MR. CLENCH: After I was awake, yes. I went down below and put my guernsey on, my round hat on, and after that I sat down on a stool having a smoke.

SENATOR BOURNE: Down in the forecastle?

MR. CLENCH: Down in the forecastle.

SENATOR BOURNE: Although you had seen this water coming in?

MR. CLENCH: I seen the water coming in, and I thought it was all right.

SENATOR BOURNE: You thought she would not sink, Mr. Clench?

MR. CLENCH: I thought she would not sink then, sir. Then after I lighted the pipe, I heard the boatswain's pipe call all hands out on deck. We went up to where he stood under the forecastle, and he ordered all hands to the boat deck. We proceeded up on the boat deck, and when we got up there he told us to go to the starboard side and uncover the boats. I went down to No. 11 boat, unlacing the cover, and just as I started to unlace, along come an officer.

SENATOR BOURNE: Were you assigned to No. 11?

MR. CLENCH: No; No. 4 was my boat. We were sent there to uncover the boat, and an officer came along and drafted me on the other side, the port side. . . .

SENATOR BOURNE: The boat that you were in—what number was that?

MR. CLENCH: No. 12, sir.

SENATOR BOURNE: How many passengers were in it?

MR. CLENCH: Between 14 and 15, in ours.

SENATOR BOURNE: And only two seamen in it?

MR. CLENCH: Two seamen.

SENATOR BOURNE: No other members of the crew?

MR. CLENCH: No members of the crew. There was only one

male passenger in our boat, and that was a Frenchman who jumped in, and we could not find him, sir.

SENATOR BOURNE: Where was he?

MR. CLENCH: Under the thwart, mixed with the women. In fact, of course, we could not look for him just as we dropped into the water.

SENATOR BOURNE: He got into the boat before you lowered her?

MR. CLENCH: Before we lowered her.

SENATOR BOURNE: Without your knowledge?

MR. CLENCH: Without our knowing it.

SENATOR BOURNE: How do you think he was able to do that?

MR. CLENCH: I could not say that, sir. We were, of course, attending to the falls and looking out to see that they went down clear.

SENATOR BOURNE: All of the rest of your passengers were women and children?

MR. CLENCH: Women and children.

SENATOR BOURNE: You rowed away from the ship about a quarter of a mile?

MR. CLENCH: About a quarter of a mile.

SENATOR BOURNE: Then you rested on your oars?

MR. CLENCH: Then we rested on our oars.

SENATOR BOURNE: According to orders?

MR. CLENCH: According to orders.

SENATOR BOURNE: What happened then? How long did you rest and what did you do after you resumed rowing?

MR. CLENCH: We was rowing up there, and up come the officer, after the ship was gone down, come up with us with his boat, and transferred some of his people he had in his boat into two boats of ours; I could not say the number of the other boats, but he transferred his people into ours so that he would have a clear boat to go around to look for the people who were floating in the water.

SENATOR BOURNE: Could you, from your boat, see anybody floating or swimming around in the water?

MR. CLENCH: Never seen anyone, sir.

SENATOR BOURNE: Did you see the ship sink?

MR. CLENCH: Yes, sir.

SENATOR BOURNE: About a quarter of a mile away?

MR. CLENCH: About a quarter of a mile away.

SENATOR BOURNE: Did she sink bow down?

MR. CLENCH: Bow down; yes, sir.

SENATOR BOURNE: Did she break in two?

MR. CLENCH: That I could not say. . . .

SENATOR BOURNE: Was the distance too great for you to see whether there were any passengers on the stern?

MR. CLENCH: You could not discern any small objects. The lights were all out.

SENATOR BOURNE: Did you hear any cries of people in the water?

MR. CLENCH: Yes, sir; there were awful cries, and yelling and shouting, and that. Of course I told the women in the boats to keep quiet, and consoled them a bit. I told them it was men in the boats shouting out to the others, to keep them from getting away from one another.

SENATOR BOURNE: You did not look around you?

MR. CLENCH: I saw no one in the water whatsoever, whether alive or dead.

SENATOR BOURNE: You did not see any wreckage around you?

MR. CLENCH: No, sir; we never seen no wreckage around us.

SENATOR BOURNE: How long did you remain about a quarter of a mile from the ship after you reached that point? Did you remain there any length of time, or did you keep on rowing away?

MR. CLENCH: No, sir; we remained there, I should say, up until about 4 o'clock.

SENATOR BOURNE: A matter of an hour and a half?

MR. CLENCH: Yes, sir; it was just after we got the women from Mr. Lowe's boat, and he said he was going around the wreckage to see if he could find anybody.

SENATOR BOURNE: How many did you have in your boat after you had taken part of the load from Mr. Lowe's boat?

MR. CLENCH: I should say we had close onto 60, then.

SENATOR BOURNE: Full up?

MR. CLENCH: Yes, sir; we were pretty well full up then.

SENATOR BOURNE: What direction did Mr. Lowe give you?

MR. CLENCH: He told us to lie on our oars and keep together until he came back to us.

SENATOR BOURNE: He, in the meantime, having gone to see if he could rescue anybody where the ship had sunk?

MR. CLENCH: Yes, sir; and while Mr. Lowe was gone I heard

shouts. Of course I looked around, and I saw a boat in the way that appeared to be like a funnel. We started to back away then. We thought it was the top of the funnel. I put my head over the gunwale and looked along the water's edge and saw some men on a raft. Then I heard two whistles blown. I sang out "Aye, aye; I am coming over," and we pulled over and found it was a raft—not a raft, exactly, but an overturned boat—and Mr. Lightoller was there on that boat, and I believe—I do not know whether I am right or not, but I think the wireless operator was on there, too. We took them on board the boat and we shared the amount of the room that was there.

SENATOR BOURNE: How many were there on this boat that was there?

MR. CLENCH: I should say about 20, sir.

SENATOR BOURNE: So that you had about 60 at the time you rescued them, and you took on approximately 10 more?

MR. CLENCH: Yes, sir; that made about 70 in my boat.

SENATOR BOURNE: The 60 were all women and children, except one man and your mate?

MR. CLENCH: Me and my mate—that is, when we came away from the boat; but when we got transferred we had some more put aboard from Mr. Lowe's boat. They were all men we picked up off of the raft, or the overturned boat. It was a raft more than anything.

SENATOR BOURNE: Was it one of the collapsible boats that had overturned?

MR. CLENCH: Some term them "collapsible" boats, and some term them "surf" boats.

SENATOR BOURNE: But she was bottom up?

MR. CLENCH: Bottom up, sir.

SENATOR BOURNE: They were all standing on the bottom?

MR. CLENCH: On the bottom of the boat, sir; and Mr. Lightoller, he came aboard of us. They were all wet through, apparently; they had been in the water.

SENATOR BOURNE: Then what did you do?

MR. CLENCH: Mr. Lightoller took charge of us and sighted the *Carpathia*'s lights. Then we started heading for that. We had to row a tidy distance to the *Carpathia*, because there was boats ahead of us, you see, and we had a boat in tow with us, besides all the people we had aboard. . . .

SENATOR BOURNE: Did you hear any shooting?

WHITE STAR LINE
ROYAL & STEAMERS — UNITED STATES MAIL

FIRST SAILING OF THE LATEST ADDITION TO THE WHITE STAR FLEET

The Queen of the Ocean

TITANIC

LENGTH 882½ FT.   OVER 45,000 TONS   BEAM 92½ FT.
TRIPLE-SCREWS

This, the Latest, Largest and Finest Steamer Afloat, will sail from

WHITE STAR LINE, PIER 59 (North River), NEW YORK

Saturday, April 20th
At 12 Noon

THIRD CLASS FOUR BERTH ROOM

Spacious Dining Saloons
Smoking Room
Ladies' Reading Room
Covered Promenade

All passengers berthed in closed rooms containing 2, 4, or 6 berths, a large number equipped with washstands, etc.

THIRD CLASS DINING SALOON

Reservations of Berths may be made direct with this Office or through any of our accredited Agents

THIRD CLASS RATES ARE:

To PLYMOUTH, SOUTHAMPTON, LONDON, LIVERPOOL and GLASGOW.	**$36.25**
To GOTHENBURG, MALMÖ, CHRISTIANIA, COPENHAGEN, ESBJERG, Etc.	41.50
To STOCKHOLM, ABO, HANGO, HELSINGFORS,	44.50
To HAMBURG, BREMEN, ANTWERP, AMSTERDAM, ROTTERDAM, HAVRE, CHERBOURG	45.00

TURIN, $48.   NAPLES, $52.50.   PIRAEUS, $55.   BEYROUTH, $61, Etc., Etc.

DO NOT DELAY: Secure your tickets through the local Agents or direct from

WHITE STAR LINE, 9 Broadway, New York

TICKETS FOR SALE HERE

Advertisement for the White Star Line's *Titanic*.
[Archive Photos]

The *Titanic* under construction in Belfast.
[UPI/Corbis-Bettmann]

The *Titanic* docked at Southampton, England, before its doomed maiden voyage. [Popperfoto/ Archive Photos]

FIRST CLASS PASSENGER LIST

PER

ROYAL AND U.S. MAIL

S.S. "Titanic,"

FROM SOUTHAMPTON AND CHERBOURG
TO NEW YORK

(Via QUEENSTOWN).

Wednesday, 10th April, 1912.

Captain, E. J. Smith, R.D. (Commr. R.N.R.).
Surgeon, W. F. N. O'Loughlin.
Asst. Surgeon, J. E. Simpson.
Pursers: H. W. McElroy.
R. L. Barker.
Chief Steward, A. Latimer.

Allen, Miss Elizabeth Walton

Allison, Mr. H. J.

Allison, Mrs. H. J. and Maid

Allison, Miss

Allison, Master and Nurse

Anderson, Mr. Harry

Andrews, Miss Cornelia I.

Andrews, Mr. Thomas

Appleton, Mrs. E. D.

Artagaveytia, Mr. Ramon

Astor, Colonel J. J. and Manservant

Astor, Mrs. J. J. and Maid

Aubert, Mrs. N. and Maid

Page one of the *Titanic*'s first-class passenger list. [Tony Stone Images]

A grimly prophetic photo of the *Titanic*'s bridge and one of its lifeboats, made by Rev. F. M. Browne, a passenger who disembarked after the short run from Southampton to Queenstown, Ireland, a few days before the disaster. [UPI/Corbis-Bettmann]

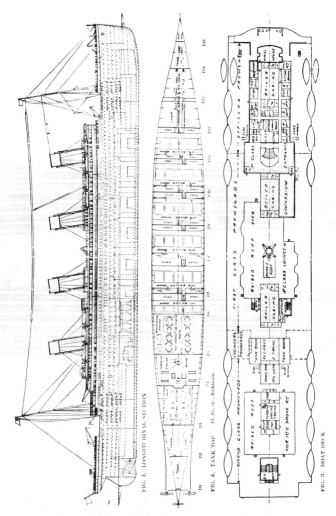

FIG. 1. LONGITUDINAL SECTION

FIG. 2. TANK TOP   Bl. Bk. &c. Bulkheads

FIG. 3. BOAT DECK

Longitudinal section, Tank Top, and Boat Deck of the *Titanic*.

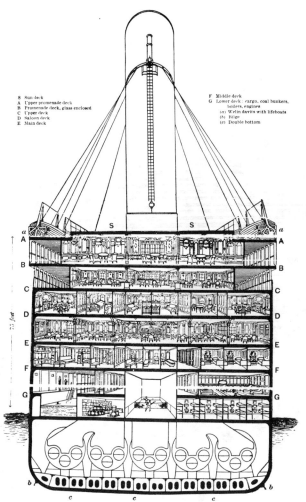

S Sun-deck
A Upper promenade deck
B Promenade deck, glass enclosed
C Upper deck
D Saloon deck
E Main deck

F Middle deck
G Lower deck : cargo, coal bunkers,
    boilers, engines
    (a) Welin davits with lifeboats
    (b) Bilge
    (c) Double bottom

FIG. 4. TRANSVERSE (AMIDSHIP) SECTION OF THE TITANIC

Transverse section of the *Titanic*.

A dining room aboard the *Titanic*.
[Express News/Archive Photos]

The *Titanic*'s Grand Staircase. [Popperfoto]

J. Bruce Ismay (facing camera, with mustache), testifies at the U.S. Senate inquiry at the Waldorf-Astoria in New York. The head of the *Titanic*'s parent company survived when many of his customers, including women and children, did not.
[UPI/Corbis-Bettmann]

BUNGLING WITH LIFEBOATS COST NEARLY 200 LIVES IN SINKING OF TITANIC

Second Officer Haltingly Tells of Sending Away Craft With Only One-Third Their Complement.

ISMAY IS RELUCTANT WITNESS

Asserts He Climbed Into Lifeboat Only When No Other Passengers on Ill-fated Titanic Were in Sight.

RAYNOR DENOUNCES ISMAY AS COWARD

Maryland Senator, in Bitter Speech on Floor of Senate, Demands Punishment for Those Found Responsible for Awful Toll of Death.

ATLANTIC SHIP LANE MOVED 180 MILES SOUTHWARD

Government Issues Order to Steamship Companies — Survivors Add to Graphic Stories of Sinking of Titanic and Rescue From Death by Carpathia.

Headlines from the April 16, 1912, edition of the *Los Angeles Times*.

The *Titanic* hearings in New York. Behind table, from left:
Senator George C. Perkins of California; Senator William A.
Smith of Michigan, Chairman of the Senate subcommittee;
Senator Francis G. Newlands, Democrat of Nevada, the
subcommittee's vice chairman; and Senator Duncan U.
Fletcher of Florida. [Stock Montage, Inc.]

Captain Arthur
Henry Rostron of
the *Carpathia* (at
right), testifies
at the *Titanic*
hearings in New
York. His ship
was the only one
to come to the
rescue of *Titanic*
survivors.
[Underwood &
Underwood/
Corbis-Bettmann]

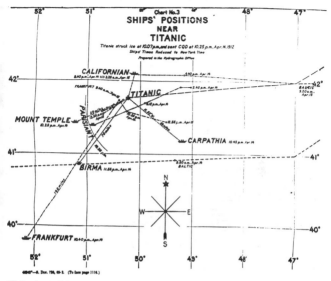

Ships' positions near the *Titanic,* from naval testimony.

Harold Bride, the *Titanic*'s wounded wireless operator, testifying at the Senate hearings at the Waldorf-Astoria on April 20, 1912. [Underwood & Underwood/Corbis-Bettmann]

Herbert John Pitman, the *Titanic*'s Third Officer, who told the Senate investigators in Washington that the men under his command lay on their oars in the lifeboat rather than return to the scene of the disaster to rescue screaming victims. [Corbis]

Guglielmo Marconi, the wireless pioneer and entrepreneur, assailed for his operators' handling of information in the disaster. [Archive Photos]

The ship's purser and Captain Edward J. Smith (right) aboard the *Titanic* on the run from Southampton to Queenstown, in a picture by Rev. Browne. [UPI/Corbis-Bettmann]

Some of the *Titanic*'s officers on the bridge before the maiden voyage. All were lost. [Archive Photos]

Isidor and Ida Straus (above). She refused to board a lifeboat without her husband and died with him. [Corbis]

Col. John Jacob Astor, who perished in the disaster. [Archive Photos]

His widow, Madeleine Astor, who survived and gave birth to a son shortly after her rescue. [Tony Stone Images]

Col. Archibald Gracie, who survived the disaster by clambering onto an overturned lifeboat. [Corbis]

A message from the *Titanic* at the end.
[Archive Photos/Express Newspapers]

Survivors in their lifeboat, in a photograph taken from aboard the *Carpathia*. [Underwood & Underwood/Corbis-Bettmann]

A lifeboat from the *Titanic* (left) being lifted aboard the rescue ship *Carpathia*. [Archive Photos/APA]

Mr. and Mrs. George A. Harder, a honeymoon couple from Brooklyn, who were rescued. Facing them, with her head in her hands, is Mrs. Charles M. Hays, whose husband was president of the Grand Trunk Railway and went down with the *Titanic*. [Underwood & Underwood/Corbis-Bettmann]

A huge crowd gathered in front of the White Star Line office on lower Broadway in New York to get the latest news on survivors of the *Titanic* disaster. [AP/Wide World]

Survivors of the *Titanic*'s crew: (first row, left to right): Archer, Fleet, Perkis, Symons, Clench; (second row, left to right): Bright, Hogg, Moore, Osman, Etches. [Stock Montage, Inc.]

Charles Lightoller, right, the *Titanic's* Second Officer, who defended Ismay in the Senate hearings, arrives in Liverpool from New York after his testimony.
[Tony Stone Images]

The *Titanic's* Fifth Officer, Harold Godfrey Lowe, who told the Senators that as his lifeboat was being lowered, he fired his pistol along each deck to prevent men from jumping on.
[Corbis]

MR. CLENCH: Yes, sir; Mr. Lowe was in No. 14 boat, and he sings out, "Anybody attempting to get into these boats while we are lowering them, I will shoot them," and he shot three shots.

SENATOR BOURNE: Did he shoot anybody?

MR. CLENCH: He shot straight down in the water.

SENATOR BOURNE: Did not fire at anybody?

MR. CLENCH: No, sir; just shot to frighten the people.

SENATOR BOURNE: Was there any effort made, after he fired three shots, by anyone to get into the boat?

MR. CLENCH: No, sir.

SENATOR BOURNE: There was no confusion at all?

MR. CLENCH: No confusion whatever, sir. Everything went as if it was boat drill in Southampton. . . .

SENATOR BOURNE: Was there any criticism on the part of any of the men that any of the officers were incompetent, or that there was any intemperance or that there was anyone to blame for the disaster?

MR. CLENCH: No; I can not say that there is.

SENATOR BOURNE: You have not heard of any?

MR. CLENCH: I have not heard of any. As for any intemperance, you seldom saw anything on a boat like that. I mean to say you can not get anything to drink there, so you are bound to be a teetotaler there. . . .

Witness: Samuel S. Hemming, 43
Seaman, from Southampton, England

Key Testimony: After the collision, a mate passed the word that Thomas Andrews, the Titanic's *designer, who perished, had confided that the ship was doomed. Hemming told of swimming 200 yards in the frigid water to a lifeboat, without a life preserver.*

. . . SENATOR SMITH: Where were you the night of this accident?

MR. HEMMING: I was in my bunk.

SENATOR SMITH: Were you asleep?

MR. HEMMING: Yes, sir.

SENATOR SMITH: Were you awakened by anybody?

MR. HEMMING: I was awakened by the impact, sir.

SENATOR SMITH: What did you do when you were awakened?

MR. HEMMING: I went out and put my head through the porthole to see what we hit. I made the remark to the storekeeper. "It must have been ice." I said, "I do not see anything."

SENATOR SMITH: What made you think it was ice?

MR. HEMMING: Because I could not see anything.

SENATOR SMITH: You mean you looked to see if you saw the lights of another boat, and, not being able to see any such thing, you thought it was ice?

MR. HEMMING: Yes, sir.

SENATOR SMITH: Had you ever seen ice in that part of the ocean before?

MR. HEMMING: No, sir.

SENATOR SMITH: Had you ever been through that part before, on your route?

MR. HEMMING: Yes, sir.

SENATOR SMITH: What did you do then?

MR. HEMMING: I went up under the forecastle head to see where the hissing noise came from.

SENATOR SMITH: What did you find?

MR. HEMMING: Nothing.

SENATOR SMITH: Go right along and tell what you did.

MR. HEMMING: I did not see anything. I opened the forepeak storeroom; me and the storekeeper went down as far as the top of the tank and found everything dry.

I came up to ascertain where the hissing noise was still coming from. I found it was the air escaping out of the exhaust of the tank.

At that time the chief officer, Mr. Wilde, put his head around the hawse pipe and says: "What is that, Hemming?" I said: "The air is escaping from the forepeak tank. She is making water in the forepeak tank, but the storeroom is quite dry." He said, "All right," and went away.

SENATOR SMITH: What did you do then?

MR. HEMMING: I went back and turned in.

SENATOR SMITH: Do you mean that you went back to your bunk and went to sleep?

MR. HEMMING: Me and the storekeeper went back and turned into our bunks.

SENATOR SMITH: How long did you stay in your bunks?

MR. HEMMING: We went back in our bunks a few minutes.

Then the joiner came in and he said: "If I were you, I would turn out, you fellows. She is making water, one-two-three, and the racket court is getting filled up."

Just as he went, the boatswain came, and he says, "Turn out, you fellows," he says; "you haven't half an hour to live." He said: "That is from Mr. [Thomas] Andrews." He said: "Keep it to yourselves, and let no one know."

SENATOR SMITH: Mr. Andrews was of the firm of Harland & Wolff, the builders of the ship?

MR. HEMMING: Yes.

SENATOR SMITH: How long was that after the ship struck this ice?

MR. HEMMING: It would be about a quarter of an hour, sir, from the time the ship struck.

SENATOR SMITH: What did you do then?

MR. HEMMING: I went on deck to help to get the boats out.

SENATOR SMITH: On which side of the deck?

MR. HEMMING: On the port side.

SENATOR SMITH: What boat did you go to? To which station did you go?

MR. HEMMING: My station was boat No. 16 on the boat list.

SENATOR SMITH: To what boat did you go?

MR. HEMMING: I went and helped turn out; started with the foremost boat, and then worked aft.

SENATOR SMITH: Did you assist in turning out the boats?

MR. HEMMING: Yes, sir. . . . I went on the boat deck. They were turning the boats out. As I went to the deck, I went there where were the least men, and helped to turn out the boats.

Then I went to the boats on the port side, to do the same, until Mr. Lightoller called me and said, "Come with me"; and he said, "Get another good man." I says, "Foley is here somewhere." He says, "I have no time to stop for Foley." So he called a man himself, and he said, "Follow me."

SENATOR SMITH: A passenger?

MR. HEMMING: No, sir; a seaman. He said: "Follow me." So we followed him, and he said: "Stand by to lower this boat." It was No. 4 boat.

We lowered the boat in line with the A deck, when I had an order come from the captain to see that the boats were properly provided with lights. . . .

SENATOR SMITH: What did you do, then, after that?

MR. HEMMING: After I had finished with the lamps, sir, when I made my last journey they were turning out the port collapsible boat. I went and assisted Mr. Lightoller to get it out.

After the boat was out I went on top of the officers' house and helped to clear away the port collapsible boat on that house. After that I went over to the starboard side. The starboard collapsible boat had just been lowered.

SENATOR SMITH: Do you mean lowered or pushed off?

MR. HEMMING: Lowered. She was away from the ship.

SENATOR SMITH: Then what?

MR. HEMMING: . . . I went to the bridge and looked over and saw the water climbing upon the bridge. I went and looked over the starboard side, and everything was black. I went over to the port side and saw a boat off the port quarter, and I went along the port side and got up the after boat davits and slid down the fall and swam to the boat and got it.

SENATOR SMITH: When you say everything looked black, you mean that there were no boats in sight?

MR. HEMMING: Everything was black over the starboard side. I could not see any boats.

SENATOR SMITH: You swam out to this boat that you saw?

MR. HEMMING: Yes, sir.

SENATOR SMITH: How far was it from the side of the *Titanic?*

MR. HEMMING: About 200 yards.

SENATOR SMITH: Did you swim that 200 yards?

MR. HEMMING: Yes.

SENATOR SMITH: Did you have a life belt on?

MR. HEMMING: No, sir.

SENATOR SMITH: When you reached the boat, what did you find?

MR. HEMMING: I tried to get hold of the grab line on the bows, and it was too high for me, so I swam along and got hold of one of the grab lines amidships.

SENATOR SMITH: What did you do then?

MR. HEMMING: I pulled my head above the gunwale, and I said, "Give us a hand in, Jack." Foley was in the boat. I saw him standing up in the boat. He said, "Is that you, Sam?" I said, "Yes"; and him and the women and children pulled me in the boat.

SENATOR SMITH: Who had charge of that boat?

MR. HEMMING: Perkis, quartermaster.

SENATOR SMITH: And they pulled you in?

MR. HEMMING: Yes, sir.

SENATOR SMITH: What did you find in the boat?

MR. HEMMING: It was full of women.

SENATOR SMITH: How many were there?

MR. HEMMING: There were about 40.

SENATOR SMITH: How many men were there?

MR. HEMMING: There were four men.

SENATOR SMITH: Who were they?

MR. HEMMING: Quartermaster Perkis, and there was Foley, the storekeeper, and McCarthy.

SENATOR SMITH: A sailor?

MR. HEMMING: A sailor, yes, sir; and a fireman.

SENATOR SMITH: What is his name?

MR. HEMMING: I do not know his name, Senator.

SENATOR SMITH: Were there any children in the boat?

MR. HEMMING: Yes, sir; there were children in the boat.

SENATOR SMITH: How many?

MR. HEMMING: Two young ladies and a little girl.

SENATOR SMITH: Altogether, then, there were how many; about 40 women and men and two or three children?

MR. HEMMING: I did not see the babies until after we got on the *Carpathia*. I did not see the babies at all when I got in the boat.

SENATOR SMITH: But they were in the boat?

MR. HEMMING: Yes.

SENATOR SMITH: And how many were there of the children?

MR. HEMMING: Three, sir. I think it was three. I would not be certain, but I think it was three.

SENATOR SMITH: I gather that there were 47 people put in the boat?

MR. HEMMING: There would not be 47 altogether, then, sir.

SENATOR SMITH: How many?

MR. HEMMING: About 40, all told, I should think, at that time, sir.

SENATOR SMITH: What was done after you got into the boat?

MR. HEMMING: They had been backing her away, to get out of the zone from the ship before the ship sank.

SENATOR SMITH: You did not return to the ship's side?

MR. HEMMING: No, sir.

SENATOR SMITH: Not at all?

MR. HEMMING: No, sir.

SENATOR SMITH: Or to the place where the ship sank?

MR. HEMMING: After the ship had gone we pulled back and picked up seven.

SENATOR SMITH: Who were they?

MR. HEMMING: I am not able to say, sir.

SENATOR SMITH: Who else?

MR. HEMMING: Stewards, firemen, seamen, and one or two men, passengers; I could not say exactly which they were; anyway, I know there were seven altogether.

SENATOR SMITH: Name what you can of them.

MR. HEMMING: There was one seaman named Lyons, and there were one or two passengers and one or two firemen. Dillon, a fireman, was one of them.

SENATOR SMITH: The others of the crew; can you recall that you picked up any of them out of the water?

MR. HEMMING: The storekeeper.

SENATOR SMITH: What is his name?

MR. HEMMING: It was the steward's storekeeper.

SENATOR SMITH: Do you remember his name?

MR. HEMMING: No, sir; I do not remember his name.

SENATOR SMITH: Who else?

MR. HEMMING: That is all I know of, sir.

SENATOR SMITH: You say there were two [male] passengers on your boat?

MR. HEMMING: I said one or two. I could not say exactly. I think there were seven men altogether. That is all I know.

SENATOR SMITH: Do you know who these passengers were?

MR. HEMMING: I know one was a third-class passenger.

SENATOR SMITH: What was his name?

MR. HEMMING: I do not know, sir.

SENATOR SMITH: Where was he from?

MR. HEMMING: That I could not tell you, sir.

SENATOR SMITH: Was he an Englishman or an American?

MR. HEMMING: I spoke to him, and I do not think he was an Englishman.

SENATOR SMITH: Do you think he was an American?

MR. HEMMING: He spoke very good English, but I have an idea that he was a foreigner of some sort.

SENATOR SMITH: You picked those seven men out of the water?

MR. HEMMING: Yes, sir.

SENATOR SMITH: Did they swim to the boat, or did the boat go to the men?

MR. HEMMING: Both. They swam toward the boat, and we went back toward them.

SENATOR SMITH: After you got these seven men in, what did you do then?

MR. HEMMING: We hung around for a bit.

SENATOR SMITH: Did you see any more men?

MR. HEMMING: No, sir.

SENATOR SMITH: Did you hear any more crying?

MR. HEMMING: We heard the cries; yes, sir.

SENATOR SMITH: Where? In what direction? Toward the *Titanic?*

MR. HEMMING: We were moving around, constantly, sir. Sometimes the stern of the boat would be toward the *Titanic,* and sometimes the bow of the boat would be toward the *Titanic.* One moment we would be facing one way, and a few moments later we would be facing another way; first the bow, and then the stern toward the ship.

SENATOR SMITH: What did you hang around for?

MR. HEMMING: We did not know what to do.

SENATOR SMITH: Did you pick up any more people in the water?

MR. HEMMING: Not from the water; no, sir.

SENATOR SMITH: Did these people that you picked up all live until you reached the *Carpathia?*

MR. HEMMING: No, sir.

SENATOR SMITH: How many died?

MR. HEMMING: Two.

SENATOR SMITH: Which two?

MR. HEMMING: Lyons and—I do not know whether it was a steward or a fireman—one more man besides Lyons.

SENATOR SMITH: Did the rest all live?

MR. HEMMING: Yes.

SENATOR SMITH: How long did you lay by at that time—after you picked these seven people out of the water?

MR. HEMMING: Not long, sir. We made for a light.

SENATOR SMITH: You saw a light?

MR. HEMMING: Yes; one of the boats' lights.

SENATOR SMITH: You mean a lifeboat light?

MR. HEMMING: Yes, sir.

SENATOR SMITH: Proceed.

MR. HEMMING: We pulled toward them and got together, and we picked up another boat and kept in her company. Then day broke and we saw two more boats.

SENATOR SMITH: Lifeboats?

MR. HEMMING: Yes. We pulled toward them and we all made fast by painters.

SENATOR SMITH: How long did you remain in that condition?

MR. HEMMING: Then we heard some hollering going on and we saw some men standing on what we thought was ice.

SENATOR SMITH: How far away?

MR. HEMMING: Half a mile, as nearly as I can judge.

SENATOR SMITH: How many men?

MR. HEMMING: A good few seemed to be standing there.

SENATOR SMITH: Give me the number approximately. About how many?

MR. HEMMING: Twenty, I should think.

SENATOR SMITH: Standing on this field of ice?

MR. HEMMING: No, sir; standing on what we thought was ice.

SENATOR SMITH: What did you do then?

MR. HEMMING: Two boats cast off—us and another boat cast off—and pulled to them, and took them in our two boats.

SENATOR SMITH: Where did you find them?

MR. HEMMING: On the bottom of this upturned boat.

SENATOR SMITH: Did you take all of the people that were on the upturned boat into your boat?

MR. HEMMING: No, sir; in the two boats.

SENATOR SMITH: You took them into the two boats?

MR. HEMMING: Yes, sir.

SENATOR SMITH: How many were there altogether?

MR. HEMMING: I could not say, sir. I guess about 20, I should say, stood up on the boat.

SENATOR SMITH: Were they standing up, or were they sitting down?

MR. HEMMING: They were standing up, sir.

SENATOR SMITH: What did you do? Did you take a portion of

them into the boat you were in, and the other portion in others?

MR. HEMMING: Yes, sir.

SENATOR SMITH: Who was the officer in charge of the boat that helped you in this?

MR. HEMMING: There was no officer, sir; a seaman.

SENATOR SMITH: What was his name?

MR. HEMMING: I think it was Poindexter. I am not sure, but I think it was.

SENATOR SMITH: Do you know what the number of the boat was?

MR. HEMMING: That I could not say, sir.

SENATOR SMITH: Did you see any officer in that boat?

MR. HEMMING: Mr. Lightoller was on the upturned boat.

SENATOR SMITH: Second Officer Lightoller was on the upturned boat?

MR. HEMMING: Yes, sir. . . .

SENATOR SMITH: What did you do then?

MR. HEMMING: We pulled away. We went away a bit. Then we pulled up until we saw the *Carpathia,* and we pulled to the *Carpathia.*

SENATOR SMITH: It was then daylight?

MR. HEMMING: Yes, sir.

SENATOR SMITH: Did you pull toward the *Carpathia?*

MR. HEMMING: Yes, sir.

SENATOR SMITH: Did all the people in your boat, then, live until they got to the *Carpathia?*

MR. HEMMING: Yes, sir. . . .

SENATOR SMITH: Do you mean to tell me that you swam from the *Titanic* two or three hundred yards?

MR. HEMMING: Two hundred yards, sir.

SENATOR SMITH: Two hundred yards without a life preserver on?

MR. HEMMING: Yes, sir.

SENATOR SMITH: Was the water cold?

MR. HEMMING: Yes, sir; it was cold, sir.

SENATOR SMITH: Did you suffer from the cold?

MR. HEMMING: It made my feet and hands sore, sir.

SENATOR SMITH: Why did you not put a life preserver on?

MR. HEMMING: After I got out of my room I never got back into my room again, sir. . . .

Witness: Frank Oliver Evans, 27
Able seaman, from Southampton, England

Key testimony: Evans recounted picking up survivors from the water in Fifth Officer Lowe's lifeboat. At dawn, under sail to the Carpathia, *a woman passenger passed a flask of whiskey around.*

. . . SENATOR SMITH: I wish you would tell what took place, so far as you know, of your own knowledge, on the *Titanic* from the time you sailed from Southampton up to the time of the accident and your rescue by the *Carpathia,* and state it in your own way and give me a connected story. . . .

MR. EVANS: . . . Sunday night was my watch on deck, and I was sitting at the table reading a book, and all of a sudden I felt a slight jar. I did not take any notice of it for a few minutes, until one of the other able seamen came down with a big lump of ice in his hands, and he said "Look what I found on the fore well deck," and he chucked it down on the deck; and I went up the ladder there and I met one officer.

SENATOR SMITH: Which officer?

MR. EVANS: The fifth officer, I think.

SENATOR SMITH: The fifth officer? Was it Lowe or Moody?

MR. EVANS: I think it was the fifth officer; the fifth or sixth officer. He told me to go down and find the carpenter and sound all the wells forward, and report to the bridge. I went down the engineer's alleyway to find him, and I met the boatswain there, and he said, "Who are you looking for, Evans?" I said "The carpenter." He said, "He has gone up." He said "What is the matter?" I said "I do not know. I think we have struck an iceberg." The boatswain went up, then. We went up and we looked down the forward hatch, where the tarpaulin was raising up with the wind, and I seen the boatswain again, and he told me to go down and tell the seamen to come up and uncover the boats, and make them ready for going out. I went up there with the remainder of the crew and uncovered all of the port boats. I then went over to the starboard side and lowered the boats there, with the assistance of the boatswain. . . .

SENATOR SMITH: What was the number of your boat?

MR. EVANS: No. 12 was my proper boat, on the port side.

SENATOR SMITH: Was No. 12 filled with women and children?

MR. EVANS: Yes, sir.

SENATOR SMITH: How many were put into it?

MR. EVANS: I should say, on a rough average, there was about 50, sir. There was one seaman standing in the stern sheets of it.

SENATOR SMITH: Were there any other men in it?

MR. EVANS: No, sir; I did not notice any other men in the boat. She was swung out on the davits. . . .

SENATOR SMITH: That boat was lowered. Were there any male passengers in there; any members of the crew, males?

MR. EVANS: I did not notice any. After we got them into that, I sung out to the seaman: "How many have you got in that boat?" I said: "Ginger, how many have you got?" He said: "There is only me here." I lowered that boat, sir, and she went away from the ship. I then went next to No. 10, sir, to that boat, and the chief officer, Mr. Murdoch, was standing there, and I lowered the boat with the assistance of a steward. The chief officer said, "What are you, Evans?" I said "A seaman, sir." He said, "All right; get into that boat with the other seamen." He said, "Get into that boat," and I got into the bows of this boat, and a young ship's baker was getting the children and chucking them into the boat, and the women were jumping. Mr. Murdoch made them jump across into the boat.

SENATOR SMITH: How far?

MR. EVANS: It was about two feet and a half, sir. He was making the women jump across, and the children he was chucking across, along with this baker. He throwed them onto the women, and he was catching the children by their dresses and chucking them in.

SENATOR SMITH: Were any children thrown overboard or any women?

MR. EVANS: One woman slipped and fell. Her heel must have caught on the rail of the deck, and she fell down and

303

some one on the deck below caught her and pulled her up. Her heel caught in the rail, I think, as she was jumping, and they pulled her in onto the next deck. She was a woman in a black dress.

SENATOR SMITH: Do you know who she was? Did you ever see her afterwards?

MR. EVANS: Yes, sir; she came up onto the boat deck again, and then jumped again, and she came into the boat that time all right.

SENATOR SMITH: Into your boat?

MR. EVANS: Yes; into No. 10 boat.

SENATOR SMITH: Who was she?

MR. EVANS: I could not distinguish her at all in the boat, and I never took no more notice of her.

SENATOR SMITH: We are talking about the No. 10 boat—the one that you were in.

MR. EVANS: Yes.

SENATOR SMITH: How many people were put into that boat with you?

MR. EVANS: There were about 60 persons, women and children.

SENATOR SMITH: How many women?

MR. EVANS: I should say about 57, sir. There were only me and another seaman and a steward, and two men besides.

SENATOR SMITH: And how many children?

MR. EVANS: Seven or eight children, sir.

SENATOR SMITH: How many men besides yourself?

MR. EVANS: I think there were one or two; there was me and another seaman and a steward, and two men.

SENATOR SMITH: Who were these men?

MR. EVANS: I do not know, sir. I think one was a foreigner that was up forward.

SENATOR SMITH: A passenger?

MR. EVANS: Yes; he was a passenger. The chief officer, Murdoch had cleared all the women and children from that side of the ship, and he asked if there was any more, and there was no reply came and the boat was packed, sir, and as this boat was being lowered this foreigner must have jumped from A deck into the boat.

SENATOR SMITH: Did he catch something and throw himself into the boat?

MR. EVANS: No; he just deliberately jumped across into the boat.

SENATOR SMITH: And saved himself?

MR. EVANS: Yes.

SENATOR SMITH: What occurred then; was it lowered?

MR. EVANS: It was lowered.

SENATOR SMITH: To the water?

MR. EVANS: Yes; to the water.

SENATOR SMITH: If I understand you correctly, Murdoch, who was chief officer, loaded that boat by having the women jump from the boat deck into the lifeboat?

MR. EVANS: Yes.

SENATOR SMITH: A distance of how much?

MR. EVANS: About 2½ or 3 feet.

SENATOR SMITH: In order to get them in there?

MR. EVANS: Yes.

SENATOR SMITH: Did the women hesitate about getting in?

MR. EVANS: One or two women did, sir; but he compelled them to jump. He told them that they must.

SENATOR SMITH: Did any women refuse to jump?

MR. EVANS: One or two women refused, in the first place, to jump; but after he told them, they finally went. . . .

SENATOR SMITH: Do you know which lifeboats you tied up to?

MR. EVANS: There was No. 12.

SENATOR SMITH: Your boat?

MR. EVANS: I was in No. 10, then.

SENATOR SMITH: Yes, I understand; but No. 12 was your own boat?

MR. EVANS: Yes, she was my original boat. That was my station.

SENATOR SMITH: What were the numbers of the other boats?

MR. EVANS: I was in No. 10, and we tied up to No. 12. We gave the man our painter and made fast, and we stopped there.

SENATOR SMITH: How long did you stop there?

MR. EVANS: We stopped there about an hour, I think it was, sir, when No. 14 boat came over with our officer.

SENATOR SMITH: What officer?

MR. EVANS: The fifth officer, I think it was.

SENATOR SMITH: Mr. Lowe, No. 14 boat?

MR. EVANS: No. 14 boat. He came over in No. 14 boat, and he says, "Are there any seamen there?" We said, "Yes, sir." He said, "All right; you will have to distribute these passengers among these boats. Tie them all together and come into my boat," he said, "to go over into the wreckage and pick up anyone that is alive there." So we got into his boat and went straight over toward the wreckage. We picked up four men there, sir, alive.

SENATOR SMITH: When you went over toward the wreckage, how many people were in your boat?

MR. EVANS: Eight or nine, sir.

SENATOR SMITH: And you picked up how many?

MR. EVANS: We picked up four persons alive.

SENATOR SMITH: Any dead?

MR. EVANS: One died on the way back, sir. There were plenty of dead bodies about us.

SENATOR SMITH: How many? Scores of them?

MR. EVANS: You couldn't hardly count them, sir. I was afraid to look over the sides because it might break my nerves down.

SENATOR SMITH: Did these bodies have life preservers on?

MR. EVANS: Yes, sir; from here upward [indicating] they were clear of the water. They were like that [indicating]. They simply had perished, sir.

SENATOR SMITH: The boat that came to you was under sail?

MR. EVANS: After we left the wreckage we made sail to another boat that was in distress, farther over.

SENATOR SMITH: That was Lowe's boat, was it not?

MR. EVANS: Yes.

SENATOR SMITH: When you picked up these four men, that left you 13 people in your boat?

MR. EVANS: Thirteen; yes, sir.

SENATOR SMITH: Did you see other people in the water, or hear their cries?

MR. EVANS: No, sir; none whatsoever, sir, other than these four persons we picked up.

SENATOR SMITH: Did you not hear the cries of anyone in distress?

MR. EVANS: No, sir.

SENATOR SMITH: For help?

MR. EVANS: In the first place, when the ship sank I was in No. 10 boat, then, sir.

SENATOR SMITH: When the ship sank you heard these cries?

MR. EVANS: We heard these cries, but we took them to be the boats that went away from the starboard side of the ship; that they were cheering one another, sir.

SENATOR SMITH: Giving them encouragement?

MR. EVANS: Giving them encouragement, sir. . . .

SENATOR SMITH: And you picked up four people?

MR. EVANS: Four people, sir.

SENATOR SMITH: One of whom died?

MR. EVANS: One died; yes, sir.

SENATOR SMITH: On the way to the *Carpathia*?

MR. EVANS: He died in the boat, sir.

SENATOR SMITH: One of whom died in the boat?

MR. EVANS: Yes.

SENATOR SMITH: Was that Mr. Hoyt?

MR. EVANS: I could not say. He was a very stout man.

SENATOR SMITH: A large man?

MR. EVANS: A large, fleshy man.

SENATOR SMITH: He was a large, fleshy man, and you had great trouble in getting him into the boat?

MR. EVANS: We had great trouble in getting him into the boat.

SENATOR SMITH: And you had to unfasten his collar to give him a chance to breathe?

MR. EVANS: Yes.

SENATOR SMITH: Why did you not go over toward the wreck quicker?

MR. EVANS: In No. 14 boat or in No. 10 boat, sir?

SENATOR SMITH: In No. 14 boat.

MR. EVANS: The officer was in command of that boat then, sir.

SENATOR SMITH: And he did not care to go over?

MR. EVANS: That I could not say, sir.

SENATOR SMITH: He did not order you to go over?

MR. EVANS: He wanted as full a crew as he could get, to go over there quicker.

SENATOR SMITH: He got the crew as soon as he got alongside of you?

MR. EVANS: Yes; he got alongside of these boats and got rid of his passengers. We never saw him before that, so that I do not know what he did.

SENATOR SMITH: How many men did he have in his crew?

MR. EVANS: In his crew in No. 14 boat, sir?

SENATOR SMITH: Yes.

MR. EVANS: Eight or nine, sir. There were stewards and firemen.

SENATOR SMITH: He had eight or nine when you went back to the wreck?

MR. EVANS: Yes.

SENATOR SMITH: But how many did he have in his crew when you first saw No. 14 boat?

MR. EVANS: I could not say, sir. I could not tell you that, sir. I never took the trouble to count them. . . .

SENATOR SMITH: After you took these four people into boat No. 14 from the water, what did you do?

MR. EVANS: I had a thorough good look around everywhere in the wreckage.

SENATOR SMITH: To see if you could see any life?

MR. EVANS: To see if I could see any live ones—any live bodies.

SENATOR SMITH: Did you see any alive?

MR. EVANS: No, sir.

SENATOR SMITH: A good many dead?

MR. EVANS: Yes.

SENATOR SMITH: Did you see any women dead in the water?

MR. EVANS: No, sir; mostly men.

SENATOR SMITH: Was it daylight at this time?

MR. EVANS: Just breaking daylight.

SENATOR SMITH: When you found there were no live persons whom you could rescue, why did you not take some of the dead ones aboard? You had lots of room.

MR. EVANS: That lay with the officer.

SENATOR SMITH: And what did he say about it?

MR. EVANS: He did not pass any remark at all, sir. He said, "Have a good look around, and see if you can see anybody alive, at all."

SENATOR SMITH: And when you did find anybody alive, what did the officer say?

MR. EVANS: The officer said, "Hoist the sail forward." I did so, and made sail.

SENATOR SMITH: Hoist the sail forward?

MR. EVANS: Yes; on the foremast; and we altered the course into the direction of this collapsible boat which had been swamped. On the way down we picked up another collapsible that had some women and children in it, and took her in tow, and then we sailed to this sinking boat.

SENATOR SMITH: What did you go out to the sinking boat for? There was nobody on it?

MR. EVANS: It was a boat that was swamped.

SENATOR SMITH: Yes; but you had taken the people off of that before.

MR. EVANS: No; we took this other boat in tow before we went to the boat that was swamped. We picked her up on our way down toward the boat that was swamped.

SENATOR SMITH: This boat that was swamped you went to after you had been around the wreck?

MR. EVANS: Yes; we came from the wreck direct in the direction of this boat that was swamped.

SENATOR SMITH: Then you took those people?

MR. EVANS: Yes; off that boat, into ours.

SENATOR SMITH: And let the collapsible drift?

MR. EVANS: Yes.

SENATOR SMITH: How many people did you find in that swamped boat?

MR. EVANS: There were about 4 of them and this 1 woman. There were about 12 men and 1 woman.

SENATOR SMITH: That made about 25 people, including the one who died?

MR. EVANS: Yes.

SENATOR SMITH: Did you take off of the swamped boat the dead bodies?

MR. EVANS: No, sir; we left them there.

SENATOR SMITH: You left them there to drift?

MR. EVANS: Yes; three of them that were dead.

SENATOR SMITH: Were those dead people passengers?

MR. EVANS: I could not say, sir. They were lying right over the thwarts, like that [indicating].

SENATOR SMITH: Did you know any of them?

MR. EVANS: No, sir.

SENATOR SMITH: Did you look at them?

MR. EVANS: No, sir, I did not particularly look at them. I was assisting the other passengers off.

SENATOR SMITH: Evidently you do not like to look at dead people very well.

MR. EVANS: No, sir.

SENATOR SMITH: Is that one of the reasons why you did not

pick up more of these dead people that were floating around there?

MR. EVANS: If the officer had given orders to pick them up, we should have picked them up.

SENATOR SMITH: But he gave no orders?

MR. EVANS: No, sir. . . .

SENATOR SMITH: After you got those people out of that swamped boat it was daylight?

MR. EVANS: Yes.

SENATOR SMITH: And you sighted the *Carpathia* coming?

MR. EVANS: Yes.

SENATOR SMITH: Did you row toward her?

MR. EVANS: We did not row toward her; we made sail.

SENATOR SMITH: You laid down your oars?

MR. EVANS: Laid down our oars and hoisted sail to make more speed, to get rid of these passengers, to get them aboard as soon as possible.

SENATOR SMITH: So that you went out with sail?

MR. EVANS: Yes.

SENATOR SMITH: To the *Carpathia?*

MR. EVANS: Yes; under sail to the *Carpathia,* with the collapsible boat in tow. One of the ladies there passed over a flash of whisky to the people who were all wet through. She asked if anybody needed the spirits, and these people were all soaking wet and nearly perished, and they passed it around between these men and women. . . .

SEVENTH DAY
Friday, April 26
Washington, D.C.

———

A major scandal was brewing over the "mystery ship" whose lights many survivors recalled seeing from the Titanic *and its lifeboats. The day's testimony brought forth clear indications that the steamer* Californian, *part of the Leyland Line, controlled by the* Titanic's *parent company, had seen the* Titanic *and heard her distress signals and done nothing.*

———

Witness: Ernest Gill, 29
Assistant engineer ("second donkeyman") on the
***Californian*, from Liverpool, England**

Key testimony: He affirmed the truth of his sworn affidavit printed the day before in the Boston American, *contradicting his captain, Stanley Lord, who had denied to the press that the* Californian *was within visual range of the* Titanic *and knew of its distress.*

... SENATOR SMITH: I want to read to you the following statement and ask you whether it is true:

I, the undersigned, Ernest Gill, being employed as second donkeyman on the steamer *Californian,* Capt. Lloyd, give the following statement of the incidents of the night of Sunday, April 14:

I am 29 years of age; native of Yorkshire; single. I was making my first voyage on the *Californian.*

On the night of April 14 I was on duty from 8 P.M. until 12 in the engine room. At 11:50 I came on deck. The stars were shining brightly. It was very clear and I could see for a long distance. The ship's engines had been stopped since 10:30, and she was drifting amid floe ice. I looked over the rail on the starboard side and saw the lights of a very large steamer about 10 miles away. I could see her broadside lights. I watched her for fully a minute. They could not have helped but see her from the bridge and lookout.

It was now 12 o'clock and I went to my cabin. I woke my mate, William Thomas. He heard the ice crunching alongside the ship and asked, "Are we in the ice?" I replied, "Yes, but it must be clear off to the starboard, for I saw a big vessel going along full speed. She looked as if she might be a big German."

I turned in, but could not sleep. In half an hour I turned out, thinking to smoke a cigarette. Because of the cargo I could not smoke 'tween decks, so I went on deck again.

I had been on deck about 10 minutes when I saw a white rocket about 10 miles away on the starboard side. I thought it must be a shooting star. In seven or eight minutes I saw distinctly a second rocket in the same place, and I said to myself, "That must be a vessel in distress."

It was not my business to notify the bridge or the lookouts; but they could not have helped but see them.

I turned in immediately after, supposing that the ship would pay attention to the rockets.

I knew no more until I was awakened at 6:40 by the chief engineer, who said, "Turn out to render assistance. The *Titanic* has gone down."

I exclaimed and leaped from my bunk. I went on deck and found the vessel under way and proceeding full speed. She was clear of the field ice, but there were plenty of bergs about.

I went down on watch and heard the second and fourth engineers in conversation. Mr. J. O. Evans is the second and Mr. Wooten is the fourth. The second was telling the fourth that the third officer had reported rockets had gone up in his watch. I knew then that it must have been the *Titanic* I had seen.

The second engineer added that the captain had been notified by the apprentice officer, whose name, I think, is Gibson, of the rockets. The skipper had told him to Morse to the vessel in distress. Mr. Stone, the second navigating officer, was on the bridge at the time, said Mr. Evans.

I overheard Mr. Evans say that more lights had been shown and more rockets went up. Then, according to Mr. Evans, Mr. Gibson went to the captain again and reported more rockets. The skipper told him to continue to Morse until he got a reply. No reply was received.

The next remark I heard the second pass was, "Why in the devil they didn't wake the wireless man up?" The entire crew of the steamer have been talking among themselves about the disregard of the rockets. I personally urged several to join me in protesting against the conduct of the captain, but they refused, because they feared to lose their jobs.

A day or two before the ship reached port the skipper called the quartermaster, who was on duty at the time the rockets were discharged, into his cabin. They were in conversation about three-quarters of an hour. The quartermaster declared that he did not see the rockets.

I am quite sure that the *Californian* was less than 20 miles from the *Titanic,* which the officers report to have been our position. I could not have seen her if she had been more than 10 miles distant, and I saw her very plainly.

I have no ill will toward the captain or any officer of the ship, and I am losing a profitable berth by making this statement. I am actuated by the desire that no captain who refuses or neglects to give aid to a vessel in distress should be able to hush up the men.

ERNEST GILL
Sworn and subscribed to before me
this 24th day of April, 1912.
SAMUEL PUTNAM, *Notary Public.*

I will ask you, witness, whether this statement is true?

MR. GILL: Yes, sir; that is correct.

SENATOR FLETCHER: What direction was the *Californian* going?

MR. GILL: We were headed for Boston, sir.

SENATOR FLETCHER: In what direction were the rockets from the *Californian* when you first saw them?

MR. GILL: On the starboard side, forward.

SENATOR FLETCHER: Was the *Californian* passed by the *Titanic,* her course being the same as the *Titanic's* course was originally?

MR. GILL: I think she must have passed the *Titanic.* The *Titanic* must have passed us first, because we were floating, and that would take a lot out of our way. We were a slower boat.

SENATOR FLETCHER: After the *Titanic* struck the iceberg did the *Californian* pass by the *Titanic*?

MR. GILL: The only way I can account for this, we were stopped in the ocean, and it is not natural for a ship to keep her head one way all the time. She must have been drifting.

SENATOR FLETCHER: How long after the rockets were sent up was it before the *Californian* got under steam and proceeded?

MR. GILL: I do not know what time she got under way, sir. It was somewhere about 5 o'clock, or in the vicinity of 5 o'clock.

SENATOR FLETCHER: Was that about daylight?

MR. GILL: Yes, sir.

SENATOR FLETCHER: Up to about that time the *Californian* was drifting?

MR. GILL: Yes, sir; with her engines stopped.

SENATOR FLETCHER: And you saw the rockets along about 2 o'clock, or before 2?

MR. GILL: About 12:30; at one bell, sir.

SENATOR FLETCHER: About 12:30 you began first to see the rockets?

MR. GILL: Yes, sir; at first, when I saw it it was not very plain.

SENATOR FLETCHER: Off on your starboard bow?

MR. GILL: Yes, sir.

SENATOR FLETCHER: What kind of rockets were they? What did they look like?

MR. GILL: They looked to me to be pale blue, or white.

SENATOR FLETCHER: Which, pale blue or white?

MR. GILL: It would be apt to be a very clear blue; I would catch it when it was dying. I did not catch the exact tint, but I reckon it was white.

SENATOR FLETCHER: Did it look as if the rocket had been sent up and the explosion had taken place in the air and the stars spangled out?

MR. GILL: Yes, sir; the stars spangled out. I could not say about the stars. I say, I caught the tail end of the rocket.

SENATOR FLETCHER: Did you see any lights on the steamer where the rockets were sent up?

MR. GILL: No, sir; no sign of the steamer at the time.

SENATOR FLETCHER: You could not see any lights at all?

Mr. GILL: No, sir.

SENATOR FLETCHER: You did not see any Morsing from that steamer?

Mr. GILL: No, sir.

SENATOR FLETCHER: Did you hear any noise; escaping steam or anything of that sort?

Mr. GILL: No, sir.

SENATOR FLETCHER: There was not much noise on the *Californian* at that time?

Mr. GILL: No, sir; not much noise on the ship.

SENATOR FLETCHER: What sort of a night was it?

Mr. GILL: It was a fine night.

SENATOR FLETCHER: No fog?

Mr. GILL: No, sir; a clear night; a very clear night.

SENATOR FLETCHER: You estimate that the rockets went up not over 20 miles away from the *Californian?*

Mr. GILL: It could not be 20 miles away, sir. I could not see 20 miles away. I seen the ship, and she had not had time to get 20 miles away by the time I got on deck again.

SENATOR FLETCHER: As I understand, you never did see the ship, did you?

Mr. GILL: No, sir; not without the one I seen, the big ship, that I told my mate was a German boat—not without that was the ship in question, the *Titanic.*

SENATOR FLETCHER: You think it may have been the *Titanic?*

Mr. GILL: Yes, sir. I am of the general opinion that the crew is, that she was the *Titanic.*

SENATOR FLETCHER: When did you first see her?

Mr. GILL: At four minutes after 12, exactly.

SENATOR FLETCHER: How do you know that?

Mr. GILL: Because at five minutes to 12 I was working with the fourth engineer at a pump that kicked, that would not work, and while we were interested in our work we forgot the time; and I looked up, and I said, "It is five minutes to 12. I haven't called my mate, Mr. Wooten. I will go call him." And I got to the ladder to climb out of the engine room and get on deck. That taken me one minute, to get up there.

SENATOR FLETCHER: Was this ship moving at that time?

Mr. GILL: I did not take particular notice of it, sir, with the rushing to call my mate. I went along the deck. It taken me about a minute, going along the deck, to get to the

315

hatch I had to go down, and I could see her as I walked along the deck. Suppose I am going forward, now; I could see her over there [indicating], a big ship, and a couple of rows of lights; so that I know it was not any small craft. It was no tramp. I did not suppose it would be a "Star" boat. I reckoned she must be a German boat. So I dived down the hatch, and as I turned around in the hatch I could not see her, so you can guess the latitude she was in. As I stood on the hatch, with my back turned, I could not see the ship. Then I went and called my mate, and that is the last I saw of it.

SENATOR FLETCHER: How long after that was it before you saw the rockets go up?

MR. GILL: About 35 minutes, sir; a little over half an hour.

SENATOR FLETCHER: Did you observe the rockets go up in the direction this ship was as you first saw her, from where the *Californian* was?

MR. GILL: It was more abeam, sir; more broadside of the ship.

SENATOR FLETCHER: In the meantime the *Californian,* as I understand, was drifting?

MR. GILL: Yes, sir.

SENATOR FLETCHER: She was not under way at all?

MR. GILL: No, sir.

SENATOR FLETCHER: Was the ship too far away, when you saw the rockets going up, for you to see the lights on her?

MR. GILL: Yes, sir; no sign of the ship.

SENATOR FLETCHER: What time was it when you heard these officers discussing this matter that was mentioned in this statement?

MR. GILL: Twenty minutes past 8 on Monday morning.

SENATOR FLETCHER: Have you been discharged or dismissed by the *Californian?*

MR. GILL: No, sir. I belong to the ship now.

SENATOR SMITH: Mr. Gill, did you ever see the North German-Lloyd ship *Frankfurt?*

MR. GILL: No, sir.

SENATOR SMITH: You did not see it that night or day?

MR. GILL: No, sir.

SENATOR SMITH: What made you think that this ship you saw, or thought you saw, was a German ship?

MR. GILL: Because the German ship would be heading to New York at about that time.

SENATOR SMITH: Heading for New York?

MR. GILL: Or from New York. It is in that vicinity we meet those boats.

SENATOR SMITH: I think that is all. . . .

Witness: Stanley Lord, 35
Captain of the *Californian*

Key testimony: In hindsight, Lord's encounter with the Senators seems bizarre. Summoned to appear under subpoena, Lord continued to maintain that the Californian *was 19½ to 20 miles away from the* Titanic, *out of visual range. But he recounted sighting and trying to signal an unidentified ship—not the* Titanic, *Lord insisted—that had earlier flashed signals that, Lord said, were not distress signals. Then, the captain said, he went to sleep. The Senators did not press Lord on this matter or confront him with assistant engineer Gill's assertions. Gill had been paid handsomely for his story and at the time Senator Smith was skeptical of it. Later, the panel would cite Lord for "reprehensible" indifference toward the* Titanic.

. . . SENATOR SMITH: Did you attempt to communicate with the vessel *Titanic* on Sunday?

MR. LORD: Yes, sir.

SENATOR SMITH: At what time of the day?

MR. LORD: Ten minutes to 11.

SENATOR SMITH: A.M.?

MR. LORD: P.M.

SENATOR SMITH: That is ship's time?

MR. LORD: At the ship's time for 47° 25' longitude.

SENATOR BURTON: That was of longitude 47° 25' west?

MR. LORD: Yes, sir.

SENATOR SMITH: What was that communication?

MR. LORD: We told them we were stopped and surrounded by ice.

SENATOR SMITH: Did the *Titanic* acknowledge that message?

MR. LORD: Yes, sir; I believe he told the operator he had

317

read it, and told him to shut up, or stand by, or something; that he was busy.

SENATOR BOURNE: That was the *Titanic's* reply?

MR. LORD: Yes, sir.

SENATOR SMITH: Did you have further communication with the *Titanic?*

MR. LORD: Not at all, sir.

SENATOR SMITH: Did the *Titanic* have further communication with you?

MR. LORD: No, sir.

SENATOR SMITH: Do you know the *Titanic's* position on the sea when she sank?

MR. LORD: I know the position given to me by the *Virginian* as the position where she struck an iceberg, 41° 56' and 50° 14'.

SENATOR SMITH: Figuring from the *Titanic's* position at the time she went down and your position at the time you sent this warning to the *Titanic,* how far were these vessels from one another?

MR. LORD: From the position we stopped in to the position at which the *Titanic* is supposed to have hit the iceberg, 19½ to 19¾ miles; south 16 west, sir, was the course. . . .

SENATOR SMITH: Do you know what time the *Titanic* sent out this C. Q. D. call?

MR. LORD: No, sir; I do not.

SENATOR SMITH: Did the *Californian* receive that call?

MR. LORD: No, sir.

SENATOR SMITH: Either from the *Titanic* or any other ship?

MR. LORD: We got it from the *Virginian.*

SENATOR SMITH: What time did you receive it?

MR. LORD: Six o'clock, sir.

SENATOR SMITH: A.M.?

MR. LORD: A.M., on the 15th. . . .

SENATOR SMITH: When you notified the *Titanic* that you were in the ice, how much ice were you in?

MR. LORD: Well, we were surrounded by a lot of loose ice, and we were about a quarter of a mile off the edge of the field.

SENATOR SMITH: Were there any icebergs in view?

MR. LORD: No; I could not see that; not then.

SENATOR SMITH: This ice that you were in was field ice?

MR. LORD: Field ice.

SENATOR SMITH: And how large an area, in your judgment, would it cover?

MR. LORD: Well, my judgment was from what I saw the next day; not what I saw that night.

SENATOR SMITH: Exactly; but how large an area would it cover the next morning?

MR. LORD: I suppose about 25 miles long and from 1 to 2 miles wide.

SENATOR SMITH: How badly were you interfered with by the ice on Sunday evening?

MR. LORD: How were we interfered with?

SENATOR SMITH: Yes.

MR. LORD: We stopped altogether.

SENATOR SMITH: What did you stop for?

MR. LORD: So we would not run over the top of it.

SENATOR SMITH: You stopped your ship so that you might avoid the ice?

MR. LORD: To avoid the ice.

SENATOR SMITH: And did you avoid it?

MR. LORD: I did.

SENATOR SMITH: When did you notify the *Titanic* of your condition? What was your purpose?

MR. LORD: It was just a matter of courtesy. I thought he would be a long way from where we were. I did not think he was anywhere near the ice. By rights, he ought to have been 18 or 19 miles to the southward of where I was. I never thought the ice was stretching that far down. . . .

SENATOR SMITH: Do you know anything regarding the *Titanic* disaster, of your own knowledge? Did you see the ship on Sunday?

MR. LORD: No, sir.

SENATOR SMITH: Or any signals from her?

MR. LORD: Not from the *Titanic*.

SENATOR SMITH: Was the *Titanic* beyond your range of vision?

MR. LORD: I should think so; 19½ or 20 miles away.

SENATOR SMITH: How long did it take you to reach the scene of the accident, from the time you steamed up and got under way Monday morning?

MR. LORD: From the time we received the message of the *Titanic*'s position?

SENATOR SMITH: Yes.

MR. LORD (reading):

Six o'clock, proceeded slow, pushing through the thick ice.

I will read this from the log book.

Six o'clock, proceeded slow, pushing through the thick ice. 6:30, clear of thickest of ice; proceeded full speed, pushing the ice. 8:30, stopped close to steamship *Carpathia*.

SENATOR SMITH: Was the *Carpathia* at that time at the scene of the wreck?

MR. LORD: Yes, sir; she was taking the last of the people out of the boats. . . .

SENATOR SMITH: I would like to ask you, Capt. Lord, to tell the committee what kind of watch you kept on Sunday night after the engines stopped. Did you keep an unusual lookout on duty?

MR. LORD: No, not after we stopped the engines.

SENATOR SMITH: Did you, up to the time you stopped?

MR. LORD: Yes.

SENATOR SMITH: Tell the committee of what that consisted.

MR. LORD: We doubled the lookout from the crew, put a man on the forecastle head—that is, right at the bow of the ship—and I was on the bridge myself with an officer, which I would not have been under ordinary conditions.

SENATOR SMITH: What time did you increase the watch?

MR. LORD: When it got dark that night.

SENATOR SMITH: As soon as it got dark?

MR. LORD: About 8 o'clock. I went on the bridge at 8 o'clock.

SENATOR SMITH: And you remained on the bridge how long?

MR. LORD: Until half past 10.

SENATOR SMITH: And this increased watch was maintained during all that time?

MR. LORD: Until half past 10.

SENATOR SMITH: You thought that was necessary in your situation at that time?

MR. LORD: Well, we had had a report of this ice three or four days before, so we were just taking the extra precautions. . . .

SENATOR SMITH: Where did you sail from on that voyage?

MR. LORD: London.

SENATOR SMITH: Bound for Boston?

MR. LORD: Boston; yes, sir. . . .

SENATOR SMITH: If you had received the C. Q. D. call of distress from the *Titanic* Sunday evening after your communication with the *Titanic,* how long, under the conditions which surrounded you, would it have taken you to have reached the scene of that catastrophe?

MR. LORD: At the very least, two hours.

SENATOR SMITH: Two hours?

MR. LORD: At the very least, the way the ice was packed around us, and it being nighttime.

SENATOR SMITH: Do you know how long it took for the *Carpathia* to reach the scene of the accident from the time the C. Q. D. call was received by Capt. Rostron?

MR. LORD: Only from what I have read in the paper.

SENATOR SMITH: You have no knowledge of your own on that?

MR. LORD: No, sir.

SENATOR SMITH: Capt. Rostron told you nothing?

MR. LORD: Oh, no. I asked him the particulars of the accident; that was all.

SENATOR SMITH: It took the *Carpathia* about four hours to reach the scene of the *Titanic*'s accident, after they received word.

MR. LORD: So I understand. . . .

SENATOR SMITH: You were about 20 miles away?

MR. LORD: Nineteen and one-half to twenty miles from the position given me by the *Titanic.*

SENATOR SMITH: At the hour the *Titanic* sank?

MR. LORD: We were 19½ to 20 miles away.

SENATOR SMITH: And the *Carpathia* was 53 miles away?

MR. LORD: Yes, sir.

SENATOR SMITH: How long after the *Carpathia* reached the scene of this accident did you reach the scene?

MR. LORD: Well, I don't know what time we got there.

SENATOR SMITH: Had the lifeboats, with their passengers, been picked up and taken aboard the *Carpathia*?

MR. LORD: I think he was taking the last boat up when I got there.

SENATOR SMITH: Did you see any of the wreckage when you got there?

321

MR. LORD: Yes, sir.

SENATOR SMITH: Tell the committee what you saw?

MR. LORD: I saw several empty boats, some floating planks, a few deck chairs, and cushions; but considering the size of the disaster, there was very little wreckage. It seemed more like an old fishing boat that had sunk.

SENATOR SMITH: Did you see any life preservers?

MR. LORD: A few life belts floating around.

SENATOR SMITH: Did you see any persons, dead or alive?

MR. LORD: No, sir. . . .

SENATOR SMITH: Captain, during Sunday, when you were in the vicinity of ice, did you give any special instructions to your wireless operator?

MR. LORD: No, sir. . . .

SENATOR SMITH: You had but one operator, had you?

MR. LORD: That is all.

SENATOR SMITH: And what was his name?

MR. LORD: Mr. Evans.

SENATOR SMITH: Is he here with you?

MR. LORD: Yes, sir; this is he [indicating].

SENATOR SMITH: Do you know whether your wireless operator was on duty Sunday night after you sent this warning message to the *Titanic?*

MR. LORD: I do not think he was.

SENATOR SMITH: You do not think he was on duty?

MR. LORD: No.

SENATOR SMITH: Then you are unable to say whether an attempt was made to communicate with the *Californian?*

MR. LORD: No; I do not know as to that. I went past his room at about a quarter to 12, and there was no light in there.

SENATOR SMITH: Does that indicate he was out, or asleep?

MR. LORD: That would indicate he was asleep. As a rule there is always a light in the accumulator burning when he is not asleep.

SENATOR SMITH: Did he have any hours particularly prescribed for him by yourself or anyone else after you became aware of your proximity to ice?

MR. LORD: No.

SENATOR SMITH: On Sunday?

MR. LORD: No.

SENATOR SMITH: Suppose your wireless operator had been at

his post in the operating room when the C. Q. D. call of distress came out from the *Titanic,* which was received by the *Carpathia* and other ships, would your ship have been apprised of the distress of the *Titanic?* I mean, have you such a wireless apparatus on that ship as would have in all probability caught this message?

MR. LORD: If the operator had been on duty?

SENATOR SMITH: Yes.

MR. LORD: Most certainly.

SENATOR SMITH: What has been the custom on your ship with reference to wireless service? Do you profess or undertake to have the operator on duty during the daytime or in the night?

MR. LORD: I have never interfered with them.

SENATOR SMITH: In any way?

MR. LORD: From what I have seen of him, he is generally around until about 10 o'clock in the morning, and next day gives me reports of things that happen after midnight, very frequently.

SENATOR SMITH: If you were to have the service of a wireless operator at a time when he might be of most service, when would it be, ordinarily, day or night?

MR. LORD: As it happens, there are so many one-operator ships around that at nighttime most of those fellows are asleep; and he would be more useful in the daytime. We would get a great deal more information in the daytime, as it happens now.

SENATOR SMITH: But at night your passengers are also asleep?

MR. LORD: Yes, sir.

SENATOR SMITH: Would it not be well to have your wireless operator at his post on duty at night, when other eyes are closed, in order that any possible signal of distress might not escape your attention?

MR. LORD: We have the officer on the bridge, who can see as far at night as in the daytime.

SENATOR SMITH: But the officer on the bridge could not see the *Titanic* even with glasses, you said, that night.

MR. LORD: No.

SENATOR SMITH: The wireless operator could have heard the call from the *Titanic* if he had been at his post of duty?

MR. LORD: Yes; he would have heard that. . . .

SENATOR BOURNE: I simply want to ask, Captain, whether the wireless operator had any regular hours or not? If so, what were they?

MR. LORD: No; I do not think there are any regular hours. I understand they are usually around from 7 in the morning to half-past 2, and then I think they lie down, because I never, as a rule, receive any messages between half-past 2 and 4. I presume they are asleep.

SENATOR BOURNE: You think it is better to have two operators on every ship, do you, so as to have continuous service?

MR. LORD: It would be much nicer. You would never miss a message, then. . . .

SENATOR SMITH: Captain, did you see any distress signals on Sunday night, either rockets or the Morse signals?

MR. LORD: No, sir; I did not. The officer on watch saw some signals, but he said they were not distress signals.

SENATOR SMITH: They were not distress signals?

MR. LORD: Not distress signals.

SENATOR SMITH: But he reported them?

MR. LORD: To me. I think you had better let me tell you that story.

SENATOR SMITH: I wish you would.

MR. LORD: When I came off the bridge, at half past 10, I pointed out to the officer that I thought I saw a light coming along, and it was a most peculiar light, and we had been making mistakes all along with the stars, thinking they were signals. We could not distinguish where the sky ended and where the water commenced. You understand, it was a flat calm. He said he thought it was a star, and I did not say anything more. I went down below. I was talking with the engineer about keeping the steam ready, and we saw these signals coming along, and I said, "There is a steamer coming. Let us go to the wireless and see what the news is." But on our way down I met the operator coming, and I said, "Do you know anything?" He said, "The *Titanic.*" So, then, I gave him instructions to let the *Titanic* know. I said, "This is not the *Titanic;* there is no doubt about it." She came and lay, at half past 11, alongside of us until, I suppose, a quarter past 1, within 4 miles of us. We could see everything on her quite distinctly; see her lights. We signaled her, at half past 11, with the Morse lamp. She did not take the slightest notice of it. That was between half past 11 and 20 minutes to 12. We signaled her again at 10 minutes past 12, half past 12, a quarter to 1, and 1 o'clock. We have a very powerful Morse lamp. I suppose you can see that about 10 miles, and she was about 4 miles off, and she did not take the slightest notice of it. When the second officer came on the bridge, at 12 o'clock, or 10 minutes past 12, I told him to watch that steamer, which was stopped, and I pointed out the ice to him; told him we were surrounded by ice; to watch the steamer that she did not get any closer to her. At 20 minutes to 1 I whistled up the speaking tube and asked him if she was getting any nearer. He said, "No; she is not taking any notice of us." So, I said, "I will go and lie down a bit." At a quarter past 1 he said, "I think she has fired a rocket." He said, "She did not answer the Morse lamp and she has commenced to go away from us." I said, "Call her up and let me know at once what her name is." So, he put the whistle back, and, apparently, he was calling. I could hear him ticking over my head. Then I went to sleep.

SENATOR SMITH: You heard nothing more about it?

MR. LORD: Nothing more until about something between then and half past 4, I have a faint recollection of the apprentice opening my room door; opening it and shutting it. I said, "What is it?" He did not answer and I went to sleep again. I believe the boy came down to deliver me the message that this steamer had steamed away from us to the southwest, showing several of these flashes or white rockets; steamed away to the southwest. . . .

Witness: Cyril Evans, 20
Marconi wireless operator on the *Californian*,
from Liverpool, England

Key testimony: Evans, who personally knew both Marconi operators on the Titanic, *said he had warned the ship of ice at about 11 P.M. Sunday night and had been told to "shut up." Evans said the ship's apprentice on the* Californian *had related telling Captain Lord three times about rockets during the night. Doubts about Lord's veracity mounted.*

. . . SENATOR SMITH: What time did you communicate with the *Titanic?*

MR. EVANS: In the afternoon, sir. I was sending a message to the *Antillian,* of our line. I was sending an ice report, handed in by the skipper, sir. I was sending to the *Antillian,* and the *Titanic* called me up and we exchanged signals, exchanged an official T R. We call it a T R when a ship gets in communication with another. I said, "Here is a message; an ice report." He said, "It's all right, old man," he said. "I heard you send to the *Antillian.*" He said, "Bi." That is an expression used among ourselves.

SENATOR SMITH: What does it mean?

MR. EVANS: It is an expression used. It means to say "enough," "finished." . . .

SENATOR SMITH: When did you next communicate with the *Titanic* and what was the message you sent or received?

MR. EVANS: 9:05 New York time, sir.

SENATOR SMITH: What day?

MR. EVANS: On the 14th, sir, the same evening, New York time, that is. I went outside of my room just before that, about five minutes before that and we were stopped, and I went to the captain and I asked him if there was anything the matter. The captain told me he was going to stop because of the ice, and the captain asked me if I had any boats, and I said the *Titanic.* He said "Better advise him we are surrounded by ice and stopped." So I went to my cabin, and at 9:05 New York time I called him up. I said, "Say, old man, we are stopped and surrounded by ice." He turned around and said "Shut up, shut up, I am busy; I am working Cape Race," and at that I jammed him.

SENATOR SMITH: What do you mean by that?

MR. EVANS: By jamming we mean when somebody is sending a message to somebody else and you start to send at the same time, you jam him. He does not get his message. I was stronger than Cape Race. Therefore my signals came in with a bang, and he could read me and he could not read Cape Race. . . .

SENATOR SMITH: What time did you retire that night?

MR. EVANS: At 11:25 I still had the phones on my ears and heard him still working Cape Race, about two or three minutes before the half hour ship's time, that was, and at

11:35 I put the phones down and took off my clothes and turned in.

SENATOR SMITH: When were you awakened?

MR. EVANS: About 3:30 A.M., New York time.

SENATOR SMITH: And who awakened you?

MR. EVANS: The chief officer.

SENATOR SMITH: What did he say to you?

MR. EVANS: He said, "There is a ship that has been firing rockets in the night. Please see if there is anything the matter."

SENATOR SMITH: What ship's officer was that?

MR. EVANS: The chief officer of our ship, Mr. Stewart.

SENATOR SMITH: He said rockets had been fired during the night?

MR. EVANS: Yes, sir.

SENATOR SMITH: And he would like to have you see if there was anything the matter?

MR. EVANS: Yes, sir.

SENATOR SMITH: What did you do?

MR. EVANS: I jumped out of bed, slipped on a pair of trousers and a pair of slippers, and I went at once to my key and started my motor and gave "C. Q." About a second later I was answered by the *Frankfurt*, "D. K. D., Dft." The "Dft," is the *Frankfurt's* call. He told me the *Titanic* had sunk.

SENATOR SMITH: He told you the *Titanic* had sunk?

MR. EVANS: Yes, sir. . . .

SENATOR FLETCHER: Do you know Gill, who was a member of the crew of the *Californian*—Ernest Gill?

MR. EVANS: I think I have seen him; yes, sir.

SENATOR FLETCHER: Do you know him when you see him? Did you see him on the ship?

MR. EVANS: Yes; I have seen him.

SENATOR FLETCHER: Did you ever have any conversation with him about that ship that was seen that night throwing up rockets?

MR. EVANS: I think so. Practically everybody on the ship— it has been common talk on the ship.

SENATOR FLETCHER: From the talk on the ship do you know when the rockets were seen that night; from what direction?

Mr. Evans: No, sir; I had turned in.

Senator Fletcher: Do you know of the conversation, or statement that was made to Gill, about which he has testified here?

Mr. Evans: I do not know, sir. Nearly everybody on the ship has talked amongst themselves, and in front of other members of the crew, about it.

Senator Fletcher: Has he ever said anything to you in reference to his statement or testimony in the case in this matter?

Mr. Evans: You mean any special statement he made to me?

Senator Fletcher: Yes. Has he ever said anything to you with reference to his statement that he has made in this matter?

Mr. Evans: No; I do not think so.

Senator Fletcher: Nothing with regard to the circumstances under which he made the statement, or how he came to make it?

Mr. Evans: No. . . .

Senator Fletcher: When the mate aroused you and spoke about a ship having been seen sending up rockets, did he make any statement about when that ship was sending, and what kind of rockets?

Mr. Evans: No. I slipped on my trousers, and got the phones on my ears inside of two minutes.

Senator Fletcher: That was at 4 A.M. on Monday morning?

Mr. Evans: That was 3:40 A.M., New York time.

Senator Fletcher: What ship's time was that?

Mr. Evans: I do not know. I have not worked out the ship's time. I do not know if the ship's clock was changed during that time.

Senator Fletcher: Did Gill, the donkeyman, ever talk to you about a story he was telling about the sending up of the rockets by a ship that night?

Mr. Evans: I think he may have mentioned it to me.

Senator Fletcher: When?

Mr. Evans: Everybody on board has been speaking about it amongst themselves.

Senator Fletcher: The captain, too?

MR. EVANS: No, sir. I have never spoken to the captain about the matter of rockets, at all.

SENATOR FLETCHER: None of this talk you have heard on the ship was in the presence of the captain?

MR. EVANS: No, sir.

SENATOR FLETCHER: In a general way, what was the talk with reference to that, that you heard on the ship?

MR. EVANS: Well, I could not say. It was just simply the usual talk about the rockets.

SENATOR FLETCHER: Were the rockets described?

MR. EVANS: Not to my knowledge, no sir. I never heard them described.

SENATOR FLETCHER: Do you know whether they were distress rockets, or some other kind of rockets?

MR. EVANS: No, sir; I do not. I did not see them, myself.

SENATOR FLETCHER: As they were mentioned in this talk on the ship?

MR. EVANS: No, sir; I do not know.

SENATOR BURTON: You say everybody was talking on board among themselves about these rockets?

MR. EVANS: Yes, sir.

SENATOR BURTON: Do you mean by that that they were saying that they themselves had seen the rockets, or that there was merely talk about it on the ship?

MR. EVANS: There was talk about it, and some of them said they had seen it, and some said they had not. . . .

SENATOR SMITH: Do you know why you were not called when the rockets were first seen?

MR. EVANS: No, sir.

SENATOR SMITH: What did the first mate or any other officer of the ship or member of the crew tell you about Capt. Lord being notified three times that a vessel was sending up rockets?

MR. EVANS: Well, we have talked among ourselves, but——

SENATOR SMITH: One minute. I do not want any idle gossip. If you can recall anything that was said by any officer of your ship about that matter, I would like to have you state it; and if you can not, say so.

MR. EVANS: I know that the mate did not say anything to me; no.

SENATOR SMITH: The mate did not?

MR. EVANS: The mate did not say anything about the captain being notified——

SENATOR SMITH: And the mate was the man that called you?

MR. EVANS: Yes; the mate was the man who called me.

SENATOR SMITH: Did any other officer of the *Californian* say anything to you about having notified the captain three times that a vessel was sending up rockets?

MR. EVANS: I think the apprentice did.

SENATOR SMITH: What is his name?

MR. EVANS: Gibson.

SENATOR SMITH: Is he now on the *Californian?*

MR. EVANS: Yes, sir.

SENATOR SMITH: What did he say to you?

MR. EVANS: I do not know, exactly. I know the effect.

SENATOR SMITH: I would rather have the language he used if you can give it.

MR. EVANS: I do not know his exact words.

SENATOR SMITH: Give it as near as you can.

MR. EVANS: Well, I think he said that the skipper was being called; called three times. I think that is all he said. . . .

SENATOR SMITH: Now, tell me if you heard anybody else say anything about the captain having been called three times and informed that rockets were being sent up, the night the *Titanic* sank?

MR. EVANS: Well, I do not remember any other special individual, but I know it was being talked about a lot.

SENATOR SMITH: Collectively?

MR. EVANS: Yes, sir.

SENATOR SMITH: There was a lot of talk about it, but you can not recall any individual who spoke to you about it?

MR. EVANS: No, sir; except the apprentice. I think he told me that he had called the captain. . . .

SENATOR SMITH: Was there any talk of this kind after you left the scene of the sinking of the *Titanic?*

MR. EVANS: Yes; it has been talked about all the time since then.

SENATOR SMITH: They have talked about it all the time since then?

MR. EVANS: Yes, sir.

SENATOR SMITH: As an unusual and extraordinary occurrence?

MR. EVANS: Yes, sir.

SENATOR SMITH: Did anybody, in the course of this conversation that you heard, say anything about having seen the Morse signals used?

MR. EVANS: Oh, no. I remember the apprentice told me that he got the Morse lamp out and called up on that, sir. But he did not get any reply on that.

SENATOR SMITH: He started to call up the *Titanic?*

MR. EVANS: I do not know whether it was the *Titanic*——

SENATOR SMITH: But the vessel from which the rockets were being fired—he tried to call her up with his Morse signals?

MR. EVANS: With his Morse lamp; yes, sir.

SENATOR SMITH: And got no Morse reply?

MR. EVANS: That is correct. . . .

SENATOR BURTON: In all this conversation, did they say these rockets came from that boat which the captain has mentioned or that they came from the *Titanic?*

MR. EVANS: They did not know which.

SENATOR BURTON: Was it said that the rockets were those which had been sent up by the *Titanic?* Was that the talk on board ship?

MR. EVANS: Some of them seemed to think so, and some not, sir.

SENATOR BURTON: Has anyone told you that he was to receive $500 for a story in regard to these rockets—anyone on your boat?

MR. EVANS: I think the donkeyman mentioned it.

SENATOR BURTON: What did he say?

MR. EVANS: He said, "I think I will make about $500 on this."

SENATOR BURTON: Did he say that to you?

MR. EVANS: Yes, sir.

SENATOR BURTON: That is the man who was a witness here this morning?

MR. EVANS: Gill, the second donkeyman. . . .

SENATOR SMITH: Did you hear the captain say that he saw rockets?

MR. EVANS: I heard so the next day. I did not hear anything about it the same day.

SENATOR SMITH: You heard him swear to it here a few moments ago?

MR. EVANS: Yes, sir.

331

SENATOR SMITH: White rockets, he said, did he not?

MR. EVANS: I think so.

SENATOR SMITH: Have you yourself been offered, or have you received, any money from any person for any information in your possession regarding this *Titanic* accident or wreck?

MR. EVANS: No, sir. . . .

EIGHTH DAY
Saturday, April 27
Washington, D.C.

Witness: James Henry Moore
Captain of the Canadian passenger ship
Mount Temple

Key testimony: Moore said his ship was 49 miles away from the Titanic *when he got its distress call, but he couldn't reach it because of ice. His ship was stopped in the wreck area doing nothing while the* Carpathia's *rescue effort was under way. Moore saw a schooner and a tramp steamer while heading toward the* Titanic's *position. He and Senator Smith explored the issue of why so few bodies were found: Did some get carried away under the ice? And the Captain offered an early and plausible theory for how the iceberg sank the* Titanic.

. . . SENATOR SMITH: I would like to have you tell in your own way what, if anything especially, occurred on that voyage of yours on Sunday and Monday. Just tell what you did, what you saw, and where you saw it.

MR. MOORE: At 12:30 A.M. on the 15th I was awakened by the steward from my sleep with a message from the Marconi operator, sir.

SENATOR SMITH: On your ship?

MR. MOORE: On my ship; yes, sir. I immediately switched on the light and took a message that the operator sent up to me which said that the *Titanic* was sending out the C. Q. D. message, and in the message it said "iceberg."

SENATOR SMITH: Have you the message?

MR. MOORE: Yes, sir.

SENATOR SMITH: Just read it, please.

MR. MOORE: *Titanic* sends——

SENATOR SMITH (interposing): Kindly give the date line, if

any; the hour, if any; and to whom that message is addressed, if to anyone.

MR. MOORE: It was a general message, sir.

> *Titanic* sends C. Q. D. Requires assistance. Position 41° 44' north, longitude 50° 24' west Come at once. Iceberg.

SENATOR SMITH: Who signed that, if anybody?

MR. MOORE: This is just a message he picked up, sir. He happened to hear it. He was sending this up at once to me. . . .

SENATOR SMITH: What did you do after receiving this message?

MR. MOORE: I immediately blew the whistle on the bridge. I have a pipe leading down from the bridge, and I blew the whistle at once, and told the second officer to put the ship on north 45° east, sir, and to come down at once, and I informed him what was the matter, and told him to get the chart out. When I was sufficiently dressed I went up to my chart room, and we computed where the ship was, and we afterwards steered east by compass.

SENATOR SMITH: Did you make any progress in your movements?

MR. MOORE: We turned her right around at once, sir, and then when he came down we took the chart out and found out where the *Titanic* was and steered her by the compass north 65° east true.

SENATOR SMITH: In the direction of the *Titanic?*

MR. MOORE: In the direction of the *Titanic;* yes, sir. After I was sufficiently dressed I went down to the chief engineer and I told him that the *Titanic* was sending out messages for help, and I said "Go down and try to shake up the fireman, and, if necessary, even give him a tot of rum if you think he can do any more." I believe this was carried out. I also told him to inform the fireman that we wanted to get back as fast as we possibly could. . . .

SENATOR SMITH: After satisfying yourself as to her position, how far was the *Titanic* from your vessel?

MR. MOORE: About 49 miles, sir. . . .

SENATOR SMITH: You say you doubled the lookout?

MR. MOORE: Yes, sir.

SENATOR SMITH: Let us get into the record exactly what you mean by that.

MR. MOORE: Before this we had only one man on the lookout, sir.

SENATOR SMITH: One man in the crow's nest?

MR. MOORE: One man in the crow's nest, and we put another man on the forward bridge, and the fourth officer we put on the forecastle head, so, if the ice was low down, he perhaps could see it farther than we could on the bridge.

SENATOR SMITH: Did you take any other precautions to avoid danger or accident?

MR. MOORE: Not at that time, sir. We had the lookout, and the engines were at "stand by," sir.

SENATOR SMITH: So you were simply protecting yourself against ice at that time?

MR. MOORE: That is all, sir.

SENATOR SMITH: And you had stopped your boat?

MR. MOORE: Oh, no, sir. We had only the engines at "stand by."

SENATOR SMITH: Were you stopped at any time?

MR. MOORE: We were stopped; yes.

SENATOR SMITH: So I understand you.

MR. MOORE: At 3:25 by our time we stopped.

SENATOR SMITH: Where were you then; in what position was your ship?

MR. MOORE: I should say we were then about 14 miles off the *Titanic's* position.

SENATOR SMITH: Can you tell me just what your position was; did you take it?

MR. MOORE: I could not; I could not take any position. There was nothing—I could not see——

SENATOR SMITH: You judged you were 14 miles from the *Titanic?*

MR. MOORE: That is what I estimate.

SENATOR FLETCHER: What time was that?

MR. MOORE: At 3:25 o'clock.

SENATOR SMITH: Was it dark or was day breaking?

MR. MOORE: It was dark, then, sir.

SENATOR SMITH: What did you do then?

MR. MOORE: I stopped the ship. Before that I want to say that I met a schooner or some small craft, and I had to get

335

out of the way of that vessel, and the light of that vessel seemed to go out.

SENATOR SMITH: The light of the schooner seemed to go out?

MR. MOORE: The light of the schooner; yes. When this light was on my bow, a green light, I starboarded my helm.

SENATOR SMITH: The schooner was between you and the *Titanic's* position?

MR. MOORE: Yes, sir. . . .

SENATOR SMITH: Was he evidently coming from the direction in which the *Titanic* lay?

MR. MOORE: Somewhere from there, sir. Of course, had he been coming straight he would have shown me his two lights, sir.

SENATOR SMITH: I have been informed that a derelict schooner was in the sea in that vicinity that night without anyone aboard her. Can you tell me whether or not this schooner was inhabited?

MR. MOORE: I could not say, sir. All I could see was the lights. It was dark.

SENATOR SMITH: You saw a light on the schooner?

MR. MOORE: A light on the schooner; yes, sir. . . .

SENATOR SMITH: I want to be certain that the schooner was as near the *Titanic* as I thought I understood you to say it was.

MR. MOORE: I should say the schooner, from the position of the *Titanic,* would be, perhaps, 12½ to 13 miles. . . .

SENATOR SMITH: What I am trying to get at is this: One or two of the ship's officers of the *Titanic* say that after the collision with the iceberg they used the Morse signals and rockets for the purpose of attracting help, and that while they were using these rockets, and displaying the Morse signals they saw lights ahead, or saw lights, that could not have been over 5 miles from the *Titanic*. What I am seeking to develop is the question as to what light that was they saw.

MR. MOORE: Well, it may have been the light of the tramp steamer that was ahead of us, because when I turned there was a steamer on my port bow.

SENATOR SMITH: Going in the same direction?

MR. MOORE: Almost in the same direction. As he went ahead, he gradually crossed our bow until he got on the starboard bow, sir—on our starboard bow.

SENATOR SMITH: Did you see that ship yourself?

MR. MOORE: I saw it myself. I was on the bridge all the time.

SENATOR SMITH: Did you communicate with it by wireless?

MR. MOORE: I do not think he had any wireless; I am sure he had no wireless, because in the daylight I was close to him. . . .

SENATOR SMITH: When you were at that point what did you do and what did you see?

MR. MOORE: I saw a large ice pack right to the east of me, sir; right in my track—right in my course.

SENATOR SMITH: How large?

MR. MOORE: In consulting my officers as to the breadth of this, one said it was 5 miles and another said it was 6 miles.

SENATOR SMITH: How wide was it?

MR. MOORE: That was the width of it.

SENATOR SMITH: How long was it?

MR. MOORE: Of course it extended as far as the eye could reach, north and south, sir.

SENATOR SMITH: Twenty miles or more?

MR. MOORE: I should say 20 miles, perhaps more than that. It was field ice and bergs.

SENATOR SMITH: Bergs also?

MR. MOORE: Yes; bergs interspersed in the pack, sir, and bowlders.

SENATOR SMITH: How many bergs were there?

MR. MOORE: I should say, altogether, there must have been between 40 and 50 I counted that morning. . . .

SENATOR SMITH: How high was the highest—the largest one?

MR. MOORE: I should say fully 200 feet high, sir.

SENATOR SMITH: Do you know the height of the *Titanic* from the water's edge?

MR. MOORE: On my boat, when she is light, it is about 50 feet from the water line to my bridge.

SENATOR SMITH: The *Titanic,* according to the testimony, was 70 feet from the water line; and you say this largest iceberg that you saw was 200 feet above the water line?

MR. MOORE: About that, I should think, sir. . . .

SENATOR SMITH: The night that you doubled your lookout did you use glasses in the crow's nest or have a searchlight, or anything of that kind?

MR. MOORE: No, sir.

SENATOR SMITH: Do you ever use glasses in the crow's nest?

MR. MOORE: Never, sir.

SENATOR SMITH: You use them on the bridge?

MR. MOORE: Yes, sir. Every officer has his own glasses, and then the ship provides glasses besides.

SENATOR SMITH: Have you ever been in the north Atlantic on a vessel equipped with searchlights?

MR. MOORE: No, sir.

SENATOR SMITH: I should like your judgment as to whether or not searchlights in darkness and in fog would prove an advantage in detecting icebergs in your path?

MR. MOORE: In fog they are utterly useless, sir.

SENATOR SMITH: And in clear weather?

MR. MOORE: If you had a very powerful projector it might be of some use, but in fog it would be just like throwing that light on a blank wall. . . .

SENATOR SMITH: I want to go back to the scene of the *Titanic* collision for a moment. When you arrived at the *Titanic*'s position, it was along after 4 in the morning?

MR. MOORE: Half past 4, sir; that is, I reckoned we were at that position at half past 4, sir.

SENATOR SMITH: Monday morning?

MR. MOORE: Yes, sir.

SENATOR SMITH: After the wreck?

MR. MOORE: Yes, sir.

SENATOR SMITH: What did you see there, if anything?

MR. MOORE: I saw nothing whatever, sir.

SENATOR SMITH: Any wreckage from the *Titanic?*

MR. MOORE: I saw nothing; but I saw this tramp steamer, sir.

SENATOR SMITH: No wreckage?

MR. MOORE: Nothing whatever, sir, in the way of wreckage.

SENATOR SMITH: Any floating corpses?

MR. MOORE: Nothing at all, sir.

SENATOR SMITH: Any abandoned lifeboats?

MR. MOORE: Nothing whatever, sir.

SENATOR SMITH: Any floating bodies?

MR. MOORE: Nothing whatever, sir.

SENATOR SMITH: How long did you stay in that position?

MR. MOORE: We searched around to see if there was a clear place we could go through, because I feared the ice was too heavy for me to push through it. Of course, I reckoned I was somewhere near, if not at, the *Titanic*'s position that he gave me, which afterwards proved correct, when I got observations in the morning, sir. I searched for a passage to get through this pack, because I realized that the *Titanic* could not have been through that pack of ice, sir. I steered away to the south-southeast true, because I thought the ice appeared thinner down there, sir. When I got down, I got within about a mile or so of this other ship, which had already stopped, finding the ice was too strong for it to go through.

SENATOR SMITH: What did you do after discovering that there was no wreckage nor any service you could render?

MR. MOORE: When I found the ice was too heavy, I stopped there and just turned around—slowed down and stopped her—and searched for a passage, and I could not see any passage whatever, sir. I had a man pulled up to the masthead in a bowline, right to the foretopmast head, and I had the chief officer at the mainmast head, and he could not see any line through the ice at all that I could go through.

SENATOR SMITH: Some passengers on your vessel, Sunday night about midnight, claim to have seen these rockets from the decks of the *Titanic*. Have you heard anything about that?

MR. MOORE: I have read it in the papers, sir; but as a matter of fact, I do not believe there was a passenger on deck at 12 o'clock at night. I am positive, because they would not know anything at all about this, and you may be sure that they would be in their beds. I know the steward tells me there was nobody on deck; that is, the night watchman at the aft end. At the forward end there was nobody on deck. The man in what we call the permanent steerage that passes under the bridge deck—we have a permanent steerage there, and the other, of course, is a portable one we can take down—and nobody saw a passenger on deck, sir. . . .

SENATOR SMITH: Do you wish to be understood as saying that you did not see, on Sunday night or Monday morning, any signal lights from the *Titanic?*

MR. MOORE: I can solemnly swear that I saw no signal lights, nor did my officers on the bridge see any signal lights.

SENATOR SMITH: What kind of wireless equipment has the *Mount Temple?*

MR. MOORE: Marconi, sir.

SENATOR SMITH: How many operators?

MR. MOORE: Only one, sir.

SENATOR SMITH: What are his hours?

MR. MOORE: He has no special hours.

SENATOR SMITH: How did he happen to be on duty at 12:30 midnight, Sunday night?

MR. MOORE: I don't know, sir. I think it was just about the time he was turning in. He just picked up the instrument just to see if there was anything coming along. It was just purely and simply an accident that he got the ship's message. . . .

SENATOR SMITH: Does the fact that you found no evidence of the wreck when you got to the *Titanic's* reported position tend to confirm you in the idea that her position was 8 miles farther to the southward?

MR. MOORE: No; to the eastward.

SENATOR SMITH: To the eastward?

MR. MOORE: Yes. . . .

SENATOR SMITH: As I recollect, the captain of the *Californian,* who was sworn yesterday, and who went to the position given by the *Titanic* in the C. Q. D., also said that he found nothing there, but cruised around this position.

MR. MOORE: I saw the *Californian* myself cruising around there, sir.

SENATOR SMITH: She was there when you were there?

MR. MOORE: She was there shortly after me, because when I came to this great pack of ice, sir, as I remarked, I went to the south-southeast to try to get around there, because I realized that if he was not in that position—I had come from the westward—he must be somewhere to the eastward of me still. Of course, I had no idea that the *Titanic* had sunk. I had not the slightest idea of that.

SENATOR SMITH: At that time?

MR. MOORE: No, sir. It was not until I received word from the *Carpathia* that she had picked up the boats and the *Titanic* had sunk.

SENATOR SMITH: And then you gave it up?

MR. MOORE: I stayed there until 9 o'clock.

SENATOR SMITH: It was not until that time that you gave the ship up?

Mr. MOORE: That I gave up hopes of seeing her, sir, because I was cruising around all that time.

SENATOR SMITH: How near the *Carpathia* did you get that morning?

Mr. MOORE: This pack of ice between us and the *Carpathia*, it is estimated, was between 5 and 6 miles. She did not communicate anything with us at all. When we sighted her she must have sighted us. . . .

SENATOR SMITH: . . . The captain of the *Carpathia* testified before the committee in New York that he saw but one body in the water.

Mr. MOORE: Yes, sir.

SENATOR SMITH: When the lifeboats came alongside.

Mr. MOORE: Yes, sir.

SENATOR SMITH: And that he cruised around for an hour or more after he took these people from the lifeboats on board and saw none. The captain of the *Californian* said yesterday he saw none. You say this morning that you saw none?

Mr. MOORE: I saw none whatever, sir.

SENATOR SMITH: Does that indicate that the *Titanic* might have sunk in a different position?

Mr. MOORE: I do not think it proves anything, as far as my going is concerned, because I must have been at least 5 miles to the westward of where the *Titanic* sank.

This great field of ice was 5 miles at least between us and the *Carpathia*, where she had picked up these lifeboats.

SENATOR SMITH: Would it have been possible—I hesitate to ask you—and do you think, from what you saw, it would have been possible after the *Titanic* sank for that field of ice to have covered the place?

Mr. MOORE: It is just possible, sir, and nothing more. Of course, that ice had been in the gulf stream and was going with the gulf stream. The gulf stream, as we know, is always flowing to the east-northeast, and it is just possible that when he struck he might have been in that ice pack. I do not know whether he got into it or not. Do the officers say they got into any field ice?

SENATOR SMITH: They say they saw field ice all about them. Do you mean the officers of the *Titanic*?

Mr. MOORE: Yes.

SENATOR SMITH: They saw considerable ice—field ice?

MR. MOORE: Did they see field ice or icebergs?

SENATOR SMITH: Both.

MR. MOORE: From the time I got there, from about 12:30—the time I received the call—until half past 4, there would be a drift there of perhaps, say, half a knot an hour.

SENATOR SMITH: There has been an impression among vessel men, and I think that same impression has extended to the American Navy, that a sinking ship—by the suction as it goes down—will draw into the vortex quite largely from the surface of the surrounding sea. That theory seems to have been exploded by the sinking of the *Titanic*, because every officer, thus far, has said that there was no suction and the wireless operator of the *Titanic*, who was the last to leave her, about 1 minute before she sank and disappeared under the water, says he left her by the starboard side and that there was an overturned, collapsible lifeboat on the starboard side that fell upon him and covered him up in the water and in that position—with the *Titanic* sinking—there was no suction.

MR. MOORE: I should hardly think that was possible, sir. Any boat sinking in the water like that, I think, is almost bound to cause suction. The time I heard there were so many people left on board I said, "then it is just possible those bodies might never be recovered," because there were so many decks, and if these people had been underneath those decks, the ship going down would cause the pressure to be very great and that pressure would have pressed them up under those decks and it is just a matter that they would never be released, because as they got lower down there would be such tremendous pressure that, even supposing the ship listed in any way, it was not possible for these bodies to withstand the pressure.

SENATOR SMITH: This theory of suction is an old theory of the sea, is it not?

MR. MOORE: Yes, sir.

SENATOR SMITH: It does not seem to have operated in this case and I think I may be pardoned for saying that when I found the *Carpathia's* captain saw no bodies, and then found from the testimony of those in the lifeboats that there were hundreds of bodies all around in the water, I came to the conclusion that they had either been sucked in with the sinking ship or that they were inclosed somewhere in the ship.

Some expressions of humor have been noted—rather unusual among the people—from an inquiry that I made as to whether or not water-tight compartments in a ship would keep out as well as hold in water. I have received many telegrams and letters from people who lost relatives in this accident, who prayed that the Government might send divers to the ship, not knowing how far she was below the surface of the water. It seemed to me that the absence on the water of these bodies that you failed to see and which the other captains failed to see might indicate that these bodies were still inclosed somewhere within the ship.

Of course, I have known for many years that a water-tight compartment is not intended as an asylum for passengers, because this same captain, who went down with the *Titanic,* showed me over his ship on one of my voyages and I am quite familiar with the uses of the water-tight compartment. But that these sorrowing people might receive some official reply as to whether that would be possible or not, I took chances of arousing the humor of people not generally accustomed to much humor, by asking that question. I assume all responsibility for it. In view of what you say and what the other two captains say perhaps it had some importance.

MR. MOORE: It may have been that these bulkheads with the water coming in had collapsed. It may have been that the pressure of the air had started something up and allowed those bodies to escape. As the water escaped they might have been disturbed by the water underneath the decks or elsewhere and that may have brought these people out, sir. Of course, she had a very heavy list, I believe. She was struck on one side. Those compartments would fill. I dare say some bulkheads would go, but if she took a list as she was falling it would give some a chance to get clear of the decks, sir.

I am almost sure that when a ship goes down like that the people underneath those decks would be held underneath them, because the ship is sinking all the time and the fact of her sinking would bring about that heavy pressure underneath those decks, as I have mentioned.

SENATOR SMITH: Would you think it a desirable thing to have as part of the equipment of a vessel a permanent buoy made, as far as it could be so made, of indestructible material, fastened to an indestructible chain or wire, so that in the event of a ship sinking at sea that buoy might register on the surface of the water its exact burial spot?

MR. MOORE: It is quite possible to do that kind of thing, unless, of course, the chain—you mean to attach that to the wreck?

SENATOR SMITH: Yes.

MR. MOORE: You see, there is such a tremendous depth——

SENATOR SMITH (interposing): I understand this boat is in 2 miles of water?

MR. MOORE: Yes, sir; over 2,000 fathoms of water. . . .

SENATOR SMITH: Can you think of anything that will throw any light on this sad affair that you have not already spoken of?

MR. MOORE: As to the way the ship struck the berg or anything of that kind?

SENATOR SMITH: Yes; any information that would help us.

MR. MOORE: My theory would be that she was going along and touched one of those large spurs from an iceberg. There are spurs projecting out beneath the water, and they are very sharp and pointed. They are like a jagged rock. My idea is that she struck one of those on her bilge, and that she ran along that, and that opened up her plates, the lining of her plates, and the water came in; and so much water got in that I think her bulkheads could not stand the strain, and she must have torn herself at a speed like that, because apparently her speed through the water was not stopped very much immediately, and, of course, that was a tremendous body, and she must have struck along on her bilge and opened herself out right along as far as the engine room, sir.

SENATOR SMITH: Have you studied the plan of the *Titanic* at all?

MR. MOORE: No, sir.

SENATOR SMITH: This opinion you are giving is the result of your own diagnosis?

MR. MOORE: Yes, sir; that is what I should say, sir. Of course, I have been fortunate myself. I have never yet had any injury from ice, although I have been master in this trade for a very long time. . . .

SENATOR SMITH: And in the ice region?

MR. MOORE: In the ice regions; yes sir.

Witness: Andrew Cunningham, 38
Stateroom steward, from Southampton, England

Key testimony: He dove off the ship after helping passengers to lifeboats and was apparently one of the few to survive in the water for a prolonged period.

. . . SENATOR SMITH: After the passengers from your staterooms had gone up, you put a life belt on yourself?

MR. CUNNINGHAM: Yes.

SENATOR SMITH: And where did you go?

MR. CUNNINGHAM: I waited on the ship until all the boats had gone and then I took to the water.

SENATOR SMITH: You waited on the ship until all the boats had gone and then threw yourself into the water?

MR. CUNNINGHAM: Yes; into the water.

SENATOR SMITH: How long was it before the boat sank?

MR. CUNNINGHAM: I went in the water about 2 o'clock, I should say.

SENATOR SMITH: How long had you been in the water before the boat sank?

MR. CUNNINGHAM: I should say about half an hour.

SENATOR SMITH: When you struck the water what did you do?

MR. CUNNINGHAM: I swam clear of the ship, I should say about three-quarters of a mile. I was afraid of the suction.

SENATOR SMITH: You were swimming away from the suction that you supposed would follow the sinking?

MR. CUNNINGHAM: Yes.

SENATOR SMITH: What did you do then?

MR. CUNNINGHAM: I had a mate with me. We both left the ship together.

SENATOR SMITH: Did he have a life preserver on?

MR. CUNNINGHAM: Yes, sir.

SENATOR SMITH: What did you do?

MR. CUNNINGHAM: We saw the ship go down then. Then we struck out to look for a boat.

SENATOR SMITH: You swam around in the water until you saw the ship go down?

MR. CUNNINGHAM: Until I saw the ship go down.

SENATOR SMITH: Then you turned to look for a lifeboat?

MR. CUNNINGHAM: Then I turned to look for a lifeboat; yes.

SENATOR SMITH: Did you see one?

MR. CUNNINGHAM: No. I heard one, and I called to it.

SENATOR SMITH: Did that lifeboat come toward you, or did you go toward it?

MR. CUNNINGHAM: I went toward it.

SENATOR SMITH: It did not come toward you?

MR. CUNNINGHAM: I do not think so.

SENATOR SMITH: When you got in it, whom did you find in it?

MR. CUNNINGHAM: There was a quartermaster in charge— Perkins or Perkis. It was No. 4 boat. They picked us up. There was also a lamp trimmer in it named Hemmings, and another sailor called Foley, and a fireman. The rest were ladies. Two of my own passengers happened to be there.

SENATOR SMITH: Two of your passengers and Hemmings and Foley and Perkis and yourself?

MR. CUNNINGHAM: And myself; yes.

SENATOR SMITH: That made six male passengers?

MR. CUNNINGHAM: Then there was a fireman there, as well.

SENATOR SMITH: What was his name?

MR. CUNNINGHAM: A fellow called Smith—F. Smith.

SENATOR SMITH: Did you see any other man in the boat?

MR. CUNNINGHAM: Yes. I think there was one of the galley hands; I am not quite sure.

SENATOR SMITH: What was his name?

MR. CUNNINGHAM: I do not know. The reason I know the names of any of them is that Mrs. Cummings, one of my passengers, sent me around to find out who was in the boat. Otherwise I would not know their names.

SENATOR SMITH: In addition to that fireman, were there any other male passengers in that boat?

MR. CUNNINGHAM: Yes; I think there was another fireman in the bottom of the boat; and besides that there was my mate, who died just after he was pulled in. . . .

Witness: Frederick D. Ray, 33
First-class steward, who waited tables in the
dining saloon

Key testimony: He shed light on the doings of some of the
Titanic's notable and well-heeled passengers, including Maj.
Archibald Butt, President William Howard Taft's close aide,
who perished. As he did throughout the hearings, Senator
Smith posed questions to learn whether Captain E. J. Smith
might have been drinking the day of the disaster. No evidence
emerged that he had been.

. . . SENATOR SMITH: Just give the location of that saloon on
the ship.

MR. RAY: As near to amidships as could be, I should
imagine; about five decks down and between fore and aft;
about amidships.

SENATOR SMITH: In the main saloon?

MR. RAY: Yes, sir.

SENATOR SMITH: Did you know the captain of the *Titanic* by
sight?

MR. RAY: Very well, sir.

SENATOR SMITH: Was he in that saloon that night?

MR. RAY: I did not notice him, sir.

SENATOR SMITH: Would you have noticed him if he had been
there?

MR. RAY: It is doubtful, sir. I was waiting on the starboard
side, quite close to him, but I can not remember whether
he was there at dinner that night or not. I did not make
any point of remembering.

SENATOR SMITH: Was it his custom to come there?

MR. RAY: Yes, sir.

SENATOR SMITH: Often?

MR. RAY: To most meals.

SENATOR SMITH: Did he dine there that night?

MR. RAY: I could not say, sir.

SENATOR SMITH: Where was his table?

MR. RAY: In the center of the saloon; the sixth table on the
forward end of the saloon; back toward the bow of the
ship.

SENATOR SMITH: Did he have a personal waiter or steward of
his own?

MR. RAY: Yes, sir.

SENATOR SMITH: Who was he?

MR. RAY: A man named Phainten, I think it was; I am almost sure.

SENATOR SMITH: Did he survive?

MR. RAY: No, sir. He was last seen on the bridge, standing by the captain.

SENATOR SMITH: Did you see Mr. Ismay in the saloon that night?

MR. RAY: I did not notice him, sir. He was on the other side. I believe he had a table on the port side of the saloon, and I was waiting on the starboard side. It being a large saloon and there being a great number of people there, I would not have noticed him, because I would not go over to the other side of the saloon. I would go right up on the starboard side.

SENATOR SMITH: Did you know him by sight?

MR. RAY: Yes, sir; very well.

SENATOR SMITH: Did you know he was on board ship?

MR. RAY: Yes, sir; I have seen him on several occasions.

SENATOR SMITH: I think I understood you to say you did not know whether the captain dined at his customary place that Sunday evening or not?

MR. RAY: Quite correct, sir.

SENATOR SMITH: If you can remember, whom did you serve on that voyage from Southampton to the place of the accident, if you know any by name?

MR. RAY: Who did I serve?

SENATOR SMITH: Yes.

MR. RAY: I waited on Maj. Butt, Mr. Moore, Mr. Millet, Mr. Clark, and Mrs. Clark.

SENATOR SMITH: Any others?

MR. RAY: That is all, sir.

SENATOR SMITH: What time did they dine on Sunday night?

MR. RAY: Mr. Moore and Mr. Millet dined together about 7:30, and finished dinner about 8:15. Maj. Butt was not down, because he was dining in the restaurant.

SENATOR SMITH: Did you know with whom he was dining?

MR. RAY: No, sir.

SENATOR SMITH: Have you since heard from anyone whether he was dining with the captain?

MR. RAY: No, sir. I heard since that he was dining with the

Wideners. I do not know whether it is true or not, though, sir; that is only what I heard.

SENATOR SMITH: From whom did you hear that? Just to refresh your recollection, let me ask whether you understood from anybody that Mrs. Widener gave a dinner in the café that night, Sunday night, to the captain of the ship, Mr. and Mrs. Carter, Mr. and Mrs. John B. Thayer, Harry Widener, jr., and Maj. Butt? Was this the report that you heard?

MR. RAY: Yes, sir. I think it was Mrs. Moore. I saw Mrs. Moore after I arrived here. I think it was. I heard Maj. Butt was dining with the Wideners. I did not hear it on the ship. . . .

SENATOR SMITH: When did you last see Maj. Butt and the other people on whom you waited at their regular table?

MR. RAY: I saw Maj. Butt for the last time at luncheon, when he left, on Sunday. Mr. Moore and Mr. Millet I saw at dinner. Mr. Moore I saw coming from the smoke room afterwards, with other people whom I did not notice, just before going to my station. Mr. Clark I did not see.

SENATOR SMITH: Just before you were going to your station?

MR. RAY: Yes, sir.

SENATOR SMITH: That is, to your lifeboat?

MR. RAY: Yes, sir.

SENATOR SMITH: Go ahead.

MR. RAY: Mr. Clark and Mrs. Clark I did not see at all after luncheon that day. . . .

SENATOR SMITH: Did you know Mr. Andrews, of the ship-building firm of Harland & Wolff, who built this vessel?

MR. RAY: Yes, sir. I was at Belfast and waited on him around there on the *Olympic* and the *Titanic*.

SENATOR SMITH: Do you know what deck his stateroom was on?

MR. RAY: No, sir; I do not know.

SENATOR SMITH: Do you know where he sat generally in the main saloon?

MR. RAY: I could not be sure, sir; but I fancy it was on the port side, aft.

SENATOR SMITH: Is that where Mr. Ismay had his table?

MR. RAY: No, sir; I do not know where Mr. Ismay sat.

SENATOR SMITH: It was not at the captain's table?

MR. RAY: No, sir.

SENATOR SMITH: Did you see Mr. Andrews after the boat struck?

MR. RAY: No, sir; I did not. . . .

SENATOR SMITH: When you got to lifeboat No. 9 . . . what took place?

MR. RAY: I went to the rail and looked over and saw the first boat leaving the ship on the starboard side. By that time I was feeling rather cold, so I went down below again, to my bedroom, the same way that I came up.

SENATOR SMITH: What did you do then?

MR. RAY: I got my overcoat on. I went along E deck. There was nobody in No. 3 when I left.

SENATOR SMITH: No. 3 room?

MR. RAY: No. 3 room, where I slept. I went along E deck and forward, and the forward part of E deck was under water. I could just manage to get through the doorway into the main stairway. I went across to the other side of the ship where the passengers' cabins were; saw nobody there. I looked to see where the water was and it was corresponding on that side of the ship to the port side. I walked leisurely up to the main stairway, passed two or three people on the way, saw the two pursers in the purser's office and the clerks busy at the safe taking things out and putting them in bags, and just then Mr. Rothschild left his stateroom and I waited for him——

SENATOR SMITH: Did you know him?

MR. RAY: Yes; I had waited on him on the *Olympic*.

SENATOR SMITH: Let us fix the place. You were still on E deck?

MR. RAY: Yes, sir.

SENATOR SMITH: And at his stateroom?

MR. RAY: I did not say that I was in any stateroom then——

SENATOR SMITH: I thought you saw Mr. Rothschild?

MR. RAY: I had come through D deck and then C deck and I saw Mr. Rothschild.

SENATOR SMITH: All right; go ahead.

MR. RAY: I spoke to him and asked him where his wife was. He said she had gone off in a boat. I said, "This seems rather serious." He said, "I do not think there is any occasion for it." So we walked leisurely up the stairs until I got to A deck and went through the door. I went out there onto the open deck and along to No. 9 boat. It was just being filled with women and children. I assisted. I saw that lowered away. Then I went along to No. 11 boat, and saw that loaded with women and children and then that was lowered away. Then I went to No. 13 boat. I saw that about half filled with women and children. They said, "A few of you men get in here." There were about nine to a dozen men there, passengers and crew. I saw Mr. Washington Dodge there, asking where his wife and child were. He said they had gone away in one of the boats. He was standing well back from the boat, and I said, "You had better get in here, then." I got behind him and pushed him and I followed. After I got in there was a rather big woman came along, and we helped her in the boat. She was crying all the time and saying, "Don't put me in the boat; I don't want to go in the boat; I have never been in an open boat in my life. Don't let me stay in." I said, "You have got to go, and you may as well keep quiet."

After that there was a small child rolled in a blanket thrown into the boat to me, and I caught it. The woman that brought it along got into the boat afterwards. We left about three or four men on the deck, at the rail, and they went along to No. 15 boat.

The boat was lowered away until we got nearly to the water, when two or three of us noticed a very large discharge of water coming from the ship's side, which I thought was the pumps working. The hole was about 2 feet wide and about a foot deep, a solid mass of water coming out from the hole. I realized that if the boat was lowered down straight away the boat would be swamped and we should all be thrown into the water. We shouted for the boat to be stopped from being lowered, and they responded promptly and stopped lowering the boat.

We got oars and pushed it off from the side of the ship. It seemed impossible to lower the boat without being swamped; we pushed it out from the side of the ship and the next I knew we were in the water free from this discharge. I do not think there were any sailors or quartermasters in the boat, because they apparently did not know how to get free from the tackle. They called for knives to cut the boat loose, and somebody gave them a knife and they cut the boat loose. In the meantime we were drifting a little aft and boat No. 15 was being lowered immediately upon us, about 2 feet over our heads, and we all shouted again, and they again replied very promptly and stopped lowering boat No. 15.

We pushed out from the side of the ship. Nobody seemed to take command of the boat, so we elected a fireman to take charge. He ordered us to put out the oars and pull straight away from the ship. We pulled all night with short intervals for rest. I inquired if the ladies were all warm, and they said they were quite warm and they had a blanket to spare. There seemed to be very little excitement in the boat. They were all quite calm and collected.

SENATOR SMITH: Did you return to the scene of the sinking of the vessel at all after you left the boat's side?

MR. RAY: No. I was not in charge of the boat, I was only pulling an oar. I objected to pulling away from the ship at all.

SENATOR SMITH: You objected?

MR. RAY: Yes. I wanted to stand by the ship, but, of course, my voice was not much against the others. We had six oars in the boat, and several times I refused to row, but eventually gave in and pulled with the others. . . .

Witness: Henry Samuel Etches, 40
Bedroom steward, from Southampton, England

Key testimony: He testified to the diligence of Thomas Andrews, the Titanic's *designer, who perished. A worried Andrews urged first-class passengers to get their life belts on, he said.*

. . . SENATOR SMITH: Did you see Mr. Andrews frequently during the voyage?

MR. ETCHES: Every morning at 7 o'clock I went to his cabin, sir.

SENATOR SMITH: For what purpose?

MR. ETCHES: I used to take him some fruit and tea.

SENATOR SMITH: When would you next see him?

MR. ETCHES: I used to see him again when he dressed at night. That would be about a quarter or 20 minutes to 7, as a rule. He was rather late in dressing.

SENATOR SMITH: Had you ever known him before this voyage?

MR. ETCHES: I had met him several times at Belfast, because I had been on the *Olympic*.

SENATOR SMITH: Did he build the *Olympic?*

MR. ETCHES: Oh, yes, sir.

SENATOR SMITH: How old a man was Mr. Andrews?

MR. ETCHES: He signed himself as 38 on a paper that I gave him.

SENATOR SMITH: Did he seem to be in good health on the voyage?

MR. ETCHES: In perfect health.

SENATOR SMITH: Did he seem to be busy?

MR. ETCHES: He was busy the whole time.

SENATOR SMITH: Did he have maps and drawings in his apartment?

MR. ETCHES: He had charts rolled up by the side of his bed, and he had papers of all descriptions on his table during the day.

SENATOR SMITH: He was apparently working?

MR. ETCHES: He was working all the time, sir. He was making notes of improvements; any improvements that could be made.

SENATOR SMITH: On the ship?

MR. ETCHES: In any of the cabins. Anything that was pointed out to him, he was making notes of it.

SENATOR SMITH: From what you saw of him, you gathered that he was giving his undivided attention to this ship on its trial trip?

MR. ETCHES: I never saw him anywhere else, but during the day I met him in all parts, with workmen, going about. I mentioned several things to him, and he was with workmen having them attended to. The whole of the day he was working from one part of the ship to the other.

SENATOR SMITH: Did you see him working nights?

MR. ETCHES: He was very late in going to bed, sir. I never saw him in the smoke room or in any other of these rooms. I happened to meet him at different parts of deck E more often than anywhere else.

SENATOR SMITH: Did you see him in the boiler room?

MR. ETCHES: He had a suit, and I have seen that suit thrown

on the bed when he had taken it off. I have seen him in the chief engineer's room.

SENATOR SMITH: You mean by that that he had a special suit which he wore when he went into the boiler room?

MR. ETCHES: It was there for the purpose. I knew exactly what it was. It was a suit the surveyors put on.

SENATOR SMITH: What did you say about a suit that he wore when he went into the engineering department?

MR. ETCHES: He had an engineering suit on then—an ordinary blue suit, sir.

SENATOR SMITH: When did you last see Mr. Andrews?

MR. ETCHES: It would be about 20 minutes past 12. He stopped me. I was going along B deck, and he asked had I waked all my passengers. Mr. Harrison came up then, and I said: "No; I am going to see if the Carter family are up." I went to open the door. Mr. Harrison said: "I can tell you they are up. I have just come out of my cabin." His cabin adjoined. Mr. Andrews then told me to come down on C deck with him, and we went down the pantry staircase together. Going down he told me to be sure and make the passengers open their doors, and to tell them the life belts were on top of the wardrobes and on top of the racks, and to assist them in every way I could to get them on, which I endeavored to do.

SENATOR SMITH: Is that the last time you ever saw him?

MR. ETCHES: No, sir. We walked along C deck together. The purser was standing outside of his office, in a large group of ladies. The purser was asking them to do as he asked them, and to go back in their rooms and not to frighten themselves, but, as a preliminary caution, to put the life belts on, and the stewards would give them every attention. Mr. Andrews said: "That is exactly what I have been trying to get them to do," and, with that, he walked down the staircase to go on lower D deck. That is the last I saw of Mr. Andrews.

SENATOR SMITH: He never asked you to put a life belt on him, did he?

MR. ETCHES: No, sir; and I never saw him with one in his own hand.

SENATOR SMITH: Was he the only passenger or the only cabin passenger in an apartment on A deck?

MR. ETCHES: No, sir; Mr. and Mrs. Carter and the two

children were occupying 98 and 96. Mr. Harrison was next door, occupying 94. Mr. Guggenheim was occupying 84, with his secretary.

SENATOR SMITH: All on A deck?

MR. ETCHES: Not on A deck. There were only two cabins on the after end of A deck. One was vacant and the other was occupied.

SENATOR SMITH: On the deck below, under your charge, what rooms did you have?

MR. ETCHES: 98, 96, 94; and then came the door. The other rooms were empty until I came to 84, occupied by Mr. Guggenheim and his secretary. Mr. Carter's valet was in 96, the inside cabin.

SENATOR SMITH: Where were you when the collision came?

MR. ETCHES: Asleep, sir. . . .

SENATOR SMITH: How were you awakened?

MR. ETCHES: I was awakened by something, but I did not know what it was, and I called to my mate and I said "What time is it that they are going to call us next?" It was then between 25 minutes and 20 minutes to 12. He said, "I don't know." I turned over to go to sleep again. At that minute I heard a loud shout, "Close water-tight bulkheads." I recognized it as our boatswain's voice; it was extra loud. I looked out and he was running from fore to aft.

SENATOR SMITH: What was he saying?

MR. ETCHES: The one shout, "Close water-tight bulkhead doors."

SENATOR SMITH: How long was that after the impact?

MR. ETCHES: That would be under 10 minutes, sir. Seven minutes, I would say, as near as possible. . . .

SENATOR SMITH: Did you arouse your passengers in their staterooms?

MR. ETCHES: I aroused the passengers in my stateroom; yes. I saw them all out, except Mr. Carter's family, and Mr. Harrison told me they were already up.

SENATOR SMITH: Did you assist in putting life belts on them?

MR. ETCHES: Yes, sir; but more on C deck. I threw the life belts down, and then threw some of them into the corridor. Mr. Andrews said to be sure there were no life belts left. The first cabin I went to was at the foot of the pantry stairs. I pulled the bottom drawer out there and

355

stood on it, and got out life belts, and as a gentleman was passing there, I gave him one of those.

SENATOR SMITH: Do you know who he was?

MR. ETCHES: No; I gave him one. He was a stout gentleman; appeared to be an Englishman. He said, "Show me how to put this on," and I showed him how; and then he said, "Tie it for me." I said, "Pull the strings around to the front and tie it," and as he was doing it I ran outside and opened other doors, and then most of the doors were opened along C deck. . . .

SENATOR SMITH: What about Mr. Guggenheim and his secretary, and others?

MR. ETCHES: They were in their room. I took the life belts out. The life belts in this cabin were in the wardrobe, in a small rack, and the cabin was only occupied by two. There were three life belts there, and I took the three out and put one on Mr. Guggenheim. He apparently had only gone to his room, for he answered the first knock. He said: "This will hurt." I said, "You have plenty of time, put on some clothes and I will be back in a few minutes."

SENATOR SMITH: Did you get back there?

MR. ETCHES: Yes, sir.

SENATOR SMITH: Was he there?

MR. ETCHES: Yes; he followed me along. I then found No. 78 cabin door shut, and I banged with both hands on the door loudly, and a voice answered, "What is it"? Then a lady's voice said, "Tell me what the trouble is." I said, "It is necessary that you should open the door, and I will explain everything, but please put the life belts on or bring them in the corridor." They said, "I want to know what is the matter." I said, "Kindly open the door," and I still kept banging. I passed along, and I found one cabin was empty, and then I came to another cabin and a lady and a gentleman stood at the door. They were swinging a life belt in their hands.

SENATOR SMITH: When you know who they were please name them.

MR. ETCHES: I do not know anyone outside of the people in my section.

SENATOR SMITH: Did this women open the door when you pounded so hard?

MR. ETCHES: I did not see the door opened.

Senator Smith: Do you know who was in that room?

Mr. Etches: Well, I don't know the name. It was a shortish name, and I fancy it began with S. They were a stiff-built gentleman and a rather short, thin lady. They were undoubtedly Americans. . . .

Senator Ismay: What did Mr. Ismay do [on the boat deck]?

Mr. Etches: Mr. Ismay, in the first place, was asking the gentlemen to kindly keep back, as it was ladies first in this boat; and they wanted to get the boat clear first.

Senator Smith: Go ahead.

Mr. Etches: After we lowered the boat——

Senator Smith: Just a moment. That boat was filled from the boat deck?

Mr. Etches: Yes, sir.

Senator Smith: Was it difficult to get into it from the deck?

Mr. Etches: There was not the slightest difficulty, sir. A child could have stepped over.

Senator Smith: Was it a full-sized lifeboat?

Mr. Etches: Yes, sir.

Senator Smith: And were the women put into it first?

Mr. Etches: Yes, sir. The gentlemen were lined up, those that were trying to assist, and Mr. Ismay said, "Kindly make a line here and allow the ladies to pass through"; and I think it was Mr. Murdoch's voice that was calling out, "Ladies, this way; is there any more ladies before this boat goes?" The boat was three parts full of ladies, to my knowledge.

Senator Smith: Were there any more to get in? Did any more get in?

Mr. Etches: There were, because No. 5 boat, which I went to next, took over 36 ladies. . . .

Senator Smith: Who was the quartermaster?

Mr. Etches: Mr. Olliver, sir.

Senator Smith: Did he survive?

Mr. Etches: Yes, sir.

Senator Smith: And two others?

Mr. Etches: Two other stewards. I have not seen then since, sir.

Senator Smith: Was the same course taken with that boat?

Mr. Etches: That was the same, sir. After getting all the women that were there they called out three times—Mr. Ismay called out twice, I know, in a loud voice—"Are there any more women before this boat goes," and there was no answer. Mr. Murdoch called out; and at that moment a female came up whom I did not recognize. Mr. Ismay said: "Come along; jump in." She said: "I am only a stewardess." He said: "Never mind, you are a woman, take your place." That was the last woman I saw get into No. 5 boat, sir. . . .

SENATOR SMITH: Was the boat lowered in safety?

MR. ETCHES: Perfect, sir.

SENATOR SMITH: What was done after you reached the water?

MR. ETCHES: Just as we got about 20 feet down a voice called out, "Be sure and see the plug is in that boat," and I passed the word around. I said, "See the plug is in that boat." Olliver crawled into the bottom of the boat, and I suppose he put the plug in, for when we touched water I crawled about in the bottom of the boat and found no water. So I took it the plug had been put in in safety.

SENATOR SMITH: Did the boat go away from the side of the *Titanic?*

MR. ETCHES: He cut the trigger that released the falls, and the order was given to pull off, to lay off from the ship. We laid off about 100 yards and waited, and the ship started going down; seemed to be going down at the head, and Mr. Pitman gave us the order to head away from the ship, and we pulled off then, I should say, about a quarter of a mile, and laid on our oars.

SENATOR SMITH: How long?

MR. ETCHES: We remained until the *Titanic* sank.

SENATOR SMITH: Did you see it go down?

MR. ETCHES: I saw it go down, sir.

SENATOR SMITH: You could not see who was on the decks from your distance?

MR. ETCHES: I saw, when the ship rose—her stern rose—a thick mass of people on the after end. I could not discern the faces, of course.

SENATOR SMITH: Did the boat go down by the head?

MR. ETCHES: She seemed to raise once as though she was going to take a violent dive, but sort of checked, as though she had scooped the water up and had leveled herself. She then seemed to settle very, very quiet, until the last, when she rose up, and she seemed to stand 20 seconds, stern in that position [indicating], and then she went down with an awful grating, like a small boat running off a shingley beach.

SENATOR SMITH: How long were you lying off, so to speak?

MR. ETCHES: Before the *Titanic* sank, sir?

SENATOR SMITH: No; after.

MR. ETCHES: We waited a few minutes after she had gone down. There was no inrush of water, or anything. Mr. Pitman then said to pull back to the scene of the wreck. The ladies started calling out. Two ladies sitting in front where I was pulling, said, "Appeal to the officer not to go back. Why should we lose all of our lives in a useless attempt to save those from the ship?" I said I had no power; an officer was in charge of the boat, and he must use his discretion.

SENATOR SMITH: As a matter of fact, you did not go back?

MR. ETCHES: We did not go back. . . .

SENATOR SMITH: Did you see lights while you were lying by, after or before the *Titanic* sank, from any other ship?

MR. ETCHES: After the *Titanic* had sunk we pulled a good distance out farther from her, after the cries were all over. We pulled away, and a light we thought was a mast headlight of a ship was across where the port bow of the *Titanic* would have been at the time. During the time the *Titanic* was there I saw no light. I was looking at the *Titanic* the whole of the time.

SENATOR SMITH: Could you see the bridge when the ship went down?

MR. ETCHES: You could see it quite plain, sir.

SENATOR SMITH: Did you see anybody on the bridge?

MR. ETCHES: Not a soul, sir.

SENATOR SMITH: You probably could not distinguish objects?

MR. ETCHES: They may have been there; they may have been near the wheel house, but not on the corner of the bridge. I did not discern anyone there, sir.

SENATOR SMITH: After you started out to sea, away from this wreck, did you see any lights of other vessels?

MR. ETCHES: Yes, sir; we saw a light that there was quite an argument over. Some said it was a star; others said it was a ship. But we pulled toward it, and we did not seem to approach it an inch nearer. It had every appearance of a masthead light of a ship, but rather a faint light. . . .

NINTH DAY
Monday, April 29
Washington, D.C.

Witness: Frederick M. Sammis, 35
**General engineer of the Marconi Wireless Telegraph
Co. of America**

*Key testimony: He took responsibility for the messages
advising the* Titanic *and* Carpathia *wireless operators to keep
quiet so they could sell their exclusives to the press. In
contentious questioning, Senator Smith hammered away at
the Marconi role in checkbook journalism. But though Smith
recalled Marconi as well as the two operators to testify again
on this day, he did not summon any representative of* The
New York Times.

... SENATOR SMITH: I will come right to the point and ask
you whether the following message, which was intercepted by the chief wireless operator, J. R. Simpson, chief
electrician United States Navy, is familiar to you:

8:30 P.M.

To Marconi officer, Carpathia and Titanic:
Arranged for your exclusive story for dollars in four
figures. Mr. Marconi agreeing. Say nothing until you see
me. Where are you now?

J. M. SAMMIS, *Opr. C.*

MR. SAMMIS: I only know about that exact message from
what I have read in the newspapers.

If you will allow me, I will describe this unpleasant
business, because it is unpleasant, as it has brought upon
me a country-wide publicity that I little desire, and has
pointed the finger of scorn at me by my neighbors, simply
because in their estimation, either intentionally or other-

360

wise, the date and time of these messages, when they were first published, at any rate, were not disclosed. In the second place because it has not been stated, I believe, thus far, that at 8:30 the ship was either across the end of her pier or nearly so.

I sat in my office at 8:10 on that night and was told by the operating department that the ship had passed the Narrows, and the Seagate Station itself is at the Narrows, New York Harbor.

It is not my desire to throw onto anybody else any responsibility for the sense of this message. Mr. Marconi did agree that the boys, when they got ashore, should be allowed to sell the report of their personal experience, which numerous other people on board the ship did. In these days, when corporations are counted as not caring very much about their employees or what happens to them, or what they get, it seemed to me that the men who had been responsible mainly and chiefly for saving 700 lives ought in some way to be recognized substantially.

It was not I who originated this scheme or this arrangement at all. The arrangement was made, however, and the information was telephoned to Seagate Station, which I say is at the Narrows, New York, to explain to these boys. In telephoning that I told them, "I know the boys are exhausted, but give them this news; maybe it will spur them on and make them feel better." I remember definitely telling them that.

SENATOR SMITH: With whom were you talking at that time?

MR. SAMMIS: To Mr. Davidson, the man temporarily in charge of Seagate Station. He is not regularly in our employ, but was sent there because he was an expert operator and one of the best men we have ever had. But he was not regularly under our control. He was sent there, and we made use of his services, and he handled the wireless entirely. I have a statement from him, and he made an affidavit, that messages about which so much noise has been made were of his own construction, and that he realizes, as we all do, that they were not gems of English literature, but they were, on the spur of the moment, instructions to the men, carrying out and explaining to them the arrangements which had been made.

SENATOR SMITH: We are not passing upon the literary

character of these productions. . . . Cottam, the regular operator of the *Carpathia*, left the ship immediately when she arrived, did he not?

MR. SAMMIS: I understand so; yes.

SENATOR SMITH: Did he do that in obedience to your request to meet you at the Strand Hotel?

MR. SAMMIS: He probably did; yes.

SENATOR SMITH: Why did you want him to meet you?

MR. SAMMIS: Simply so that he could get in touch with the New York Times reporter, with whom the arrangement had been made, and give him the story.

SENATOR SMITH: Then we may presume the arrangement he made with the Times and carried out was with your consent?

MR. SAMMIS: With the consent of the company, Mr. Marconi, and Mr. Bottomley, as well. I simply passed along the arrangement which had been made.

SENATOR SMITH: But with your consent?

MR. SAMMIS: Yes. I had not very much to say. He did not need my consent.

SENATOR SMITH: With your concurrence?

MR. SAMMIS: With my approval; yes, sir. My unofficial approval.

SENATOR SMITH: Did he meet you at the Strand Hotel, or was he to meet you?

MR. SAMMIS: No.

SENATOR SMITH: Were you there?

MR. SAMMIS: I was at the Strand Hotel; yes. That was the headquarters of the New York Times.

SENATOR SMITH: Five hundred and two West Fourteenth Street?

MR. SAMMIS: Yes, sir.

SENATOR SMITH: Whom did you go there to meet—Mr. Cottam?

MR. SAMMIS: I went there to meet the operators; yes.

SENATOR SMITH: To meet Mr. Cottam?

MR. SAMMIS: Not Mr. Cottam any more than Mr. Bride, particularly, but to meet both of them.

SENATOR SMITH: Did you go to the side of the *Carpathia* at all when she docked?

MR. SAMMIS: Yes.

SENATOR SMITH: At what time?

MR. SAMMIS: I have not the least idea. It took me 45 minutes to get across the street. At the time I got to the *Carpathia* I lost all sense of time. I should say, roughly, it might have been a couple of hours after she had docked.

SENATOR SMITH: Did you find Mr. Bride there?

MR. SAMMIS: Yes.

SENATOR SMITH: But had you seen Mr. Cottam in the meantime?

MR. SAMMIS: No.

SENATOR SMITH: Did you go to the Cunard Dock with Mr. Marconi?

MR. SAMMIS: Yes.

SENATOR SMITH: Was that the first time he had been there that evening?

MR. SAMMIS: I assume so.

SENATOR SMITH: Was he with you at the Strand Hotel?

MR. SAMMIS: No.

SENATOR SMITH: Was anybody with you?

MR. SAMMIS: You could not be in the Strand Hotel that night without having somebody with you. There were Times men and all the other newspaper men.

SENATOR SMITH: Yes; but who went with you to the Strand Hotel?

MR. SAMMIS: Nobody.

SENATOR SMITH: Who left the Strand Hotel with you?

MR. SAMMIS: One of the Times men; I have forgotten his name. [It was Jim Speers, a reporter, according to one account.]

SENATOR SMITH: How much was Mr. Cottam, the operator on the *Carpathia*, to get for that story?

MR. SAMMIS: The Times agreed to pay $1,000 for the two stories. I do not know how they were going to divide it; I did not interest myself in it.

SENATOR SMITH: For his and Cottam's story of the loss of the *Titanic*?

MR. SAMMIS: Yes.

SENATOR SMITH: With whom was that arrangement made?

MR. SAMMIS: With the New York Times.

SENATOR SMITH: I know; but who made it in behalf of these boys?

MR. SAMMIS: You mean what representative of the Times?

SENATOR SMITH: No; who made the arrangement on behalf of the company?

MR. SAMMIS: Well, everybody had something to do with it. I had something to do with it; Mr. Bottomley had something to do with it; it was a general conversation carried on by the New York Times office and our office and Mr. Bottomley's house.

SENATOR SMITH: Was the contract on the part of the operators completed? Did they give their stories?

MR. SAMMIS: I think they did.

SENATOR SMITH: Both to the same paper?

MR. SAMMIS: I think so.

SENATOR SMITH: Did they receive their money?

MR. SAMMIS: I understand they did, and more besides.

SENATOR SMITH: How much more?

MR. SAMMIS: I understand they got $250 more apiece than was promised them.

SENATOR SMITH: That is, they got $750 apiece?

MR. SAMMIS: That is my rough recollection: I did not see the money or handle it, and do not wish to. That is hearsay. [Later, Bride testified that he got $1,000 and Cottam said he got $750.]

SENATOR SMITH: In order that we may clear this up as we go along, were you to have any part in this yourself?

MR. SAMMIS: Absolutely none.

SENATOR SMITH: Was Mr. Bottomley to have any part in it?

MR. SAMMIS: Absolutely none.

SENATOR SMITH: And you have had no part in it?

MR. SAMMIS: No.

SENATOR SMITH: Mr. Cottam says he has not yet received his money.

MR. SAMMIS: Perhaps that is Mr. Cottam's fault. Perhaps he has not been accessible.

SENATOR SMITH: Is the money being held for him by anybody, to your knowledge?

MR. SAMMIS: I presume, if anybody were holding it, it would be the Times.

SENATOR SMITH: Nobody else?

MR. SAMMIS: I understood Mr. Cottam had received his money.

SENATOR SMITH: He had not when he was on the stand a day or two ago.

MR. SAMMIS: I understand that he has since.

SENATOR SMITH: Were these payments made through yourself or any other officer of the Marconi Co.?

MR. SAMMIS: I have already stated that I did not see the money, did not expect to, and did not wish to.

SENATOR SMITH: Do you mean that you did not see a check or an envelope containing the money?

MR. SAMMIS: I have not taken part in the transaction one iota, one way or the other.

SENATOR SMITH: Let us clear this up as we go along. I think it is a most distasteful matter to you, as it is to the committee, and I think to the public.

MR. SAMMIS: I have not done anything I am ashamed of, and if I can clear my record, that the newspapers have impugned, I want to do it, and I am sure you want to help me.

SENATOR SMITH: Have you done anything in this matter, about which we have just been speaking, that you are very proud of?

MR. SAMMIS: I have not done anything I am ashamed of.

SENATOR SMITH: I did not ask you that. I want to know whether you are proud of it?

MR. SAMMIS: Yes; I am proud of the fact that, being an employer of labor, and being the superior of poorly paid men, or mediumly paid men—men who do not see very much of this world's goods—I will do them a good turn honestly if I can, and that I consider I have done. I know of no law that can forbid a man selling his personal experience, after he comes ashore, and we have no rule by which we could prevent them from doing it.

SENATOR SMITH: Then am I to understand from what you say that, so far as your opinion goes, this practice to which I am calling attention will be continued?

MR. SAMMIS: I should consider it very dangerous indeed— and I had intended to bring it to your attention—to forbid them, by some hard and fast rule, which you have indicated, along that line, because the result would be that you would obtain the very results you now have. It would seem only reasonable that if no recognition whatsoever, in standing or financially, should be made of the efforts of these men to get the news off the ships, they would not stir themselves very much to do it. I believe it could be regulated. I believe an error was made. I believe it would have been better to have sent this news to the Associated Press and let them settle with the boys, if they liked. The news then would have had more general distribution, and there would not have been any sore toes.

SENATOR SMITH: I have not seen any sore toes, and I do not know of anybody who is complaining of any, myself. But do you not think it would have been better to communicate this intelligence to your office, in answer to the numerous inquiries made by Mr. Marconi, from the time of the accident until the arrival of the *Carpathia*, and then disseminate it to the public, that they might be relieved of the anxiety under which they were suffering?

MR. SAMMIS: With all due deference to the question, my judgment would not be that that was the best course to pursue, for this reason, that the international telegraph convention has already placed itself on record as putting news dispatches last in the list; ship service telegrams first, paid passenger telegrams second, and then press messages.

SENATOR SMITH: How general is this custom of receiving and accepting money for exclusive stories of sea disasters?

MR. SAMMIS: I should say it was quite general. I perused the copies of messages from the shore stations. I saw messages from practically every paper in New York City asking practically everybody, from the captain down to the survivors, for exclusive stories. Whether they got them or not I am unable to say, except that I did see in the New York World, on the day after the *Carpathia* arrived, that they had published an exclusive story two hours and a half before the New York Times had theirs on the street.

SENATOR SMITH: The committee are not very much concerned with that. . . . I am asking you whether or not this custom or habit or practice, of which you do not seem to wholly disapprove, of selling the experiences of operators at sea in disasters of that kind, had anything to do with the failure to get that information here promptly?

MR. SAMMIS: Absolutely nothing whatever. I should say that the boys obeyed their rules, the rules of conscience and the rules of the international telegraph convention, which they were forced to do. They followed them blindly. I believe I should have done the same in their place.

SENATOR SMITH: I will let this personal eulogy stand for itself and ask you how you happened to go to the Strand Hotel with the Times representative that night?

MR. SAMMIS: Simply to get him in touch with the men when they came off the ship.

SENATOR SMITH: And to see that this news was obtained by the New York Times?

MR. SAMMIS: Yes.

SENATOR SMITH: You have spoken of rewarding the service of these operators. Mr. Bride is here, and at the risk of saying something that I am not called upon to say, I want to observe that Mr. Bride was so loyal to the *Titanic* and so obedient to its commander and so courageous in its distress, that he refused to leave the *Titanic* in a lifeboat, and stayed on the ship until one minute before she sank, because the captain had not given him permission to leave; and he remained at his apparatus all that time ticking off the fate of that ship. I want to know whether it would not be more creditable to you and to your company to encourage that kind of gallantry and heroism and fidelity by leaving the question of reward for such service to the public, rather than to seal his lips with an injunction of secrecy, so that he might receive a pittance from some private source?

MR. SAMMIS: We did not seal his lips. We provided the means for unsealing them.

SENATOR SMITH: Did you tell him to shut his mouth?

MR. SAMMIS: I did not.

SENATOR SMITH: Did you tell him to agree to nothing until he saw you?

MR. SAMMIS: Not in those words. I have told you I——

SENATOR SMITH (interposing): Answer me, now. Did you tell him to say nothing until he saw you?

MR. SAMMIS: I gave him the information that I have already stated—that the Times wanted him to tell the story of his own personal experiences after he got ashore.

SENATOR SMITH: Did you tell him in any wireless message the New York Times wanted this story?

MR. SAMMIS: No.

SENATOR SMITH: Did you tell him to "say nothing until you see me."

MR. SAMMIS: I gave the information which probably was responsible for that message; yes, sir.

SENATOR SMITH: In other words, you put an injunction on him?

MR. SAMMIS: No; I did not.

SENATOR SMITH: You expected him to disregard it?

MR. SAMMIS: He did exactly what I told him to do. There was no injunction on him whatever. He could not possibly have sent a message, had I desired it or had anybody desired it, in the time available before he got to the dock. It was absurd to think such a thing would be possible. . . .

Witness: Hugh Woolner
Businessman and first-class passenger, from London

Key testimony: He witnessed Ida Straus refusing to leave her husband. He and a Scandinavian acquaintance together made a jump for it as a lifeboat was being lowered past them.

. . . SENATOR SMITH: Tell us in your own way whether you paid any special attention to the movements of the ship, to the weather, to the equipment, and any circumstance that may tend to throw light upon this calamity up to the time of the collision?

MR. WOOLNER: I took the ordinary passenger's interest in the number of miles we did each day. Beyond that I did not take any note of the speed of the ship.

SENATOR SMITH: What were your observations?

MR. WOOLNER: I noticed that, so far as my memory serves me, the number of miles increased per day as we went on. If I remember right, one day it was 314, and the next day was 356, and that was the last number I remember. I think that was the last number that was put up on the ship's chart, or whatever it is called. . . .

SENATOR SMITH: If you can, I would like to have you tell the committee where you were on Sunday preceding that accident?

368

MR. WOOLNER: I was in the smoking room at the time of the shock. . . .

SENATOR SMITH: When did you first know of the impact?

MR. WOOLNER: We felt it under the smoking room. We felt a sort of stopping, a sort of, not exactly shock, but a sort of slowing down; and then we sort of felt a rip that gave a sort of a slight twist to the whole room. Everybody, so far as I could see, stood up and a number of men walked out rapidly through the swinging doors on the port side, and ran along to the rail that was behind the mast—I think there was a mast standing out there—and the rail just beyond.

SENATOR SMITH: What did you do?

MR. WOOLNER: I stood hearing what the conjectures were. People were guessing what it might be, and one man called out, "An iceberg has passed astern," but who it was I do not know. I never have seen the man since.

SENATOR SMITH: What did you do then?

MR. WOOLNER: I then went to look for Mrs. Candee, because she was the lady in whom I was most interested, and I met her outside her stateroom.

SENATOR SMITH: What took place? Just detail what you did?

MR. WOOLNER: I said: "Some accident has happened, but I do not think it is anything serious. Let us go for a walk." We walked the after deck for quite a considerable time. As we passed——

SENATOR SMITH (interposing): For how long a time?

MR. WOOLNER: I should think for 10 minutes or more. As we passed one of the entrances to the corridor, I saw people coming up with life belts; so I went inside and asked the steward: "Is this orders?"

SENATOR SMITH: That is, you asked him if the life belts were ordered?

MR. WOOLNER: Yes. I shouted to some one going by.

SENATOR SMITH: An employee with a life belt on?

MR. WOOLNER: No; standing at the entrance; and he said, "Orders."

I went back to Mrs. Candee and took her to her stateroom, and we got her life belt down from the top of the wardrobe, and tied hers onto her, and then she chose one or two things out of her baggage, little things she could put into her pocket, or something of that sort, and I said, "We will now go up on deck and see what has really happened."

SENATOR SMITH: Did you yourself put a life belt on?

MR. WOOLNER: Yes, sir. I missed that. I went back to my cabin and brought out and put one on myself, and I took the other one—there were two in the room—with me. I met some one in the passage who said, "Do you want that?" and I said "No," and gave it to him. . . .

SENATOR SMITH: Was there any difficulty in getting [people] to enter the lifeboat?

MR. WOOLNER: Yes; there was a certain amount of reluctance on the part of the women to go in, and then some officer said, "It is a matter of precaution," and then they came forward rather more freely. . . .

SENATOR SMITH: Do you recall how many men were put into that boat?

MR. WOOLNER: No; I can not. There were very few, I think.

SENATOR SMITH: Or how many women?

MR. WOOLNER: Oh, I did not count them, but it struck me as not being very full, but it was rather difficult to get it filled.

SENATOR SMITH: Mrs. Candee got in that boat?

MR. WOOLNER: Yes.

SENATOR SMITH: After you had put her in the boat, what did you do?

MR. WOOLNER: I looked around to see what else I could do.

SENATOR SMITH: Did you find anything to do?

MR. WOOLNER: I did what a man could. It was a very distressing scene—the men parting from their wives.

SENATOR SMITH: Did you assist in loading the boats?

MR. WOOLNER: Yes, sir.

SENATOR SMITH: How many boats?

MR. WOOLNER: I think nearly all, except one on the port side, and Mr. Steffanson stayed by me all the time, also.

SENATOR SMITH: This Swedish acquaintance you formed stayed by you?

MR. WOOLNER: Yes, sir.

SENATOR SMITH: What, if any, order was given by officers, or what did you hear regarding the filling of the lifeboats?

MR. WOOLNER: I do not think I remember any orders. I do not think any orders were necessary.

SENATOR SMITH: You mean that the men stood back and passed the women and children forward?

MR. WOOLNER: Yes.

SENATOR SMITH: There was no crowding?

MR. WOOLNER: None.

SENATOR SMITH: No jostling?

MR. WOOLNER: None.

SENATOR SMITH: Were these boats all filled in your presence?

MR. WOOLNER: On the port side?

SENATOR SMITH: On the port side.

MR. WOOLNER: Not all. I think we missed one, because I said to Steffanson: "Let us go down on the deck below and see if we can find any people waiting about there." So we went down onto A deck and we found three women who did not seem to know their way, and we brought them up. . . .

SENATOR SMITH: From your own observation are you enabled to say that, so far as you know, the women and children all got aboard these lifeboats?

MR. WOOLNER: So far as I could see, with the exception of Mrs. Straus.

SENATOR SMITH: Did you see her get into the boat?

MR. WOOLNER: She would not get in. I tried to get her to do so and she refused altogether to leave Mr. Straus. The second time we went up to Mr. Straus, and I said to him: "I am sure nobody would object to an old gentleman like you getting in. There seems to be room in this boat." He said: "I will not go before the other men."

SENATOR SMITH: What happened then?

MR. WOOLNER: Then they eventually lowered all the wooden lifeboats on the port side, and then they got out a collapsible and hitched her onto the most forward davits and they filled that up, mostly with steerage women and children, and one seaman, and a steward, and I think one other man—but I am not quite certain about that—and when that boat seemed to be quite full, and was ready to be swung over the side, and was to be lowered away, I said to Steffanson: "There is nothing more for us to do here." Oh, no; something else happened while that boat was being loaded. There was a sort of scramble on the starboard side, and I looked around and I saw two flashes of a pistol in the air.

SENATOR SMITH: Two flashes of a pistol?

MR. WOOLNER: Yes.

SENATOR SMITH: Pistol shots?

MR. WOOLNER: Yes; but they were up in the air, at that sort of an angle [indicating]. I heard Mr. Murdoch shouting out, "Get out of this, clear out of this," and that sort of thing, to a lot of men who were swarming into a boat on that side.

SENATOR SMITH: Swarming into the boat?

MR. WOOLNER: Yes.

SENATOR SMITH: Was that into this collapsible boat?

MR. WOOLNER: It was a collapsible; yes, sir.

SENATOR SMITH: That was the first collapsible that was lowered on the port side?

MR. WOOLNER: On the starboard side. That was the other side.

SENATOR SMITH: You were across the ship?

MR. WOOLNER: Yes.

SENATOR SMITH: You were then on the starboard side?

MR. WOOLNER: Yes. We went across there because we heard a certain kind of shouting going on, and just as we got around the corner I saw these two flashes of the pistol, and Steffanson and I went up to help to clear that boat of the men who were climbing in, because there was a bunch of women—I think Italians and foreigners—who were standing on the outside of the crowd, unable to make their way toward the side of the boat.

SENATOR SMITH: Because these men had gathered around this collapsible boat?

MR. WOOLNER: Yes, sir. So we helped the officer to pull these men out, by their legs and anything we could get hold of.

SENATOR SMITH: You pulled them out of the boat?

MR. WOOLNER: We pulled out several, each.

SENATOR SMITH: How many?

MR. WOOLNER: I should think five or six. But they were really flying before Mr. Murdoch from inside of the boat at the time.

SENATOR SMITH: They were members of the crew?

MR. WOOLNER: I could not tell. No; I do not think so. I think they were probably third-class passengers. It was awfully difficult to notice very carefully. I got hold of them by their feet and legs. Then they cleared out, practically all the men, out of that boat, and then we lifted in these Italian women, hoisted them up on each side and put them into the boat. They were very limp. They had not much spring in them at all. Then that boat was finally filled up and swung out, and then I said to Steffanson: "There is nothing more for us to do. Let us go down onto A deck again." And we went down again, but there was nobody there that time at all. It was perfectly empty the whole length. It was absolutely deserted, and the electric lights along the ceiling of A deck were beginning to turn red, just a glow, a red sort of glow. So I said to Steffanson: "This is getting rather a tight corner. I do not like being inside these closed windows. Let us go out through the door at the end." And as we went out through the door the sea came in onto the deck at our feet.

SENATOR SMITH: You were then on A deck?

MR. WOOLNER: Yes, sir.

SENATOR SMITH: And did you look on both sides of the deck to see whether there were people?

MR. WOOLNER: Yes, sir.

SENATOR SMITH: You say there were none?

MR. WOOLNER: None, the whole length of it.

SENATOR SMITH: The whole length of A deck you saw no people?

MR. WOOLNER: Not a soul.

SENATOR SMITH: How long was that after the collapsible lifeboat that you have just referred to was lowered?

MR. WOOLNER: Oh, quite a few minutes; a very few minutes.

SENATOR SMITH: You remained down there with your friend until the sea came in—water came in—on A deck?

MR. WOOLNER: On that A deck. Then we hopped up onto the gunwale preparing to jump out into the sea, because if we had waited a minute longer we should have been boxed in against the ceiling. And as we looked out we saw this collapsible, the last boat on the port side, being lowered right in front of our faces.

SENATOR SMITH: How far out?

MR. WOOLNER: It was about 9 feet out?

SENATOR SMITH: Nine feet out from the side of A deck?

MR. WOOLNER: Yes.

SENATOR SMITH: You saw a collapsible boat being lowered?

MR. WOOLNER: Being lowered; yes.

SENATOR SMITH: Was it filled with people?

MR. WOOLNER: It was full up to the bow, and I said to Steffanson: "There is nobody in the bows. Let us make a jump for it. You go first."

And he jumped out and tumbled in head over heels into the bow, and I jumped too, and hit the gunwale with my chest, which had on this life preserver, of course, and I sort of bounced off the gunwale and caught the gunwale with my fingers, and slipped off backwards.

SENATOR SMITH: Into the water?

MR. WOOLNER: As my legs dropped down I felt that they were in the sea.

SENATOR SMITH: You are quite sure you jumped 9 feet to get that boat?

MR. WOOLNER: That is my estimate. By that time, you see, we were jumping slightly downward.

SENATOR SMITH: Did you jump out or down?

MR. WOOLNER: Both.

SENATOR SMITH: Both out and down?

MR. WOOLNER: Slightly down and out.

SENATOR SMITH: It could not have been very far down if the water was on A deck; it must have been out.

MR. WOOLNER: Chiefly out; but it was sufficiently down for us to be able to see just over the edge of the gunwale of the boat.

SENATOR SMITH: You pulled yourself up out of the water?

MR. WOOLNER: Yes; and then I hooked my right heel over the gunwale, and by this time Steffanson was standing up, and he caught hold of me and lifted me in. Then we looked over into the sea and saw a man swimming in the sea just beneath us, and pulled him in.

SENATOR SMITH: Who was he?

MR. WOOLNER: I do not know.

SENATOR SMITH: Did you pull anybody else in?

MR. WOOLNER: No; by that time we were afloat.

SENATOR SMITH: Did anybody leave your lifeboat?

MR. WOOLNER: Leave it?

SENATOR SMITH: Yes; after you got in.

MR. WOOLNER: No.

SENATOR SMITH: Or attempt to leave it?

MR. WOOLNER: No. By that time we were bumping against the side of the ship.

SENATOR SMITH: Against the *Titanic's* side?

MR. WOOLNER: She was going down pretty fast by the bow. . . .

SENATOR SMITH: Who took charge of that boat?

MR. WOOLNER: There was a seaman in the stern who steered her with an oar, but when we got out among the other boats, we obeyed the orders of the officer who was in charge of the bunch of boats.

SENATOR SMITH: Who was that, if you know?

MR. WOOLNER: I think it was Mr. Lowe, the man who got his sail up.

SENATOR SMITH: He got his sail up?

MR. WOOLNER: Afterwards; not then, but later. I think his name was Lowe.

SENATOR SMITH: How far out from the side of the *Titanic* did you go before you stopped?

MR. WOOLNER: We got out three oars first, and shoved off from the side of the ship. Then we got her head more or less straightaway, and then we pulled as hard as we could, until, I should think, we were 150 yards away, when the *Titanic* went down.

SENATOR SMITH: Did you see her go down?

MR. WOOLNER: Yes.

SENATOR SMITH: Were you near enough to recognize people on deck?

MR. WOOLNER: No.

SENATOR SMITH: As she went down did you see or feel any suction?

MR. WOOLNER: I did not detect any; she seemed to me to stop for about 30 seconds at one place before she took the final plunge, because I watched one particular porthole, and the water did not rise there for at least half a minute, and then she suddenly slid under with her propellers under the water.

SENATOR SMITH: She went down bow first.

MR. WOOLNER: Yes.

SENATOR SMITH: Did you hear any explosion?

MR. WOOLNER: No; a sort of rumbling roar, it sounded to me, as she slid under.

SENATOR SMITH: What, if anything, can you say to the committee regarding the discipline or absence of discipline on the part of the officers or crew after the impact?

MR. WOOLNER: I saw no want of discipline.

SENATOR SMITH: Was there any warning or signal given, to your knowledge, after the boat struck, to passengers in their rooms?

MR. WOOLNER: I can not tell you, because I simply went to my room and got my life belt and came away—— . . .

SENATOR SMITH: Who fired those two shots, do you know?

MR. WOOLNER: Mr. Murdoch, so far as I can tell. . . .

SENATOR SMITH: After pulling out for 15 minutes or so, what took place?

MR. WOOLNER: Then some officer came along and said: "I want all these boats tied up by their painters, head and tail, so as to make a more conspicuous mark"; and we did that; and there was no call to row much after that because we were simply drifting about.

SENATOR SMITH: Did you go back to the scene of the wreck after pulling out this 150 or 200 yards?

MR. WOOLNER: No.

SENATOR SMITH: Was there any attempt made by your boat to go back, so far as you know?

MR. WOOLNER: Not by our boat; no.

SENATOR SMITH: Did the women urge that the boat be taken back?

MR. WOOLNER: No.

SENATOR SMITH: Did you hear any officer say that the boat should be taken back to the scene of the wreck?

MR. WOOLNER: I did not.

SENATOR SMITH: After you got tied together, what did you do?

MR. WOOLNER: We drifted about for a long time.

SENATOR SMITH: Drifted?

MR. WOOLNER: Yes; just drifted about. There was nothing to do.

SENATOR SMITH: And waited until daylight?

MR. WOOLNER: Yes; and then dawn began to break very slowly, and we could see more. . . .

Witness: Joseph Groves Boxhall
Titanic's Fourth Officer

Key testimony: Since the captain of the Mount Temple *had testified that the* Titanic's *stated position was 8 miles off,*

Boxhall was recalled to defend his navigational calculations. Boxhall also affirmed in detail his sighting of a ship in the distance that turned away.

... SENATOR BURTON: The captain of the *Mount Temple* maintains that the course as conveyed by the distress signal was wrong; that the *Titanic* was actually eight miles distant from the place indicated. What do you say as to that?

MR. BOXHALL: I do not know what to say. I know our position, because I worked the position out, and I know that it is correct. One of the first things that Capt. Rostron said after I met him was, "What a splendid position that was you gave us."

SENATOR BURTON: You gave them what position?

MR. BOXHALL: 41° 46′, and 50° 14′.

SENATOR BURTON: And you are satisfied that was correct?

MR. BOXHALL: Perfectly.

SENATOR BURTON: You computed it yourself, did you?

MR. BOXHALL: I computed it myself, and computed it by star observations that had been taken by Mr. Lightoller that same evening; and they were beautiful observations.

SENATOR BURTON: Who made the computations on them?

MR. BOXHALL: I did. You asked me if the officer who took the observations and the one who made the computations compared their results?

SENATOR BURTON: Yes.

MR. BOXHALL: I do not see what there is to compare. The officer who takes the observations always is the senior officer.

SENATOR BURTON: He writes those down, does he?

MR. BOXHALL: He simply takes the observations with his sextant. The junior officer takes the time with the chronometer, and then is told to work them out.

SENATOR BURTON: That is, another person works them out?

MR. BOXHALL: Yes. If he does not think these things are correct, he tells you to work them over, and you have to do it.

SENATOR BURTON: Would there not be some danger of your mistaking a figure, or something of that kind, that is written down by another person?

MR. BOXHALL: When you take stars you always endeavor, as they did that night, to take a set of stars. One position checks another. You take two stars for latitude, and two for longitude, one star north and one star south, one star east and one star west. If you find a big difference between eastern and western stars, you know there is a mistake somewhere. If there is a difference between these two latitude stars you know there is a mistake somewhere. But, as it happened, I think I worked out three stars for latitude and I think I worked out three stars for longitude.

SENATOR BURTON: And they all agreed?

MR. BOXHALL: They all agreed. . . .

MR. BOXHALL: I judge so.

SENATOR BURTON: How much did the *Titanic* draw at that time?

MR. BOXHALL: I could not say what the draft was when we left Southampton; probably 33 feet.

SENATOR BURTON: You are very positive you saw that ship ahead on the port bow, are you?

MR. BOXHALL: Yes, sir; quite positive.

SENATOR BURTON: Did you see the green or red light?

MR. BOXHALL: Yes; I saw the side lights with my naked eye.

SENATOR BURTON: When did you see them?

MR. BOXHALL: From our ship, before I left the ship. I saw this steamer's stern light before I went into my boat, which indicated that the ship had turned around. I saw a white light, and I could not see any of the masthead lights that I had seen previously, and I took it for a stern light.

SENATOR BURTON: Which light did you see first?

MR. BOXHALL: I saw the masthead lights first, the two steaming lights; and then, as she drew up closer, I saw her side lights through my glasses, and eventually I saw the red light. I had seen the green, but I saw the red most of the time. I saw the red light with my naked eye.

SENATOR BURTON: Did she pull away from you?

MR. BOXHALL: I do not know when she turned; I can not say when I missed the lights, because I was leaving the bridge to go and fire off some more of those distress rockets and attend to other duties.

SENATOR BURTON: Then your idea is that she was coming toward you on the port side?

MR. BOXHALL: Yes.

SENATOR BURTON: Because you saw the red light and the masthead lights?

MR. BOXHALL: Yes, sir.

SENATOR BURTON: Afterward you saw the green light, which showed that she had turned?

MR. BOXHALL: I think I saw the green light before I saw the red light, as a matter of fact. But the ship was meeting us. I am covering the whole thing by saying the ship was meeting us.

SENATOR BURTON: Your impression is she turned away, or turned on a different course?

MR. BOXHALL: That is my impression. . . .

MR. BOXHALL: That is my idea, sir.

SENATOR BURTON: She kept on a general course toward the east, and then bore away from you, or what?

MR. BOXHALL: I do not think she was doing much steaming. I do not think the ship was steaming very much, because after I first saw the masthead lights she must have been still steaming, but by the time I saw her red light with my naked eye she was not steaming very much. So she had probably gotten into the ice, and turned around.

SENATOR BURTON: What do you think happened after she turned around? Do you think she went away to avoid the ice?

MR. BOXHALL: I do not know whether she stayed there all night, or what she did. I lost the light. I did not see her after we pulled around to the starboard side of the *Titanic*.

SENATOR BURTON: Then you lost track of her?

MR. BOXHALL: Yes.

SENATOR BURTON: And you saw her no more after that?

MR. BOXHALL: No, sir. As a matter of fact, Capt. Smith was standing by my side, and we both came to the conclusion that she was close enough to be signaled by the Morse lamp. So I signaled to her. I called her up, and got no answer. The captain said, "Tell him to come at once, we are sinking." So I sent that signal out, "Come at once, we are sinking."

SENATOR BURTON: And you kept firing up those rockets?

MR. BOXHALL: Then leaving off and firing rockets. There were a lot of stewards and men standing around the bridge and around the boat deck. Of course, there were quite a lot of them quite interested in this ship, looking from the bridge, and some said she had shown a light in reply, but I never saw it. I even got the quartermaster who was working around with me—I do not know who he was—to fire off the distress signal, and I got him to also signal with the Morse lamp—that is just a series of dots with short intervals of light—whilst I watched with a pair of glasses to see whether this man did answer, as some people said he had replied.

SENATOR BURTON: You saw nothing of the hull of the boat?

MR. BOXHALL: Oh, no; it was too dark.

I have already stated, in answer to a question, how far this ship was away from us, that I thought she was about 5 miles, and I arrived at it in this way. The masthead lights of a steamer are required by the board of trade regulations to show for 5 miles, and the signals are required to show for 2 miles.

SENATOR BURTON: You could see that distance on such a night as this?

MR. BOXHALL: I could see quite clearly.

SENATOR BURTON: You are very sure you are not deceived about seeing these lights?

MR. BOXHALL: Not at all. . . .

TENTH DAY
Tuesday, April 30
Washington, D.C.

Witness: J. Bruce Ismay
Managing director of the White Star Line and
first-class passenger

Key testimony: Summoned back for further grilling, Ismay steadfastly denied urging the captain on to greater speeds. He denied press accounts quoting a passenger, Emily Ryerson, from a prominent Pennsylvania steel family, as saying that he had shown her a telegraphed warning of ice and said the ship would speed up to get through it. He again explained the circumstances of his climbing into the lifeboat. He filled in details of the ship's conception and construction. And, while clearly chafing at being detained by the Senators, he bit his tongue.

. . . SENATOR SMITH: I desire to ask you a few questions in addition to those I asked you the other day. . . .

    What mail contracts have you with the British Government or any other Government?

MR. ISMAY: We have a mail contract for carrying the mails from Southampton to New York, for which we receive a lump-sum payment of £70,000 a year; $350,000 a year.

SENATOR SMITH: £70,000?

MR. ISMAY: That is the maximum payment that we can receive.

SENATOR SMITH: For that payment what are you supposed to do?

MR. ISMAY: We carry the mails from Southampton. We pick up the mails at Southampton, and then we go on to

Queenstown and pick up any mails that are there, and land them in New York.

SENATOR SMITH: In that contract is there any condition that you shall make any specific speed between Southampton and New York?

MR. ISMAY: No, sir. We are supposed to use the fastest ships we have in our fleet for the conveyance of the mails, but there is absolutely no penalty attached to our not making any special speed.

SENATOR SMITH: Is there any minimum?

MR. ISMAY: I think there is. I think there is a minimum; or we are not allowed to put the mails into ships that will go less than 16 knots, or something like that. . . .

SENATOR SMITH: Have you any contract with the United States Government for mail service between New York or Boston and other ports than Southampton?

MR. ISMAY: No, sir.

SENATOR SMITH: Is there any speed condition in the contract of the United States Government?

MR. ISMAY: I am really not conversant with that contract, sir. . . .

SENATOR SMITH: Who of your company directed the Harland & Wolff Co. to build the *Titanic?*

MR. ISMAY: I did, sir.

SENATOR SMITH: What did you say to them?

MR. ISMAY: It is very difficult for me to say what I said. It would be in a conversation with Lord [W. J.] Pirrie [chairman of Harland & Wolff], that we had decided to build the *Olympic* and the *Titanic.*

SENATOR SMITH: Were both ships ordered at the same time?

MR. ISMAY: Yes, sir.

SENATOR SMITH: What did you say to them? Did you say, "We want the largest and best ship that you can build safely"?

MR. ISMAY: We would naturally try to get the best ship we possibly could. We wanted the best ship crossing the north Atlantic when we built her.

SENATOR SMITH: And when you gave the order that was your instruction?

MR. ISMAY: Yes, sir.

SENATOR SMITH: And you made no limitation as to cost?

MR. ISMAY: Absolutely none.

SENATOR SMITH: You were content that they should build that ship at whatever it cost to build it?

MR. ISMAY: Yes, sir. What we wanted was the very best ship they could possibly produce.

SENATOR SMITH: You examined this ship, I assume, on the voyage from Liverpool to the place of the accident, from time to time?

MR. ISMAY: I was never outside the first-class passenger accommodations on board the ship, sir. I never went in any part of that ship that any other first-class passenger had not a perfect right to go to. I had not made any inspection of the ship at all.

SENATOR SMITH: From that do you wish to be understood as saying that you were not officially on board the ship for the purpose of inspecting?

MR. ISMAY: No, sir; I do not. I was there to inspect the ship and see if there were any defects in her, with the idea of not repeating them in the other ship which we are now building at Belfast.

SENATOR SMITH: You are building another ship of the same type now?

MR. ISMAY: We are now building a sister ship to the *Olympic*.

SENATOR SMITH: Did you make these observations?

MR. ISMAY: No, sir; I had not been around the ship.

SENATOR SMITH: Did you have it in mind to do so?

MR. ISMAY: Yes. I should have gone around the ship before we arrived at New York.

SENATOR SMITH: Did Mr. Andrews go about the ship?

MR. ISMAY: He was about the ship all the time, I believe.

SENATOR SMITH: Inspecting and examining her?

MR. ISMAY: I think so. Naturally, in a ship of that size, there were a great many minor defects on board the ship, which he was rectifying. I think there were probably three or four apprentices on board from Messrs. Harland & Wolff's shipbuilding yard, who were there to right any small detail which was wrong.

SENATOR SMITH: On the spot?

MR. ISMAY: Yes. A door might jam, or a pipe might burst, or anything like that, and they were there to make it good at once.

SENATOR SMITH: Did Mr. [Thomas] Andrews [the ship's designer] bring these men for that purpose?

MR. ISMAY: Yes, sir.

SENATOR SMITH: Did you yourself have opportunity to confer with Mr. Andrews during the voyage from Southampton to the place of this accident?

MR. ISMAY: No, sir; I did not. Mr. Andrews dined with me one night. We had no conversation, really, in regard to the ship. Indeed, the only plan which Mr. Andrews submitted to me was a plan where he said he thought the writing room and reading room was unnecessarily large, and he said he saw a way of putting a stateroom in the forward end of it. That was a matter which would have been taken up and thoroughly discussed after we got back to England.

SENATOR SMITH: Were you in conference with the captain during this journey from Southampton?

MR. ISMAY: I was never in the captain's room the whole voyage over, sir, and the captain was never in my room. I never had any conversation with the captain except casual conversation on the deck.

SENATOR SMITH: Were you on the bridge at any time?

MR. ISMAY: I was never on the bridge until after the accident.

SENATOR SMITH: How long after the accident?

MR. ISMAY: I should think it might have been 10 minutes.

SENATOR SMITH: Was the captain there at that time?

MR. ISMAY: The captain was there; yes.

SENATOR SMITH: Was that the only time you saw the captain on the bridge?

MR. ISMAY: I saw him afterwards, when I went up the second time to the bridge.

SENATOR SMITH: How long after?

MR. ISMAY: I should think it might be 35 minutes. It is very difficult to place the time.

SENATOR SMITH: After the impact?

MR. ISMAY: Yes, sir.

SENATOR SMITH: What, if anything, did he say to you about the collision?

MR. ISMAY: The only conversation I had with Capt. Smith was when I went up on the bridge. I asked him what had happened, and he said we had struck ice.

SENATOR SMITH: I believe you said you dined on Sunday evening with the surgeon of the *Titanic?*

MR. ISMAY: Yes. I was all alone, so I asked Dr. O'Loughlin to come and dine with me, and he dined with me in the restaurant at half-past 7.

SENATOR SMITH: And no other person was present at that table except yourself and him?

MR. ISMAY: No other persons were present excepting the doctor and myself, sir.

SENATOR SMITH: Did the doctor survive?

MR. ISMAY: No, sir.

SENATOR SMITH: Do you know where the captain dined on Sunday evening?

MR. ISMAY: He dined in the restaurant.

SENATOR SMITH: The same place that you dined?

MR. ISMAY: In the same room; yes.

SENATOR SMITH: At the same hour?

MR. ISMAY: I do not know what time he dined. I saw him in the room dining.

SENATOR SMITH: With whom?

MR. ISMAY: I believe he dined with Mr. and Mrs. [George] Widener. . . .

SENATOR SMITH: Did you dine with the captain at all on the trip from Southampton to the place of the accident?

MR. ISMAY: I think he dined with me on Friday night.

SENATOR SMITH: Is that the only time?

MR. ISMAY: The only time. He left us immediately after dinner. I went into my own room with the people who were dining with me, and we sat in my room and played bridge. But I never saw the captain after we left the restaurant. He never came near my room.

SENATOR SMITH: Had you known the captain of that ship some time?

MR. ISMAY: Yes; I had known him a great many years.

SENATOR SMITH: On what ships of your line had he been captain?

MR. ISMAY: I think he had been commander of a great many of them. The first time I remember Capt. Smith being commander of one of our ships was when he was in command of one of our cargo boats called the *Cufic,* a great many years ago. He was in command of the *Olympic,* he was in the *Adriatic,* the *Baltic,* and the old

Brittanic. I can not remember them all, sir. We have a record in the office of every ship he has commanded.

SENATOR SMITH: In this journey from Southampton to the place of the accident did he seem to be in good health?

MR. ISMAY: As far as I saw, sir; as far as I was able to judge, at least.

SENATOR SMITH: Do you know his age?

MR. ISMAY: I would not like to be absolutely certain about it, but I think he was about 62. . . .

SENATOR SMITH: In ordering that vessel, did you give Harland & Wolff any special instructions with reference to her safety?

MR. ISMAY: We were very anxious indeed to have a ship which would float with her two largest water-tight compartments full of water. What we wanted to guard against was any steamer running into the ship and hitting her on a bulkhead, because if the ship ran into her broadside on and happened to hit her right on a bulkhead, that would open up two big compartments, and we were anxious to guard against the possibility of that happening; and the *Olympic* and *Titanic* were so constructed that they would float with the two largest compartments full of water.

SENATOR SMITH: You remember, I think, the statement of the wheelman, Hitchens, that the last thing he did before striking the iceberg was to so turn his wheel as to avoid contact directly with the bow, the extreme bow?

MR. ISMAY: Yes, sir.

SENATOR SMITH: Do you recall that?

MR. ISMAY: I think he said he was told "Hard aport," and then "Hard astarboard," if I remember rightly.

SENATOR SMITH: And then that threw the vessel——

MR. ISMAY (interposing). He wanted to throw his quarter up.

SENATOR SMITH: Suppose that had not been done, Mr. Ismay, and the ship had met this iceberg bows on; what would have been the effect, in your judgment?

MR. ISMAY: It is really impossible to say. It is only a matter of opinion. I think the ship would have crushed her bows in, and might not have sunk.

SENATOR SMITH: She might not have sunk?

MR. ISMAY: She might not have sunk. I think it would have

taken a very brave man to have kept his ship going straight on an iceberg. I think he should have endeavored to avoid it.

SENATOR SMITH: What I am getting at is this, whether in the construction of this ship, which was intended for the North Atlantic and in which naturally the designers and builders had planned for such exigencies as might occur off the Grand Banks of Newfoundland, she was built with special reference to her resistance at the bow?

MR. ISMAY: No, sir.

SENATOR SMITH: For that purpose?

MR. ISMAY: No, sir. I think the only ships in which they do that are ships trading to the St. Lawrence. I understand that on the forward end those ships are very often fitted with double plates because they have to go through field ice. . . .

SENATOR SMITH: There has been considerable confusion about the cost of the *Titanic*. I will take the liberty of asking you to state it.

MR. ISMAY: She cost $7,500,000, sir.

SENATOR SMITH: And for how much was she insured?

MR. ISMAY: For $5,000,000, I understand, sir.

SENATOR SMITH: Did you have anything to do with the insurance?

MR. ISMAY: No; very little. That is done in New York; that is dealt with and handled in New York.

SENATOR SMITH: I will ask you whether you know of any attempt being made to reinsure any part of the vessel on Monday, the 14th of April?

MR. ISMAY: Absolutely none, sir; and I can not imagine anybody connected with the International Mercantile Marine Co. endeavoring to do such a dishonorable thing.

SENATOR SMITH: I do not want you to understand me to assert that it was attempted.

MR. ISMAY: I know, sir; but it is such a horrible accusation to have been made.

SENATOR SMITH: You would regard it as a very dishonorable thing to do?

MR. ISMAY: It would have been taking advantage of private knowledge which was in my possession; yes, sir. Yes, sir; I should so regard it.

SENATOR SMITH: Was the knowledge of the sinking of the *Titanic* that was in your possession communicated by you to your company in Liverpool or to your offices in New York on the journey from the place of the collision to New York?

MR. ISMAY: Yes, sir. I sent the message on Monday morning, very shortly after I got on board the *Carpathia*. The captain came down to me and said, "Don't you think, sir, you had better send a message to New York, telling them about this accident?" I said, "Yes." I wrote it out on a slip of paper, and I turned to the commander of the *Carpathia* and I said, "Captain, do you think that is all I can tell them?" He said, "Yes." Then he took it away from the room. . . .

SENATOR SMITH: Some little confusion has arisen over your statement in your testimony as to the number of revolutions made by the *Titanic*. I understood you to say that at certain times she made 70 revolutions, at another time 75, and, finally, 80. Am I incorrect?

MR. ISMAY: Yes, sir; I do not think I said that. If I did, I had no intention of doing so.

SENATOR SMITH: How would you wish to be understood on that matter?

MR. ISMAY: My recollection is that between Southampton and Cherbourg we ran at 60 revolutions, from Cherbourg to Queenstown at 70 revolutions, and when we left Queenstown we were running at 72 revolutions, and I believe that the ship was worked up to 75 revolutions, but I really have no accurate knowledge of that.

SENATOR SMITH: How many knots per hour would that indicate at her maximum speed?

MR. ISMAY: I could not tell you that, sir.

SENATOR SMITH: How many knots per hour?

MR. ISMAY: The whole thing has been absolutely worked out.

SENATOR SMITH: But you yourself are unable to answer?

MR. ISMAY: Yes; that has all been worked out, the speed of the ship has been worked out at a certain number of revolutions. Her speed would depend absolutely on the slip, as I understand.

SENATOR SMITH: Was she running at her maximum speed at the time she was making 75 revolutions?

MR. ISMAY: No, sir. My understanding is, or I am told—because I really have no technical knowledge—that the engines were balanced, and would run their best, at 78 revolutions. They were built for 78 revolutions.

SENATOR SMITH: How many knots per hour would that indicate her speed to be?

MR. ISMAY: I heard one gentleman here on the stand say that he expected the ship to go 25 knots, sir. All that we expected the *Titanic* to do was to have the same speed as the *Olympic*.

SENATOR SMITH: You were not looking for any greater speed, and were not crowding her for that purpose?

MR. ISMAY: We did not expect the ship to make any better speed than the *Olympic;* no, sir. . . .

SENATOR SMITH: Did you have any talk with the captain with reference to the speed of the ship?

MR. ISMAY: Never, sir.

SENATOR SMITH: Did you, at any time, urge him to greater speed?

MR. ISMAY: No, sir.

SENATOR SMITH: Do you know of any one who urged him to greater speed than he was making when the ship was making 70 revolutions?

MR. ISMAY: It is really impossible to imagine such a thing on board ship.

SENATOR SMITH: Did you, in your position of general manager of this company, undertake in any way to influence or direct the management of that ship, from the time she left Southampton until the time of the accident?

MR. ISMAY: No, sir; I did not. The matter would be entirely out of my province. . . .

SENATOR SMITH: How does it happen that the *Titanic* had but 20 lifeboats, including lifeboats, emergency boats, and collapsibles?

MR. ISMAY: That was a matter for the builders, sir, and I presume that they were fulfilling all the requirements of the board of trade.

SENATOR SMITH: Do you know whether they were?

MR. ISMAY: I do not know of my own knowledge, but I am convinced that they must have done so, because otherwise the ship never could have left port. We never could have gotten our clearance.

SENATOR SMITH: How is the apportionment of lifeboats made, do you know?

MR. ISMAY: No, sir.

SENATOR SMITH: Is it made on tonnage?

MR. ISMAY: It is based on tonnage.

SENATOR SMITH: On tonnage entirely?

MR. ISMAY: On tonnage entirely, I believe.

SENATOR SMITH: That would not include passenger capacity?

MR. ISMAY: No, sir; it is on the tonnage of the ship. I think the boatage is determined by the register of the ship—the tonnage register of the ship.

SENATOR SMITH: Let me ask you, Mr. Ismay, whether in view of this experience you have just gone through you would not consider it desirable to have the apportionment of lifeboats based upon passenger capacity rather than tonnage?

MR. ISMAY: I think the result of this horrible accident is that the whole question of life-saving appliances on board vessels and ships will be very carefully gone through and receive the most full and careful consideration to see what is the best thing to be done. . . .

SENATOR SMITH: Are you familiar with a paper read at the spring meeting of the fifty-third session of the Institution of Naval Architects, March 19, 1912, entitled, "The Arrangement of Boat Installations on Modern Ships," by Axel Welin?

MR. ISMAY: No, sir. I know Mr. Welin.

SENATOR SMITH: You do know Mr. Welin?

MR. ISMAY: He is the davit man, the man who has these patent davits, is he not?

SENATOR SMITH: I think he is the same man.

MR. ISMAY: I think they are called the Welin davits.

SENATOR SMITH: Yes. Do you know him?

MR. ISMAY: I met him once, I think.

SENATOR SMITH: I desire to read into the record a very short quotation from that article:

On the boat deck of the White Star Liner *Olympic* and also of the *Titanic* this double-acting type of davit has been fitted throughout in view of coming changes in official regulations. It was considered wise by the owners that these changes should be thus anticipated and so make it possible to double, or even treble, the number of boats without any structural alterations should such increase ultimately prove to be necessary.

Will you kindly explain, if you can, what the White Star Line had in contemplation in so arranging the davits?

MR. ISMAY: Nothing that I know of, sir.

SENATOR SMITH: Had the *Titanic* carried double the number of lifeboats or treble the number of lifeboats, do you consider that there might have been an increase in the number of passengers and crew saved?

MR. ISMAY: I think that is quite probable, sir.

SENATOR SMITH: I do not want to commit you to any special course in your company, and presume I will not do so, by this inquiry; but in view of all that has occurred, are you willing to say that the proportion of lifeboats should be increased to more approximately meet such exigencies as you have just passed through?

MR. ISMAY: I think, having regard to our experience, there is no question that that should be done; but I think it may be quite possible to improve on the construction of the ship.

SENATOR SMITH: Also?

MR. ISMAY: Yes, sir.

SENATOR SMITH: Have you given any instructions to increase the lifeboat capacity of other White Star ships?

MR. ISMAY: We have given instructions that no ship belonging to the I. M. M. Co. is to leave any port unless she has sufficient boats on board for the accommodation of all the passengers and the whole of the crew.

SENATOR SMITH: Who gave those instructions?

MR. ISMAY: I did, sir.

SENATOR SMITH: When?

MR. ISMAY: The day after I landed from the *Carpathia*. . . .

SENATOR SMITH: I think in my prior examination in New York you said you entered the lifeboat from the A deck?

MR. ISMAY: From the boat deck, sir.

SENATOR SMITH: And that at the time there were no other persons around; no women, particularly?

MR. ISMAY: Absolutely none that I saw, sir.

SENATOR SMITH: Was that the last lifeboat or the last collapsible boat to leave?

MR. ISMAY: It was the last collapsible boat that left the starboard side of the ship.

SENATOR SMITH: Was it filled to its capacity?

MR. ISMAY: No; it was not.

SENATOR SMITH: Why?

MR. ISMAY: I understand the full capacity of one of those boats is about 60 to 65.

SENATOR SMITH: Of the collapsible?

MR. ISMAY: I do not know whether the capacity of the collapsible is the same as that of the wooden boat.

SENATOR SMITH: It was not filled to its capacity?

MR. ISMAY: No, sir.

SENATOR SMITH: Do you know how many people were in it?

MR. ISMAY: I should think there were about 40 women in it, and some children. There was a child in arms. I think they were all third-class passengers, so far as I could see.

SENATOR SMITH: And this boat was from the starboard side of the boat deck, or top deck, near the bridge?

MR. ISMAY: Yes, sir.

SENATOR SMITH: At the time you entered it, did you say anything to the captain about entering it?

MR. ISMAY: No, sir: I did not. I never saw the captain.

SENATOR SMITH: Did he say anything to you about your entering it?

MR. ISMAY: No, sir.

SENATOR SMITH: Who, if anyone, told you to enter that lifeboat?

MR. ISMAY: No one, sir.

SENATOR SMITH: Why did you enter it?

MR. ISMAY: Because there was room in the boat. She was being lowered away. I felt the ship was going down, and I got into the boat. . . .

SENATOR SMITH: Not desiring to be impertinent at all, but in order that I may not be charged with omitting to do my duty, I would like to know where you went after you boarded the *Carpathia,* and how you happened to go there?

MR. ISMAY: Mr. Chairman, I understand that my behavior on board the *Titanic,* and subsequently on board the

Carpathia, has been very severely criticized. I want to court the fullest inquiry, and I place myself unreservedly in the hands of yourself and any of your colleagues, to ask me any questions in regard to my conduct: so please do not hesitate to do so, and I will answer them to the best of my ability. So far as the *Carpathia* is concerned, sir, when I got on board the ship I stood up with my back against the bulkhead, and somebody came up to me and said, "Will you not go into the saloon and get some soup, or something to drink?" "No," I said, "I really do not want anything at all." He said, "Do go and get something." I said, "No. If you will leave me alone I will be very much happier here." I said, "If you will get me in some room where I can be quiet, I wish you would." He said, "Please go in the saloon and get something hot." I said, "I would rather not." Then he took me and put me into a room. I did not know whose the room was, at all. This man proved to be the doctor of the *Carpathia*. I was in that room until I left the ship. I was never outside the door of that room. During the whole of the time I was in this room, I never had anything of a solid nature, at all; I lived on soup. I did not want very much of anything. The room was constantly being entered by people asking for the doctor. The doctor did not sleep in the room the first night. The doctor slept in the room the other nights that I was on board that ship. Mr. Jack Thayer was brought into the room the morning we got on board the *Carpathia*. He stayed in the room for some little time, and the doctor came in after he had been in, I should think, about a quarter of an hour, and he said to this young boy, "Would you not like something to eat?" He said, "I would like some bacon and eggs;" which he had. The doctor did not have a suite of rooms on the ship. He simply had this one small room, which he himself occupied and dressed in every night and morning. . . .

SENATOR SMITH: In view of your statement, I desire to say that I have seen none of these comments to which you refer. In fact, I have not read the newspapers since I started for New York; I have deliberately avoided it; so that I have seen none of these reports, and you do not understand that I have made any criticism upon your conduct aboard the *Carpathia?*

MR. ISMAY: No, sir. On the contrary, I do not say that anybody has. But I am here to answer any questions in regard thereto.

SENATOR SMITH: What can you say, Mr. Ismay, as to your treatment at the hands of the committee since you have been under our direction?

MR. ISMAY: I have no fault to find. Naturally, I was disappointed in not being allowed to go home; but I feel quite satisfied you have some very good reason in your own mind for keeping me here.

SENATOR SMITH: You quite agree now that it was the wisest thing to do?

MR. ISMAY: I think, under the circumstances, it was.

SENATOR SMITH: And even in my refusal to permit you to go you saw no discourtesy?

MR. ISMAY: Certainly not, sir.

SENATOR SMITH: Do you know of any unfair or discourteous or inconsiderate treatment upon the part of the committee of any of your officers connected with this investigation?

MR. ISMAY: No; I do not. . . .

SENATOR FLETCHER: Mr. Ismay, I believe some passengers state that Capt. Smith gave you a telegram reporting ice.

MR. ISMAY: Yes, sir.

SENATOR FLETCHER: On Sunday afternoon?

MR. ISMAY: Sunday afternoon, I think it was.

SENATOR FLETCHER: Is that true?

MR. ISMAY: Yes, sir.

SENATOR FLETCHER: What became of that telegram?

MR. ISMAY: I handed it back to Capt. Smith. I should think about 10 minutes past 7 on Sunday evening. I was sitting in the smoking room when Capt. Smith happened to come in the room for some reason what it was I do not know and on his way back he happened to see me sitting there and came up and said, "By the way, sir, have you got that telegram which I gave you this afternoon?" I said, "Yes." I put my hand in my pocket and said, "Here it is." He said, "I want it to put up in the officers' chart room." That is the only conversation I had with Capt. Smith in regard to the telegram. When he handed it to me, he made no remark at all.

394

SENATOR FLETCHER: Can you tell what time he handed it to you and what its contents were?

MR. ISMAY: It is very difficult to place the time. I do not know whether it was in the afternoon or immediately before lunch; I am not certain. I did not pay any particular attention to the Marconi message—it was sent from the *Baltic*—which gave the position of some ice. It also gave the position of some steamer which was short of coal and wanted to be towed into New York, and I think it ended up by wishing success to the *Titanic*. It was from the captain of the *Baltic*. . . .

SENATOR SMITH: Would you not regard it as an exercise of proper precaution and care to lessen the speed of a ship crossing the Atlantic when she had been warned of the presence of ice ahead?

MR. ISMAY: I am afraid that question I can not give any opinion on. We employ the very best men we possibly can to take command of these ships, and it is a matter entirely in their discretion. . . .

SENATOR BURTON: Did you have any conversation with a passenger on the *Titanic* about slackening or increasing speed when you heard of the ice?

MR. ISMAY: No, sir; not that I have any recollection of. I presume you refer to what Mrs. Ryerson said. I testified in New York, the day after we arrived, that it was our intention on Monday or Tuesday, assuming the weather conditions to suit, and everything was working satisfactorily down below, to probably run the ship for about four or six hours full speed to see what she could do.

SENATOR PERKINS: You did not have any conversation on that Sunday about increasing the speed, did you?

MR. ISMAY: Not in regard to increasing the speed going through the ice, sir.

SENATOR BURTON: That is all.

SENATOR SMITH: Did you have any talk with Capt. Rostron from the time you went on board the *Carpathia* with reference to communication of information with New York, or with Liverpool, or with other ships, regarding the loss of the *Titanic*?

MR. ISMAY: No, sir. The only conversation I had with the captain of the *Carpathia* was that he came to me and told me he had a Marconi message from Capt. Haddock to say that he was coming to him. At that time the *Carpathia* was bound for New York. The captain of the *Carpathia* came to the conclusion there was no use in the *Olympic* coming to the *Carpathia,* because he could render absolutely no assistance, and he said he thought it was very undesirable that the unfortunate passengers from the *Titanic* should see her sister ship so soon afterwards. That is the only conversation I had with the captain, except that he asked me to send a message to our office in New York to have the tug boats and some White Star sailors at quarantine to relieve him of those boats about his deck.

SENATOR BURTON: But you yourself did not attempt to put any embargo upon news of any kind while you were on board the *Carpathia?*

MR. ISMAY: Absolutely none, sir; and I asked for no preferential treatment for any messages that I sent. I do not know that any was given. . . .

Witness: C. E. Henry Stengel
Leather manufacturer and first-class passenger,
from Newark, N.J.

Key testimony: He told of shots being fired to deter men from jumping into lifeboats. A mechanical buff, he wagered in a pool to guess the ship's speed, which he concluded was quite fast. He reported hearsay from Mrs. G. Thorne, a dining companion of E. J. Smith, who said the captain "did not drink a drop."

. . . SENATOR SMITH: Were you a passenger on board the *Titanic* on the ill-fated voyage from Southampton to the place of the accident?

MR. STENGEL: Yes, sir.

SENATOR SMITH: While you were on that voyage did you familiarize yourself with the speed of the *Titanic?*

MR. STENGEL: I did, the last day; particularly the last day. I did.

SENATOR SMITH: Particularly the day of the accident?

MR. STENGEL: The day of the accident; that is, from Saturday noon to Sunday noon.

SENATOR SMITH: Will you kindly tell the committee how you familiarized yourself with the speed, and what the speed was when you last informed yourself about it?

MR. STENGEL: As is usual in these voyages, there were pools made to bet on the speed that the boat would make, and at 12 o'clock, after the whistle blew, the people who had bet went to the smoking room, and came out and reported she had made 546 knots. I figured then that at 24 hours to a day we made 22¾ knots; but I was told I was mistaken; that I should have figured 25 hours.

SENATOR SMITH: Twenty-five hours for the day?

MR. STENGEL: Yes, on account of the elapsed time, I believe, which made it almost 22 knots an hour. At the same time a report came—this was the report that came from the engine room—that the engines were turning three revolutions faster than at any time on the voyage.

SENATOR SMITH: What time was that on Sunday?

MR. STENGEL: I should say about between 1 and 2 o'clock Sunday afternoon.

SENATOR SMITH: Did you have occasion to consult with anyone as to, or did you familiarize yourself with, the speed of the ship after that time?

MR. STENGEL: Not after that time, any more than that I called my wife's attention to the fact that the engines were running very fast. That was when I retired, about 10 o'clock. I could hear the engines running when I retired, and I noticed that the engines were running fast. I said I noticed that they were running faster than at any other time during the trip.

SENATOR SMITH: How could you tell that?

MR. STENGEL: Just through being familiar with engines in the manufacturing business. We have bought a great many engines in 28 or 29 years, and we generally take the speed of the engine. We want to buy an engine that will run a certain speed to do a certain amount of work. It was just natural instinct, that was all.

SENATOR SMITH: Where were you when the accident happened?

MR. STENGEL: I had retired. My wife called me. I was

moaning in my sleep. My wife called me, and says, "Wake up, you are dreaming"; and I was dreaming, and as I woke up I heard a slight crash. I paid no attention to it until I heard the engines stop. When the engines stopped I said, "There is something serious; there is something wrong. We had better go up on deck." I just put on what clothes I could grab, and my wife put on her kimono, and we went up to the top deck and walked around there. There were not many people around there. That was where the lifeboats were. We came down to the next deck, and the captain came up. I supposed he had come up from investigating the damage. He had a very serious and a very grave face. I then said to my wife, "This is a very serious matter, I believe." . . .

Shortly after that the orders were given to have the passengers all put on life preservers. I went back to my stateroom and put a life preserver on my wife, and then she tied mine on. We went back up to the top deck. Then I heard the orders given to put all the women and children in the boats and have them go off about 200 yards from the vessel.

SENATOR SMITH: Who gave that order?

MR. STENGEL: It seemed to me an officer. Of course I was a little bit agitated, and I heard them and I did not look particularly to see who it was. While they were loading the lifeboats, the officers or men who had charge of loading the lifeboats said, "There is no danger; this is simply a matter of precaution." After my wife was put in a lifeboat she wanted me to come with them, and they said, "No; nothing but ladies and children." After the five boats, I think it was, or the boats as far as I could see on the starboard side, were loaded. I turned toward the bow. I do not know what led me there, but there was a small boat that they called an emergency boat, in which there were three people, Sir Duff Gordon and his wife and Miss Francatelli. I asked the officer—I could not see them, it was so dark, and I presume I was agitated somewhat—I asked him if I could not get into that boat. There was no one else around, not a person I could see except the people working at the boats, and he said, "Jump in." The railing was rather high—it was an emergency boat and was always swung over toward the water—I jumped onto the railing and rolled into it. The officer then said, "That is the funniest sight I have seen to-night," and he laughed quite heartily. That rather gave me some encouragement. I thought perhaps it was not so dangerous as I imagined. After getting down part of the way there was a painter on the boat, and we were beginning to tip, and somebody hollered to stop lowering. Somebody cut that line and we went on down.

SENATOR SMITH: Describe this rail if you can. Was it a guard?

MR. STENGEL: I do not know what they call it; a fence, like, on the side. The other lifeboats were all loaded from the floor. You could step right from the floor into the lifeboats.

SENATOR SMITH: That was on the upper deck?

MR. STENGEL: That was on the boat deck; yes, sir; toward the bow.

SENATOR SMITH: And this rail was at the outside of the boat deck?

MR. STENGEL: It was just at the edge of the deck, just to keep people from falling over.

SENATOR SMITH: How high was it?

MR. STENGEL: I should judge it was about three feet and a half, or so.

SENATOR SMITH: Was there any opening in it?

MR. STENGEL: No, sir.

SENATOR SMITH: Persons entering that boat were obliged to go over that rail?

MR. STENGEL: Yes, sir.

SENATOR SMITH: Did your wife go over that rail?

MR. STENGEL: No, sir; my wife was loaded three or four boats previous to that. We were up there quite early; that is, we were up there almost the first on the deck.

SENATOR SMITH: When you got down to the water, what happened?

MR. STENGEL: Just as I jumped into the boat some one else, a man named A. L. Solomon, appeared. I do not know where he appeared from, but he asked to get in and jumped in the boat with us. There were five passengers and, I understand, three stokers and two seamen; that is, five of the crew.

SENATOR SMITH: How many women?

MR. STENGEL: There were two ladies. Sir Duff Gordon's wife

and Miss Francatelli—in that boat. There was no one else in sight at that time. . . .

SENATOR SMITH: Your five passengers included the two women?

MR. STENGEL: Yes, sir; the five passengers included the two women.

SENATOR SMITH: Did any others of the passengers or crew board that boat?

MR. STENGEL: Besides the 10 that I say were on it?

SENATOR SMITH: Yes.

MR. STENGEL: No, sir.

SENATOR SMITH: Who was in charge of that boat?

MR. STENGEL: I do not know. As I said, there were two seamen, one at the bow and one at the rudder at the stern, and the other three were rowing, with myself, as I was rowing with one of the stokers.

SENATOR SMITH: Do you know who gave directions?

MR. STENGEL: I think between Sir Duff Gordon and myself we decided which way to go. We followed a light that was to the bow of the boat, which looked like in the winter, in the dead of winter, when the windows are frosted with a light coming through them. It was in a haze. Most of the boats rowed toward that light, and after the green lights began to burn I suggested it was better to turn around and go toward the green lights, because I presumed there was an officer of the ship in that boat, and he evidently knew his business.

SENATOR SMITH: That was evidently from another lifeboat?

MR. STENGEL: Yes, sir; it was from another lifeboat.

SENATOR SMITH: Did you go toward it?

MR. STENGEL: Yes, sir; we did.

SENATOR SMITH: Did you reach its side?

MR. STENGEL: We did not reach its side. It was toward morning that we turned, and by that time another man and myself thought we saw rockets—one rocket; that is, a rocket explode and I said, "I think I saw a rocket," and another one said, "I think I saw a rocket," and one of the stokers, I think it was, said, "I see two lights. I believe that is a vessel." Then, after that, when another green light was burned, there was a flashlight from a boat, and I said, "Now, I am pretty positive that is a boat, because that is an answer to the green signal," and one of the stokers said, "The green light is the company's color," I understood him to say. That is what he said. Whether he was right or not, I do not know. When we saw that flashlight, it was like powder was set off. I said, "Now let us give it to her and let us steer in between the green light where we saw the green light and that boat," and that being a very light boat we left the other boats quite a way behind. I felt somewhat enthused to see the boat, and I began to jolly them along to pull. I said, "Keep pulling." We kept pulling, and I thought we were the first boat aboard, but I found that the boat that had the green lights burning was ahead of us. We were the second boat aboard.

SENATOR SMITH: What was the number of this emergency boat?

MR. STENGEL: I do not know sir, I did not look at that.

SENATOR SMITH: How far out from the side of the upper deck did that boat hang when you got into it?

MR. STENGEL: It was right up against the side. If it had not been I would have gone down into the water, because I rolled. I did not step into it; I just simply rolled.

SENATOR SMITH: There was no difficulty in entering it when you got over this rail?

MR. STENGEL: No. There was a partition of canvas or something or other like that to keep it from scraping the sides.

SENATOR SMITH: Did you see icebergs the next morning?

MR. STENGEL: I guess you could. They were all around. You could see them. As soon as we landed down into the water, as soon as we were afloat, you could see icebergs all around, because we thought they were sailing vessels at first, and began pulling this way, and then turning around and going the other way. They were in sight all along the horizon.

SENATOR SMITH: Were you menaced in any way, after you got into the water in this emergency boat, by ice?

MR. STENGEL: No, sir.

SENATOR SMITH: How far away was it from you, apparently?

MR. STENGEL: It was quite a ways, but you could see the outline in the dusk.

SENATOR SMITH: Describe these icebergs. How large were they?

MR. STENGEL: There was one of them, particularly, that I noticed, a very large one, which looked something like the Rock of Gibraltar; it was high at one point, and another point came up at the other end, about the same shape as the Rock of Gibraltar.

SENATOR SMITH: How did it compare with the size of the *Titanic?*

MR. STENGEL: I was a good ways off. It was not quite as large as the *Titanic,* but it was an enormous, large iceberg.

SENATOR SMITH: Can you approximate its height from the water?

MR. STENGEL: Of course I might. At such a distance I should judge it was 250 feet high at the highest point.

SENATOR SMITH: Where was the field ice—back of these icebergs or to the east of them?

MR. STENGEL: The field ice I did not see much of until we got aboard the *Carpathia.* Then there was a floe there that I should think was about 5 miles long, and I should say it would take 20 minutes by the *Carpathia* to get by that field ice. It was ice all covered with snow.

SENATOR SMITH: How high above the water?

MR. STENGEL: Not very high above the water.

SENATOR SMITH: Five or ten feet, or something like that?

MR. STENGEL: I should judge not over 2 feet; 2 or 3 feet.

SENATOR SMITH: Do you think of anything more you care to say in addition to what you have already said that might throw any light on the subject of this inquiry?

MR. STENGEL: No. There is only one thing that I would like to say, and that is that evidently, when they struck the iceberg, the ice came on the deck, and there was one of the passengers had a handful of ice when we were up there, and showed it. Another passenger said that the ice came into his porthole. His porthole was open.

SENATOR SMITH: How long after the impact was it before the engines were stopped?

MR. STENGEL: A very few minutes.

SENATOR SMITH: Give the number of minutes, if you can. You are accustomed to machinery and matters of this kind.

MR. STENGEL: I should say two or three minutes, and then they started again just slightly; just started to move again. I do not know why; whether they were backing off, or not.

I do not know. I hardly thought they were backing off, because there was not much vibration to the ship.

SENATOR SMITH: Did you hear or see anyone arousing passengers from their rooms after the impact?

MR. STENGEL: I heard the order given to the stewards to arouse the passengers, and afterwards I heard somebody remark, "Did you ever see such actions," or some remark like that—"Did you ever see such actions as the stewards are showing." It seems they were not arousing the people.

SENATOR BURTON: They were not, do you say?

MR. STENGEL: Yes, sir. There was a remark made like that, "Did you ever see such actions of the stewards," or some remark like that, indicating they were not doing their duty.

SENATOR SMITH: What is your judgment about it?

MR. STENGEL: My judgment about the officers is that when they were loading I think they were cool. I think so far as the loading of the boats after the accident was concerned, sir, they showed very good judgment. I think they were very cool. They calmed the passengers by making them believe it was not a serious accident. In fact, most of them, after they got on board the *Carpathia,* said they expected to go back the next day and get aboard the *Titanic* again. I heard that explained afterwards by an officer of the ship, when he said, "Suppose we had reported the damage that was done to that vessel; there would not be one of you aboard. The stewards would have come up"—not the stewards, but the stokers— "would have come up and taken every boat, and no one would have had a chance of getting aboard of those boats."

SENATOR SMITH: Did you see any man attempt to enter these lifeboats who was forbidden to do so?

MR. STENGEL: I saw two, a certain physician in New York and his brother, jump into the same boat my wife was in. Then the officer, or the man that was loading the boat, said "I will stop that. I will go down and get my gun." He left the deck momentarily and came right back again. Afterwards I heard about five shots; that is, while we were afloat. Four of them I can account for in this way, that when the green lights were lit on the boat they were lashed to—my wife's boat—the man shot off a revolver four times, thinking it was a vessel. The man in charge said, "You had better save all your revolver shots, you had better save all your matches, and save everything. It may be the means of saving your life." After that I heard another shot that seemed to be aboard the *Titanic*. It was explained to me afterwards that that was the time that one of the men shot off his revolver—that is, the mate or whoever had charge of the boat shot off his revolver—to show the men that his revolver was loaded and he would do what he said; that any man who would step into the lifeboat he would shoot.

SENATOR SMITH: But you saw no attempt by a man to enter a lifeboat, except in the manner you have described?

MR. STENGEL: No, sir; I saw no attempt of anyone to get into the lifeboats except these two gentlemen that jumped in the boat after the boat was lowered; that is, started to lower. . . .

SENATOR BOURNE: The emergency boat that you got into had a capacity for how many passengers?

MR. STENGEL: I do not think it had a capacity for any more than were in it. It was just a small boat. In fact, when we arrived at the *Carpathia* it was never taken aboard the *Carpathia*. It was too small and too light a boat, and they just set it adrift. The other large lifeboats were taken aboard the *Carpathia*. . . .

SENATOR FLETCHER: How far were you from the *Titanic* when she went down?

MR. STENGEL: I could not say the distance. I saw all the movements. I saw her first row of port lights go under the water; I saw the next port lights go under the water; and finally the bow was all dark. When the last lights on the bow went under, I said, "There is danger here; we had better row away from here. This is a light boat, and there may be suction when the ship goes down. Let us pull away." The other passengers agreed, and we pulled away from the *Titanic*, and after that we stopped rowing for awhile, and she was going down by the bow most all the time, and all of a sudden there were four sharp explosions about that far apart, just like this [the witness indicating by snapping his fingers four times], and then she dipped and the stern stood up in the air, and then the cries began for help. I should think that the people who were left on the boat began to jump over. There was an awful wail like.

SENATOR FLETCHER: Could you see the people?

MR. STENGEL: No, sir; I could not see any of the people, but I could hear them.

SENATOR FLETCHER: What was the character of these explosions?

MR. STENGEL: I do not know, but I should judge it would be a battery of boilers going.

SENATOR FLETCHER: Might it have been bulkheads giving way?

MR. STENGEL: I do not know. I have never been familiar with bulkheads giving way; but they were quite hard explosions. She dipped, then, forward, and all you could see was the stern sticking up. When I heard the cries I turned my back. I said, "I can not look any longer."

SENATOR FLETCHER: You did not attempt to go back to get any of those people?

MR. STENGEL: We could not. We were quite a ways away, and the suggestion was not made, and we did not; that is all there is about that. I do not know why we did not, but we did not.

SENATOR SMITH: Was there any evidence of intoxication among the officers or crew that night?

MR. STENGEL: No, sir. I have a distinct recollection of a Mrs. Thorne stating, while talking about the captain being to dinner, that she was in that party, and she said, "I was in that party, and the captain did not drink a drop." He smoked two cigars, that was all, and left the dining room about 10 o'clock.

SENATOR SMITH: You have spoken of this betting pool. Was any officer or member of the crew engaged in this pool, that you know of?

MR. STENGEL: No, sir; not that I know of. I just happened to be in the party. I had been watching a game of cards most of the trip, and Mr. Harris, one of the ill-fated passengers, had won the hat pool.

SENATOR SMITH: This was a pastime among the passengers?

MR. STENGEL: Yes.

SENATOR SMITH: And you are quite certain that no officer or director took any part in it?

MR. STENGEL: I did not see any of them, sir; and I did not

even go and look at the names of those who were on the list.

SENATOR SMITH: You did not see Mr. Ismay there?

MR. STENGEL: No, sir; I do not know Mr. Ismay.

SENATOR SMITH: Or the captain?

MR. STENGEL: No, sir.

SENATOR SMITH: There is Mr. Ismay, sitting back at the wall there [indicating].

MR. STENGEL: (after looking at Mr. Ismay). I do not think I saw Mr. Ismay but one evening, I think, while the band was playing after dinner. . . .

Witness: Col. Archibald Gracie
Historian and first-class passenger, from
Washington, D.C.

Key testimony: He gave a vivid account of the scene in first class—and of passengers swarming up to the ship's rear decks from below. He made a jump for it, saving himself by climbing atop the by-now famous overturned collapsible lifeboat. He was one of the numerous survivors who later wrote memoirs of the disaster.

. . . SENATOR SMITH: Colonel, you were one of the passengers on the ill-fated *Titanic*. Will you kindly, as succinctly and as tersely as possible, in your own way, trace the principal events leading up to the sinking of that ship on Sunday night, April 14? . . .

MR. GRACIE: I was awakened in my stateroom at 12 o'clock. The time, 12 o'clock, was noted on my watch, which was on my dresser, which I looked at promptly when I got up. At the same time, almost instantly, I heard the blowing off of steam, and the ship's machinery seemed to stop.

It was so slight I could not be positive of it. All through the voyage the machinery did not manifest itself at all from my position in my stateroom, so perfect was the boat. I looked out of the door of my stateroom, glanced up and down the passageway to see if there was any commotion, and I did not see anybody nor hear anybody moving at all; but I did not like the sound of it, so I thought I would partially dress myself, which I did, and went on deck.

I went on what they call the A deck. Presently some passengers gathered around. We looked over the sides of the ship to see whether there was any indication of what had caused this noise. I soon learned from friends around that an iceberg had struck us.

Presently along came a gentleman, described by Mr. Stengel here, who had ice in his hands. Some of this ice was handed to us with the statement that we had better take this home for souvenirs. Nobody had any fear at that time at all. I looked on deck outside to see if there was any indication of a list. I could not distinguish any. At that time I joined my friend, Mr. Clint Smith, and he and I in the cabin did notice a list, but thought it best not to say anything about it for fear of creating some commotion. Then we agreed to stick by each other through thick and thin if anything occurred, and to meet later on. He went to his cabin and I went to mine. In my cabin I packed my three bags very hurriedly. I thought if we were going to be removed to some other ship it would be easy for the steward to get my luggage out.

As I went up on deck the next time I saw Mr. Ismay with one of the officers. He looked very self contained, as though he was not fearful of anything, and that gave encouragement to my thought that perhaps the disaster was not anything particularly serious.

Presently I noticed that women and men had life preservers on, and under protest, as I thought it was rather previous, my steward put a life preserver around myself and I went up on deck, on the A deck. Here I saw a number of people, among others some ladies whom I had told when I first came on the ship at Southampton that I hoped they would let me do anything I could for them during the voyage. These ladies were Mrs. E. D. Appleton, Mrs. Cornell, and Mrs. Browne, the publisher's wife, of Boston, and Miss Evans. They were somewhat disturbed, of course. I reassured them and pointed out to them the lights of what I thought was a ship or steamer in the distance.

Mr. Astor came up and he leaned over the side of the deck, which was an inclosed deck, and there were windows and the glass could be let down. I pointed toward the bow, and there were distinctly seen these lights—or a light, rather one single light. It did not seem to be a star, and that is what we all thought it was, the light of some steamer.

SENATOR SMITH: How far away?

MR. GRACIE: I could not judge, only by what they told me. I should say it could not have been more than 6 miles away.

SENATOR SMITH: Was it ahead?

MR. GRACIE: Ahead toward the bow, because I had to lean over, and here was this lifeboat down by the side at that time, and I pointed right ahead and showed Mr. Astor so he could see, and he had to lean away over.

Some time elapsed, I should say from three-quarters of an hour to an hour before we were ordered to the boats. Then a young English officer of the ship, a tall thin chap, whose name was Murphy—I think it was Officer Murphy——

SENATOR FLETCHER: Murdoch?

MR. GRACIE: No; not Murdoch. Murphy, I think it was. He was the sixth officer, or something of that sort.

SENATOR SMITH: Moody, was it not?

MR. GRACIE: Moody was his name. He said, "No man beyond this line." Then the women went beyond that line. I saw that these four ladies, with whose safety I considered myself intrusted, went beyond that line to get amidships on this deck, which was A deck. Then I saw Mr. Straus and Mrs. Straus, of whom I had seen a great deal during the voyage. I had heard them discussing that if they were going to die they would die together. We tried to persuade Mrs. Straus to go alone, without her husband, and she said no. Then we wanted to make an exception of the husband, too, because he was an elderly man, and he said no, he would share his fate with the rest of the men, and that he would not go beyond. So I left them there. . . .

Just about the time we were ordered to take the boats, I passed through the A deck, going from the stern toward the bow. . . .

Then I found my friend Smith, and on deck A, on the bow side, we worked together under the second officer in loading and helping the women and babies and children aboard the different boats. I think we loaded about two boats there.

This was on the enclosed deck.

SENATOR SMITH: On which side did you say, Colonel?

MR. GRACIE: This was the port side.

The only incident I remember in particular at this point is when Mrs. Astor was put in the boat. She was lifted up through the window, and her husband helped her on the other side, and when she got in, her husband was on one side of this window and I was on the other side, at the next window. I heard Mr. Astor ask the second officer whether he would not be allowed to go aboard this boat to protect his wife. He said, "No, sir; no man is allowed on this boat or any of the boats until the ladies are off." Mr. Astor then said, "Well, tell me what is the number of this boat so I may find her afterwards," or words to that effect.

The answer came back, "No. 4."

The next scene was on the deck above.

SENATOR SMITH: Was there a special reason why Mr. Astor asked to get into that boat with his wife?

MR. GRACIE: Yes; I think it was on account of the condition of his wife. If that had been explained to the second officer, possibly he might have been allowed to get in that boat.

SENATOR SMITH: But that was the reason he gave?

MR. GRACIE: The second officer did not know that it was Mr. Astor at all. He did not know. I believe he told me that he testified before this committee to the effect that he did not know Mr. Astor, and when I recalled the circumstance to him and the conversation that passed between them he said, "Oh, is that the man?" He said, "Was that Mr. Astor." That was the conversation that took place.

Then we went to the boat deck, which was the deck above. There were no men allowed in the boats that were loaded below, not one, except the crews necessary to man the boats. On the deck above we loaded about two boats, at least two boats. That deck was above deck A, at the bow on the port side. When we were loading the last boat, just a short time before it was fully loaded, a palpable list toward the port side began, and the officer called out, "All passengers to the starboard side," and Smith and myself went to the starboard side, still at the bow of the ship. Prior to our going to the starboard side we had rushed up and down in the vicinity of the bow, calling out, "Any more ladies? Any more ladies?" Then we went to the starboard side. On the starboard side, to my surprise, I found there were ladies still there, and Mrs. Browne and Miss Evans particularly, the ones whom I supposed had been loaded into a boat from A deck, below, about three-quarters of an hour before. There I saw also Mr. George Widener and Mr. John B. Thayer. I speak of them particularly, because I knew them, and of course, Mr. Clint Smith was there with me, too.

As to what happened on the other side during our departure, the information I was given by the second officer was that some of the steerage passengers tried to rush the boat, and he fired off a pistol to make them get out, and they did get out.

SENATOR SMITH: Who fired that pistol?

MR. GRACIE: Lightoller. That is what he told me. He is the second officer.

SENATOR SMITH: Are you sure it was not Murdoch?

MR. GRACIE: I am sure it was not Murdoch.

SENATOR SMITH: Or Lowe?

MR. GRACIE: I am sure it was not. That is what Mr. Lightoller himself told me. I did not hear the pistol. That is what I was told by Lightoller himself. That is all hearsay, Senator.

I want to say that there was nothing but the most heroic conduct on the part of all men and women at that time, where I was at the bow on the port side. There was no man who asked to get in a boat, with the single exception that I have already mentioned. No woman even sobbed or wrung her hands, and everything appeared perfectly orderly. Lightoller was splendid in his conduct with the crew, and the crew did their duty. It seemed to me it was rather a little bit more difficult than it should have been to launch the boats alongside the ship. I do not know the cause of that. I do not know whether it was on account of the newness of it all, the painting, or something of that sort. I know I had to use my muscle as best I could in trying to push those boats so as to get them over the gunwale.

SENATOR SMITH: You refer now to the tackle?

MR. GRACIE: I refer to the port bow, at the side.

SENATOR SMITH: Do you refer now to the tackle or to the davits or to any particular part of the mechanism?

MR. GRACIE: No; I do not. I refer to it in a general way, as to there being difficulty at that point in that way, in trying to lift them and push them over the gunwale.

The crew seemed to resent my working with them, but they were very glad when I worked with them later on. Every opportunity I got to help, I helped.

When I arrived on the other side, as I have said, there were these women, and of a sudden I heard the cry that there was room for more women on the port side; so I grabbed by the arm these two ladies, Miss Evans and Mrs. Browne, and conducted them to the port side. But I did not get but half way—that is, directly at the bow—when the crew made what you might call a dead line, and said, "No men are allowed beyond this line." So I let the ladies go beyond, and then about six ladies followed after the two that I had particular charge of.

From Mrs. Browne I learned what happened thereafter; that she was after Miss Evans, and Miss Evans could have gotten over first, and could possibly have been pulled into the boat and gotten away; but she sacrificed her own life in order that Mrs. Browne might go first. Mrs. Browne was able to board the boat; but this young lady I think must have collapsed and lost her nerve, and could not climb over the gunwale in order to get in. If there had been some man there to help her, she possibly would have been saved.

SENATOR SMITH: Describe this gunwale, as you call it?

MR. GRACIE: This gunwale is the side of the deck which prevents people from falling into the sea.

SENATOR SMITH: A rail?

MR. GRACIE: The rail, yes.

SENATOR SMITH: How high from the deck?

MR. GRACIE: I should think it was about 3 feet or 3½ feet high from the deck.

SENATOR SMITH: And it was of wood?

MR. GRACIE: It was of wood.

SENATOR SMITH: Was there more than one rail on it?

MR. GRACIE: There was this one rail that was about so thick [indicating] on the top.

SENATOR SMITH: What else was there between there and the floor of the deck?

MR. GRACIE: Between there and the floor was part of the ship that was underneath.

SENATOR SMITH: But would it have been possible to crawl under that rail?

MR. GRACIE: Oh, no; no, indeed. There was no open space underneath the rail. It was solid.

Meanwhile the crew were trying to launch a boat, a collapsible canvas boat, as they call it, that was on the hurricane deck, or the bridge deck. This was let down from the bridge deck, and we tried to slide it along those oars that they put in there for that purpose. There was no other boat at that time being lowered from the deck davits.

Finally this boat came down on the deck. I do not know whether it was injured or not by the fall, but we were afraid that it had been injured.

I may say that before this happened one of the men on the deck, when loosening this boat from the hurricane deck, called out, "Is there any passenger who has a knife?" I said I had my penknife, if that would do, and I passed that up. For just what purpose it was used I do not know. It struck me as rather peculiar that they should find the want of some tool for the purposes for which it was intended.

SENATOR SMITH: How long after this did the boat go down?

MR. GRACIE: Soon after that the water came up on the boat deck. We saw it and heard it. I had not noticed in the meantime that we were gradually sinking. I was engaged all the time in working, as I say, at those davits, trying to work on the falls to let this boat down. Mr. Smith and myself thought then that there was no more chance for us there, there were so many people at that particular point, so we decided to go toward the stern, still on the starboard side, and as we were going toward the stern, to our surprise and consternation, up came from the decks below a mass of humanity, men and women—and we had thought that all the women were already loaded into the boats. The water was then right by us, and we tried to jump, Mr. Smith and myself did. We were in a sort of cul-de-sac which was formed by the cabin and the bridge, the structure that is right on the boat deck. We were right in this cul-de-sac. I have a diagram here which may explain the position better. The top of the page is the bow [indicating on diagram], and on the right, or on the starboard side, is where this last boat that I speak of was, where the first officer, Murdoch, was at work trying to launch the boat. I would like to point out to you there my position with Mr. Smith. I will put a star there on the diagram and then you can see it better [marking on diagram]. It was where that star is, where I put that cross. That is the port side and this is the starboard side, and this is the structure that was on the boat deck, and this is the top of the hurricane deck or the bridge deck, where the funnels came down to the top and where I was was right where that cross is [indicating on diagram].

SENATOR SMITH: What occurred there?

MR. GRACIE: Mr. Smith jumped to try to reach the deck. I jumped also. We were unsuccessful. Then the wave came and struck us, the water came and struck us, and then I rose as I would rise in bathing in the surf, and I gave a jump with the water, which took me right on the hurricane deck, and around that was an iron railing, and I grabbed that iron railing and held tight to it and I looked around, and the same wave which saved me engulfed everybody around me. I turned to the right and to the left and looked. Mr. Smith was not there, and I could not see any of this vast mass of humanity. They had all disappeared. Officer Lightoller tells me that at that same time he was on the bridge deck, where I have marked it "L," and that the first officer, Murdoch, was about 15 feet away, where you see that boat near the davits there. That boat, I understand, was thrown overboard.

SENATOR BURTON: What do you say became of that boat?

MR. GRACIE: It was thrown overboard.

SENATOR FLETCHER: It was never launched?

MR. GRACIE: It was never launched; no, sir.

SENATOR SMITH: That is not the boat that was taken from the top of the officers' quarters, the collapsible?

MR. GRACIE: There were two; one on the port side and this one on the starboard side. This knife which was called for may have been wanted for the boat on the other side, on the bridge deck there. I heard that they called for two knives. There is where the officers' quarters were, possibly.

SENATOR SMITH: So far as you know, was this boat to which you have referred put to any use that night?

MR. GRACIE: Yes.

SENATOR SMITH: Describe it.

MR. GRACIE: That is the boat that I came to when I came up from below. I was taken down with the ship, and hanging on to that railing, but I soon let go. I felt myself whirled around, swam under water, fearful that the hot water that came up from the boilers might boil me up—and the second officer told me that he had the same feeling—swam it seemed to me with unusual strength, and succeeded finally in reaching the surface and in getting a good distance away from the ship.

SENATOR SMITH: How far away?

MR. GRACIE: I could not say, because I could not see the ship. When I came up to the surface there was no ship there. The ship would then have been behind me, and all around me was wreckage. I saw what seemed to be bodies all around. Do you want me to go through the harrowing details?

SENATOR SMITH: No; I am not particular about that. I would like to know specifically whether, while this ship was sinking, and you were in close proximity to it, you noticed any special suction?

MR. GRACIE: No; I noticed no suction, and I did not go down so far as that it would affect my nose or my ears. My great concern was to keep my breath, which I was able to do, and being able to do that was what I think saved me.

SENATOR SMITH: Was the water cold?

MR. GRACIE: I did not notice any coldness of the water at that time. I was too much preoccupied in getting away.

SENATOR SMITH: Did it have any bad effect on you?

MR. GRACIE: No, not then, but afterwards, on the raft. I was on the raft, which I will speak of, all night; and I did not notice how cold the water was until I got on the raft. There was a sort of gulp, as if something had occurred, behind me, and I suppose that was where the water was closing up, where the ship had gone down; but the surface of the water was perfectly still; and there were, I say, this wreckage and these bodies, and there were the horrible sounds of drowning people and people gasping for breath.

While collecting the wreckage together I got on a big wooden crate, some sort of wooden crate, or wood of that sort. I saw an upturned boat, and I struck out for that boat, and there I saw what I supposed were members of the crew on this upset boat. I grabbed the arm of one of them and pulled myself up on this boat.

SENATOR SMITH: Did anybody resist you at all?

MR. GRACIE: What is that?

SENATOR SMITH: Was there any resistance offered?

MR. GRACIE: Oh, no; none whatever. I was among the first. I suppose the boat was then about half full.

SENATOR SMITH: How many were on it?

MR. GRACIE: I suppose there must have been between 15 and 20.

SENATOR SMITH: Was Officer Lightoller on it?

MR. GRACIE: Yes; Officer Lightoller was on that same boat.

SENATOR SMITH: At that time?

MR. GRACIE: At that same time. Then I came up to the surface and was told by Lightoller what had occurred. One of the funnels fell from the steamer, and was falling toward him, but when it was going to strike him, young Mr. Thayer, who was also on the same boat, said that it splashed near him, within 15 yards, he said, and it splashed him toward this raft. We climbed on this raft. There was one man who was in front, with an oar, and another man in the stern with what I think was a piece of a board, propelling the boat along. Then we loaded the raft, as we now call it, with as many as it would contain, until she became under water, until we could take no more, because the water was up to our waists.

SENATOR SMITH: Just one moment. That was while you were on the bottom of the overturned boat?

MR. GRACIE: Of the overturned boat; yes, sir.

SENATOR SMITH: Was that a collapsible?

MR. GRACIE: That was a collapsible canvas boat.

SENATOR SMITH: What was the bottom, oval or flat?

MR. GRACIE: The top was irregular, and about 3½ feet wide,

I should say. It was like a canoe—distinct, therefore, from the lifeboats—and it was about, I should say, between 25 and 30 feet long.

SENATOR SMITH: Were you standing on top of this overturned boat?

MR. GRACIE: Not at first. We did not stand on it until just before sun up. Our concern now was to get out of the wreckage and to get away from the swimmers in the water before they tried to get on the boat, and all of us would be lost. You do not want the details of that, nor the horrors of it! That does not concern you.

SENATOR SMITH: No; that does not concern us much. I will change that. That will not be helpful to us in our deliberations.

MR. GRACIE: We were taken through the wreckage and away from the screams of the drowning people, and we were on the lookout then in every direction for lights and ships to come to our rescue, hallooing all the time "Boat ahoy," or "Ship ahoy," our spirits kept up all the time by what we thought were steamship lights and boat lights; but I think most of those lights we saw were the lights of the lifeboats of the *Titanic*, particularly one that was steering ahead of us, with green lights, and throwing up rockets, I think, or making lights every little while—not rockets, but making a light. I do not know what kind of light they had, but it was a green light that was every little while conspicuous from some lifeboat directly ahead of us.

SENATOR SMITH: There were no explosions of any kind from that lifeboat?

MR. GRACIE: Which lifeboat, the lifeboat we saw ahead?

SENATOR SMITH: The one with the green light. Was the green light the only light you saw?

MR. GRACIE: No; the only light that was right straight ahead of us; and then right to the port side we finally did see the lights of a ship, and that was finally the *Carpathia*, and the Marconi man who was on the raft said he thought this was the *Carpathia*, because he had conversed with the operator on the *Carpathia*. That was the nearest ship, he thought, to us at the time. We had to keep the equilibrium of the boat all night long, from half past 2. I say half past 2; I might say from 2:22, because my watch, that I spoke of before, when I looked at it afterwards on the *Carpathia*, had stopped, and the time indicated was 2:22. So that would indicate the time between the collision and the time that I went down with the ship. We stood upon this collapsible boat in the early morn, just before dawn, so that we might be seen the better, and also, it was not quite so cold, although our feet were in the water. Then, as the sun came up, a welcome sight was the four lifeboats of the *Titanic* on our starboard side. Lightoller blew his whistle and ordered them to come over and take us off of our upset boat. "Aye, aye, sir," they replied, and immediately turned toward us, and two boats came right up close and then began the difficult task of a transfer, and some were loaded. We got on the nearest lifeboat, the bow of this, and some went on this one and some went on the one adjoining. The complement of the lifeboat I was on was filled up to 65. . . .

Away off in the distance we saw these icebergs, in the direction from which we had come during the night, and toward the port side. We were transferred successfully from the raft. The second officer stayed until the last, lifting up the body of one of the crew and putting it right down by me, where I chafed his temples and his wrists to see whether there was any life in him. Then rigor mortis set in and I thought the man was dead, and there was no more use trying to resuscitate him. Then it seemed an interminable time before we got to the *Carpathia*, the boat I was in towing another boat behind, and after two hours, possibly, we finally reached the *Carpathia*, and the women were put in these seats and lifted up to the deck. I got hold of one of the ladders that was hanging down the side and I ran up that ladder.

SENATOR SMITH: Do you know any of the women in your lifeboat by name?

MR. GRACIE: No; I do not. There was a splendid Frenchwoman, who was very kind to us, who loaned us one of her blankets to put over our heads—that is, four of us. One poor Englishman, who was the only other passenger besides Mr. Thayer and myself who was saved on this raft—he was bald, and for that reason he needed this protection, which was very grateful to him. It was very grateful to me, too. The people on the *Carpathia* received us with open arms, and provided us with hot comforts, and acted as ministering angels.

SENATOR SMITH: Is that all?

MR. GRACIE: I have here some pictures that were taken by a cousin of mine on the *Carpathia*, who had a very good camera, which will show you the lifeboats, or some of them, as they arrived on the *Carpathia*. I hand these to you, with the distinct understanding that they are to be returned to me immediately, if that is agreeable to you.

SENATOR SMITH: We are greatly obliged to you for your courtesy in responding to the committee's wish. . . .

Witness: Helen W. Bishop
First-class passenger, from Dowagiac, Mich.

Key testimony: "The conduct of the crew . . . was absolutely beyond criticism."

. . . SENATOR SMITH: I wish you would tell the committee what you did after learning of this accident.

MRS. BISHOP: My husband awakened me at about a quarter of 12 and told me that the boat had struck something. We both dressed and went up on deck, looked around, and could find nothing. We noticed the intense cold; in fact, we had noticed that about 11 o'clock that night. It was uncomfortably cold in the lounge. We looked all over the deck; walked up and down a couple of times, and one of the stewards met us and laughed at us. He said, "You go back downstairs. There is nothing to be afraid of. We have only struck a little piece of ice and passed it." So we returned to our stateroom and retired. About 15 minutes later we were awakened by a man who had a stateroom near us. We were on B deck, No. 47. He told us to come upstairs. So we dressed again thoroughly and looked over all our belongings in our room and went upstairs. After being there about 5 or 10 minutes one of the men we were with ran up and spoke to the captain, who was just then coming down the stairs.

SENATOR SMITH: Who was the man?

MRS. BISHOP: Mr. Astor.

SENATOR SMITH: Col. Astor?

MRS. BISHOP: Yes. The captain told him something in an undertone. He came back and told six of us, who were standing with his wife, that we had better put on our life belts. I had gotten down two flights of stairs to tell my husband, who had returned to the stateroom for a moment, before I heard the captain announce that the life belts should be put on. That was about three or four minutes later that the captain announced the life belts should be put on. We came back upstairs and found very few people up.

SENATOR SMITH: When you say upstairs, which deck do you mean?

MRS. BISHOP: We were on B deck, and we came back up to A deck. There was very little confusion; only the older women were a little frightened. They were up, partially dressed. So I sent a number of them back and saw that they were thoroughly dressed before they came up again. Then we went up onto the boat deck on the starboard side. We looked around, and there were so very few people up there that my husband and I went to the port side to see if there was anyone there. There were only two people, a young French bride and groom, on that side of the boat, and they followed us immediately to the starboard side. By that time an old man had come upstairs and found Mr. and Mrs. [George] Harder, of New York. He brought us all together and told us to be sure and stay together; that he would be back in a moment. We never saw him again. About five minutes later the boats were lowered, and we were pushed in. At the time our lifeboat was lowered I had no idea that it was time to get off.

SENATOR SMITH: Tell me which lifeboat you refer to?

MRS. BISHOP: The first lifeboat that was taken off the *Titanic* on the starboard side. I think it was No. 7. Officer Lowe told us that.

SENATOR SMITH: All right. Proceed.

MRS. BISHOP: We had no idea that it was time to get off, but the officer took my arm and told me to be very quiet and get in immediately. They put the families in the first two boats. My husband was pushed in with me, and we were lowered away with 28 people in the boat.

SENATOR SMITH: Was that a large lifeboat?

419

MRS. BISHOP: Yes; it was a wooden lifeboat.

SENATOR SMITH: And there were 28 people in it?

MRS. BISHOP: Yes. We counted off after we reached the water.

SENATOR SMITH: How many women were there?

MRS. BISHOP: There were only about 12 women.

SENATOR SMITH: And the rest were——

MRS. BISHOP: (interposing). Were men.

SENATOR SMITH: Yes; but I want to divide the rest into two classes, the crew and the passengers.

MRS. BISHOP: There were three of the crew. The rest of them were passengers. We had no officer in our boat.

SENATOR SMITH: Three of the crew?

MRS. BISHOP: Three of the crew.

SENATOR SMITH: And 13 passengers?

MRS. BISHOP: Thirteen passengers; yes. Among those there were several unmarried men in our boat, I noticed, and three or four foreigners in our boat. After we had been out in the water about 15 minutes—the *Titanic* had not yet sunk—five boats were gathered together, and five people were put into our boat from another one, making 33 people in our boat.

SENATOR SMITH: Do you know from what boat these persons were transferred to your boat?

MRS. BISHOP: No; I can not say. The man in charge was an officer with a mustache. I have never seen him since.

SENATOR SMITH: Did the boat from which these people were transferred seem to have more people than yours?

MRS. BISHOP: Yes, sir; they had 38, I believe, or 37, or something like that.

SENATOR SMITH: Do you remember the number of the boat?

MRS. BISHOP: No; I do not.

SENATOR SMITH: Go ahead.

MRS. BISHOP: We had been rowing for some time when the other people were transferred into our boat. Then we rowed still farther away, as the women were nervous about the suction. We waited out in the water perhaps three-quarters of an hour after we had rowed this distance when we saw the *Titanic* sink. For some time after that we were separated from all of the boats except one; that tied to us and stayed with us. We found we had no compass, no light, and I do not know about the crackers

420

or water; but we had no compass and no light. We were out there until just before daylight, I think it was, when we saw the lights of the *Carpathia* and rowed as hard as we could and arrived at the *Carpathia* 5 or 10 minutes after 5 o'clock in the morning.

SENATOR SMITH: I suppose your experience was the same as that of the others as to the presence of ice and your proximity to icebergs?

MRS. BISHOP: Yes; we saw a number of icebergs.

SENATOR SMITH: Is there anything else you care to say which will throw any light upon our inquiry as to the causes of this catastrophe or the conduct of the officers and crew of the *Titanic*?

MRS. BISHOP: The conduct of the crew, as far as I could see, was absolutely beyond criticism. It was perfect. The men in our boat were wonderful. One man lost his brother. When the *Titanic* was going down I remember he just put his hand over his face; and immediately after she sank he did the best he could to keep the women feeling cheerful all the rest of the time. We all thought a great deal of that man.

SENATOR SMITH: What was his name?

MRS. BISHOP: I do not know. . . .

ELEVENTH DAY
Thursday, May 2
Waldorf-Astoria Hotel, New York

Senator Smith returned to New York to take testimony separately from two witnesses.

Witness: Mrs. J. Stuart White
First-class passenger, from New York

Key testimony: Mrs. White (hobbled by a foot injury at the time) said the women rowed—"Countess Rothes stood at the tiller"—while boorish men smoked.

... SENATOR SMITH: Do you make the Waldorf-Astoria your permanent home, Mrs. White?

MRS. WHITE: My home really is Briarcliffe Lodge; Briarcliff Manor, N. Y. That is my summer home. When I am in New York, I am always here at the Waldorf-Astoria. ...

SENATOR SMITH: Where did you get aboard the ship?

MRS. WHITE: At Cherbourg.

SENATOR SMITH: Where were your apartments on the *Titanic*? What deck were you on?

MRS. WHITE: We were on deck C.

SENATOR SMITH: Do you remember the number of the room?

MRS. WHITE: I do not believe I could tell you with any degree of certainty, at all. Miss [Marie] Young [first-class passenger from New York] and my maid could tell you.

SENATOR SMITH: Miss Young or your maid would know the number of your room?

MRS. WHITE: Yes. I never went out of my room from the time I went into it. I was never outside of the door until I came off the night of the collision.

SENATOR SMITH: That was due, I believe, to a little accident that you had on entering the ship?

MRS. WHITE: Yes, sir.

422

SENATOR SMITH: You went directly to your apartment and remained there?

MRS. WHITE: Yes; I remained in my room until I came out that night. I never took a step from my bed until that night.

SENATOR SMITH: Were you aroused especially by the impact?

MRS. WHITE: No; not at all. I was just sitting on the bed, just ready to turn the lights out. It did not seem to me that there was any very great impact at all. It was just as though we went over about a thousand marbles. There was nothing terrifying about it at all.

SENATOR SMITH: Were you aroused by any one of the ship's officers or crew?

MRS. WHITE: No.

SENATOR SMITH: Do you know whether there was any alarm turned in for the passengers?

MRS. WHITE: We heard no alarm whatever. We went immediately on deck ourselves.

SENATOR SMITH: You went on deck?

MRS. WHITE: We went right up on deck ourselves.

SENATOR SMITH: On the upper deck?

MRS. WHITE: Yes, sir.

SENATOR SMITH: And Miss Young and your maid were with you?

MRS. WHITE: Yes; and my manservant.

SENATOR SMITH: What were they doing then?

MRS. WHITE: Simply all standing around.

SENATOR SMITH: Was anything being done about the lifeboats?

MRS. WHITE: No; we were all standing around inside, waiting to know what the result was.

SENATOR SMITH: The lifeboats had not then been cleared?

MRS. WHITE: Nothing had been said about the lifeboats in any way, when suddenly Capt. Smith came down the stairway and ordered us all to put on our life preservers, which we did. We stood around for another 20 minutes, then, I should think.

SENATOR SMITH: Still on that deck?

MRS. WHITE: No; on deck B.

SENATOR SMITH: You went down to deck B?

MRS. WHITE: Yes; he said we must go back again, then, to deck A, which we did, to get into the boats.

SENATOR SMITH: Where did you enter the lifeboat?

MRS. WHITE: I entered the lifeboat from the top deck, where the boats were. We had to enter the boat there. There was no other deck to the steamer except the top deck. It was a perfect rat trap. There was no other deck that was open, at all.

SENATOR SMITH: Do you recollect what boat you entered?

MRS. WHITE: Boat 8, the second boat off.

SENATOR SMITH: On which side of the ship?

MRS. WHITE: I could not tell you. It was the side going this way—the left side, as we were going.

SENATOR SMITH: That would be the port side?

MRS. WHITE: Yes. I got in the second boat that was lowered.

SENATOR SMITH: What officer stood there?

MRS. WHITE: I could not tell you that; I have no idea.

SENATOR SMITH: What officer supervised this work?

MRS. WHITE: I have no idea. I could not even tell whether it was an officer or the captain. I know we were told to get into the boat.

SENATOR SMITH: Did you have any difficulty in getting into the boat?

MRS. WHITE: None whatever. They handled me very carefully, because I could hardly step. They lifted me in very carefully and very nicely.

SENATOR SMITH: How far out from the side of the ship did the lifeboat hang? Were you able to step into it?

MRS. WHITE: Oh, yes.

SENATOR SMITH: Or were you passed into it?

MRS. WHITE: No; we stepped into it. It did not hang far out.

SENATOR SMITH: Did you see how far out it was?

MRS. WHITE: No, sir; I have no idea. We got into it very easily. We got into the lifeboat without any inconvenience whatever. As I said, my condition was such that I had to be handled rather carefully, and there was no inconvenience at all.

SENATOR SMITH: Did you see anything after the accident bearing upon the discipline of the officers or crew, or their conduct, which you desire to speak of?

MRS. WHITE: Yes; lots about them.

SENATOR SMITH: Tell me about that.

MRS. WHITE: For instance, before we cut loose from the ship two of the seamen with us—the men, I should say; I do

424

not call them seamen; I think they were dining-room stewards—before we were cut loose from the ship they took out cigarettes and lighted them; on an occasion like that! That is one thing that we saw. All of those men escaped under the pretense of being oarsmen. The man who rowed me took his oar and rowed all over the boat, in every direction. I said to him, "Why don't you put the oar in the oarlock?" He said, "Do you put it in that hole?" I said, "Certainly." He said, "I never had an oar in my hand before." I spoke to the other man and he said, "I have never had an oar in my hand before, but I think I can row." Those were the men that we were put to sea with at night—with all those magnificent fellows left on board, who would have been such a protection to us. Those were the kind of men with whom we were put out to sea that night.

SENATOR SMITH: How many were there in your boat?

MRS. WHITE: There were 22 women and 4 men.

SENATOR SMITH: None of the men seemed to understand the management of a boat?

MRS. WHITE: Yes; there was one there, one who was supposed to be a seaman, up at the end of our boat, who gave the orders.

SENATOR SMITH: Do you know who he was?

MRS. WHITE: No; I do not know. I do not know the names of any of those men. But he seemed to know something about it.

SENATOR SMITH: I wish you would describe, as nearly as you can, just what took place after your lifeboat got away from the *Titanic*.

MRS. WHITE: What took place between the passengers and the seamen?

SENATOR SMITH: Yes.

MRS. WHITE: We simply rowed away. We had the order, on leaving the ship, to do that. The officer who put us in the boat—I do not know who he was—gave strict orders to the seamen, or the men, to make for the light opposite and land the passengers and get back just as soon as possible. That was the light that everybody saw in the distance.

SENATOR SMITH: Did you see it?

MRS. WHITE: Yes; I saw it distinctly.

425

SENATOR SMITH: What was it?

MRS. WHITE: It was a boat of some kind.

SENATOR SMITH: How far away was it?

MRS. WHITE: Oh, it was 10 miles away, but we could see it distinctly. There was no doubt but that it was a boat. But we rowed and rowed and rowed, and then we all suggested that it was simply impossible for us to get to it; that we never could get to it, and the thing to do was to go back and see what we could do for the others. We only had 22 in our boat.

Then we turned and went back, and lingered around there for a long time, trying to locate the other boats, but we could not locate them except by hearing them. The only way they could locate us was by my electric light. The lamp on the boat was absolutely worth nothing. They tinkered with it all along, but they could not get it in shape. I had an electric cane—a cane with an electric light in it—and that was the only light we had. We sat there for a long time, and we saw the ship go down, distinctly.

SENATOR SMITH: What was your impression of it as it went down?

MRS. WHITE: It was something dreadful.

Nobody ever thought the ship was going down. I do not think there was a person that night, I do not think there was a man on the boat who thought the ship was going down. They speak of the bravery of the men. I do not think there was any particular bravery, because none of the men thought it was going down. If they had thought the ship was going down, they would not have frivoled as they did about it. Some of them said, "When you come back you will need a pass," and "You can not get on tomorrow morning without a pass." They never would have said those things if anybody had had any idea that the ship was going to sink.

In my opinion the ship when it went down was broken in two. I think very probably it broke in two.

I heard four distinct explosions, which we supposed were the boilers. Of course, we did not know anything about it.

SENATOR SMITH: How loud were those explosions?

MRS. WHITE: They were tremendous.

We did what we were ordered to do. We went toward

426

the light. That seemed to be the verdict of everybody in the boat. We had strict orders to do that from the officer or whoever started us off—to row as fast as possible for that boat, land the passengers and come right back for the others. We all supposed that boat was coming toward us, on account of all the rockets that we had sent up.

SENATOR SMITH: Did you urge the man in charge of your lifeboat to go back?

MRS. WHITE: One of us did.

SENATOR SMITH: Did you urge him to go back to seek to pick up more people?

MRS. WHITE: Not until we had gone out for half an hour and found it perfectly useless to attempt to reach that boat or that light. Then everybody suggested going back and we did, too, but we could not get there.

SENATOR SMITH: You went back?

MRS. WHITE: Yes. The sailor changed our course and tried to go back. That was after trying to reach that light for three-quarters of an hour. It was evidently impossible to reach it. It seemed to be going in the same direction in which we were going, and we made no headway toward it at all. Then we turned and tried to go back.

SENATOR SMITH: Did anybody try to get in or get out of your boat?

MRS. WHITE: No.

SENATOR SMITH: Did you land alongside the *Carpathia* with the same party with which you started from the boat deck of the *Titanic?*

MRS. WHITE: Exactly.

SENATOR SMITH: You all landed safely?

MRS. WHITE: We all landed safely. We had a great deal of trouble, but we all landed safely.

SENATOR SMITH: How many were there in your party?

MRS. WHITE: Three; Miss Young, myself, and my maid. My valet was lost.

SENATOR SMITH: Did you make any attempt to communicate with your friends, after you got aboard the *Carpathia,* by wireless or otherwise?

MRS. WHITE: That was the first thing we did.

SENATOR SMITH: Did you succeed?

MRS. WHITE: No; we did not succeed. They never received the telegram until last Monday night in this hotel. They took our telegram the first thing when we got on board the *Carpathia,* Monday morning. They took our marconigram. I think the people on land had a much more serious time than we had, so far as real suffering was concerned.

SENATOR SMITH: Will you describe what you saw after daybreak, with regard to ice or icebergs?

MRS. WHITE: We saw one iceberg in front of us. Of course, I could not see it, because I was standing this way [indicating]. I did not even see the *Carpathia* until my attention was called to her. I stood up all night long because I could not get up onto the seats, which were very high, on account of my foot being bound up. I had no strength in my foot, and I stood all night long.

After we got aboard the *Carpathia,* we could see 13 icebergs and 45 miles of floating ice, distinctly, right around us in every direction.

Everybody knew we were in the vicinity of icebergs. Even in our staterooms it was so cold that we could not leave the port hole open. It was terribly cold. I made the remark to Miss Young, on Sunday morning: "We must be very near icebergs to have such cold weather as this." It was unusually cold.

It was a careless, reckless thing. It seems almost useless to speak of it.

No one was frightened on the ship. There was no panic. I insisted on Miss Young getting into something warm, and I got into something warm, and we locked our trunks and bags and went on deck.

There was no excitement whatever. Nobody seemed frightened. Nobody was panic-stricken. There was a lot of pathos when husbands and wives kissed each other good-by, of course.

We were the second boat pushed away from the ship, and we saw nothing that happened after that. We were not near enough. We heard the yells of the steerage passengers as they went down, but we saw none of the harrowing part of it at all.

As I have said before, the men in our boat were anything but seamen, with the exception of one man. The women all rowed, every one of them. Miss Young rowed every minute. The men could not row. They did not know the first thing about it. Miss Swift, from Brooklyn, rowed every minute, from the steamer to the *Carpathia*. Miss Young rowed every minute, also, except when she was throwing up, which she did six or seven times. Countess Rothes [Lucy-Noel Martha, Countess of Rothes] stood at the tiller. Where would we have been if it had not been for our women, with such men as that put in charge of the boat? Our head seaman would give an order and those men who knew nothing about the handling of a boat would say, "If you don't stop talking through that hole in your face there will be one less in the boat." We were in the hands of men of that kind. I settled two or three fights between them, and quieted them down. Imagine getting right out there and taking out a pipe and filling it and standing there smoking, with the women rowing, which was most dangerous; we had woolen rugs all around us.

Another thing which I think is a disgraceful point. The men were asked, when they got into our boat, if they could row. Imagine asking men that who are supposed to be at the head of lifeboats—imagine asking them if they can row.

There is another point that has never been brought out in regard to this accident and that is that that steamer had no open decks except the top deck. How could they fill the lifeboats properly? They could not lower a lifeboat 70 feet with any degree of safety with more than 20 people in it. Where were they going to get any more in them on the way down? There were no other open decks.

Just to think that on a beautiful starlit night—you could see the stars reflected in the water—with all those Marconi warnings, that they would allow such an accident to happen, with such a terrible loss of life and property.

It is simply unbearable, I think.

SENATOR SMITH: There were no male passengers in your boat?
MRS. WHITE: Not one. . . .

Witness: John Bottomley, 63
General manager of the Marconi Wireless
Telegraph Co. of America

Key testimony: To Senator Smith's pointed questions, he defended Marconi's role in handling the dissemination of information in ship disasters. More details were elicited about the Marconi operators' deal to sell their stories to The New York Times.

... SENATOR SMITH: Where were you on Sunday night, the 14th of April, and Monday, Tuesday, Wednesday, and Thursday following?

MR. BOTTOMLEY: In various places in New York.

SENATOR SMITH: Were you at the office of the Marconi Co.?

MR. BOTTOMLEY: Not on Sunday. I was on the other days.

SENATOR SMITH: Did you have anything to do with the sending or receipt of messages concerning the loss of the *Titanic?*

MR. BOTTOMLEY: No, sir.

SENATOR SMITH: Did you attempt to put yourself in communication with the operator of the *Carpathia?*

MR. BOTTOMLEY: I did, to the best of my ability.

SENATOR SMITH: Just tell what you did in that regard.

MR. BOTTOMLEY: I sent a memorandum—what we call a memorandum—to the operator of the *Carpathia* on Monday night through our office—or, rather, instructed our office to send it—asking the operator of the *Carpathia* to send at least 500 words of good news to your office.

SENATOR SMITH: Did you do anything else in connection with this matter?

MR. BOTTOMLEY: On Tuesday I called up the traffic managers of the Western Union and Postal Telegraph Cos. and asked them to hold their lines as clear as possible, so that communication might readily be made, as I expected a large rush of business—private messages and also messages for the press—and they agreed to do so.

I further sent memoranda to the stations at Cape Race, Sable Island, and Halifax, asking them to furnish us any information that they could.

SENATOR SMITH: Did you have anything else to do with the receipt or sending of messages by wireless telegraphy or cable connected with that?

MR. BOTTOMLEY: No, sir. You mean the actual sending?

SENATOR SMITH: Or instructions pertaining thereto?

MR. BOTTOMLEY: I did not send any other message that I remember.

SENATOR SMITH: Have you knowledge regarding any being sent?

MR. BOTTOMLEY: Yes.

SENATOR SMITH: Did you in any manner undertake to influence the course of Cottam, the operator on the *Carpathia,* or of Bride, the surviving operator of the *Titanic,* regarding the sending or receipt of information concerning this catastrophe?

MR. BOTTOMLEY: In no way did I do so until the vessel had passed quarantine, when, having heard from the New York Times that it would be willing to give the operator or operators, whose names I did not know at that time, a sum of money for their story, I said if Mr. Marconi, whom I was to meet shortly at a social function, consented, I would consent thereto. At about a quarter to 8 Mr. Marconi, at my house, said that while he did not altogether care for the business, he saw no objection to the operator giving his story to the New York Times newspaper. But little conversation passed as the matter was at a dinner party, and all the persons were waiting. I immediately, however, rang up the office and told them that Mr. Marconi did not object and that I did not object either. . . .

SENATOR SMITH: Do you consider it proper to encourage wireless operators in the manner referred to?

MR. BOTTOMLEY: I think it more advisable that the operators should give their story to one paper than to have it scattered piece-meal, and written up by various reporters for various newspapers.

SENATOR SMITH: Might not this custom or habit lead to a general understanding among operators, and tend to influence them in their course following calamities of this character?

MR. BOTTOMLEY: No, sir; I do not think so.

SENATOR SMITH: If it were understood that they should have the right to exclusively sell the information in their possession, would it not weaken the confidence of the public in the accuracy and completeness of published information?

MR. BOTTOMLEY: Admitted that operators are proper people to give out information, it might do so; but operators are not capable of giving out any proper information. That has been established by us in the last 10 or 12 years. There is hardly an operator crossing the ocean who can give out any news in a decent way for publication, and, in

431

addition, the operators are not permitted to send from the ships anything of their own volition touching the working or operation of the ship, or any accident or matter in relation to the ship.

SENATOR SMITH: Would not the fact that that is so give additional valuation to their own observation and experience in cases of great horror, like the *Titanic* disaster, which, if made their own exclusive property, would operate to public disadvantage?

MR. BOTTOMLEY: Not in my opinion.

SENATOR SMITH: Do you admit that the wages of wireless operators are very low?

MR. BOTTOMLEY: I think they get a fair wage, considering that they are kept at virtually no expense whatsoever. Several of our operators are married men, living comfortably on their pay.

SENATOR SMITH: If they get just compensation, why should rewards of this character, which may be of doubtful propriety, be held out to them as one of the inducements for their service?

MR. BOTTOMLEY: Absolutely no such rewards are held out, nor has this ever been offered to any operator as an inducement for him to come into the service.

SENATOR SMITH: Did not [Jack] Binns, in the *Republic* disaster [off Nantucket several years earlier] receive considerable remuneration for his personal observations and experience?

MR. BOTTOMLEY: I do not know what Binns received. I think he received a very small amount indeed at that time. I believe he afterwards received an immense amount of money from various sources, such as lectures, theatrical entertainments, magazines, etc.

SENATOR SMITH: Do you know what Bride, the *Titanic* operator, received?

MR. BOTTOMLEY: Mr. [Carr] Van Ander, managing editor of the New York Times, told me he was giving $1,000, to be equally divided between the two boys; that a London paper had since given, unsolicited, $250 for Bride; and it is said—although I have no personal knowledge on the subject—that Bride also received another $250. I believe that he admitted on the stand that he received $1,000,

432

and that Cottam has admitted on the stand that he received $1,250.

SENATOR SMITH: Mr. Marconi, in his testimony, admitted that this practice might be of doubtful wisdom, and that it was his purpose to discourage it in the future. What have you to say about that?

MR. BOTTOMLEY: Anything that Mr. Marconi requests the American company to do will be done without demur or hesitation.

SENATOR SMITH: Did you have anything to do with arranging for this exclusive story through the New York Times?

MR. BOTTOMLEY: No, sir; nothing further than what I have said.

SENATOR SMITH: Mr. Bottomley, is this true, as reported in the London Daily Telegraph:

The Marconi Co. will give no information to any ship not fitted with the Marconi wireless system, nor will it consider its calls?

MR. BOTTOMLEY: It is absolutely untrue as far as the American company is concerned.

SENATOR SMITH: A passenger on the Russian ship *Birma*, fitted with another wireless system, reported, on reaching London, that the ship's offers to help care for the survivors on board the *Carpathia* were met by repeated signals to "Shut up." Were those answers in consonance with the general orders of the Marconi Co.?

MR. BOTTOMLEY: Most certainly not. The absolute order is that everything must be communicated with, ships or anywhere, in any time of danger or distress. That is one of the first provisions of our general orders.

SENATOR SMITH: That passenger gave the London Daily Telegraph a statement, attested by the officers and wireless operators of the *Birma*, that on the day of the disaster and on days following the ship was refused any information whatever with regard to the wreck survivors. Was that refusal in obedience to orders or instructions given by the Marconi Co.?

MR. BOTTOMLEY: Most certainly not.

SENATOR SMITH: Do you think that there is any justification for such suppression of information of world-wide importance at such a time?

MR. BOTTOMLEY: There would be none.

SENATOR SMITH: Is it not true that if the operator on the *Carpathia* had acquainted the operator on the *Birma* with some details concerning the disaster the world would not have been kept in suspense for many days?

MR. BOTTOMLEY: I can not answer that question. I know nothing about the *Birma,* or where she was.

SENATOR SMITH: Was there anything to prevent the operator on the *Carpathia* from giving the *Birma* a few details?

MR. BOTTOMLEY: As I have said before, the operator can only send such news as is authorized by the captain of a ship.

SENATOR SMITH: Are Marconi operators absolutely under the control of the captains of the ships on which they serve?

MR. BOTTOMLEY: To the best of my knowledge, they are as long as they are on board ship. The captain is the absolute ruler of his ship.

SENATOR SMITH: Is it not true that your operators can talk to each other and that, as a matter of fact, they are almost constantly chatting when in touch with each other?

MR. BOTTOMLEY: There is an absolute rule against such chatting or talking or exchanging matters not of proper business connected with wireless, but it would be impossible to follow each operator and find that he did not chat or speak with another. As a general rule they do not do so. None of our best men follow that practice. If it was discovered, the operator would be severely reprimanded, and many times shore stations have picked up chatting between operators which was led, in some instances to discharge, and in others to very severe reprimanding of the offenders. It is one of the rules which should be most strictly observed by operators. They are not there for their own purposes at all.

SENATOR SMITH: You must admit, Mr. Bottomley, that no captain can know of these personal messages between operators.

MR. BOTTOMLEY: Oh, no; of course not.

SENATOR SMITH (continuing): Unless informed by the operator himself.

MR. BOTTOMLEY: No, sir; he would not know anything about it.

SENATOR SMITH: The testimony in this case clearly shows

that there is more or less social and personal communication between operators on shipboard and at coast stations as well.

MR. BOTTOMLEY: If that is so, it is very much to be deplored, and any instance brought to our notice will be severely dealt with. I speak for the whole allied Marconi companies in that respect.

SENATOR SMITH: Do you not think this practice should be regulated by law; that it ought to be made the subject of inquiry by the Berlin convention, in order to insure the proper transaction of public business?

MR. BOTTOMLEY: I think the matter might be brought up at the Berlin conference or convention. I presume it will be.

SENATOR SMITH: Mr. Bottomley, Mr. Marconi said he sent a personal message to the operator of the *Carpathia* two nights before that ship reached New York, ordering him to send to the Associated Press a description of what happened to the *Titanic*. Can you give any reason why this request was not complied with?

MR. BOTTOMLEY: None but that the operator was unable to cope with the business which he had in hand.

SENATOR SMITH: And as to that you are not fully advised?

MR. BOTTOMLEY: As to that I am not fully advised.

SENATOR SMITH: Can the orders of the president of your company, or of any of its general officers, be disregarded with impunity?

MR. BOTTOMLEY: The circumstances are so exceptional that I would be unable to answer that question properly. I think that an operator should do as I would do—give every possible attention to any request sent out by Mr. Marconi; but an officer of this company is of no greater importance than the smallest person on board the boat who has friends ashore.

SENATOR SMITH: So far as I have been able to observe during the hearings before the committee, I have as yet seen no one whose message was either delivered to or sent from the *Carpathia* for a passenger. How can you account for that?

MR. BOTTOMLEY: I am unable to account for it at all. We do not control the operator of the *Carpathia* in any way. He is under the direction of Marconi's International Marine Communication Co.

SENATOR SMITH: Do you know whether he received any injunction of silence from that company?

MR. BOTTOMLEY: I know that he received no injunction of silence from that company so far as any man can know that, because I am confident the company sent out no such injunction.

SENATOR SMITH: Do you think that your operator on the *Carpathia* should have put aside important messages, such as this, in order that he might send messages bearing upon the personal comfort of passengers of that ship?

MR. BOTTOMLEY: That would be my opinion. I think the people on the ship were suffering tremendously, and the matter of news was of next to no importance except to satisfy the cravings of the public. That is my honest opinion.

SENATOR SMITH: Do you believe that the failure to respond to this request was due entirely to the operator?

MR. BOTTOMLEY: I think so.

SENATOR SMITH: What influence, in your opinion, did the plan of Bride and Cottam to market the news which was in their possession have in this case?

MR. BOTTOMLEY: Absolutely none, in my opinion, because they knew nothing about any plan to market the news until after it was too late to send anything to the press or anywhere else.

SENATOR SMITH: Do you not think they were aware of the success of Operator Binns in disposing of information in his possession at the time of the *Republic* disaster?

MR. BOTTOMLEY: They may have been. I do not know that they were. It was common talk. What one operator does not know about another one is very little. Still, I do not believe it would influence them in any way.

SENATOR SMITH: Do you not think such matters should be under better control by your company, or by the owners of the ships?

MR. BOTTOMLEY: If a way could be devised to find that better control, I think so; but I doubt if it can be done.

SENATOR SMITH: Would you favor an international agreement for the control of information of disasters at sea?

MR. BOTTOMLEY: Yes.

SENATOR SMITH: Are you willing to submit the complete record of all messages sent by operators of your company

from the first message of the *Titanic* until the arrival of
the *Carpathia* in New York?

MR. BOTTOMLEY: So far as we are permitted by law, we will
give every record in our office. We will throw our records
open to Senator Smith or any member of the committee,
provided promises of secrecy will first be made. . . .

TWELFTH DAY
Friday, May 3
New York

Witness: Daniel Buckley, 21
Irish immigrant and steerage passenger

Key testimony: The disaster was something of an equalizer between the aristocracy and hoi polloi. Buckley described the chaotic scene in steerage when passengers were briefly kept below; later, in his lifeboat, he apparently sat next to young Madeleine Astor, pregnant with the child of her husband, Col. John Jacob of New York, who perished. Buckley said the woman wrapped him in her shawl.

... SENATOR SMITH: How did you happen to come over to America?

MR. BUCKLEY: I wanted to come over here to make some money. I came in the *Titanic* because she was a new steamer.

This night of the wreck I was sleeping in my room on the *Titanic*, in the steerage. There were three other boys from the same place sleeping in the same room with me.

I heard some terrible noise and I jumped out on the floor, and the first thing I knew my feet were getting wet; the water was just coming in slightly. I told the other fellows to get up, that there was something wrong and that the water was coming in. They only laughed at me. One of them says: "Get back into bed. You are not in Ireland now."

I got on my clothes as quick as I could, and the three other fellows got out. The room was very small, so I got out, to give them room to dress themselves.

Two sailors came along, and they were shouting: "All up on deck! unless you want to get drowned."

When I heard this, I went for the deck as quick as I could. When I got up on the deck I saw everyone having

438

those life belts on only myself; so I got sorry, and said I would go back again where I was sleeping and get one of those life preservers; because there was one there for each person.

I went back again, and just as I was going down the last flight of stairs the water was up four steps, and dashing up. I did not go back into the room, because I could not. When I went back toward the room the water was coming up three steps up the stairs, or four steps; so I did not go any farther. I got back on the deck again, and just as I got back there, I was looking around to see if I could get any of those life belts, and I met a first-class passenger, and he had two. He gave me one, and fixed it on me.

Then the lifeboats were preparing. There were five lifeboats sent out. I was in the sixth. I was holding the ropes all the time, helping to let down the five lifeboats that went down first, as well as I could.

When the sixth lifeboat was prepared, there was a big crowd of men standing on the deck. And they all jumped in. So I said I would take my chance with them.

SENATOR SMITH: Who were they?

MR. BUCKLEY: Passengers and sailors and firemen, mixed. There were no ladies there at the same time.

When they jumped, I said I would go too. I went into the boat. Then two officers came along and said all of the men could come out. And they brought a lot of steerage passengers with them; and they were mixed, every way, ladies and gentlemen. And they said all the men could get out and let the ladies in. But six men were left in the boat. I think they were firemen and sailors.

I was crying. There was a woman in the boat, and she had thrown her shawl over me, and she told me to stay in there. I believe she was Mrs. Astor. Then they did not see me, and the boat was lowered down into the water, and we rowed away out from the steamer.

The men that were in the boat at first fought, and would not get out, but the officers drew their revolvers, and fired shots over our heads, and then the men got out. When the boat was ready, we were lowered down into the water and rowed away out from the steamer. We were only about 15 minutes out when she sank.

SENATOR SMITH: What else happened?

MR. BUCKLEY: One of the firemen that was working on the *Titanic* told me, when I got on board the *Carpathia* and he was speaking to me, that he did not think it was any iceberg; that it was only that they wanted to make a record, and they ran too much steam and the boilers bursted. That is what he said.

We sighted the lights of the big steamer, the *Carpathia*. All the women got into a terrible commotion and jumped around. They were hallooing and the sailors were trying to keep them sitting down, and they would not do it. They were standing up all the time.

When we got into the *Carpathia* we were treated very good. We got all kinds of refreshments.

SENATOR SMITH: Did you feel a shock from the collision when the ship struck?

MR. BUCKLEY: Yes; I did.

SENATOR SMITH: And did that wake you up?

MR. BUCKLEY: It did. I did not feel any shock in the steamer; only just heard a noise. I heard a kind of a grating noise.

SENATOR SMITH: Did you get right out of bed?

MR. BUCKLEY: Yes; I did.

SENATOR SMITH: When you got out, you got into the water? There was water in your compartment in the steerage?

MR. BUCKLEY: Yes; water was there slightly. There was not very much.

SENATOR SMITH: How much?

MR. BUCKLEY: The floor was only just getting wet. It was only coming in under the door very slightly.

SENATOR SMITH: You had two or three boys with you?

MR. BUCKLEY: Yes; three boys that came from the same place in Ireland.

SENATOR SMITH: What became of those other three boys?

MR. BUCKLEY: I can not say. I did not see them any more after leaving the room where I parted from them.

SENATOR SMITH: They were lost?

MR. BUCKLEY: Yes; they were lost.

SENATOR SMITH: Was there any effort made on the part of the officers or crew to hold the steerage passengers in the steerage?

MR. BUCKLEY: I do not think so.

SENATOR SMITH: Were you permitted to go on up to the top deck without any interference?

MR. BUCKLEY: Yes, sir. They tried to keep us down at first on our steerage deck. They did not want us to go up to the first-class place at all.

SENATOR SMITH: Who tried to do that?

MR. BUCKLEY: I can not say who they were. I think they were sailors.

SENATOR SMITH: What happened then? Did the steerage passengers try to get out?

MR. BUCKLEY: Yes; they did. There was one steerage passenger there, and he was getting up the steps, and just as he was going in a little gate a fellow came along and chucked him down; threw him down into the steerage place. This fellow got excited, and he ran after him, and he could not find him. He got up over the little gate. He did not find him.

SENATOR SMITH: What gate do you mean?

MR. BUCKLEY: A little gate just at the top of the stairs going up into the first-class deck.

SENATOR SMITH: There was a gate between the steerage and the first-class deck?

MR. BUCKLEY: Yes. The first-class deck was higher up than the steerage deck, and there were some steps leading up to it; 9 or 10 steps, and a gate just at the top of the steps.

SENATOR SMITH: Was the gate locked?

MR. BUCKLEY: It was not locked at the time we made the attempt to get up there, but the sailor, or whoever he was, locked it. So that this fellow that went up after him broke the lock on it, and he went after the fellow that threw him down. He said if he could get hold of him he would throw him into the ocean.

SENATOR SMITH: Did these passengers in the steerage have any opportunity at all of getting out?

MR. BUCKLEY: Yes; they had.

SENATOR SMITH: What opportunity did they have?

MR. BUCKLEY: I think they had as much chance as the first and second class passengers.

SENATOR SMITH: After this gate was broken?

MR. BUCKLEY: Yes; because they were all mixed. All the steerage passengers went up on the first-class deck at this

441

time, when the gate was broken. They all got up there. They could not keep them down.

SENATOR SMITH: How much water was there in the steerage when you got out of the steerage?

MR. BUCKLEY: There was only just a little bit. Just like you would throw a bucket of water on the floor; just very little, like that.

SENATOR SMITH: But it was coming in, was it?

MR. BUCKLEY: Yes; it was only just commencing to come in. When I went down the second time, to get one of the life preservers, there was a terrible lot of water there, in a very short time.

SENATOR SMITH: How much?

MR. BUCKLEY: It was just about three steps up the stairs, on the last flight of stairs that I got down.

SENATOR SMITH: Did you find any people down in the steerage when you went back the second time?

MR. BUCKLEY: There were a number, but I can not say how many. All the boys and girls were coming up against me. They were all going for the deck.

SENATOR SMITH: Were they excited?

MR. BUCKLEY: Yes; they were. The girls were very excited, and they were crying; and all the boys were trying to console them and saying that it was nothing serious.

SENATOR SMITH: Were you crying at the time?

MR. BUCKLEY: Not at this time. There was a girl from my place, and just when she got down into the lifeboat she thought that the boat was sinking into the water. Her name was Bridget Bradley. She climbed one of the ropes as far as she could and tried to get back into the *Titanic* again, as she thought she would be safer in it than in the lifeboat. She was just getting up when one of the sailors went out to her and pulled her down again.

SENATOR SMITH: How many people were there in the steerage when you got out of bed?

MR. BUCKLEY: I can not say.

SENATOR SMITH: Could you see many people around?

MR. BUCKLEY: Yes, sir; there was a great crowd of people. They were all terribly excited. They were all going for the decks as quick as they could. The people had no difficulty in stepping into the lifeboat. It was close to the ship.

SENATOR SMITH: I want to ask you whether, from what you saw that night, you feel that the steerage passengers had an equal opportunity with other passengers and the crew in getting into the lifeboats?

MR. BUCKLEY: Yes; I think they had as good a chance as the first and second class passengers.

SENATOR SMITH: You think they did have?

MR. BUCKLEY: Yes. But at the start they tried to keep them down on their own deck.

SENATOR SMITH: But they broke down this gate to which you have referred?

MR. BUCKLEY: Yes, sir.

SENATOR SMITH: And then they went on up as others did, mingling all together?

MR. BUCKLEY: Yes; they were all mixed up together.

SENATOR SMITH: Have you told all you know, of your own knowledge, about that?

MR. BUCKLEY: Yes.

SENATOR SMITH: Were you where you could see the ship when she went down?

MR. BUCKLEY: Yes; I saw the lights just going out as she went down. It made a terrible noise, like thunder. . . .

Witness: George A. Harder, 25
Brooklyn manufacturer and first-class passenger

Key testimony: On their honeymoon, the Harders found themselves confronted with the wrenching question about whether they could have rowed back and saved lives.

. . . SENATOR SMITH: What occurred Sunday night between the hours of 11 and 12 o'clock?

MR. HARDER: About a quarter to 11 I went down to my stateroom with Mrs. Harder and retired for the night; and at 20 minutes to 12 we were not asleep yet, and I heard this thump. It was not a loud thump; just a dull thump. Then I could feel the boat quiver and could feel a sort of rumbling, scraping noise along the side of the boat.

When I went to the porthole I saw this iceberg go by. The porthole was closed. The iceberg was, I should say, about 50 to 100 feet away. I should say it was about as high as the top deck of the boat. I just got a glimpse of it, and it is hard to tell how high it was.

SENATOR SMITH: What did you do then?

MR. HARDER: I thought we would go up on deck to see what had happened; what damage had been done. So we dressed fully and went up on deck, and there we saw quite a number of people talking; and nobody seemed to think anything serious had happened. There were such remarks as "Oh, it will only be a few hours before we will be on the way again."

I walked around the deck two or three times, when I noticed that the boat was listing quite a good deal on the starboard side; so Mrs. Harder and myself thought we would go inside and see if there was any news. We went in there and talked to a few people, and all of them seemed of the opinion that it was nothing serious.

SENATOR SMITH: Who were these people with whom you talked? Do you know?

MR. HARDER: I do not know. I do not know the names.

SENATOR SMITH: Were Mr. and Mrs. Bishop there?

MR. HARDER: Yes. I saw Mr. and Mrs. Bishop, and I saw Colonel and Mrs. Astor, and they all seemed to be of the opinion that there was no danger.

A little while after that an officer appeared at the foot of the stairs, and he announced that everybody should go to their staterooms and put on their life belts.

SENATOR SMITH: How long was that after the collision?

MR. HARDER: That, I think, was a little after 12—about 12 o'clock; that is, roughly.

So, we immediately went down to our stateroom and took our life belts and coats and started up the stairs and went to the top deck. There we saw the crew manning the lifeboats; getting them ready; swinging them out. So we waited around there, and we were finally told "Go over this way; go over this way." So we followed and went over toward the first lifeboat, where Mr. and Mrs. Bishop were. That boat was filled, and so they told us to move on to the next one.

SENATOR SMITH: On which side?

MR. HARDER: The starboard side.

SENATOR SMITH: So that the first boat was filled?

MR. HARDER: Yes. Somebody told us to move down toward

the second one. We got to the second one, and we were told to go right in there. I have been told that Mr. Ismay took hold of my wife's arm—I do not know him, but I have been told that he did—and pushed her right in. Then I followed.

SENATOR SMITH: How far did you have to step from the side of the ship into the lifeboat?

MR. HARDER: I should say it was about a foot and a half. Anyway, you had to jump. When I jumped in there, one foot went in between the oars, and I got in there and could not move until somebody pulled me over. . . .

SENATOR SMITH: Proceed to tell us regarding the lifeboat.

MR. HARDER: We got into the lifeboat, which was either No. 7 or No. 5, I do not know which.

SENATOR SMITH: Who was in charge of it?

MR. HARDER: Mr. Pitman. That was the second boat to leave on the starboard side, as far as I could see.

As we were being lowered, they lowered one side quicker than the other, but we finally reached the water safely, after a few scares. When we got down into the water, somebody said the plug was not in; so they fished around to see if that was in, and I guess it was in. Then, they could not get the boat detached from the tackle, so they fussed around there for a while, and finally they asked if anybody had a knife, and nobody seemed to have a knife. Finally, one of the passengers had a knife in his possession, and they cut some rope; what it was I do not know.

SENATOR SMITH: Do you know what passenger that was?

MR. HARDER: No, sir; I do not. I can not remember his name.

SENATOR SMITH: Do you wish to be understood as saying that the tackle or gear by which this boat was lowered did not work properly?

MR. HARDER: You mean when we lowered down? No. That was on account of the crew up on the deck. They had two or three men on each side, letting out the rope, and they let out the rope on one side faster than the other. That caused the boat to assume this position going down [indicating] and we thought for a time that we were all going to be dumped out. We finally reached the water all right.

Then the next job was to get the ropes at each end of

the boat, the bow and the stern of the lifeboat, detached. I understand there was some new patented lever on there some device that you pull, and that would let loose the whole thing. Whether they did not know that was there or not, I do not know; I presume they did not, because they did not seem to get it to work, and they finally had to resort to this knife.

SENATOR SMITH: You got away from the side of the boat?

MR. HARDER: Yes; and we started to pull away from the ship. We had, as I learned afterwards, about 42 people in the boat.

SENATOR SMITH: How many women were in the boat?

MR. HARDER: I should say, roughly, about 30 women. That is just a guess.

SENATOR SMITH: And who composed the remainder of the people in the boat?

MR. HARDER: There was this officer, and there was a sailor, and then there were about three men in the boat; as far as I could judge some kind of seamen. I do not know whether they were stewards or whether they were seamen, they were not dressed as sailors. There was only one man there with a regular sailor's hat and blouse.

SENATOR SMITH: Did they know anything about handling the boat?

MR. HARDER: Yes; they seemed to be able to row as well as possible. Of course, those boats are very unwieldly sort of things, and have great big long oars.

SENATOR SMITH: I want to call your attention specifically to a statement made by Mr. Pitman, officer in charge of that boat. He says that they rowed off some distance from the side of the ship. Is that correct?

MR. HARDER: Yes, sir.

SENATOR SMITH: And that there were cries for help, and the passengers in that boat would not permit him, Pitman, to go to their relief.

MR. HARDER: This is the way it was, Senator: We rowed out there some distance from the ship. How far it was, I do not know. It may have been as far as a quarter of a mile and it may have been one-eighth of a mile. At any rate, we were afraid of the suction. So the passengers said, "Let us row out a little farther." So they rowed out farther

446

perhaps about a half a mile; it may have been three-quarters of a mile. There we waited, and after waiting around a while, there was this other boat that came alongside, that Pitman hailed alongside; and that was either boat No. 7 or boat No. 5, I do not know which, in which Mr. and Mrs. Bishop were. We tied alongside of that, and they had 29 people in their boat, and we counted the number of people in our boat; and at that time we only counted, I think it was, 36. So we gave them four or five of our people in order to make it even, as we were kind of crowded.

SENATOR SMITH: This was a large lifeboat that you were in?

MR. HARDER: Yes, sir; it was the regular size lifeboat.

They say those boats hold 60 people, but we had only the number of people I have mentioned; and, believe me, we did not have room to spare.

Then we waited out there until the ship went down. We were out there until the ship went down. After it went down, we heard a lot of these cries and yells. You could not hear any shouts for help, or anything like that. It was a sort of continuous yelling or moaning. You could not distinguish any sounds. It was more like—what I thought it was—the steerage on rafts, and that they were all hysterical. That is the way it sounded in the distance.

Then we stayed around there until daybreak, when we saw the *Carpathia,* and we rowed the distance; I do not know how far it was; probably 2 miles; it might have been less. . . .

SENATOR SMITH: Is there anything else you can say bearing on this matter that will be helpful to the committee in its endeavors to get all the facts and circumstances leading up to and subsequent to this accident?

MR. HARDER: No, sir; there is nothing else that I can think of.

Our boat was managed very well. It is true this officer did want to go back to the ship, but all the passengers held out and said: "Do not do that. Do not do that. It would only be foolish if we went back there. There will be so many around they will only swamp the boat." And, at the time, I do not think those people appreciated that there were not sufficient lifeboats to go around. I never paid any attention to how many lifeboats there were. I did not know.

Witness: John R. (Jack) Binns
Reporter for the *New York American* and former
Marconi wireless operator

Key testimony: Binns became a hero in the press in 190[?]
when he sold his story of how his wits as a Marconi wireles[?]
operator helped save all aboard the wreck of the White Sta[?]
liner Republic off Nantucket. Now a journalist, he face[?]
Senator Smith's pointed questions about shipboard wireles[?]
communications and checkbook journalism, offering an ex[?]
pert critique of the Titanic's *design as well.*

... SENATOR SMITH: Were you the wireless operator at th[?]
time of the disaster to the *Republic*?

MR. BINNS: I was; yes, sir.

SENATOR SMITH: Will you state to the committee whethe[?]
news concerning that disaster was promptly sent out fror[?]
the *Republic* immediately following the disaster?

MR. BINNS: Yes; the news was sent out immediately.

SENATOR SMITH: And in detail?

MR. BINNS: Not exactly in detail, but the exact details of th[?]
accident, in so far as they referred to the *Republi[?]*
generally.

SENATOR SMITH: As I have been informed, you gave you[?]
personal experiences to some newspaper on your arriv[?]
in New York?

MR. BINNS: Yes, sir.

SENATOR SMITH: Will you state the circumstances und[?]
which that was done?

MR. BINNS: After the sinking of the *Republic* we we[?]
transferred to the United States revenue cutter *Greshar[?]*
and thence to the United States revenue cutter *Seneca.*

Coming up the coast I received wireless messages fro[?]
various newspapers asking me for my own personal stor[?]
This I submitted to Capt. Sealby, and asked his opinic[?]
about the matter. He said that should the White Star Lir[?]
have no objection to it, he certainly would not.

During the voyage I also received a message from t[?]
Marconi Co. asking me to reserve the story, if possib[?]
for the New York Times, owing to their friendly conne[?]

tion with the Marconi Co., by whom I was employed at that time.

I arrived in New York, and made a report to the White Star Line, and asked Mr. Franklin if he had any objection to my writing my own personal story to the New York Times, to which he said "no."

I had the story already written out, and I had already submitted it to Capt. Sealby, and also to Mr. Franklin, and the story was then handed over to the New York Times. This story, by the way, was handed over a day and a half after the passengers on the *Republic* had been landed in New York City.

SENATOR SMITH: Is there anything else connected with that matter which will be useful to the committee?

MR. BINNS: I handed in the story to the New York Times Tuesday evening, the 26th of January, and then immediately left for Mr. Bottomley's house, where I was staying at that time.

There was some dispute with the New York Times the following morning regarding the price to be paid for this story, which, I understood, was $500. They offered me a check for $100, which I refused. I then mentioned the matter to Mr. Bottomley, the vice president of the Marconi Co., who took the matter up with the editor of the New York Times, and a check for $250 was eventually sent me, with an explanation saying that had the story been handed in on Monday evening instead of Tuesday evening it would have been worth the amount they originally offered.

SENATOR SMITH: From your experience as a wireless operator, can you account for the failure to give to the public promptly this information pertaining to the disaster to the *Titanic?*

MR. BINNS: The only explanation that I could give is the general inadequacy of the set installed on board the *Carpathia* to cover the distances required in communication with the land stations in that vicinity. The set on the *Carpathia* is what is known as a coil set, and the combination used is what is known as plain aerial. In this combination the antenna between the masts is joined directly to one side of the spark gap and grounded to the other.

449

In the event of damp or rainy weather the insulators holding the antenna between the masts, becoming moist, allow a great leakage, and this leakage dissipates the energy produced by the coil, and consequently reduces the radius of communication.

At the time of the *Titanic* disaster the atmosphere in the vicinity was rather moist, and the probability is that the *Carpathia* was unable to attain more than 75 miles communicating radius. . . .

SENATOR SMITH: Mr. Binns, do you not think it would be more serviceable if, on ships where it is impracticable to have two operators, the watch of the single operator should be from 6 o'clock at night until 6 o'clock in the morning, in order that he might always be ready to take communications from other ships at a time when other means of observation are most difficult?

MR. BINNS: In cases where it is impossible or impracticable to have two operators, I think that the operator himself should be on duty during the night watch, and that a cadet or wireless-telegraph learner should be supplied to take the day watch. . . . However, I think, and I always have thought that in all cases two operators should be supplied to every vessel.

SENATOR SMITH: Let me call your attention to the fact that the *Californian* was but 14 miles from the *Titanic* when it sank. If there had been a wireless operator on duty on the *Californian*, in all probability every passenger and member of the crew of the *Titanic* could have been saved.

MR. BINNS: Yes; that is so. . . .

SENATOR SMITH: Have you observed any part of the construction of the *Olympic*, on which you served, which was followed in the construction of her sister ship, the *Titanic*, which you think would be of interest to the committee?

MR. BINNS: The *Olympic* has what is known as two expansion joints. These joints are composed in this way: The ship is split completely through the deck and also through the sides of the ship to a point above the water line; the split is then joined over by a curved piece of steel, which is riveted to each side of the severed part of the ship. The idea of this joint is to reduce the excessive vibration caused by the high speed of the ship. In my opinion this is an element of weakness and tends to detract from its structural strength. This I observed on the *Olympic;* and the *Titanic* was built in the same way. The same feature was followed in the *Titanic*, which vessel I observed prior to her launching and the launching of which I also witnessed in Belfast.

I have observed steamship construction, and am quite familiar with the plans of the *Olympic* and the *Titanic*, and with those of the *Mauritania* and the *Lusitania* of the Cunard Line.

From the plans of the *Olympic* and the *Titanic* the vessel has been built to meet every possible accident with the exception of a glancing blow such as the *Titanic* received. The ship has a certain number of water-tight compartments and also a double bottom; but according to the plans the sides of the ship are just a single shell under the water line, and in the event of a glancing blow extending from one end of the ship to the other the water-tight compartments would be rendered absolutely useless, owing to the fact that there is no side protection.

In the plans of the *Mauritania* and *Lusitania,* of the Cunard Line, these vessels are shown to have double cellular sides as well as a double cellular bottom. Also, on the inside of the inner plating of the cellular sides are the coal bunkers, which can also be turned into water-tight compartments. In the event of a glancing blow ripping up the side of one of these vessels, they would still remain afloat, owing to the presence of the inner shell of the vessel's cellular sides. . . .

Witness: Olaus Abelseth, 26
Norwegian immigrant and steerage passenger

Key testimony: He provided a harrowing account of diving off the Titanic's *plunging stern at the last minute.*

. . . SENATOR SMITH: I wish you would tell the reporter when you first knew of this collision, and what you did, and where you were in the ship. I believe you were a steerage passenger?

MR. ABELSETH: Yes, sir.

SENATOR SMITH: In the forward part of the ship?

MR. ABELSETH: Yes. I was in compartment G on the ship.

SENATOR SMITH: Go ahead and tell us just what happened.

MR. ABELSETH: I went to bed about 10 o'clock Sunday night, and I think it was about 15 minutes to 12 when I woke up; and there was another man in the same room—two of us in the same room—and he said to me, "What is that?" I said, "I don't know, but we had better get up." So we did get up and put our clothes on, and we two went up on deck in the forward part of the ship.

Then there was quite a lot of ice on the starboard part of the ship. They wanted us to go down again, and I saw one of the officers, and I said to him: "Is there any danger?" He said, "No." I was not satisfied with that, however, so I went down and told my brother-in-law and my cousin, who were in the same compartment there. They were not in the same room, but they were just a little ways from where I was. I told them about what was happening, and I said they had better get up. Both of them got up and dressed, and we took our overcoats and put them on. We did not take any life belts with us. There was no water on the deck at that time.

We walked to the hind part of the ship and got two Norwegian girls up. One was in my charge and one was in charge of the man who was in the same room with me. He was from the same town that I came from. The other one was just 16 years old, and her father told me to take care of her until we got to Minneapolis. The two girls were in a room in the hind part of the ship, in the steerage.

We all went up on deck and stayed there. We walked over to the port side of the ship, and there were five of us standing, looking, and we thought we saw a light.

SENATOR SMITH: On what deck were you standing?

MR. ABELSETH: Not on the top deck, but on—I do not know what you call it, but it is the hind part, where the sitting room is; and then there is a kind of a little space in between, where they go up on deck. It was up on the boat deck, the place for the steerage passengers on the deck. We were then on the port side there, and we looked out at this light. I said to my brother-in-law: "I can see it plain, now. It must be a light."

SENATOR SMITH: How far away was it?

MR. ABELSETH: I could not say, but it did not seem to be so very far. I thought I could see this mast light, the front mast light. That is what I thought I could see.

A little while later there was one of the officers who came and said to be quiet, that there was a ship coming. That is all he said. He did not say what time, or anything. That is all he said.

So I said to them, we had better go and get the life belts, as we had not brought them with us. So my cousin and I went down to get the life belts for all of us. When we came up again we carried the life belts on our arms for a while.

There were a lot of steerage people there that were getting on one of these cranes that they had on deck, that they used to lift things with. They can lift about two and a half tons, I believe. These steerage passengers were crawling along on this, over the railing, and away up to the boat deck. A lot of them were doing that.

SENATOR SMITH: They could not get up there in any other way?

MR. ABELSETH: This gate was shut.

SENATOR SMITH: Was it locked?

MR. ABELSETH: I do not know whether it was locked, but it was shut so that they could not go that way.

A while later these girls were standing there, and one of the officers came and hollered for all of the ladies to come up on the boat deck. The gate was opened and these two girls went up.

We stayed a little while longer, and then they said, "Everybody." I do not know who that was, but I think it was some of the officers that said it. I could not say that, but it was somebody that said "everybody." We went up. We went over to the port side of the ship, and there were just one or two boats on the port side that were lost. Anyway, there was one. We were standing there looking at them lowering this boat. We could see them, some of the crew helping take the ladies in their arms and throwing them into the lifeboats. We saw them lower this boat, and there were no more boats on the port side.

So we walked over to the starboard side of the ship, and just as we were standing there, one of the officers came up and he said just as he walked by, "Are there any sailors here?"

I did not say anything. I have been a fishing man for six years, and, of course, this officer walked right by me and asked: "Are there any sailors here?" I would have gone, but my brother-in-law and my cousin said, in the Norwegian language, as we were speaking Norwegian: "Let us stay here together." I do not know, but I think the officer wanted some help to get some of these collapsible boats out. All he said was: "Are there any sailors here?" I did not say anything, but I have been used to the ocean for a long time. I commenced to work on the ocean when I was 10 years old with my dad fishing. I kept that up until I came to this country.

Then we stayed there, and we were just standing still there. We did not talk very much. Just a little ways from us I saw there was an old couple standing there on the deck, and I heard this man say to the lady, "Go into the lifeboat and get saved." He put his hand on her shoulder and I think he said: "Please get into the lifeboat and get saved." She replied: "No; let me stay with you." I could not say who it was, but I saw that he was an old man. I did not pay much attention to him, because I did not know him.

I was standing there, and I asked my brother-in-law if he could swim and he said no. I asked my cousin if he could swim and he said no. So we could see the water coming up, the bow of the ship was going down, and there was a kind of an explosion. We could hear the popping and cracking, and the deck raised up and got so steep that the people could not stand on their feet on the deck. So they fell down and slid on the deck into the water right on the ship. Then we hung onto a rope in one of the davits. We were pretty far back at the top deck.

My brother-in-law said to me, "We had better jump off or the suction will take us down." I said, "No. We won't jump yet. We ain't got much show anyhow, so we might as well stay as long as we can." So he stated again, "We must jump off." But I said, "No; not yet." So, then, it was only about 5 feet down to the water when we jumped off. It was not much of a jump. Before that we could see the people were jumping over. There was water coming onto the deck, and they were jumping over, then, out in the water.

My brother-in-law took my hand just as we jumped off, and my cousin jumped at the same time. When we came into the water, I think it was from the suction—or anyway we went under, and I swallowed some water. I got a rope tangled around me, and I let loose of my brother-in-law's hand to get away from the rope. I thought then, "I am a goner." That is what I thought when I got tangled up in this rope. But I came on top again, and I was trying to swim, and there was a man—lots of them were floating around—and he got me on the neck like that [illustrating] and pressed me under, trying to get on top of me. I said to him, "Let go." Of course, he did not pay any attention to that, but I got away from him. Then there was another man, and he hung on to me for a while, but he let go. Then I swam; I could not say, but it must have been about 15 or 20 minutes. It could not have been over that. Then I saw something dark ahead of me. I did not know what it was, but I swam toward that, and it was one of those collapsible boats.

When we jumped off of the ship, we had life preservers on. There was no suction from the ship at all. I was lying still, and I thought "I will try to see if I can float on the life belt without help from swimming," and I floated easily on the life belt.

When I got on this raft or collapsible boat, they did not try to push me off, and they did not do anything for me to get on. All they said when I got on there was, "Don't capsize the boat." So I hung onto the raft for a little while before I got on.

Some of them were trying to get up on their feet. They were sitting down or lying down on the raft. Some of them fell into the water again. Some of them were frozen; and there were two dead, that they threw overboard.

I got on this raft or collapsible boat and raised up, and then I was continually moving my arms and swinging them around to keep warm. There was one lady aboard this raft, and she got saved. I do not know her name. I saw her on board the *Carpathia,* but I forgot to ask her name. There were also two Swedes, and a first-class passenger— I believe that is what he said—and he had just his underwear on. I asked him if he was married, and he said he had a wife and a child. There was also a fireman named Thompson on the same raft. He had burned one of his hands. Also there was a young boy, with a name that sounded like Volunteer. He was at St. Vincent's Hospital afterwards. Thompson was there, too.

The next morning we could see some of the lifeboats. One of the boats had a sail up, and he came pretty close, and then we said, "One, two, three"; we said that quite often. We did not talk very much, except that we would say, "One, two, three," and scream together for help.

SENATOR SMITH: Was this collapsible boat that you were in filling with water?

MR. ABELSETH: There was water on the top.

SENATOR SMITH: Were you on the top of the overturned collapsible boat?

MR. ABELSETH: No. The boat was not capsized. We were standing on the deck. In this little boat the canvas was not raised up. We tried to raise the canvas up but we could not get it up. We stood all night in about 12 or 14 inches of water on this thing and our feet were in the water all the time. I could not say exactly how long we were there, but I know it was more than four hours on this raft.

This same boat I was telling about——

SENATOR SMITH: The sailboat?

MR. ABELSETH: Yes; when the *Carpathia* came she was picked up. There were several boats there then. It was broad daylight and you could see the *Carpathia*. Then this boat sailed down to us and took us aboard, and took us in to the *Carpathia*. I helped row in to the *Carpathia*.

SENATOR SMITH: Did you see any icebergs on that morning?

MR. ABELSETH: We saw three big ones. They were quite a ways off.

SENATOR SMITH: I want to direct your attention again to the steerage. Do you think the passengers in the steerage and in the bow of the boat had an opportunity to get out and up on the decks, or were they held back?

MR. ABELSETH: Yes, I think they had an opportunity to get up.

SENATOR SMITH: There were no gates or doors locked, or anything that kept them down?

MR. ABELSETH: No, sir; not that I could see.

SENATOR SMITH: You said that a number of them climbed up one of these cranes?

MR. ABELSETH: That was on the top, on the deck; after they

got on the deck. That was in order to get up on this boat deck.

SENATOR SMITH: Onto the top deck?

MR. ABELSETH: Onto the top deck; yes. But down where we were, in the rooms, I do not think there was anybody that held anybody back.

SENATOR SMITH: You were not under any restraint? You were permitted to go aboard the boats the same as other passengers?

MR. ABELSETH: Yes, sir.

SENATOR SMITH: Do you think the steerage passengers in your part of the ship all got out?

MR. ABELSETH: I could not say that for sure; but I think the most of them got out.

SENATOR SMITH: Did that part of the ship fill rapidly with water?

MR. ABELSETH: Oh, yes; I think that filled up; yes. There was a friend of mine told me that he went back for something he wanted, and then there was so much water there that he could not get to his room.

SENATOR SMITH: Were the three relatives of yours from Norway lost?

MR. ABELSETH: Yes; they were lost. . . .

THIRTEENTH DAY
Saturday, May 4
Waldorf-Astoria Hotel, New York

On Day 13, Senator Smith on his own called several witnesses, mainly to elicit details filling in the byzantine story of wireless telegraphy in the disaster. That testimony is omitted here.

Witness: Berk Pickard, 32
Steerage passenger and immigrant living in
New York

Key testimony: He saved himself by rising in class, so to speak.

... SENATOR SMITH: State your name, age, residence, and occupation.

MR. PICKARD: Berk Pickard; No. 229, Hebrew Immigrant Society. At the time I took passage on the *Titanic* I came from London. I am 32 years old. I am a leather worker; a bag maker. I was born in Russia, in Warsaw. My name was Berk Trembisky. I was for a long time in France and I assumed a French name. As regards private business, I am Pickard.

I was one of the third-class passengers on the *Titanic*. My cabin was No. 10 in the steerage, at the stern. I first knew of the collision when it happened, about 10 minutes to 12. We had all been asleep, and all of a sudden we perceived a shock. We did not hear such a very terrible shock, but we knew something was wrong, and we jumped out of bed and we dressed ourselves and went out, and we could not get back again. I wanted to go back to get my things but I could not. The stewards would not allow us to go back. They made us all go forward on the deck. There were no doors locked to prevent us from going back. I did not take much notice of it, and I went to the deck. The other passengers started in arguing. One said that it was dangerous and the other said that it was not; one said white and the other said black. Instead of arguing with those people, I instantly went to the highest spot.

I said to myself that if the ship had to sink, I should be one of the last. That was my first idea, which was the best. I went and I found the door. There are always a few steps from this third class, with a moveable door, and it is marked there that second-class passengers have no right to penetrate there. I found this door open so that I could go into the second class, where I did not find many people, only a few that climbed on the ladder and went into the first class, which I did. I found there only a few men and about two ladies. They had been putting them into lifeboats and as no women were there, we men sprang in the boat. We had only one woman and another young girl. There were two women. They stood just in front of me. We were lowered down, and when I was lowered down I saw the whole ship, as big as she was, the right side a little bit sinking, and I was far from imagining that it was the beginning of the end. When I was going away from the ship, of course I was rather frightened; I was sorry at not being on the ship, and I said to the seaman, "I would rather be on the ship." He was laughing at me, and he said, "Do you not see we are sinking?" I was rather excited, and I said, "It is fortunate that now the sea is nice, but perhaps in five minutes we will be turned over." So I was in the boat until 5 o'clock in the morning.

In regard to the ship, I saw the ship very quickly started sinking, and one rail went under and then another, until in a half an hour, from my point of view, the ship sank altogether.

The steerage passengers, so far as I could see, were not prevented from getting up to the upper decks by anybody, or by closed doors, or anything else. While I was on the ship no one realized the real danger, not even the stewards. If the stewards knew, they were calm. It was their duty to try to make us believe there was nothing serious. Nobody was prevented from going up. They tried to keep us quiet. They said, "Nothing serious is the matter." Perhaps they did not know themselves. I did not realize it, the whole time, even to the last moment. Of course, I would never believe such a thing could happen.

The lifeboat I got into was an ordinary lifeboat. I do not know what number it was; I am sorry to say I did not look at it. There was some seaman in charge of it, who belonged to the ship. What kind of employment the seamen were in I do not know, but they belonged to the ship.

The only warning given to the steerage passengers after the collision was that we were ordered to take our life belts and go to the deck. There was no water in the steerage when I left.

That is all I know about it. I was one of the first to go. Of course, if I had stayed until a little bit later, I would have seen a little bit more. I was one of the luckiest ones, I think.

FOURTEENTH DAY
Thursday, May 9
Washington, D.C.

Witness: Maurice L. Farrell, 35
Managing editor of Dow, Jones & Co.

Key testimony: It is an understatement to say that the disaster was not journalism's finest hour. At Senator Smith's behest, Farrell listed the embarrassing inaccuracies moving over the Dow, Jones news service's ticker on the day after one of the century's signal catastrophes. The statement appended to Farrell's testimony is a remarkable study in editorial hemming and hawing without actually admitting error.

. . . SENATOR SMITH: I want to direct your attention specifically to two things.

In your bulletin, or ticker original—is that the proper expression?

MR. FARRELL: Yes. . . .

SENATOR SMITH: From your bulletin Local "A"-3, headed "Bulletin," I read as follows:

> NEW YORK, *April 15.*
> A dispatch received here from Halifax, N. S., this morning reports that all the passengers of the *Titanic* had left the steamship after 3:30 o'clock this morning.
> 9:33 A.M.

Following that on your original memoranda appears the following:

> *Titanic*—A dispatch from Halifax reports that all passengers had left the *Titanic* in boats shortly after 3:30 this morning.

Have you that?

461

MR. FARRELL: We published that dispatch on our ticker at 8:58 on the morning of April 15. We received it from the Boston News Bureau, our Boston correspondent.

SENATOR SMITH: Did you make any attempt to verify that statement at the White Star Line offices or through Mr. Franklin personally?

MR. FARRELL: We did.

SENATOR SMITH: With what results?

MR. FARRELL: Prior to that we had received from the White Star offices a statement somewhat similar.

SENATOR SMITH: Have you got it there?

MR. FARRELL: I have; and with your permission I will read it.

SENATOR SMITH: Please do so.

MR. FARRELL: This was published at our tickers at 8:35, or thereabouts. It was obtained by Mr. Gingold, one of our reporters, who is now in London. He went to London on a vacation very shortly after that. I will read the statement as it appeared on our tickers, headed *"Titanic."* I reads:

Officers of White Star Line stated at 8 o'clock this morning that passengers on the *Titanic* were being taken off in boats and that there was no danger of loss of life. The *Baltic* and the *Virginian*, they stated, were standing by to assist in the rescue work.

SENATOR SMITH: Is that the end of that?

MR. FARRELL: Then there are two more items running along on the same story:

On *Titanic* there were 300 first class, 320 second class, 800 third class passengers, and a crew of 900 men.

It is not yet known whether the vessel will be saved. White Star people are in something of a quandary if she should be saved, as it is said there is no dry dock on this side of the Atlantic to take care of her.

SENATOR SMITH: From whom was that information received?

MR. FARRELL: That was received at the White Star office from some of the junior officials. Mr. [P. A. S.] Franklin [American vice president of International Mercantile Marine] had not yet arrived at the office.

SENATOR SMITH: Can you give me the name of your informant?

MR. FARRELL: No, sir; I can not. Let me explain the relation of this. This was early in the morning. The early newspaper accounts had been published. There was a great crowd, and there was great excitement at the White Star offices. Dozens of newspaper men and also the relatives of passengers on the *Titanic* were all clamoring for information. In response to questions, this was the information given out by some of the representatives of the White Star Line. This particular information was not given by Mr. Franklin.

SENATOR SMITH: Did you make any attempt to verify it?

MR. FARRELL: Yes; we made every attempt we could.

SENATOR SMITH: What did you do?

MR. FARRELL: Then, subsequent to that, came the dispatch from Boston which you have just mentioned:

A dispatch from Halifax reports that all passengers had left the *Titanic* in boats shortly after 3:30 this morning.

SENATOR SMITH: Did you regard that as confirmatory?

MR. FARRELL: We did.

SENATOR SMITH: Did you talk with Mr. Franklin later in the day about the information you had gotten from his office at the time just referred to?

MR. FARRELL: We had reporters at the White Star offices all day long seeking information from Mr. Franklin and other officials, and the bulk of the news we published came from the White Star offices.

SENATOR SMITH: Did it come from Mr. Franklin?

MR. FARRELL: Most of it from Mr. Franklin; some of it from some of his subordinates.

SENATOR SMITH: I call your attention to a bulletin which we will designate as No. 3, 9:43 A.M., April 15 [reading]:

MONTREAL, *April 15.*

The Montreal Star to-day says that an unofficial dispatch from Halifax stated that word had been received there that the *Titanic* was still afloat and was making her way slowly toward Halifax.

Do you know anything about that?

MR. FARRELL: No, sir; I do not find such a dispatch in our

record here on our ticker tape. If the stenographer wi
note it, I will subsequently go over the bulletins.

SENATOR SMITH: I am quoting from the bulletins.

MR. FARRELL: From the bulletins?

SENATOR SMITH: Yes. That was from a bulletin. Have you g
them numbered?

MR. FARRELL: Yes.

SENATOR SMITH: What is that one you are looking at?

MR. FARRELL: This is No. 20. Is your memorandum nun
bered?

SENATOR SMITH: My memorandum starts with No. 1. What
have just read was from No. 3.

MR. FARRELL: We printed nothing about the *Titanic* o
bulletin No. 1. We printed nothing on bulletin No. 3—

SENATOR SMITH: Perhaps you will find under this Montrea
date this dispatch which I have just read.

MR. FARRELL: No, sir; I do not find that.

SENATOR SMITH: Do you find at 9:53 A.M. an optimisti
statement by Mr. Franklin in which he said, as will b
seen on page 2, which I have already quoted:

The *Olympic* has just been reported as having been i
direct communication by wireless with the *Titanic*.

MR. FARRELL: No; I do not find that either, Senator. Are yo
sure you have not got our bulletins confused with som
one else's?

SENATOR SMITH: No; I wanted to know about these tw
things. I have here your original memorandum, fro
which I will now read:

Titanic.—Dispatch from Montreal received by Whi
Star officials says *Titanic* was afloat at 8:30, and th
women and children had not yet been taken off, thoug
lifeboats were ready in case of emergency.

The steamship is heading in direction of Halifax, fro
which the *Virginian* is approaching. It is thought tha
bulkheads will prevent ship from sinking. *Titanic*
moving under her own engines.

This is dated 11:03 A.M., Monday, April 15.

MR. FARRELL: I think I recall such a dispatch as that.

SENATOR SMITH: This is your original note, I think.

MR. FARRELL: That is ours, yes; that is our tape.

464

SENATOR SMITH: I would like to ask where you got that information?

MR. FARRELL: I will tell you in just a moment. [After examining papers.] That previous one which you read was as follows:

White Star officials report *Olympic* was in communication with *Titanic* at 8:24 this morning, and *Titanic* was still afloat.

I find that on the record here. I received that from the Boston News Service.

SENATOR SMITH: Referring to the Montreal dispatch which I just read, where did you get that information?

MR. FARRELL (reading):

Dispatch from Montreal received by White Star officials says *Titanic* was afloat at 8:30 and that women and children had not yet been taken off, though lifeboats were ready in case of emergency.

The steamship is heading in direction of Halifax, from which the *Virginian* is approaching. It is thought that bulkheads will prevent ship from sinking. *Titanic* is moving under her own engines.

We received that from Mr. Franklin. Mr. Byrne, one of our reporters, got that from Mr. Franklin.

SENATOR SMITH: At the time indicated?

MR. FARRELL: Approximately; yes. Of course all these were rush stuff. It was telephoned into the office and slapped on the ticker as quickly as possible. We published it about 10:45.

SENATOR SMITH: Monday morning?

MR. FARRELL: Yes.

SENATOR SMITH: April 15?

MR. FARRELL: Yes.

SENATOR SMITH: I now call your attention to a bulletin of Monday, April 15. I am now reading from your original. It reads as follows:

10:49 A.M.—*Titanic.*—Montreal.—Wireless message received 10 o'clock this morning said that two vessels were standing by *Titanic* and that the big vessel's passengers had been taken off.

MR. FARRELL: That was published on our ticker tape; time 10:49. We received it from the Laffan News Bureau, New York.

SENATOR SMITH: Have you in your bulletin of April 15, at 12:07 P.M., the following:

The local office of Horton Davidson, one of the *Titanic* passengers, has received the following wireless message: "All passengers are safe and *Titanic* taken in tow by the *Virginian.*"

MR. FARRELL: What time was that, Senator Smith?

SENATOR SMITH: 12:07 P.M.

MR. FARRELL: No, sir; we have no dispatch on our ticker tape of that character at that time. At 12:12 we published this:

Wireless says *Titanic* is under way and proceeding to New York.

SENATOR SMITH: From whom did you receive that message?

MR. FARRELL: From the Laffan News Bureau, New York.

SENATOR SMITH: Have you a complete transcript or copy of news published by your company regarding the *Titanic* disaster, which you now hold in your hand?

MR. FARRELL: Not complete. I have the ticker tape in my hand.

SENATOR SMITH: And you have the bulletins?

MR. FARRELL: The bulletins we published contained some non-essential statements which did not appear on the ticker, but all of the important items appeared on the ticker.

SENATOR SMITH: I would like to have you read into the record that statement, and indicate, with each item of news quoted, the sources of your information.

MR. FARRELL: The first item we published was at approximately 8:10 A.M., April 15, as follows:

At 10:25 Sunday night new White Star liner *Titanic* called C. Q. D. [the pre-S.O.S. distress signal] and reported having struck an iceberg. Wireless received stated steamship needed immediate assistance as she was sinking at the bow.

Another message received half hour later reported the women were being put off in lifeboats. Marconi station at

466

Cape Race notified Allan Line steamship *Virginian*, which immediately headed for the *Titanic*. At midnight the *Virginian* was about 170 miles distant from the *Titanic* and expected to reach that vessel about 10 o'clock this morning. Steamship *Baltic* is headed toward the disaster, being 200 miles away at midnight.

Last word received from sinking *Titanic* was a wireless heard by the *Virginian* at 12:27. The operator on board the *Virginian* said these signals were blurred and ended abruptly.

Among those on board are J. J. Astor, J. Bruce Ismay, Benjamin Guggenheim, George B. Widener, and Isidor Straus.

You understand we begin business at 8 o'clock in the morning. This was a brief summary of what appeared in the morning papers, principally taken from the Herald.

SENATOR SMITH: Some of that information, however, you obtained direct from the White Star office—that to which I have previously called your attention?

MR. FARRELL: I believe that one of our men, about 7:30 in the morning, went to the White Star office and got some information there, but as I recall it, he did not get much additional to what had been published in the morning papers. The Herald, the Times, and some of the other papers had rather complete accounts of it up to that time.

At 8:25 or thereabouts, in what we call our summary, which consists of the important developments over night, taken from various sources——

SENATOR SMITH: That was on April 15?

MR. FARRELL: Yes; we printed this line:

White Star Liner *Titanic*, on maiden westward voyage, hit by iceberg and reported to be sinking. Passengers being taken off.

That was taken from the general news which appeared in the morning papers.

At 8:35, or approximately that time, April 15, we published the following:

Officers of White Star Line stated at 8 o'clock this morning that passengers on the *Titanic* were being taken off in boats and that there was no danger of loss of life. The *Baltic* and the *Virginian* they stated were standing by to assist in the rescue work.

On *Titanic* there were 300 first class, 320 second class, 800 third class passengers, and a crew of 900 men.

It is not yet known whether the vessel will be saved. White Star people are in something of a quandary if she should be saved, as it is said there is no dry dock on this side of the Atlantic to take care of her.

That was obtained by Mr. Gingold, one of our reporters, from the White Star office.

SENATOR SMITH: From Mr. Franklin?

MR. FARRELL: No; this was not from Mr. Franklin.

SENATOR SMITH: From some other of the subordinates?

MR. FARRELL: From some of the junior officers or employees. Mr. Franklin had not yet arrived at his office.

At 8:58, or thereabouts, on April 15, we published the following:

A dispatch from Halifax reports that all passengers had left the *Titanic* in boats shortly after 3:30 this morning.

That was received from the Boston News Bureau, our Boston correspondent.

At 9:02 A.M., April 15, we published the following:

An official of White Star Line said: "There is no danger that *Titanic* will sink. The boat is unsinkable, and nothing but inconvenience will be suffered by the passengers."

Latest information which has come to White Star office is that the *Virginian* is due alongside the *Titanic* at 10 A.M., the *Olympic* at 3 P.M., and the *Baltic* at 4 P.M.

That was obtained from Mr. Franklin by two of our reporters, Mr. Smallwood and Mr. Byrne, who both saw him at the time.

At 9:22 A.M., or thereabouts, April 15, we published the following:

Vice President Franklin, of International Mercantile Marine, says, regarding reported accident to *Titanic*: "I is unbelievable that *Titanic* could have met with accident without our being notified. We had a wireless from her late Sunday giving her position, and are absolutely satisfied that if she had been in collision with an iceberg we should have heard from her at once. In any event, the ship is unsinkable, and there is absolutely no danger to passengers."

That was received from Mr. Franklin by Mr. Trebell, one of our reporters.

At 9:25 A.M., April 15, we published the following:

CAPE RACE.

Wireless advices from steamship *Virginian* said last word from wireless telegrapher on *Titanic* was received at 3:05 o'clock this morning. He said women and children were being taken off in calm sea. It is thought that *Titanic* wireless has failed, due to some local cause.

That was received from the Laffan News Bureau, of New York.

At 9:27 we published the following:

LONDON.

Lloyd's were . . . reinsuring *Titanic's* cargo to-day, but demanding premium of 50 per cent.

That was received from the Laffan News Bureau.

SENATOR SMITH: At what hour?

MR. FARRELL: We published it at 9:47; so it was a few minutes before that that it came in.

SENATOR SMITH: Did you make any attempt to verify the Laffan News Bureau item that an attempt was being made to reinsure the cargo with Lloyd's?

MR. FARRELL: No.

SENATOR SMITH: Did you send one of your reporters to Lloyd's, after receiving this information, where he had an interview with the representative of that firm?

MR. FARRELL: I am not sure but that a reporter may have gone to Lloyd's. Personally I did not send any, but of course the reporter may have gone on his own initiative.

SENATOR SMITH: Do you know what he ascertained the fact to be?

MR. FARRELL: No; I do not.

SENATOR SMITH: Did he ever report to you?

MR. FARRELL: Not to my recollection.

SENATOR SMITH: I wish you would think rather carefully about this, because I do not want any mistake about it.

MR. FARRELL: I do not recollect any reports having been made to me about the result of any investigation.

SENATOR SMITH: Or to anyone else in your company or to any other officer of your company?

MR. FARRELL: There might have been; but I could not say definitely as to that.

SENATOR SMITH: It was the subject of some speculation and conversation in your office, was it not?

MR. FARRELL: Yes; it was.

SENATOR SMITH: And was regarded as rather an unusual circumstance in connection——

MR. FARRELL: At that time it was not regarded as so unusual, because of our information that the boat was unsinkable; and we believed that she was not going to go down.

SENATOR SMITH: Subsequently it became rather important?

MR. FARRELL: Subsequently it became very important.

SENATOR SMITH: Have you taken any pains to ascertain the truthfulness of that publication?

MR. FARRELL: I do not recollect any specific inquiry which we made regarding that.

SENATOR SMITH: Did you make any general inquiry of any representative of Lloyd's or the White Star Line regarding it?

MR. FARRELL: We made inquiries, as I recall, from the White Star Line.

SENATOR SMITH: When?

MR. FARRELL: I do not recall whether we published anything about it or not, but the other newspapers had had, as I recall, emphatic statements from the White Star Line that they had made no attempt to reinsure or anything of that sort; and of course it was our custom, where all the other papers had something, to let it go at that.

SENATOR SMITH: In Wall Street, where your Journal is supposed to reflect the opinion of financiers, that item was calculated to create considerable controversy, was it not?

MR. FARRELL: Much controversy subsequently did arise on that item.

SENATOR SMITH: Were you criticized or threatened for publishing that reinsurance story?

MR. FARRELL: Not to my knowledge. Any criticism of a serious nature certainly would come to my knowledge. I would be the one to whom it should be made.

SENATOR SMITH: Have you since been criticized for it?

MR. FARRELL: Not directly. We have received no direct criticism. There may have been talk, but no direct criticism has come to my knowledge.

SENATOR SMITH: Where is the office of Lloyd's in New York?

MR. FARRELL: I really do not know where their agent is in New York.

SENATOR SMITH: It is in Wall Street, is it not?

MR. FARRELL: Some place in that neighborhood. I do not know where their New York office is.

SENATOR SMITH: Where is your own office in New York?

MR. FARRELL: At No. 44 Broad Street.

SENATOR SMITH: In the center of the financial district?

MR. FARRELL: Yes; approximately.

SENATOR SMITH: It would have been rather easy to have sent some one to the office of Lloyd's that morning, would it not, to have ascertained that important fact?

MR. FARRELL: It would; but that morning we were working under tremendous pressure, and every man we had was bent on getting the news as to what was likely to happen to the *Titanic*, and at the time we considered the matter of reinsurance a relatively unimportant matter.

SENATOR SMITH: That is, you thought at the time that it was a rather desirable hazard?

MR. FARRELL: Yes; we thought Lloyd's were willing to gamble on it. They wanted a high premium, but were willing to gamble, nevertheless.

SENATOR SMITH: But from your own knowledge, or from any information you have received from your associates in the publication of the Wall Street Journal, you do not know whether this was proposed or consummated or not?

MR. FARRELL: I do not; no.

SENATOR SMITH: Is there any officer or stockholder of your company who is also a stockholder or officer of the White Star Line?

MR. FARRELL: No, sir.

SENATOR SMITH: Or of Lloyd's?

MR. FARRELL: No.

SENATOR SMITH: Or of the Western Union Co., of the Postal Telegraph Co., of the Marconi companies, or the cable companies?

MR. FARRELL: I could not say as to that. I know none of them are officers or directors, I believe. Some of them may own 10 or 100 shares of stock in those companies, but not enough to be of any consequence. In ordinary investments a man might own almost anything, probably, but they have no official connection.

SENATOR SMITH: Can you give the name of any stockholder——

MR. FARRELL: No; I could not give any names. We have some 70 or 80 or 100 men—I guess, more than that—in our employ, and some of them may have taken some Western Union stock as an investment, or some Postal Telegraph stock or Marconi stock as an investment. That is none of our business. They are private investments.

SENATOR SMITH: Proceed with your reading of the messages.

MR. FARRELL: At 9:28 A.M., or thereabouts, we published this item.

SENATOR SMITH: I am going to assume, Mr. Farrell, that when you state the time as 9:28, or any other time, you are now speaking of the 15th of April?

MR. FARRELL: Oh, yes; April 15.

SENATOR SMITH: And that when you get beyond the 15th you will indicate that fact?

MR. FARRELL: Yes. At 9:28 A.M. on April 15 we published the following:

Additional passengers on *Titanic* are Washington Dodge, Henry H. Harris, Col. Washington Roebling, T. Stead, Alfred G. Vanderbilt, J. Stuart White, John B. Thayer, vice president of the Pennsylvania Railroad, and Henry Harper.

That was obtained from the passenger list.

At 10:29, or thereabouts, on April 15, we published the following:

STASCONSET, MASS.

Wireless station here early to-day got message from S. S. *Olympic* stating damage to *Titanic* was great.

That was received from the Boston News Bureau. Directly afterwards we published the following:

White Star officials report *Olympic* was in communication with *Titanic* at 4:24 this morning, when *Titanic* was still afloat.

That also came from the Boston News Bureau.

At 10:45, or thereabouts, on April 15, we published the following:

Dispatch from Montreal received by White Star officials says *Titanic* was afloat at 8:30 and that women and children had not yet been taken off, though lifeboats were ready in case of emergency.

The steamship is heading in direction of Halifax, from which the *Virginian* is approaching. It is thought that bulkheads will prevent ship from sinking. *Titanic* is moving under her own engines.

That was received from Mr. Franklin by Mr. Byrne, one of our reporters.

At 10:49 or thereabouts, on April 15, we published the following:

MONTREAL

Wireless message received 10 o'clock this morning said that two vessels were standing by *Titanic* and the big vessel's passengers had been taken off.

That was received from the Laffan News Bureau.

About 10:53, I should think, we published the following:

Possibility of losing *Titanic* is severe blow to International Mercantile Marine. Like its sister ship, the *Olympic*, the *Titanic* started in with a run of hard luck. However, this loss will not be shown in forthcoming annual report, to be issued in June, as company's year closed December 31. It is expected that Mercantile Marine will earn about $38,000,000 for year ended December 31 last, a net of about $8,500,000 and final surplus of about $4,500,000. However, it is expected company will write off at least $3,500,000 of this amount for depreciation, leaving about $1,000,000 surplus for year.

473

Both the *Titanic* and *Olympic* are fully covered by a combination of company and outside insurance.

Of course, that had no direct bearing on the *Titanic*.

SENATOR SMITH: From whom did you get that information?

MR. FARRELL: That was written, I believe, by Mr. Trebell. I do not know where he got that information. Of course, it had nothing to do with the disaster.

SENATOR SMITH: I would like, if you could get it, to know the source of that information, whether it was official or was from some other news agency.

MR. FARRELL: We did not receive it from any other news agency. This may have been his estimate, you know. Of course, our reporters are supposed to keep very close track of the earnings of these various companies, and frequently they are able of their own knowledge to make an estimate without official information.

SENATOR SMITH: Then you think this information was probably put together in your office?

MR. FARRELL: Yes; I know it was put together in our office.

SENATOR SMITH: In the item which you read just preceding that, I did not catch the expression, "Women and children had not yet been taken off, though lifeboats were ready in case of emergency." Was that in there?

MR. FARRELL: That was not on the ticker tape in that message.

SENATOR SMITH: It is in your original memorandum.

MR. FARRELL: It may be on the bulletin.

SENATOR SMITH: It is in your original memorandum.

MR. FARRELL: I was looking at the wrong one, I see. Yes; it is here [indicating].

At 10:55, or thereabouts, on April 15, we published the following:

A wireless message to White Star Line office states that the *Virginian* is now alongside the *Titanic*.

That was received from the Laffan News Bureau.

At 11:12 A.M., or thereabouts, on April 15, we published the following:

P. A. S. Franklin, of International Mercantile Marine, says:

"We can not state too strongly our belief that the ship is

474

unsinkable and passengers perfectly safe. The ship is reported to have gone down several feet by the head. This may be due from water filling forward compartments, and ship may go down many feet by the head and still keep afloat for an indefinite period."

Interruption of wireless communication with the ship, according to company officials, does not indicate danger.

That was received from Mr. Franklin by Mr. Byrne and Mr. Smallwood, two of our reporters.

At 11:15 A.M., on April 15, we published the following:

LONDON.

Information given out here states *Titanic* carried about $5,000,000 in bonds and diamonds.

That was received from the Laffan News Service.

At 11:25 A.M., on April 15, we published the following:

Dispatch received at White Star offices from Capt. Haddock, of steamship *Olympic,* says that both the *Parisian* and *Carpathia* are in attendance on the *Titanic*. *Carpathia* has taken off 20 boatloads of passengers. The *Baltic* is expected on the scene shortly.

That was received from Mr. Franklin by Mr. Byrne, one of our reporters, and substantially the same message at practically the same hour was received from Mr. Bottomley, an official of the Marconi Co., by Mr. Smallwood, one of our reporters.

At 12:12 P.M., or thereabouts, on April 15, we published the following:

The Sandy Hook marine operator received the following wireless on his machine at 11:22 o'clock this morning:

"Wireless says *Titanic* is under way and proceeding to New York."

That came from the Laffan News Bureau.

At 3:01 P.M., April 15, we published the following:

P. A. S. Franklin, vice president International Mercantile Marine, says arrangements have been made with New Haven road to send special train to Halifax to meet passengers of the *Titanic*. Train will consist of 23 sleepers, 2 diners, and coaches sufficient for 710 people.

That was received by Mr. Byrne, one of our reporters, from Mr. Franklin.

SENATOR SMITH: That was at what hour?

MR. FARRELL: One minute past 8 o'clock P.M.

SENATOR SMITH: On Monday?

MR. FARRELL: April 15; yes.

SENATOR SMITH: You say this information came from Mr. Franklin?

MR. FARRELL: Yes, sir.

SENATOR SMITH: Directly to one of your reporters?

MR. FARRELL: Yes.

SENATOR SMITH: That would seem to indicate that he had at that time absolute information as to the loss of the *Titanic* and the survival of only about 700 passengers from the ship's people, passengers and crew?

MR. FARRELL: Taken at the face value, the statement would seem to indicate that, but I will explain to you later what the White Star people explained to me the following day.

SENATOR SMITH: Let us get this just right. This is a direct statement from Mr. Franklin, on Monday afternoon following the accident, that arrangements had been made for the survivors, indicating that he had some information——

MR. FARRELL: I would not want you to put that in my mouth, Senator, because——

SENATOR SMITH: No; I am just construing this, by way of asking you a question.

That would indicate that he had some information upon which he based the necessity for caring for about 700 people. What did you publish after that?

MR. FARRELL: About 3:15 P.M. or thereabouts, on April 15, we published the following:

CARSO, NOVA SCOTIA.

At 2 o'clock the *Titanic*, having transferred her passengers to the *Parisian* and *Carpathia*, was being towed to Halifax by the *Virginian*.

That came to us from the Laffan News Bureau.

SENATOR SMITH: Of course, Mr. Farrell, you note the inconsistency between that news item and the one that just precedes it?

MR. FARRELL: Yes.

SENATOR SMITH: If her passengers had been transferred, as that last item would seem to suggest, there would be two thousand and odd passengers, while the only provision in the former item was for 700 survivors. Between the time of the publication of that information from Mr. Franklin and the publication of the last item to which you have referred, did you have any personal talk with Mr. Franklin?

MR. FARRELL: I did not.

SENATOR SMITH: What was the time of that item?

MR. FARRELL: 3:15 o'clock.

SENATOR SMITH: And that came from the Laffan News Bureau?

MR. FARRELL: Yes. That is all we published in our news ticker on April 15 concerning this accident.

SENATOR SMITH: Do your bulletins for that day and the days following, up to the time of the arrival of the *Carpathia,* contain substantially the same information?

MR. FARRELL: The bulletins contain substantially the same information.

SENATOR SMITH: As that contained on the ticker tape?

MR. FARRELL: As that contained on the ticker tape; yes.

SENATOR SMITH: Of Monday?

MR. FARRELL: Yes.

SENATOR SMITH: Do you call that the ticker tape?

MR. FARRELL: Yes.

SENATOR SMITH: That is the ticker tape of Monday?

MR. FARRELL: Yes.

SENATOR SMITH: And the same would be reflected in the bulletins of the succeeding days?

MR. FARRELL: Only the story was entirely changed on the succeeding days when we got it. . . .

SENATOR SMITH: Let us see what you have for Tuesday and Wednesday. Had we better go through the bulletins for that day, or have you compared them?

MR. FARRELL: It is substantially the same stuff. All the important stuff appeared on the ticker also.

SENATOR SMITH: Can you let me see the bulletins of Monday?

MR. FARRELL: Yes. Of course, we have the full list, and I picked out the particular stuff pertaining to the *Titanic.*

SENATOR SMITH: Let me ask what the effect was, upon the

stock of the International Mercantile Marine Co., of the information published in the Wall Street Journal on Monday?

MR. FARRELL: As I remember it, the stock declined about two points. I think we have a record of it in the bulletins here. I am quite sure we have.

SENATOR SMITH: If you can give that accurately, I would like to have it.

MR. FARRELL: I know that from time to time during the day we published it. Here it is: International Mercantile Marine; common 2,100 shares were dealt in; opened at $6 a share. The high was $6; the low was $5.50; the close was $6.

SENATOR SMITH: That was on Monday?

MR. FARRELL: Yes; there was no net change.

The preferred opened at 20, rose to 23⅛, and closed at 23⅛. That was off seven-eighths for the day, net.

SENATOR SMITH: What time does that indicate that the exchange opened?

MR. FARRELL: Ten o'clock. The movements occurred between 10 A.M. and 3 P.M., so that there was that substantial change in the market value.

SENATOR SMITH: I take it from the publication which you manage that you are somewhat familiar with the movements of stocks.

MR. FARRELL: Yes, sir.

SENATOR SMITH: What, in your opinion, was the effect upon the market value of the stock, both preferred and common, of the International Mercantile Marine Co., of the reports printed in the Wall Street Journal and upon your bulletins and ticker tape that day, giving assurance of the safety of the *Titanic*?

MR. FARRELL: There was, you might say, virtually no market influence, because the trading was very light, and, as I just pointed out, the net change in the trades for the day on the preferred was only seven-eighths down and there was no net change for the common. At one time the preferred was down about three points. It was down about three points from the previous day's close and then recovered. The transactions were comparatively light and it really seemed to have very little market.

SENATOR SMITH: Suppose you had printed on that day the information that was obtained that day by Mr. Franklin, of the White Star Co., over the telephone from Montreal at 2:30 o'clock Monday morning, indicating that the *Titanic* was sinking and had not bolstered up the unfavorable news by the optimistic reports which your ticker and bulletin indicate, what, in your opinion, would have been the effect?

MR. FARRELL: Probably about the same, because after the full extent of the case became known the Mercantile Marine market price changed very little.

SENATOR SMITH: Of course it was filtered out so slowly that the actual loss of the *Titanic* was not fully known to the public for two days——

MR. FARRELL: It was known the next day, Tuesday.

SENATOR SMITH (continuing): After the accident occurred?

MR. FARRELL: Yes.

SENATOR SMITH: That would have a tendency to strengthen the market somewhat, would it not?

MR. FARRELL: It might have. A sudden and unexpected shock sometimes has more effect on the market than the same shock for which the market has been prepared.

SENATOR SMITH: But notwithstanding the belated news, the preferred stock of the International Mercantile Marine Co. went off on Monday about seven points?

MR. FARRELL: No.

SENATOR SMITH: How much?

MR. FARRELL: I think the maximum decline was about three points, all of which, except seven-eighths, had been recovered before the close, as I recall it. Maybe I can give that exactly here.

SENATOR SMITH: What I am seeking to show, which of course you can see very readily, is the effect of these false reports that were being constantly sent broadcast, through your paper and your ticker and your bulletins——and not alone by you——

MR. FARRELL: And by others.

SENATOR SMITH (continuing): But also by others——on the market for this company's shares. I would like to have you help me as much as you can with any information you have there.

MR. FARRELL: The comparatively small trading in the shares showed clearly enough that there was no suppression of news for market purposes, I should judge.

SENATOR SMITH: Although it might have operated to affect the market that way? That might, however, have been the effect of the course pursued, whether intentional or otherwise?

MR. FARRELL: That might have been the effect on a more active stock than International Mercantile Marine, and one more widely distributed. But, you understand, Mercantile Marine is a very inactive stock.

SENATOR SMITH: It is closely held?

MR. FARRELL: It is closely held, and never has been widely distributed, so far as I have been able to learn.

SENATOR SMITH: I suppose you would like to be understood as saying that the loss of the single ship, quite fully insured, would not necessarily break the price of the stock very much?

MR. FARRELL: Exactly; yes. You see, the ship cost about $8,000,000; I believe it was insured for something like $5,000,000 or $6,000,000; and the net loss might be $2,000,000 to $3,000,000, which would not break a company like the International Mercantile Marine Co., or ought not to do so, at any rate. . . .

SENATOR SMITH: Mr. Farrell, the bulletins which you have handed me are all that contain news items regarding the *Titanic*, which items appeared on the ticker?

MR. FARRELL: I think, Senator, there is one item—one bulletin—which we lost. This item which appears on the ticker, and which has already been incorporated in the record, was on one bulletin which was lost, somehow or other:

Officers of the White Star Line stated at 8 o'clock this morning that passengers of the *Titanic* were being taken off in boats and that there was no danger of loss of life. The *Baltic* and the *Virginian*, they said, were standing by to assist in the rescue.

Substantially the same thing was published in the bulletin.

SENATOR SMITH: In all other respects these bulletins which you have handed to the committee contain all the information that appeared on the ticker and, I assume, in the Wall Street Journal as well?

MR. FARRELL: Yes.

SENATOR SMITH: Regarding the *Titanic?*

MR. FARRELL: They contain more than appeared in the Wall Street Journal, because in making up the Wall Street Journal we rewrote the statement, partially, so as to make it more readable. . . .

THE STATEMENT SUBMITTED BY MR. FARRELL.

Maurice I. Farrell, managing news editor of Dow, Jones & Co., news agency, of New York, made the following statement to the Senate subcommittee investigating the *Titanic* disaster:

Reports published by Dow, Jones & Co. on Monday, April 15, regarding the *Titanic* disaster came chiefly from three sources—office of the White Star Line, the Laffan News Bureau, and the Boston News Bureau. At 8 A.M. on that day, upon interviewing representatives of the White Star Line in their New York office, a reporter received information which was summarized on the Dow, Jones & Co. news tickers as follows:

"Officers of the White Star Line stated at 8 o'clock this morning that passengers on the *Titanic* were being taken off in boats and that there was no danger of loss of life. The *Baltic* and the *Virginian*, they stated, were standing by to assist in the rescue."

On account of a misconstruction of the expression "standing by," this item may have given rise to subsequent erroneous reports. To the lay mind "standing by" conveyed the meaning that the vessels were in the immediate vicinity, holding themselves in readiness to render aid. Its use, however, appears to have been in the technical sense, indicating that the vessels had received the C. Q. D., responded to it, and had headed their course toward the *Titanic*. The expression used in its nautical sense meant response to direction or the setting a course toward, rather than being in the immediate presence of the *Titanic*.

The statement was cabled to London, and later in the day at least two dispatches of similar purport, but different verbiage, were received from different quarters, and may have represented merely a return of the same report from other parts of the world. In New York they were at the time taken as confirming the earlier statement made at the White

Star office. No one was willing to believe, and, in fact, at the time could believe, that the *Titanic* had sunk. Every scrap of what purported to be news indicating safety of the passengers was seized with avidity and rushed by telephone, telegraph, or cable to all parts of America and Europe. This process doubtless entailed duplication of the same messages flying back and forth, which was erroneously construed as confirmatory evidence.

As an example of the misunderstandings arising, I am informed that the White Star office at Boston called up the Allen Line in Montreal by telephone to get confirmation of a report that all *Titanic* passengers were transferred to the *Virginian* and the *Titanic* was proceeding to Halifax under her own steam. The Allen Line replied that they had such a statement, meaning that they had heard such a report. The White Star Boston office took this as substantiating the rumor, and accordingly called up the White Star office in New York confirming the message to Vice President Franklin. Doubtless many similar cases of unintentional errors occurred in the same way, the chances of error, of course, being increased as the reports went through different channels. . . .

Affidavit: A. H. Weikman
Barber on the *Titanic*

Key testimony: He saved himself by swimming to deck chairs. In his affidavit, the questions apparently posed to him by investigators were run together with his recollections and filed as one statement.

SENATOR SMITH: I . . . received the following affidavit made by A. H. Weikman, who was a barber on the *Titanic*, which covers his observations:

APRIL 24, 1912.

MR. A. H. WEIKMAN:

I certify that my occupation on the *Titanic* was known as the saloon barber. I was sitting in my barber shop on Sunday night, April 14, 1912, at 11:40 P.M., when the collision occurred. I went forward to the steerage on "G" deck and saw one of the baggage-masters, and he told me that water was coming in in the baggage room on the deck below. I think the baggageman's name was Bessant. I then went upstairs and met Mr. Andrews, the "builder," and he was giving instructions to get the steerage passengers "on deck." I proceeded along "E" deck to my room on "C" deck. I went on the main deck and saw some ice laying there. Orders were given, "All hands to man the lifeboats, also to put on life belts." Who gave the orders? "Mr. Dodd, second steward."

I helped to launch the boats, and there seemed to be a shortage of women. When I was on "E" deck I met the captain returning from "G" deck, who had been there with Mr. Andrews, and the captain was on the bridge at that time. I did not think there was any danger. What happened after the orders were given? Instructions were given to get the passengers into life belts and get on deck from all the staterooms. Did you see Mr. Ismay? Yes. I saw Mr. Ismay helping to load the boats. Did you see him get in a boat? Yes; he got in along with Mr. Carter, because there were no women in the vicinity of the boat. This boat was the last to leave, to the best of my knowledge. He was ordered into the boat by the officer in charge. I think that Mr. Ismay was justified in leaving in that boat at that time.

I was proceeding to launch the next boat when the ship suddenly sank at the bow and there was a rush of water that washed me overboard, and therefore the boat was not launched by human hands. The men were trying to pull up the sides when the rush of water came, and that was the last moment it was possible to launch any more boats, because the ship was at an angle that it was impossible for anybody to remain on deck. State further what you know about the case. After I was washed overboard I started to swim, when there was a pile of ropes fell upon me, and I managed to get clear of these and started to swim for some dark object in the water. It was dark. This was about 1:50 A.M., toward the stern. How do you know it was 1:50 A.M.? Because my watch was stopped at that time by the water. Did you hear any noise? Yes; I was about 15 feet away from the ship when I heard a second explosion. What caused the explosion? I think the boilers blew up about in the middle of the ship. The explosion blew me along with a wall of water toward the dark object I was swimming to, which proved to be a bundle of deck chairs, which I managed to climb on. While on the chairs I heard terrible groans and cries coming from people in the water. Was it possible to help them? No; it was not. The lifeboats were too far away. Do you think if the lifeboats were nearer they could render any assistance? Yes; had the lifeboats remained close to the *Titanic* they could have taken 10 to 15 or maybe 20 more passengers in each boat. There was a great number of people killed by the explosion, and there was a great number that managed to get far enough away that the explosion did not injure them, and these are the people that I think could have been saved had the lifeboats been closer. Did you see the ship go down? I mean the *Titanic*. Yes; I was afloat on some chairs about 100 feet away, looking toward the ship. I seen her sink. Did you feel any suction? No; but there was some waves come toward me caused by the ship going down, and not enough to knock me off of the chairs. How many lifeboats were there on the *Titanic?* About 18 or 20 and four collapsible boats, and the best equipment possible to put on a ship. Do you think there was enough lifeboats? No. Do you know anything about the water-tight doors? Yes; she had self-closing doors of the latest type, and they all worked, to the best of my knowledge. How fast was she going when she struck the iceberg? I think about 20 knots per hour. I was told by Mr. Ismay that she was limited to 75 revolutions several days before.

A. H. Weikman.

Affidavit: Harold Godfrey Lowe
Fifth Officer

Key testimony: Under Italian pressure, he retracts an earlier disparaging remark about Italians.

Senator Smith: I have also a statement from Officer Lowe, of the *Titanic*, which I have been requested to put into the record. This comes to me through the Italian ambassador and contains an explanation by Mr. Lowe of the testimony which he gave that he fired his gun, as his boat was being lowered into the water, because of the glaring eyes of Italian immigrants, who he was afraid menaced his safety in lowering the lifeboat. Mr. Lowe wants this statement to go into the record, and the Italian ambassador wants it to go in.

The statement referred to is as follows:

This is to certify that I, Harold Godfrey Lowe . . . fifth officer of the late steamship *Titanic*, in my testimony at the Senate of the United States stated that I fired shots to prevent Italian immigrants from jumping into my lifeboat.

I do hereby cancel the word "Italian" and substitute the words "immigrants belonging to Latin races." In fact, I did not mean to infer that they were especially Italians, because I could only judge from their general appearance and complexion, and therefore I only meant to imply that they were of the types of the Latin races. In any case, I did not intend to cast any reflection on the Italian nation.

This is the real truth, and therefore I feel honored to give out the present statement.

H.G. LOWE,
Fifth Officer late "Titanic."
WASHINGTON, D. C., *April 30, 1912.*

[On the reverse.]

The declaration on the other side was made and confirmed this day by Harold Godfrey Lowe, fifth officer of the late steamship *Titanic*, in my presence and in the presence of Signor Guido di Vincenzo, secretary of the legal office of the royal embassy.

Washington, this 30th day of April, 1912.

The Royal Ambassador of Italy,
CUSANI.

[Seal]

THE SECRETARY OF THE LEGAL OFFICE OF THE ROYAL
EMBASSY, G. DI. VINCENZO.

Affidavit: Mahala D. Douglas
First-class passenger, from Minneapolis

Key testimony: She quotes Emily Ryerson of Philadelphia as saying aboard the Carpathia *(just as she was later quoted in*

485

the press) that Ismay had dismissed an ice warning with
vow to speed up the ship. Yet, curiously, in Mrs. Ryerson
sworn affidavit filed on Day 15 of the hearings, she makes
mention of any such encounter with Ismay.

SENATOR SMITH: I have also an affidavit, filed at my reques
of Mrs. Mahala D. Douglas, of Minneapolis, Minn.
interrogated Mrs. Douglas in New York after the arriv
of the *Carpathia.* Her grief was so great over the loss
her husband that I concluded not to attempt to take h
testimony at that time. On the 2d day of May, at n
request, she made an affidavit, and I present it for tl
record. Her husband's name was Walter D. Douglas, b
she has signed the affidavit as Mahala D. Douglas.

The affidavit of Mrs. Douglas is as follows:

We left Cherbourg late on account of trouble at Sout
ampton, but once off, everything seemed to go perfectl
The boat was so luxurious, so steady, so immense, and su
a marvel of mechanism that one could not believe he was
a boat—and there the danger lay. We had smooth se
clear, starlit nights, fresh favoring winds; nothing to m
our pleasure.

On Saturday, as Mr. Douglas and I were walking forwar
we saw a seaman taking the temperature of the water. Tl
deck seemed so high above the sea I was interested to kno
if the tiny pail could reach it. There was quite a breeze, ar
although the pail was weighted, it did not. This I watch
from the open window of the covered deck. Drawing up t
pail the seaman filled it with water from the stand pip
placed the thermometer in it, and went with it to the offic
in charge.

On Sunday we had a delightful day; everyone in the be
of spirits; the time the boat was making was consider
very good, and all were interested in getting into New Yo
early. We dined in the restaurant, going in about
o'clock. . . .

As far as I have been able to learn, not a man in th
room; all those who served, from the head steward dov
including Mr. Gattie, in charge; the musicians who play
in the corridor outside, and all the guests were lost exce
Sir Cosmo Gordon Duff, Mr. [William] Carter, and N

Ismay. All stories of excessive gaiety are, to my mind, absolutely unfounded. We did not leave the tables until most of the others had left, including Mr. Ismay, Mr. and Mrs. [Harry] Widener, and their guests, and the evening was passed very quietly. As we went to our stateroom . . . we both remarked that the boat was going faster than she ever had. The vibration as one passed the stairway in the center was very noticeable. The shock of the collision was not great to us; the engines stopped, then went on for a few moments, then stopped again. We waited some little time. Mr. Douglas reassuring me that there was no danger before going out of the cabin. But later Mr. Douglas went out to see what had happened, and I put on my heavy boots and fur coat to go up on deck later. I waited in the corridor to see or hear what I could. We received no orders; no one knocked at our door; we saw no officers nor stewards—no one to give an order or answer our questions. As I waited for Mr. Douglas to return I went back to speak to my maid, who was in the same cabin as Mrs. Carter's maid. Now people commenced to appear with life preservers, and I heard from some one that the order had been given to put them on. I took three from our cabin, gave one to the maid, telling her to get off in the small boat when her turn came. Mr. Douglas met me as I was going up to find him and asked, jestingly, what I was doing with those life preservers. He did not think even then that the accident was serious. We both put them on, however, and went up on the boat deck. Mr. Douglas told me if I waited we might both go together, and we stood there waiting. We heard that the boat was in communication with three other boats by wireless: we watched the distress rockets sent off—they rose high in the air and burst.

No one seemed excited. Finally, as we stood by a collapsible boat lying on the deck and an emergency boat swinging from the davits was being filled, it was decided I should go. Mr. Boxhall was trying to get the boat off, and called to the captain on the bridge, "There's a boat coming up over here." The captain said, "I want a megaphone." Just before we got into the boat the captain called, "How many of the crew are in that boat? Get out of there, every man of you"; and I can see a solid row of men, from bow to stern, crawl over on to the deck. We women then got in. I asked Mr.

Douglas to come with me, but he replied, "No; I must be a gentleman," turning away. I said, "Try and get off with Mr. Moore and Maj. [Archibald] Butt [President Taft's aide]. They will surely make it." Maj. Butt and Clarence Moore were standing together near us, also Mr. Meyer, and I remember seeing Mr. Ryerson's face in the crowd. There were many people about. I got into the boat and sat under the seats on the bottom, just under the tiller. Mr. Boxhall had difficulty about getting the boat loose and called for a knife. We finally were launched. . . . The rowing was very difficult, for no one knew how. I tried to steer, under Mr. Boxhall's orders, and he put the lantern—an old one, with very little light in it—on a pole which I held up for some time. Mr. Boxhall got away from the ship and we stopped for a time. Several times we stopped rowing to listen for the lapping of the water against the icebergs. In an incredibly short space of time, it seemed to me, the boat sank. I heard no explosion. I watched the boat go down, and the last picture to my mind is the immense mass of black against the star-lit sky, and then—nothingness.

Mrs. Appleton and some of the other women had been rowing and did row all of the time. Mr. Boxhall had charge of the signal lights on the *Titanic*, and he had put in the emergency boat a tin box of green lights, like rockets. These he commenced to send off at intervals, and very quickly we saw the lights of the *Carpathia*, the captain of which stated he saw our green lights 10 miles away, and, of course, steered directly to us, so we were the first boat to arrive at the *Carpathia*.

When we pulled alongside Mr. Boxhall called out, "Shut down your engines and take us aboard. I have only one sailor." At this point I called out, "The *Titanic* has gone down with everyone on board," and Mr. Boxhall told me to "shut up." This is not told in criticism; I think he was perfectly right. We climbed a rope ladder to the upper deck of the *Carpathia*. I at once asked the chief steward, who met us, to take the news to the captain. He said the officer was already with him.

The history of our wonderful treatment on the *Carpathia* is known to the world. It has been underestimated.

We reached the *Carpathia* at 4:10, and I believe by 10 o'clock all of the boats had been accounted for. We sailed away, leaving the *Californian* to cruise about the scene. We circled the point where the *Titanic* had gone down, and I saw nothing except quantities of cork, loose cork floating in the current, like a stream—nothing else.

In the afternoon I sent a brief Marconigram with the news that Mr. Douglas was among the missing. I went myself to the purser several times every day, and others also made inquiries for me in regard to it, but it was not sent.

We heard many stories of the rescue from many sources. These I tried to keep in my mind clearly, as they seemed important. Among them I will quote Mrs. Ryerson, of Philadelphia. This story was told in the presence of Mrs. Meyers, of New York, and others.

(Mrs. Ryerson speaking.) "Sunday afternoon Mr. Ismay, whom I know very slightly, passed me on the deck. He showed me, in his brusque manner, a Marconigram, saying, 'We have just had news that we are in the icebergs.' 'Of course, you will slow down,' I said. 'Oh, no,' he replied, 'we will put on more boilers and get out of it.'"

An Englishwoman, who was going to her sons in Dakota, told me: "I was in a boat with 5 women and 50 men—they had been picked up from London unemployed to fill out the crew. They would not row, told frightful stories to alarm the women, and when the *Carpathia* was sighted, said: 'We are jolly lucky. No work to-night; nothing to do but smoke and yarn. Back in London next week with the unemployed.'"

The history of the quartermaster's conduct was told by many women; his brutality is known. His inefficiency is shown by his asking "Is that a buoy?" when they were out in the small boat on the ocean. . . .

All the women told of insufficient seamen to man the boats; all women rowed; some had to bail water from their boats. Mrs. Smith was told to watch a cork in her boat, and if it came out to put her finger in place of it.

When we arrived in New York the crew of the *Titanic* was ordered to get off in the lifeboats before we could dock.

I sat in a deck chair and listened and looked. The unseamanlike way of going at their simple tasks without excitement showed me more plainly than anything I had seen or heard the inefficiency of the crew, and accounted, in some measure, for the number of the crew saved and the unfilled lifeboats. A passenger on the *Carpathia* also spoke to me of this.

Mr. Lightoller and Mr. Boxhall were extremely courteous and kind on board the *Carpathia*. I think them both capable seamen and gentlemen.

MAHALA D. DOUGLAS.

FIFTEENTH DAY

Friday, May 10

Washington, D.C.

Affidavit: Emily B. Ryerson
First-class passenger, from Philadelphia

Key testimony: She chose not to swear to accounts attributed to her of Ismay's dismissal of ice warnings. She mentions that the Titanic's *band kept playing after the collision, and recounts "the cries for help of people drowning all around us, which seemed to go on forever."*

SENATOR SMITH: I desire printed in the record also an affidavit received by me made by Mrs. E. B. Ryerson, of Chicago, Ill.

The affidavit referred to is as follows:

STATE OF NEW YORK, *County of Otsego, as*:

Emily Bosie Ryerson, being duly sworn, deposes and says, I reside in the city of Chicago, Ill. I was a passenger on the steamship *Titanic* on April 14, 1912. At the time of collision I was awake and heard the engines stop, but felt no jar. My husband was asleep, so I rang and asked the steward, Bishop, what was the matter. He said, "There is talk of an iceberg, ma'am, and they have stopped, not to run into it." I told him to keep me informed if there were any orders. It was bitterly cold, so I put on a warm wrapper and looked out the window (we were in the large cabins on the B deck, very far aft) and saw the stars shining and a calm sea, but heard no noise. It was 12 o'clock. After about 10 minutes I went out in the corridor, and saw far off people hurrying on deck. A passenger ran by and called out, "Put on your life belts and come up on the boat deck." I said, "Where did you get those orders?" He said, "From the captain." I went back then and told Miss Bowen and my daughter, who were

491

in the next room, to dress immediately, roused my husband and the two younger children, who were in a room on the other side, and then remembered my maid, who had a room near us. Her door was locked and I had some difficulty in waking her. By this time my husband was fully dressed, and we could hear the noise of feet tramping on the deck overhead. He was quite calm and cheerful and helped me put the life belts on the children and on my maid. I was paralyzed with fear of not all getting on deck together in time, as there were seven of us. I would not let my younger daughter dress, but she only put on a fur coat, as I did over her nightgown. My husband cautioned us all to keep together, and we went up to A deck, where we found quite a group of people we knew. Everyone had on a life belt, and they all were very quiet and self-possessed.

We stood about there for quite a long time—fully half an hour, I should say. I know my maid ran down to the cabin and got some of my clothes. Then we were ordered to the boat deck. I only remember the second steward at the head of the stairs, who told us where to go. My chief thought and that of everyone else was, I know, not to make a fuss and to do as we were told. My husband joked with some of the women he knew, and I heard him say, "Don't you hear the band playing?" I begged him to let me stay with him, but he said, "You must obey orders. When they say, 'Women and children to the boats' you must go when your turn comes I'll stay with John Thayer. We will be all right. You take a boat going to New York." This referred to the belief that there was a circle of ships around waiting. The *Olympic*, the *Baltic*, were some of the names I heard. All this time we could hear the rockets going up—signals of distress. Again we were ordered down to A deck, which was partly enclosed. We saw people getting into boats, but waited our turn. There was a rough sort of steps constructed to get up to the window. My boy, Jack, was with me. An officer at the window said, "That boy can't go." My husband stepped forward and said, "Of course, that boy goes with his mother; he is only 13." So they let him pass. They also said "No more boys." I turned and kissed my husband, and as we left he and the other men I knew—Mr. Thayer, Mr. Widener, and others—were all standing there together very quietly. The decks were lighted, and as you went through

492

the window it was as if you stepped out into the dark. We were flung into the boats. There were two men—an officer inside and a sailor outside—to help us. I fell on top of the women who were already in the boat, and scrambled to the bow with my eldest daughter. Miss Bowen and my boy were in the stern and my second daughter was in the middle of the boat with my maid. Mrs. Thayer, Mrs. Widener, Mrs. Astor, and Miss Eustis were the only others I knew in our boat.

Presently an officer called out from the upper deck, "How many women are there in that boat?" Someone answered, "Twenty-four." "That's enough; lower away."

The ropes seemed to stick at one end and the boat tipped, some one called for a knife, but it was not needed until we got into the water, as it was but a short distance, and I then realized for the first time how far the ship had sunk. The deck we left was only about 20 feet from the sea. I could see all the portholes open and water washing in, and the decks still lighted. Then they called out, "How many seamen have you," and they answered one. "That is not enough," said the officer, "I will send you another," and he sent a sailor down the rope. In a few minutes after several other men not sailors came down the ropes over the davits and dropped into our boat. The order was given to pull away, then they rowed off—the sailors, the women, anyone—but made little progress; there was a confusion of orders; we rowed toward the stern, some one shouted something about a gangway, and no one seemed to know what to do. Barrels and chairs were being thrown overboard. Then suddenly, when we still seemed very near, we saw the ship was sinking rapidly. I was in the bow of the boat with my daughter and turned to see the great ship take a plunge toward the bow, the two forward funnels seemed to lean and then she seemed to break in half as if cut with a knife, and as the bow went under the lights went out; the stern stood up for several minutes, black against the stars, and then that, too, plunged down, and there was no sound for what seemed like hours, and then began the cries for help of people drowning all around us, which seemed to go on forever. Some one called out, "Pull for your lives, or you'll be sucked under," and everyone that could rowed like mad. I could see my younger daughter and Mrs. Thayer and Mrs. Astor rowing, but there seemed to be no suction. Then we turned to pick up some of those in the water. Some of the women protested, but others persisted, and we dragged in six or seven men; the men we rescued were principally stokers, stewards, sailors, etc., and were so chilled and frozen already they could hardly move. Two of them died in the stern later and many were raving and moaning and delirious most of the time. We had no lights or compass. There were several babies in the boat, but there was no milk or water. (I believe these were all stowed away somewhere, but no one knew where, and as the bottom of the boat was full of water and the boat full of people it was very difficult to find anything.)

After the *Titanic* sank we saw no lights, and no one seemed to know what direction to take. Lowe, the officer in charge of the boat, had called out earlier for all to tie together, so we now heard his whistle, and as soon as we could make out the other boats in the dark, five of us were tied together, and we drifted about without rowing, as the sea was calm, waiting for the dawn. It was very cold, and soon a breeze sprang up, and it was hard to keep our heavy boat bow on; but as the cries died down we could see dimly what seemed to be a raft with about 20 men standing on it, back to back. It was the overturned boat; and as the sailors on our boat said we could still carry 8 or 10 more people, we called for another boat to volunteer and go to rescue them. So we two cut loose our painters and between us got all the men off. They were nearly gone and could not have held out much longer. Then, when the sun rose we saw the *Carpathia* standing up about 5 miles away, and for the first time saw the icebergs all around us. The *Carpathia* steamed toward us until it was full daylight; then she stopped and began picking up boats, and we got on board about 8 o'clock. Very soon after we got on board they took a complete list of the names of all survivors. The kindness and the efficience of all the arrangements on the *Carpathia* for our comfort can never be too highly praised.

The foregoing affidavit is made at the request of William Alden Smith, chairman of the Senate investigating committee, in relation of the *Titanic* disaster.

EMILY BOSIE RYERSON.

Affidavit: Daisy Minahan
First-class passenger, from Wisconsin

Key testimony: Fifth Officer Lowe resisted going back to pick up survivors in the water, but eventually did, she said. She quoted him as telling the women in his lifeboat: "You ought to be damn glad you are here and have got your own life."

Senator Smith: I offer also to be printed in the record, an affidavit made by Daisy Minahan, and also a letter received from her by me.

The affidavit and letter referred to are as follows:

AFFIDAVIT AT REQUEST OF SENATOR SMITH.

State of Wisconsin, *Wood County, as*:

Daisy Minahan, being first duly sworn, upon oath deposes and says: I was asleep in stateroom C-78; I was awakened by the crying of a woman in the passageway. I roused my brother and his wife, and we began at once to dress. No one came to give us warning. We spent five minutes in dressing and went on deck to the port side. The frightful slant of the deck toward the bow of the boat gave us our first thought of danger.

An officer came and commanded all women to follow, and he led us to the boat deck on the starboard side. He told us there was no danger, but to get into a lifeboat as a precaution only. After making three attempts to get into boats, we succeeded in getting into lifeboat No. 14. The crowd surging around the boats was getting unruly.

Officers were yelling and cursing at men to stand back and let the women get into the boats. In going from one lifeboat to another we stumbled over huge piles of bread lying on the deck.

When the lifeboat was filled there were no seamen to man it. The officer in command of No. 14 called for volunteers in the crowd who could row. Six men offered to go. At times when we were being lowered we were at an angle of 45° and expected to be thrown into the sea. As we reached the level of each deck men jumped into the boat until the officer threatened to shoot the next man who jumped. We landed in the sea and rowed to a safe distance from the sinking ship. The officer counted our number and found us to be 48. The officer commanded everyone to feel in the bottom of the boat for a light. We found none. Nor was there bread or water in the boat. The officer, whose name I learned afterwards to be Lowe, was continually making remarks such as, "A good song to sing would be, Throw Out the Life Line," and "I think the best thing for you women to do is to take a nap."

The *Titanic* was fast sinking. After she went down the cries were horrible. This was at 2:20 A.M. by a man's watch who stood next to me. At this time three other boats and ours kept together by being tied to each other. The cries continued to come over the water. Some of the women implored Officer Lowe, of No. 14, to divide his passengers among the three other boats and go back to rescue. His first answer to those requests was, "You ought to be damn glad you are here and have got your own life." After some time he was persuaded to do as he was asked. As I came up to him to be transferred to the other boat he said, "Jump, God damn you, jump." I had showed no hesitancy and was waiting only my turn. He had been so blasphemous during the two hours we were in his boat that the women at my end of the boat all thought he was under the influence of liquor. Then he took all of the men who had rowed No. 14, together with the men from the other boats, and went back to the scene of the wreck. We were left with a steward and a stoker to row our boat, which was crowded. The steward did his best, but the stoker refused at first to row, but finally helped two women, who were the only ones pulling on that side. It was just 4 o'clock when we sighted the *Carpathia*, and we were three hours getting to her. On the *Carpathia* we were treated with every kindness and given every comfort possible.

A stewardess who had been saved told me that after the *Titanic* left Southampton that there were a number of carpenters working to put the doors of the air-tight compartments in working order. They had great difficulty in making them respond, and one of them remarked that they would be of little use in case of accident, because it took so long to make them work.

Daisy Minahan.

May 11, 1912

Hon. Wm. Alden Smith,
Washington, D. C.

Dear Sir: I have given you my observations and experiences after the disaster, but want to tell you of what occurred on Sunday night, April 14.

My brother, his wife, and myself went to the café for dinner at about 7:15 p.m. (ship's time). When we entered there was a dinner party already dining, consisting of perhaps a dozen men and three women. Capt. Smith was a guest, as also were Mr. and Mrs. Widener, Mr. and Mrs. Blair, and Maj. Butt. Capt. Smith was continuously with his party from the time we entered until between 9:25 and 9:45, when he bid the women good night and left. I know this time positively, for at 9:25 my brother suggested my going to bed. We waited for one more piece of the orchestra, and it was between 9:25 and 9:45 (the time we departed), that Capt. Smith left.

Sitting within a few feet of this party were also Sir Cosmo and Lady Duff-Gordon, a Mrs. Meyers, of New York, and Mrs. Smith, of Virginia. Mr. and Mrs. Harris also were dining in the café at the same time.

I had read testimony before your committee stating that Capt. Smith had talked to an officer on the bridge from 8:45 to 9:25. This is positively untrue, as he was having coffee with these people during this time. I was seated so close to them that I could hear bits of their conversation.

Yours,

Daisy Minahan.

SIXTEENTH DAY
Saturday, May 18

Witness: Capt. John J. Knapp
United States Navy hydrographer

Key testimony: Referring to charts and abundant ice warnings from ships that were available to the Titanic—*including one describing ice in the North Atlantic "as far as the eye could see"—Knapp described the* Titanic's *predictable course to doom. He also presented a detailed argument— damning for Captain Lord of the* Californian—*that the* Titanic *and* Californian *were in sight of each other. The* Californian *could have reached the* Titanic *well before she sank and, Knapp implied, all might have been saved.*

... SENATOR SMITH: Will you tell the committee what special branch of the public service you have in charge?

CAPT. KNAPP: I am in charge of the Hydrographic Office, which is under the Bureau of Navigation of the Navy Department. . . .

For more than a quarter of a century the Hydrographic Office of the Bureau of Navigation, Navy Department, has been publishing graphically from month to month a series of charts known as the Pilot Chart of the North Atlantic Ocean, depicting thereon the physical conditions of the ocean and of the atmosphere for the current month, as well as the location of dangers to navigation as reported by incoming ships. A summary of these dangers and a more detailed description than the space on the pilot chart would permit was in time given from week to week on a printed sheet known as the Hydrographic Bulletin. These publications were circulated freely among the shipmasters and shipping people in return for their news of the sea, the point of contact between the office at Washington and the marine world being a chain of branch hydrographic offices at the principal seaports.

Practically all the captains in the trans-Atlantic trade

cooperate in this work by handing in their information upon arrival in port to the branch hydrographic offices. In recent years the collection of marine data has been immensely accelerated by the use of radio telegraphy and the Hydrographic Office is thereby enabled to publish daily in a so-called daily memorandum whatever important reports of dangers have been received. This sheet is prepared every afternoon and is mailed to the branch hydrographic offices and there given publicity to all concerned. . . . Thus in the case of the recent loss of the *Titanic*, the shipping companies and shipmasters had been put in possession of the experience and judgment of a trained staff in the Hydrographic Office as summarized in a pamphlet printed in April, 1909, entitled "North Atlantic ice movements," giving a study of the entire question with diagrams to show the usual limits of ice for a period of 10 years. More specifically, the shipping community had been provided from month to month with the pilot chart showing the conditions of ice up to the time of printing and with the weekly Hydrographic Bulletin giving all pertinent details in regard to ice and derelicts and also the daily memorandum summarizing the collected reports of each day. . . .

SENATOR SMITH: Captain, have you any means of knowing the ice conditions in the North Atlantic Ocean in the vicinity of the Grand Banks of Newfoundland on the 14th day of April last, or on any preceding day of that week?

CAPT. KNAPP: The Hydrographic Office, prior to the 14th of April, was constantly receiving reports of ice in the North Atlantic. These reports began to come in early in the winter, as the ice moved down to the eastward of Newfoundland. These ice reports as received, as heretofore stated, are given out to the maritime world daily, and prior to the 14th of April, in what is called the Daily Memorandum issued by the office, there had been on several days ice so published that had been reported near the spot of the *Titanic* disaster.

The April Pilot Chart, which was issued March 28, 1912, showed that in March ice had come as far south as latitude 44° N. The Daily Memorandum prior to the 13th instant showed that the trend of ice was to the southward,

499

icebergs being sighted below the forty-third parallel on April 7, 8, 9, and 11; on the 9th and 11th it had reached the forty-second parallel, and on the 11th some of it was seen south of latitude 42°.

The Daily Memorandum of April 15 contains a message from the steamship *Amerika* via steamship *Titanic* and Cape Race, Newfoundland, April 14, 1912, to the Hydrographic Office, Washington, D. C.:

Amerika has passed two large icebergs in 41° 27′ N., 50° 8′ W., on the 14th of April.

KNUTH.

On the morning of the 15th of April, the day following the accident, the office received a radiogram sent by the steamship *Amerika* via the *Titanic* to Cape Race, and from there forwarded to Washington, reporting ice in latitude 41° 27′ N., longitude 50° 8′ W. The ice so reported was about 19 miles to the southward of where the *Titanic* struck.

SENATOR SMITH: Have you the message sent to you by the *Amerika* through the steamship *Titanic*, to which you refer?

CAPT. KNAPP: Yes. It was as follows:

S. S. "AMERIKA" VIA S. S. "TITANIC" AND
CAPE RACE, N. F.,
April 14, 1912.

HYDROGRAPHIC OFFICE, *Washington, D. C.*:
Amerika passed two large icebergs in 41° 27′ N., 50° 8′ W., on the 14th of April.

KNUTH.

Upon request, the Hamburg-American Line, to which line the steamship *Amerika* belongs, furnished to the Hydrographic Office this copy (hereunto appended). As will be seen by a reference thereto, the wireless message was sent from the *Amerika* to the *Titanic* at 11:45 A.M. (New York time, it is understood):

HYDROGRAPHIC OFFICE, *Washington, D. C.*:
Amerika passed two large icebergs in 41° 27′ N., 50° 8′ W., on the 14th of April.

KNUTH.

SENATOR SMITH: Captain, will you kindly tell the committee how extensive this ice flow was, to which you have just referred?

CAPT. KNAPP: I submit to the committee ... the following copies of ice reports made by said steamers.

The ice reports referred to are here printed in the record, as follows:

MARINE DATA FOR THE UNITED STATES HYDROGRAPHIC OFFICE.

REPORTS OF WRECKS, DERELICTS, ICE, AND OTHER OBSTRUCTIONS TO NAVIGATION.

British S. S. *Californian*. Master, Lord. Received in branch hydrographic office, Boston, Mass., April 22. Received in Hydrographic Office April 23:

April 14, 6:30 P.M., latitude 42.05 N., longitude 49.10 W., sighted two large icebergs 5 miles south of the above position. At 7:15 P.M., latitude 42.05 N., longitude 49.20 W., two bergs, and 7:30 P.M. two bergs. At 10:20 P.M., latitude 42.05 N., longitude 50.07 W., encountered heavy packed field ice, extending north and south as far as the eye could see and about 5 miles wide; also numerous bergs could be seen. From above position until April 15, 2:30 P.M., latitude 41.33 N., longitude 50.42 W., almost continuously in field ice. At the last position sighted two bergs and cleared the field ice.

From Greek S. S. *Athinai*. Master, John Coulonlound. Received in branch hydrographic office, New York, April 25. Forwarded and received in Hydrographic Office April 26:

April 14, 11:45 A.M., 41° 50′ 48″ N., 49° 34′ 15″ W., passed several (about 6) icebergs about 50–60 feet high and large quantity of field ice.

From *Perisian*, British S. S. Master, William Hains. Received in branch hydrographic office, Boston, Mass., April 24, and forwarded to Hydrographic Office. Received April 25:

April 14, 4:30 P.M., latitude 41° 55′ N., longitude 49°
02′ W., passed first iceberg. 8 P.M., latitude 41° 42′ N.,
longitude 49° 55′ W., passed last iceberg. Between positions passed 14 medium and large icebergs and numerous
growlers.

From German S. S. *Paula*. Master, H. Rieke. Received at
branch hydrographic office, Norfolk, Va., April 20, and
forwarded to Hydrographic Office. Received in Hydrographic Office April 22:

April 14, 11:40 A.M., latitude 41° 54′ N., longitude 40°
32′ W., one large iceberg. April 14, 11:40 A.M., latitude
41° 50′ N., longitude 49° 33′ W., one large iceberg. Apr.
14, noon, latitude 41° 53′ N., longitude 49° 36′ W., one
large iceberg. April 14, forenoon, from latitude 41° 58′,
longitude 49° 30′ W., till 41° 56′, 49° 52′, heavy pack ice
(one field). April 14, 5:30 P.M., from latitude 41° 55′,
longitude 50° 13′, till latitude 41° 40′, longitude 50° 30′,
heavy pack ice and 30 large icebergs in one field.

From German S. S. *Trautenfels*. Master, Hupers. Received
in branch hydrographic office, Boston, Mass., April 18,
and forwarded to Hydrographic Office. Received in Hydrographic Office April 19:

April 14, 5:05 A.M., latitude 42° 01′ N., longitude 49°
53′ W., passed two large icebergs about 200 feet long and
40 feet high.

April 14, 5:40 A.M., latitude 42° 01′ N., longitude 50°
06′ W., to 8 A.M., latitude 41° 40′ N., longitude 50° 22′ W.,
passing along a field of heavy, closely packed ice, with no
openings in the field. The ice field could be seen extending
far to the northward. During this time sighted about 30
large bergs.

Copy of telegram received from the Branch Hydrographic
Office, New York, on Apr. 17:

Steamer *La Bretagne* from Havre reports, April 14,
latitude 41° 39′, longitude 49° 21′ and 50° 21′, steamed
through an ice field with numerous icebergs for four
hours—7:30 to 11:38 A.M.

Steamer *Hellig Olav* from Copenhagen reports, April 13, latitude 41° 43', longitude 49° 51', passed three large icebergs; same date, latitude 41° 39', longitude 50° 81', medium-size berg and field ice.

From S. S. *Meeba*. Master, O. P. Clarke. Received in Hydrographic Office Apr. 19, 1912. From Branch Hydrographic Office, New York, N. Y.:

April 14, 11 A.M., latitude 41° 50' north, longitude 49° 15' west, passed a quantity of bergs, some very large; also, a field of pack ice about 5 miles long. April 14, 2 P.M., 42° north, longitude 50°, passed another field of pack ice with numerous bergs intermixed, and extended from 4 points on the starboard bow to abeam on the port side. Had to steer about 20 miles south to clear it. Ice seemed to be one solid wall of ice, at least 16 feet high, as far as could be seen. In latitude 41° 35' north, longitude 50° 30 west, we came to the end of it, and at 4 P.M. we were able to again steer to the westward. Saw no more ice after this. Weather clear and bright.

Telegram received by Hydrographic Office Apr. 15 from S. S. *Amerika*, via S. S. *Titanic* and Cape Race, Newfoundland, Apr. 14:

Amerika passed two large icebergs in 41° 27' north, 50° 8' west, on the 14th of April. Knuth, 10:51 p.

Copy of telegram received in Hydrographic Office Apr. 15 from S. S. *Pisa* via Halifax:

In latitude 42° 6' north and longitude 49° 43' west met with extensive field ice, and sighted seven bergs of considerable sizes on both sides of track.

In this connection the attention of the committee is especially invited to the report made by the master of the steamship *Mesaba*, wherein he reports on April 14, at 2 P.M., in latitude 42° north, longitude 50° west, that he "passed another field of pack ice, with numerous bergs intermixed, and extended from four points on the starboard bow to abeam on the port side. Had to steer about 20 miles south to clear it. Ice seemed to be one solid wall of ice at least 16 feet high, as far as could be seen. In latitude 41° 35' north, longitude 50° 30' west, we came to the end of it, and at 4 P.M.—April 14—we were able to again steer to the westward."

The ice so reported by the master of the steamship *Mesaba* was directly in the track on which the *Titanic* is reported to have been steaming when she met with the accident.

Chart No. 2, submitted to the committee, shows the ice barrier as it was on April 14, judging from the various reports made to the office, and from the testimony as given before your committee by the master of the steamship *Mount Temple*, Capt. Moore.

The attention of the committee is further invited to the report made by the steamship *Athinai*. This is the same steamer whose report by radio of icebergs and field ice was received by the steamship *Baltic*, as testified to before your committee by wireless operator Balfour, and which was transmitted by him to the steamship *Titanic* on April 14, 1912, at about 11:50 A.M., receipt of which was acknowledged at 12:05 P.M. on the 14th of April by Capt. Smith of the *Titanic*. This ice, as shown on our chart, was on or near the track of the *Titanic*.

SENATOR SMITH: Have you any means, from the description of the ice to which you have just referred and the speed of the *Titanic*, which was at that time making about 75 revolutions of her propeller per minute, of knowing the force of the impact?

CAPT. KNAPP: It is impossible, under the testimony as given, to state just how direct a blow the *Titanic* struck the ice, but an idea may be formed as to the possible blow by using the accepted formula, the weight multiplied by the square of the velocity divided by twice the gravity. Multiplying the weight of the ship by the square of its speed in feet per second and dividing by twice the force of gravity will give the blow that would have been struck if she had kept straight on her course against this apparently solid mass of ice, which, at a speed of 21 knots would have been equal to 1,173,200 foot tons, or energy enough to lift 14 monuments the size of the Washington Monument in one second of time. I think from the evidence before your committee it is shown that the ship struck the berg before she had appreciably lost any headway, due either to change of helm or stoppage or reversal of engines, in which event her striking energy would be practically that given above.

SENATOR SMITH: Captain, in view of the strength of this blow, can you account for the apparent absence of shock, the shock seeming to have been scarcely noticeable by the passengers and crew?

CAPT. KNAPP: A comparison might be made to striking a sharp instrument a glancing blow with the hand. There would be no apparent resisting shock. That part of the ice which cut into its outer skin was struck by the ship very much like the edge of a knife would be so struck by the hand. If the ship had struck end on solidly against the mass of ice, then there would have been the shock that takes place when a moving body meets an immovable body. . . .

SENATOR SMITH: Captain, can you think of anything else that you desire to say that will tend to throw any light upon the inquiry being made by the committee into the causes leading up to this wreck, and subsequent events, including any memorandum or data bearing upon the position of the steamship *Californian* on the night of this accident?

CAPT. KNAPP: I desire to submit the following "Memorandum on chart," marked "*Titanic*—Ice barrier—Near-by ships," which is explanatory of chart No. 2, which I have introduced in evidence.

The memorandum referred to is as follows:

HYDROGRAPHIC OFFICE.
Washington, D. C., May 14, 1912.

MEMORANDUM ON CHART.

"TITANIC"—ICE BARRIER—NEAR-BY SHIPS.

The chart bearing the above heading shows the ice barrier into which the *Titanic* undoubtedly steamed. The ice as shown on this chart, it will be noted, is grouped in one

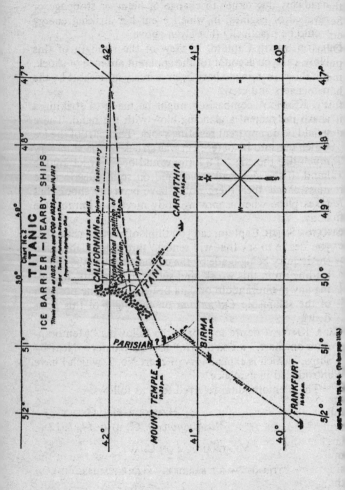

Chart No.2
TITANIC
ICE BARRIER — NEARBY SHIPS

Times struck her at 11.40Z. Titanic sent CQD at 10.25 pm Apr.14,1912
Ships' Times Reduced to New York Time
Prepared at the Hydrographic Office

8.00 p.m. 3.21 am. Apr.15
Hypothetical position of
Californian as given in testimony

CALIFORNIAN
11.15 pm

CARPATHIA
10.05 pm

TITANIC

PARISIAN ?
11.45 pm

BIRMA
11.53 p.m.

MOUNT TEMPLE
10.30 p.m.

FRANKFURT
10.40 p.m.

4865°—A. Doc. 726. 62-2.   (To face page 112.)

barrier, and not shown scattered as on the chart headed "Ice as reported near *Titanic*." From all the evidence before the Hydrographic Office—that is, the hearings before the Senate committee and the various reports made by steamers of ice in the locality in question—the Hydrographic Office deems that the ice barrier was, to all intents and purposes, as shown on this chart. Copies of the above-mentioned ice reports are forwarded herewith. There may have been, and probably were, other ice fields or bergs in this general locality, but they are not shown on the chart, as it is desired to bring out clearly, without other confusing details, the barrier into which the *Titanic* steamed.

An inspection of this chart will show that the *Mount Temple* ran into the southwestern end of this ice field at 12:55 A.M. (New York time), April 15. Thereafter to have reached the *Titanic* it would have been necessary for the *Mount Temple* to have steamed around the southern end of this ice barrier, and around it to the northward and eastward over 30 miles. As her highest speed does not exceed 13 knots (Lloyds Register) she could not have reached the scene of the *Titanic* disaster earlier than 3:15 A.M. (New York time) of that morning, or about 2 hours and 18 minutes after the *Titanic* sank (12:57 A.M., New York time).

A further inspection of this chart shows the *Californian* as located by the master thereof.

A still further inspection of the chart will show certain arcs of circles, shown in dotted lines drawn from the following centers: The position of the *Californian*, the position of the *Titanic*, the "hypothetical" position of the *Californian*. These arcs are drawn to represent the following: The radii of the arcs drawn about the *Titanic* as a center and the *Californian* as a center are identical, the larger radius being 16 miles and the smaller radius being 7 miles. Sixteen miles represents the distance at which the side lights of the *Titanic* could be seen from one standing on the *Californian* at the height of the latter ship's side lights, or the reverse, the 7 miles radius being the distance at which the side lights of the *Californian* would cease to be seen by a person from a boat in the water. A further reference to the chart will show, midway between the plotted positions of the *Californian* and *Titanic*, a plotted "hypothetical position of the *Californian*." With the hypothesis that the *Californian* was in this plotted position, a dotted line is drawn on a bearing SSE given by the master of the *Californian* as the bearing in which he sighted a large steamer. This dotted line is drawn to intersect the track of the *Titanic*. A line parallel thereto is drawn to also intersect the track of the *Titanic* at a point at which the *Titanic* appears to have been at 10:06 P.M., New York time, April 14—at 11:56 P.M. of that date by the *Californian's* time—at which time the large steamer is testified to have been seen by Ernest Gill, of the *Californian*. It thus appears that the bearings of the steamer given by the master of the *Californian* and the testimony of Ernest Gill of that ship will fix the *Californian's* position near or about the hypothetical position shown on the chart, if the lights seen on that ship were those of the *Titanic*.

A still further inspection of the chart will show that the *Californian*, if located in the position given by the master thereof, could have reached the scene of the disaster in about two hours, and, if located in the hypothetical position shown on the chart, the *Californian* certainly could have reached the *Titanic* in a little over an hour after she struck. The evidence taken in the hearings shows that the *Titanic* floated for two and a half hours after she struck the barrier.

JOHN J. KNAPP.

I invited especial attention to that part of the memorandum referring to the hypothetical position of the *Californian*, as shown on that chart, and, in connection therewith, it is desirable to explain that the arcs of circles drawn about the position of the steamship *Titanic* and about the position of the steamship *Californian* were drawn to graphically illustrate the testimony of certain witnesses before your committee.

SENATOR SMITH: What do these arcs indicate?

CAPT. KNAPP: The outer arc around each ship is drawn with a radius of 16 miles, which is approximately the farthest distance at which the curvature of the earth would have permitted the side lights of the *Titanic* to be seen by a person at the height of the side lights of the *Californian*, or at which the side lights of the *Californian* could have been seen by a person at the height of the side lights of the *Titanic*. The inner circle around each ship is drawn with a radius of 7 miles. This is approximately the distance after reaching which the curvature of the earth would have shut out the side lights of the *Californian* from the view of one in a lifeboat in the water. It appears, therefore, that if the *Titanic*'s position at the time of the accident was as fixed by the testimony and if it was the side light of the *Californian* that was seen from the boat deck of the *Titanic*, the *Californian* was somewhere inside of the arc of the 16-mile circle drawn about the *Titanic*. It further appears that if the above hypothesis be correct and if the side light of the other steamer could not be seen, as is testified to, from one of the lifeboats of the *Titanic* after being lowered, the *Californian* was somewhere outside of the circle with the 7-mile radius drawn about the *Titanic*.

In the case of the *Californian*, if the steamer which in the testimony given by members of the crew of the *Californian*, including the captain and the donkey engine-man and others, is said to have been seen by them, was the *Titanic*, she must have been somewhere inside of the circle with the 16-mile radius drawn around the *Californian*. If that be the case, as the *Californian*'s side light was shut out by the curvature of the earth from the view of anyone in a lifeboat of the *Titanic* after being lowered into the water, then the *Titanic* must have been outside of the circle drawn with the 7-mile radius around the *Californian*.

Further reference to this chart will show plotted a hypothetical position of the *Californian*. On the hypothesis that the *Californian* was in this position, a dotted line is drawn on the chart on the bearing given by the captain of the *Californian* as that on which the steamer was sighted. This bearing is drawn on the chart to intersect the track of the *Titanic*. Another dotted line is drawn parallel thereto from a point on the course of the *Titanic* where she apparently was at 10:06 P.M., New York time, April 14, that being 11:56 P.M. of that date of the *Californian*'s time, at which Ernest Gill, a member of the crew of the *Californian*, in his testimony before your committee, stated that the large steamer was seen by him. If the *Californian* was in the hypothetical position shown on the chart, the *Titanic* could have been seen by the officers and crew of the *Californian* at the time mentioned.

SENATOR SMITH: Captain, are you able to state to the committee whether there was any vessel between the position of the *Titanic* just preceding and following the accident and the position of the *Californian* at that time?

CAPT. KNAPP: From being present at hearings before your committee and from reading the printed testimony of witnesses examined by the committee I am led to the conclusion that if there was any vessel between the *Californian* and the *Titanic* at the time referred to she does not seem to have been seen by any of the ships near there on the following morning, nor have there been any reports submitted to the Hydrographic Office which would indicate that there was any such steamer in that locality. The evidence does not indicate to me that there was any such third steamer in those waters, especially in view of the fact that no such steamer was seen by other steamers or by those in the lifeboats the following morning, and as the ice barrier, from all reports, between the reported position of the *Californian* and that of the *Titanic* was impassable to a vessel proceeding to the westward, and there is no testimony to show that if such a steamer was between the *Californian* and the *Titanic* she proceeded to the eastward, the captain of the *Californian* having testified that he last saw the said steamer proceeding to the westward and being on a bearing to the westward of the *Californian*. Nothing appears in the testimony to show that the steamer so seen reversed its course and proceeded to the eastward.

Letter: George Otis Smith
Director of the United States Geological Survey

Key testimony: The Titanic *could have had its hull torn open by rock embedded in the iceberg underwater.*

510

SENATOR SMITH: I also submit a letter received by the committee from the Director of the United States Geological Survey, bearing date May 16, 1912, having special reference to the composition of icebergs.

The letter referred to is here printed in the record as follows:

DEPARTMENT OF THE INTERIOR,
UNITED STATES GEOLOGICAL SURVEY,
Washington, May 16, 1912.

HON. WILLIAM ALDEN SMITH,
Chairman Subcommittee United States Senate,
Washington, D. C.

MY DEAR SIR: Replying to a letter of May 8 requesting information concerning the possibility of the *Titanic* having had its hull torn open by a mass of rock imbedded in the submerged portion of the iceberg with which it collided:

As Prof. E. H. Williams, Jr., suggests, in his card which you inclose, such may possibly have been the case. It certainly appears that such an ice mass, around with embedded rock fragments, would be much more effective in ripping open the plates of a ship's hull than a mass of clear ice. It is a well-known fact, as reported by numerous Arctic explorers, that some at least of the Greenland icebergs transport rock masses. In one of his addresses delivered in Washington last year, either that before the Geological Society of Washington, or one before the National Academy of Sciences, Sir John Murray referred to the abundant bowlders found by the dredging of the *Challenger* expedition, scattered over parts of the bottom of the North Atlantic. He referred to these as being so numerous in places that were the sea bottom elevated and drained so as to become land he thought geologists would be inclined to refer the deposit to a continental ice sheet, as has been done with the drift spread over the north half of the North American Continent.

Dr. Elisha Kent Kane, in his volume on the "U. S. Grinnell Expedition," 1854, p. 113, describes bergs covered with detritus or rock fragments, varying in size from mere pebbles to large blocks. He writes of one as follows:

"The berg had evidently changed its equilibrium, and it seemed as if these rocks had been cemented in its former base and had there been subjected to attrition during its rotary oscillations against the bottom of the sea."

On page 455 he describes the overturning of bergs due to changes in their equilibrium, and, referring to rock-studded ice, states (p. 456):

"In such cases the deeply embedded position of the larger fragments spoke of their having been there from the original structure of the berg."

Further (p. 457):

"Of nearly 5,000 bergs which I have seen there was perhaps not one that did not contain fragmentary rock."

In his Arctic Expeditions: The Second Grinnell Expedition (vol. 2, 1856, pp. 156, 157), Dr. Kane describes ice in Marshall Bay covered with millions of tons of rock debris. Concerning this he writes:

"I have found masses that had been detached in this way floating many miles out to sea—long symmetrical tables, 200 feet long by 80 broad, covered with large angular rocks and bowlders, and seemingly impregnated throughout with detrital matter. These rafts in Marshall Bay were so numerous that could they have melted as I saw them the bottom of the sea would have presented a more curious study for the geologist than the bowlder-covered lines of our middle latitudes."

It should be noted, however, that these ice rafts probably do not transport their loads to such low latitudes as are reached by the more massive bergs.

Dr. I. I. Hayes, in his volume on The Open Polar Sea, a narrative of a voyage of discovery toward the North Pole (1867, pp. 403, 404), describes the rock debris dropped upon the ice from cliffs along the shore and thence drifted away. He writes:

"The amount of rock thus transported to the ocean is immense, and yet it falls far short of that which is carried by the icebergs, the rock and sand embedded in which, as they lay in the parent glacier, being sometimes sufficient to bear them down under the weight until but the merest fragments rise above the surface. As the berg melts, the rock and sand fall to the bottom of the ocean; and, if the place of their deposit should one day rise above the sea level, some geological students of future ages may, perhaps, be as much puzzled to know how they came there as those of the present generation are to account for the bowlders of the Connecticut Valley."

The amount of rock in any one iceberg is, however, probably small, so that it is not generally noticeable in the bergs which reach the lower latitudes, at least in those parts of the bergs which extend above the water level. Holland (1877), as quoted by James D. Dana (Manual of Geology, Fourth Edition, 1895, p. 252), states that most of the Greenland icebergs are clean, but "now and then one is seen with bowlders upon it, and here and there small bergs that are quite covered with stones and gravel." . . .

The Greenland glaciers, extending from the great ice cap down the valleys which notch the margin of the interior up and, as described by other observers, do not carry a great amount of rock debris, and most of this is embedded in the lower part of the ice. When these glaciers extend into water sufficiently deep for icebergs to break off, most of the debris would thus be in the basal part of the ice and, since but one-ninth of the mass of floating ice extends above the water level, most of the debris in a berg standing 50 to 100 feet above the surface of the sea would at first be far below the depth at which a ship's hull would encounter it. With the melting of the ice as it floats southward, the rock fragments are released and dropped to the sea bottom. The most distant of this glacio-natant deposition is said to take place about the banks of Newfoundland, or between meridians 44 and 52 and north of parallel 40° 30'. Some of the rock is probably carried still farther south, especially in such a year as 1912, when the icebergs are reported as having been seen much farther south than is customary. It is thus quite possible that rock masses may have been embedded in the berg which the *Titanic* encountered. While most of the debris is probably embedded in the basal part of such ice masses, melting of the part of the ice exposed above the water would cause the basal part to be gradually raised toward the surface. Moreover, the tilting of icebergs from their original positions results from the change of the center of gravity, due to disruption and unequal melting of different parts of the mass. Such bergs are also known to turn over, so that even though the upper part of the berg were at first free from rock debris, the rock-shod part might be brought up to a level where a ship's hull would encounter it.

Masses of rock 50 feet or more in circumference are known to have been transported by continental glaciers, and it is quite possible that large masses of rock may be carried by some of the icebergs, though probably most of the stones are comparatively small. However, one large rock firmly embedded in the ice at the point of contact would certainly be most effective in ripping open a ship's hull under the force of a glancing impact. Ice in such a great mass as the berg which was encountered is, however, probably quite competent to produce disastrous results experienced without calling for the presence of any included mass of rock.

Very respectfully,

GEO. OTIS SMITH, *Director.*

FINAL DAY
Saturday, May 25
New York

Senator Smith visited the Olympic, *the* Titanic's *sister ship, at port in New York to interview its captain and wireless operator as well as its new fireman, from the* Titanic. *When the* Titanic *sank, the* Olympic *was some 500 miles southwest.*

Witness: E. J. Moore
Wireless operator on the *Olympic*

Moore submitted his log illustrating the early and prolonged confusion about the fate of the Titanic *and those aboard. Since the rescue ship* Carpathia *had only a short-range wireless, it had to use other ships like the* Olympic *as intermediaries for relaying information ashore about survivors. (Even President William Howard Taft was unsuccessful in messaging the* Carpathia *to learn the fate of his aide Archie Butt, who died.) The log reflects the exhaustion of the* Carpathia's *wire operators (Cottam as well as Bride from the* Titanic, *on duty now on the rescue ship) as well as the willingness of the New York press to pay for stories. On the* Carpathia, *Ismay was said to be "under opiate." The* Carpathia's *captain, Henry Rostron, and the* Olympic's *captain agreed that it would not be a good idea to bring* Titanic *survivors to the* Olympic, *a virtually identical ship.*

LOG AS MADE BY WIRELESS OPERATOR MOORE ON
S. S. "OLYMPIC."

SUNDAY, APRIL 14, 1912—NEW YORK TIME.

10:15 A.M.: Standing by for Cape Cod.
10:45 P.M.: Received four messages from Cape Cod.

10:50 P.M.: Hear *Titanic* signaling to some ship about striking an iceberg. Am not sure it is the *Titanic* who has struck an iceberg. Am interfered by atmospherics and many stations working.

11 P.M.: . . . *Titanic* sending out signals of distress and I answered his calls immediately.

11: . . . P.M.: *Titanic* replies and gives me his position . . . and says, "We have struck an iceberg." Reported this information to bridge immediately. Our distance from the *Titanic* . . . miles.

11: . . . P.M.: Signals with the *Titanic*. He says, "Tell captain get your boats ready and what is your position?"

11 . . . P.M.: Sent message to *Titanic*: "Commander, *Titanic*, 4:24 A.M. G.M.T. 40.52 N., 61.1 . . . W. "Are you steering southerly to meet us? [*Olympic* captain, Herbert] Haddock."

11:00 P.M.: *Titanic* says, "Tell captain we are putting the passengers off in small boats."

11:45 P.M.: Asked *Titanic* what weather he had had. He says, "Clear and calm."

11:50 P.M.: Message to *Titanic*: "Commander, *Titanic*. Am lighting up all possible boilers as fast as can. Haddock."

11:56 P.M.: Sable Island [relay station] calling me with traffic. Told him to stand by for a while, as having urgent communication with *Titanic*.

MONDAY, APRIL 15, 1912—NEW YORK TIME.

12:30 A.M.: Signals with the S. S. *Hellig Olav*, His signals strong. Asked if he knows anything of *Titanic*. He says, "No." Keeping strict watch, but hear nothing more from *Titanic*. Calling Sable Island at intervals. No reply from him.

4:15 A.M. to 5:20 A.M.: Calling *Titanic*. Now daylight: no reply. Sable Island calls up with traffic. Received following:

NEW YORK.

CAPT. HADDOCK, *Olympic*:

Endeavor communicate *Titanic* and ascertain time and position. Reply as soon as possible to Ismay, New York [White Star Offices].

F. W. REDWAY.

Sent following service via Sable Island:

PERATOR, *Cape Reid*:
Have you any particulars of the *Titanic*?

COMMANDER.

5:30 A.M.: Communication with *La Bretagne*, west bound.
sk him for news of *Titanic*, but he knows nothing.

5:40 A.M.: Signals with S. S. *Asian* with German oil tank
a tow for Halifax. Says, "We are only going 5 knots." Ask
im for news of *Titanic*. Says, "I think the *Baltic* was some
ay ahead of us, say about 200 miles. He would be passed
er (*Titanic*) same way, I should think, but our ship
ntillian (Leyland), if he was on watch, should have got
itanic. He was only about 60 miles astern, so the captain
alculated. Who is 'M. G. Y.'? I informed him 'M. G. Y.' is
ae *Titanic*." Continues: "I last heard him at 11:52 P.M.
alling 'S. O. S.' Had heard him previous to that, very faint,
orking to Cape Race [Newfoundland]." (This was sent
fficially again later.)
Calling *Titanic* at intervals until—

7 A.M.: Exchanged signals with Sable Island. Distance,
05 SSM.

7:10 A.M.: Exchanged signals with *Asian*.

7:35 A.M.: Received following service message from Sable
land:

NEW YORK.

OMMANDER OLYMPIC:
Keep us posted fully regarding *Titanic*.

FRANKLIN [P.A.S. Franklin, International
Mercantile Marine's top American executive].

7:40 A.M.: Service from Cape Race via Sable, received as
llows:

Your signals good here. Watch and tune for us.

CAPE RACE.

7:45 A.M.: Following message sent via Sable Island:

MAY, *New York*:
Since midnight, when her position was 41.46 north 50.14
est, have been unable to communicate. We are now 310
iles from her. 9 A.M., under full power. Will inform you at
ace if hear anything.

COMMDR.

Called Cape Race several times, but unable to hear him
7:50 A.M.: Following message sent:

CAPTAIN ASIAN:
Can you give me any information *Titanic*, and if an
ships standing by her?

COMMANDER.

8:05 A.M.: Communication with S. S. *Atkenei*. He know
nothing of *Titanic*.
8:06 A.M.: Communication with S. S. *Scandinavian*
bound east. He can give me no information either.
8:15 A.M.: Again called Cape Race, but can not hear him
8:30 A.M.: Following service messages received from
Asian confirming previous information:

CAPTAIN OLYMPIC:
Asian heard *Titanic* signalling Cape Race on and o
from 8 to 10 P.M., local time, Sunday. Messages too faint t
read. Finished calling S. O. S. midnight. Position given a
latitude 41.40, longitude 50.14. No further information
Asian then 500 miles west of *Titanic* and towing oil tank t
Halifax.

WOOD [*Asian* captain].

13th April: iceberg reported in latitude 41.50, longitud
50.30.

WOOD.

Keeping close watch until—
9:25 A.M.: Communication with S. S. *Parisian*. He says: "
sent traffic to the *Titanic* at 8:50 last night, and I heard him
send traffic just before I went to bed to Cape Race. I turne
in at 11:15, ship's time. The *Californian* was about 50 mile
astern of us. I heard following this morning, 6 o'clock:
"Would you like me to send service message to you
commander? According to information picked up the *Ca
pathia* has picked up about 20 boats with passengers. Th
Baltic is returning to give assistance. As regards *Titanic*
have heard nothing—don't know if she is sunk."
(This information was given to the commander immed
ately verbally.)
10:10 A.M.: Sent two messages to the S. S. *Berlin*.

10:12 A.M.: Communication with S. S. *Mesaba*. Can give no information of *Titanic*. Sends following service:

CAPTAIN OLYMPIC:
In lat. 42 to lat. 41.25 N., long 49 W. to long 50.35 W. saw heavy pack ice and a large number of icebergs; also some field ice; weather has been very fine and clear.

CLARK [*Mesaba* captain].

10:17 A.M.: Received following service from Cape Race, via Sable Island:

"No further news *Titanic*; we have batch traffic for you and your sigs. Good readable here."

10:25 A.M.: Sent following service message via Sable Island:

ISMAY, *New York*:
Parisian reports *Carpathia* in attendance and picked up 20 boats of passengers and *Baltic* returning to give assistance. Position not given.

HADDOCK.

10:35 A.M.: Received following message from the *Parisian*:

CAPTAIN OLYMPIC:
Field ice extends to lat 41.22; heavy to the northwest of that and bergs very numerous of all sizes: had fine clear weather.

HAINS [*Parisian* captain].

10:55 A.M.: Communication with Cape Race; distance, 450 miles. He is just audible, and knows nothing more of *Titanic*; working Cape Race for next hour. Sent his three and received five messages, with assistance from the *Scandinavian*, who is able to read Cape Race. The S. S. *Berlin* working to other ships and interfering with us considerably.
Noon: *Scandinavian* gives "B1" for lunch, Cape Race having no important traffic.
12:35 P.M.: Following are two messages sent to the *Parisian*:

CAPTAIN PARISIAN:
Many thanks for message. Can we steer to 41.22 north,

50.14 west from westward, and then north to *Titanic* fairly free from ice. We are due there midnight. Should appreciate *Titanic*'s current position if you can give it to me.

HADDOCK.

12:50 P.M.: Receiving following service message from *Parisian*:

CAPTAIN OLYMPIC:

Safe from field ice to 41.22, 30.14; as the ice was yesterday, you would need to steer from that position about northeast and north to about lat. 41.42 and 50, then approach his position from the westward, steering about west northwest. My knowledge of the *Titanic*'s position at midnight was derived from your own message to New York in which you gave it as 41.47, 50.20; if such were correct she would be in heavy field ice and numerous bergs. Hope and trust matters are not as bad as they appear.

HAINS.

1:25 P.M.: Trying to receive from Cape Race his sign dead week, and the *Berlin* is interfering with me badly; told the *Berlin* that it would be a serious matter for him if he kept on interfering. *Scandinavian* assists me in receiving from Cape Race.

1:40 P.M.: Succeeded in receiving the following message from Cape Race:

NEW YORK.

WIRELESS OPERATOR, *Olympic*:

We will pay you liberally for story of rescue of *Titanic*' passengers any length possible for you to send earliest possible moment. Mention prominent persons.

THE WORLD.

I then informed Cape Race that it was no use sending me messages from newspapers asking us to send news of *Titanic*, as we had no news to give. If he had no important traffic he had better stand-by, as it was most important that I should get hold of some ship who has news of the *Titanic* Cape Race says, "We must clear traffic, so all the message are paid for."

Called "CQ" to stand-by.

2 P.M.: Establish communication with the S. S. *Carpathia*

ask him for news of the *Titanic*. He says, "I can't do everything at once. Patience, please." Then continues, "I received distress signals from the *Titanic* at 11:20, and we proceeded right to the spot mentioned. On arrival at day-break we saw field ice 25 miles, apparently solid, and a quantity of wreckage and a number of boats full of people. We raised about 670 souls. The *Titanic* has sunk. She went down in about two hours. Captain and all engineers lost. Our captain sent order that there was no need for *Baltic* to come any farther. So with that she returned on her course to Liverpool. Are you going to resume your course on that information? We have two or three officers aboard and the second Marconi operator, who had been creeping his way through water 30° sometime. Mr. Ismay aboard." This information was reported to the commander immediately. I informed the *Carpathia* that if he had any important traffic to get through I would take it for him, as I was then in communication with Cape Race.

Carpathia . . . [operator] informs me that he has had nothing to eat since 5:30 P.M., yesterday.

2:35 P.M.: Sent following to *Carpathia*:

CAPTAIN CARPATHIA:

7:35 P.M.: G. M. T. Our position 41.17 N. 53.53 W. Steering east, true; shall I meet you and where.

HADDOCK.

2:40 P.M.: Communication with the S. S. *Virginian* (Allan). He says please tell *Carpathia* we have been standing by for him since he asked us to resume our course at 9 A.M., when we were within 25 miles of him. Have message for him. I told the *Virginian* to give the *Carpathia* a chance, as he was so busy.

3:15 P.M.: Received the following from the *Carpathia*:

CARPATHIA.

CAPTAIN OLYMPIC:

7:30: G. M. T. Lat. 41.15 north, long. 51.45 west. Am steering south 87 west, true. Returning to New York with *Titanic*'s passengers.

ROSTRON.

521

CARPATHIA.

CAPTAIN OLYMPIC:
Bruce Ismay is under opiate.

ROSTRON.

CARPATHIA.

CAPTAIN OLYMPIC:
Do you think it is advisable *Titanic*'s passengers see *Olympic*? Personally I say not.

ROSTRON.

CARPATHIA.

CAPTAIN OLYMPIC:
Sir Ismay orders *Olympic* not to be seen by *Carpathia*. No transfer to take place.

ROSTRON.

Following message sent:
CAPTAIN CARPATHIA:
Kindly inform me if there is the slightest hope of searching *Titanic* position at daybreak. Agree with you on not meeting. Will stand on present course until you have passed and will then haul more to southward. Does this parallel of 42.17 N. lead clear of the ice? Have you communicated the diameter to our people at New York or Liverpool, or shall I do so, and what particulars can you give me to send?

Sincere thanks for what you have done.

HADDOCK.

4 P.M.: Following from *Carpathia*:

CARPATHIA.

CAPT. HADDOCK, *Olympic*:
South point pack ice 41.16 north. Don't attempt to go north until 49.30 west. Many bergs, large and small amongst pack. Also for many miles to eastward. Fear absolutely no hope searching *Titanic*'s position. Left Leyland S. S. *Californian* searching around. All boats accounted for. About 675 souls saved, crew and passengers latter nearly all women and children. *Titanic* foundered about 2:20 A.M., 5.47 G. M. T., in 41.16 north, 50.14 west not certain of having got through. Please forward to White Star, also to Cunard, Liverpool and New York, that I am returning to New York. Consider this most advisable for many considerations.

ROSTRON.

4:15 P.M.: Told *Carpathia* that we would report the information to White Star and Cunard immediately.

4:25 P.M.: Following service messages sent to Cape Race:

OLYMPIC.

ISMAY, *New York and Liverpool*:

Carpathia reached *Titanic* position at daybreak. Found boats and wreckage only. *Titanic* had foundered about 2:20 A.M. in 41.16 N., 50.14 W. All her boats accounted for. About 675 souls saved, crew and passengers; latter nearly all women and children. Leyland Line S. S. *Californian* remaining and searching position of disaster. *Carpathia* returning to New York with survivors. Please inform Cunard.

HADDOCK.

OLYMPIC.

FRANKLIN, ISMAY, *New York*:

Inexpressible sorrow. Am proceeding straight on voyage. *Carpathia* informs me no hope in searching. Will send names survivors as obtainable. Yamsi [Ismay] on *Carpathia*.

HADDOCK.

4:50 P.M.: Following service message sent to *Carpathia*:

CAPTAIN CARPATHIA:

Can you give me names survivors forward?

HADDOCK.

. . . P.M.: Signals with *Californian*, who says: "We were second boat on the scene of disaster. All we could see there were some boxes and coats and a few empty boats and what looked like oil on the water. When we were near the *Carpathia* he would not answer me, though I kept on calling him, as I wanted the position. We kept on talking to the *Baltic*. The latter says he is going to report me for jamming. We were the nearer boat to the *Carpathia*. A boat called the *Birma* was still looking."

Informed the *Californian* that would take note of fact that in case of distress [sinking] ships should have precedence.

. . . :30 P.M.: *Californian* sends through following ice report: Icebergs and . . . ice in 42 . . . north 4 . . . west; 41 . . . north, 50.00 west. He tells us he is 200 miles out of his course.

5:4.. P.M.: Received following from the *Carpathia*:

(Private to Capt. Haddock, *Olympic*.)

Captain: Chief, first, and sixth officers, and all engineers gone; also doctor; all persons; one Marconi operator, and chief steward gone. We have second, third, fourth, and fifth officers and one Marconi operator on board.

ROSTRON.

CARPATHIA.

Captain *Olympic*:

Will send names immediately we can. You can understand we are working under considerable difficulty. Everything possible being done for comfort of survivors. . . .

ROSTRON.

Carpathia then starts sending names of survivors. He says: "Please excuse sending, but am half asleep."

7:35 P.M.: Received 333 first and second class passengers' names from him. During the transmission of the names it was evident that the operator on *Carpathia* was tired out.

7:40 P.M.: Sent five private messages to the *Carpathia*. He says the third-class passengers' names and list of crew will follow later.

7:50 P.M.: Trying to read Cape Race, who has a bunch of traffic for us. His signals very weak and am interfered with by atmospherics. We try for some time, but his signals so weak impossible to hear him.

8:35 P.M.: Received following messages from the *Carpathia* for retransmission to Cape Race:

CARPATHIA.

Cunard, *New York and Liverpool*.

Titanic struck iceberg Monday 3 A.M., 41.46 north, 50.14 west. *Carpathia* picked up many passengers in boats. Will wire further particulars later. Proceeding back to New York

ROSTRON.

Carpathia, Associated Press, New York. (Text same as last message.)

Asked *Carpathia* if he had list of third-class and crew survivors ready. He says: "No: will send them soon."

8:35 P.M.: Sent one private message to *Californian* asking if they had any survivors on board from the *Titanic*.

8:45 P.M.: Private message from the *Californian* saying no *Titanic* survivors on board. Standing by for the *Carpathia* and calling him frequently. Hear nothing from him. I informed the commander that I was unable to hear anything more of *Carpathia* and asked, "Should I start sending list of names to Cape Race?" He instructed me to send them.

10 P.M.: Calling Cape Race with list of survivors, but can not hear him.

10:30 P.M.: Sable Island answers me and offers traffic. Told him I have list of survivors here and ask him to take them. Sable Island gives "O. K.," and I commence sending them to him.

TUESDAY, APRIL 16, 1912.

12:30 A.M.: Cape Race breaks in. His signals good; says he can read me OK and that he has already been receiving names I have been sending to Sable Island; so as Cape Race is strong and Sable Island very difficult to read on account of atmospherics, I send the remaining names to Cape Race.

2:50 A.M.: Completed sending list of survivors' names through to Cape Race, and then start sending *Carpathia*'s service messages, after which received the following from him:

NEW YORK.

Capt. HADDOCK, *Olympic*:

It is vitally important that we have names of every survivor on *Carpathia* immediately. If you can expedite this by standing by the *Carpathia* please do so.

FRANKLIN.

2:55 A.M.:

NEW YORK.

CAPTAIN OLYMPIC:

Wireless name of every passenger, officer, crew of *Car-*

pathia; it is most important. Keep in communication with the *Carpathia* to accomplish this. Instruct *Californian* stand by scene of wreck until she hears from us or is relieved or her coal supply runs short. Ascertain *Californian*'s coal and how long she can stand by. Has life raft been accounted for? Are you absolutely satisfied that *Carpathia* has all survivors, as we heard a rumor that *Virginian*, *Parisian* also had survivors? Where is *Baltic*?

FRANKLIN.

NEW YORK.

CAPTAIN OLYMPIC:

Distressed to learn from your message that *Carpathia* is only steamer with passengers. We understand *Virginian* and *Parisian* also has passengers, and are you in communication with them and can you get any information?

FRANKLIN.

3:10 A.M.: Now daylight. Cape Race's signals die off.

3:35 A.M.: Signals with the *Virginian*. He says, "We were requested by *Carpathia* to resume our course at the same time as the *Baltic*. We got within 25 miles of the *Titanic*. I heard her distress signal calls, and we went to her right away. We had 200 miles to go."

Received following service message:

8:45 A.M.:

VIRGINIAN.

CAPTAIN OLYMPIC:

Hear rumors that we have survivors of *Titanic* on board. This is not so. I have none. At 10 A.M. yesterday, when 30 miles from position of disaster, received Marconi from Marconi, as follows:

'Turn back now. Everything O. K. We have 800 aboard. Return to your northern track.' I consequently proceeded on my course to Liverpool. Similar instructions were sent at same time to the *Baltic* from *Carpathia*. I passed a large quantity of heavy field ice and bergs. Compliments.

GAMBELL.

Witness: Frederick Barrett
Coal fireman

Key testimony: Barrett, now employed as fireman on the nearly identical Olympic and interviewed there, described the sudden inrush of water down in the Titanic's firerooms and getting out just before the watertight doors shut.

Q: You were a fireman on the *Titanic*?

A: I was leading fireman.

Q: Were you on duty on the night of the accident?

A: Yes.

Q: Where?

A: In 6 section.

Q: Were you there when the accident occurred?

A: Yes. I was standing talking to the second engineer. The bell rang, the red light showed. We sang out shut the doors [indicating the ash doors to the furnaces] and there was a crash just as we sung out. The water came through the ship's side. The engineer and I jumped to the next section. The next section to the forward section is No. 5.

Q: Where did the water come through?

A: About 2 feet above the floor plates, starboard side.

Q: How much water?

A: A large volume of water came through.

Q: How big was this hole in the side?

A: About 2 feet above the floor plates.

Q: You think it was a large tear?

A: Yes; I do.

Q: All along the side of No. 6?

A: Yes.

Q: How far along?

A: Past the bulkhead between sections 5 and 6, and it was a hole 2 feet into the coal bunkers. She was torn through No. 6 and also through 2 feet abaft the bulkhead in the bunker at the forward head of No. 5 section. We got through before the doors broke, the doors dropped instantly, automatically from the bridge. I went back to No.

6 fireroom and there was 8 feet of water in there. I went to No. 5 fireroom when the lights went out. I was sent to find lamps, as the lights were out, and when we got the lamps we looked at the boilers and there was no water in them. I ran to the engineer and he told me to get some firemen down to draw the fires. I got 15 men down below.

Q: Did you not have fires in No. 6?

A: Yes, the fires were lit when the water came.

Q: I would like to know how many boilers were going that night?

A: There were five boilers not lit.

Q: How many were there going?

A: There was 24 boilers lit and five without. Fires were lighted in three boilers for the first time Sunday, but I don't know whether they were connected up or not.

Q: This tear went a couple of feet past the bulkhead in No. 5. How were you able to keep the water from reaching——

A: It never came above the plates, until all at once I saw a wave of green foam come tearing through between the boilers and I jumped for the escape ladder.

Q: Was there any indication of any explosion of a boiler?

A: There was a knocking noise, but no explosion, only when the ship was sinking a volume of smoke came up. . . .

Affidavit: Imanita Shelley
Second-class passenger, from Montana

Key testimony: Not only did the Titanic *sink but the accommodations and service were bad.*

STATE OF MONTANA, *County of Powell, ss.*

Mrs. Imanita Shelley, of lawful age, being first duly sworn as regards the *Titanic* disaster, on her oath deposes and says:

That her mother, Mrs. Lutle Davis Parrish, of Woodford County, Ky., and herself embarked on the White Star Steamship *Titanic* at Southampton, England, upon the 10th day of April, 1912, having purchased the best second-class accommodation sold by said company.

That instead of being assigned to the accommodation purchased, were taken to a small cabin many decks down in the ship, which was so small that it could only be called a cell. It was impossible to open a regulation steamer trunk in said cabin. It was impossible for a third person to enter said cabin unless both occupants first of all crawled into their bunks.

That the stewardess was sent to the chief purser demanding transfer to accommodation purchased. That he replied he could do nothing until the boat had left Queenstown, Ireland, when he would check up all tickets and find out if there was any mistake.

That after leaving Queenstown Mrs. L. D. Parrish made 11 trips herself to the purser asking for transfer, only to be put off with promises. That at 9 o'clock P.M., no one having come to take them to better quarters, Mrs. Shelley wrote a note to the purser to the effect that she had paid for the best second-class accommodation on the ship and had the receipts to prove it; that she was very ill and, owing to the freezing cold of the cabin, was in great danger; that if he, the purser, refused to act she, Mrs. Shelley, would appeal to the captain; that if neither would act she realized she would have to wait until reaching America for redress, but most assuredly would claim damages if she lived to reach her native land.

That the result of this letter was the arrival of four stewards to carry her to the room paid for, who offered apology after apology.

That the stewardess, on being asked what the purser had said on reading the note, replied: "He asked first if you were really so very sick, to which I answered there was no doubt about that. Then the purser asked me if there was such a cabin on board the *Titanic* where a cabin trunk could not be opened; to which I replied in the affirmative. I also told him that the cabin was entirely too small for two women, and that two men could not hardly fit in; that it was impossible for myself or the steward to enter the cabin to wait upon the occupants unless both of them first climbed into their berths. The purser then told me that he would have to act at once, or the company would get into trouble."

That after being transferred to this new cabin the second-class physician, Dr. Simpson, called from three to four times a day; that he feared the attack of tonsillitis brought on by the chill would become diphtheretic and ordered Mrs. Shelley to remain in her cabin.

That this cabin, though large and roomy, was not furnished in the comfortable manner as the same accommodation procured on the Cunard and other lines; that it looked in a half-finished condition; that this room was just as cold as the cell from which we had been removed, and on asking the steward to have heat turned on, he answered that it was impossible, as the heating system for the second-class cabins refused to work. That of all the second-class cabins, only three—the three first cabins to be reached by the heat—had any heat at all, and that the heat was so intense there that the occupants had complained to the purser, who had ordered the heat shut off entirely; consequently the rooms were like ice houses all of the voyage, and Mrs. L. D. Parrish, when not waiting on her sick daughter, was obliged to go to bed to keep warm.

That afterwards, when on board the *Carpathia,* Mrs. Shelley took pains to inquire of steerage passengers as to whether or not they had heat in the steerage of the *Titanic* and received the answer that there was the same trouble with their heating plant, too.

That although the servants on board were most willing, they had a hard time to do their work; that the stewardess could not even get a tray to serve Mrs. Shelley's meals and had to bring the plates and dishes one at a time in her hands, making the service very slow and annoying. The food, though good and plentiful, was ruined by this trouble in serving. That although both steward and stewardess appealed time and time again to the heads of their departments, no relief was obtained; there seemed to be no organization at all.

That in the ladies' toilet room only part of the fixtures had been installed, some of the said fixtures being still in crates.

That in the early evening of the night of the accident the temperature had fallen considerably, so that all on board realized we were in the ice belt. There were rumors of wireless messages from other ships warning of icebergs close at hand. It was also reported that certain first-class passengers had asked if the ship was to slow down whilst going through the ice belts and had been told by the captain that, on the contrary, the ship would be speeded through.

That at the moment of the collision we were awakened out of sleep by the shock, and especially by the stopping of the engines. That excited voices were heard outside in the passage saying that an iceberg had been run into. That after continued ringing of the steward bell a steward, but not the regular one, came and insisted that all was well and for all passengers to go back to bed. Afterwards, on board the *Carpathia,* a first-cabin passenger, a Mme. Baxter, of Montreal, Canada, told Mrs. Shelley that she had sent her son to the captain at the time of the collision to find out what to do. That her son had found the captain in a card game, and he had laughingly assured him that there was no danger and to advise his mother to go back to bed.

That about three-quarters of an hour after returning to their berths a steward came running down the passage bursting open the cabin doors and calling "All on deck with life belts on." That this steward brought Mrs. Parrish and Mrs. Shelley each a life belt and showed them how to tie them on. That they were told to go up to the top deck, the boat deck. That as Mrs. Shelley was very weak, it took several minutes to reach the upper deck. That Mr. and Mrs. Isidor Straus, who had known of Mrs. Shelley being so ill, met them on the way and helped them to the upper deck, where they found a chair for her and made her sit down.

That owing to the great number of persons on the deck Mrs. Shelley was not able to see anything of the handling of boats except the one she herself was placed in. There was practically no excitement on the part of anyone during this time, the majority seeming to think that the big boat could not sink altogether, and that it was better to stay on the steamer than trust to the little boats. After sitting in the chair for about five minutes one of the sailors ran to Mrs. Shelley and implored her to get in the lifeboat that was then being launched. He informed Mrs. Shelley that it was the last boat on the ship, and that unless she got into this one she would have to take her chances on the steamer, and that as she had been so sick she ought to take to the boat and make sure. Mrs. Straus advised taking to the boats, and, pushing her mother toward the sailor, Mrs. Shelley made for the davits where the boat hung. It was found impossible to swing the davits in, which left a space of between 4 and 5 feet between the edge of the deck and the suspended boat. The sailor picked up Mrs. Parrish and threw her bodily into the boat. Mrs. Shelley jumped and landed safely. That two men of the ship's crew manned this boat at the time of launching, one of whom said he was a stoker and the other a ship's baker. That at the time of launching these were the only men in the boat. That at the time of lowering the boat it seemed to be as full of passengers as the seating capacity called for, but owing to the excitement no thought of numbers entered Mrs. Shelley's head. The boat appeared to be filled with as many as could get in without overcrowding, all of them women and children, with the exception of the two mentioned above.

That on trying to lower the boat the tackle refused to work and it took considerable time, about 15 minutes, it is believed, to reach the water. That on reaching the water the casting-off apparatus would not work and the ropes had to be cut.

That just as they reached the water a crazed Italian jumped from the deck into the lifeboat, landing on Mrs. Parrish, severely bruising her right side and leg. This gave them one extra man.

After cutting loose from the ship the orders were to pull out toward the other boats and get as far away from the probable suction which would ensue if the steamer should sink. Orders were also given to keep in sight of the green light of the ship's boat which had been sent out ahead to look for help. That on reaching a distance of about 100 yards from the *Titanic* a loud explosion or noise was heard, followed closely by another, and the sinking of the big vessel began.

Throughout the entire period from the striking of the icebergs and taking to the boats the ship's crew behaved in an ideal manner. Not a man tried to get into a boat unless ordered to, and many were seen to strip off their clothing and wrap around the women and children who came up half

532

lad from their beds. Mrs. Shelley feels confident that she peaks the truth when she says that with the exception of hose few men ordered to man the boats all other sailors aved had gone down with the ship and were miraculously aved afterwards. Mrs. Shelley says that no crew could have ehaved in a more perfect manner and that they proved hemselves men in every sense of the word. That after the inking of the ship the boat they were in picked up several truggling in the water and were fortunate enough to rescue 0 sailors who had gone down with the ship, but who had een most miraculously blown out of the water after one of he explosions and been thrown near a derelict collapsible oat to which they had managed to cling. That after taking ll these men on board the boat was so full that many feared hey would sink, and it was suggested that some of the other oats should take some of these rescued ones on board; but hey refused, for fear of sinking. . . .

Affidavit: Eleanor Widener
First-class passenger, from Philadelphia

Key testimony: The captain hadn't been drinking.

STATE OF PENNSYLVANIA, *County of Philadelphia, ss:*

Mrs. George D. Widener, being duly sworn according to aw, deposes and says as follows:

I was a passenger with my husband, George D. Widener, nd my son, Harry Widener, on the steamship *Titanic* of the White Star Line on her voyage from Southampton on the 10th lay of April, 1912. On the night of Sunday, the 14th day of April, 1912, my husband and I gave a dinner at which Capt. mith was present. Capt. Smith drank absolutely no wine or ntoxicating liquor of any kind whatever at the dinner.

ELEANOR ELKINS WIDENER.

Letter: H. C. Wolfe
New York World correspondent

Key testimony: Many appeared to have died from exposure, ot drowning. Currents carried bodies from the scene.

SENATOR WILLIAM ALDEN SMITH,
Washington, D.C.

That many of the victims of the *Titanic* disaster die
from exposure and not from drowning was quite evident
from an examination of the bodies recovered from the se
by the ships sent to search in the vicinity of the disaster
This fact was first brought to light when the steamer *Mini*
returned to Halifax on May 6 with 15 bodies and reporte
having buried 2 others at sea. A careful examination of th
17 bodies recovered by Dr. Mosher, the *Minia's* physiciar
showed that only 1 of bodies had water on the lungs, th
other unfortunates having died from exposure.

While I have not been able to communicate with D
Mosher, above statement was made by Rev. H. W. Cur
ningham, chaplain on *Minia*, on her return to Halifax, wh
repeated it to-night and gave as his authority Dr. Moshe
ship's physician. I have, however, positive knowledge tha
Capt. Decarterett, of *Minia*, in report of his trip to Whi
Star Line and to Anglo-American Cable Co., owners (
Minia, used practically same words regarding condition (
bodies recovered.

H. C. WOLFE.
New York World Correspondent.

EPILOGUE

Excerpts from the Senate subcommittee's final report on the *Titanic* disaster, issued May 28, 1912:

INVESTIGATION INTO LOSS OF
S. S. "TITANIC."

MR. SMITH of Michigan, from the Committee on Commerce, submitted the following

REPORT

[Pursuant to S. Res. 283.]

The Committee on Commerce, which was authorized and directed to inquire into the loss of the British steamship *Titanic,* respectfully reports that that duty has been performed, and the committee has reached its conclusions thereon. . . .

WITNESSES EXAMINED.

We examined 82 witnesses upon various phases of this catastrophe, including the examination of 53 British subjects or residents of Great Britain and 29 citizens of the United States or residents thereof.

We interrogated 2 general officers of the International Mercantile Marine Co., which owned the steamship *Titanic*—J. Bruce Ismay, of Liverpool, England, president, also a passenger on the ship on this voyage, and P. A. S. Franklin, of New York, vice president in the United States of the International Mercantile Marine Co.; all the surviving officers, 4 in number—Charles Herbert Lightoller, second officer, of Netley Abbey, Hampshire, England; Third Officer Herbert John Pitman, of Somerset, England; Fourth Officer Joseph Groles Boxhall, of Hull, England; and Fifth Officer Harold Godfrey Lowe, of North Wales; and 34 members of the crew. . . .

We took the testimony of 21 passengers of all classes (including President Ismay) and of 23 other witnesses on subjects related to our inquiry (including Vice President Franklin).

We held our sessions in New York and in Washington, and took testimony by deposition in other parts of the country and in the Dominion of Canada.

The results of our investigation may be stated as follows:

OWNERSHIP OF STEAMSHIP "TITANIC."

We find that the *Titanic* was a White Star steamer and was owned by the Oceanic Steam Navigation Co., of England, all the stock of which company is in turn owned by the International Navigation Co. (Ltd.), of England, and the stock of that company, in turn, is owned by the International Mercantile Marine Co., an American corporation, organized under the laws of New Jersey.

INTERNATIONAL MERCANTILE MARINE CO.

Mr. J. Bruce Ismay, of Liverpool, England, is president of the International Mercantile Marine Co., and Mr. P. A. S. Franklin, of New York City, is vice president of that company in the United States.

The board of directors of the International Mercantile Marine Co. is composed of the following persons:

C. A. Griscom, chairman.	J. Bruce Ismay, president.
E. C. Grenfell.	Percy Chubb.
John F. Archbold.	E. J. Berwind.
John I. Waterbury.	Harold A. Sanderson.
The Right Hon. Lord Pirrie.	P. A. B. Widener.
George W. Perkins.	Charles F. Torrey.
Charles Steele.	J. P. Morgan, jr.

The International Mercantile Marine Co., through its various ramifications and constituent companies, owns the White Star Line, the American Line, the Red Star Line, the Atlantic Transport Line, the National Line, and the majority of the stock of the Leyland Line. . . .

The *Titanic* was built by Harland & Wolff, of Belfast, Ireland. No restriction as to limit of cost was placed upon the builders. She was launched May 31, 1911. She was a vessel of 46,328 tons register; her length was 882.6 feet, and her breadth was 92.6 feet. Her boat deck and bridge were 70 feet above the water line. She was, according to the testimony of President Ismay, "especially constructed to float with her two largest water-tight compartments full of water."

The vessel, fully equipped, cost £1,500,000 sterling, or about $7,500,000.

At the time of the accident the vessel carried insurance of £1,000,000 sterling or about $5,000,000, the remaining risk being carried by the company's insurance fund.

The *Titanic* was a duplicate of the *Olympic,* which is owned by the same company, with the single exception of her passenger accommodations, and was built to accommodate 2,599 passengers, with additional accommodations for officers and crew numbering 903 persons.

TRIAL TESTS STEAMSHIP "TITANIC."

The committee finds from the evidence that between six and seven hours was spent in making trial tests of this vessel at Belfast Lough on Monday, the 1st day of April last. A few turning circles were made, compasses adjusted, and she steamed a short time under approximately a full head of steam, but the ship was not driven at her full speed. One general officer of the steamship company was on board during the trial tests, while the builders were represented by Mr. Thomas Andrews, who had superintended the building of the vessel. Mr. Andrews conducted certain tests at Southampton and represented the builders both at Southampton and on the first voyage.

With a partial crew, the ship sailed from Belfast, immediately after the trial, for Southampton, where she arrived on Wednesday, April 3, about midnight. She made fast with her port side to the wharf, where she remained until April 10, about 12 o'clock noon, when she sailed for Cherbourg, Queenstown, and New York.

Many of the crew did not join the ship until a few hours before sailing, and the only drill while the vessel lay at Southampton or on the voyage consisted in lowering two lifeboats on the starboard side into the water, which boats were again hoisted to the boat deck within a half hour. No boat list designating the stations of members of the crew was posted until several days after sailing from Southampton, boatmen being left in ignorance of their proper stations until the following Friday morning.

CERTIFICATE OF BRITISH BOARD OF TRADE.

On Wednesday morning, the day the ship sailed from Southampton, Capt. Clark, a representative of the British Board of Trade, came aboard and, after spending a brief time, issued the necessary certificate to permit sailing.

Boat davits and lifeboats of the steamship "Titanic."

The *Titanic* was fitted with 16 sets of double-acting boat davits of modern type, capable of handling 2 or 3 boats per set of davits. The davits were thus capable of handling 48 boats, whereas the ship carried but 16 lifeboats and 4 collapsibles, fulfilling all the requirements of the British Board of Trade. The *Titanic* was provided with 14 lifeboats, of capacity for 65 persons each, or 910 persons; 2 emergency sea boats, of capacity for 35 persons each, or 70 persons; 4 collapsible boats, of capacity for 49 persons each, or 196 persons. Total lifeboat capacity, 1,176. There was ample life-belt equipment for all.

DEPARTURE OF THE STEAMSHIP "TITANIC."

The ship left Southampton Wednesday, April 10, at 12:15 P.M., with the ship's complement of officers and crew (see Exhibit A) numbering 899 persons. As the *Titanic* left the wharf at Southampton the moorings of the *New York* were carried away by the backwash from the *Titanic's* starboard propeller, causing a delay of about half an hour.

The *Titanic* arrived at Cherbourg late the same afternoon. The *Titanic* left Cherbourg and proceeded to Queenstown, Ireland, arriving there on Thursday about midday, departing for New York immediately after embarking the mails and passengers. . . .

SUMMARY OF PASSENGERS AND SURVIVORS.

Including the crew, the *Titanic* sailed with 2,223 persons aboard, of whom 1,517 were lost and 706 were saved. It will be noted in this connection that 60 per cent of the first-class passengers were saved, 42 per cent of the second-class passengers were saved, 25 per cent of the third-class passengers were saved, and 24 per cent of the crew were saved.

WEATHER CONDITIONS DURING VOYAGE.

During the entire voyage the weather was clear, with the single exception of 10 minutes of fog, and the sea was calm throughout the voyage, with sunshine the whole of each day and bright starlight every night. No untoward incident marred the trip. Greetings were frequently exchanged with passing vessels by appropriate signals.

ICE WARNINGS.

On the third day out ice warnings were received by the wireless operators on the *Titanic,* and the testimony is conclusive that at least three of these warnings came direct to the commander of the *Titanic* on the day of the accident, the first about noon, from the *Baltic,* of the White Star Line. It will be noted that this message places icebergs within 5 miles of the track which the *Titanic* was following, and near the place where the accident occurred. The message from the commander of the *Baltic* is as follows:

STEAMSHIP "BALTIC," *April 14, 1912.*
CAPT. SMITH, *Titanic:*
Have had moderate variable winds and clear fine weather since leaving. Greek steamer *Athinai* reports

passing icebergs and large quantity of field ice to-day in latitude 41.51 north, longitude 49.52 west. Last night we spoke German oil tank *Deutschland,* Stettin to Philadelphia, not under control; short of coal; latitude 40.42 north, longitude 55.11. Wishes to be reported to New York and other steamers. Wish you and *Titanic* all success.

COMMANDER.

The second message was received by the *Titanic* from the *Californian,* of the Leyland Line, at 5:35 P.M. New York time, Sunday afternoon, reporting ice about 19 miles to the northward of the track which the *Titanic* was following. This message was as follows:

Latitude 42.3 north, longitude 49.9 west. Three large bergs 5 miles to southward of us. Regards. (Sig.) Lord.

The third message was transmitted from the *Amerika* via the *Titanic* and Cape Race to the Hydrographic Office in Washington, D. C., reporting ice about 19 miles to the southward of the course being followed by the *Titanic,* and reads as follows:

STEAMSHIP "AMERIKA," VIA "TITANIC" AND
CAPE RACE, N. F.,
April 14, 1912.

HYDROGRAPHIC OFFICE, *Washington, D. C.:*
Amerika passed two large icebergs in 41.27 N., 50.8 W., on the 14th of April.

K. N. U. T.

This message was actually received at the Hydrographic Office in Washington at 10:51 P.M., April 14.

The fourth message was sent to the *Titanic* at 9:05 P.M. New York time, on Sunday, the 14th of April, approximately an hour before the accident occurred. The message reads as follows:

We are stopped and surrounded by ice.

To this the operator of the *Titanic* replied:

Shut up. I am busy. I am working Cape Race [the wireless station in Newfoundland].

While this was the last message sent by the *Californian* to the *Titanic,* the evidence shows that the operator of the *Californian* kept the telephones on his head, and heard the *Titanic* talking to Cape Race up to within a few minutes of the time of the accident, when he "put the phones down, took off his clothes, and turned in."

The *Baltic's* operator on that Sunday overheard ice reports going to the *Titanic* from the *Prinz Friedrich Wilhelm,* and from the *Amerika,* while the *Carpathia* on the same day overheard the *Parisian* talking about ice with other ships.

ICE BOTH TO NORTHWARD AND SOUTHWARD STEAMSHIP "TITANIC'S" TRACK.

This enables the committee to say that the ice positions so definitely reported to the *Titanic* just preceding the accident located ice on both sides of the track or lane which the *Titanic* was following, and in her immediate vicinity. No general discussion took place among the officers; no conference was called to consider these warnings; no heed was given to them. The speed was not relaxed, the lookout was not increased, and the only vigilance displayed by the officer of the watch was by instructions to the lookouts to keep "a sharp lookout for ice." It should be said, however, that the testimony shows that Capt. Smith remarked to Officer Lightoller, who was the officer doing duty on the bridge until 10 o'clock ship's time, or 8:27 o'clock New York time, "If it was in a slight degree hazy there would be no doubt we would have to go very slowly" and "If in the slightest degree doubtful, let me know." The evidence is that it was exceptionally clear. There was no haze, and the ship's speed was not reduced.

SPEED.

The speed of the *Titanic* was gradually increased after leaving Queenstown. The first day's run was 464 miles, the second day's run was 519 miles, the third day's run was 546 miles. Just prior to the collision the ship was making her

maximum speed of the voyage—not less than 21 knots, o
24¼ miles per hour.

At 11:46 P.M. ship's time, or 10:13 P.M. New York time
Sunday evening, April 14, the lookout signaled the bridg
and telephoned the officer of the watch, "Iceberg righ
ahead." The officer of the watch, Mr. Murdoch, immedi
ately ordered the quartermaster at the wheel to put the helm
"hard astarboard," and reversed the engines; but while th
sixth officer standing behind the quartermaster at the whee
reported to officer Murdoch "The helm is hard astarboard,
the *Titanic* struck the ice. The impact, while not violen
enough to disturb the passengers or crew, or to arrest th
ship's progress, rolled the vessel slightly and tore the ste
plating above the turn of the bilge.

FIRST DAMAGE REPORTED.

The testimony shows that coincident with the collisio
air was heard whistling or hissing from the overflow pipe t
the forepeak tank, indicating the escape of air from th
tank because of the inrush of water. Practically at once, th
forepeak tank, No. 1 hold, No. 2 hold, No. 3 hold, and th
forward boiler room, filled with water, the presence c
which was immediately reported from the mail room an
the racquet court and trunk room in No. 3 hold, and als
from the firemen's quarters in No. 1 hold. Leading Firema
Barret saw the water rushing into the forward fireroom fron
a tear about two feet above the stokehold floor plates an
about twenty feet below the water line, which tear extende
two feet into the coal bunker at the forward end of th
second fireroom.

SERIOUS NATURE OF DAMAGE REALIZED.

The reports received by the captain after various inspe
tions of the ship must have acquainted him promptly wit
its serious condition, and when interrogated by Presider
Ismay, he so expressed himself. It is believed, also, that th
serious condition was promptly realized by the chief eng

...eer and by the builders' representative, Mr. Andrews, none
of whom survived.

FLOODING OF THE VESSEL.

Under this added weight of water the bow of the ship sank
deeper and deeper into the water, and through the open
hatch leading from the mail room, and through other
openings, water promptly overflowed E deck, below which
deck the third, fourth, fifth, sixth, seventh, and eighth
transverse bulkheads ended, and thus flooded the compartments abaft No. 3 hold.

WATER-TIGHT COMPARTMENTS.

The *Titanic* was fitted with 15 transverse water-tight
bulkheads, only 1, the first bulkhead from forward, extended to the uppermost continuous deck, C; bulkheads
Nos. 2, 10, 11, 12, 13, 14, and 15 extended to the second
continuous deck, D; and bulkheads Nos. 3, 4, 5, 6, 7, 8, and
extended only to the third continuous deck, E. The
openings through deck E were not designed for water-tight
closing, as the evidence shows that flooding over deck E
contributed largely to the sinking of the vessel. The bulkheads above described divided the ship into 16 main water-
tight compartments, and the ship was so arranged that any
main compartments might be flooded without in any way
involving the safety of the ship. As before stated, the
testimony shows that the 5 extreme forward compartments
were flooded practically immediately, and under such circumstances, by reason of the nonwater-tight character of
the deck at which the transverse bulkheads ended, the
supposedly water-tight compartments were NOT water-
tight, and the sinking of the vessel followed.

DISTRESS CALLS SENT OUT.

No general alarm was sounded, no whistle blown, and no
systematic warning was given the passengers. Within 15 or
20 minutes the captain visited the wireless room and
instructed the operator to get assistance, sending out the
distress call, C. Q. D.

This distress call was heard by the wireless station at Cape Race that evening at 10:25 P.M. New York time, together with the report that she had struck an iceberg, and at the same time was accidentally overheard by the *Mount Temple*, which ship was immediately turned around toward the *Titanic*. Within two or three minutes a reply was received from the *Frankfurt*. Within 10 minutes the wireless operator of the *Carpathia* fortunately and largely by chance heard the *Titanic's* C. Q. D. call, which he reported at once to the bridge and to the captain. The *Carpathia* was immediately turned around and reported her latitude and longitude to the *Titanic*, together with the fact that she was steaming full speed toward the stricken ship. The *Frankfurt*, however, did not give her latitude or longitude, and after waiting 20 minutes asked the operator of the *Titanic*, "What is matter?" To this the *Titanic* operator replied that he was a fool.

In view of the fact that no position had been given by the *Frankfurt*, and that her exact distance from the *Titanic* was unknown at that time, the answer of the operator of the *Titanic* was scarcely such as prudence would have dictated. Notwithstanding this, however, the *Frankfurt* was overheard by the *Mount Temple* to report "Our captain will go for you." Communication was promptly established with the *Olympic* and the *Baltic*, and the *Caronia*, some 800 miles to the eastward, overheard the *Titanic's* C. Q. D. call. The wireless messages of the *Titanic* were recorded in part by the Cape Race station and by the *Mount Temple*, and in part by the *Baltic*. The *Mount Temple* last heard the *Titanic* after the accident at 11:47 P.M. New York time. The *Baltic* and the *Carpathia* lost touch about the same time, the last message they received being "Engine room getting flooded." The *Virginian* last heard the *Titanic's* signals at 12:27 New York time, and reported them blurred, and ending abruptly.

FIRST PRESS REPORT.

This information is contained in a report received by the Associated Press from Cape Race, and communicated by them to the public, and also to Vice President Franklin of the White Star Line, and later verified from his office in Montreal, as follows:

CAPE RACE, NEW BRUNSWICK,
Sunday night, April 14.

At 10:25 o'clock to-night the White Star Line steamship *Titanic* called "C. Q. D." to the Marconi wireless station here and reported having struck an iceberg. The steamer said that immediate assistance was required.

Half an hour afterwards another message came, reporting that they were sinking by the head, and that women were being put off in the lifeboats.

The weather was calm and clear, the *Titanic's* wireless operator reported, and gave the position of the vessel as 41.46 north latitude and 50.14 west longitude.

The Marconi station at Cape Race notified the Allan liner *Virginian,* the captain of which immediately advised that he was proceeding for the scene of the disaster.

The *Virginian* at midnight was about 170 miles distant from the *Titanic* and expected to reach that vessel about 10 A.M. Monday.

2 A.M. MONDAY.

The *Olympic* at an early hour this (Monday) morning was in latitude 40.32 north and longitude 61.18 west. She was in direct communication with the *Titanic* and is now making all haste toward her.

The steamship *Baltic* also reported herself as about 200 miles east of the *Titanic* and was making all possible speed toward her.

The last signals from the *Titanic* were heard by the *Virginian* at 12:27 A.M.

The wireless operator on the *Virginian* says these signals were blurred and ended abruptly.

VESSELS IN VICINITY OF STEAMSHIP "TITANIC."

At this time the committee thinks it advisable to invite attention to the reported positions of the vessels in the vicinity of the *Titanic* when her calls of distress were being sent out.

The *Californian,* of the Leyland Line, west-bound, was in latitude 42° 05′ north, longitude 50° 07′ west, and was

545

distant in a northerly direction 19½ miles according to the captain's figures.

The *Mount Temple,* of the Canadian Pacific Railroad line, west-bound, was in latitude 41° 25′ north, longitude 51° 14′ west, and was about 49 miles to the westward of the *Titanic* and on her return to the *Titanic's* position passed an unknown schooner.

The *Carpathia,* of the Cunard Line, east-bound, was 58 miles away, and she steered a course north 52° west to reach the *Titanic.*

The *Birma,* a Russian ship, was 70 miles off at 12:25 A.M. on Monday, the 15th of April.

The *Frankfurt,* of the North German Lloyd Line, east-bound, was in latitude 39° 47′ north, longitude 52° 10′ west, 153 miles to the southwest.

The *Virginian* at midnight was about 170 miles distant from the *Titanic.*

The *Baltic,* of the White Star Line, east-bound, was about 243 miles southeast of the *Titanic's* position at about 11 o'clock Sunday evening, New York time.

The *Olympic,* of the White Star Line, east-bound, at 12:14, New York time, was about 512 miles to the westward, in latitude 40° 22′ north, longitude 61° 18′ west.

STEAMSHIP LIGHT SEEN FROM STEAMSHIP "TITANIC."

Sixteen witnesses from the *Titanic,* including officers and experienced seamen, and passengers of sound judgment testified to seeing the light of a ship in the distance, and some of the lifeboats were directed to pull for that light, to leave the passengers and to return to the side of the *Titanic.* The *Titanic* fired distress rockets and attempted to signal by electric lamp and Morse code to this vessel. At about the same time the officers of the *Californian* admit seeing rockets in the general direction of the *Titanic* and say that they immediately displayed a powerful Morse lamp, which could be easily seen a distance of 10 miles, while several of the crew of the *Californian* testify that the side lights of a large vessel going at full speed were plainly visible from the lower deck of the *Californian* at 11:30 P.M., ship's time, just before the accident. There is no evidence that any rocket were fired by any vessel between the *Titanic* and th

Californian, although every eye on the *Titanic* was searching the horizon for possible assistance.

THE STEAMSHIP "CALIFORNIAN'S" RESPONSIBILITY.

The committee is forced to the inevitable conclusion that the *Californian,* controlled by the same company, was nearer the *Titanic* than the 19 miles reported by her captain, and that her officers and crew saw the distress signals of the *Titanic* and failed to respond to them in accordance with the dictates of humanity, international usage, and the requirements of law. The only reply to the distress signals was a counter signal from a large white light which was flashed for nearly two hours from the mast of the *Californian.* In our opinion such conduct, whether arising from indifference or gross carelessness, is most reprehensible, and places upon the commander of the *Californian* a grave responsibility. The wireless operator of the *Californian* was not aroused until 3:30 A.M., New York time, on the morning of the 15th, after considerable conversation between officers and members of the crew had taken place aboard that ship regarding these distress signals or rockets, and was directed by the chief officer to see if there was anything the matter, as a ship had been firing rockets during the night. The inquiry thus set on foot immediately disclosed the fact that the *Titanic* had sunk. Had assistance been promptly proffered, or had the wireless operator of the *Californian* remained a few minutes longer at his post on Sunday evening, that ship might have had the proud distinction of rescuing the lives of the passengers and crew of the *Titanic.* . . .

STEAMSHIP "TITANIC'S" LIFEBOATS CLEARED AWAY.

When Captain Smith received the reports as to the water entering the ship, he promptly gave the order to clear away the lifeboats, and later orders were given to put women and children into the boats. During this time distress rockets were fired at frequent intervals.

The lack of preparation was at this time most noticeable. There was no system adopted for loading the boats; there was great indecision as to the deck from which boats were to be loaded; there was wide diversity of opinion as to the number of the crew necessary to man each boat; there was no direction whatever as to the number of passengers to be carried by each boat, and no uniformity in loading them. On one side only women and children were put in the boats, while on the other side there was almost an equal proportion of men and women put into the boats, the women and children being given the preference in all cases. The failure to utilize all lifeboats to their recognized capacity for safety unquestionably resulted in the needless sacrifice of several hundred lives which might otherwise have been saved.

CAPACITY OF LIFEBOATS NOT UTILIZED.

The vessel was provided with lifeboats, as above stated, for 1,176 persons, while but 706 were saved. Only a few of the ship's lifeboats were fully loaded, while others were but partially filled. Some were loaded at the boat deck, and some at the A deck, and these were successfully lowered to the water. The twentieth boat was washed overboard when the forward part of the ship was submerged, and in its overturned condition served as a life raft for about 30 people, including Second Officer Lightoller, Wireless Operators Bride and Phillips (the latter dying before rescue), passengers Col. [Archibald] Gracie and Mr. Jack Thayer, and others of the crew, who climbed upon it from the water at about the time the ship disappeared.

LIFEBOAT DEVICES.

Had the sea been rough it is questionable whether any of the lifeboats of the *Titanic* would have reached the water without being damaged or destroyed. The point of suspension of the *Titanic*'s boats was about 70 feet above the level of the sea. Had the ship been rolling heavily the lifeboats as they were lowered would have swung out from the side of the ship as it rolled toward them and on the return roll would have swung back and crashed against its side. It is evident from the testimony that as the list of the *Titanic* became noticeable the lifeboats scraped against the high side as they were being lowered. Every effort should be

ade to improve boat-handling devices, and to improve the
ntrol of boats while being lowered.

CONFLICT IN LIFEBOAT REPORTS.

In the reports of the survivors there are marked differ-
ces of opinion as to the number carried by each lifeboat.
lifeboat No. 1, for instance, one survivor reports 10 in
. The seaman in charge reports 7 of the crew and 14 to 20
ssengers. The officer who loaded this boat estimated that
m 3 to 5 women and 22 men were aboard. Accepting the
nimum report as made by any one survivor in every boat,
e total far exceeds the actual number picked up by the
rpathia.

NO DISTINCTION BETWEEN PASSENGERS.

The testimony is definite that, except in isolated in-
nces, there was no panic. In loading boats no distinction
s made between first, second, and third class passengers,
hough the proportion of lost is larger among third-class
ssengers than in either of the other classes. Women and
ildren, without discrimination, were given preference.
Your committee believes that under proper discipline the
vivors could have been concentrated into fewer boats
er reaching the water, and we think that it would have
en possible to have saved many lives had those in charge
boats thus released returned promptly to the scene of the
aster.

CONDUCT ON LIFEBOATS.

After lowering, several of the boats rowed many hours in
direction of the lights supposed to have been displayed
the *Californian*. Other boats lay on their oars in the
inity of the sinking ship, a few survivors being rescued
m the water. After distributing his passengers among the
r other boats which he had herded together, and after the
es of distress had died away, Fifth Officer Lowe, in boat
. 14, went to the scene of the wreck and rescued four
ng passengers from the water, one of whom afterwards
d in the lifeboat, but was identified. Officer Lowe then

set sail in boat No. 14, took in tow one collapsible boat, a proceeded to the rescue of passengers on another collapsi lifeboat.

The men who had taken refuge on the overturned colla ible lifeboat were rescued, including Second Officer Li toller and passengers Gracie and Thayer, and Wirel Operators Bride and Phillips, by lifeboats No. 4 and No. before the arrival of the *Carpathia*. The fourth collapsi lifeboat was rowed to the side of the *Carpathia*, a contained 28 women and children, mostly third-class p sengers, 3 firemen, 1 steward, 4 Filipinos, President Ism and Mr. Carter, of Philadelphia, and was in charge Quartermaster Rowe.

SHIP SINKING.

The ship went down gradually by the bow, assuming almost perpendicular position just before sinking at 12 A.M., New York time, April 15. There have been many c flicting statements as to whether the ship broke in two, but preponderance of evidence is to the effect that she assumed almost end-on position and sank intact. [The conclusion refuted after the ship's remains were found in 1985.]

NO SUCTION.

The committee deems it of sufficient importance to attention to the fact that as the ship disappeared under water there was no apparent suction or unusual disturba of the surface of the water. Testimony is abundant t while she was going down there was not sufficient suction be manifest to any of the witnesses who were in the water on the overturned collapsible boat or on the floating déb or to the occupants of the lifeboats in the vicinity of vessel, or to prevent those in the water, whether equipp with life belts or not, from easily swimming away from ship's side while she was sinking.

CAPTAIN ROSTRON.

The committee invites your attention to the course lowed by Captain Rostron, commanding the *Carpat.*

Immediately upon the receipt of the wireless call of distress Captain Rostron gave the order to turn the ship around and set a definite course toward the *Titanic* and instructed the chief engineer to call another watch of stokers and make all possible speed to that ship.

Realizing the possible presence of ice, because of the collision, Captain Rostron doubled his lookouts and exerted extra vigilance, putting an extra lookout on duty forward and having another officer on the bridge. The captain immediately instructed the first officer to "prepare all our lifeboats and have them all ready for turning outboard." . . .

The committee deems the course followed by Captain Rostron of the *Carpathia* as deserving of the highest praise and worthy of especial recognition. . . .

ON THE SCENE OF THE WRECK.

The first boat was picked up at 4:10 A.M. Monday, and the last of the survivors was on board by 8:30 A.M., after which Captain Rostron made arrangements "to hold service, a short prayer of thankfulness for those rescued, and a short burial service for those who were lost."

Upon the arrival of the *Californian* upon the scene, about 3 o'clock in the morning, the captain of the *Carpathia* communicated with her commander, stating that all of the passengers had been rescued from the boats but that he thought one was still unaccounted for; and arrangements were made whereby the *Californian* made an exhaustive search in the vicinity for this missing boat.

Captain Rostron stated that the *Carpathia* picked up 15 lifeboats and 2 collapsible boats. Evidence was given before the committee by at least one occupant of every lifeboat, satisfying the committee that the 16 lifeboats with which the *Titanic* was equipped were all accounted for. Thirteen of these lifeboats were hoisted on board and carried to New York by the *Carpathia*.

After arranging for a thorough search of the vicinity by the *Californian,* Captain Rostron headed his vessel for New York, reporting immediately by wireless to the officials of his company in New York, as follows:

New York, latitude 41.45; longitude 50.20 west.—An
proceeding New York unless otherwise ordered, with
about 800, after having consulted with Mr. Ismay and
considering the circumstances. With so much ice about
consider New York best. Large number icebergs, and 2
miles field ice with bergs amongst.

BODIES NOT VISIBLE.

The committee directs attention to the fact that Captain
Rostron, of the *Carpathia,* although four hours in the
vicinity of the accident, saw only one body, and that
Captain Lord, of the *Californian,* who remained three hour
in the vicinity of the wreckage, saw none. The failure of the
captain of the *Carpathia,* of the captain of the *Californian*
and of the captain of the *Mount Temple* to find bodie
floating in that vicinity in the early morning of the da
following can only be accounted for on the theory that thos
who went down with the ship either did not rise to the
surface or were carried away or hidden by the extensive ic
floe which during the night came down over the spot wher
the ship disappeared, while those bodies which have bee
found remote from the place where the ship went dow
were probably carried away from the scene by the current
or by the movement of the ice.

WIRELESS SERVICE.

Numerous wireless messages of an official character wer
given to the operator on the *Carpathia* on Monday mornin
April 15, with explicit instructions from the captain to sen
them immediately, and, if necessary, relay through othe
vessels. . . .

Notwithstanding the specific instructions of the captai
to the wireless operator on the morning of April 15 regar
ing the transmission of Mr. Ismay's message to Mr. Fran
lin in New York, the evidence shows that the message i
question was not received by Mr. Franklin until about
o'clock Wednesday morning, April 17. The original me
sage, in the possession of the committee, shows that th
message was transmitted from the *Carpathia,* April 17, v
Halifax. Our investigation discloses the fact that the me

age was delivered to Mr. Franklin in New York promptly
after its receipt by the Postal Telegraph & Cable Co.

The message in question is as follows:

STEAMSHIP CARPATHIA, *April 17, 1912 (via Halifax)*.
ISLEFRANK, *N. Y. C.*:

Deeply regret advise you *Titanic* sank this morning,
after collision iceberg, resulting serious loss life. Further
particulars later.

BRUCE ISMAY.

This message was received by Mr. Franklin in New York
about 9 A.M. April 17.

PUBLIC INFORMATION.

The record further discloses the first official information
concerning the disaster communicated to the public by the
officials of the White Star Line was received from Capt.
Haddock, of the *Olympic*, at 6:16 P.M. Monday, April 15, as
follows:

Carpathia reached *Titanic's* position at daybreak.
Found boats and wreckage only. *Titanic* had foundered
about 2:20 A.M. in 41.16 north, 50.14 west. All her boats
accounted for. About 675 souls saved, crew and passengers, latter nearly all women and children. Leyland Line
steamship *Californian* remaining and searching position
of disaster. *Carpathia* returning to New York with survivors; please inform Cunard.

HADDOCK.

Notwithstanding this information in possession of the
officials of that company, a telegram was sent to Representative J. A. Hughes, Huntington, W. Va., dated New York,
April 15, 1912, reading as follows:

Titanic proceeding to Halifax. Passengers will probably
land there Wednesday all safe.

WHITE STAR LINE.

8:27 P.M.

The committee have been unable to fix the identity of the
author of this telegram. We find, however, that this message
was delivered to the Western Union branch office, in the

same building as the offices of the White Star Line, 1 [
Broadway, at 7:51 P.M., on that day, but are left wholly in
doubt as to the person who sent it or the purpose of the
author in sending such a message. Whoever sent this
message, under the circumstances, is guilty of the most
reprehensible conduct.

INFORMATION WITHHELD.

The committee does not believe that the wireless operator
on the *Carpathia* showed proper vigilance in handling the
important work confided to his care after the accident.
Information concerning an accident at sea had been used by
a wireless operator prior to this accident for his own advan
tage. That such procedure had been permitted by the Marconi
ni Co. may have had its effect on this occasion. The
disposition of officials of the Marconi Co. to permit this
practice and the fact of that company's representative
making the arrangements for the sale of the experiences of
the operators of the *Titanic* and *Carpathia* subjects the
participants to criticism, and the practice should be prohib
ited. The committee are pleased to note that Mr. Marcon
approves of such prohibition.

RECOMMENDATIONS.

The committee finds that this accident clearly indicates the
necessity of additional legislation to secure safety of life at sea
By statute the United States accepts reciprocally the in
spection certificates of foreign countries having inspection
laws approximating those of the United States. Unless there
is early revision of inspection laws of foreign countries along
the lines laid down hereinafter, the committee deems it
proper that such reciprocal arrangements be terminated, and
that no vessel shall be licensed to carry passengers from port
of the United States until all regulations and requirements of
the laws of the United States have been fully complied with
The committee recommends that sections 4481 and
4488, Revised Statutes, be so amended as to definitely
require sufficient lifeboats to accommodate every passenger
and every member of the crew. That the importance of this
feature is recognized by the steamship lines is indicated by

the fact that on many lines steps are being taken to provide lifeboat capacity for every person on board, including crew; and the fact of such equipment is being widely advertised. The president of the International Mercantile Marine Co., Mr. Ismay, definitely stated to the committee:

We have issued instructions that none of the ships of our lines shall leave any port carrying more passengers and crew than they have capacity for in the lifeboats.

Not less than four members of the crew, skilled in handling boats, should be assigned to every boat. All members of the crew assigned to lifeboats should be drilled in lowering and rowing the boats, not less than twice each month and the fact of such drill or practice should be noted in the log.

The committee recommends the assignment of passengers and crew to lifeboats before sailing; that occupants of certain groups of staterooms and the stewards of such groups of rooms be assigned to certain boats most conveniently located with reference to the rooms in question; the assignment of boats and the shortest route from stateroom to boat to be posted in every stateroom.

The committee recommends that every ocean steamship carrying 100 or more passengers be required to carry 2 electric searchlights.

The committee finds that this catastrophe makes glaringly apparent the necessity for regulation of radiotelegraphy. There must be an operator on duty at all times, day and night, to insure the immediate receipt of all distress, warning, or other important calls. Direct communication either by clear-speaking telephone, voice tube, or messenger must be provided between the wireless room and the bridge, so that the operator does not have to leave his station. There must be definite legislation to prevent interference by amateurs, and to secure secrecy of radiograms or wireless messages. There must be some source of auxiliary power, either storage battery or oil engine, to insure the operation of the wireless installation until the wireless room is submerged.

The committee recommends the early passage of S. 6412, already passed by the Senate and favorably reported by the House.

The committee recommends that the firing of rockets or

candles on the high seas for any other purpose than as a signal of distress be made a misdemeanor.

The committee recommends that the following additional structural requirements be required as regards ocean-going passenger steamers the construction of which is begun after this date:

All steel ocean and coastwise seagoing ships carrying 100 or more passengers should have a water-tight skin inboard of the outside plating, extending not less than 10 per cent of the load draft above the full-load waterline, either in the form of an inner bottom or of longitudinal water-tight bulkheads, and this construction should extend from the forward collision bulkhead over not less than two-thirds of the length of the ship.

All steel ocean and coastwise seagoing ships carrying 100 or more passengers should have bulkheads so spaced that any two adjacent compartments of the ship may be flooded without destroying the flotability or stability of the ship. Water-tight transverse bulkheads should extend from side to side of the ship, attaching to the outside shell. The transverse bulkheads forward and abaft the machinery spaces should be continued water-tight vertically to the uppermost continuous structural deck. The uppermost continuous structural deck should be fitted water-tight. Bulkheads within the limits of the machinery spaces should extend not less than 25 per cent of the draft of the ship above the load waterline and should end at a water-tight deck. All water-tight bulkheads and decks should be proportioned to withstand, without material permanent deflection, a water pressure equal to 5 feet more than the full height of the bulkhead. Bulkheads of novel dimensions or scantlings should be tested by being subjected to actual water pressure.

A quotation from Senator William Alden Smith's address to the Senate in delivering the *Titanic* panel's report on May 28, 1912:

. . . In our imagination we can see again the proud ship instinct with life and energy, with active figures again swarming upon its decks; musicians, teachers, artists, an authors; soldiers and sailors and men of large affairs; brave men and noble women of every land. We can see the unpretentious and the lowly, progenitors of the great and strong, turning their back upon the Old World, where endurance is to them no longer a virtue, and looking hopefully to the new. At the very moment of their greatest joy the ship suddenly reels, mutilated and groaning. With splendid courage the musicians fill the last moments with sympathetic melody. The ship wearily gives up the unequal battle. Only a vestige remains of the men and women that but a moment before quickened her spacious apartments with human hopes and passions, sorrows, and joys. Upon that broken hull new vows were taken, new fealty expressed, old love renewed, and those who had been devoted in friendship and companions in life went proudly and defiantly on the last life pilgrimage together. In such a heritage we must feel ourselves more intimately related to the sea than ever before, and henceforth it will send back to us on its rising tide the cheering salutations from those we have lost. . . .

Summary of Passengers and Survivors
from the Senate subcommittee's final report

Including the crew, the *Titanic* sailed with 2,223 persons aboard, of whom 1,517 were lost and 706 were saved. It will be noted in this connection that 60 per cent of the first-class passengers were saved, 42 per cent of the second-class passengers were saved, 25 per cent of the third-class passengers were saved, and 24 per cent of the crew were saved.

	On board.			Saved.			Lost.			Per cent saved.
	Women and children.	Men.	Total.	Women and children.	Men.	Total.	Women and children.	Men.	Total.	
Passengers:										
First class	156	173	329	145	54	199	11	119	130	60
Second class	128	157	285	104	15	119	24	142	166	42
Third class	224	486	710	105	69	174	119	417	536	25
Total passengers.	508	816	1,324	354	138	492	154	678	832	....
Crew	23	876	899	20	194	214	3	682	685	24
Total.............	531	1,692	2,223	374	332	706	157	1,360	1,517	32

LIST OF WITNESSES

(* denotes testimony included in this book)

560

DIGEST OF TESTIMONY

Editor's note: The Senate subcommittee's digest is here adapted to the excerpts included in this book. There are some inconsistencies between the digest and actual testimony; for example, steerage passengers did testify that they had been briefly prevented from moving up to lifeboats from below. But that testimony is not reflected in the subcommittee's digest.

—T.K.